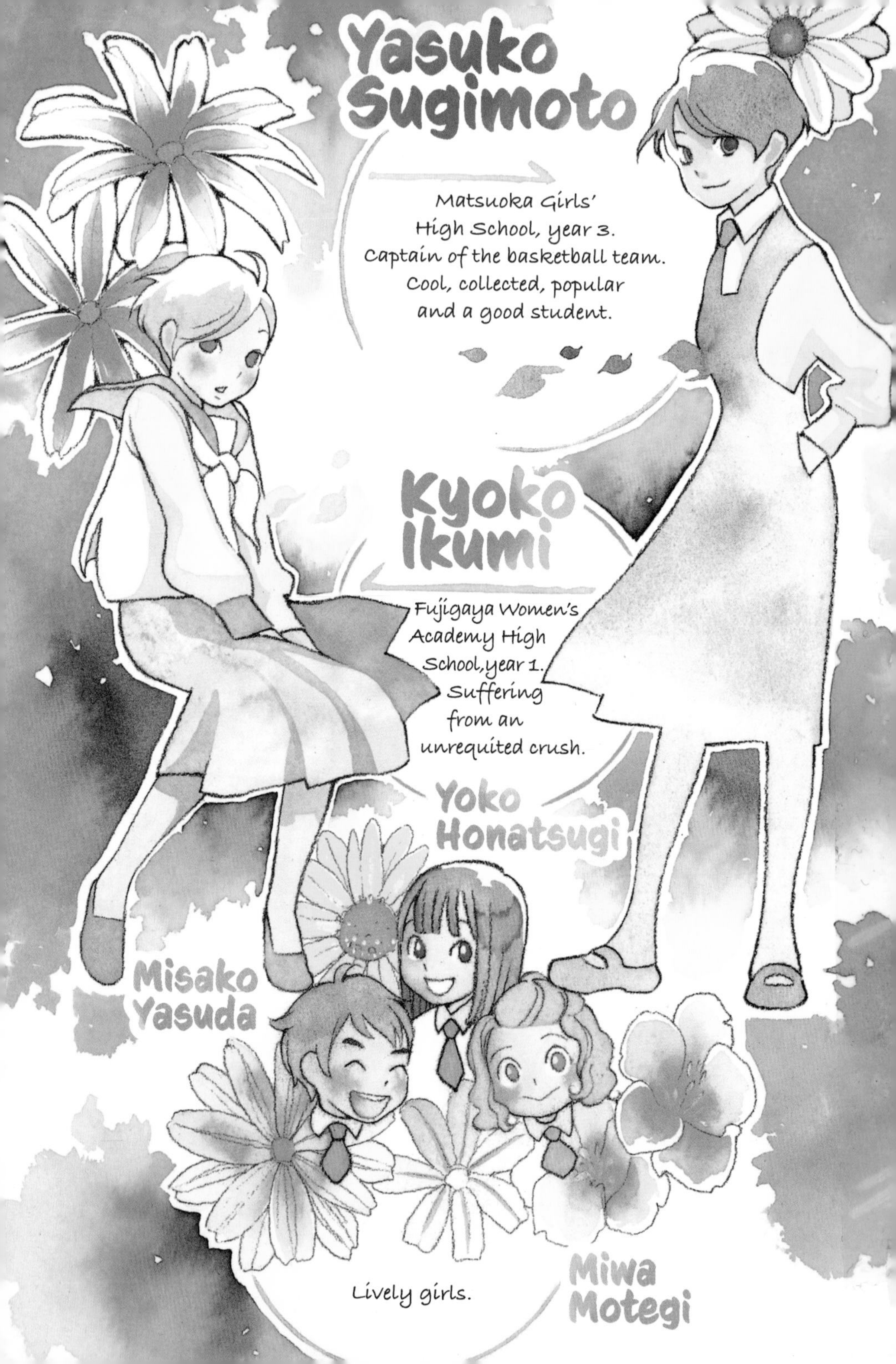
Yasuko Sugimoto
Matsuoka Girls' High School, year 3. Captain of the basketball team. Cool, collected, popular and a good student.
Kyoko Ikumi
Fujigaya Women's Academy High School,year 1. Suffering from an unrequited crush.
Yoko Honatsugi
Misako Yasuda
Miwa Motegi
Lively girls.

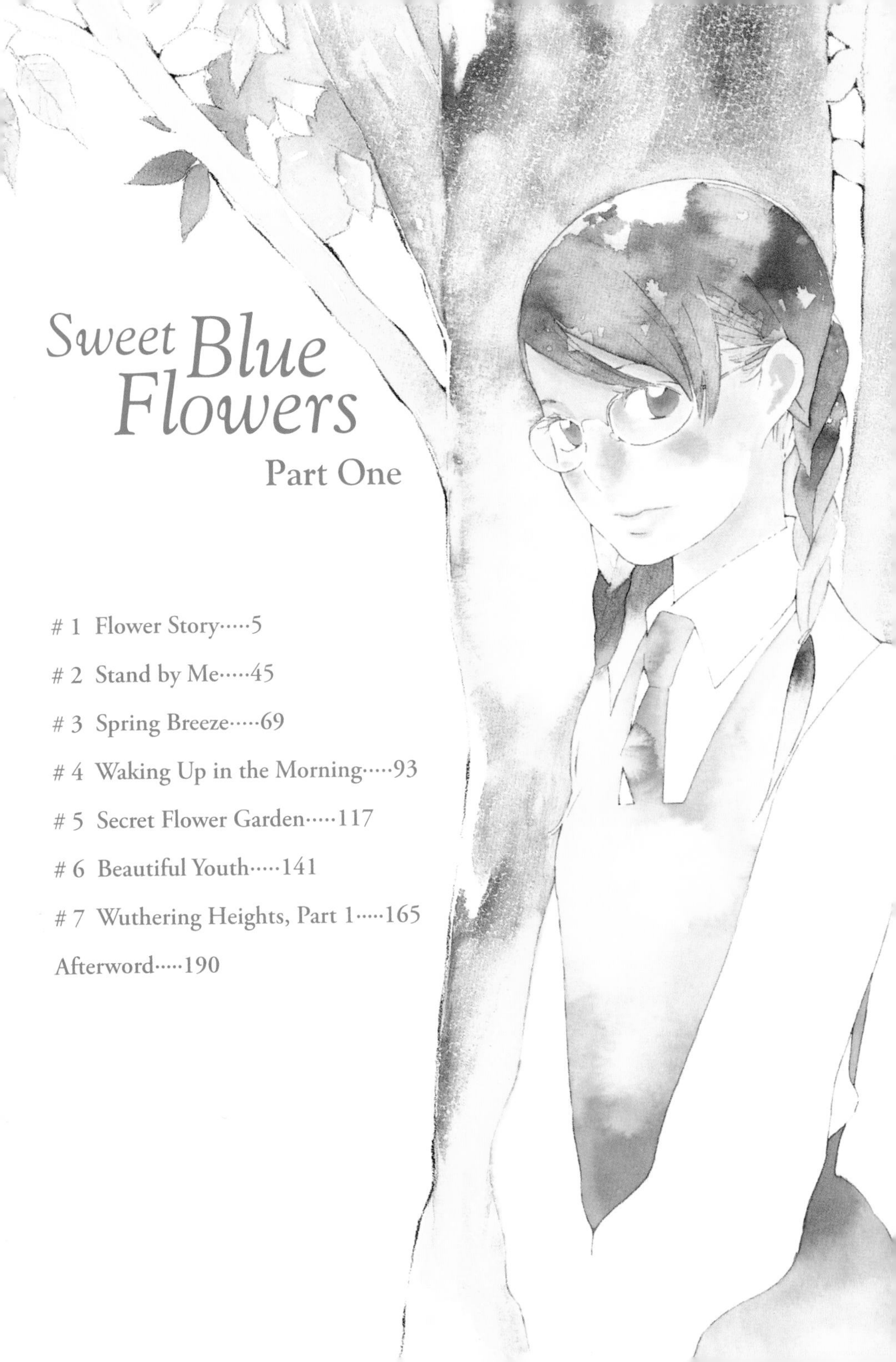

# Sweet Blue Flowers

## Part One

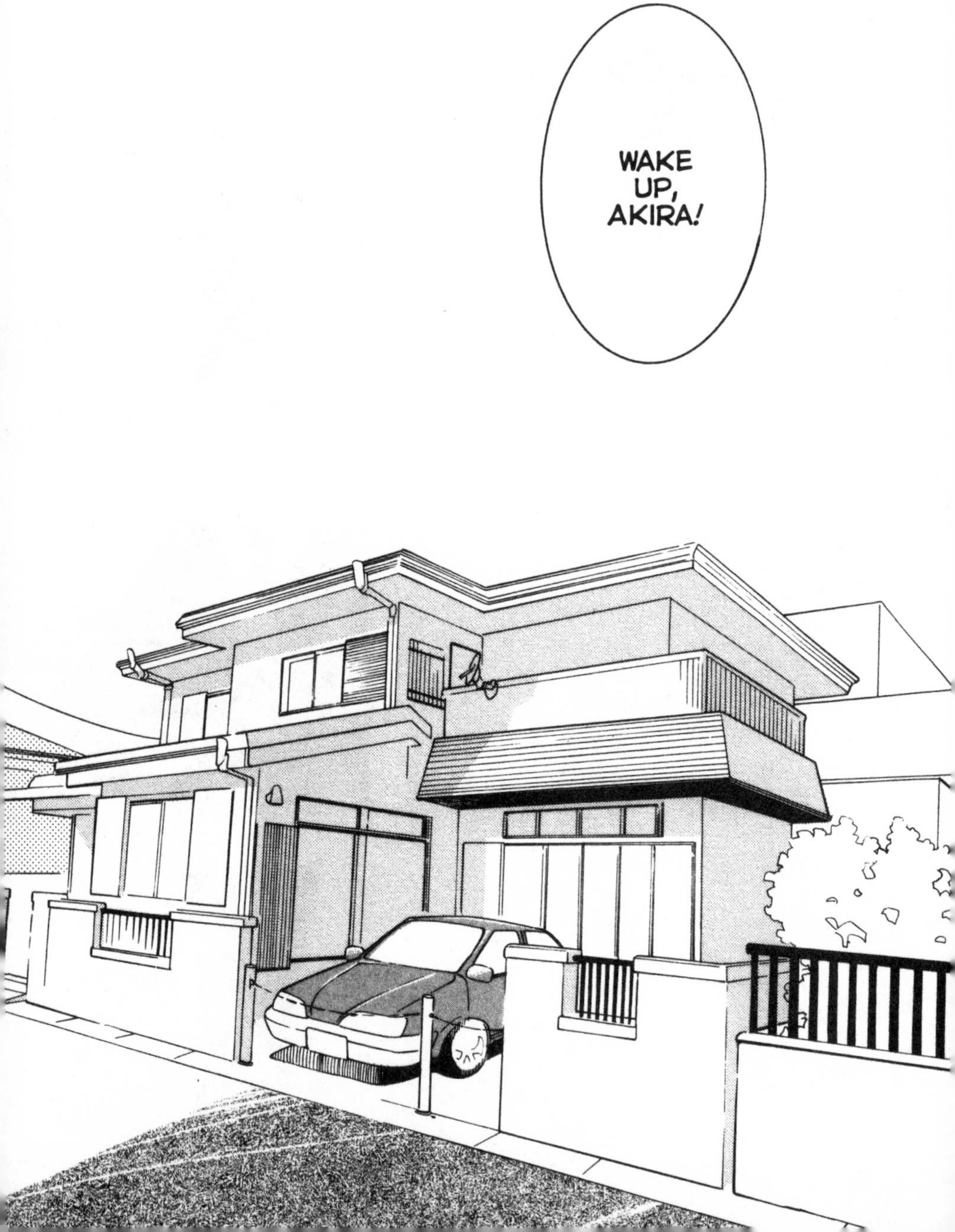
WAKE UP, AKIRA!

# Sweet *Blue Flowers*

## #1 Flower Story

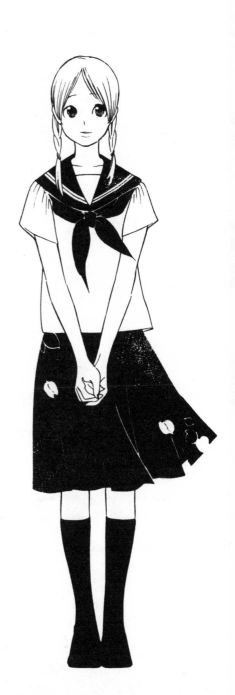

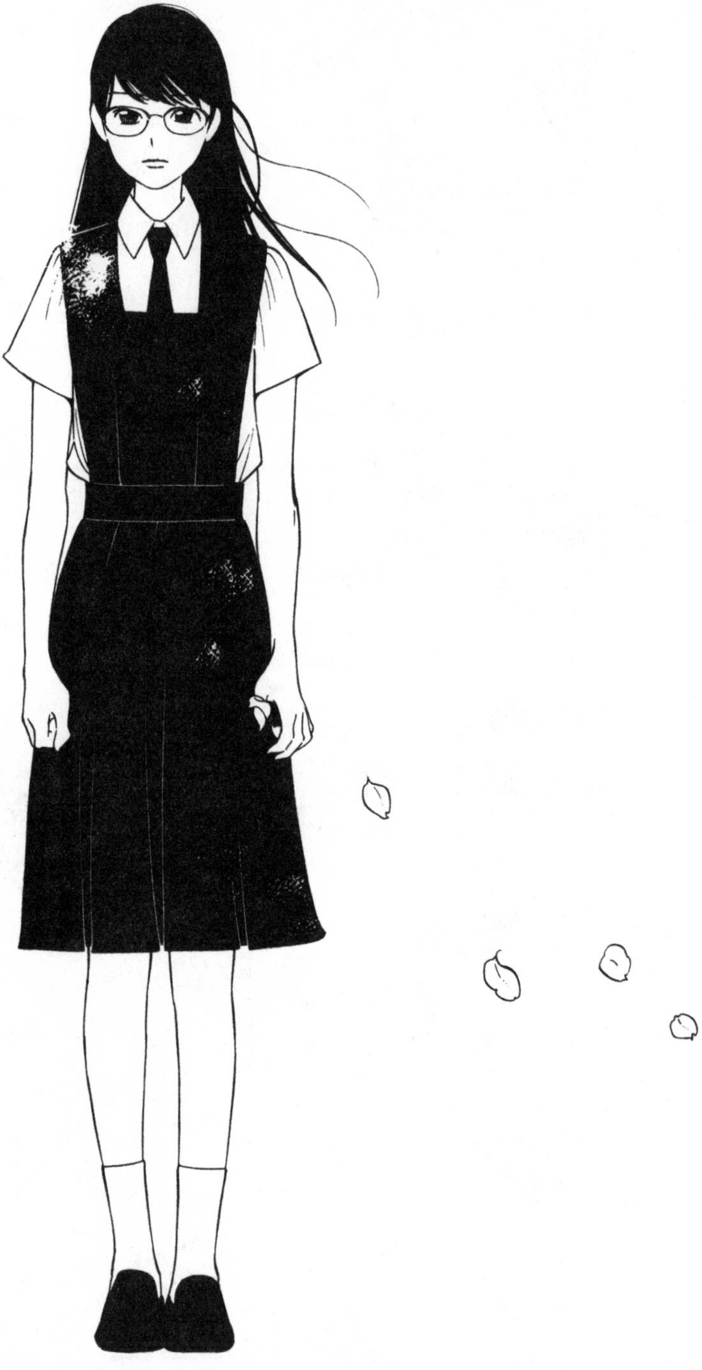

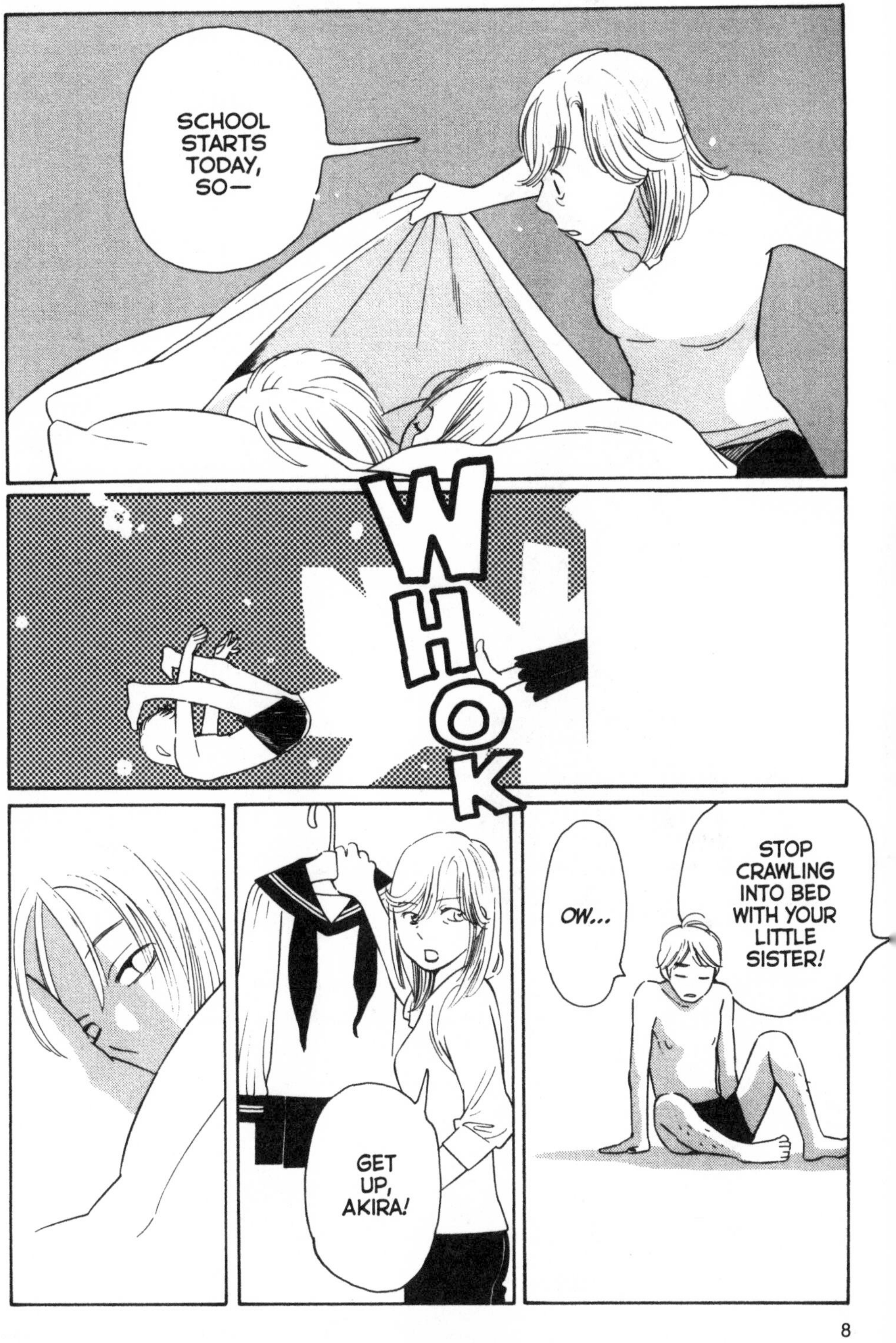
SCHOOL STARTS TODAY, SO—
WHOK
STOP CRAWLING INTO BED WITH YOUR LITTLE SISTER!
OW...
GET UP, AKIRA!

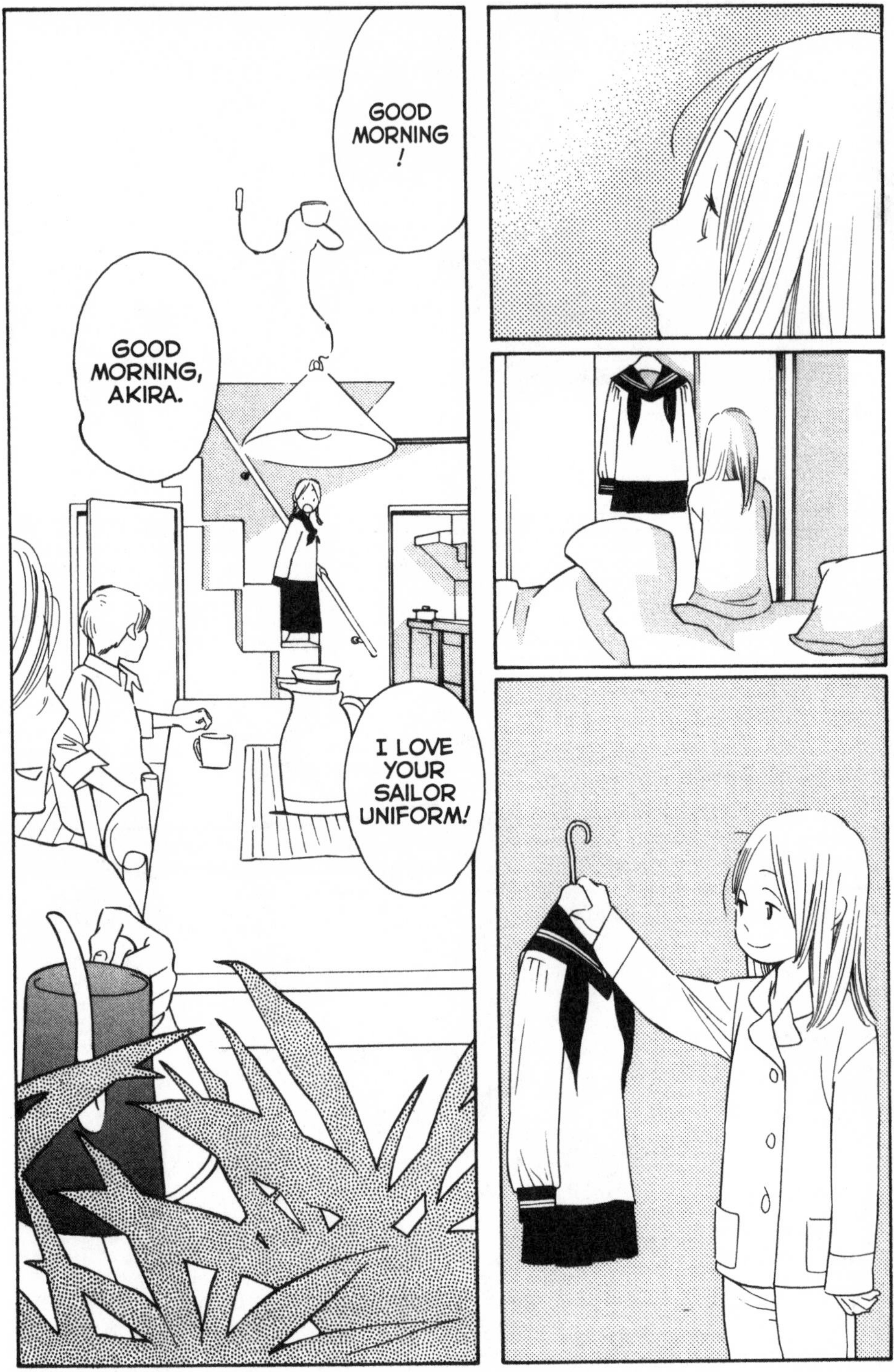
GOOD MORNING!
GOOD MORNING, AKIRA.
I LOVE YOUR SAILOR UNIFORM!

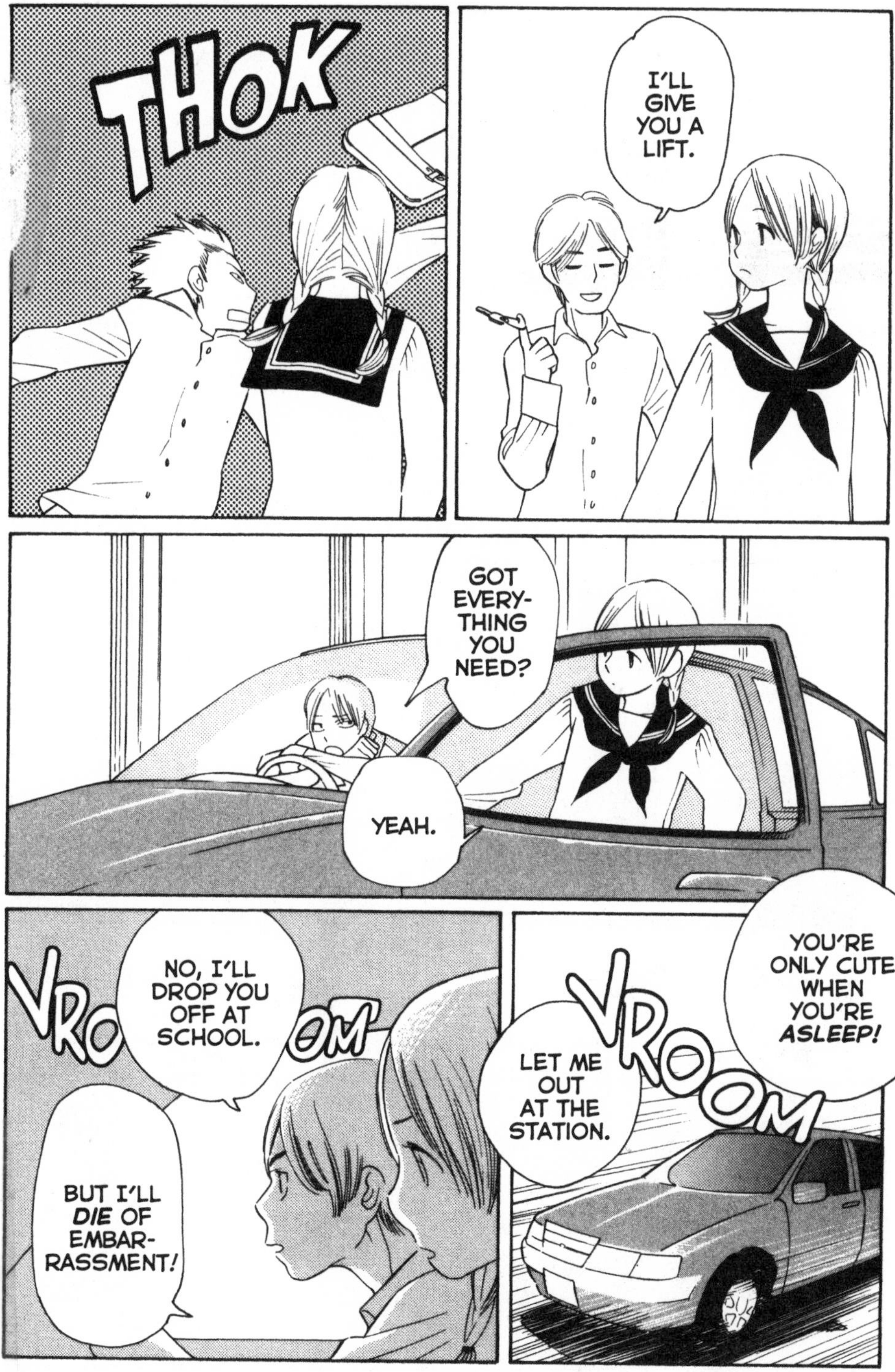
I'LL GIVE YOU A LIFT.
THOK
GOT EVERY-THING YOU NEED?
YEAH.
YOU'RE ONLY CUTE WHEN YOU'RE *ASLEEP!*
VROOM
LET ME OUT AT THE STATION.
VRO OM
NO, I'LL DROP YOU OFF AT SCHOOL.
BUT I'LL *DIE* OF EMBAR-RASSMENT!

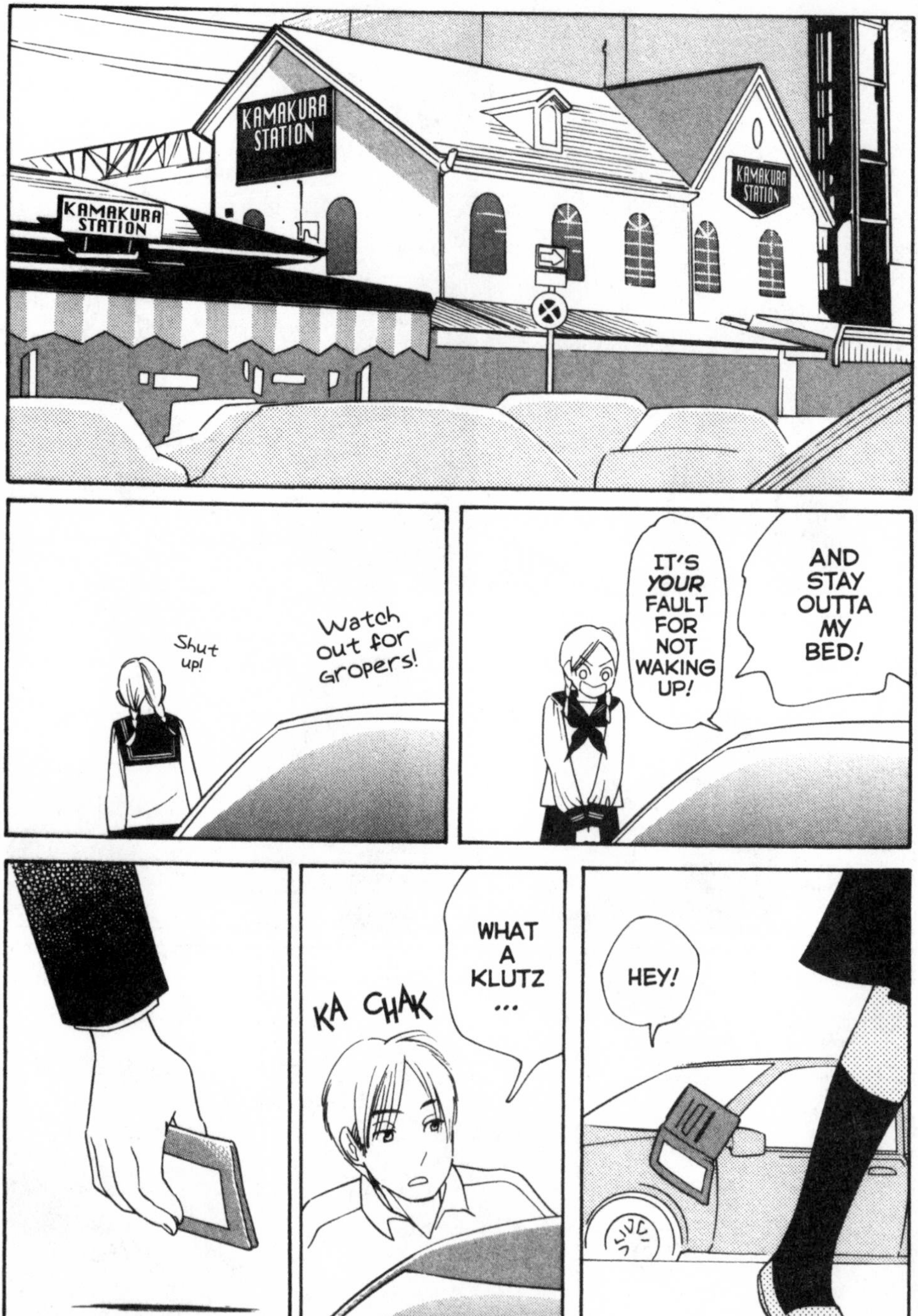
KAMAKURA STATION
KAMAKURA STATION
KAMAKURA STATION
AND STAY OUTTA MY BED!
IT'S *YOUR* FAULT FOR NOT WAKING UP!
Watch out for gropers!
Shut up!
HEY!
WHAT A KLUTZ ...
KA CHAK

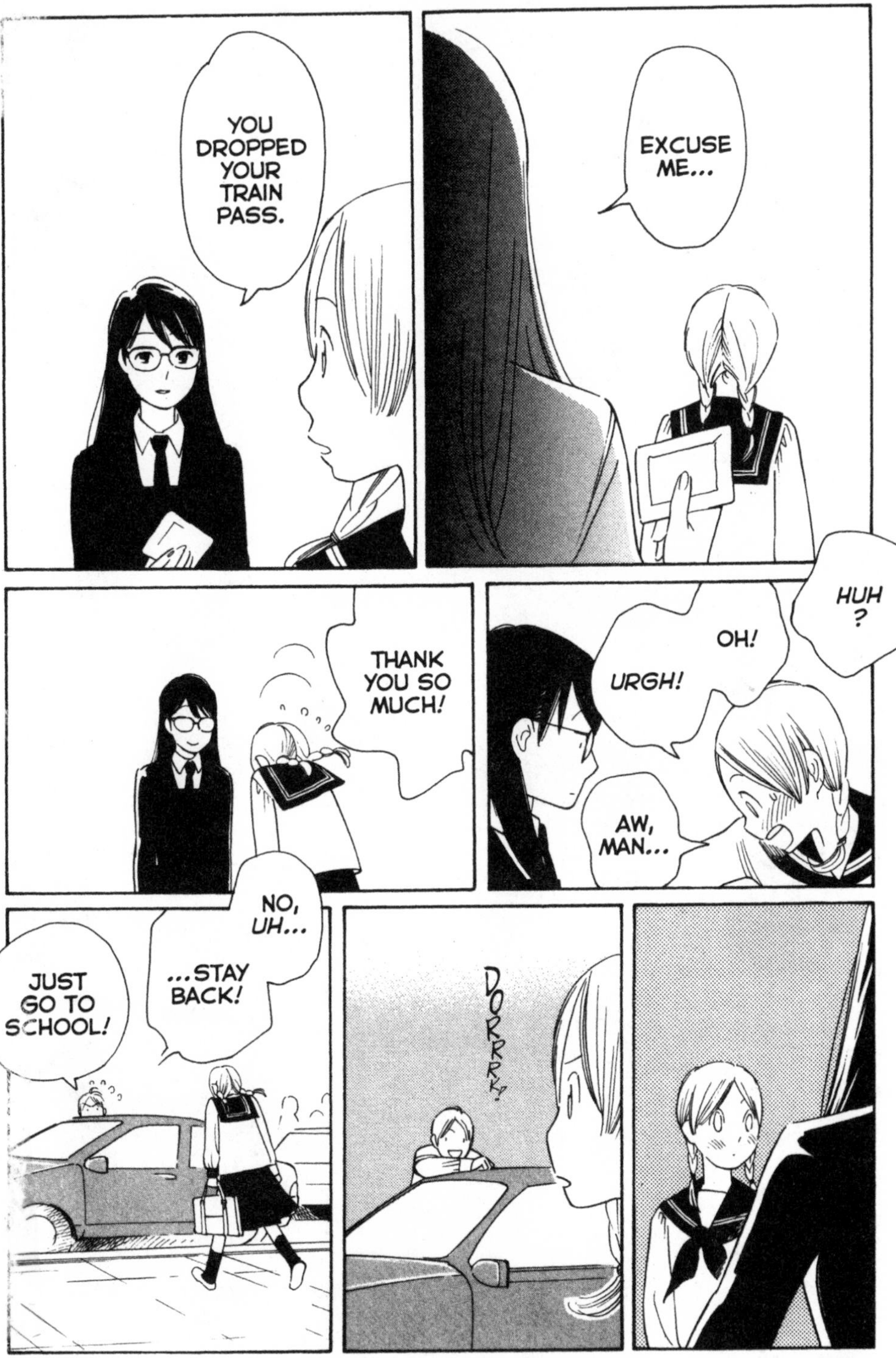
EXCUSE ME...
YOU DROPPED YOUR TRAIN PASS.
HUH?
OH!
URGH!
AW, MAN...
THANK YOU SO MUCH!
DORRRK
NO, UH...
...STAY BACK!
JUST GO TO SCHOOL!

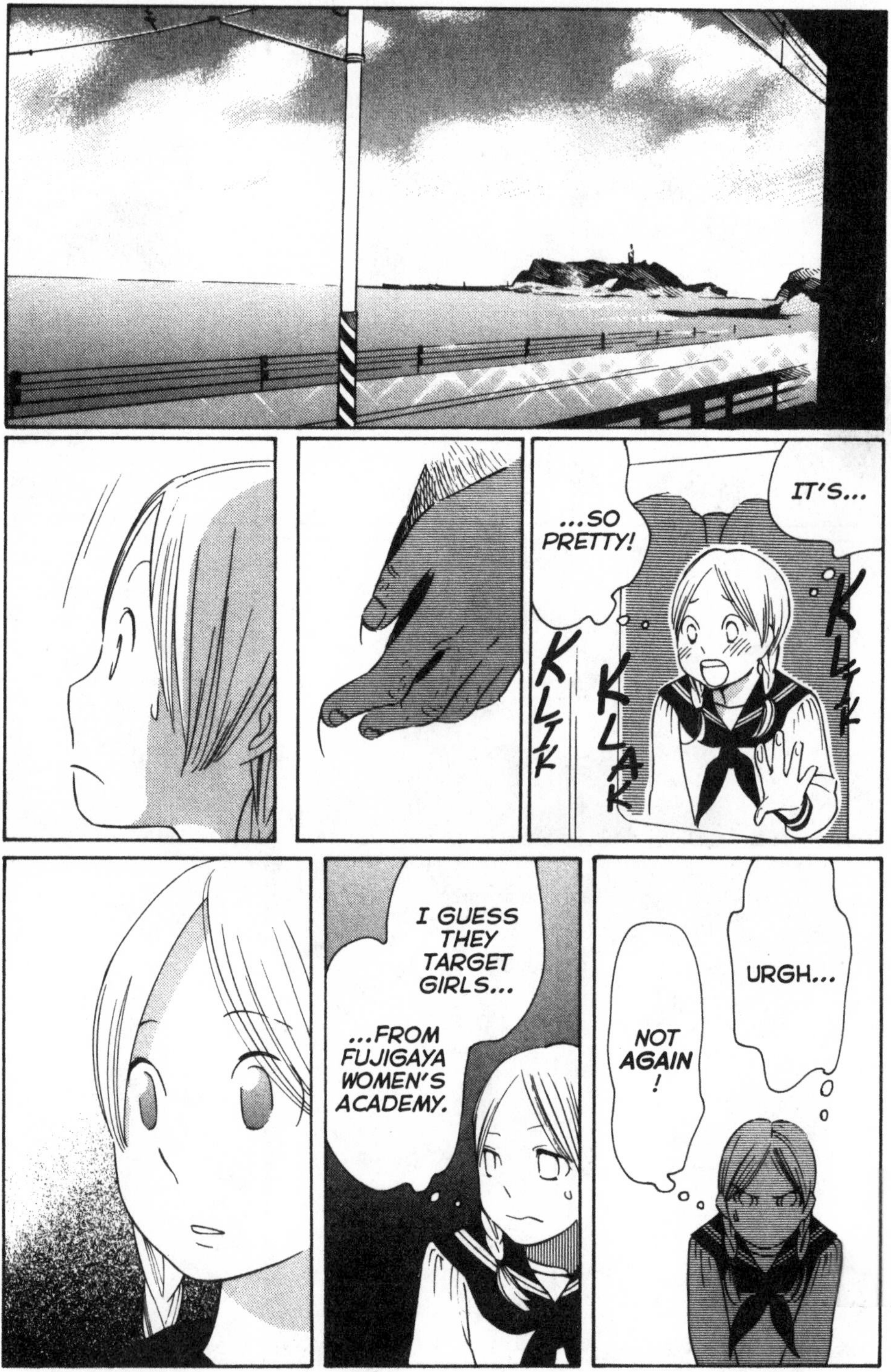
IT'S...
...SO PRETTY!
KLIK
KLAK
KLIK
URGH...
NOT AGAIN!
I GUESS THEY TARGET GIRLS...
...FROM FUJIGAYA WOMEN'S ACADEMY.

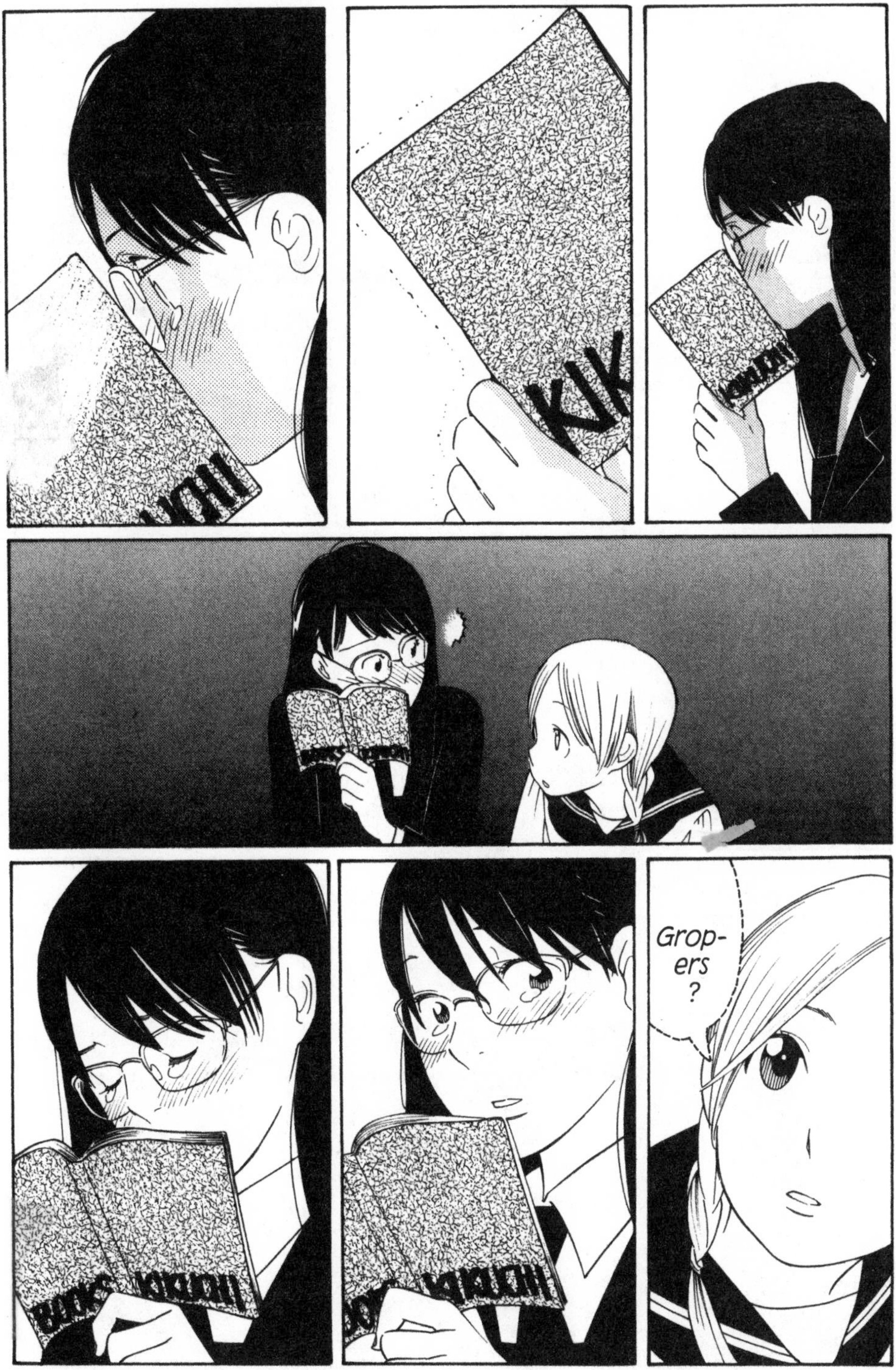
Grop-ers?

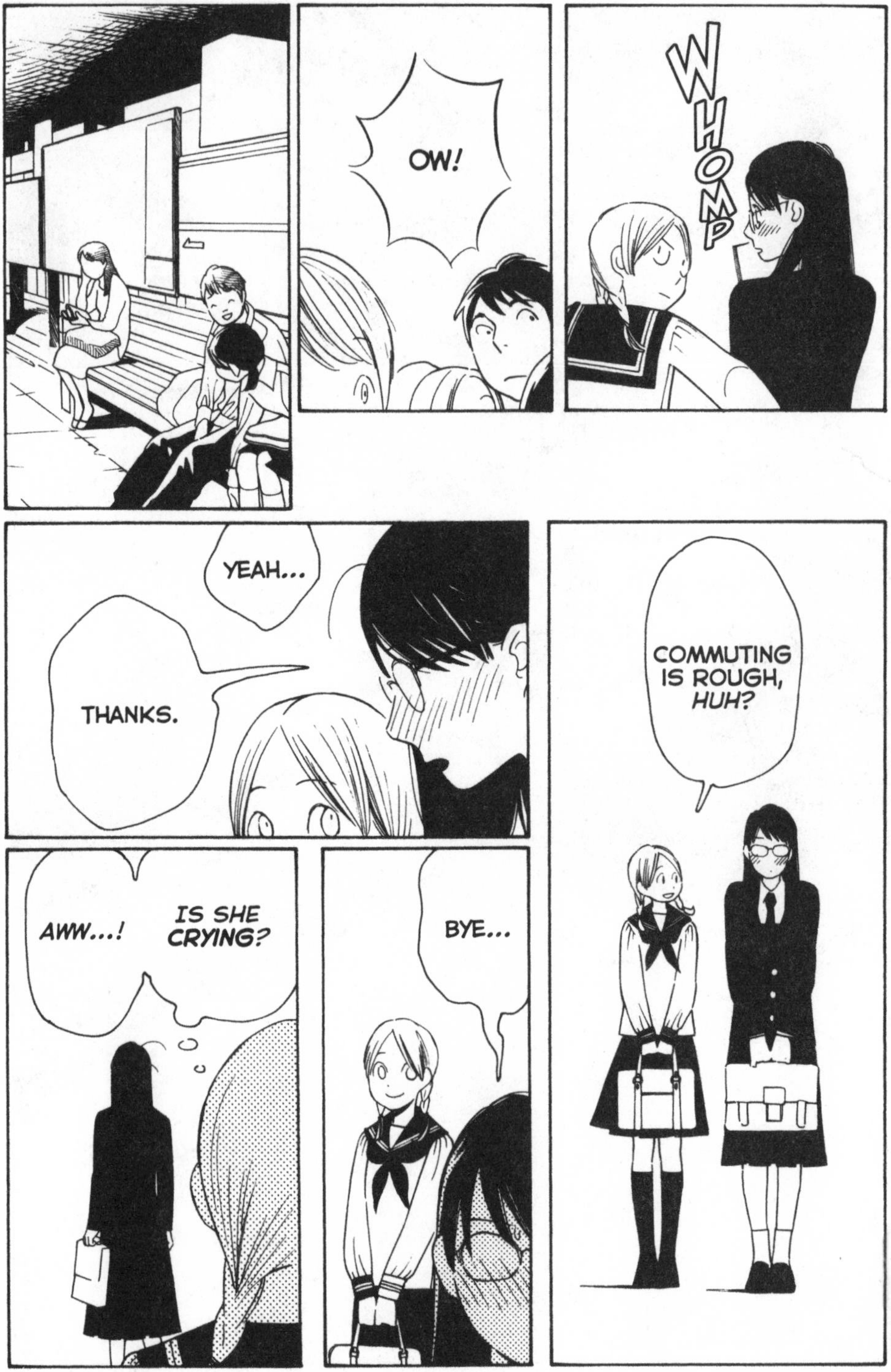
WHOMP
OW!
COMMUTING IS ROUGH, HUH?
YEAH...
THANKS.
BYE...
AWW...! IS SHE CRYING?

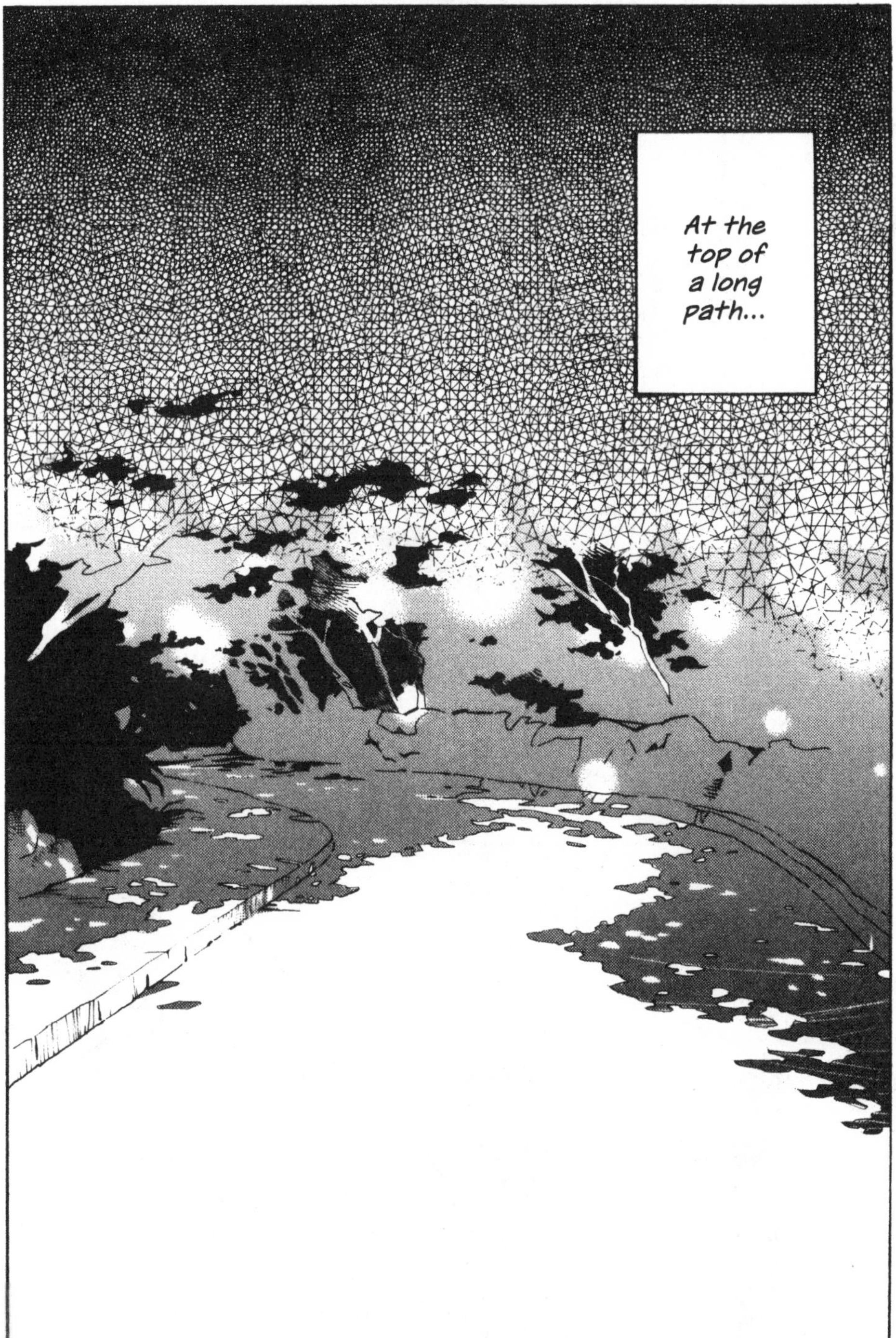
At the top of a long path...

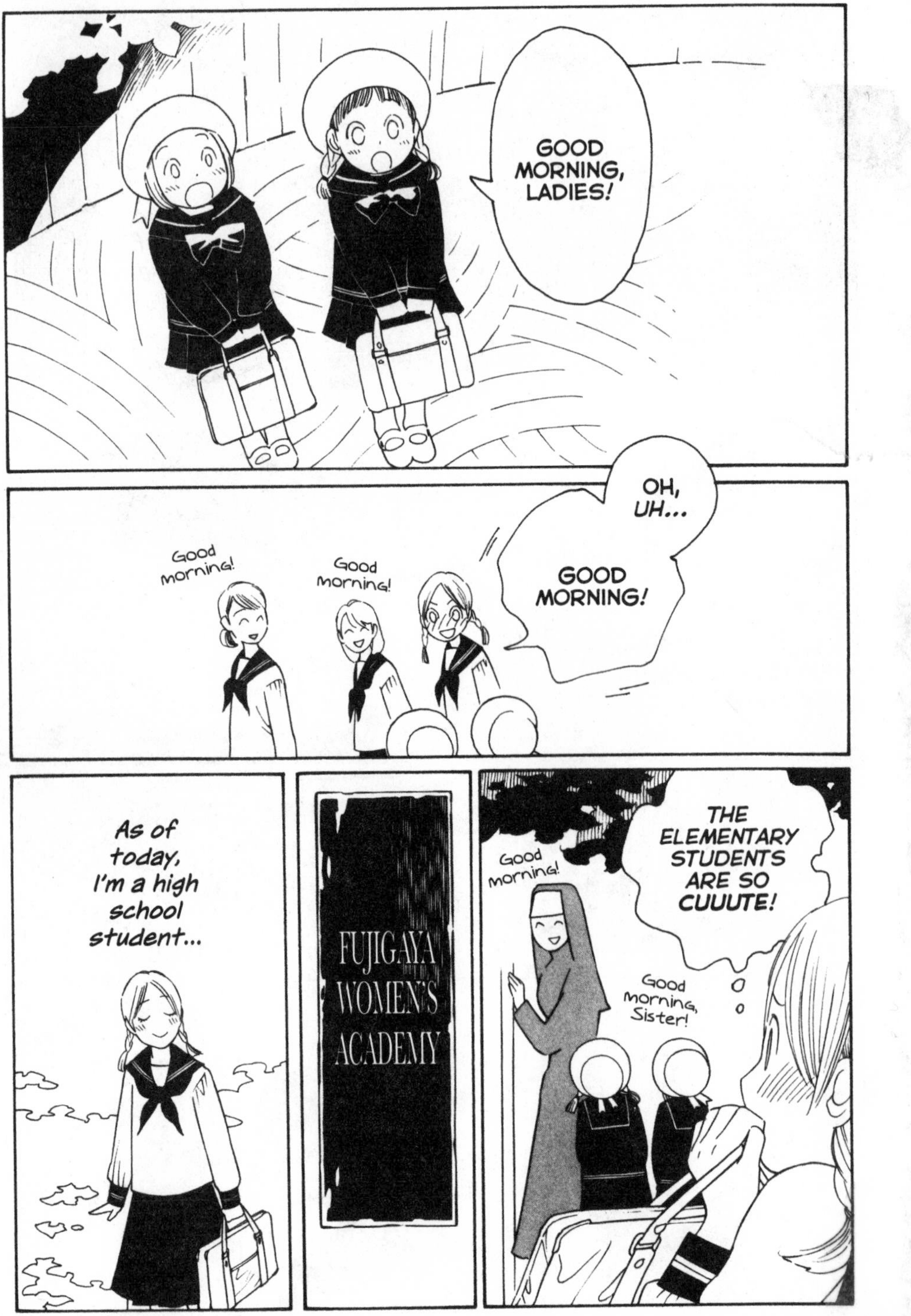
GOOD MORNING, LADIES!
OH, UH... GOOD MORNING!
Good morning!
Good morning!
THE ELEMENTARY STUDENTS ARE SO CUUUTE!
Good morning!
Good morning, Sister!
FUJIGAYA WOMEN'S ACADEMY
As of today, I'm a high school student...

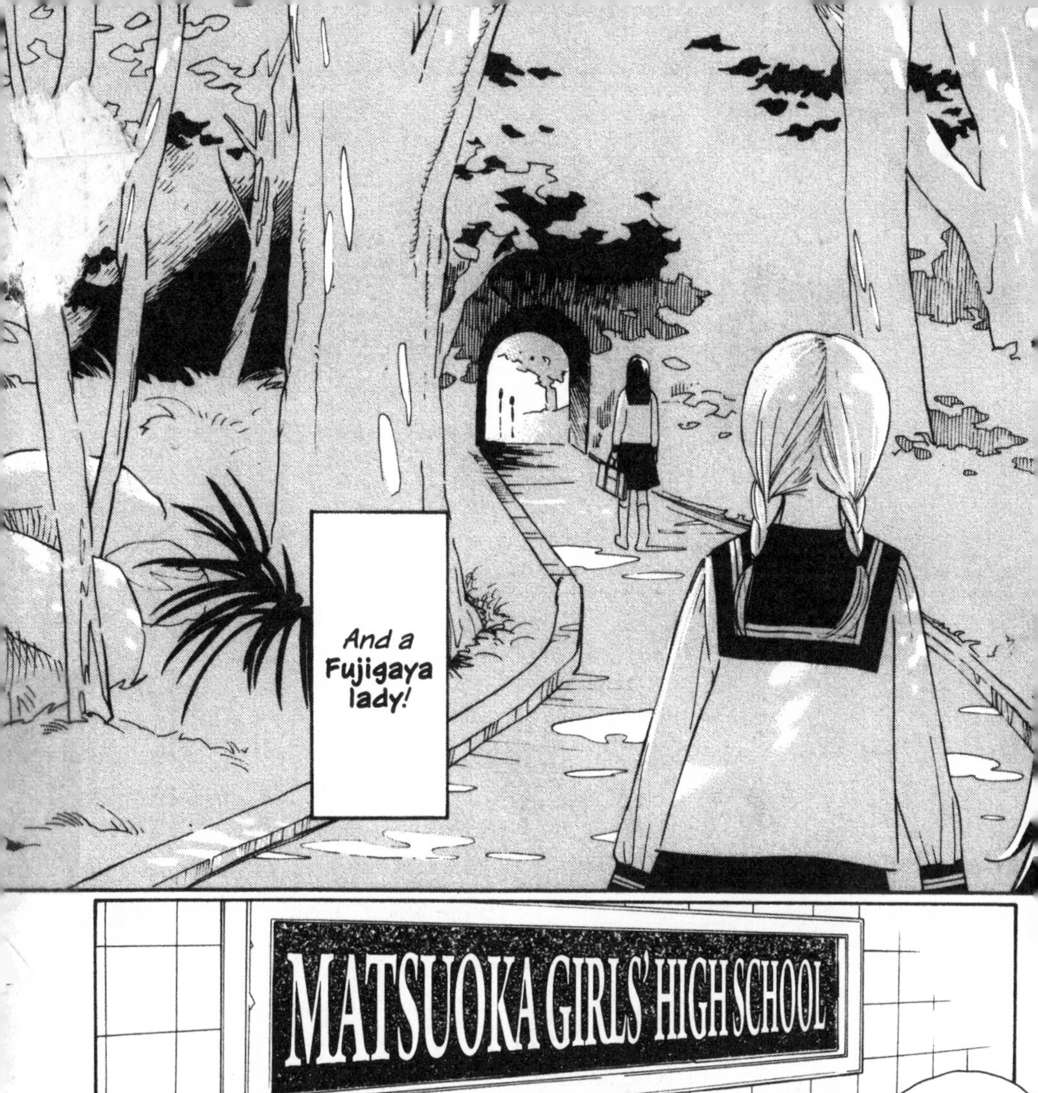
And a Fujigaya lady!

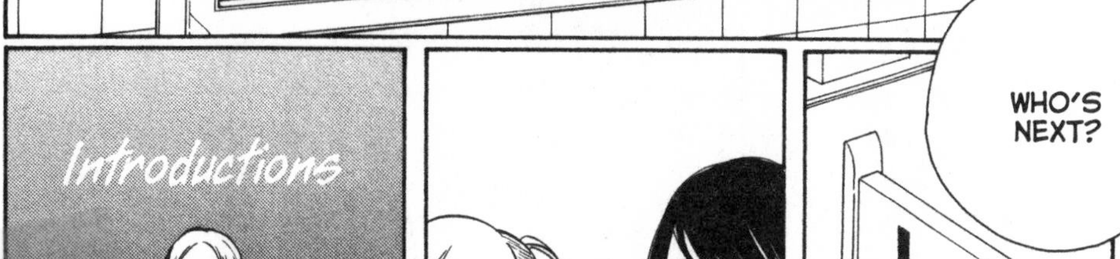
MATSUOKA GIRLS' HIGH SCHOOL

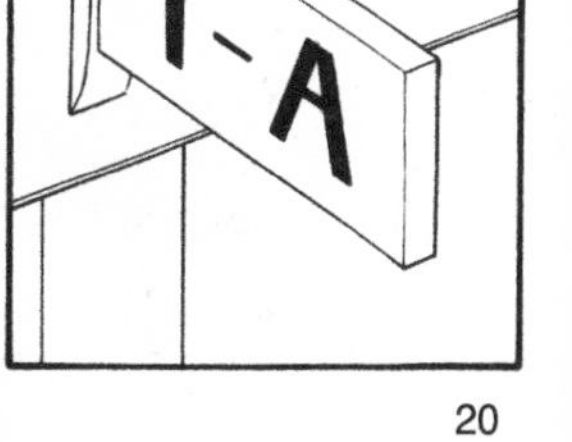
WHO'S NEXT?
I-A

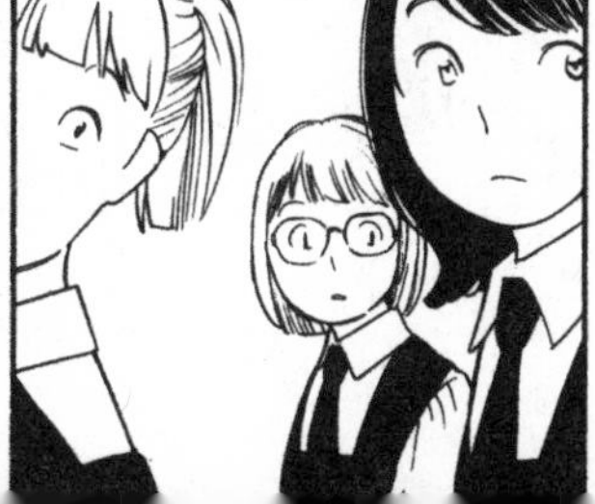

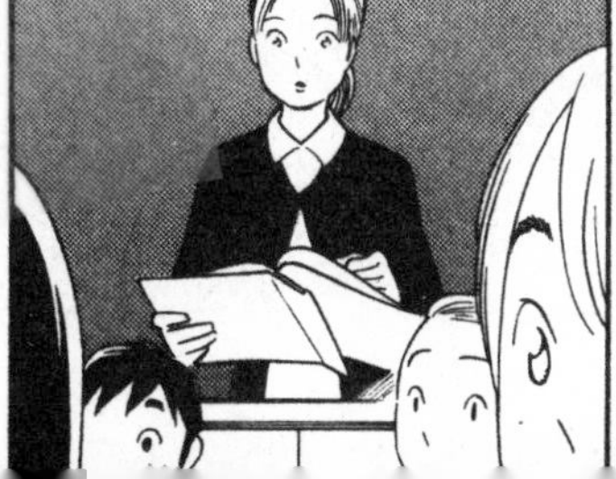
Introductions

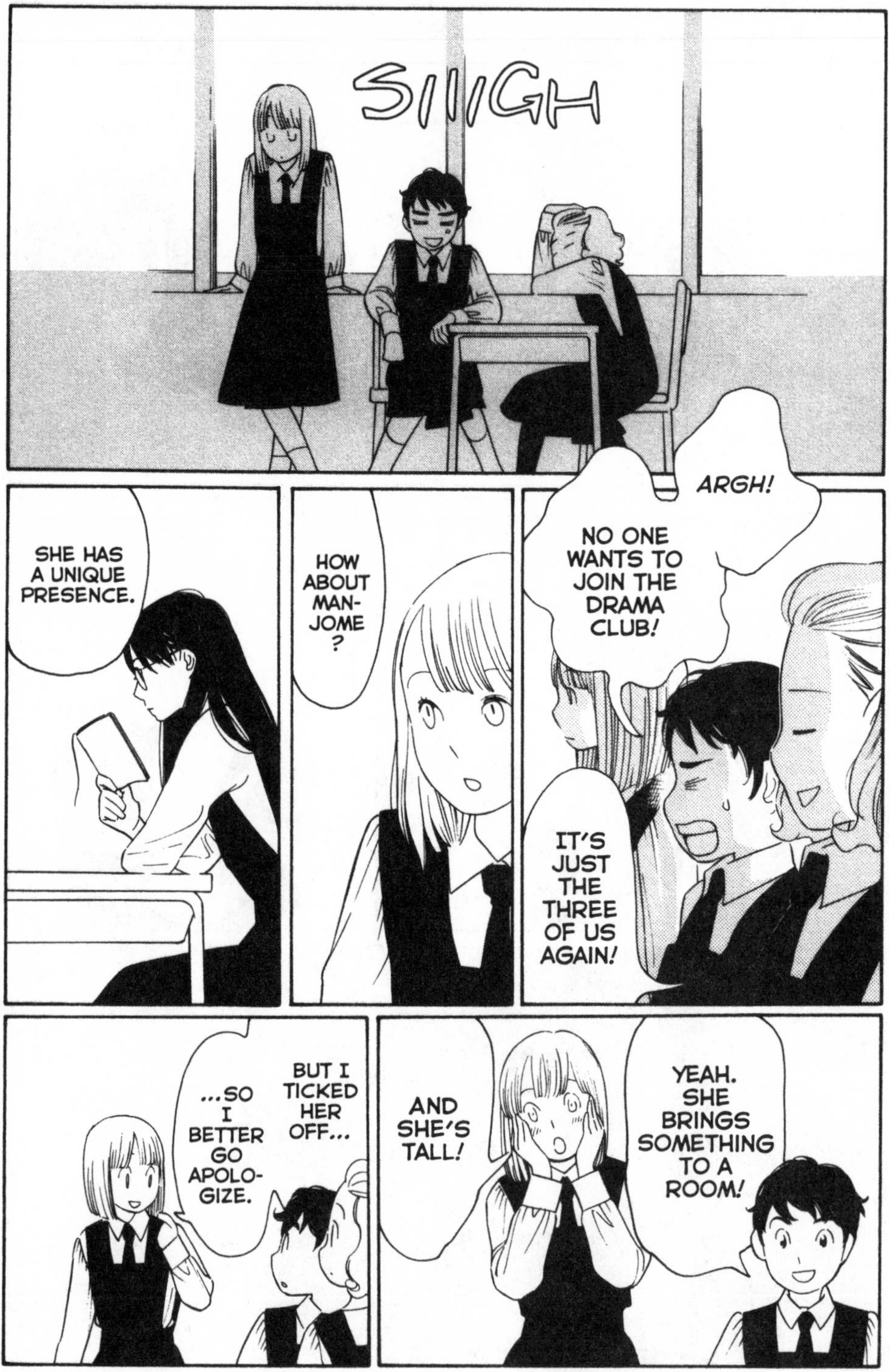
SIIIGH
ARGH!
NO ONE WANTS TO JOIN THE DRAMA CLUB!
IT'S JUST THE THREE OF US AGAIN!
HOW ABOUT MAN-JOME?
SHE HAS A UNIQUE PRESENCE.
YEAH. SHE BRINGS SOMETHING TO A ROOM!
AND SHE'S TALL!
BUT I TICKED HER OFF...
...SO I BETTER GO APOLO-GIZE.

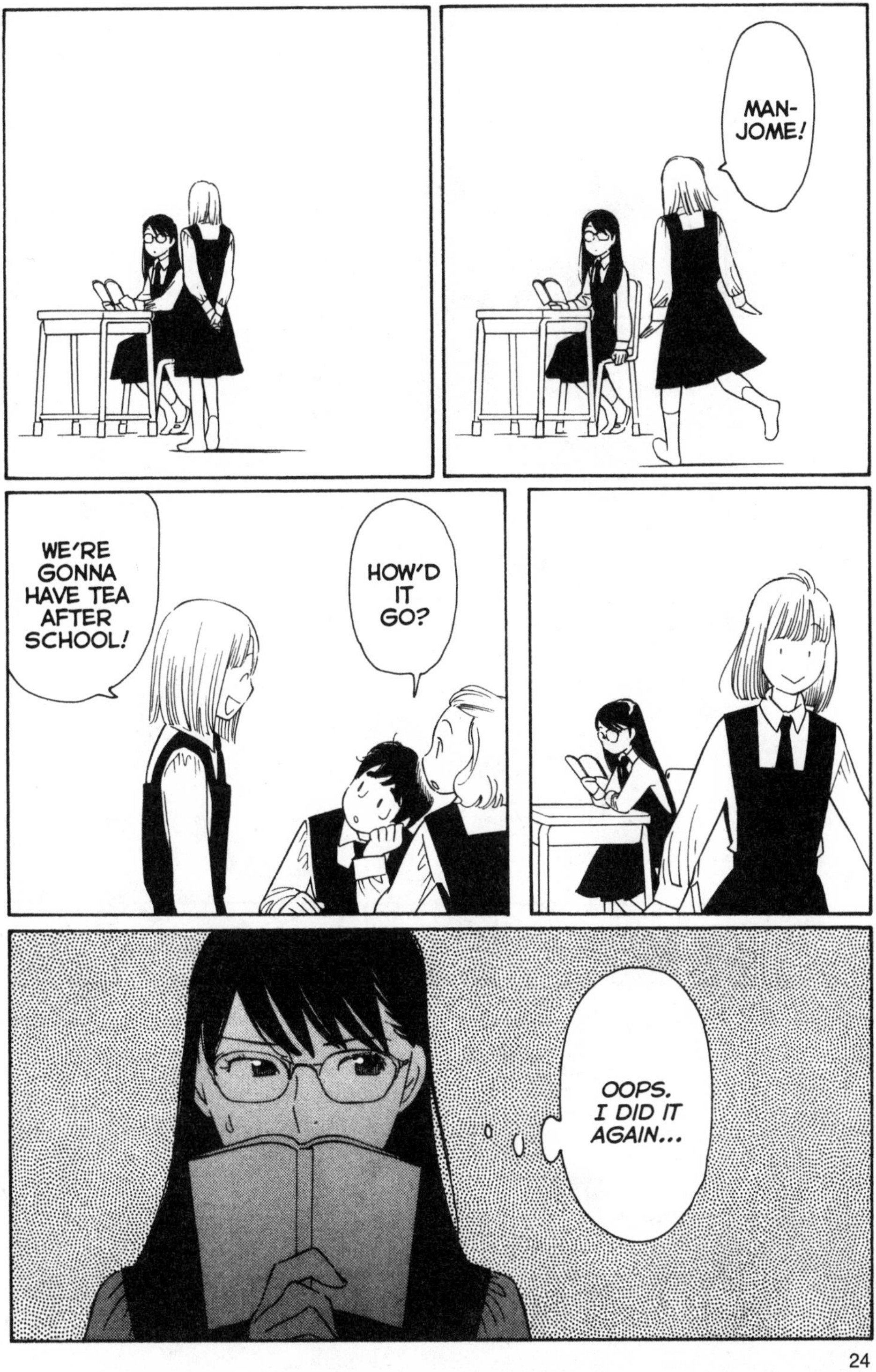
MAN-
JOME!
HOW'D
IT
GO?
WE'RE
GONNA
HAVE TEA
AFTER
SCHOOL!
OOPS.
I DID IT
AGAIN...

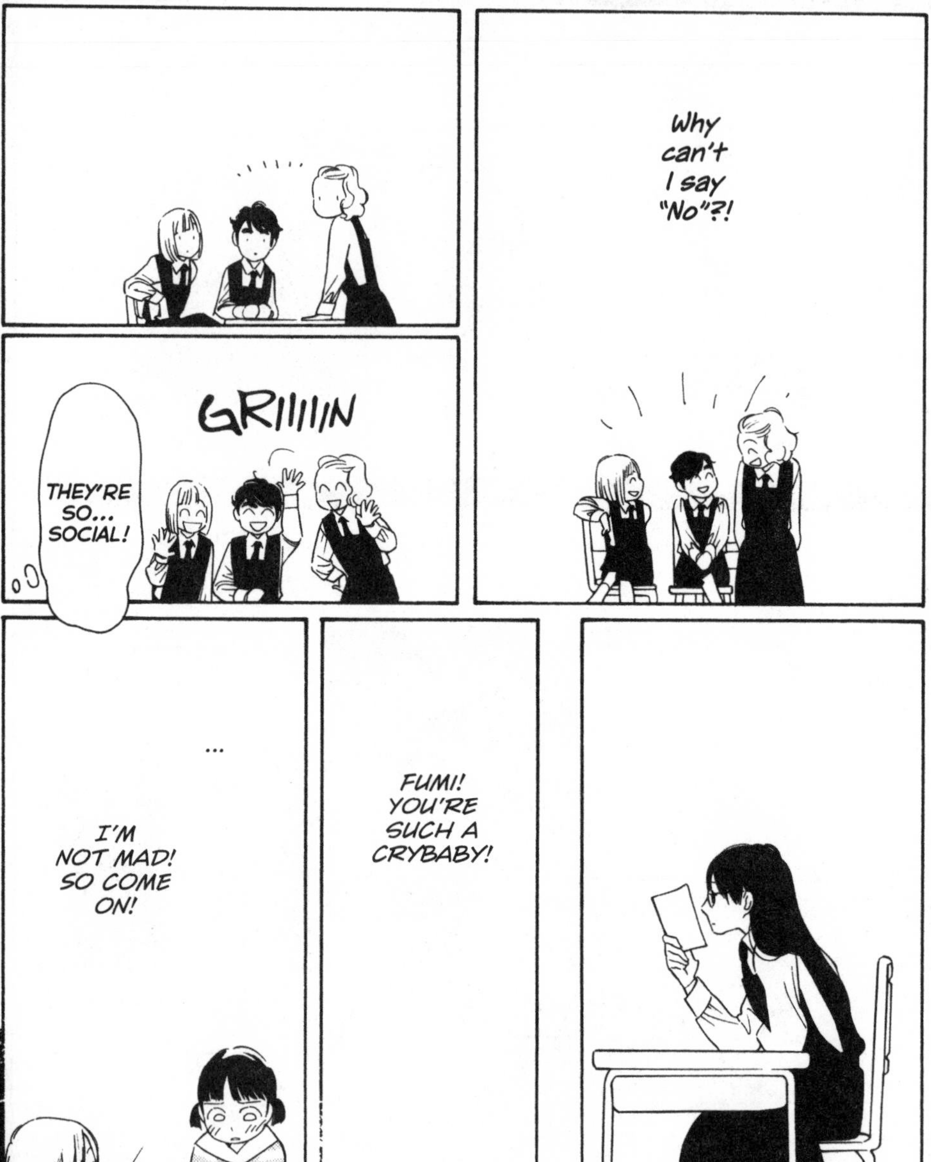
Why can't I say "No"?!
GRIIIIIN
THEY'RE SO... SOCIAL!
FUMI! YOU'RE SUCH A CRYBABY!
...
I'M NOT MAD! SO COME ON!

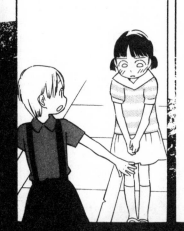

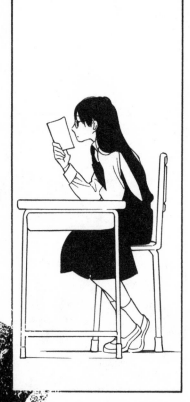

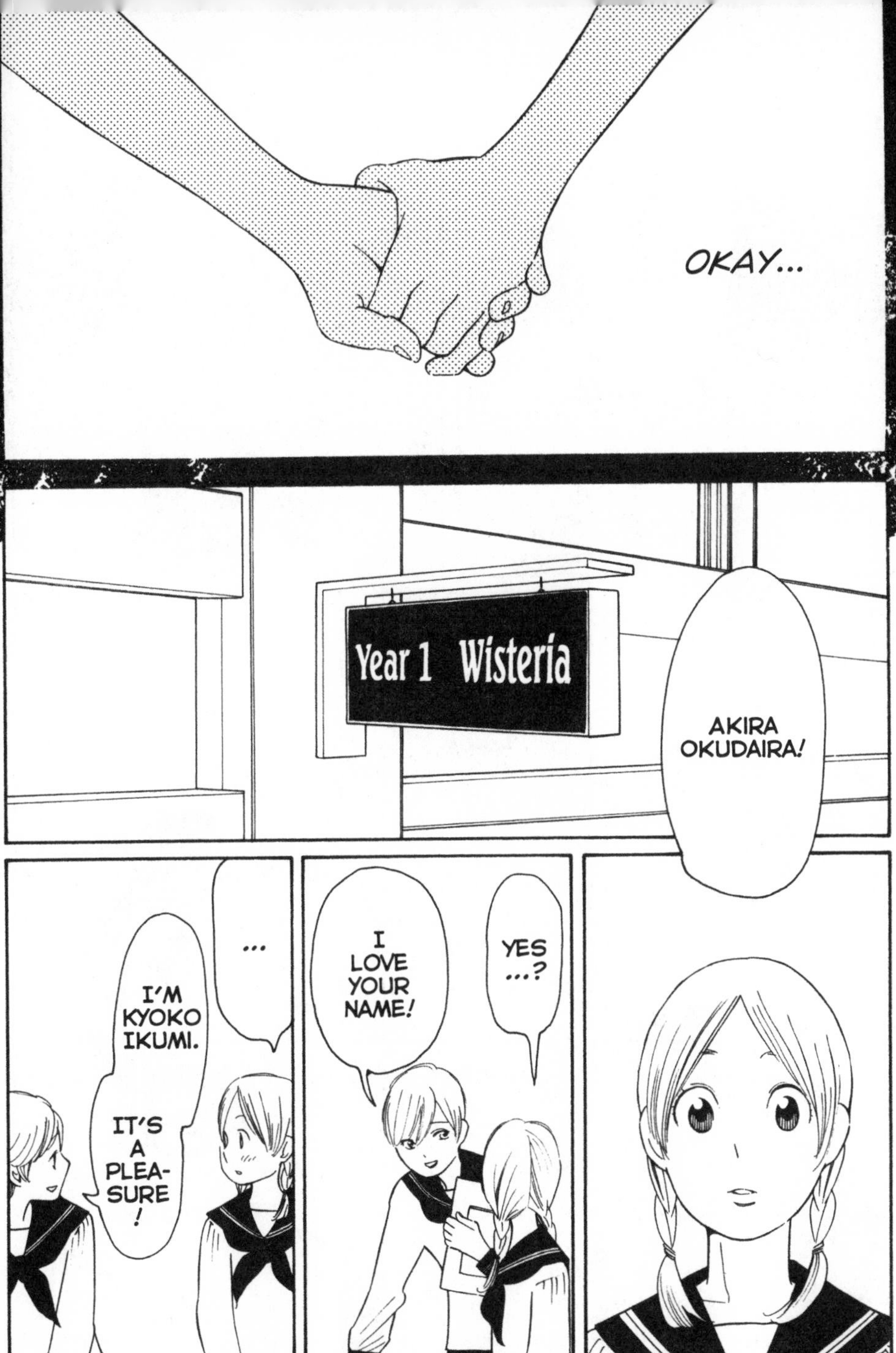
OKAY...
Year 1 Wisteria
AKIRA OKUDAIRA!
YES ...?
I LOVE YOUR NAME!
...
I'M KYOKO IKUMI.
IT'S A PLEASURE!

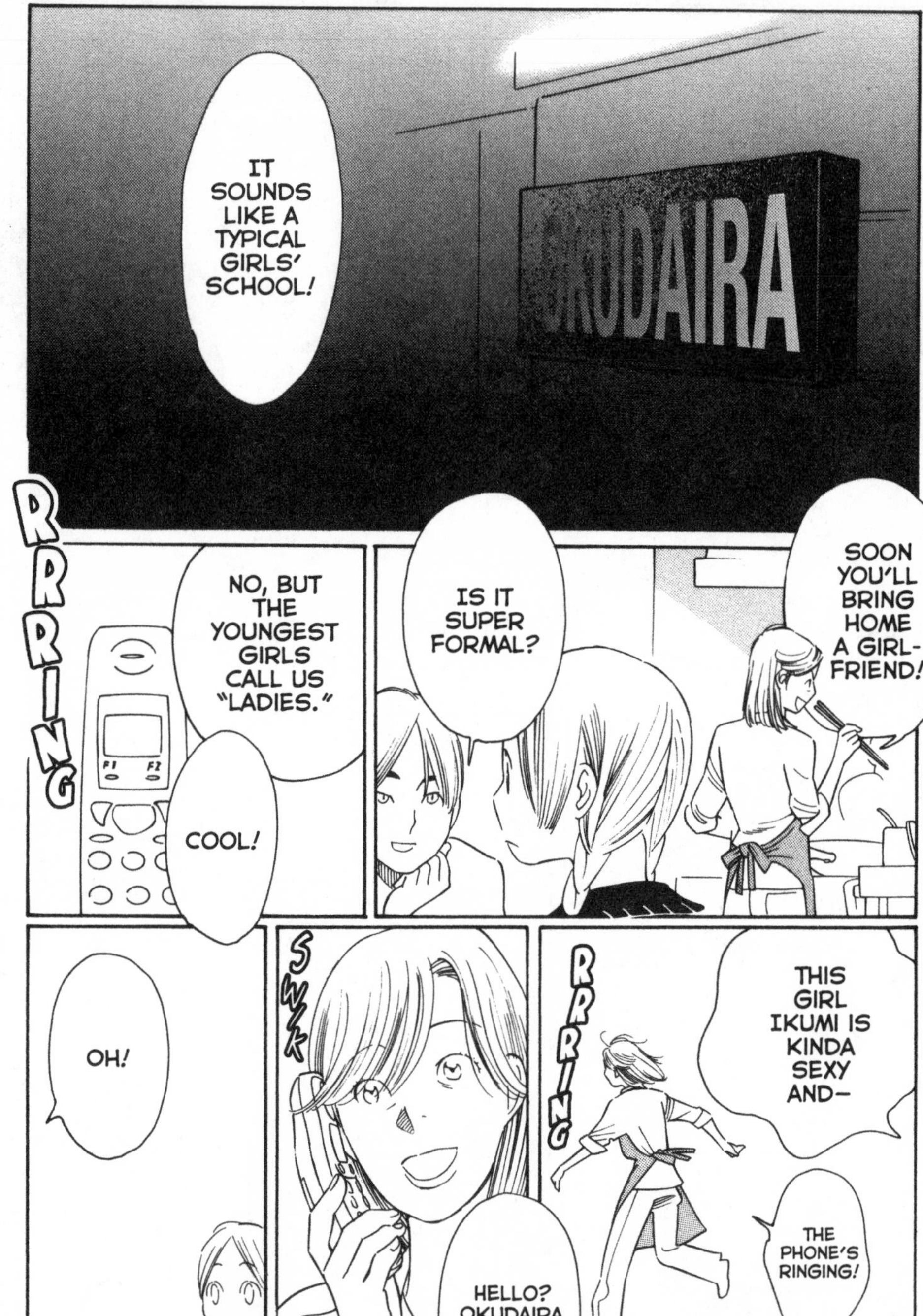
IT SOUNDS LIKE A TYPICAL GIRLS' SCHOOL!
OKUDAIRA
SOON YOU'LL BRING HOME A GIRL-FRIEND!
IS IT SUPER FORMAL?
NO, BUT THE YOUNGEST GIRLS CALL US "LADIES."
COOL!
RRRING
THIS GIRL IKUMI IS KINDA SEXY AND—
RRRING
THE PHONE'S RINGING!
SWK
HELLO? OKUDAIRA RESIDENCE.
OH!

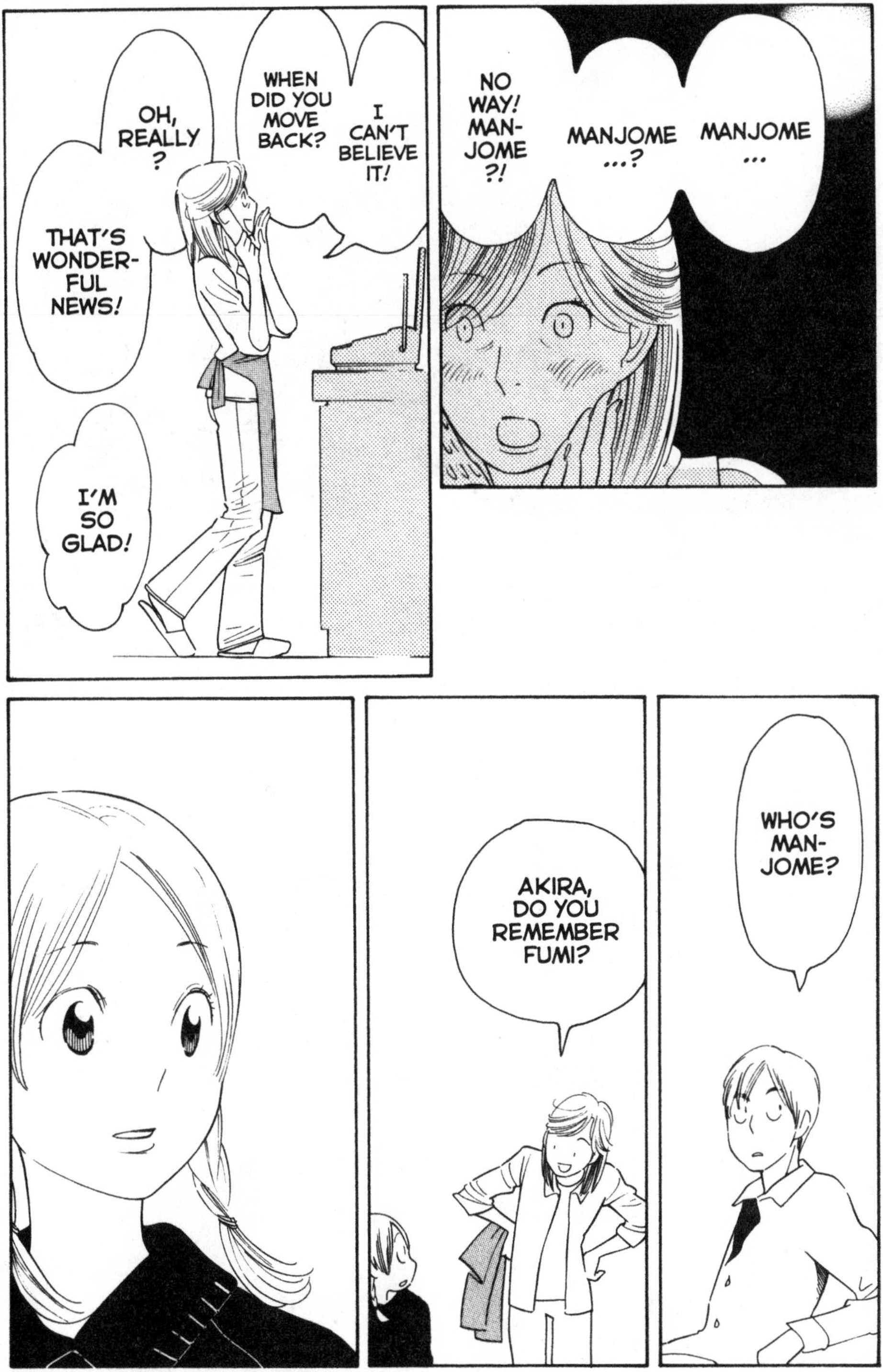
MANJOME ...
MANJOME ...?
NO WAY! MANJOME ?!
I CAN'T BELIEVE IT!
WHEN DID YOU MOVE BACK?
OH, REALLY?
THAT'S WONDERFUL NEWS!
I'M SO GLAD!
WHO'S MANJOME?
AKIRA, DO YOU REMEMBER FUMI?

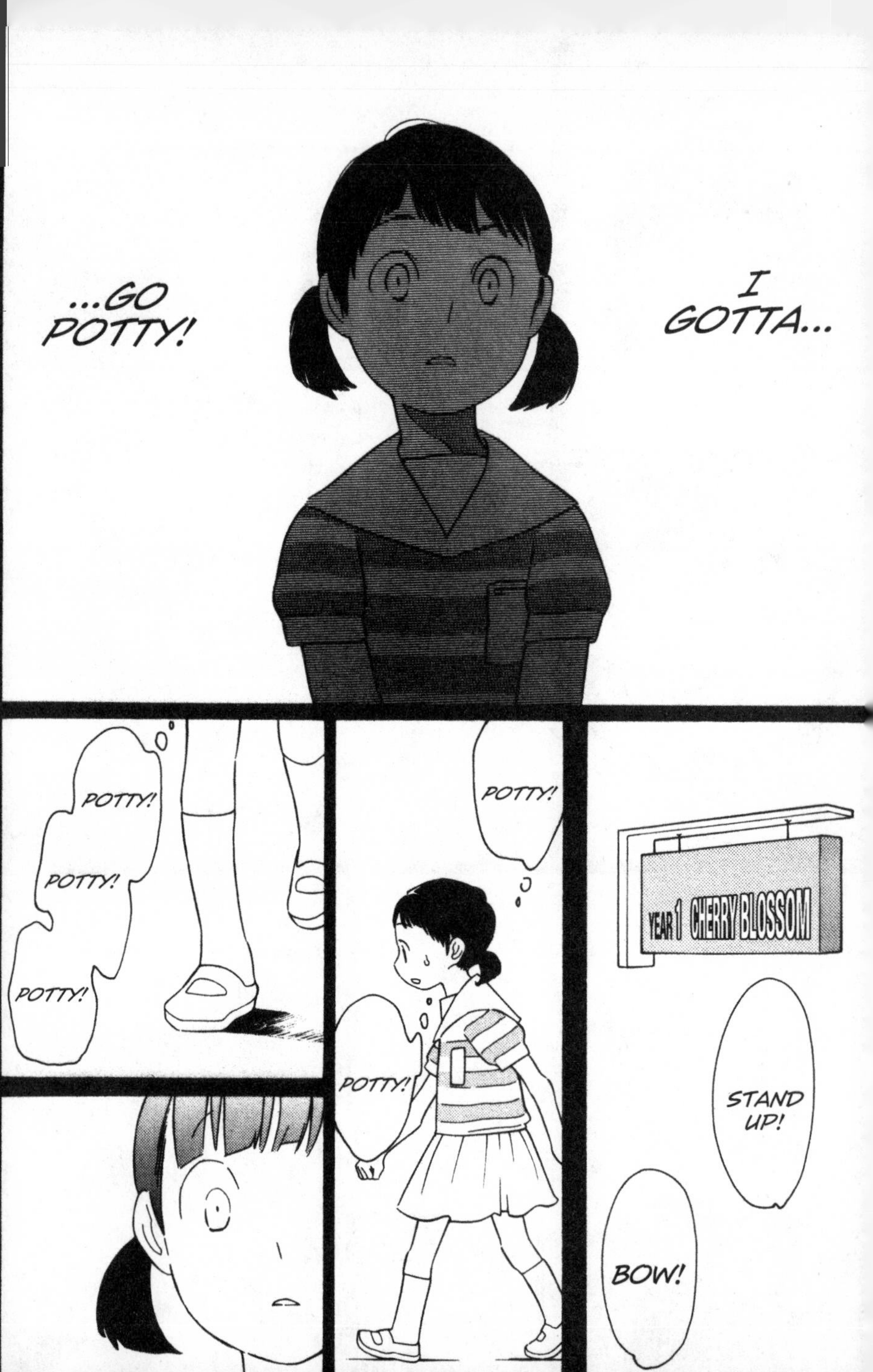
I GOTTA...
...GO POTTY!
YEAR 1 CHERRY BLOSSOM
STAND UP!
BOW!
POTTY!
POTTY!
POTTY!
POTTY!
POTTY!

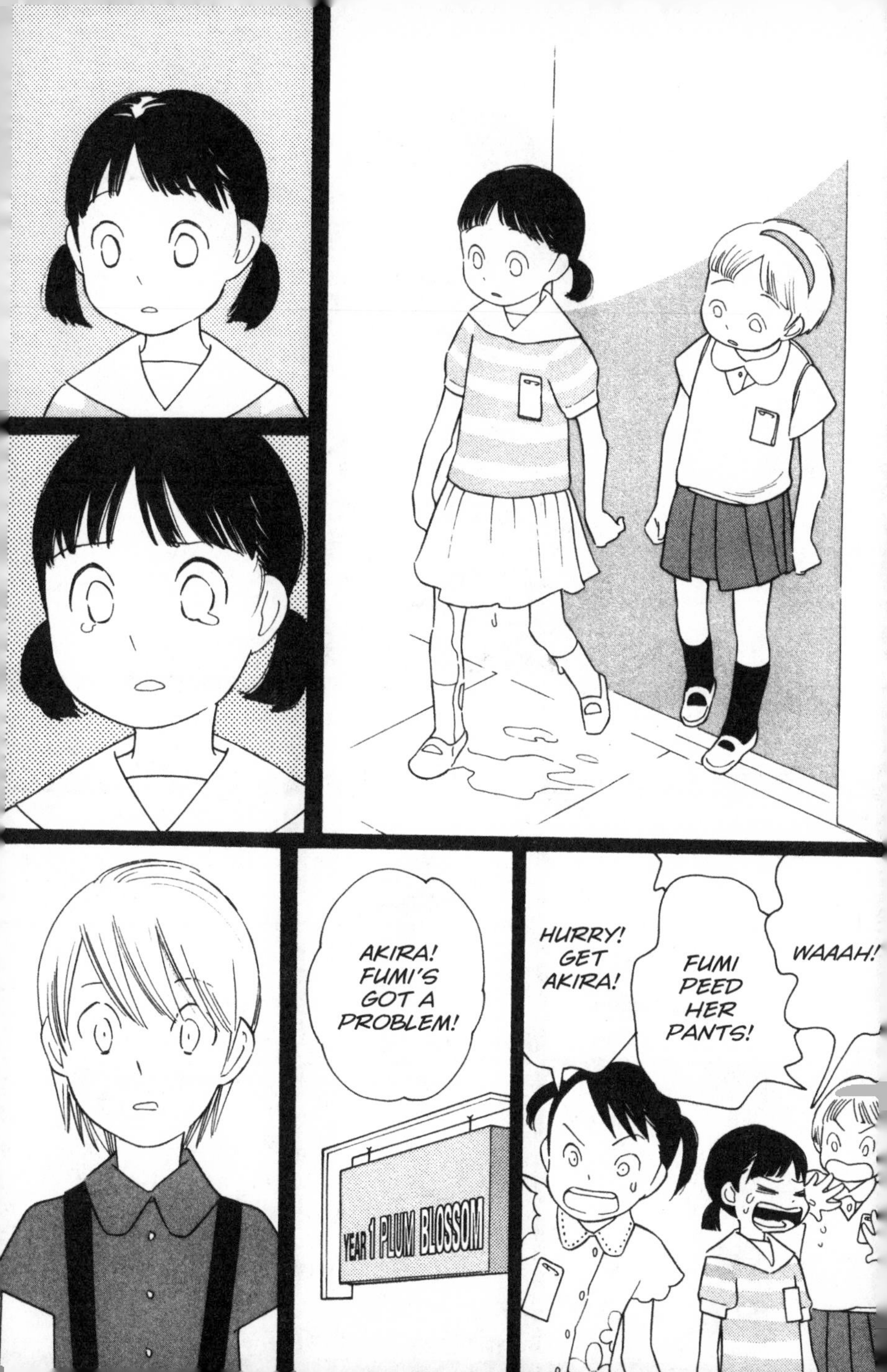
WAAAH!
FUMI PEED HER PANTS!
HURRY! GET AKIRA!
AKIRA! FUMI'S GOT A PROBLEM!
YEAR 1 PLUM BLOSSOM

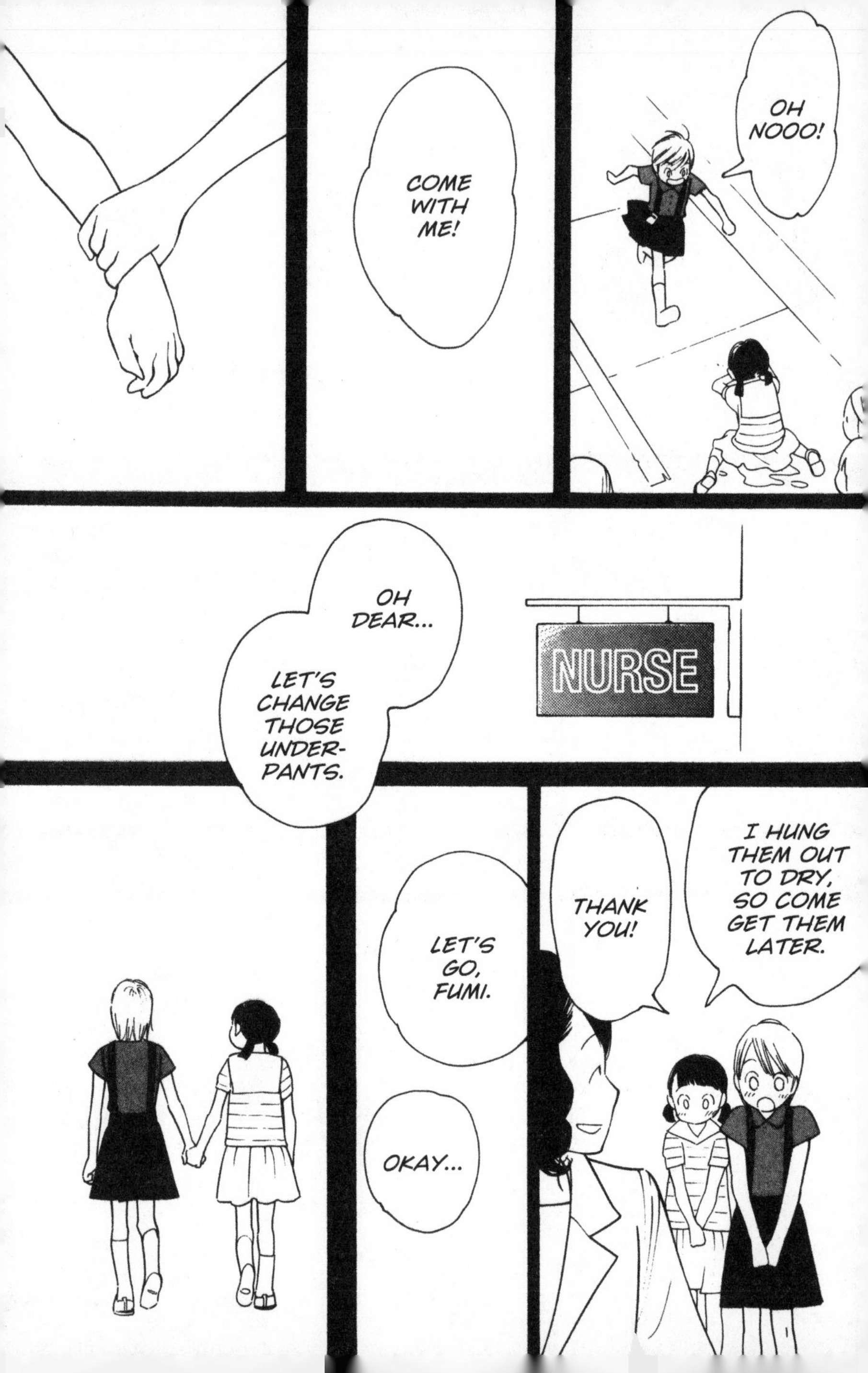
OH NOOO!
COME WITH ME!
NURSE
OH DEAR...
LET'S CHANGE THOSE UNDER-PANTS.
I HUNG THEM OUT TO DRY, SO COME GET THEM LATER.
THANK YOU!
LET'S GO, FUMI.
OKAY...

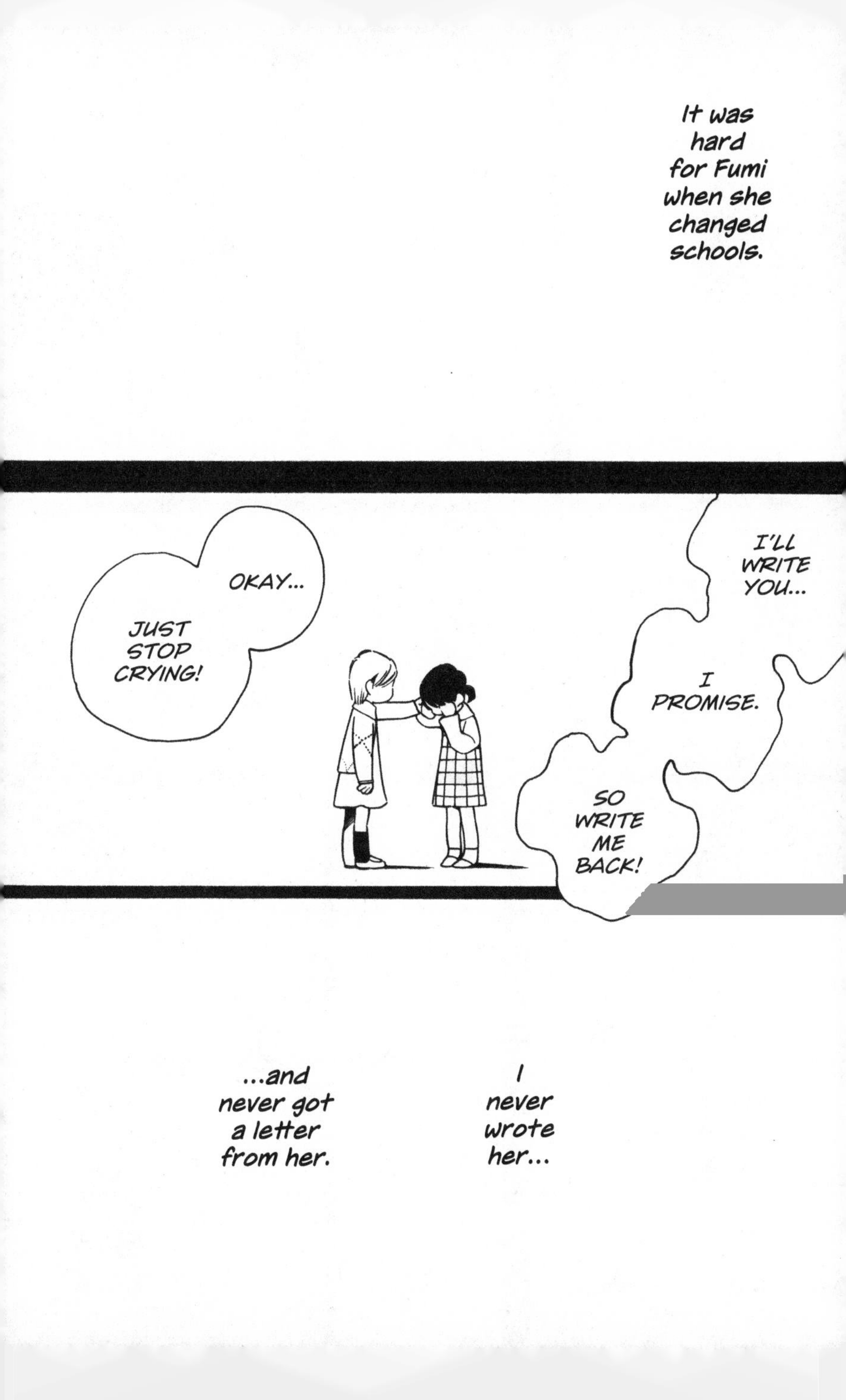
It was hard for Fumi when she changed schools.
I'LL WRITE YOU...
I PROMISE.
SO WRITE ME BACK!
OKAY...
JUST STOP CRYING!
I never wrote her...
...and never got a letter from her.

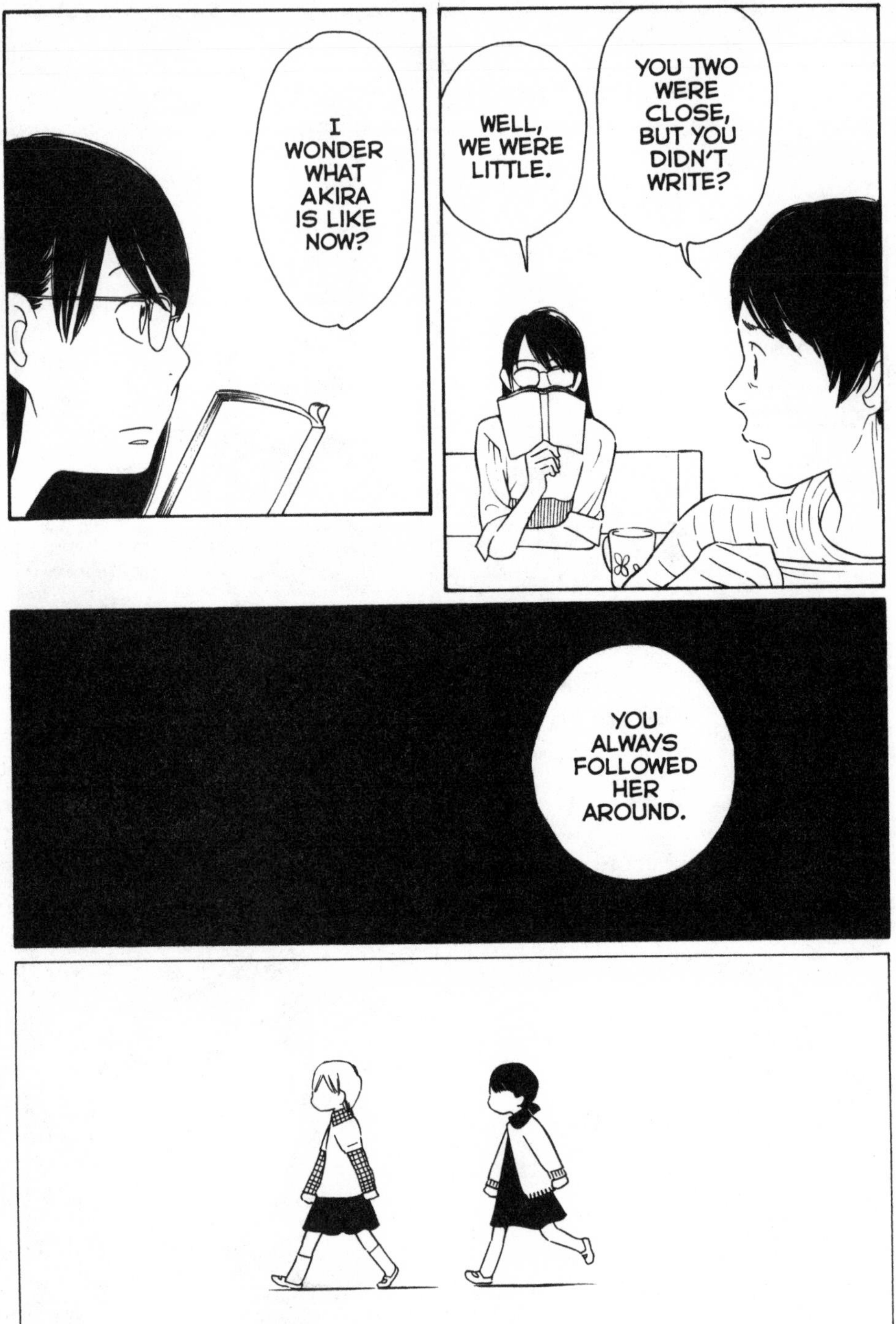
YOU TWO WERE CLOSE, BUT YOU DIDN'T WRITE?
WELL, WE WERE LITTLE.
I WONDER WHAT AKIRA IS LIKE NOW?
YOU ALWAYS FOLLOWED HER AROUND.

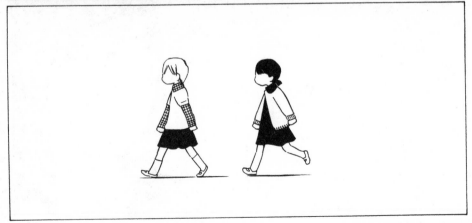

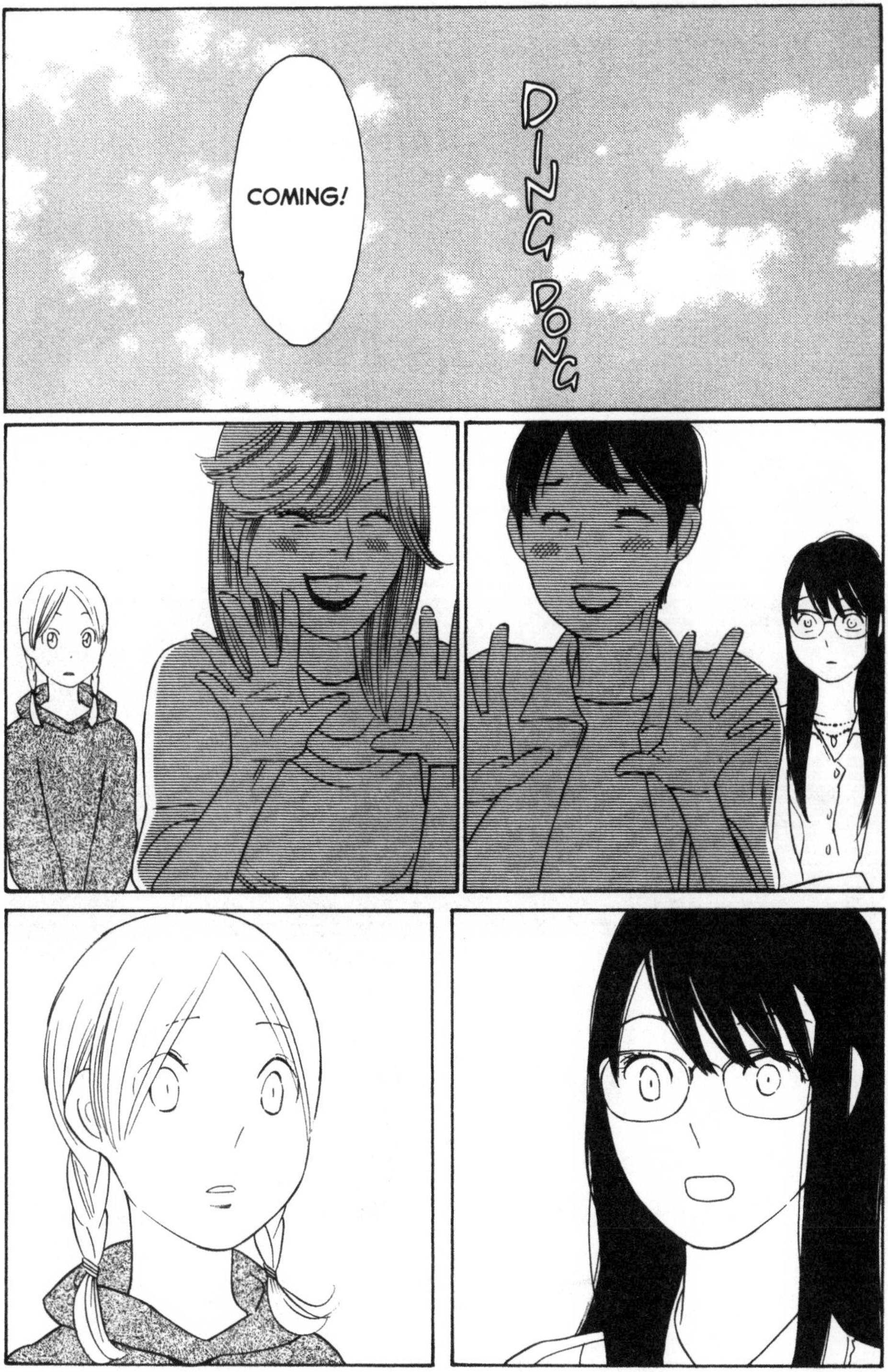
DING DONG
COMING!

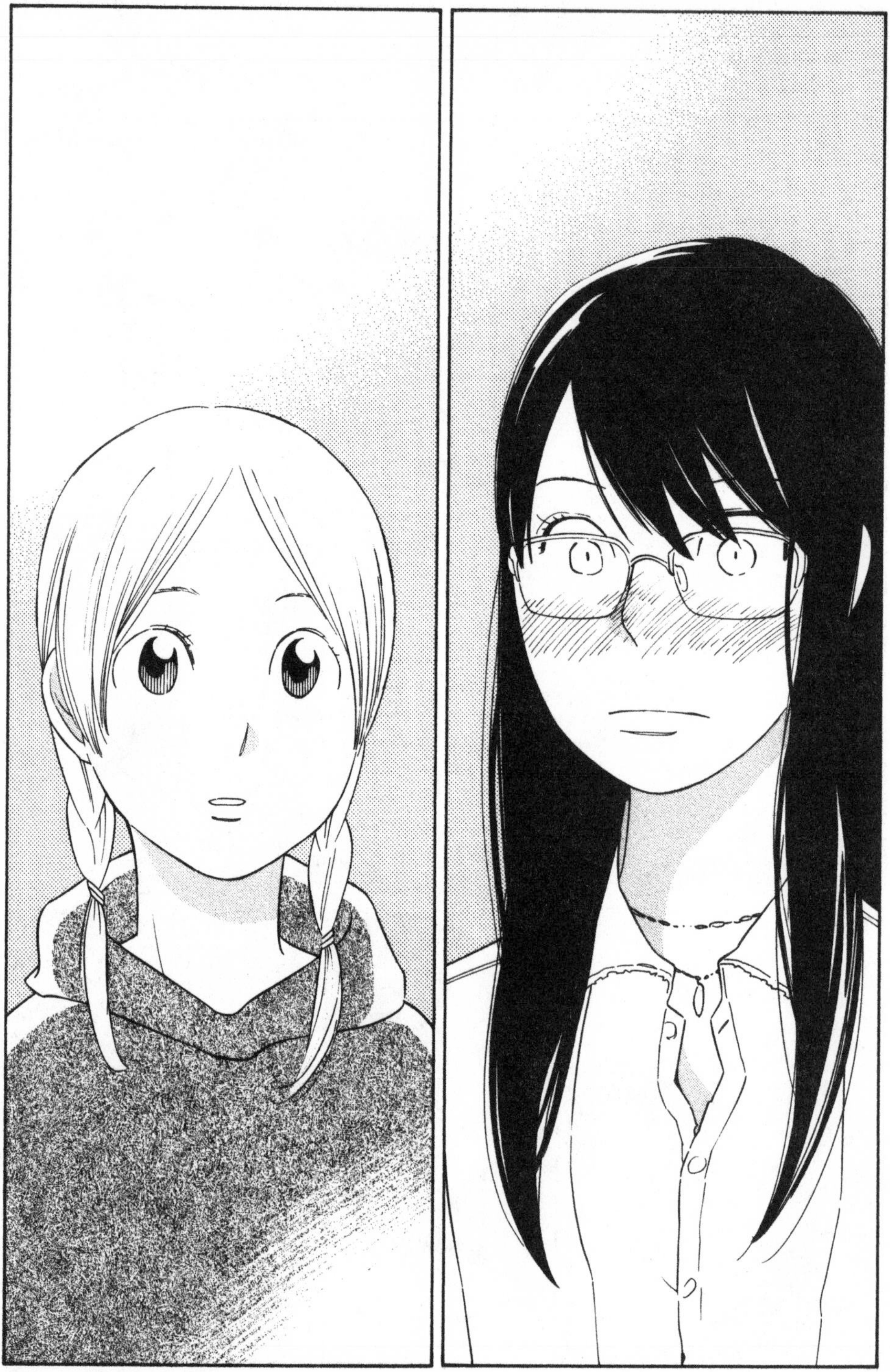

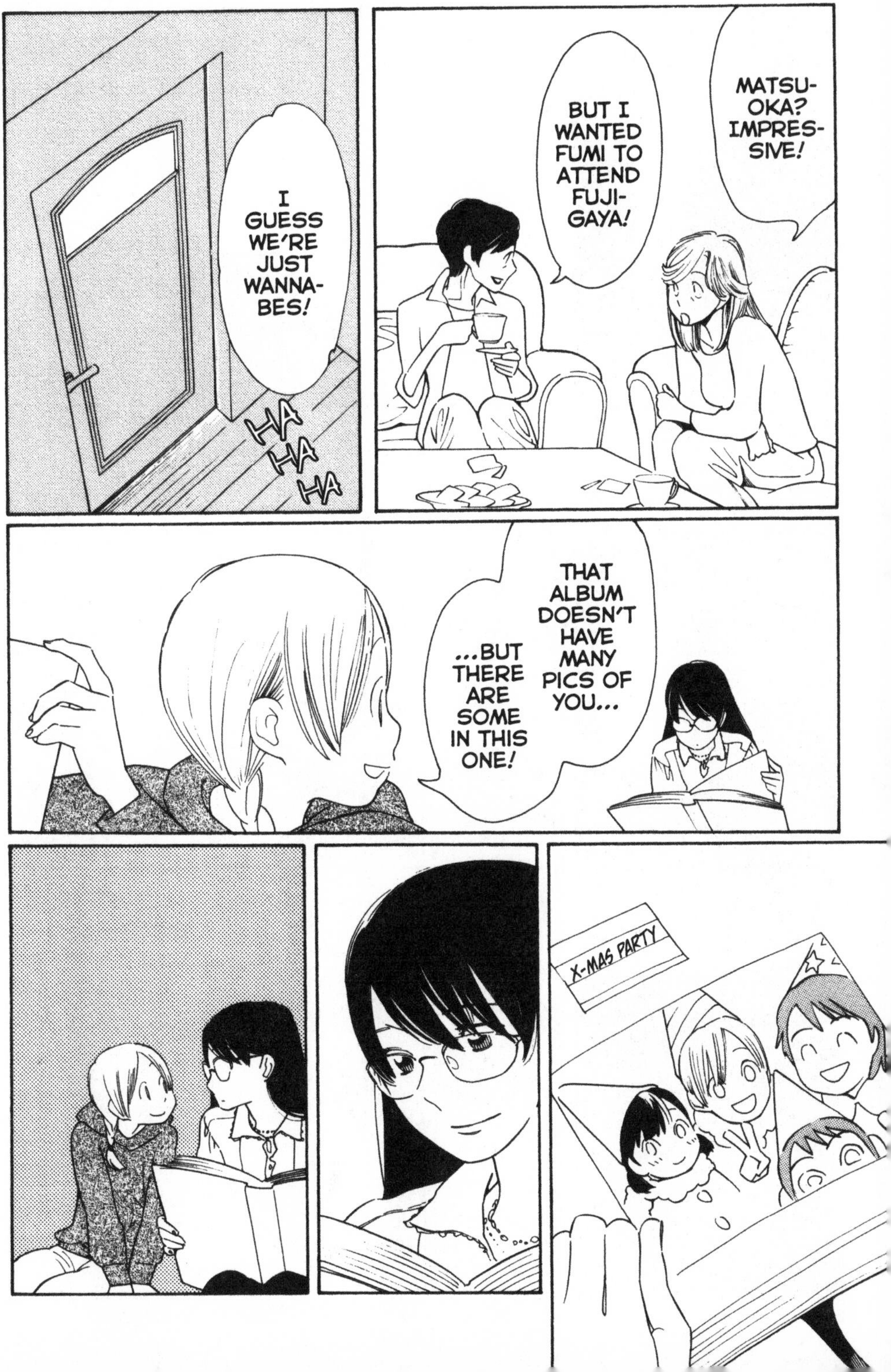
MATSU-OKA? IMPRES-SIVE!
BUT I WANTED FUMI TO ATTEND FUJI-GAYA!
I GUESS WE'RE JUST WANNA-BES!
HA HA HA
THAT ALBUM DOESN'T HAVE MANY PICS OF YOU...
...BUT THERE ARE SOME IN THIS ONE!
X-MAS PARTY

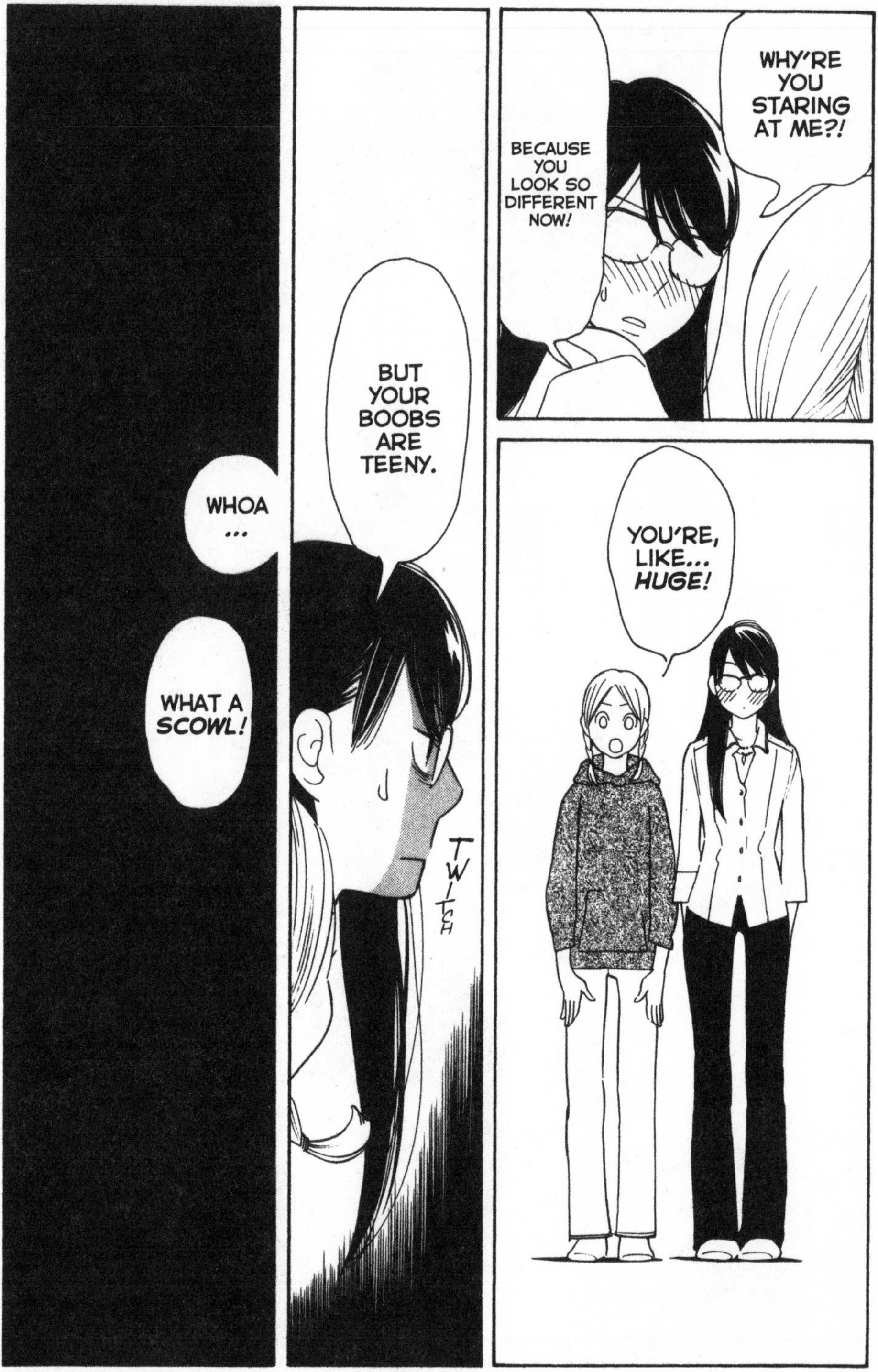
WHY'RE YOU STARING AT ME?!
BECAUSE YOU LOOK SO DIFFERENT NOW!
YOU'RE, LIKE... *HUGE!*
BUT YOUR BOOBS ARE TEENY.
TWITCH
WHOA...
WHAT A *SCOWL!*

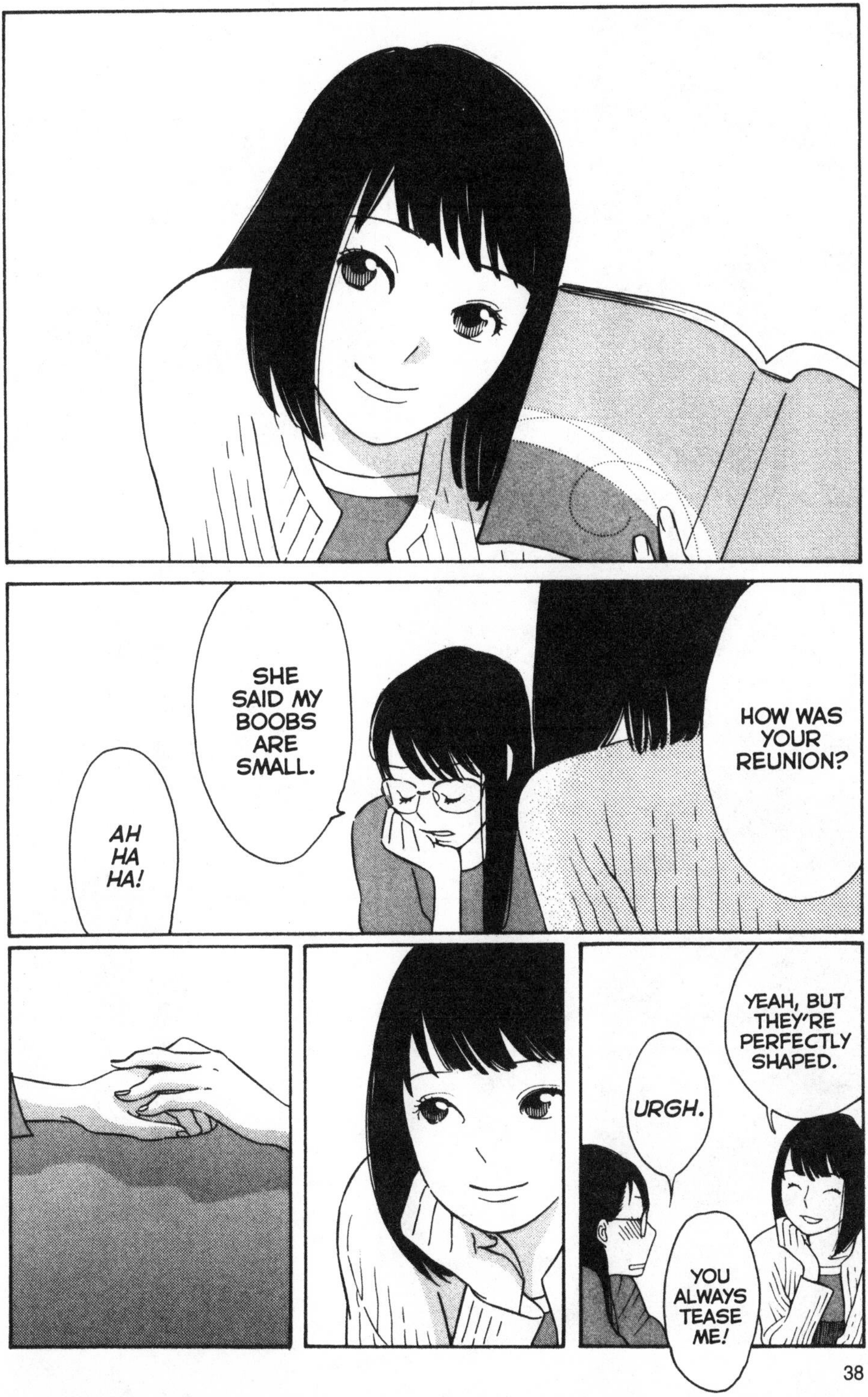
HOW WAS YOUR REUNION?
SHE SAID MY BOOBS ARE SMALL.
AH HA HA!
YEAH, BUT THEY'RE PERFECTLY SHAPED.
URGH.
YOU ALWAYS TEASE ME!

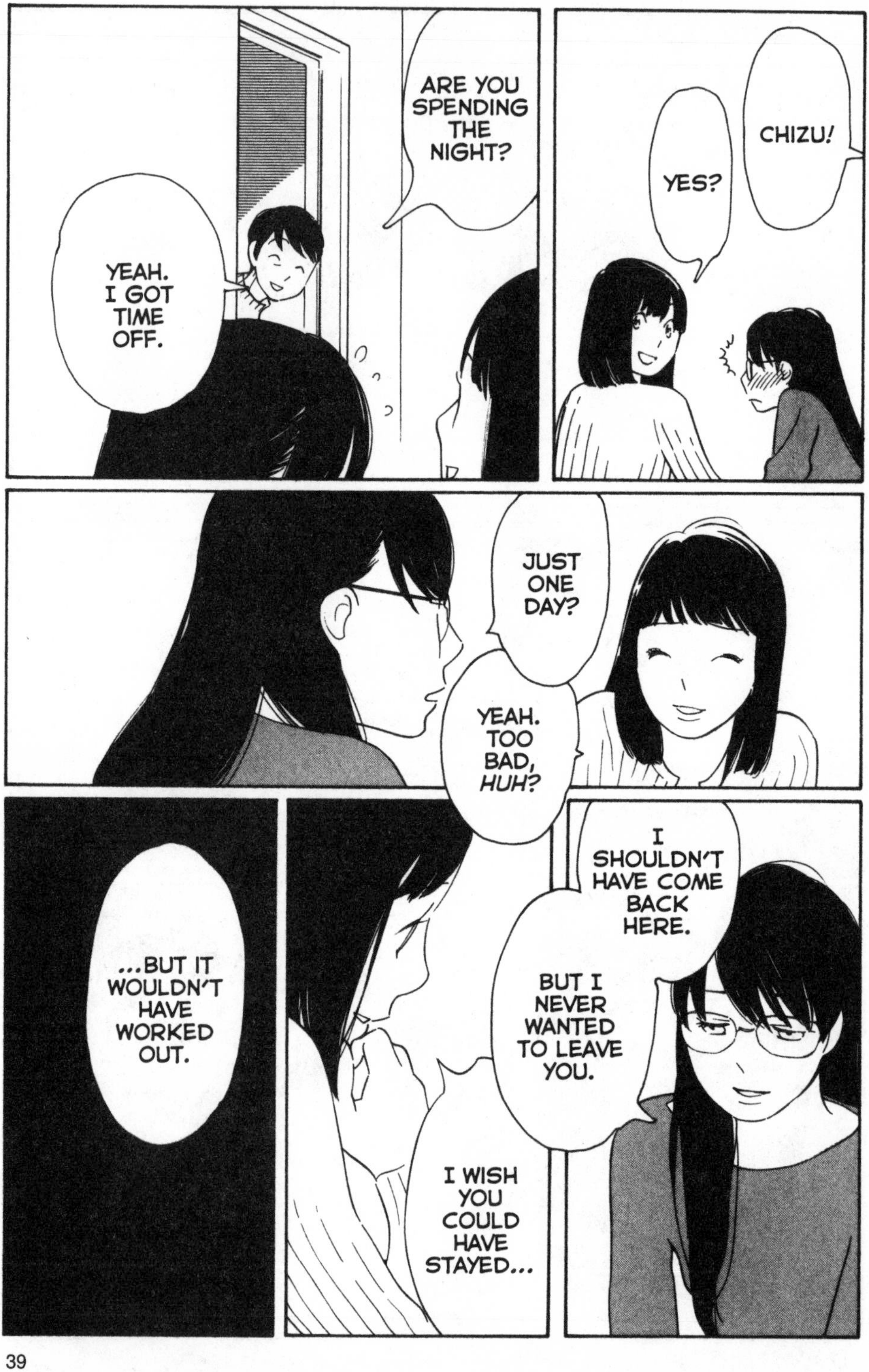
CHIZU!
YES?
ARE YOU SPENDING THE NIGHT?
YEAH. I GOT TIME OFF.
JUST ONE DAY?
YEAH. TOO BAD, *HUH*?
I SHOULDN'T HAVE COME BACK HERE.
BUT I NEVER WANTED TO LEAVE YOU.
I WISH YOU COULD HAVE STAYED...
...BUT IT WOULDN'T HAVE WORKED OUT.

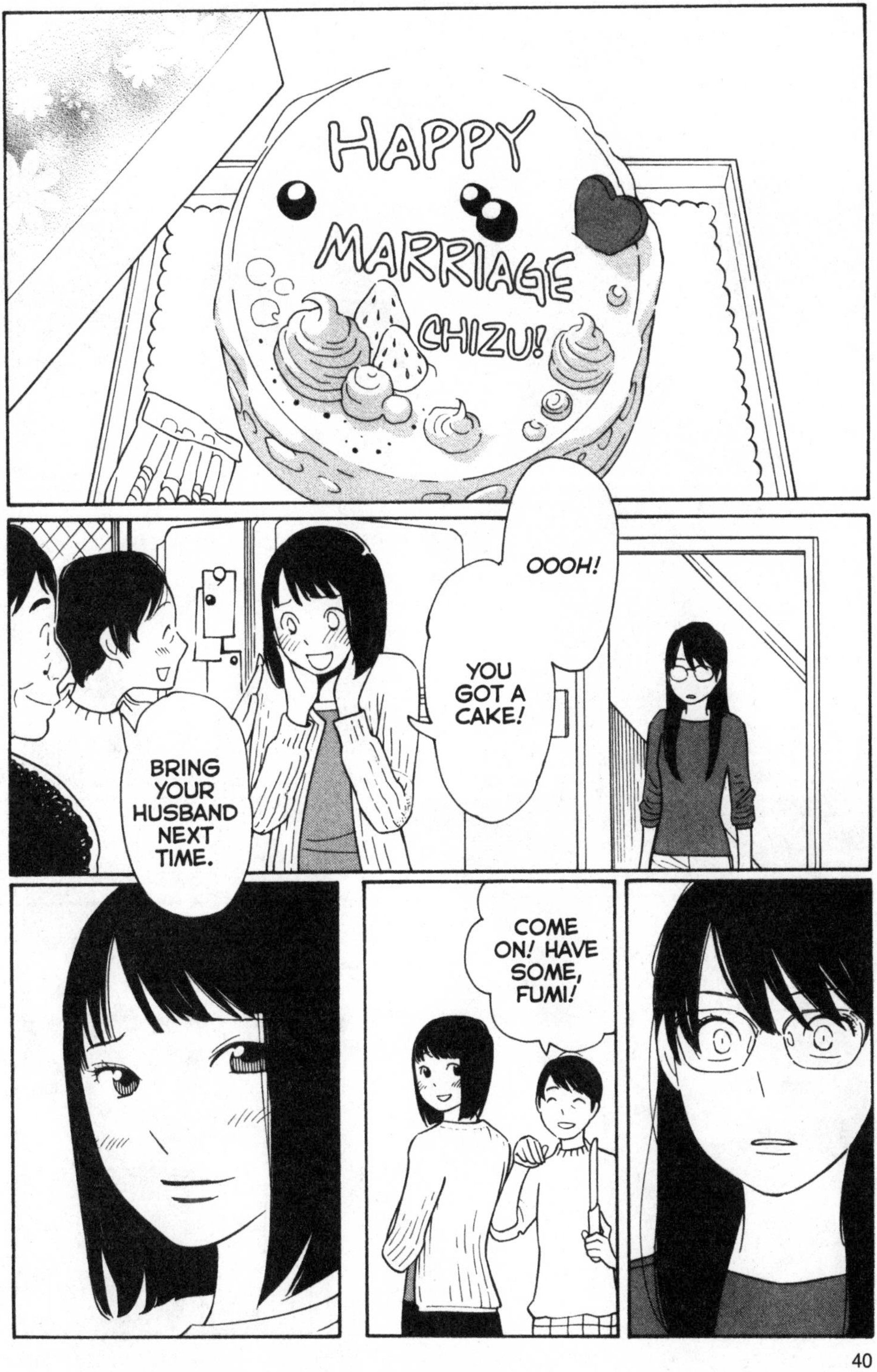
HAPPY MARRIAGE CHIZU!
OOOH! YOU GOT A CAKE!
BRING YOUR HUSBAND NEXT TIME.
COME ON! HAVE SOME, FUMI!

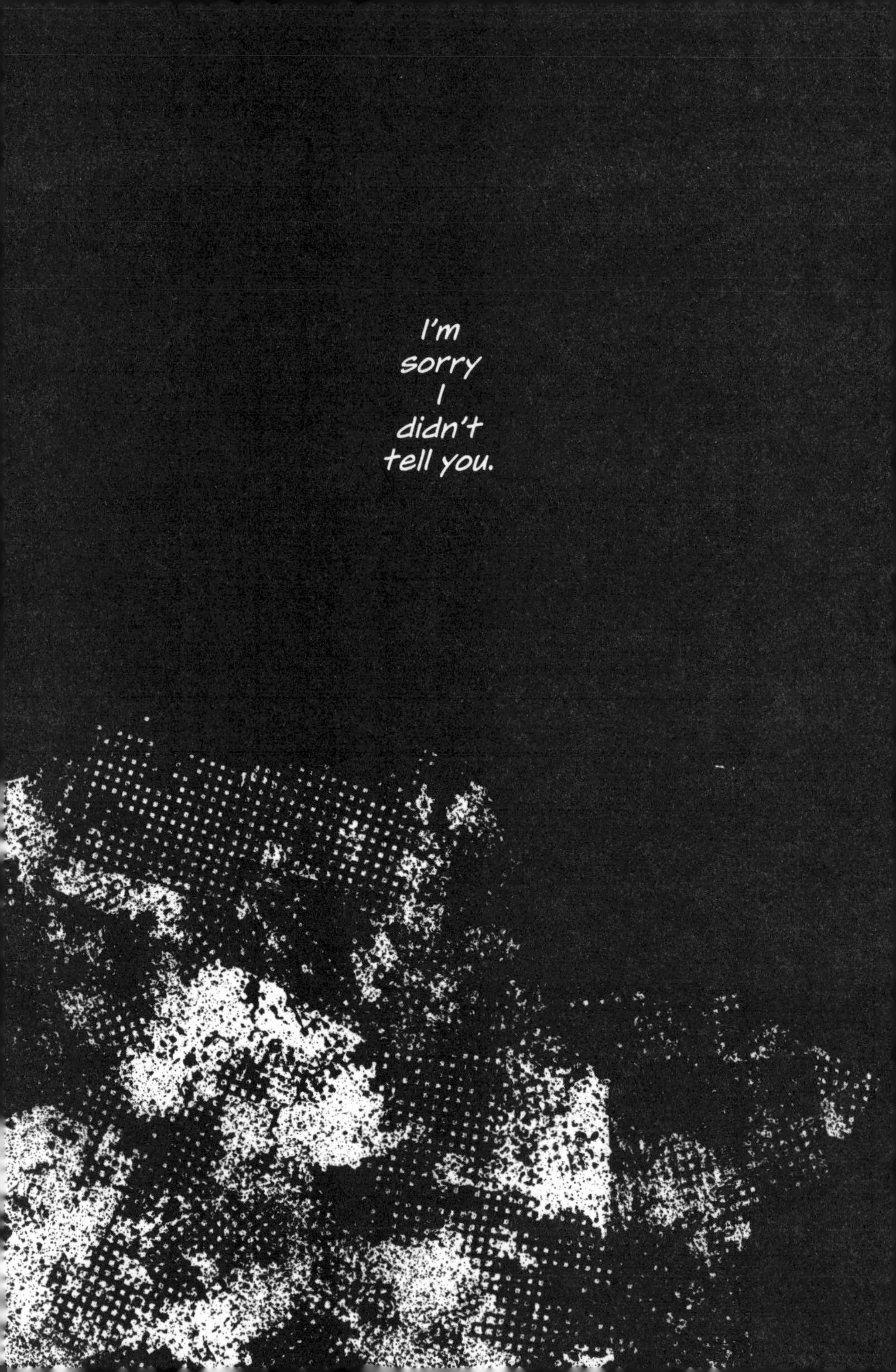
I'm sorry I didn't tell you.

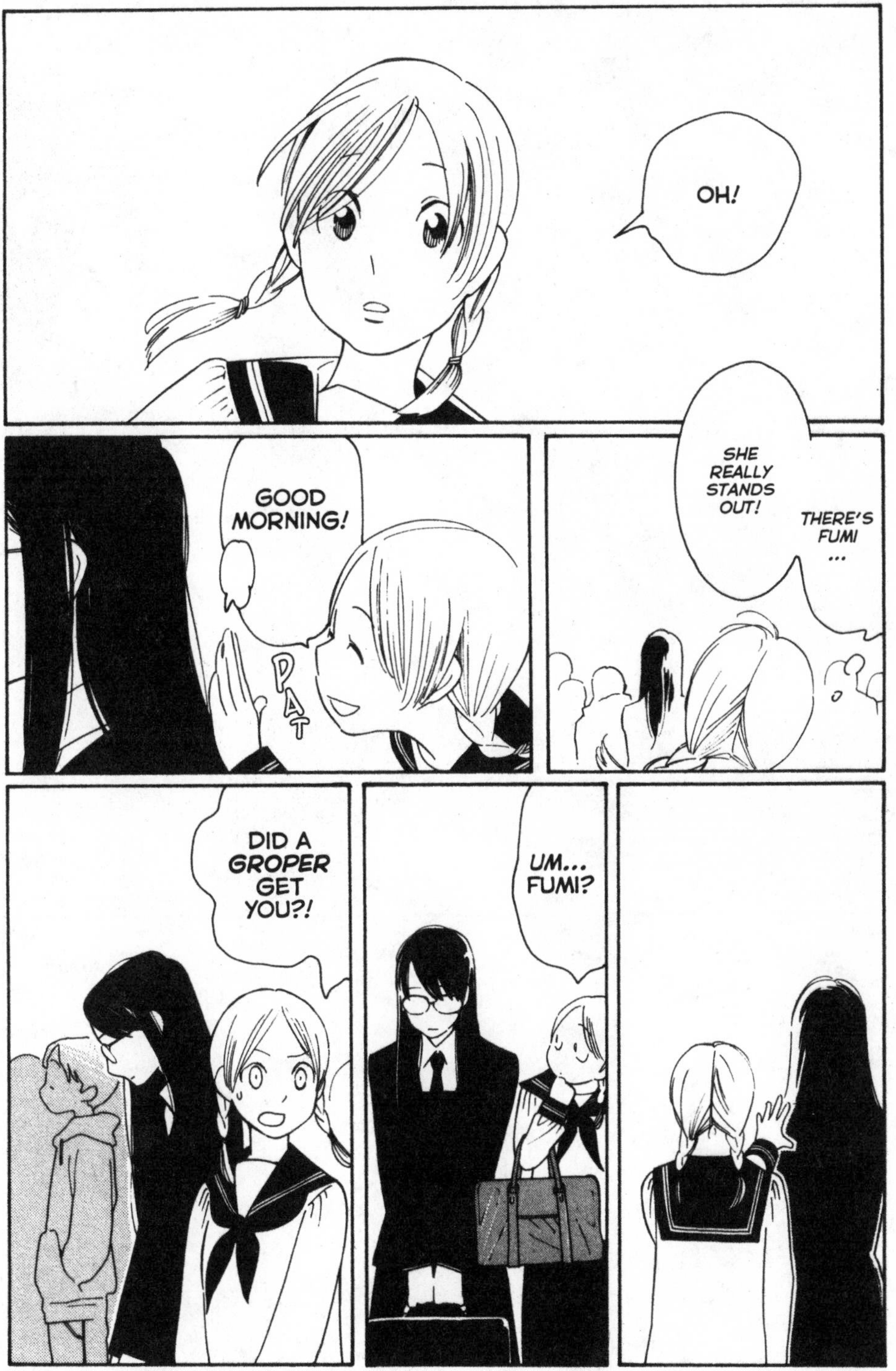
OH!
THERE'S FUMI ...
SHE REALLY STANDS OUT!
GOOD MORNING!
PAT
UM... FUMI?
DID A GROPER GET YOU?!

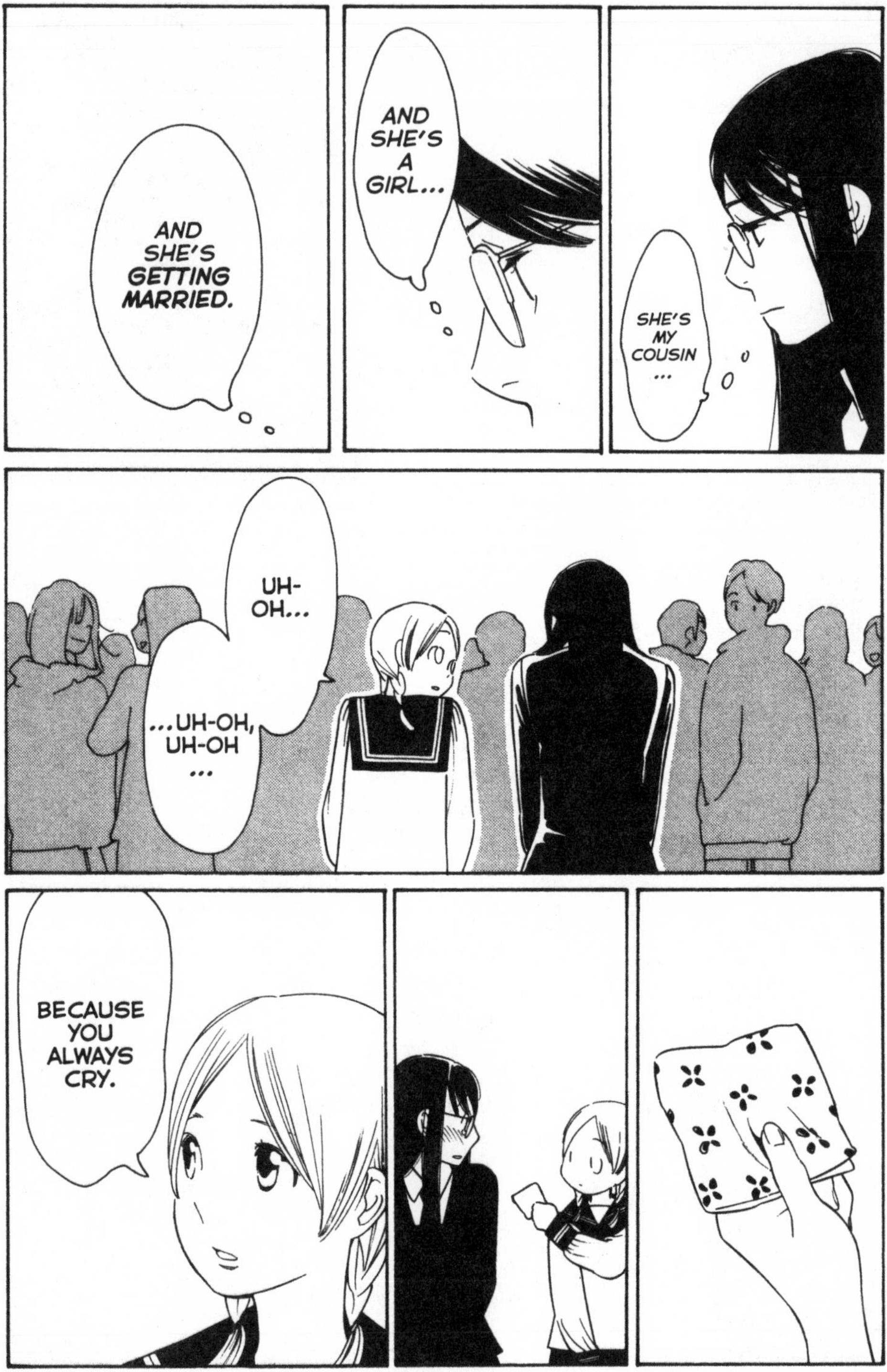
SHE'S MY COUSIN ...
AND SHE'S A GIRL...
AND SHE'S GETTING MARRIED.
UH-OH...
...UH-OH, UH-OH ...
BECAUSE YOU ALWAYS CRY.

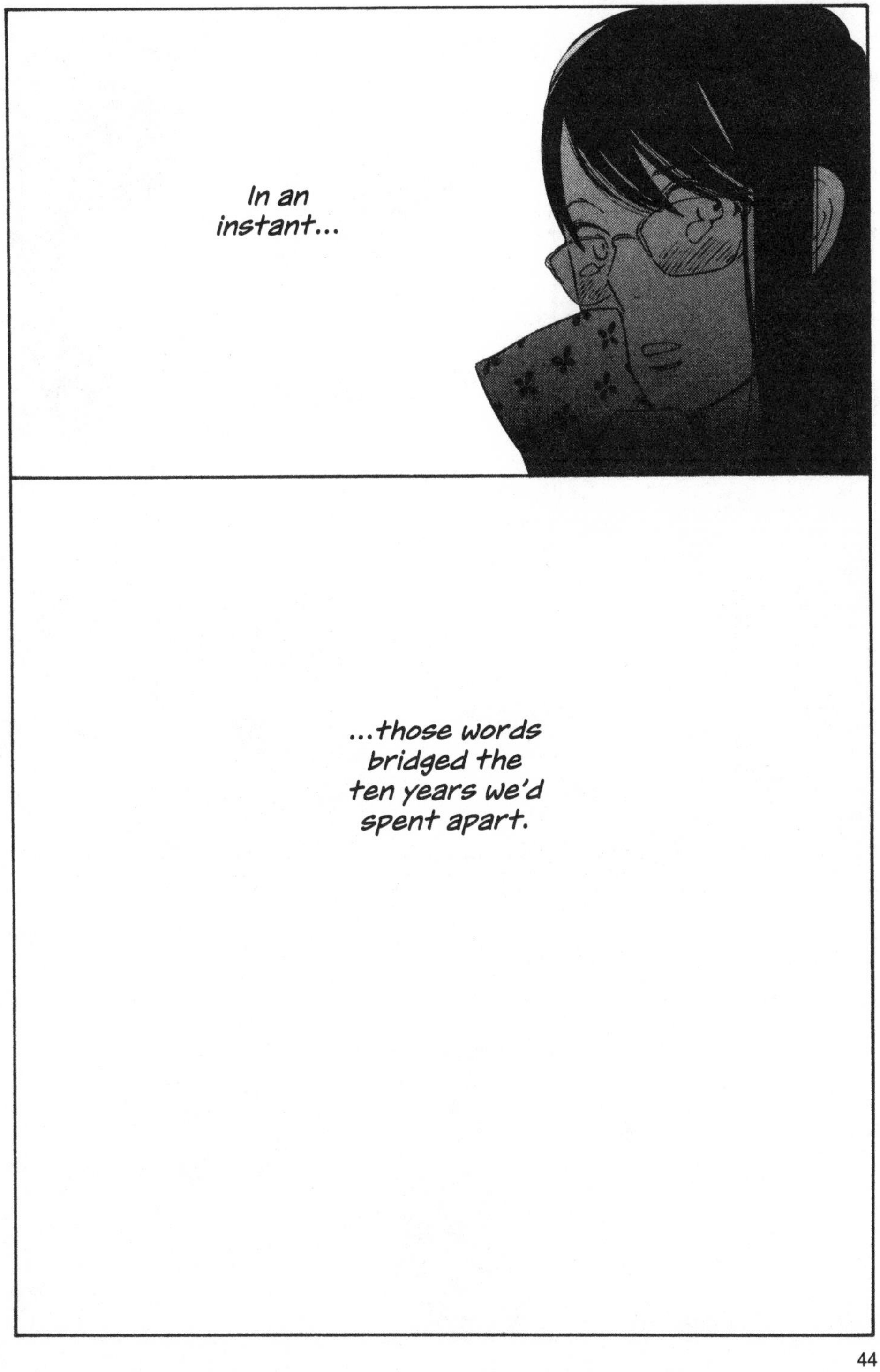
In an instant...
...those words bridged the ten years we'd spent apart.

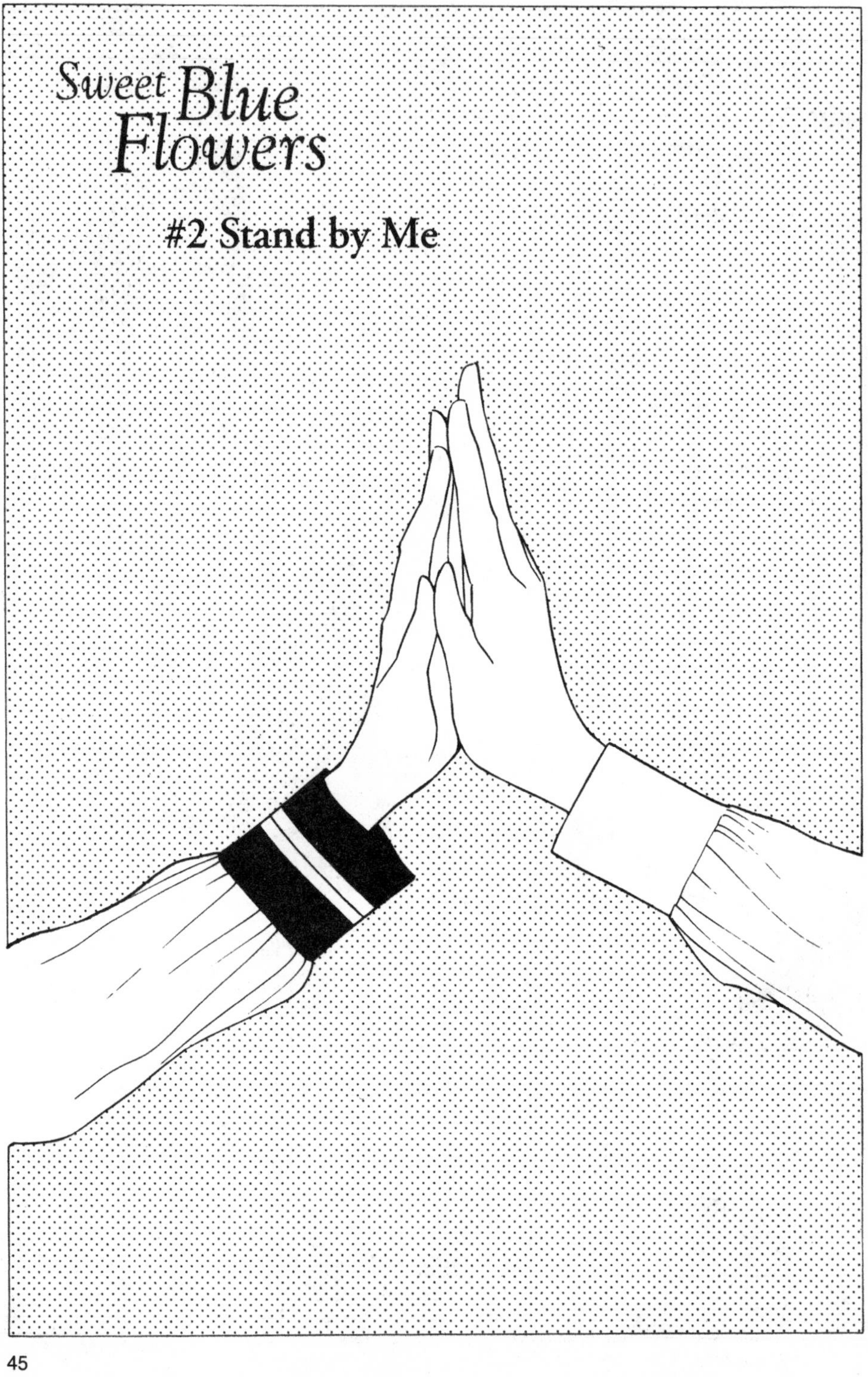
Sweet Blue Flowers
#2 Stand by Me

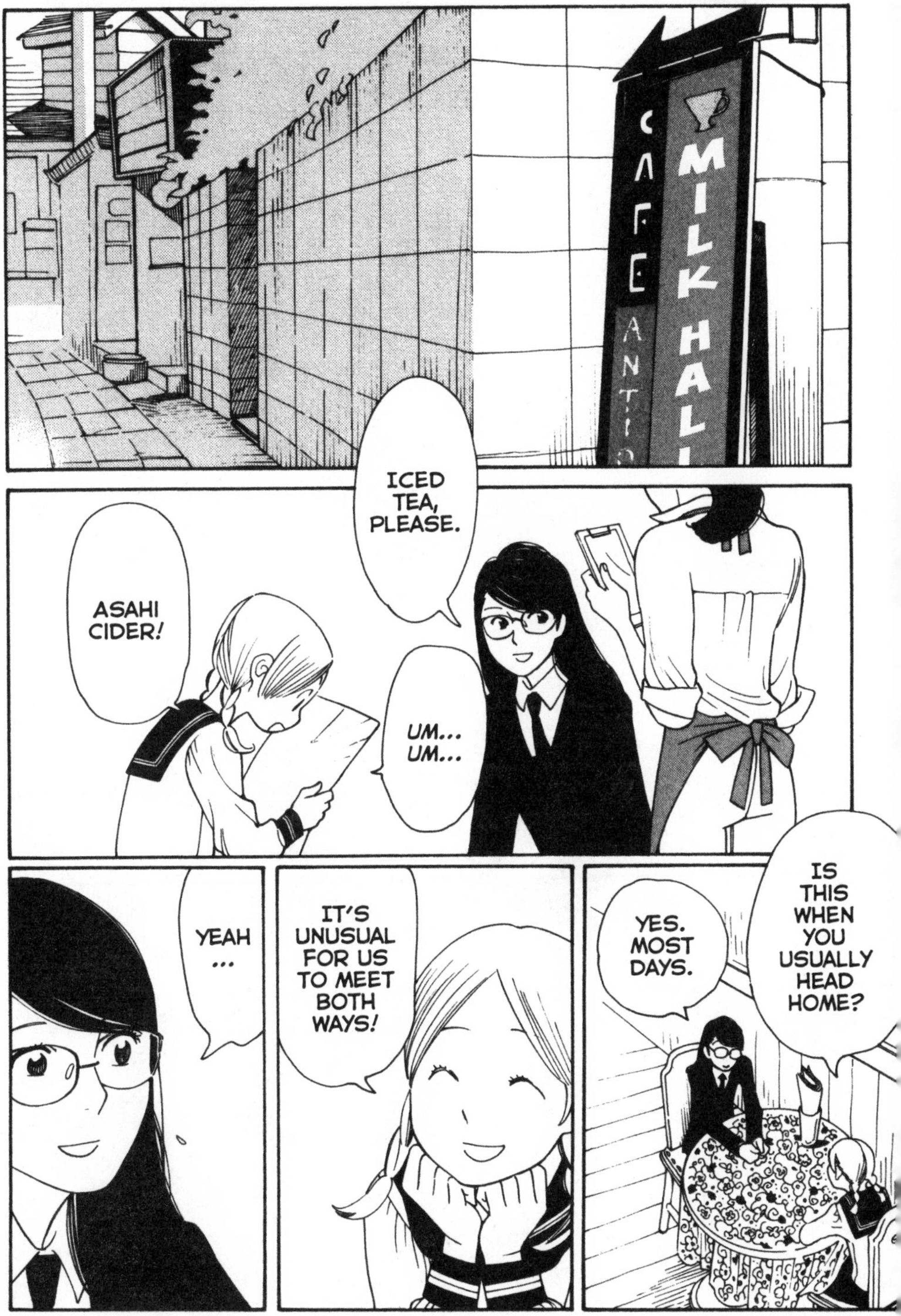
CAFE
MILK HALL
ICED TEA, PLEASE.
UM... UM...
ASAHI CIDER!
IS THIS WHEN YOU USUALLY HEAD HOME?
YES. MOST DAYS.
IT'S UNUSUAL FOR US TO MEET BOTH WAYS!
YEAH ...

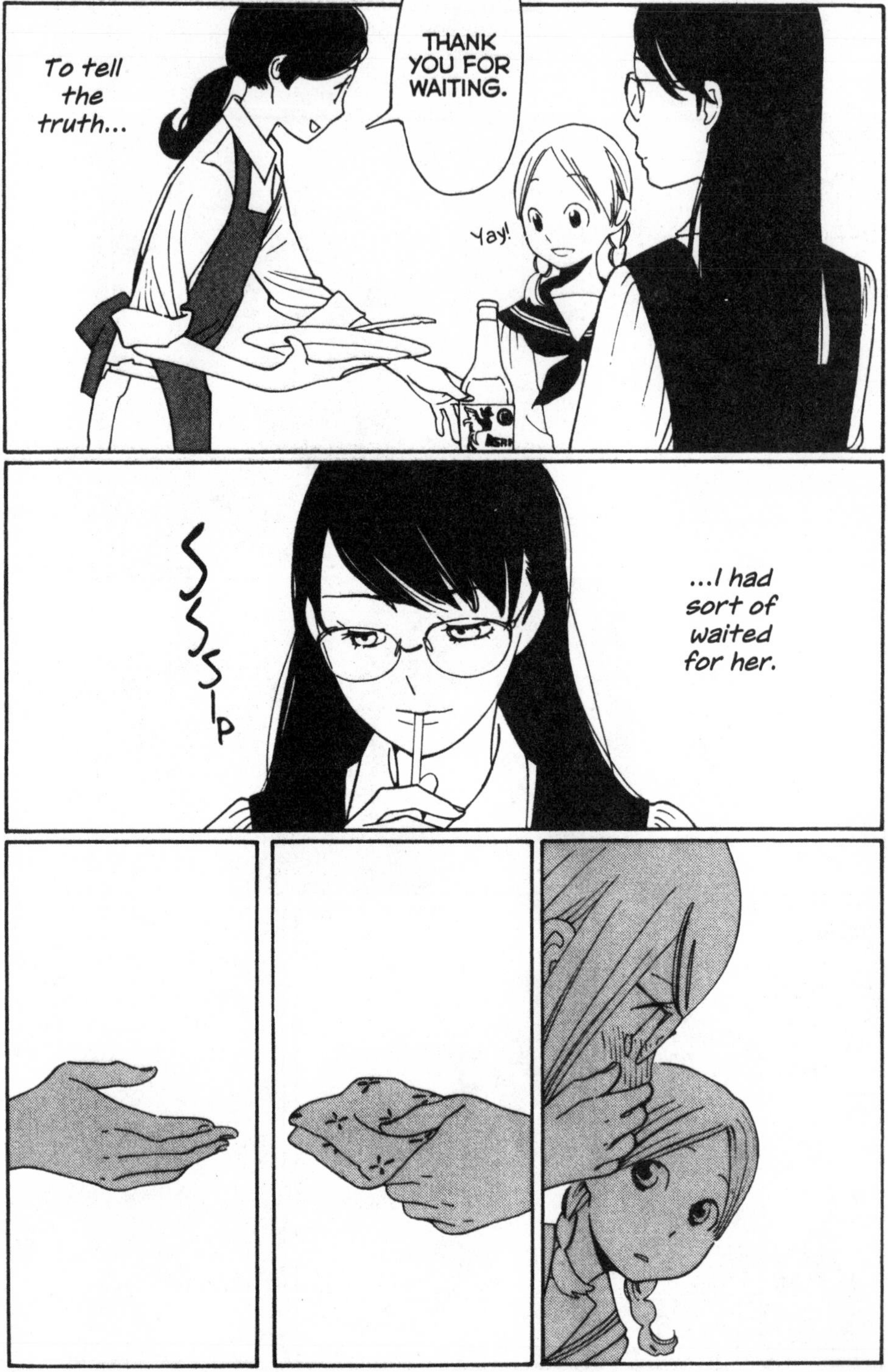
THANK YOU FOR WAITING.
To tell the truth...
Yay!
...I had sort of waited for her.
SSSlip

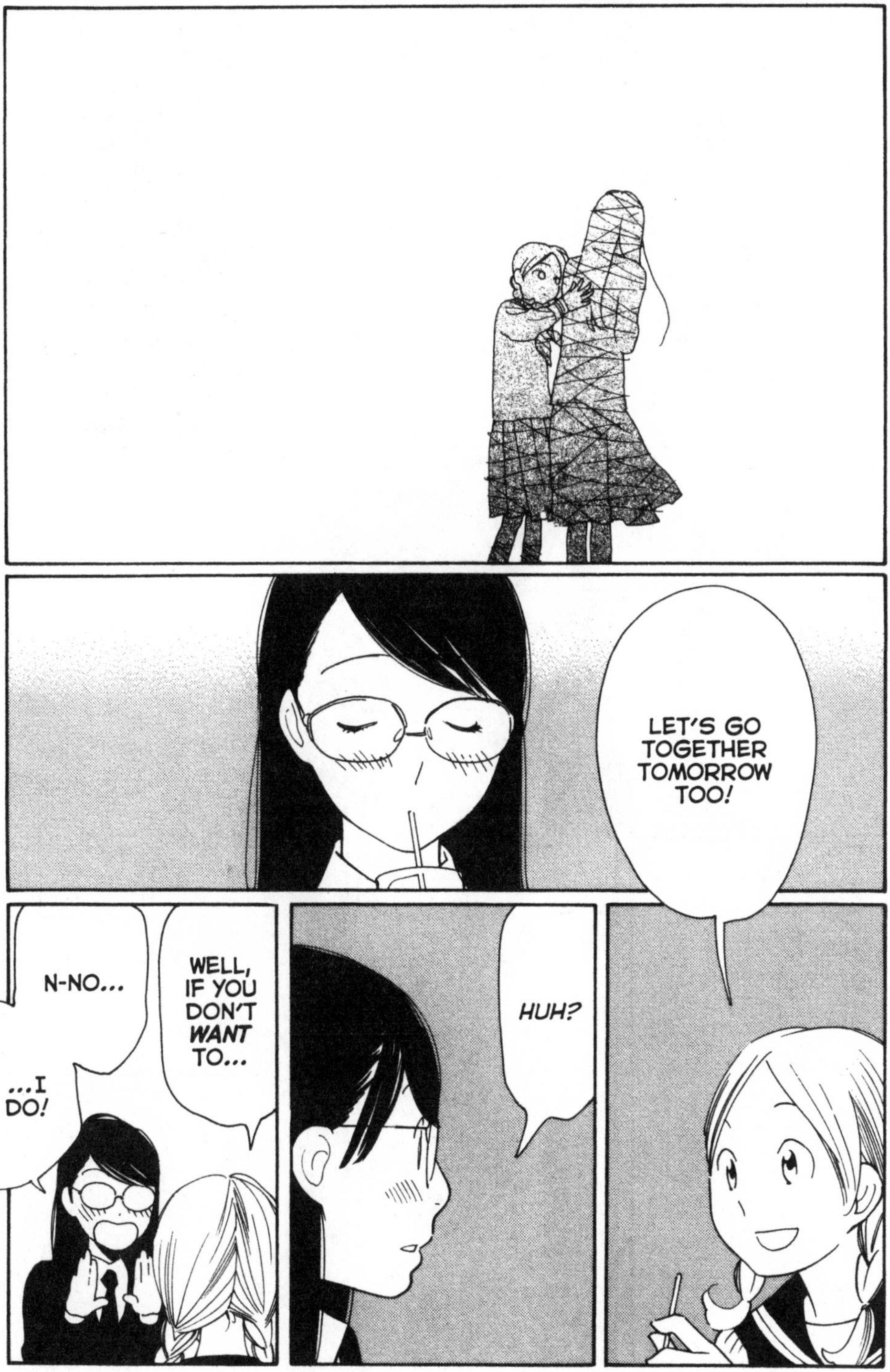
LET'S GO TOGETHER TOMORROW TOO!
HUH?
WELL, IF YOU DON'T *WANT* TO...
N-NO...
...I DO!

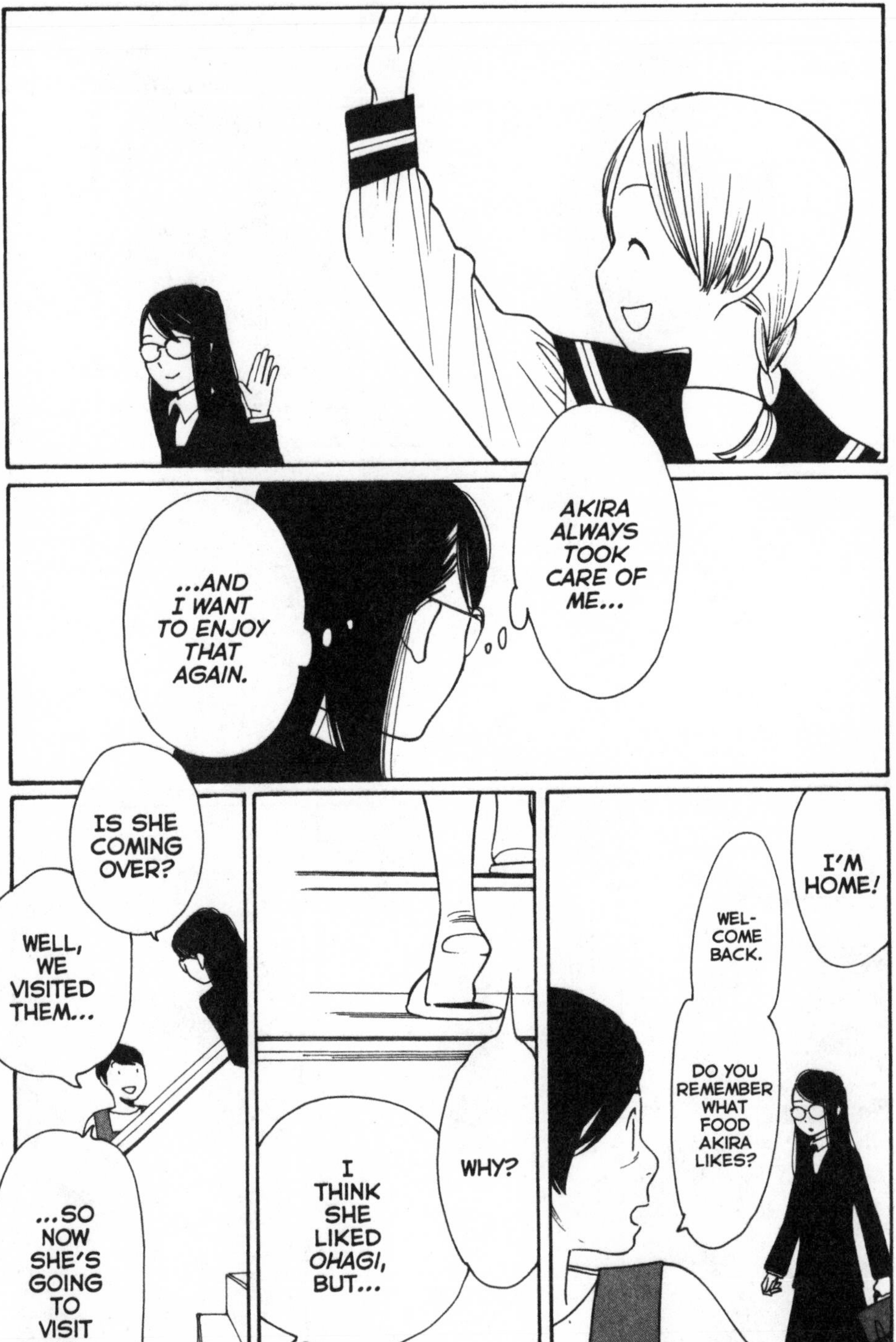
AKIRA ALWAYS TOOK CARE OF ME...
...AND I WANT TO ENJOY THAT AGAIN.
I'M HOME!
WEL-COME BACK.
DO YOU REMEMBER WHAT FOOD AKIRA LIKES?
WHY?
I THINK SHE LIKED *OHAGI*, BUT...
IS SHE COMING OVER?
WELL, WE VISITED THEM...
...SO NOW SHE'S GOING TO VISIT US.

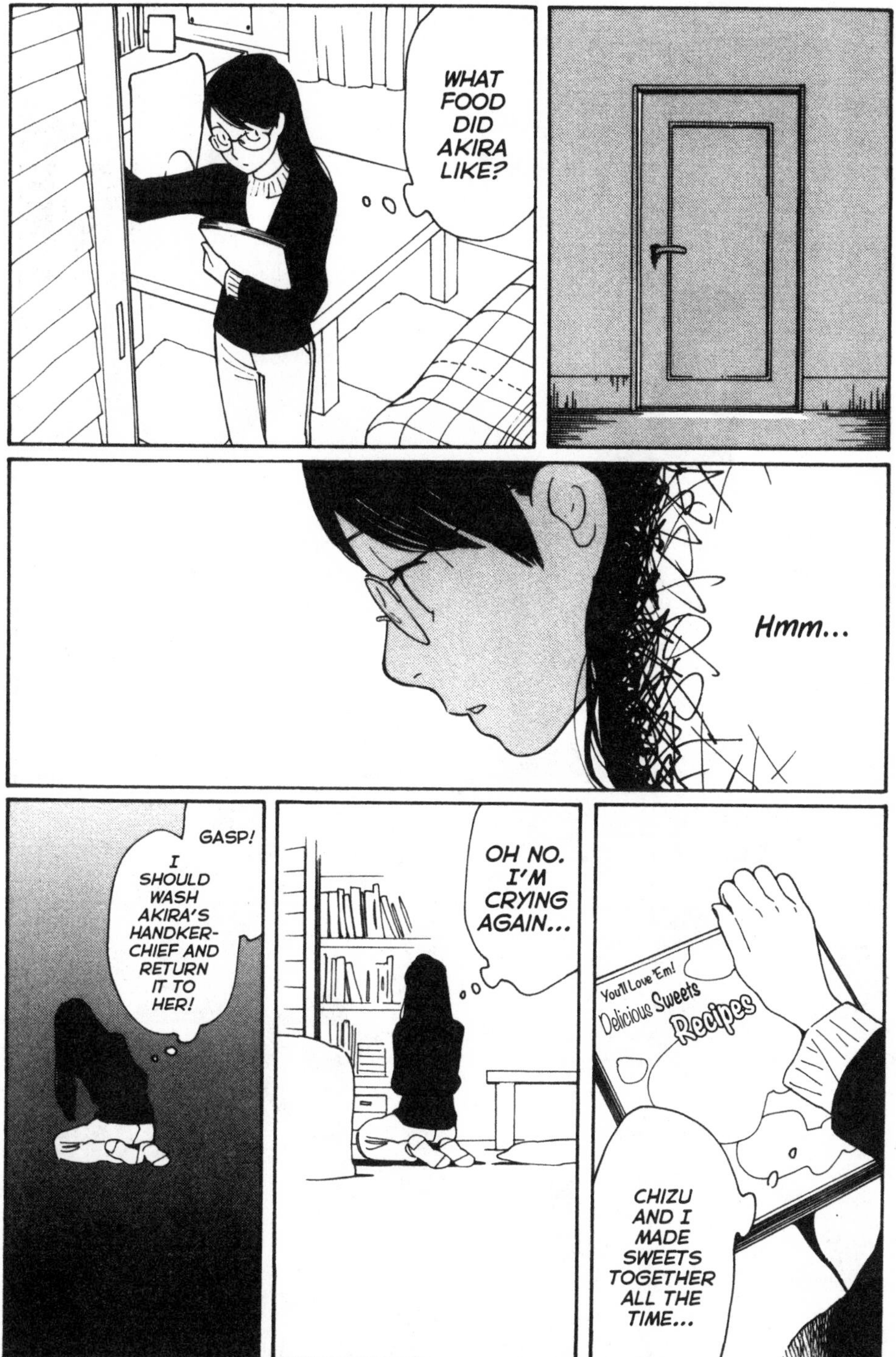
WHAT FOOD DID AKIRA LIKE?
Hmm...
You'll Love 'Em!
Delicious Sweets Recipes
CHIZU AND I MADE SWEETS TOGETHER ALL THE TIME...
OH NO. I'M CRYING AGAIN...
GASP!
I SHOULD WASH AKIRA'S HANDKERCHIEF AND RETURN IT TO HER!

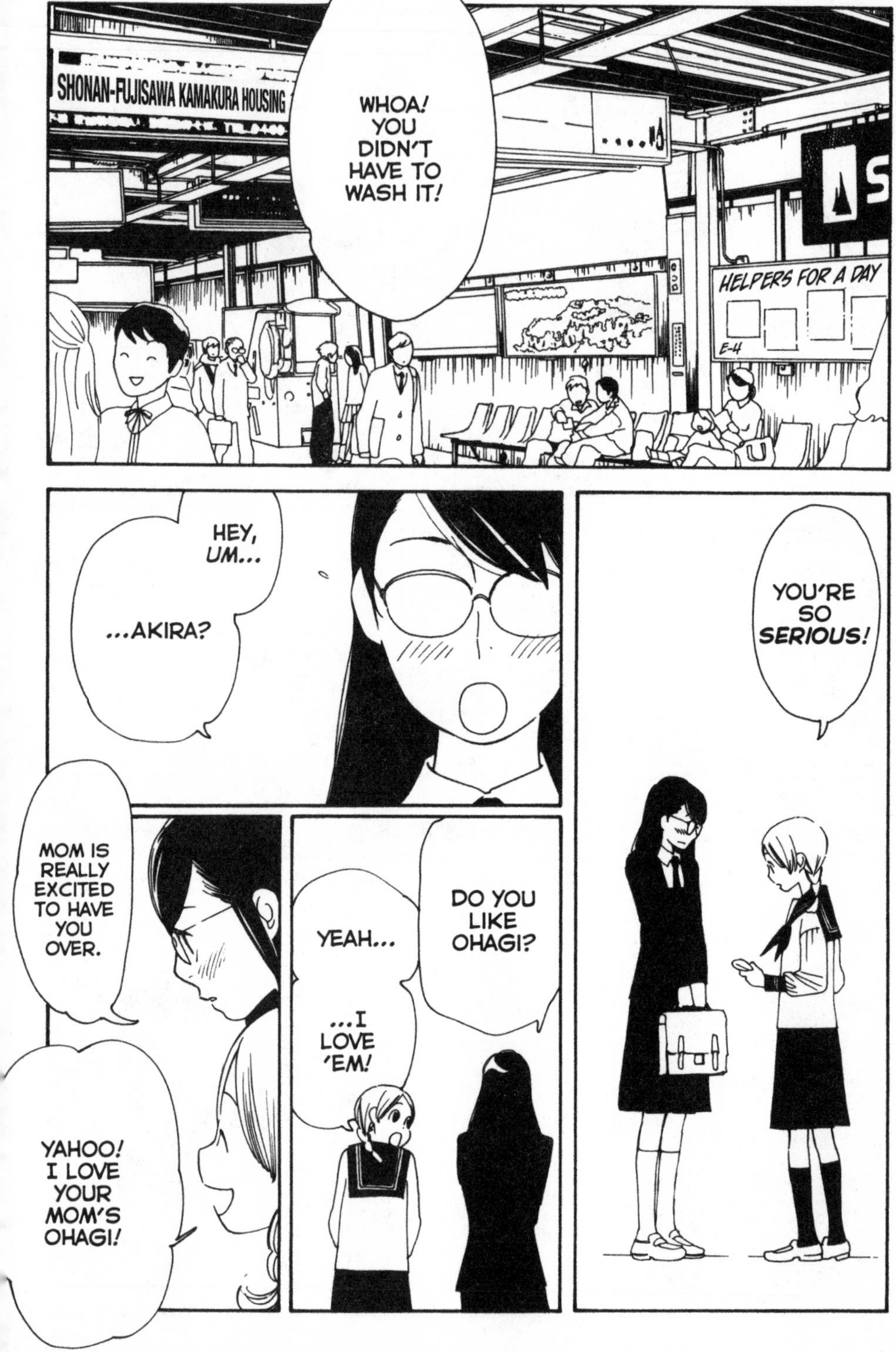
SHONAN-FUJISAWA KAMAKURA HOUSING
WHOA! YOU DIDN'T HAVE TO WASH IT!
HELPERS FOR A DAY
E-4
YOU'RE SO SERIOUS!
HEY, UM...
...AKIRA?
DO YOU LIKE OHAGI?
YEAH...
...I LOVE 'EM!
MOM IS REALLY EXCITED TO HAVE YOU OVER.
YAHOO! I LOVE YOUR MOM'S OHAGI!

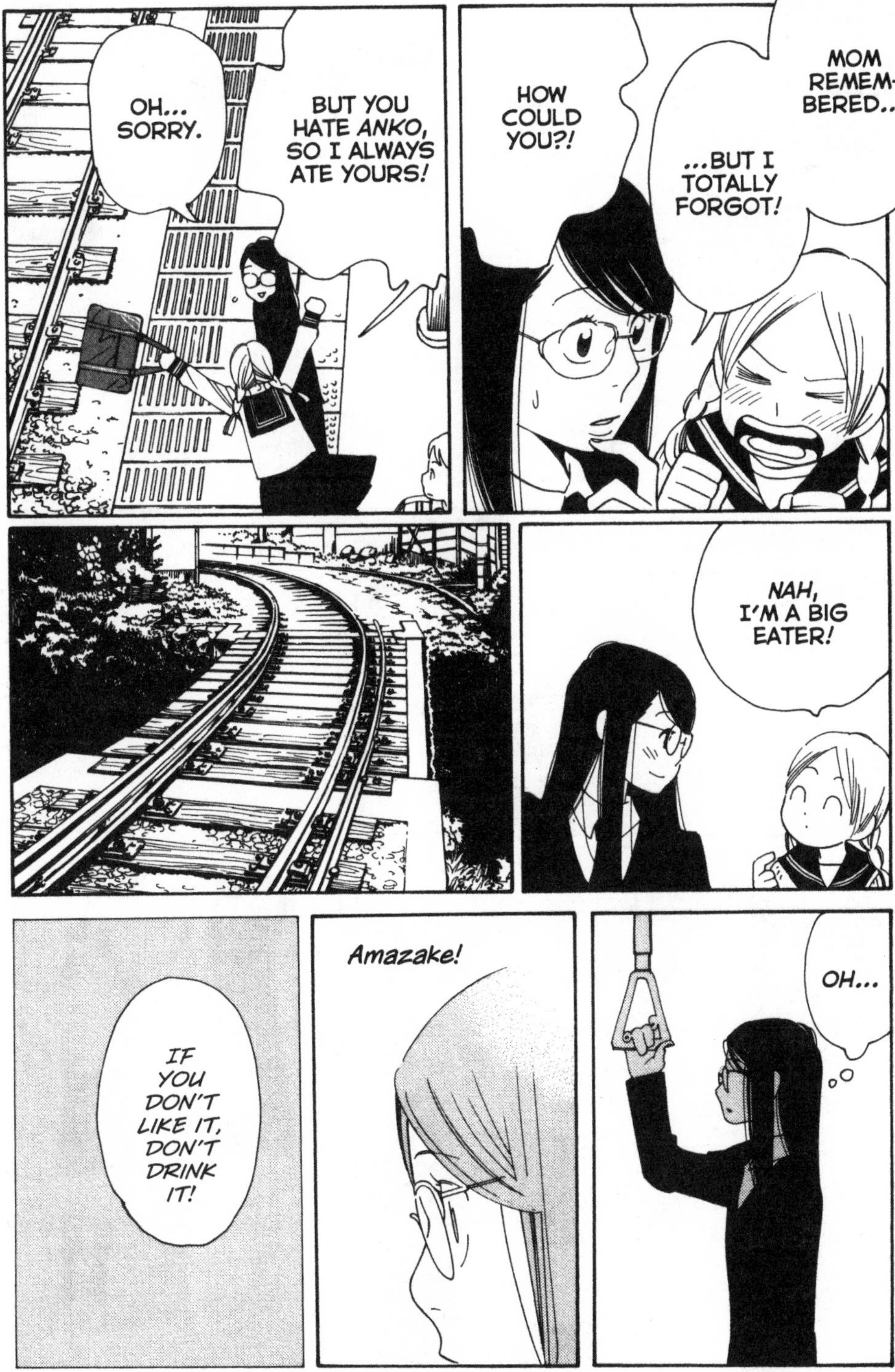
MOM REMEM-BERED...
...BUT I TOTALLY FORGOT!
HOW COULD YOU?!
BUT YOU HATE *ANKO*, SO I ALWAYS ATE YOURS!
OH... SORRY.
*NAH*, I'M A BIG EATER!
OH...
*Amazake!*
*IF YOU DON'T LIKE IT, DON'T DRINK IT!*

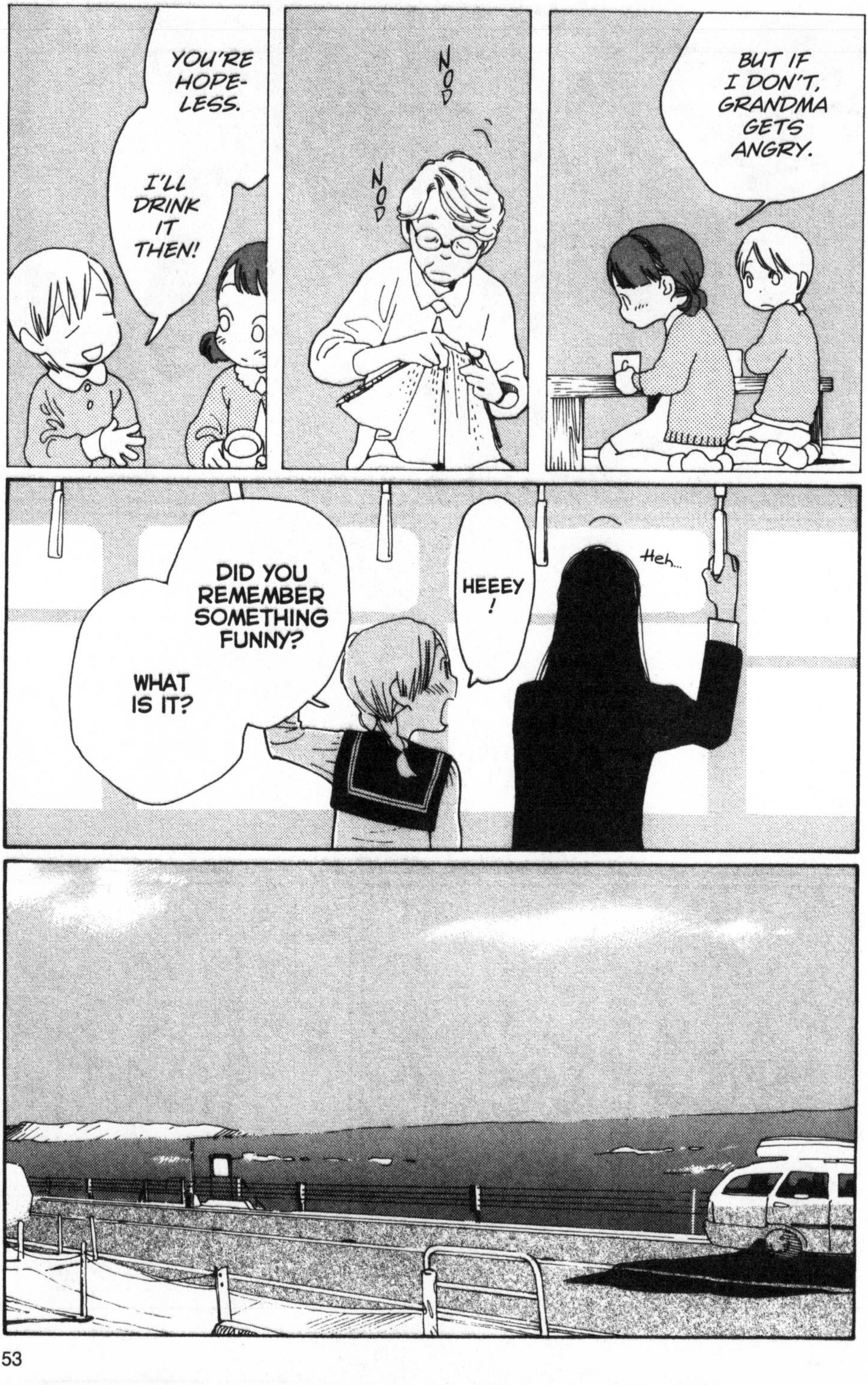
BUT IF I DON'T, GRANDMA GETS ANGRY.
NOD
NOD
YOU'RE HOPE-LESS.
I'LL DRINK IT THEN!
Heh...
HEEEY!
DID YOU REMEMBER SOMETHING FUNNY?
WHAT IS IT?

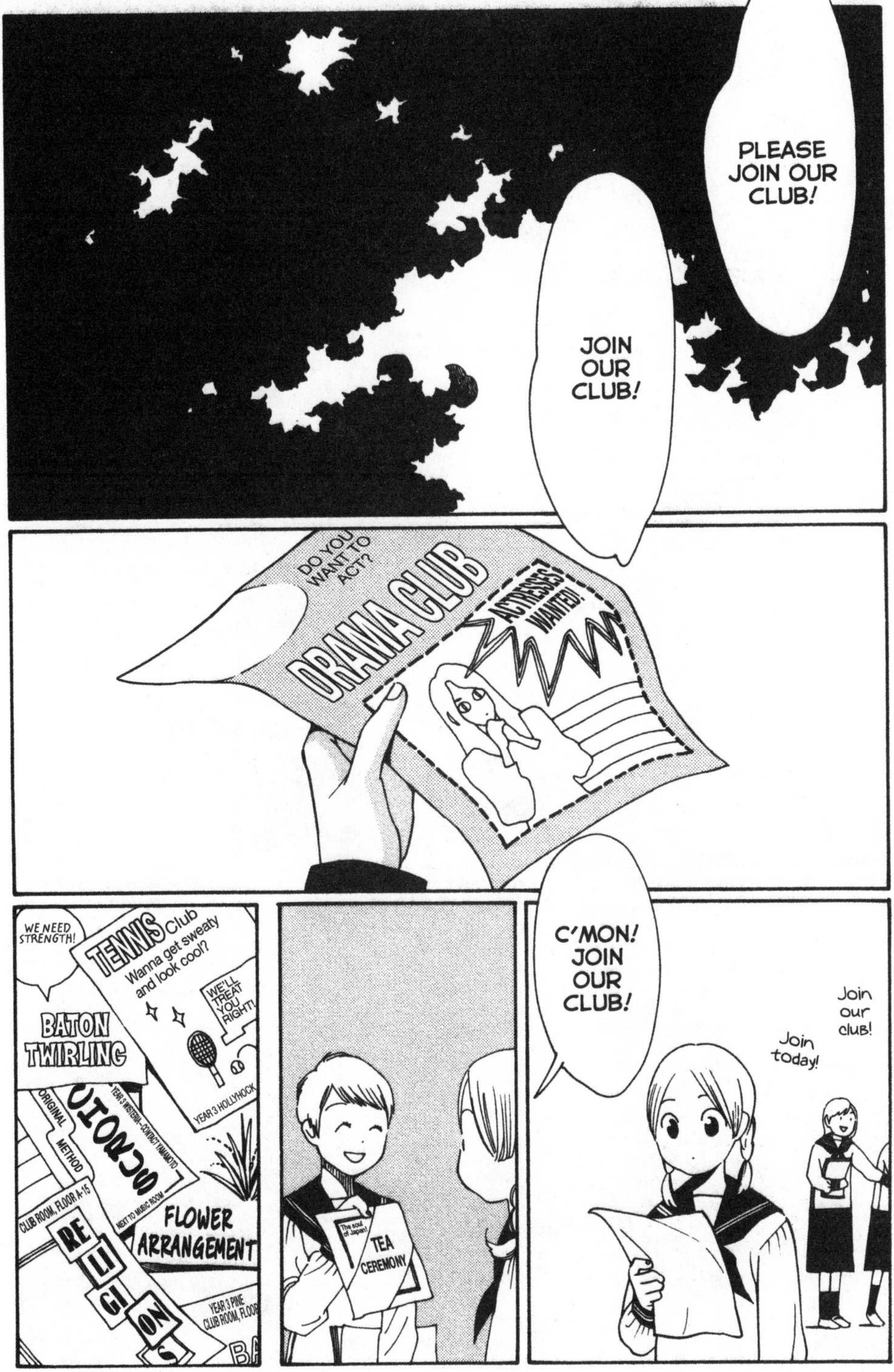
PLEASE JOIN OUR CLUB!
JOIN OUR CLUB!
DO YOU WANT TO ACT?
DRAMA CLUB
ACTRESSES WANTED!
C'MON! JOIN OUR CLUB!
Join our club!
Join today!
The soul of Japan!
TEA CEREMONY
WE NEED STRENGTH!
TENNIS Club
Wanna get sweaty and look cool?
WE'LL TREAT YOU RIGHT!
YEAR 3 HOLLYHOCK
BATON TWIRLING
ORIGINAL
METHOD
YEAR 3 WISTERIA—CONTACT YAMAMOTO
CLUB ROOM, FLOOR A-15
NEXT TO MUSIC ROOM
FLOWER ARRANGEMENT
RELIGION
YEAR 3 PINE

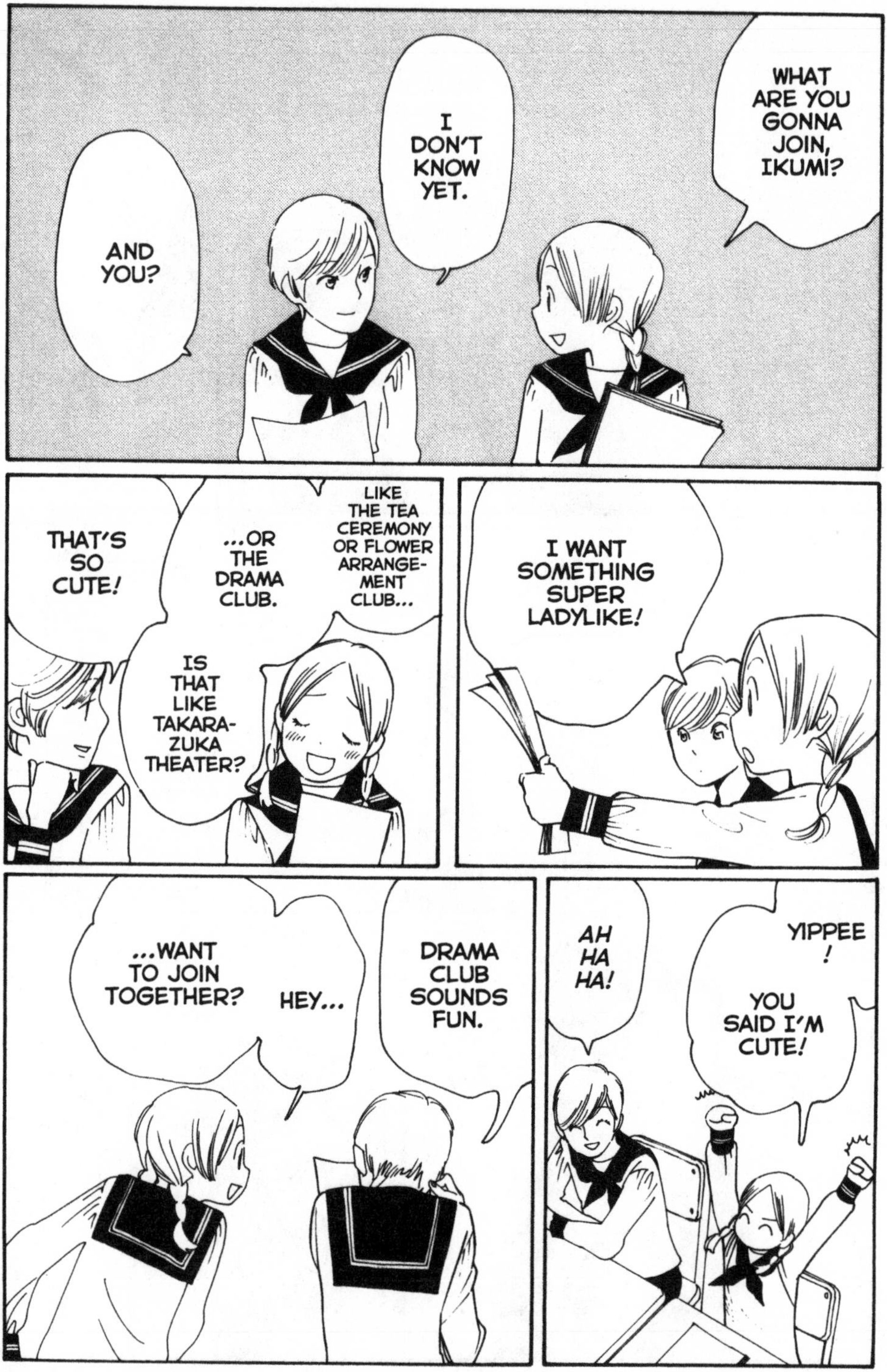
WHAT ARE YOU GONNA JOIN, IKUMI?
I DON'T KNOW YET.
AND YOU?
I WANT SOMETHING SUPER LADYLIKE!
LIKE THE TEA CEREMONY OR FLOWER ARRANGE-MENT CLUB...
...OR THE DRAMA CLUB.
THAT'S SO CUTE!
IS THAT LIKE TAKARA-ZUKA THEATER?
YIPPEE!
YOU SAID I'M CUTE!
AH HA HA!
DRAMA CLUB SOUNDS FUN.
HEY...
...WANT TO JOIN TOGETHER?

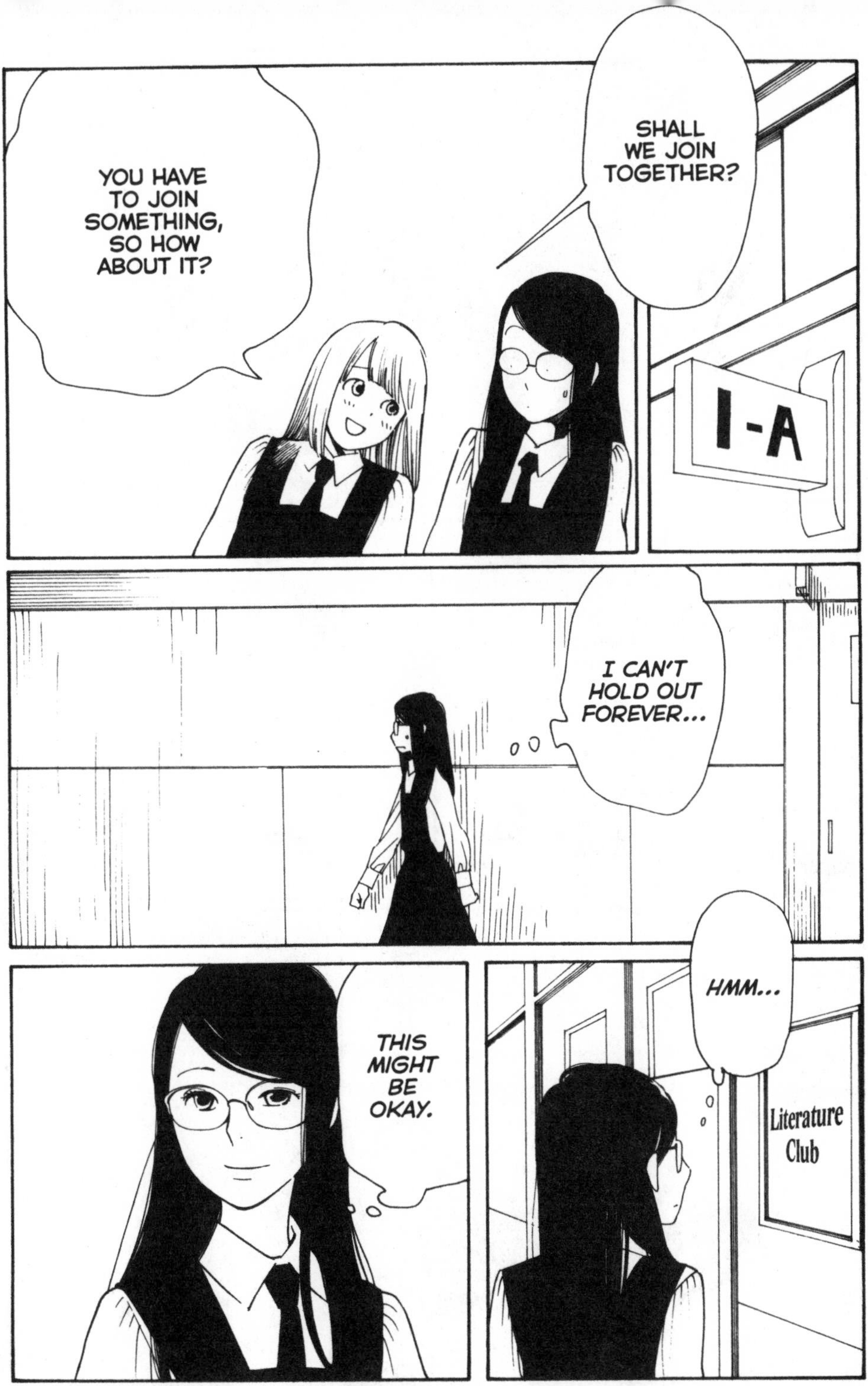
I-A
SHALL WE JOIN TOGETHER?
YOU HAVE TO JOIN SOMETHING, SO HOW ABOUT IT?
I CAN'T HOLD OUT FOREVER...
HMM...
Literature Club
THIS MIGHT BE OKAY.

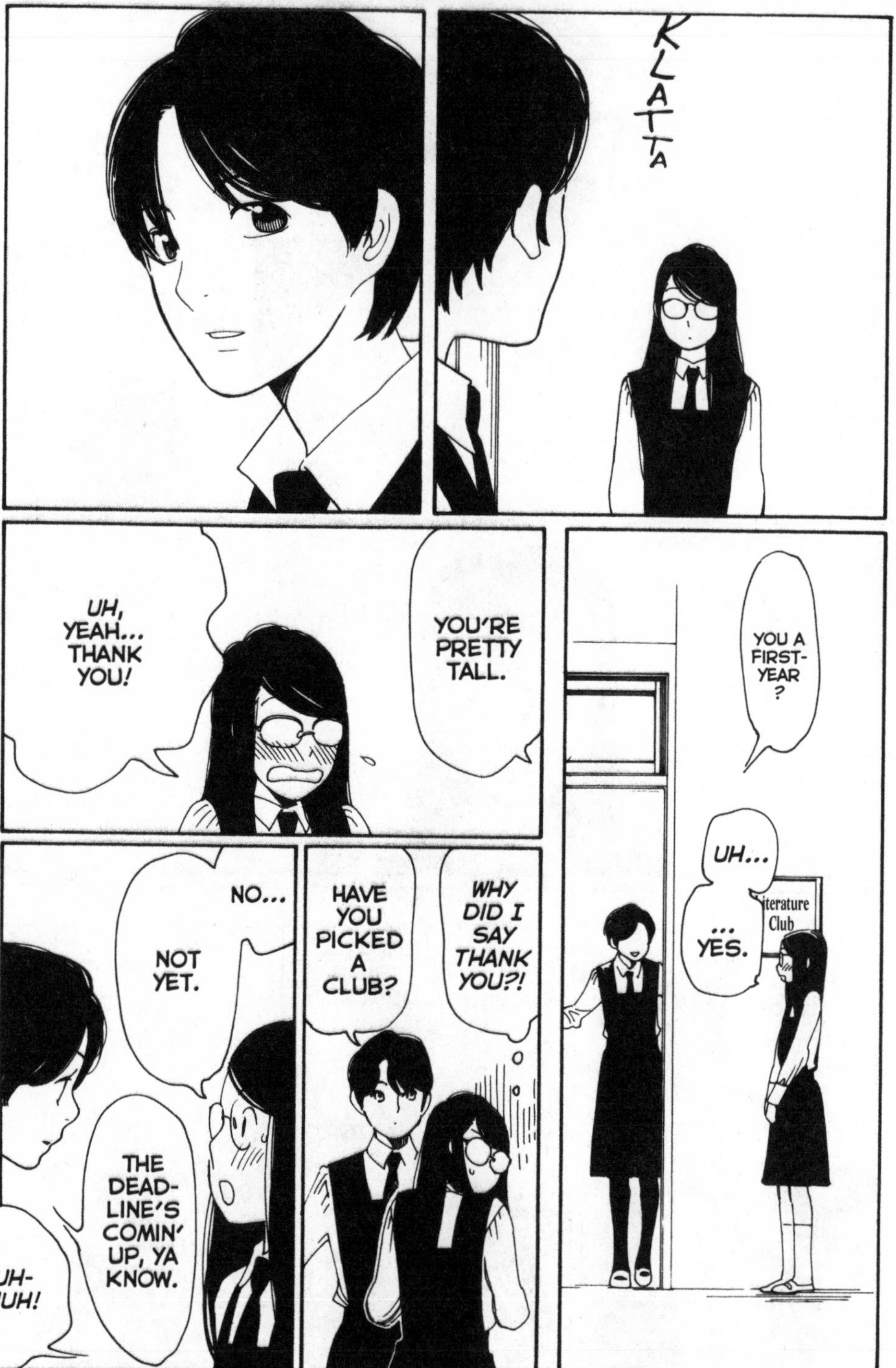
KLATTA
YOU A FIRST-YEAR?
UH...
... YES.
iterature Club
YOU'RE PRETTY TALL.
UH, YEAH... THANK YOU!
WHY DID I SAY THANK YOU?!
HAVE YOU PICKED A CLUB?
NO...
NOT YET.
THE DEAD-LINE'S COMIN' UP, YA KNOW.
UH-HUH!

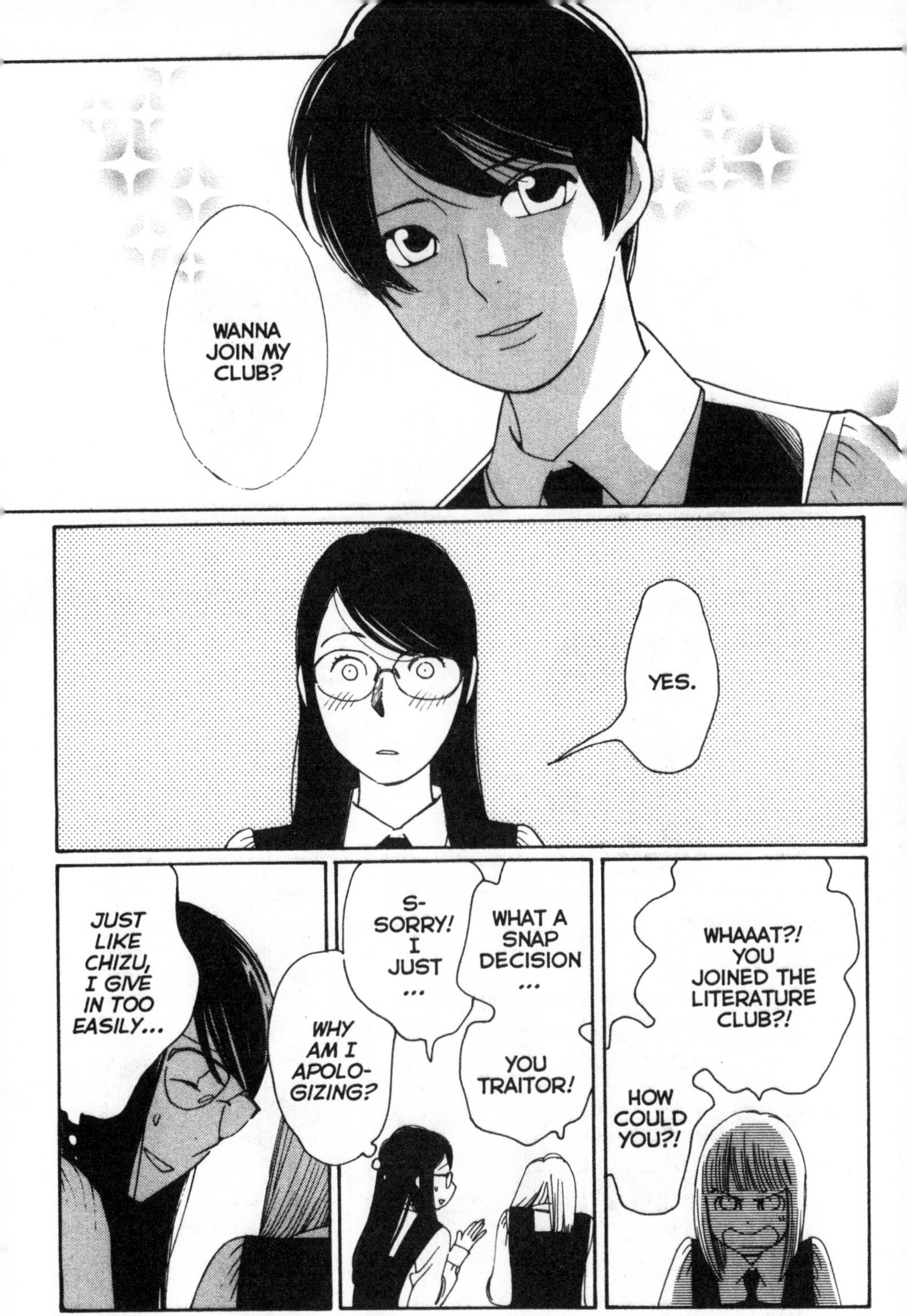
WANNA JOIN MY CLUB?
YES.
WHAAAT?! YOU JOINED THE LITERATURE CLUB?!
HOW COULD YOU?!
WHAT A SNAP DECISION ...
YOU TRAITOR!
S-SORRY! I JUST ...
WHY AM I APOLOGIZING?
JUST LIKE CHIZU, I GIVE IN TOO EASILY...

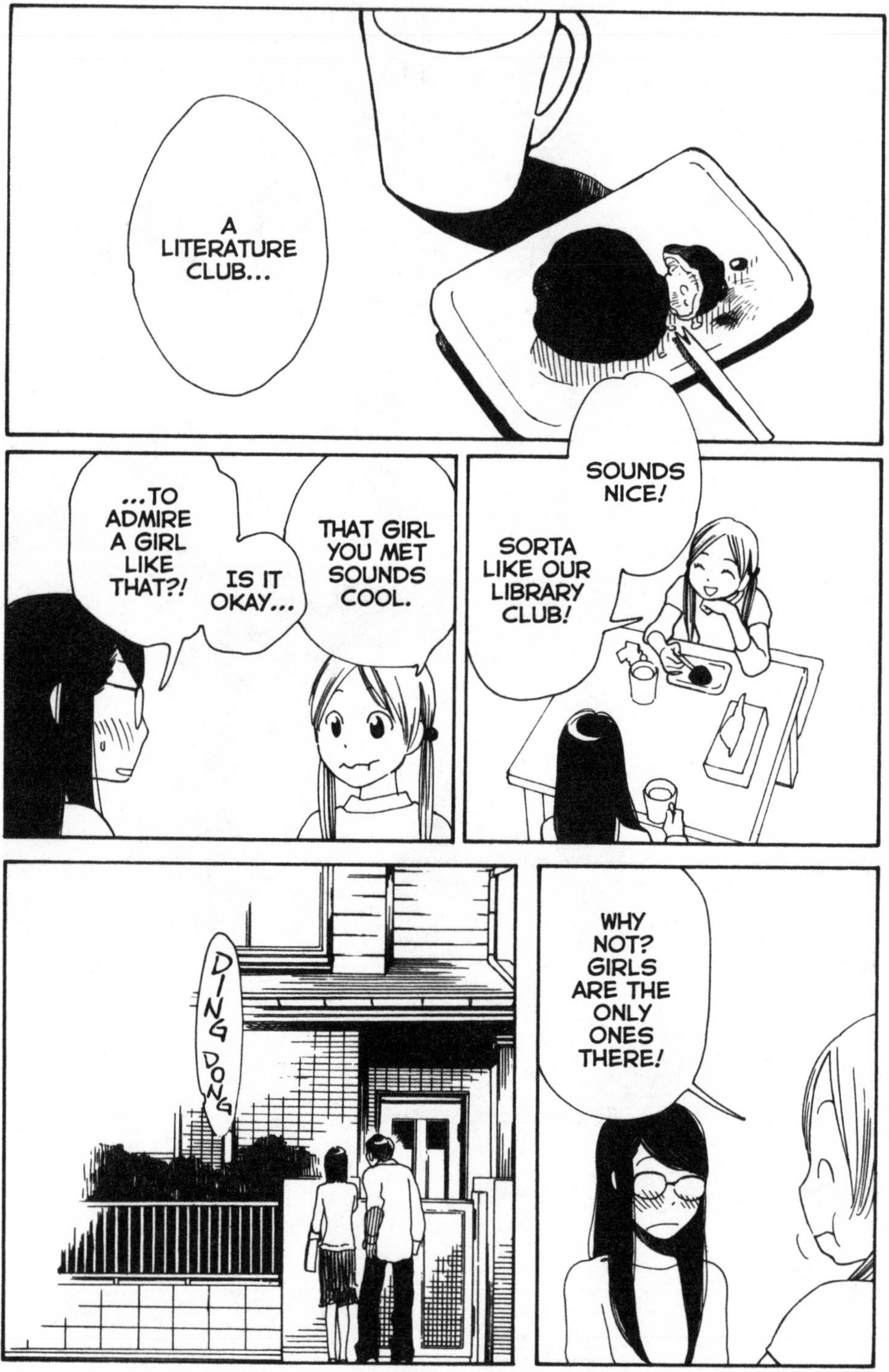
A LITERATURE CLUB...
SOUNDS NICE!
SORTA LIKE OUR LIBRARY CLUB!
THAT GIRL YOU MET SOUNDS COOL.
IS IT OKAY...
...TO ADMIRE A GIRL LIKE THAT?!
WHY NOT? GIRLS ARE THE ONLY ONES THERE!
DING DONG

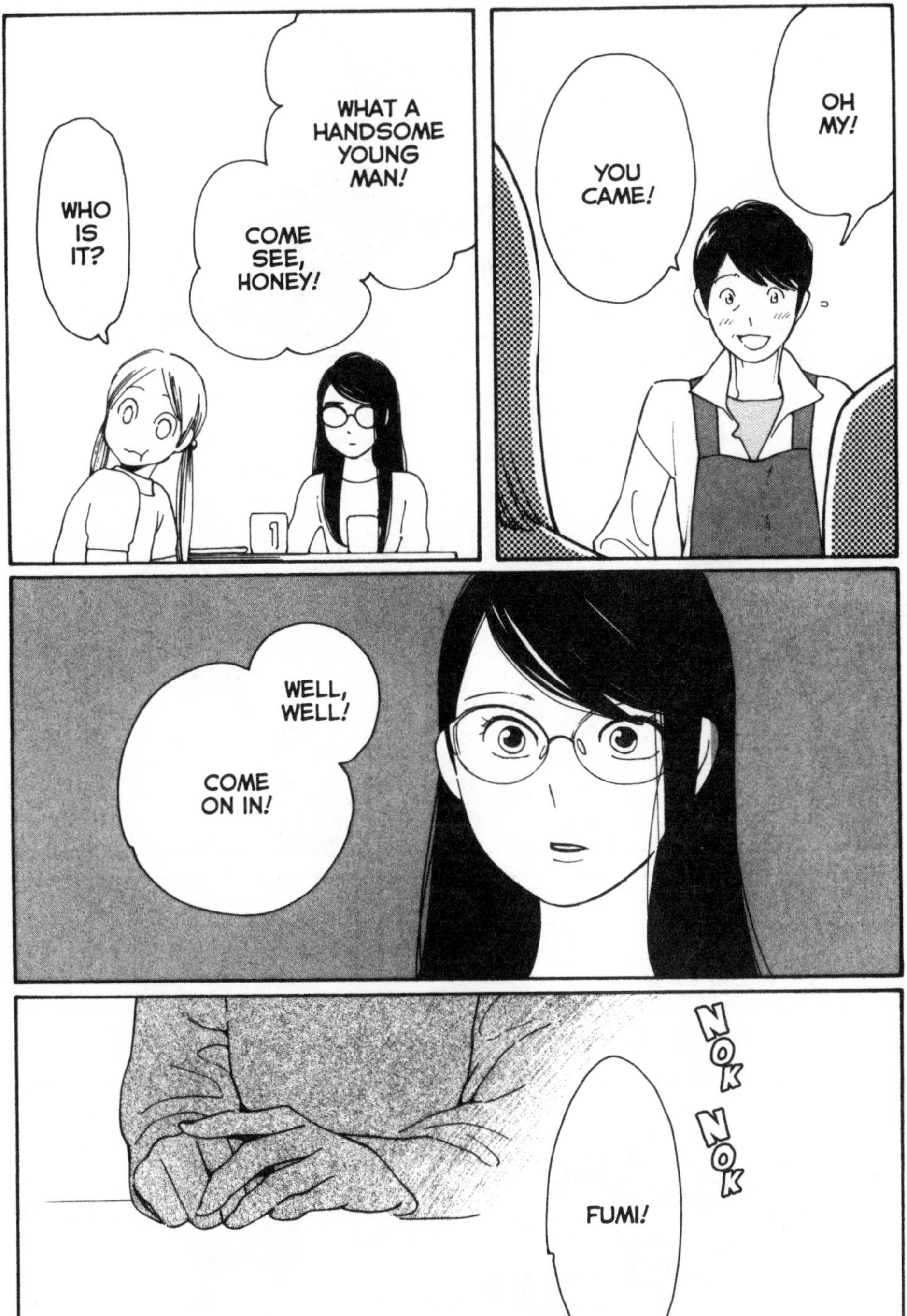
OH MY!
YOU CAME!
WHAT A HANDSOME YOUNG MAN!
COME SEE, HONEY!
WHO IS IT?
WELL, WELL!
COME ON IN!
NOK NOK
FUMI!

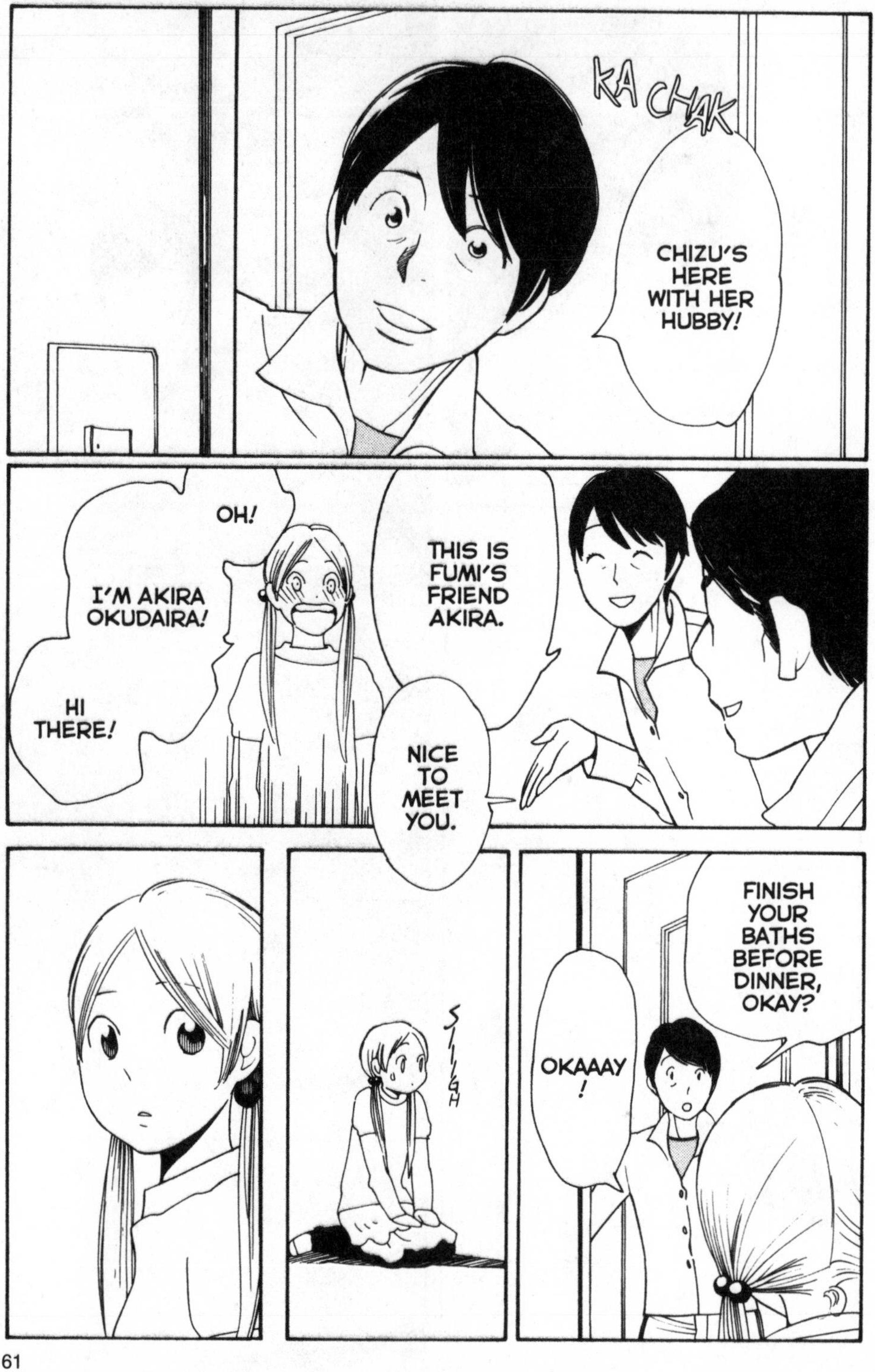
KA CHAK
CHIZU'S HERE WITH HER HUBBY!
THIS IS FUMI'S FRIEND AKIRA.
NICE TO MEET YOU.
OH!
I'M AKIRA OKUDAIRA!
HI THERE!
FINISH YOUR BATHS BEFORE DINNER, OKAY?
OKAAAY!
SIIIGH

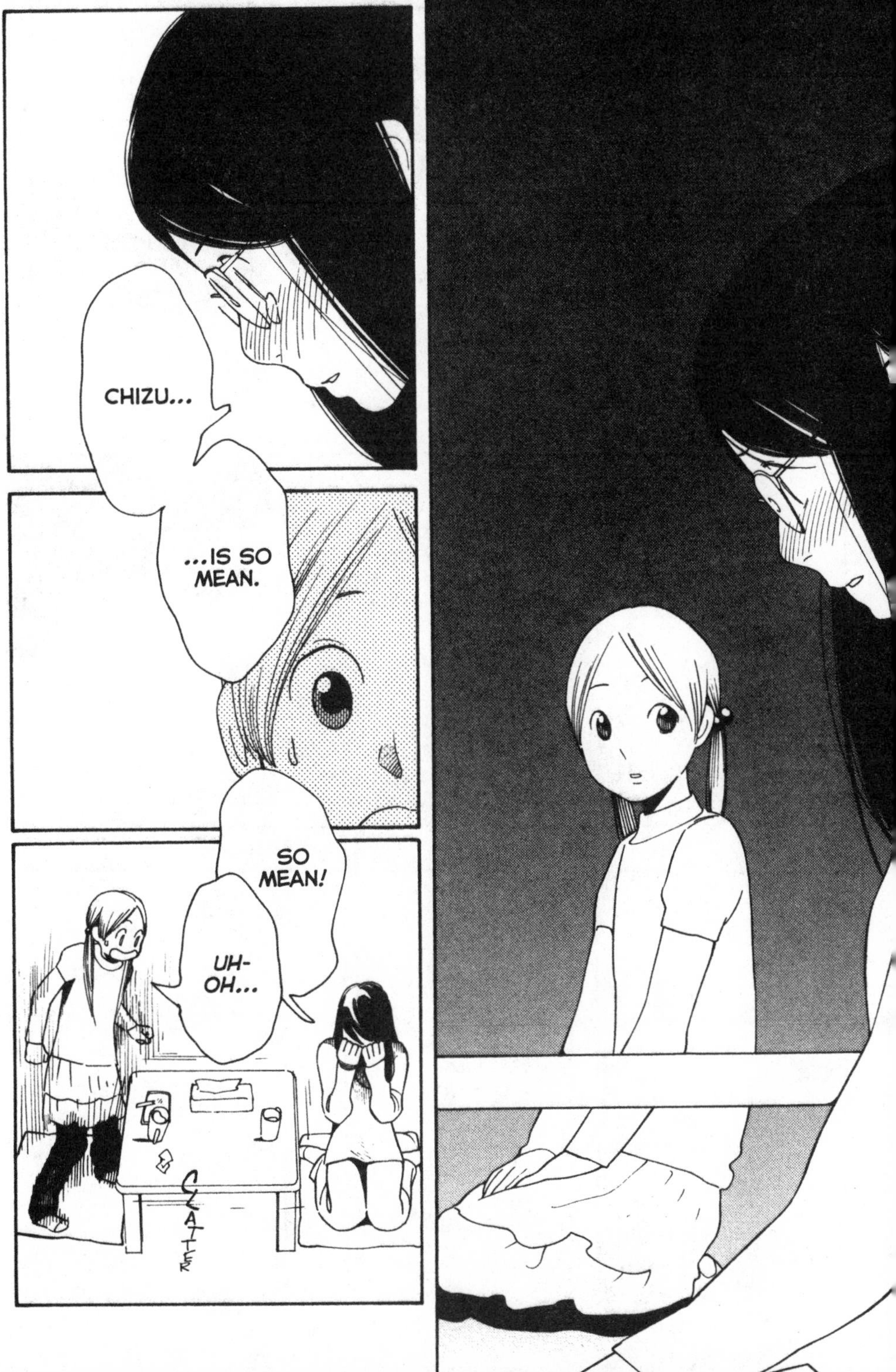
CHIZU...
...IS SO MEAN.
SO MEAN!
UH-OH...
CLATTER

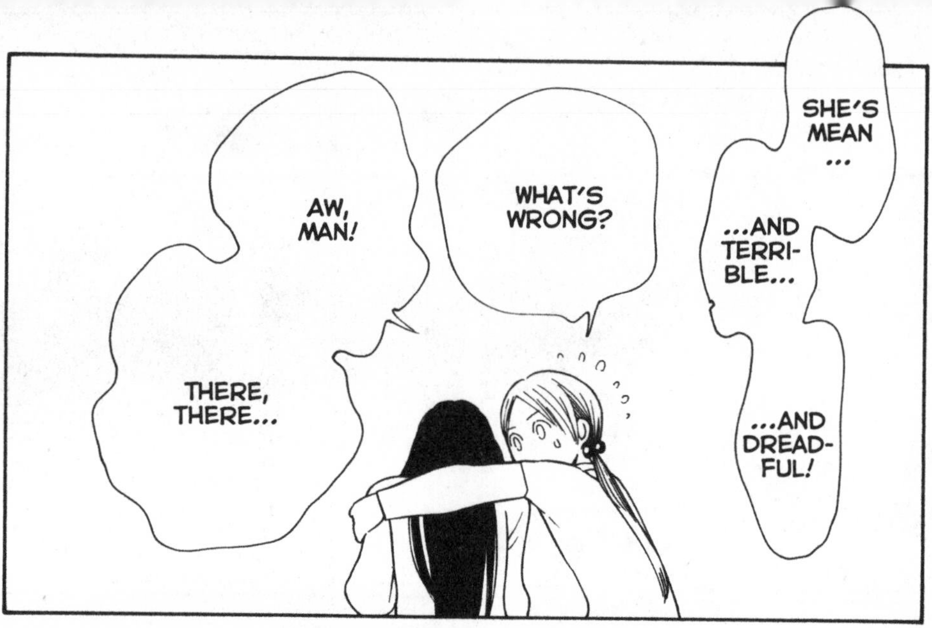
SHE'S MEAN ...
...AND TERRIBLE...
...AND DREADFUL!
WHAT'S WRONG?
AW, MAN!
THERE, THERE...

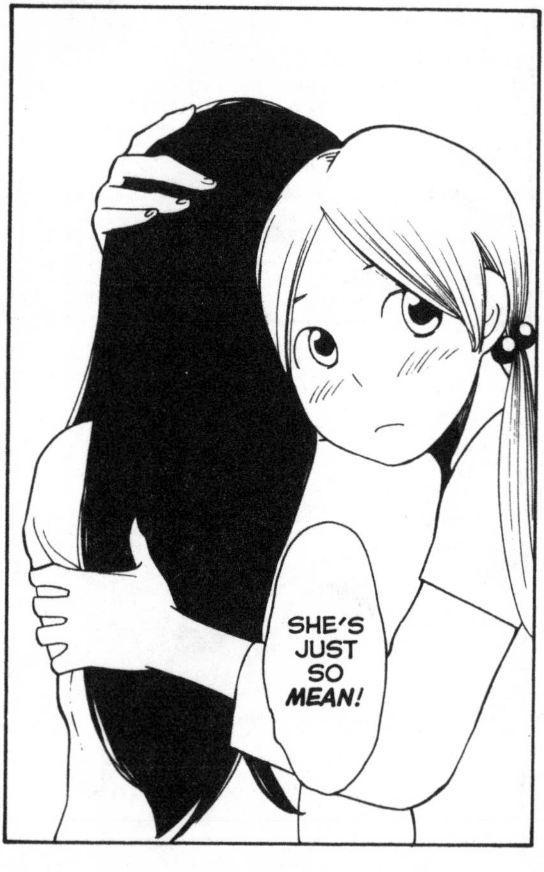
SHE'S JUST SO MEAN!

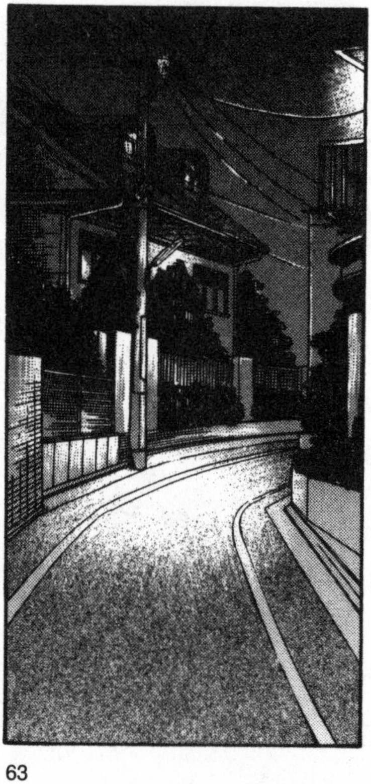

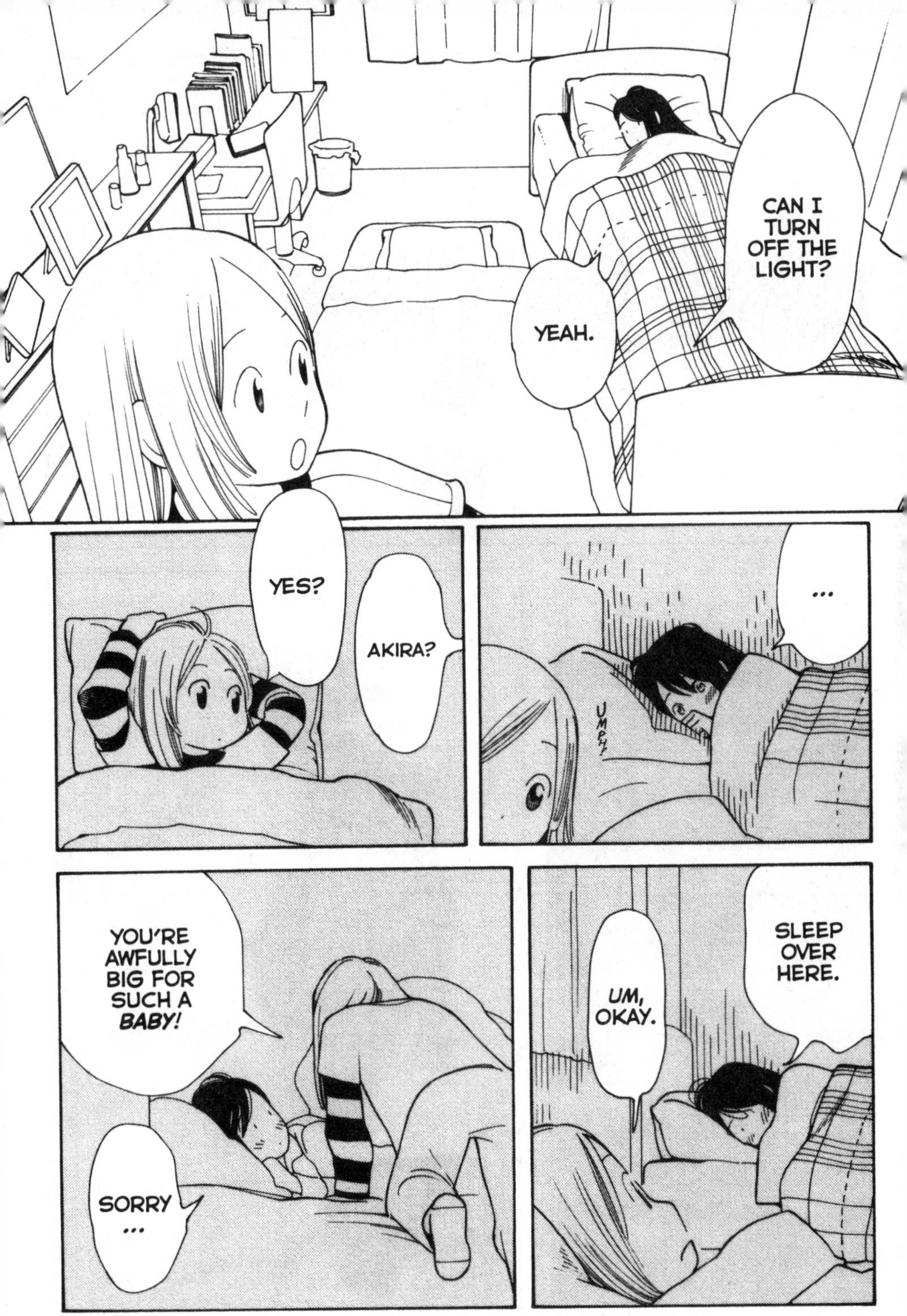
CAN I TURN OFF THE LIGHT?
YEAH.
...
UMPH!
AKIRA?
YES?
SLEEP OVER HERE.
UM, OKAY.
YOU'RE AWFULLY BIG FOR SUCH A *BABY!*
SORRY ...

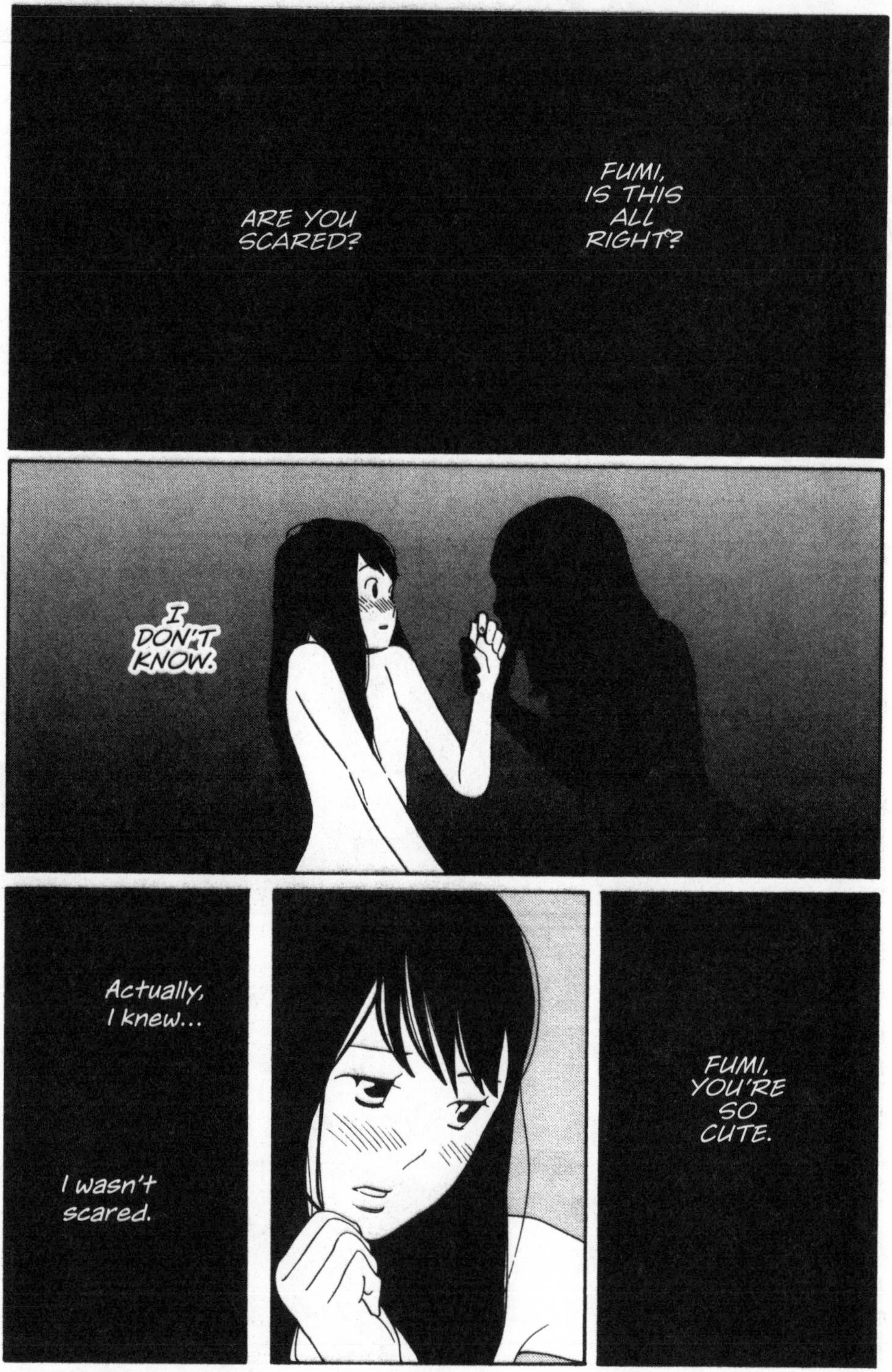
FUMI, IS THIS ALL RIGHT?
ARE YOU SCARED?
I DON'T KNOW.
FUMI, YOU'RE SO CUTE.
Actually, I knew...
I wasn't scared.

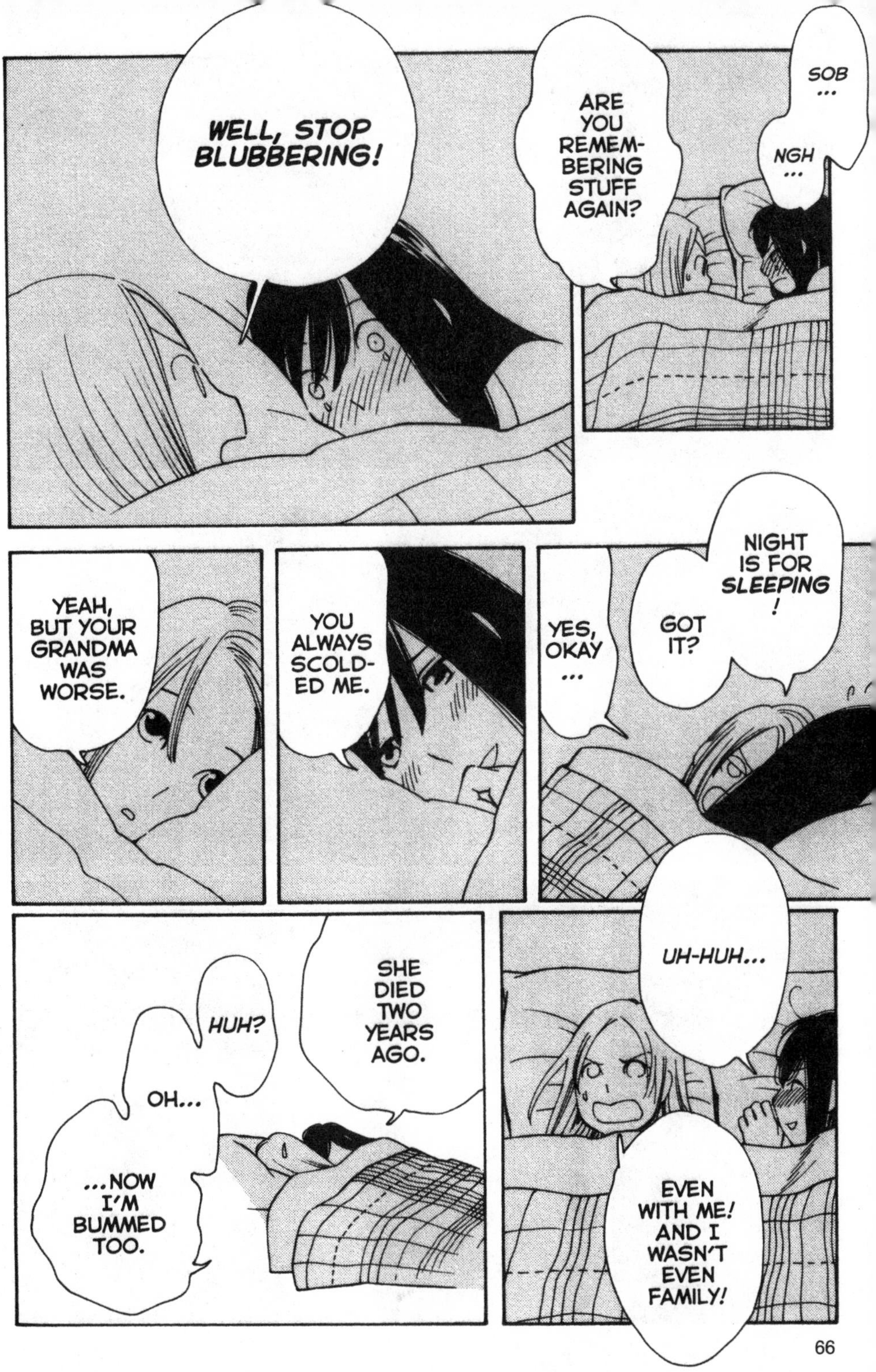
SOB... NGH...
ARE YOU REMEMBERING STUFF AGAIN?
WELL, STOP BLUBBERING!
NIGHT IS FOR SLEEPING!
GOT IT?
YES, OKAY...
YOU ALWAYS SCOLDED ME.
YEAH, BUT YOUR GRANDMA WAS WORSE.
UH-HUH...
EVEN WITH ME! AND I WASN'T EVEN FAMILY!
SHE DIED TWO YEARS AGO.
HUH?
OH...
...NOW I'M BUMMED TOO.

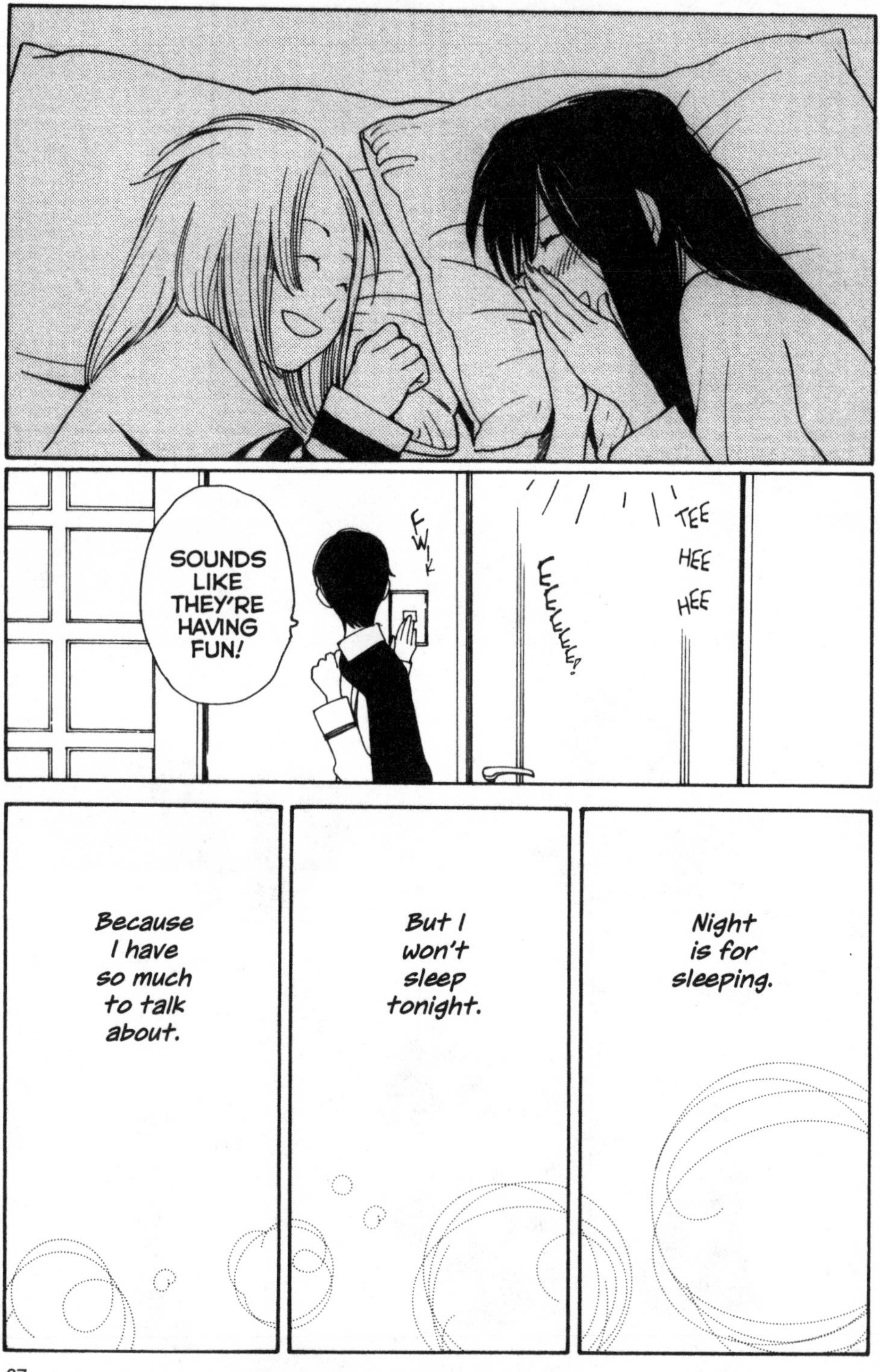
TEE
HEE
HEE
FWIK
SOUNDS LIKE THEY'RE HAVING FUN!
Night is for sleeping.
But I won't sleep tonight.
Because I have so much to talk about.

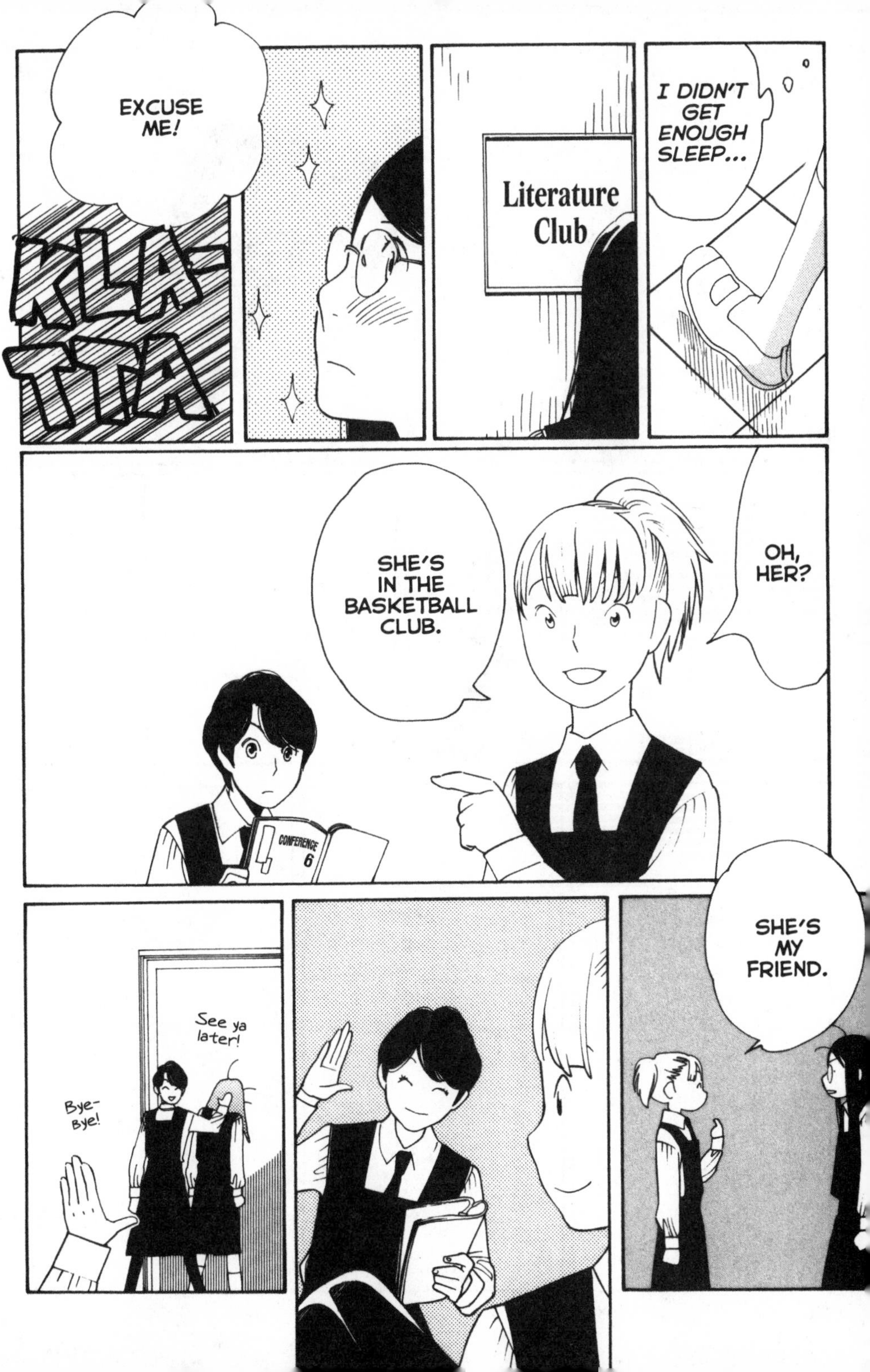
I DIDN'T GET ENOUGH SLEEP...
Literature Club
EXCUSE ME!
KLA-TTA
OH, HER?
SHE'S IN THE BASKETBALL CLUB.
CONFERENCE 6
SHE'S MY FRIEND.
See ya later!
Bye-Bye!

# Sweet Blue Flowers

## #3 Spring Breeze

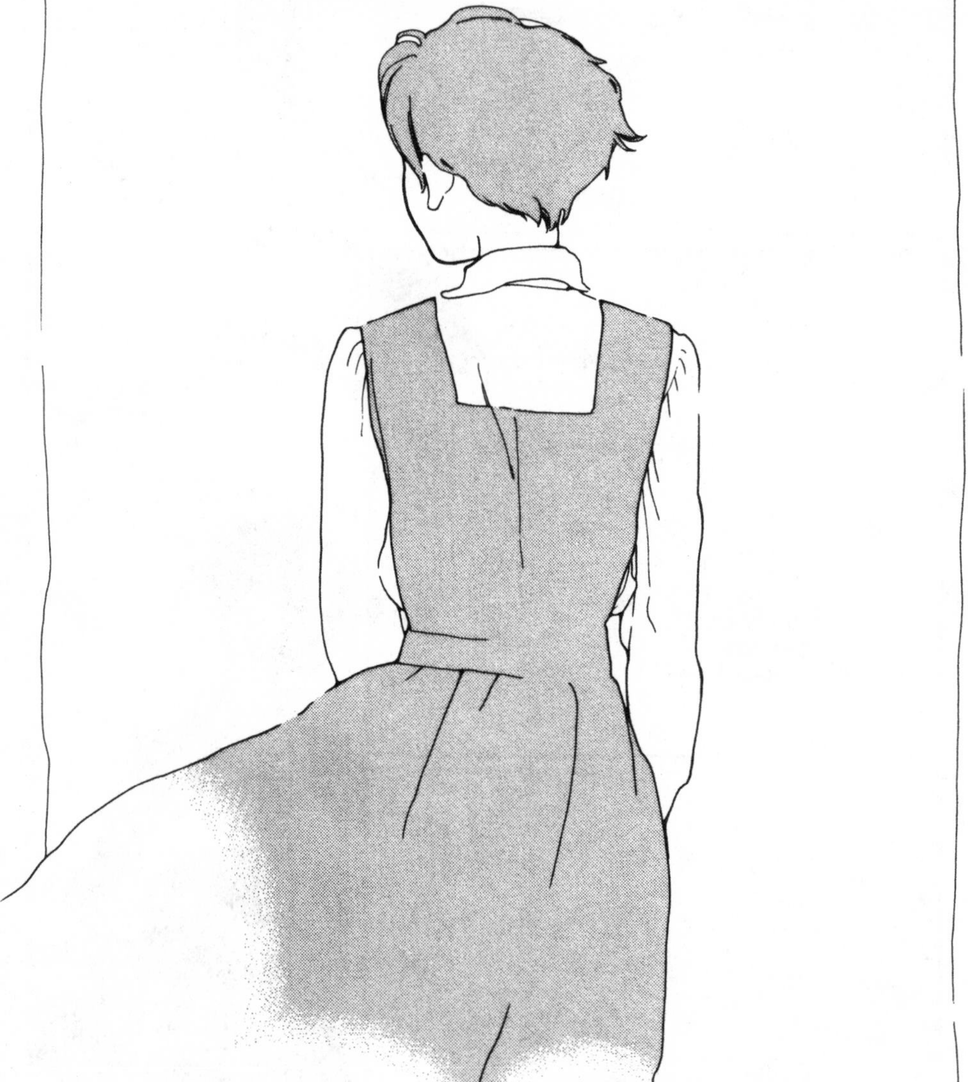

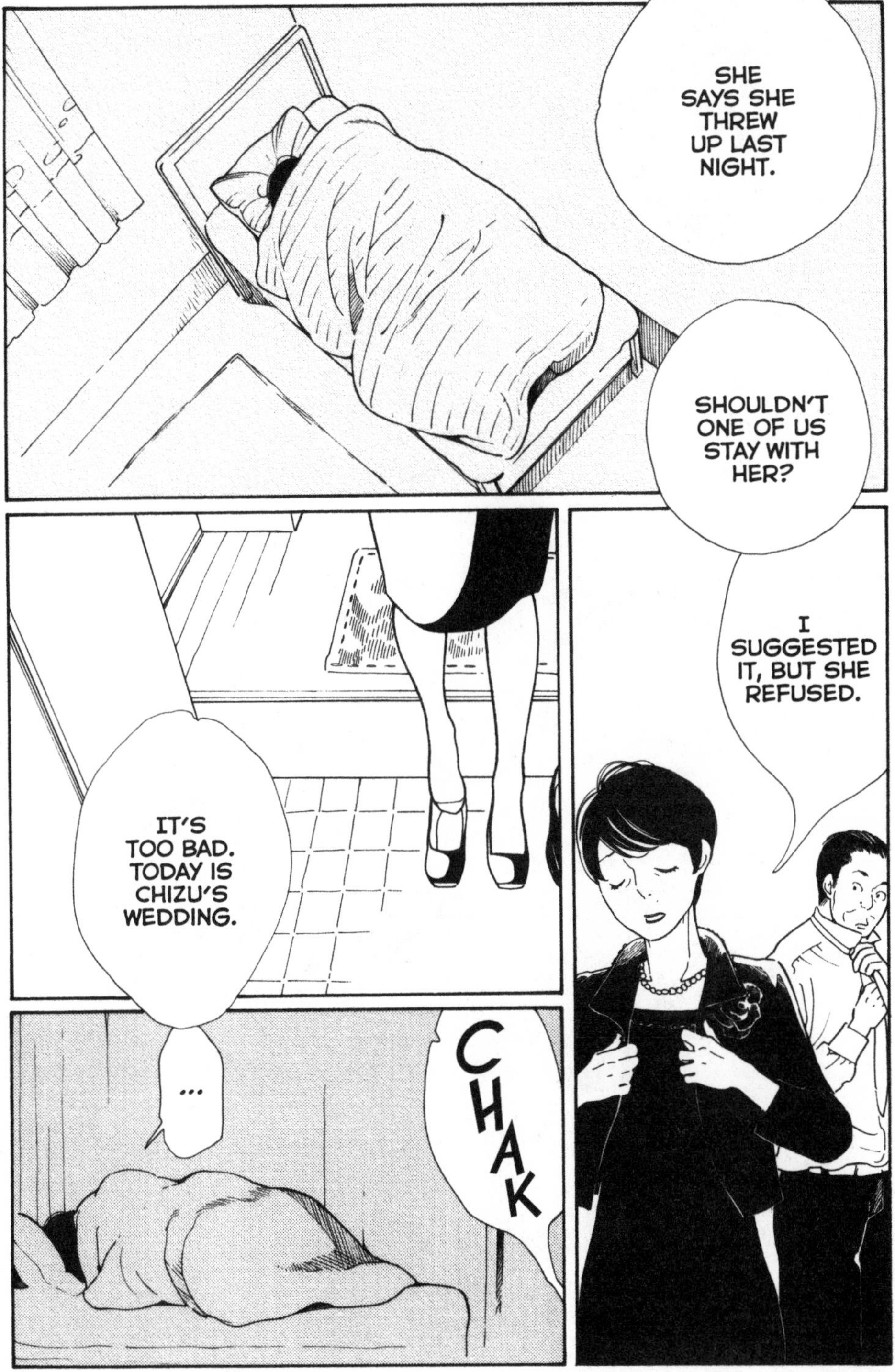

SHE SAYS SHE THREW UP LAST NIGHT.
SHOULDN'T ONE OF US STAY WITH HER?
I SUGGESTED IT, BUT SHE REFUSED.
IT'S TOO BAD. TODAY IS CHIZU'S WEDDING.
CHAK
...

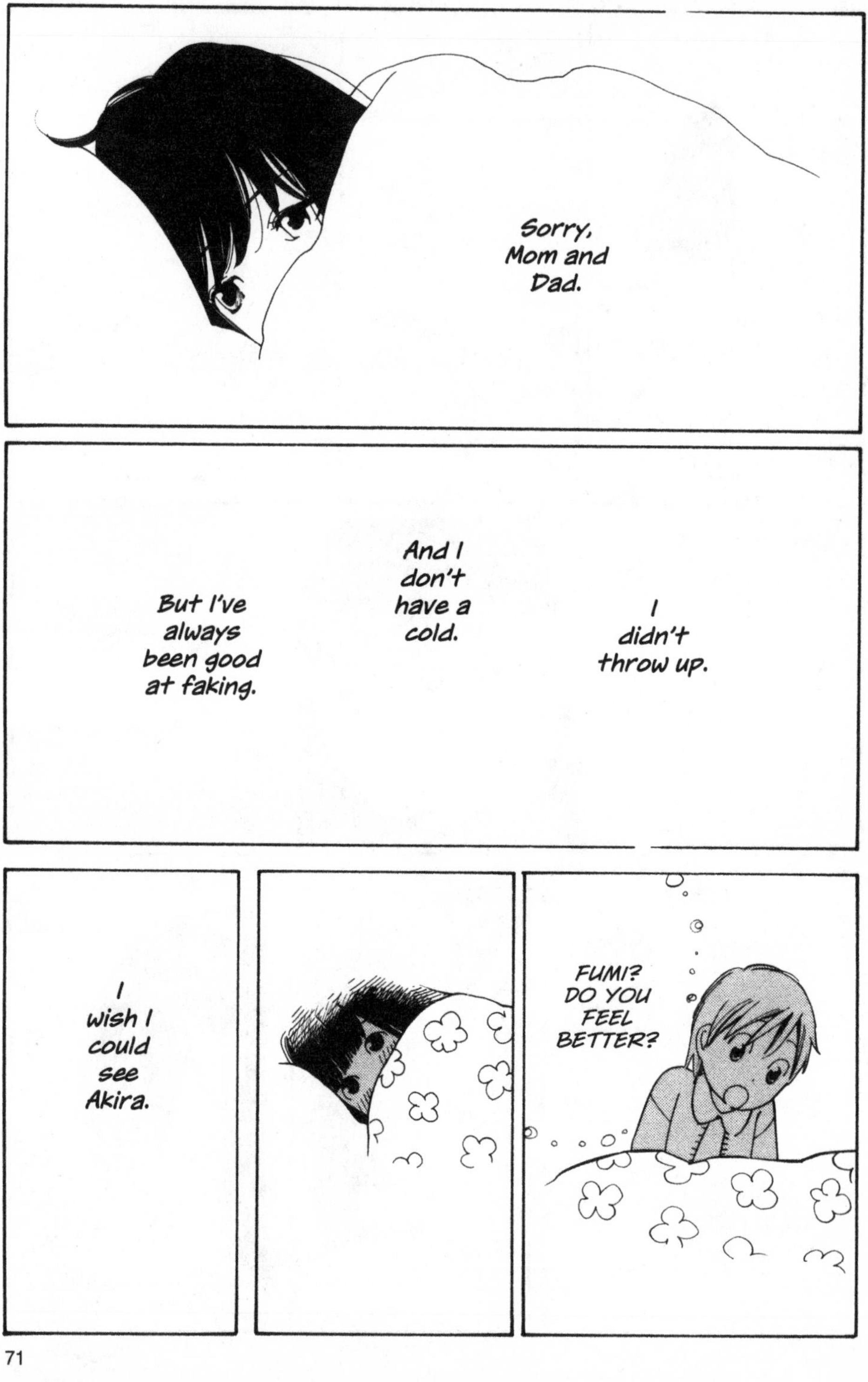
Sorry, Mom and Dad.
I didn't throw up.
And I don't have a cold.
But I've always been good at faking.
FUMI? DO YOU FEEL BETTER?
I wish I could see Akira.

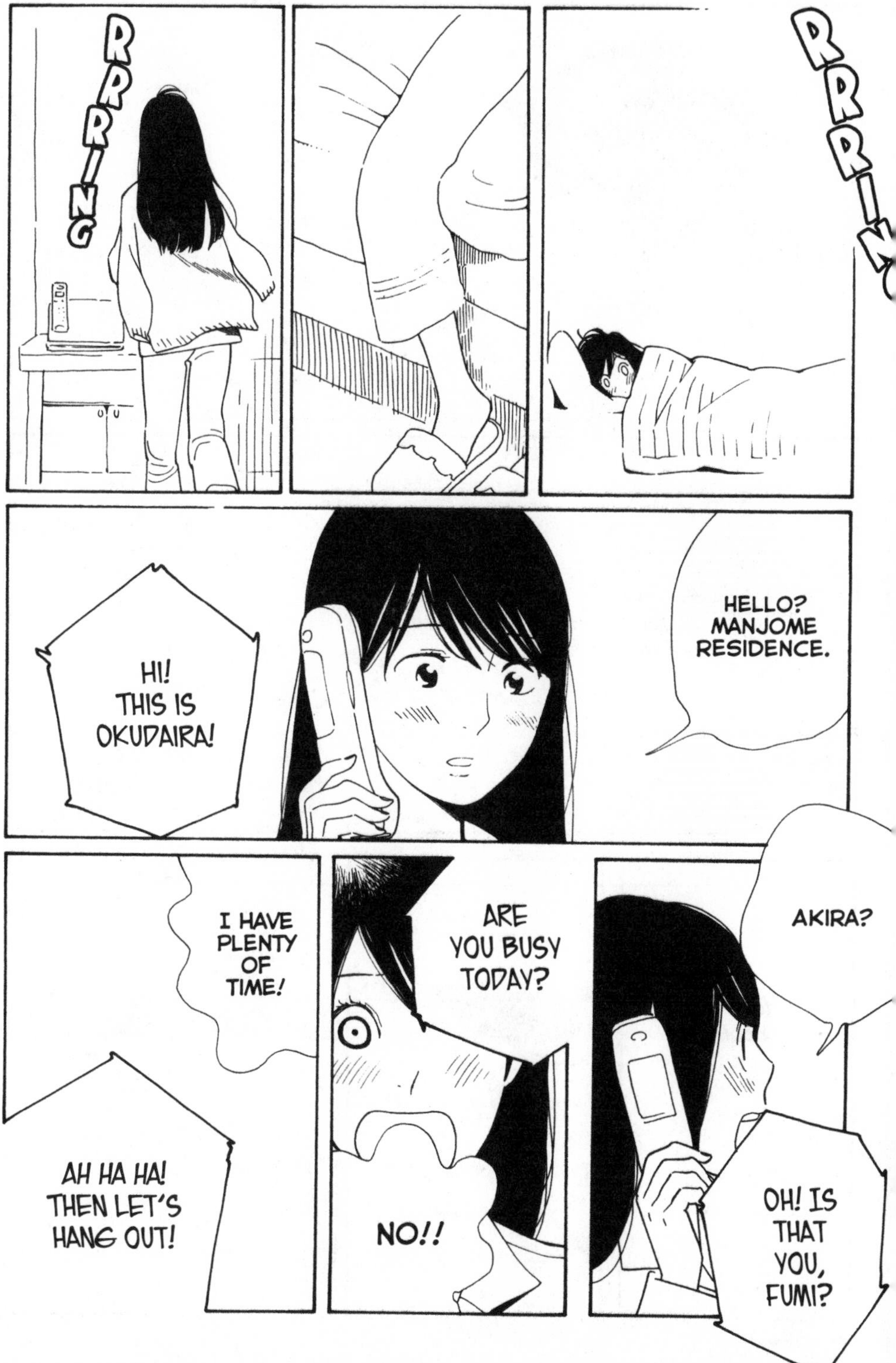
RRRIN
RRRING
HELLO? MANJOME RESIDENCE.
HI! THIS IS OKUDAIRA!
AKIRA?
OH! IS THAT YOU, FUMI?
ARE YOU BUSY TODAY?
NO!!
I HAVE PLENTY OF TIME!
AH HA HA! THEN LET'S HANG OUT!

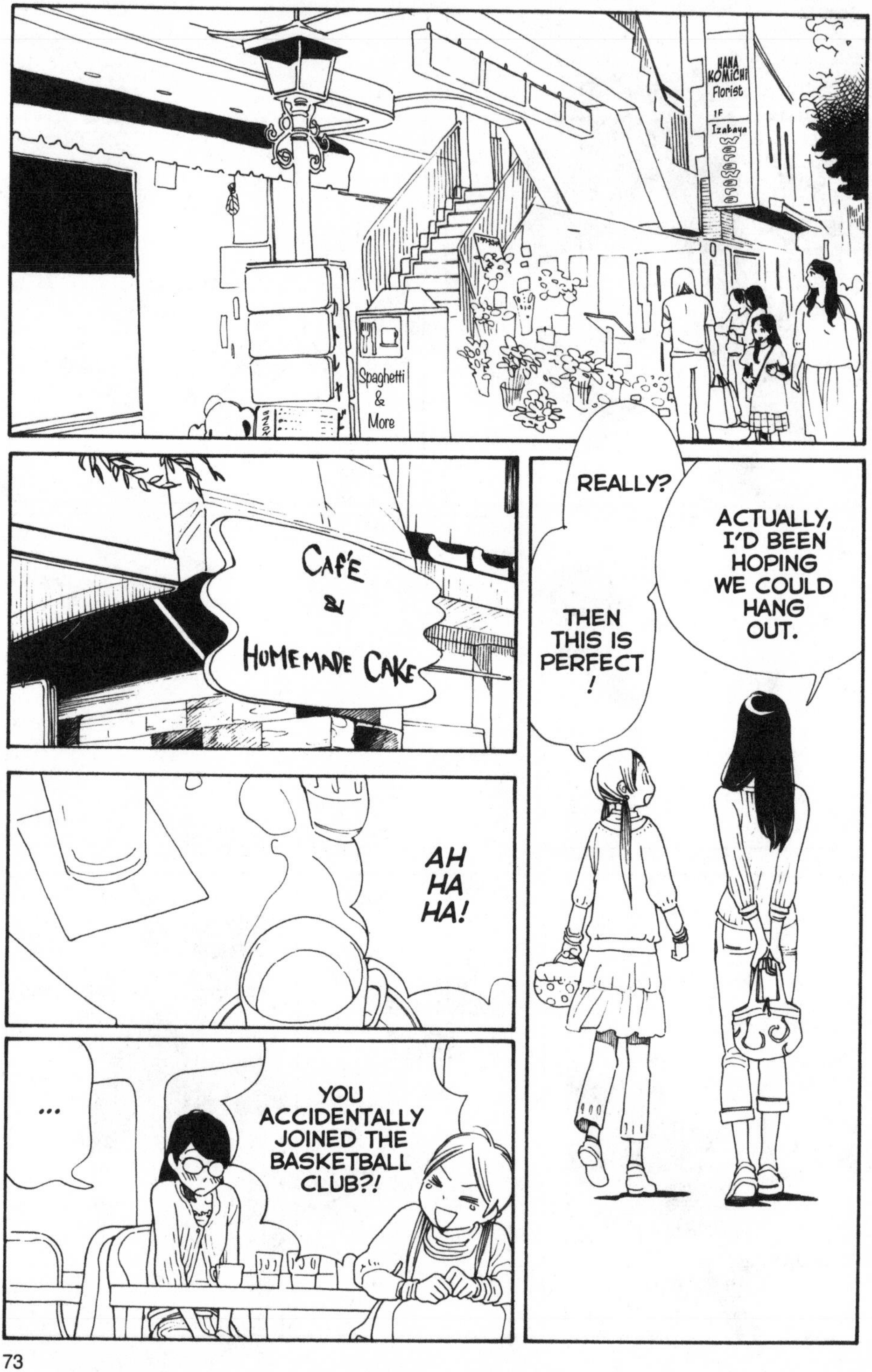
HANA KOMICHI Florist
1F Izakaya Warawara
Spaghetti & More
ACTUALLY, I'D BEEN HOPING WE COULD HANG OUT.
REALLY? THEN THIS IS PERFECT!
CAFÉ & HOMEMADE CAKE
AH HA HA!
YOU ACCIDENTALLY JOINED THE BASKETBALL CLUB?!
...

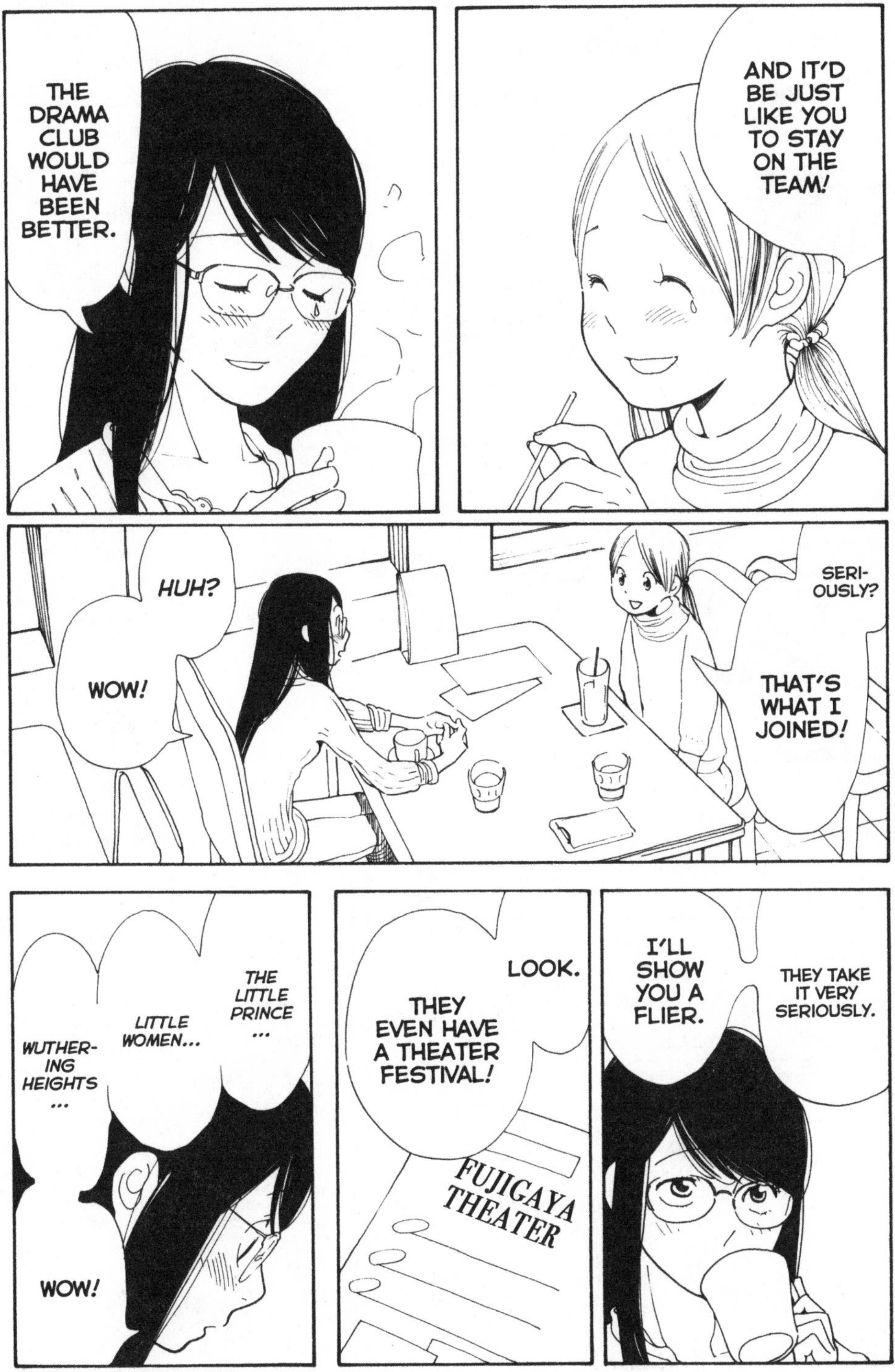
AND IT'D BE JUST LIKE YOU TO STAY ON THE TEAM!
THE DRAMA CLUB WOULD HAVE BEEN BETTER.
SERI-OUSLY?
THAT'S WHAT I JOINED!
HUH?
WOW!
THEY TAKE IT VERY SERIOUSLY.
I'LL SHOW YOU A FLIER.
LOOK.
THEY EVEN HAVE A THEATER FESTIVAL!
FUJIGAYA THEATER
THE LITTLE PRINCE...
LITTLE WOMEN...
WUTHER-ING HEIGHTS...
WOW!

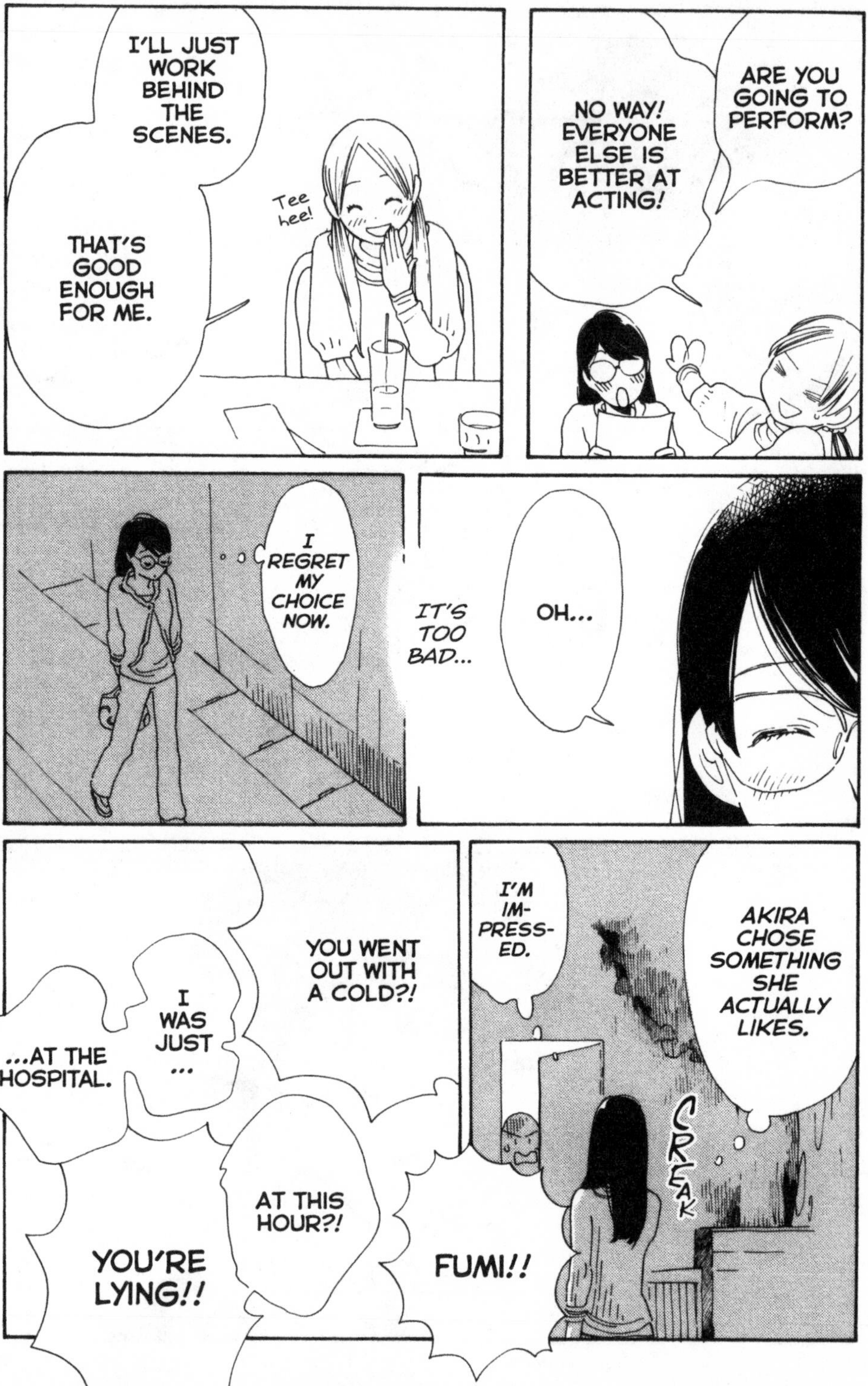
ARE YOU GOING TO PERFORM?
NO WAY! EVERYONE ELSE IS BETTER AT ACTING!
I'LL JUST WORK BEHIND THE SCENES.
Tee hee!
THAT'S GOOD ENOUGH FOR ME.
OH...
IT'S TOO BAD...
I REGRET MY CHOICE NOW.
AKIRA CHOSE SOMETHING SHE ACTUALLY LIKES.
I'M IM-PRESS-ED.
CREAK
FUMI!!
YOU WENT OUT WITH A COLD?!
I WAS JUST...
...AT THE HOSPITAL.
AT THIS HOUR?!
YOU'RE LYING!!

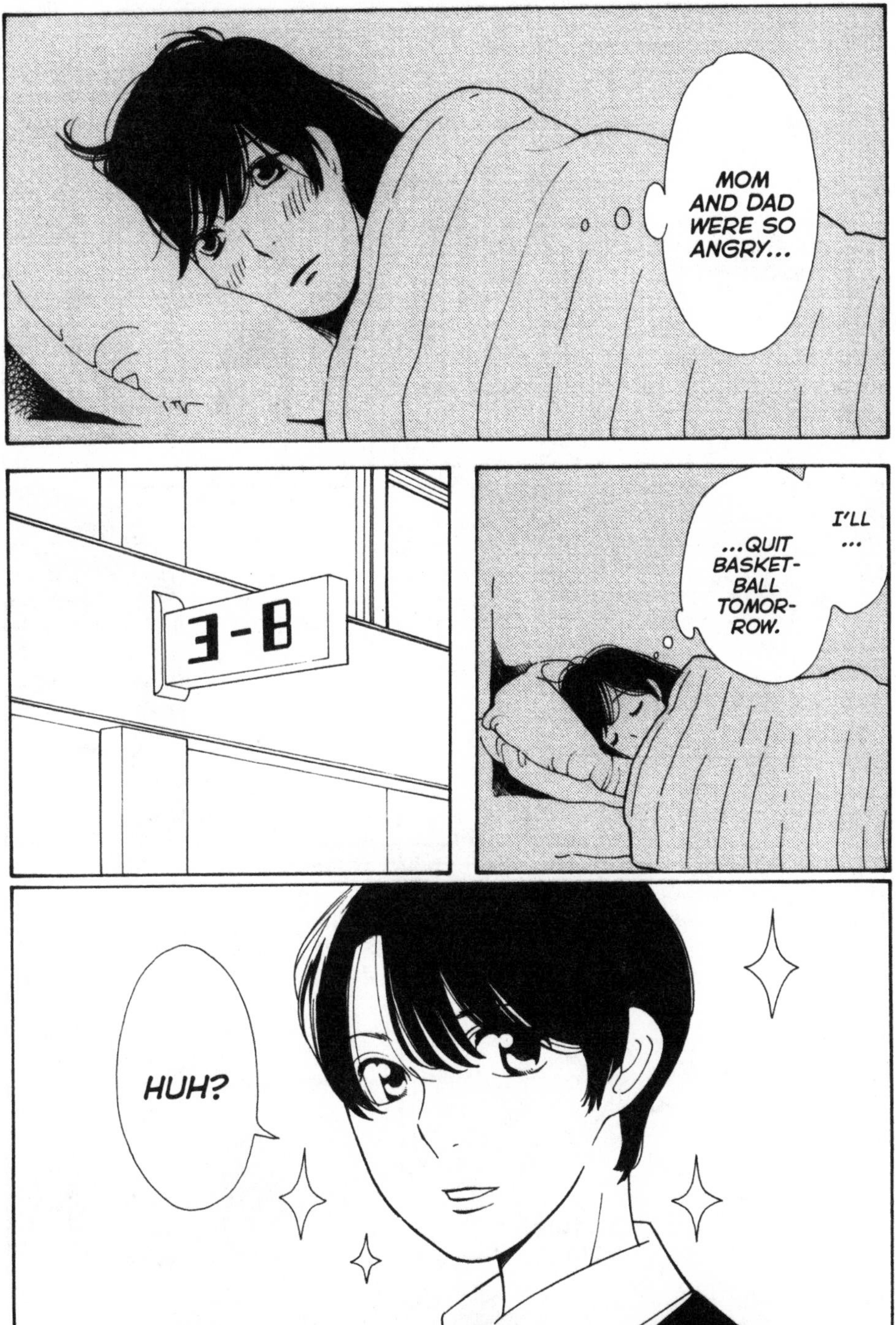
MOM AND DAD WERE SO ANGRY...
I'LL... ...QUIT BASKETBALL TOMORROW.
3-B
HUH?

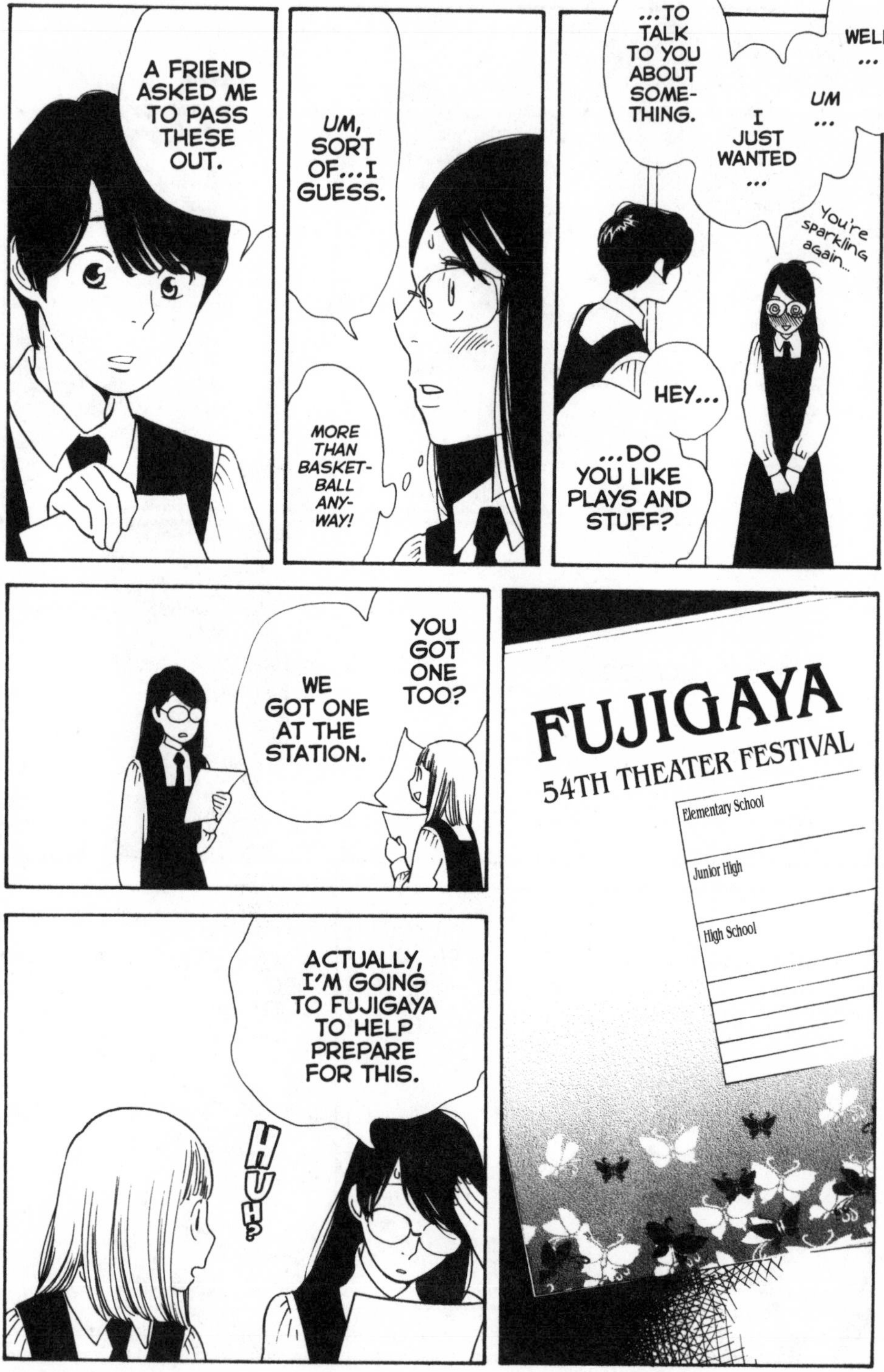
WELL... UM... I JUST WANTED...
...TO TALK TO YOU ABOUT SOME-THING.
You're sparkling again...
HEY...
...DO YOU LIKE PLAYS AND STUFF?
UM, SORT OF...I GUESS.
MORE THAN BASKET-BALL ANY-WAY!
A FRIEND ASKED ME TO PASS THESE OUT.
FUJIGAYA
54TH THEATER FESTIVAL
Elementary School
Junior High
High School
YOU GOT ONE TOO?
WE GOT ONE AT THE STATION.
ACTUALLY, I'M GOING TO FUJIGAYA TO HELP PREPARE FOR THIS.
HUH?

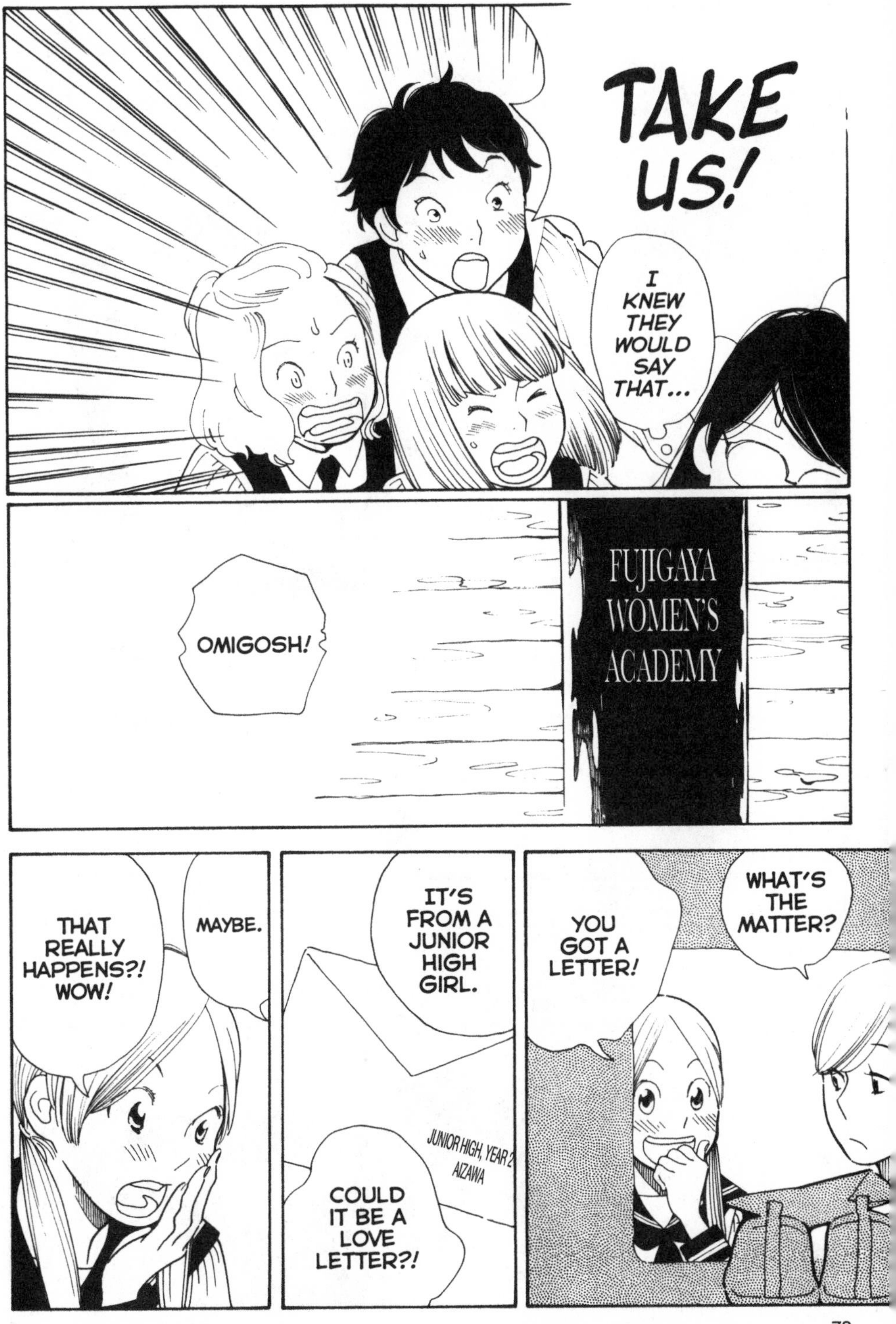

TAKE US!
I KNEW THEY WOULD SAY THAT...
FUJIGAYA WOMEN'S ACADEMY
OMIGOSH!
WHAT'S THE MATTER?
YOU GOT A LETTER!
IT'S FROM A JUNIOR HIGH GIRL.
JUNIOR HIGH, YEAR 2 AIZAWA
COULD IT BE A LOVE LETTER?!
MAYBE.
THAT REALLY HAPPENS?! WOW!

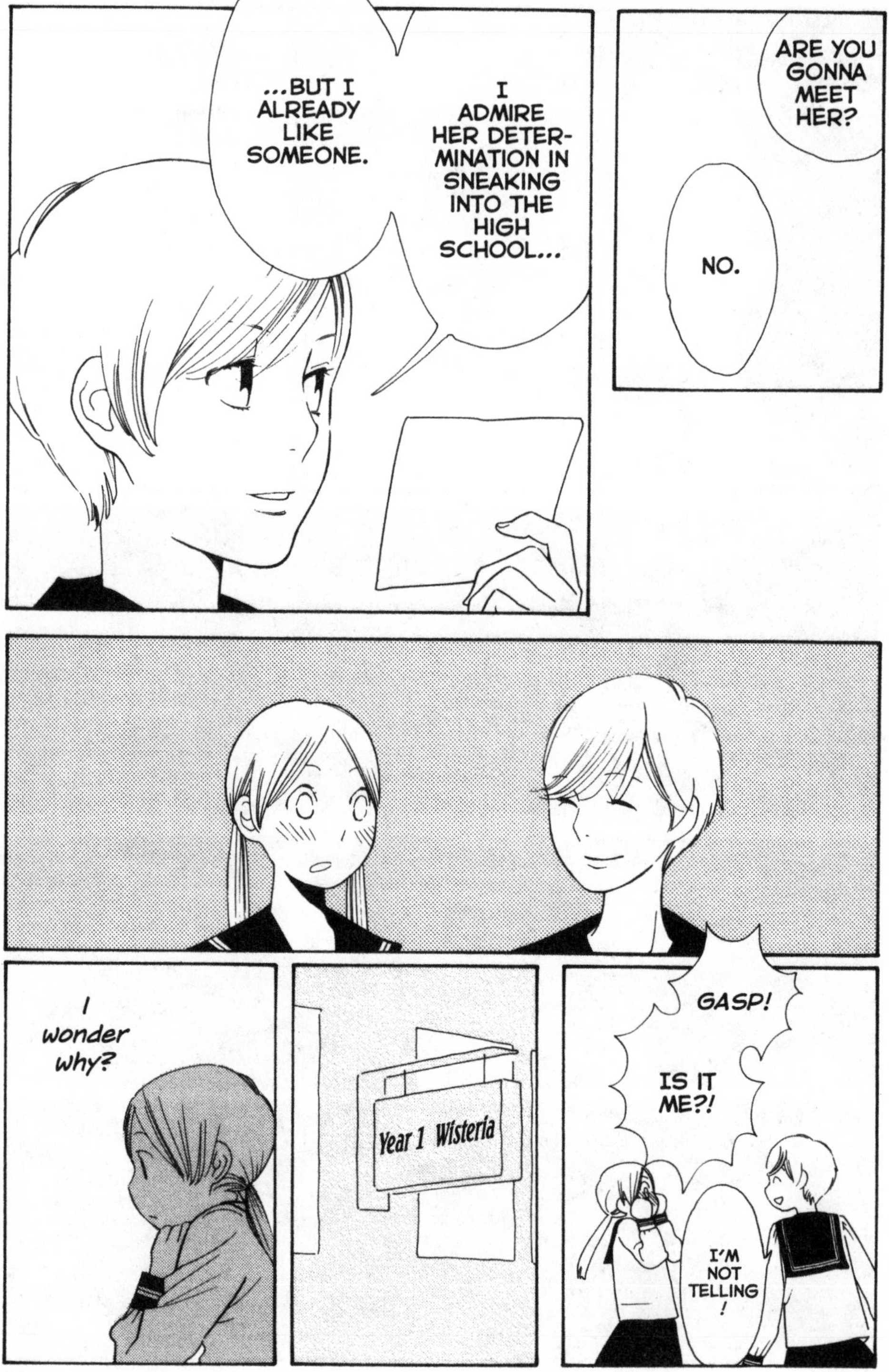
ARE YOU GONNA MEET HER?
NO.
I ADMIRE HER DETERMINATION IN SNEAKING INTO THE HIGH SCHOOL...
...BUT I ALREADY LIKE SOMEONE.
GASP!
IS IT ME?!
I'M NOT TELLING!
Year 1 Wisteria
I wonder why?

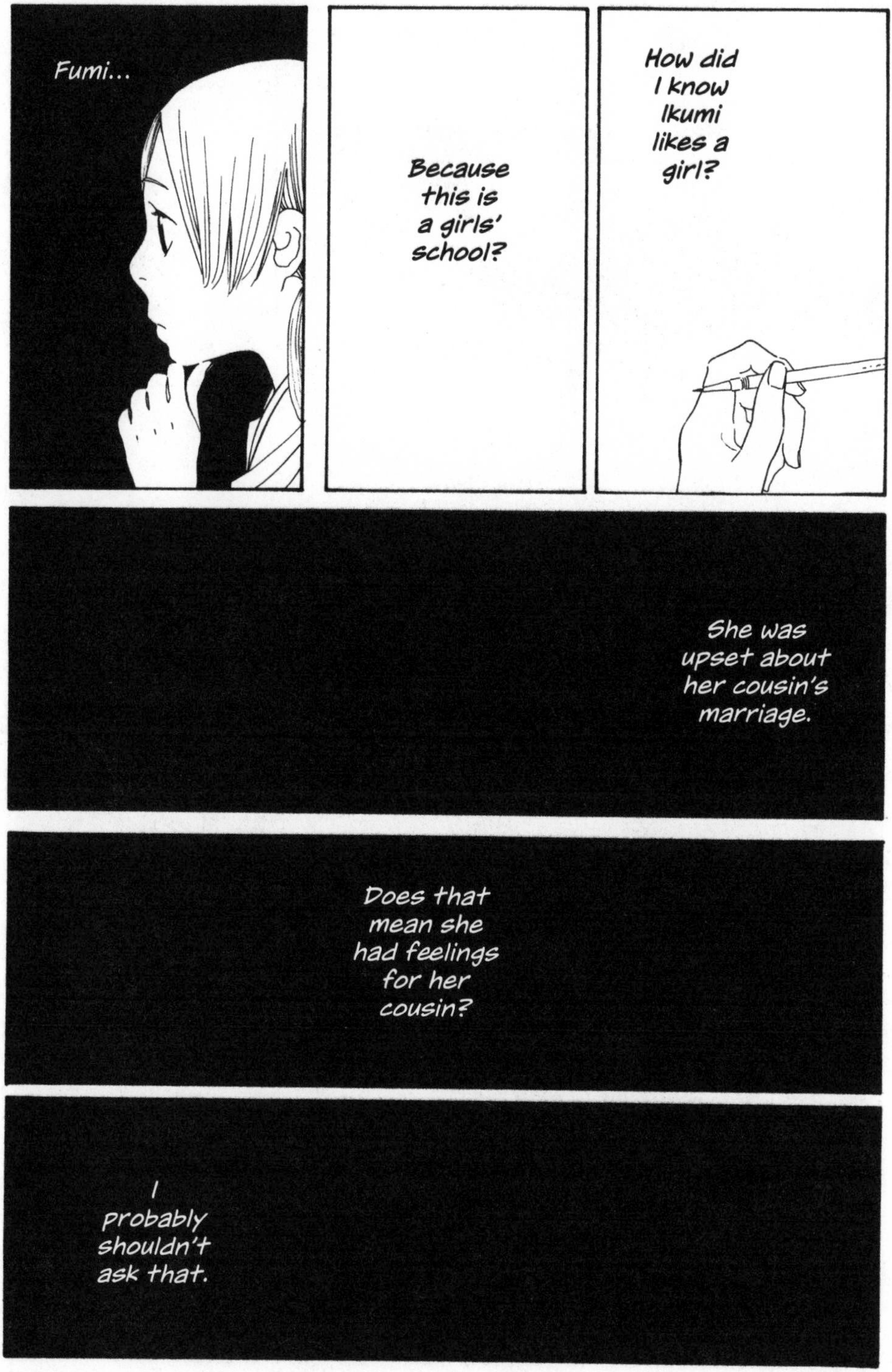
How did I know Ikumi likes a girl?
Because this is a girls' school?
Fumi...
She was upset about her cousin's marriage.
Does that mean she had feelings for her cousin?
I probably shouldn't ask that.

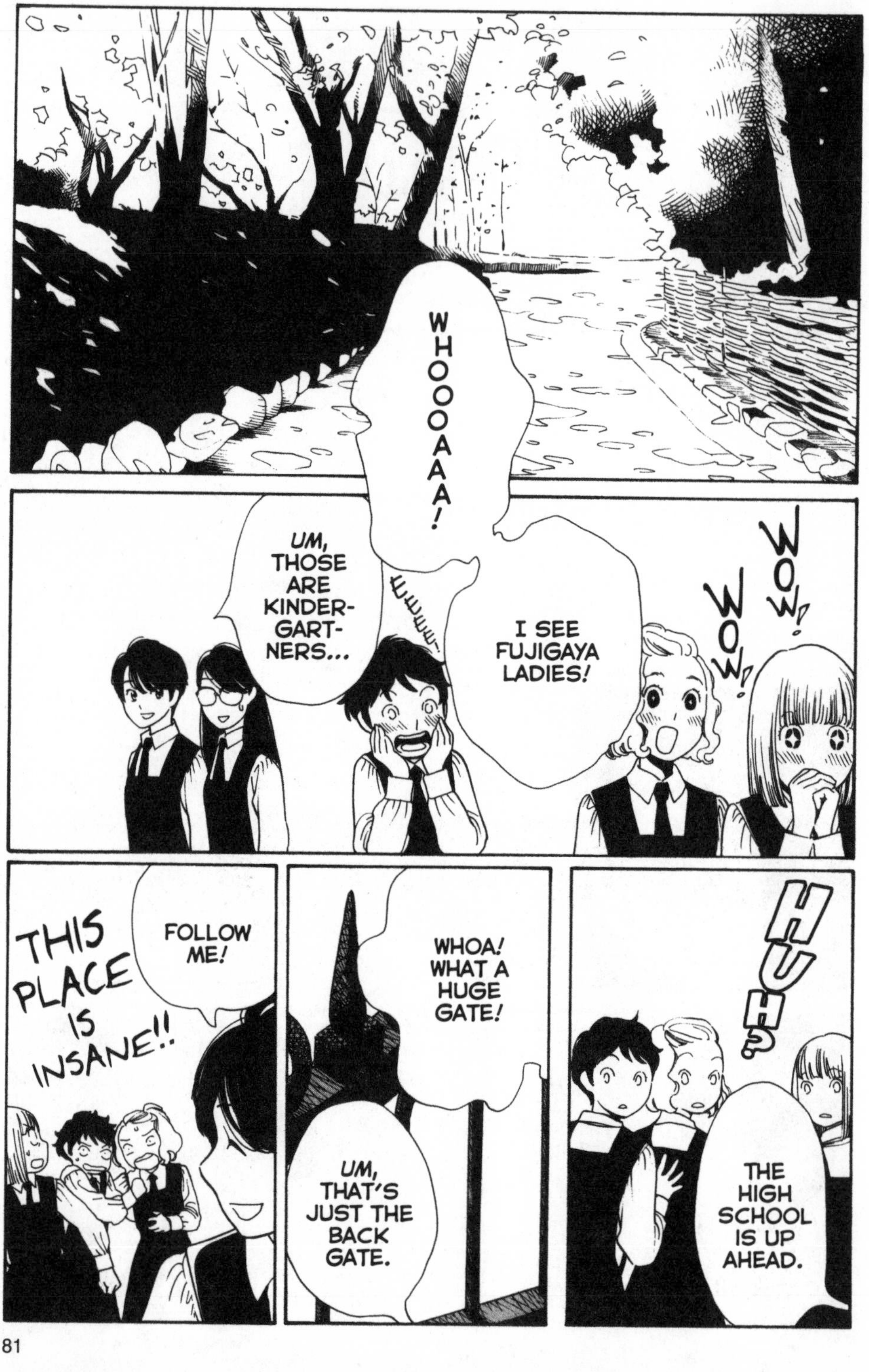
WHOOOAAA!
WOW WOW!
I SEE FUJIGAYA LADIES!
UM, THOSE ARE KINDERGARTNERS...
HUH?
THE HIGH SCHOOL IS UP AHEAD.
WHOA! WHAT A HUGE GATE!
UM, THAT'S JUST THE BACK GATE.
FOLLOW ME!
THIS PLACE IS INSANE!!

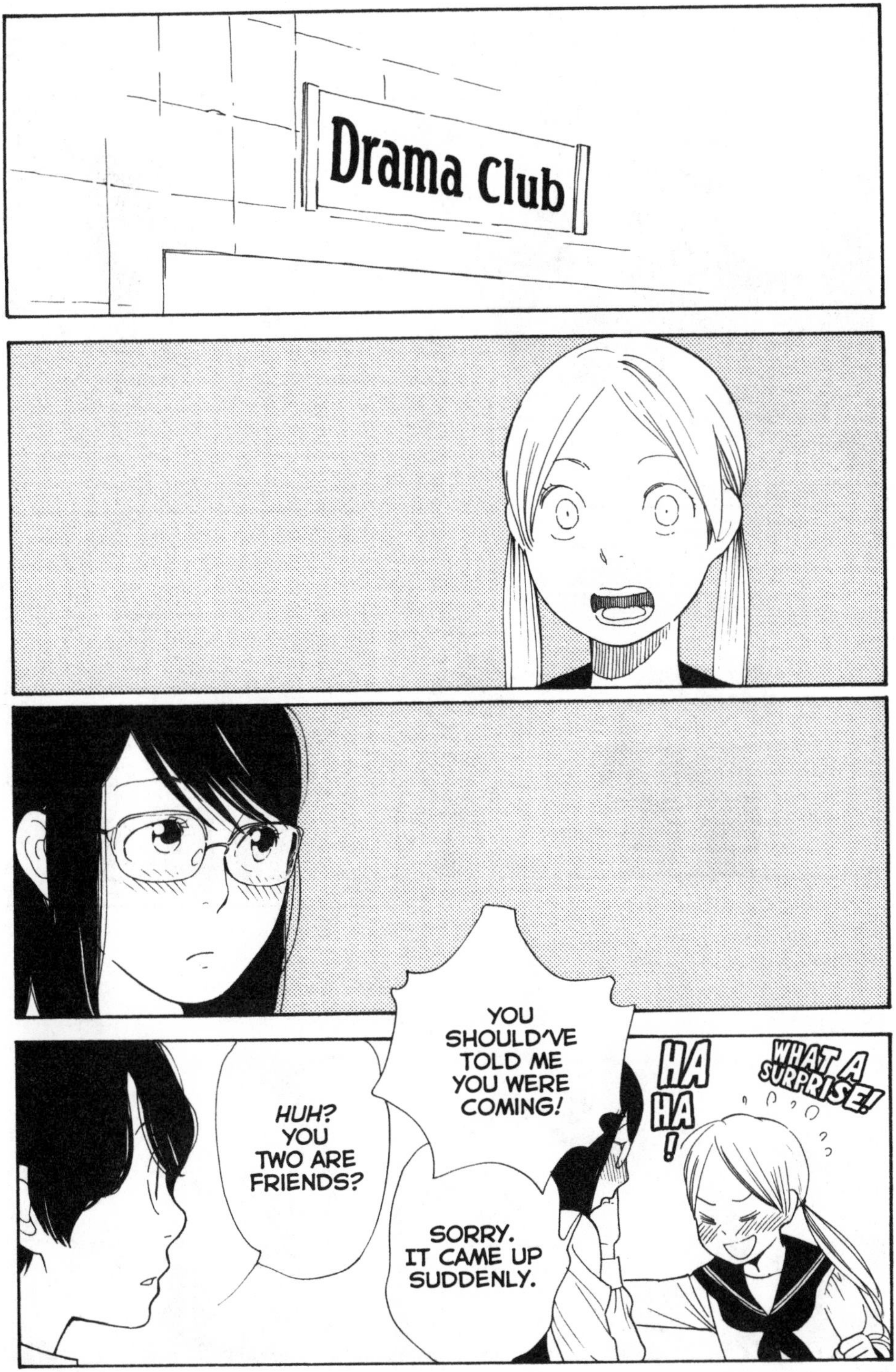
Drama Club
WHAT A SURPRISE!
HA HA!
YOU SHOULD'VE TOLD ME YOU WERE COMING!
SORRY. IT CAME UP SUDDENLY.
HUH? YOU TWO ARE FRIENDS?

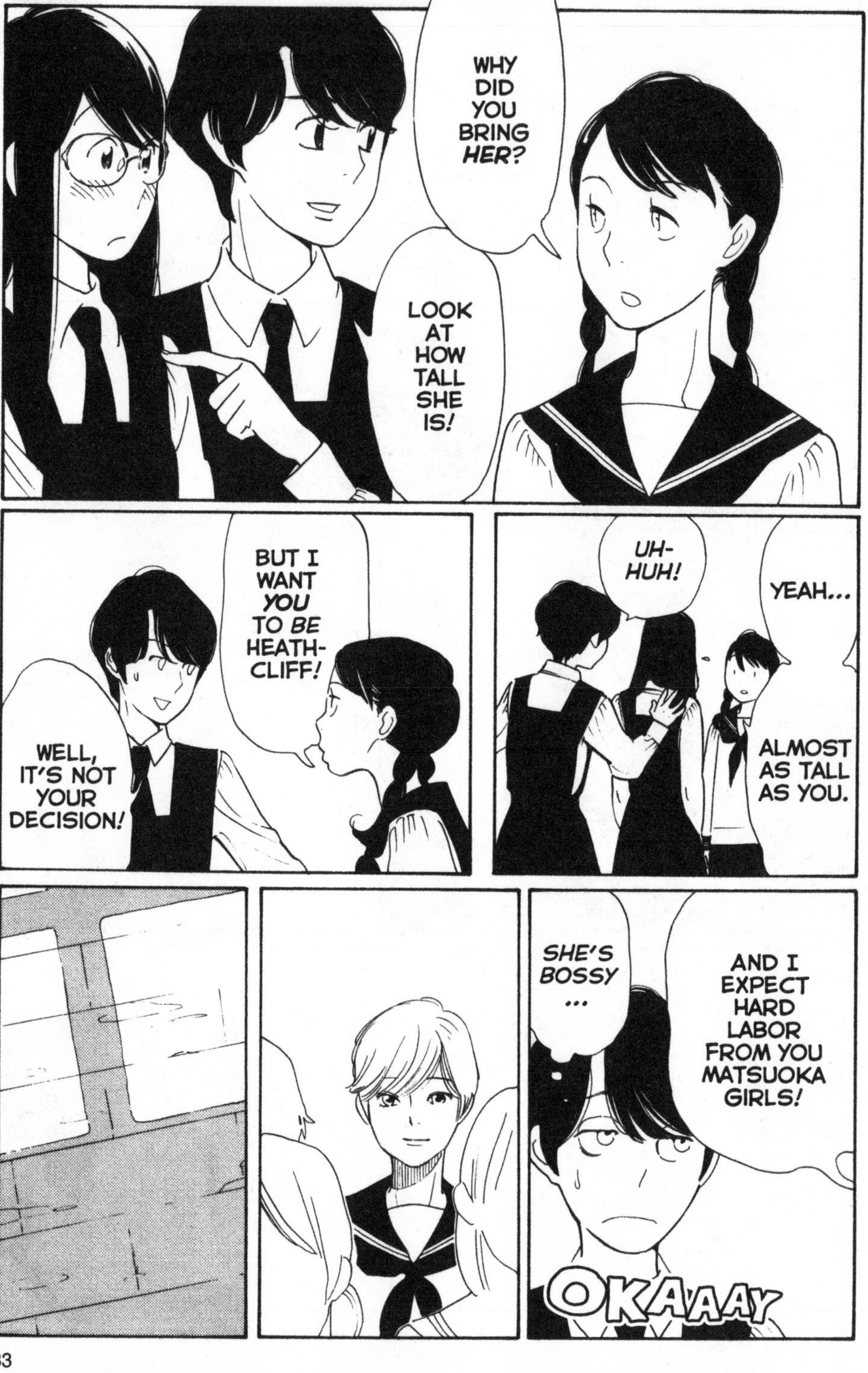
WHY DID YOU BRING HER?
LOOK AT HOW TALL SHE IS!
YEAH...
ALMOST AS TALL AS YOU.
UH-HUH!
BUT I WANT YOU TO BE HEATH-CLIFF!
WELL, IT'S NOT YOUR DECISION!
AND I EXPECT HARD LABOR FROM YOU MATSUOKA GIRLS!
SHE'S BOSSY ...
OKAAAY

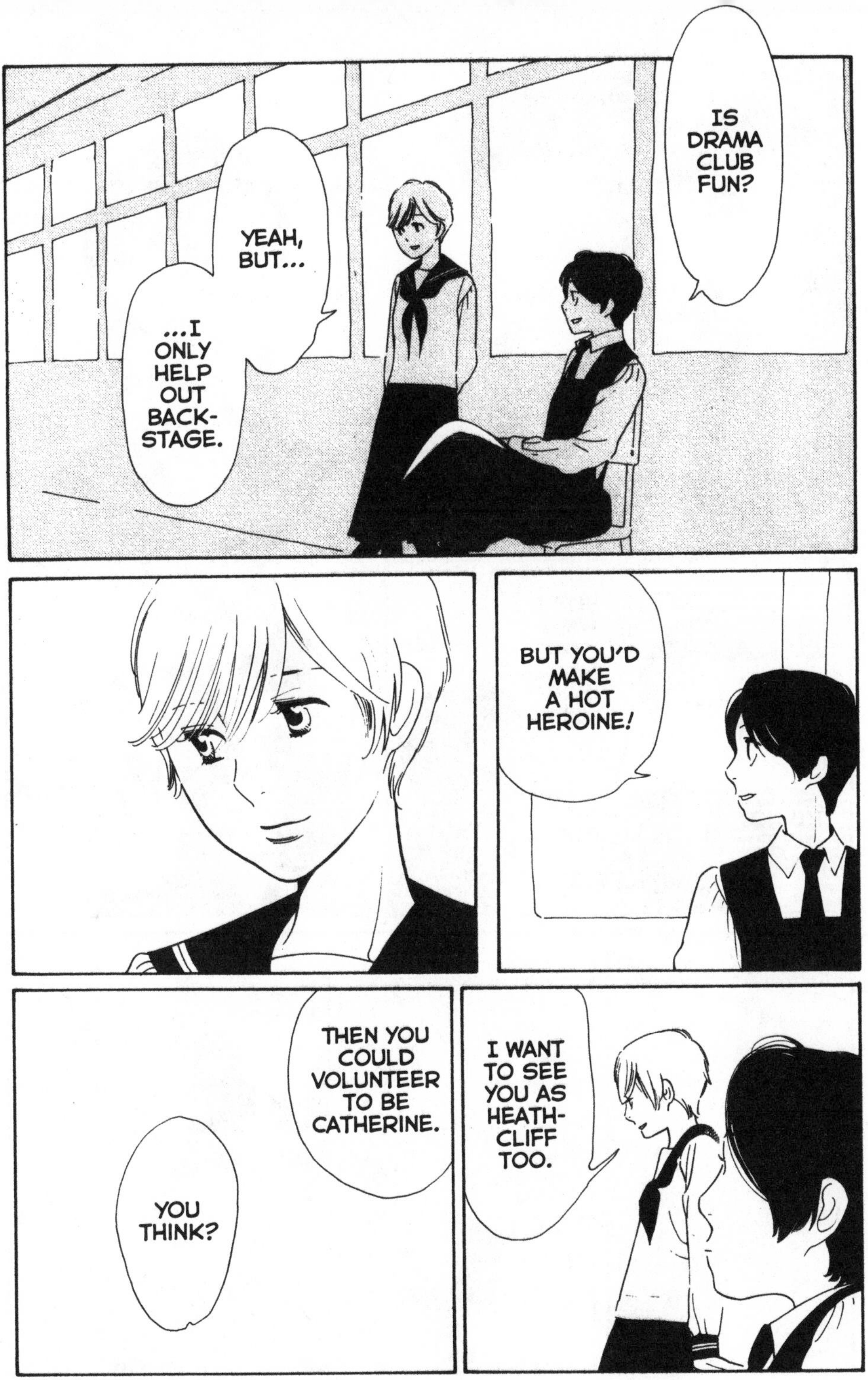
IS DRAMA CLUB FUN?
YEAH, BUT...
...I ONLY HELP OUT BACK-STAGE.
BUT YOU'D MAKE A HOT HEROINE!
I WANT TO SEE YOU AS HEATH-CLIFF TOO.
THEN YOU COULD VOLUNTEER TO BE CATHERINE.
YOU THINK?

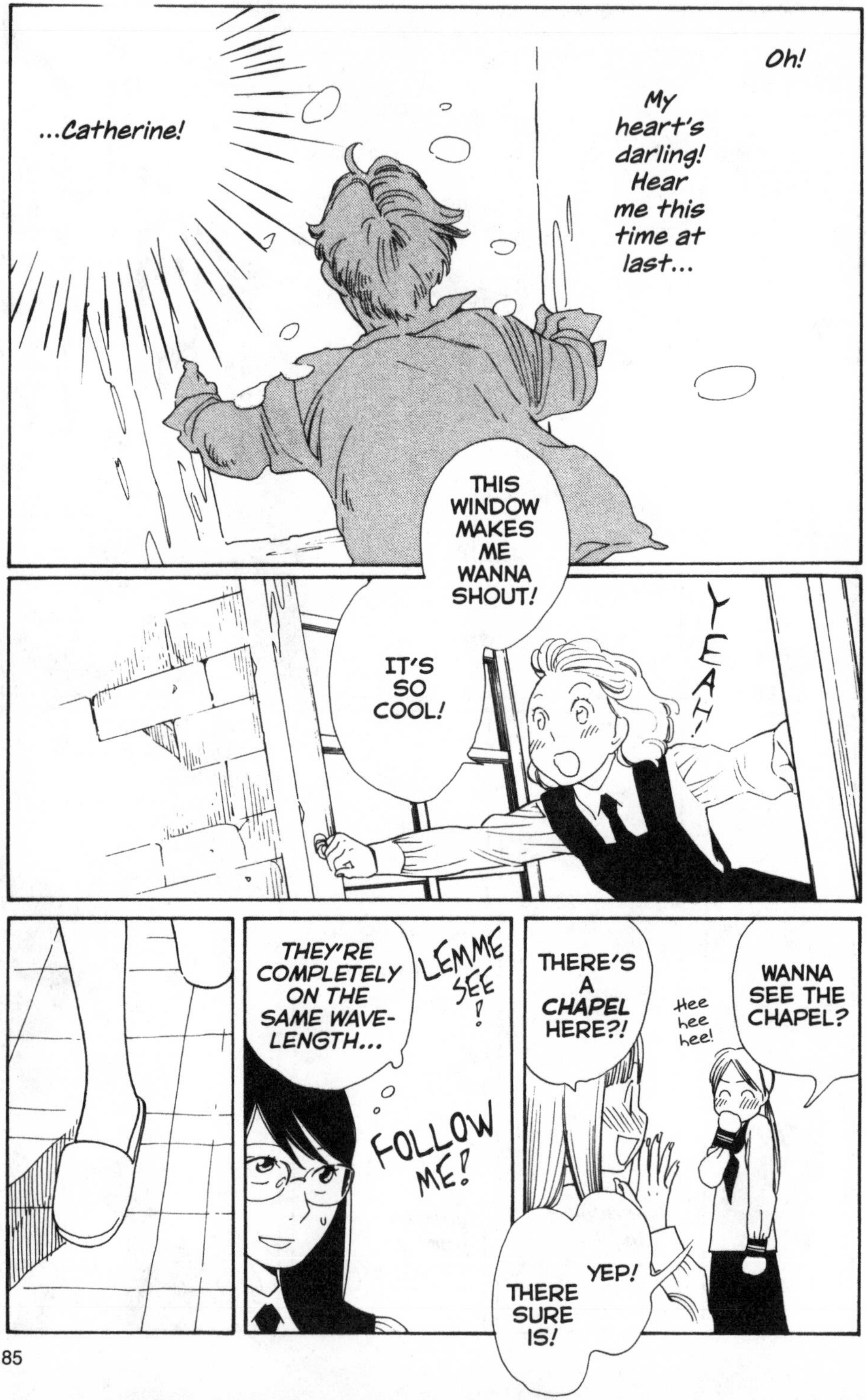
Oh!
My heart's darling! Hear me this time at last...
...Catherine!
THIS WINDOW MAKES ME WANNA SHOUT!
YEAH!
IT'S SO COOL!
WANNA SEE THE CHAPEL?
Hee hee hee!
THERE'S A CHAPEL HERE?!
YEP! THERE SURE IS!
LEMME SEE!
THEY'RE COMPLETELY ON THE SAME WAVE-LENGTH...
FOLLOW ME!

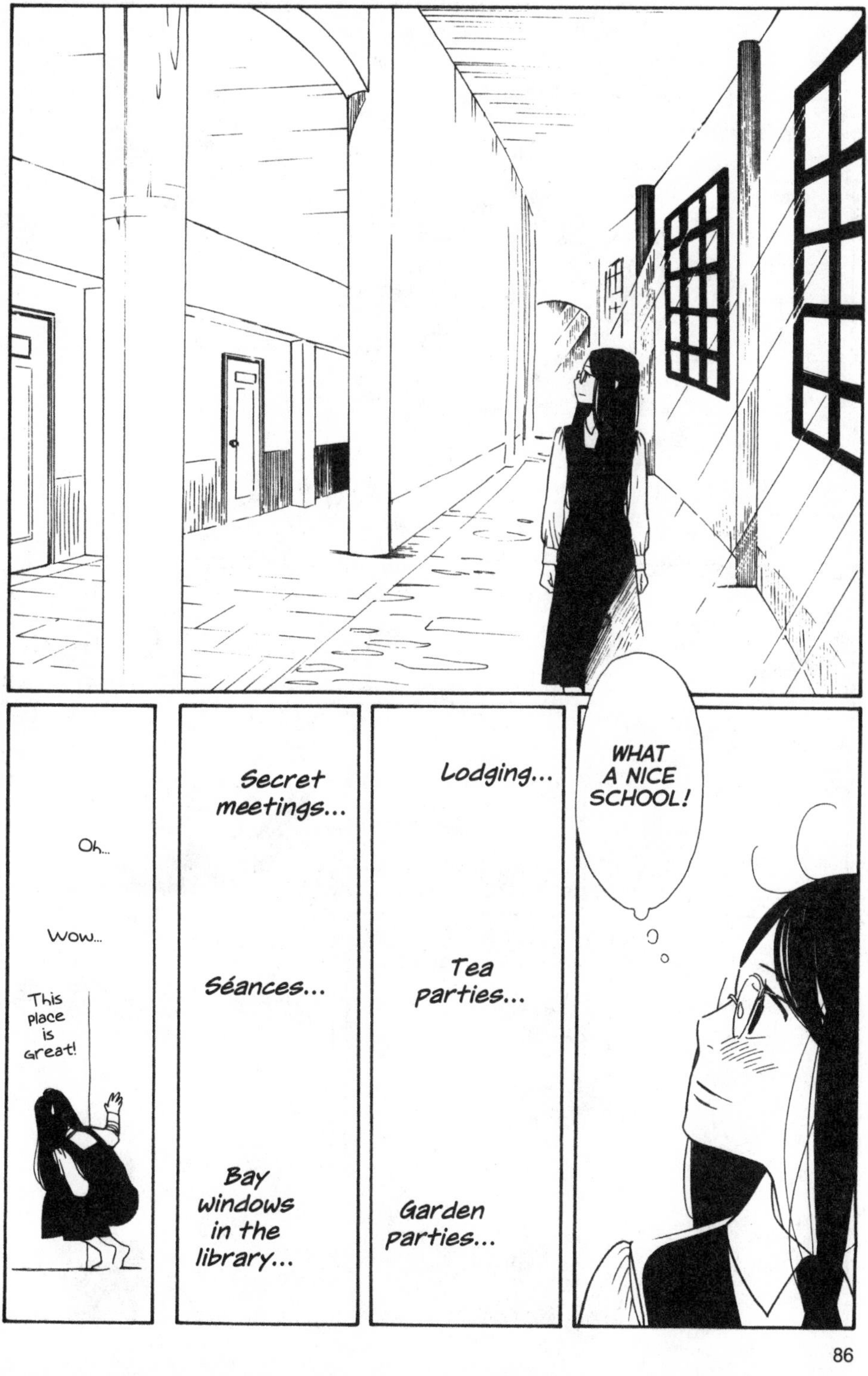
WHAT A NICE SCHOOL!
Lodging...
Tea parties...
Garden parties...
Secret meetings...
Séances...
Bay windows in the library...
Oh...
Wow...
This place is Great!

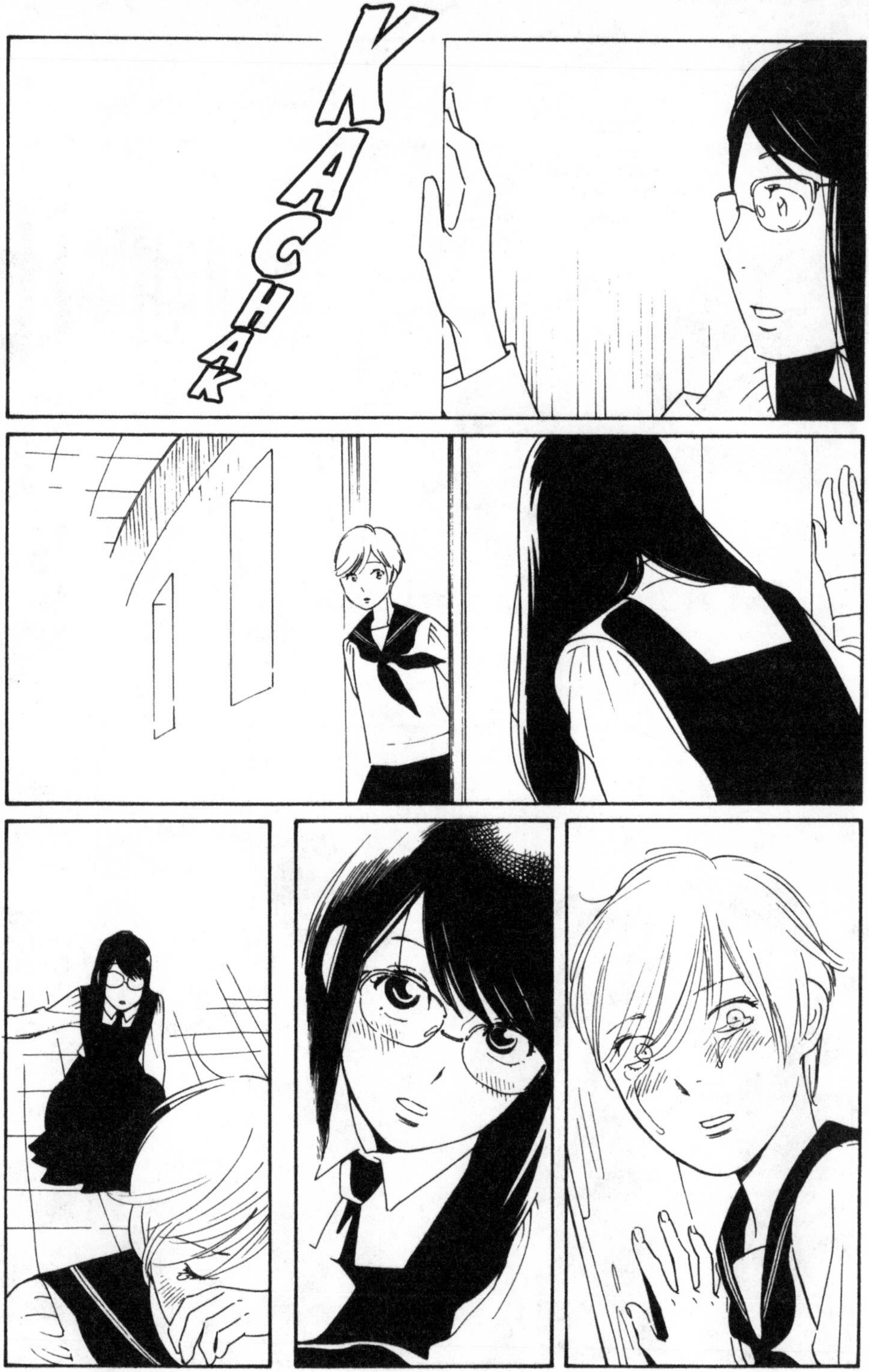
KACHAK

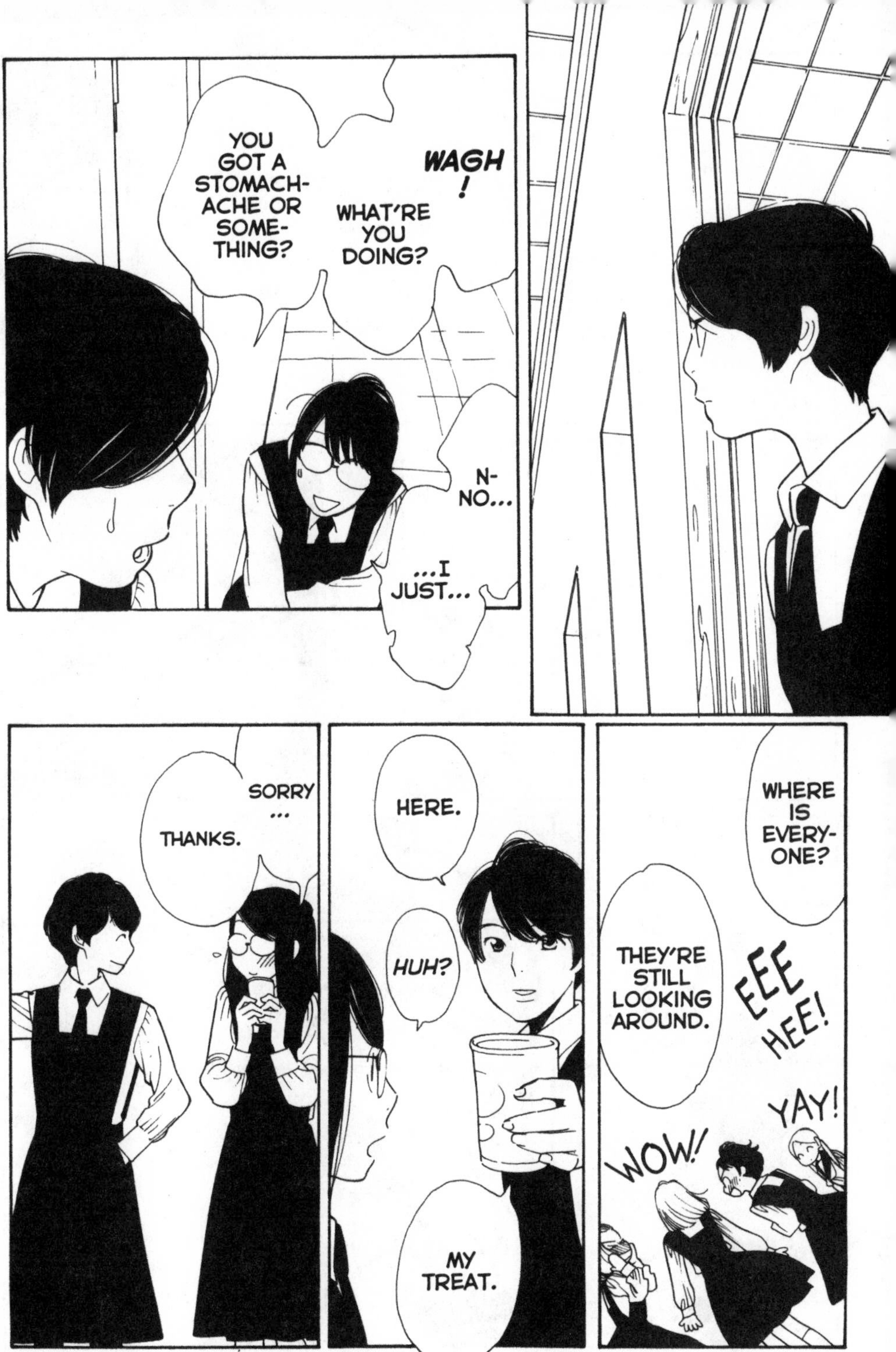
WAGH!
WHAT'RE YOU DOING?
YOU GOT A STOMACH-ACHE OR SOME-THING?
N-NO...
...I JUST...
WHERE IS EVERY-ONE?
THEY'RE STILL LOOKING AROUND.
EEE HEE!
YAY!
WOW!
HERE.
HUH?
MY TREAT.
SORRY...
THANKS.

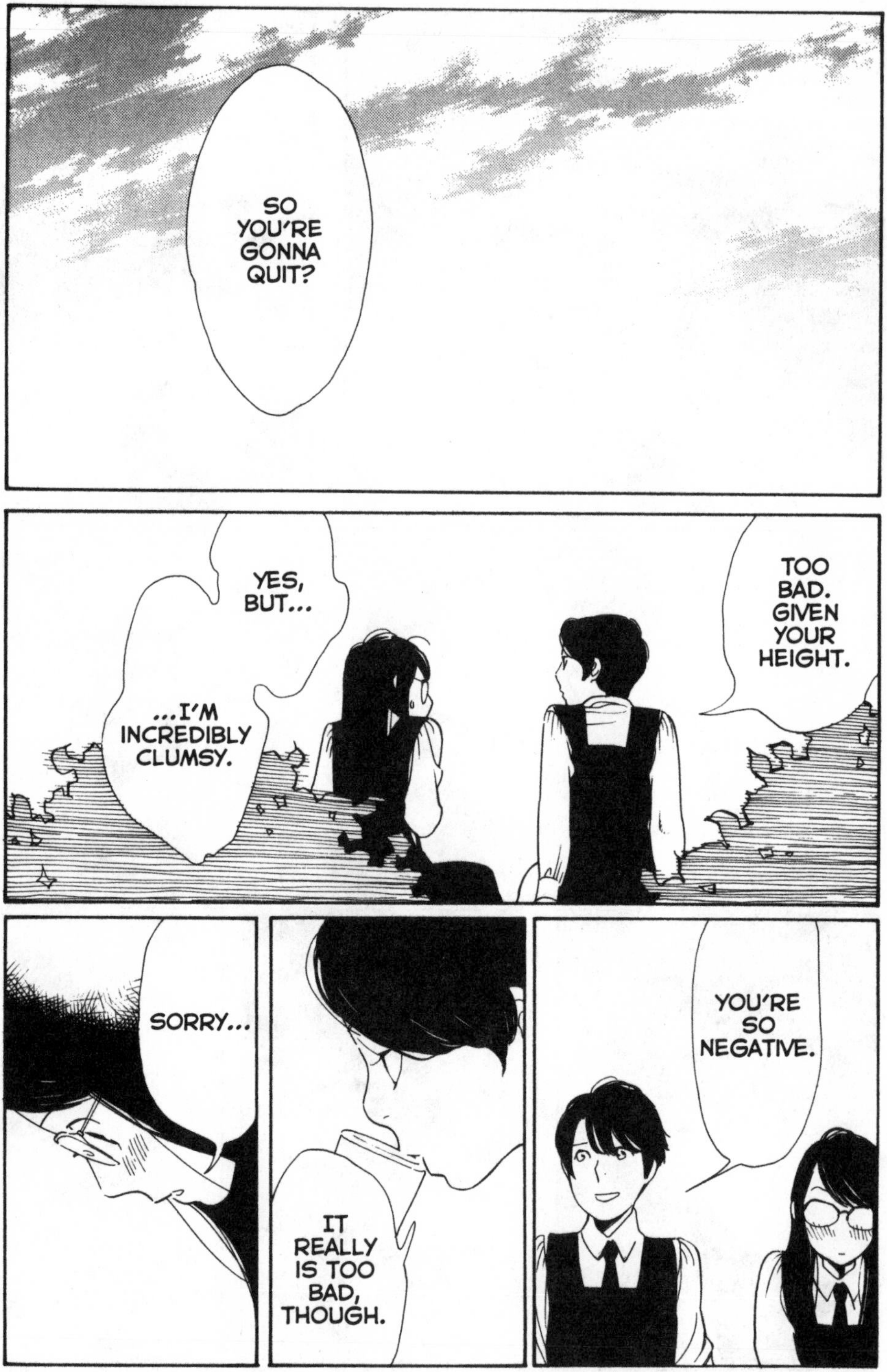
SO YOU'RE GONNA QUIT?
TOO BAD. GIVEN YOUR HEIGHT.
YES, BUT...
...I'M INCREDIBLY CLUMSY.
YOU'RE SO NEGATIVE.
IT REALLY IS TOO BAD, THOUGH.
SORRY...

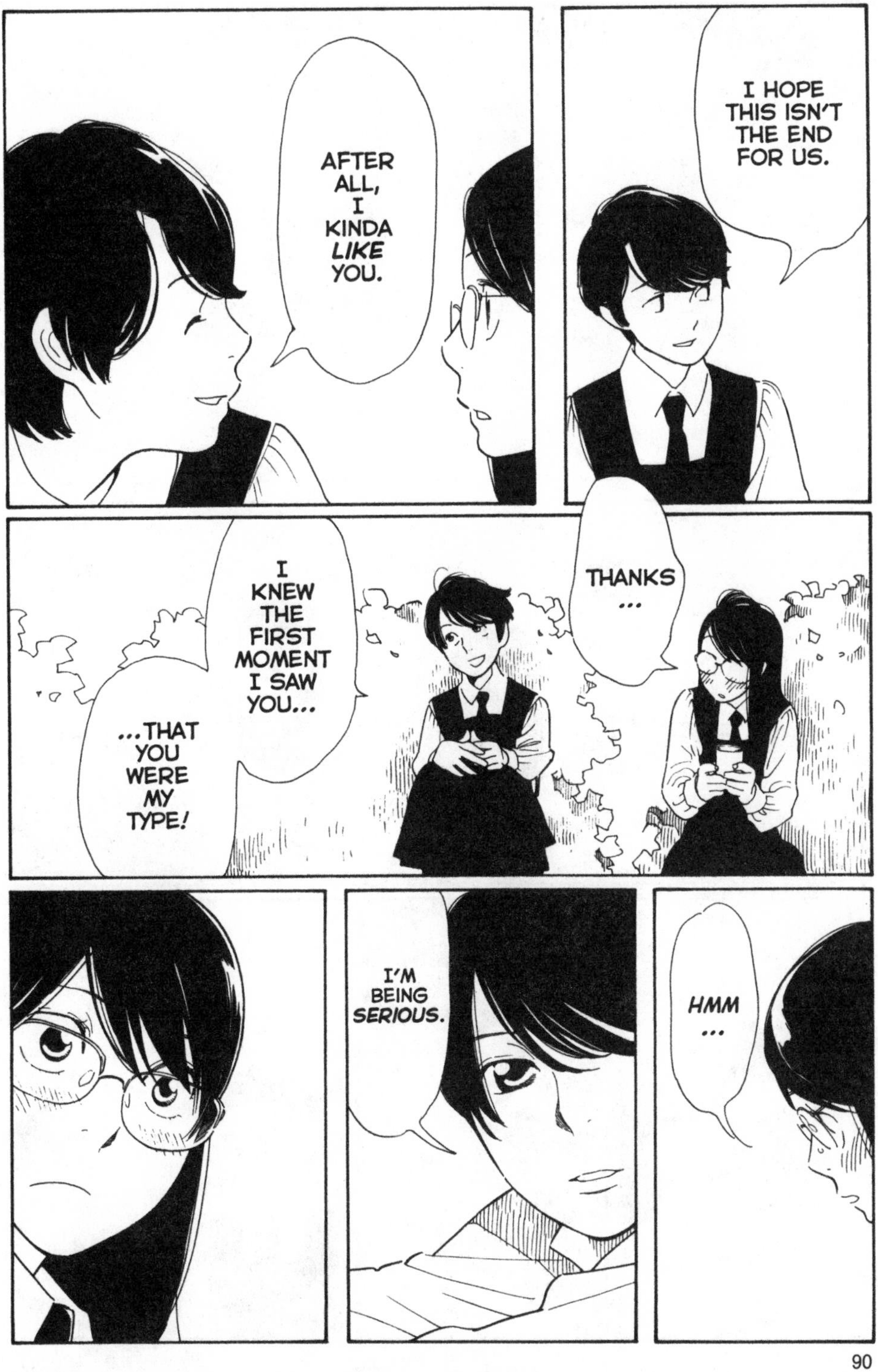
I HOPE THIS ISN'T THE END FOR US.
AFTER ALL, I KINDA *LIKE* YOU.
I KNEW THE FIRST MOMENT I SAW YOU...
...THAT YOU WERE MY TYPE!
THANKS...
*HMM*...
I'M BEING *SERIOUS*.

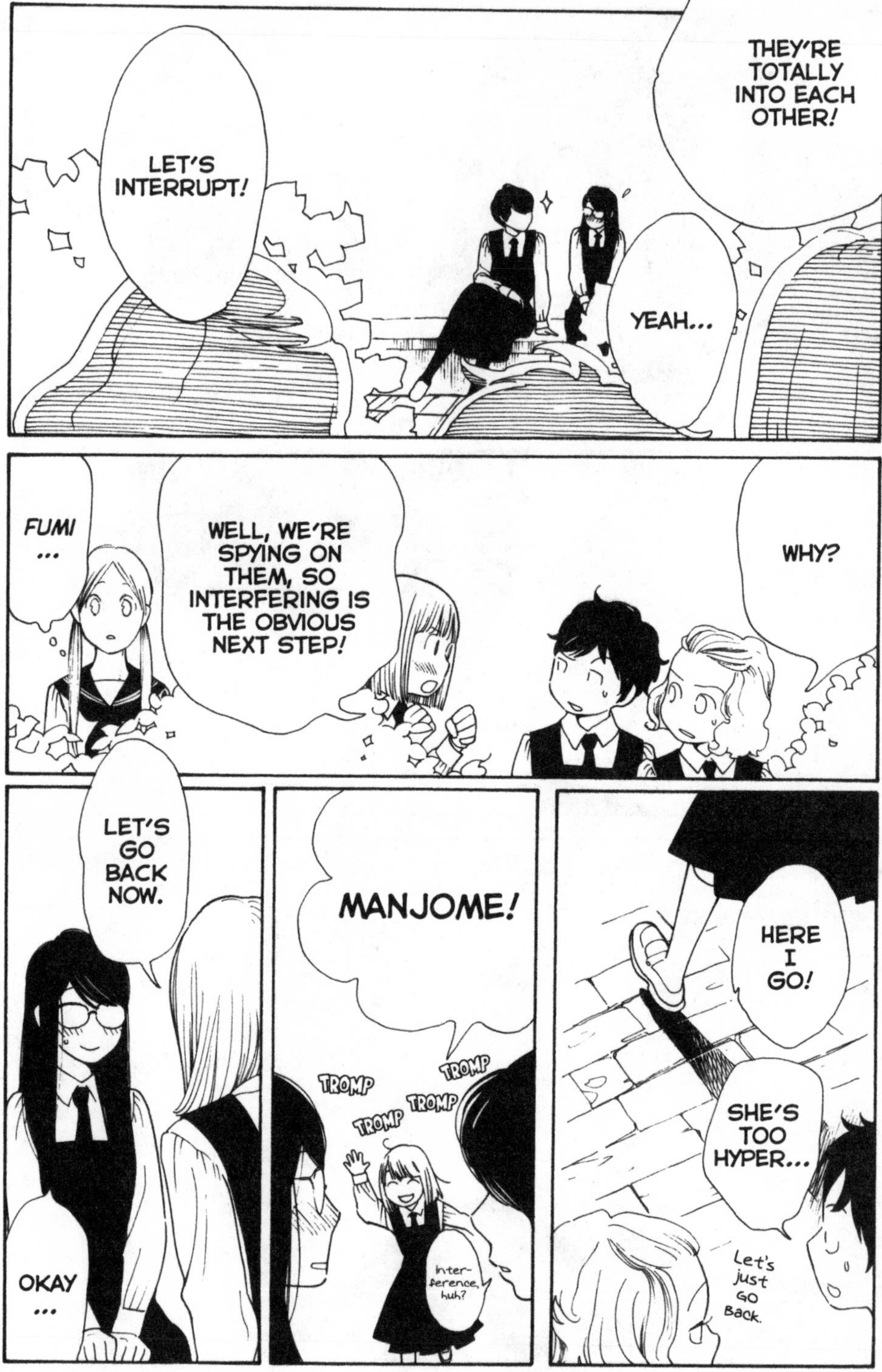

THEY'RE TOTALLY INTO EACH OTHER!
YEAH...
LET'S INTERRUPT!
WHY?
WELL, WE'RE SPYING ON THEM, SO INTERFERING IS THE OBVIOUS NEXT STEP!
FUMI ...
HERE I GO!
SHE'S TOO HYPER...
Let's just go back.
MANJOME!
TROMP
TROMP
TROMP
TROMP
Inter-ference, huh?
LET'S GO BACK NOW.
OKAY ...

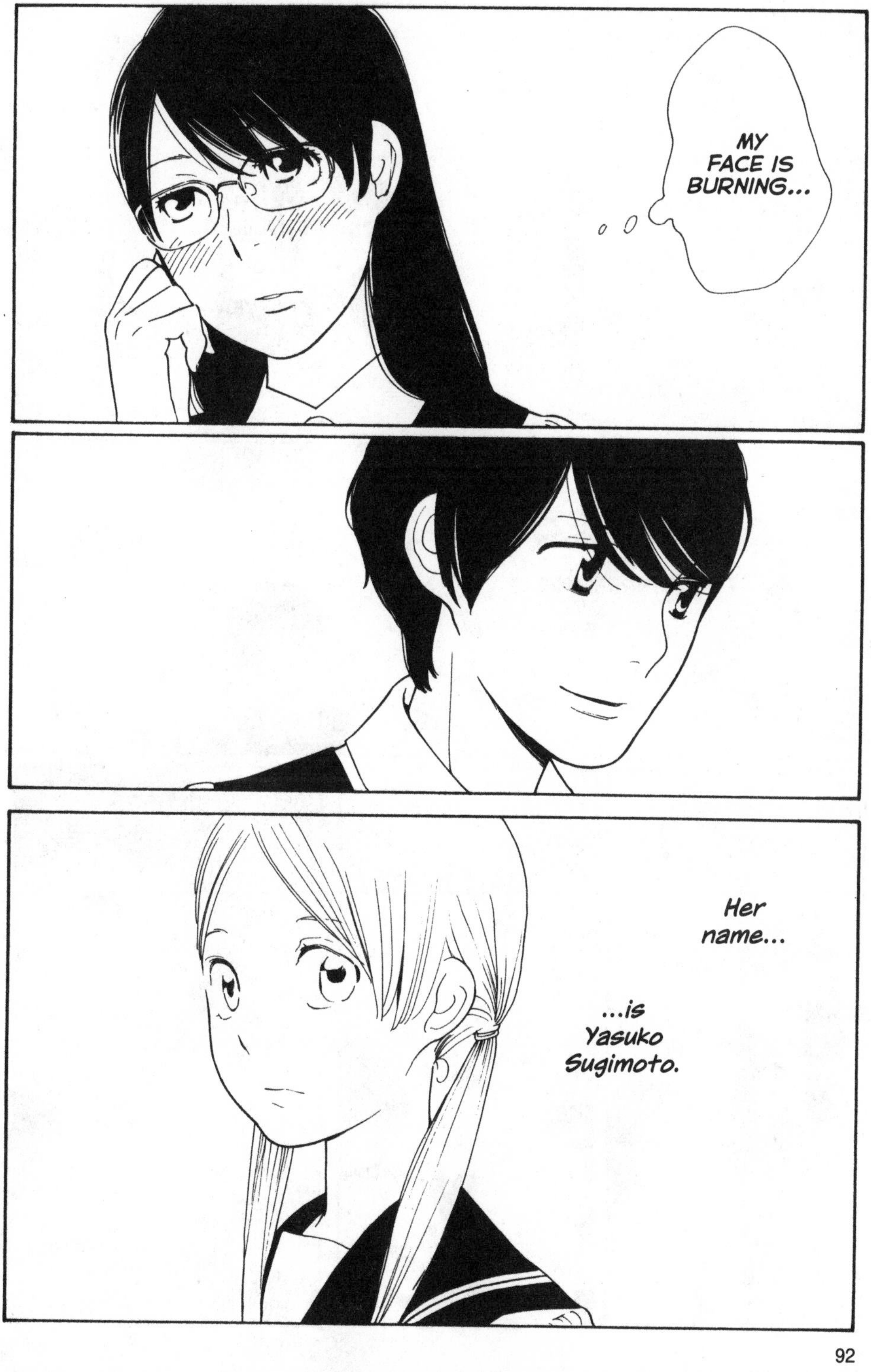
MY FACE IS BURNING...
Her name...
...is Yasuko Sugimoto.

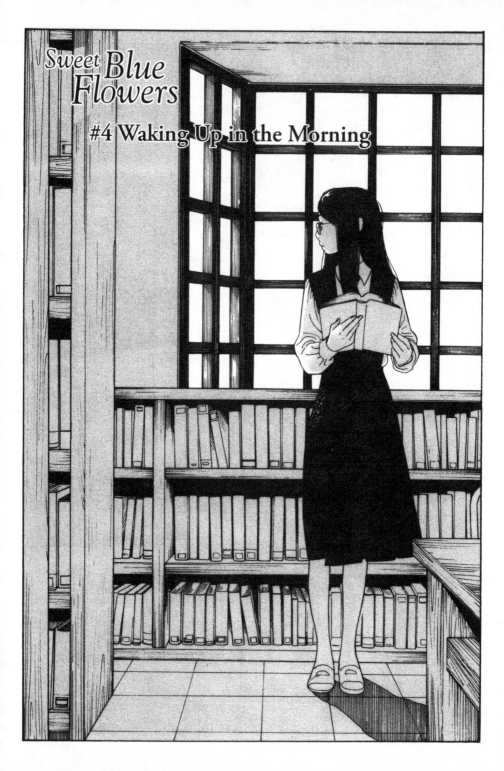

Sweet *Blue Flowers*

#4 Waking Up in the Morning

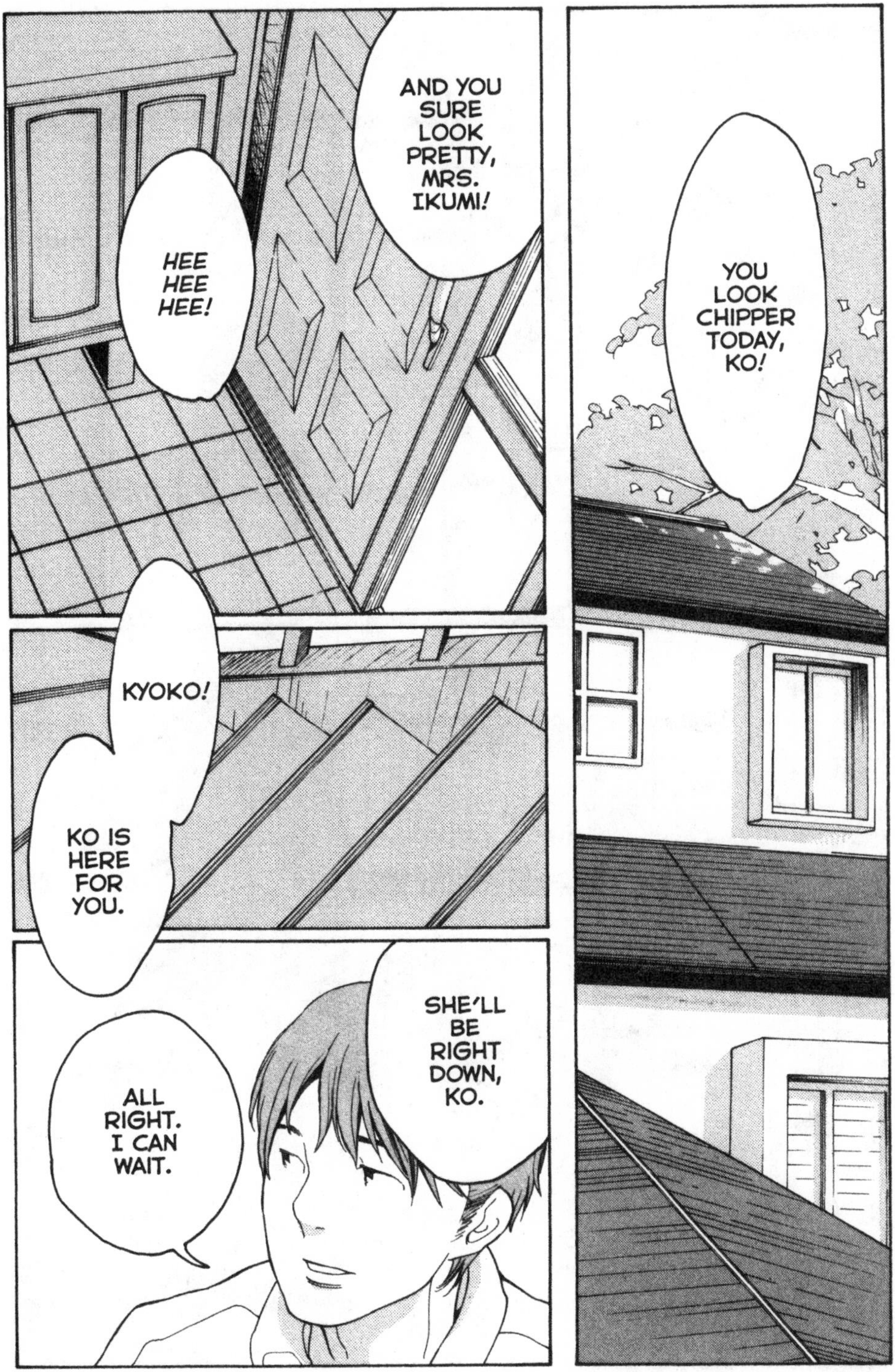
YOU LOOK CHIPPER TODAY, KO!
AND YOU SURE LOOK PRETTY, MRS. IKUMI!
HEE HEE HEE!
KYOKO!
KO IS HERE FOR YOU.
SHE'LL BE RIGHT DOWN, KO.
ALL RIGHT. I CAN WAIT.

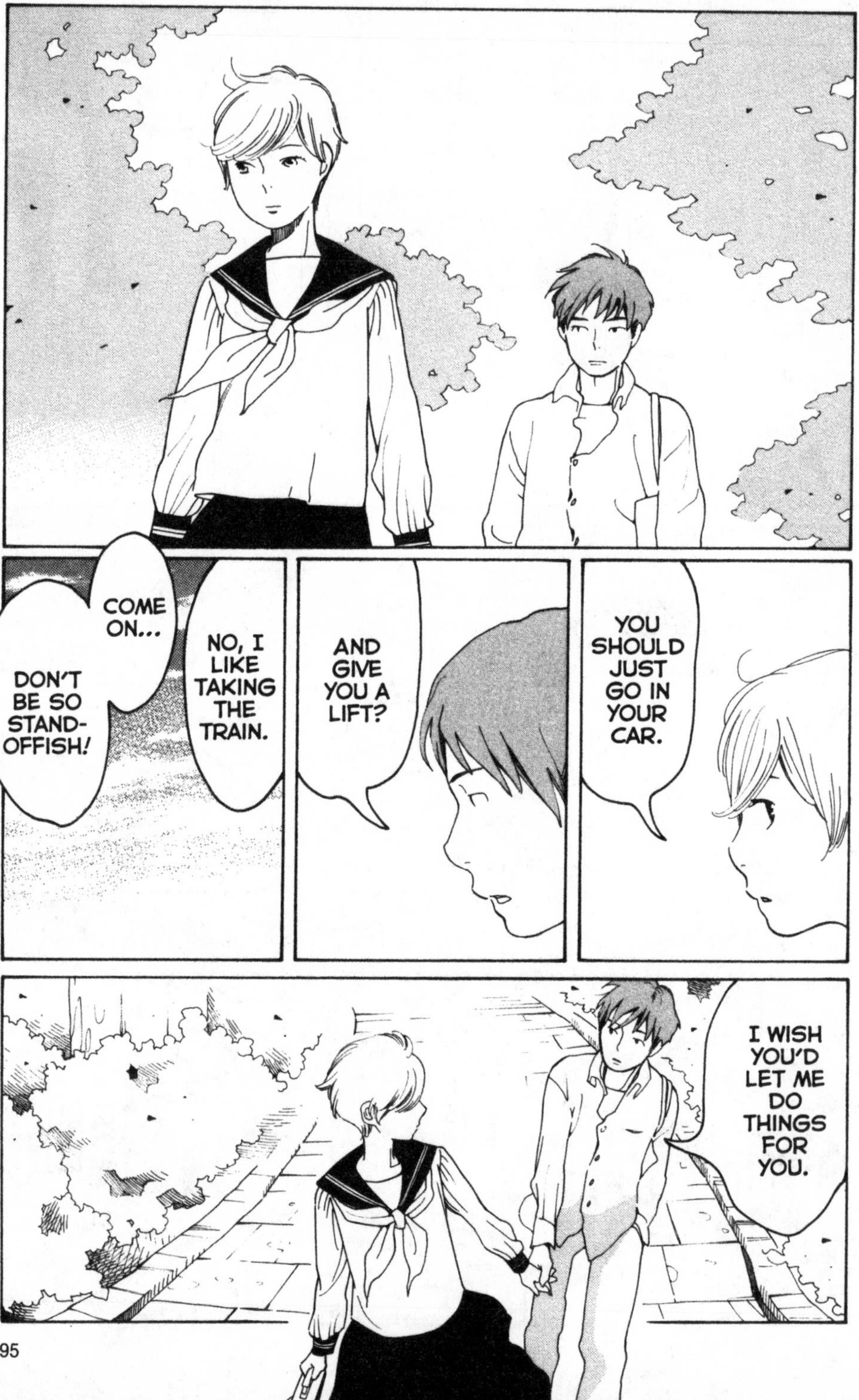
YOU SHOULD JUST GO IN YOUR CAR.
AND GIVE YOU A LIFT?
NO, I LIKE TAKING THE TRAIN.
COME ON...
DON'T BE SO STAND-OFFISH!
I WISH YOU'D LET ME DO THINGS FOR YOU.

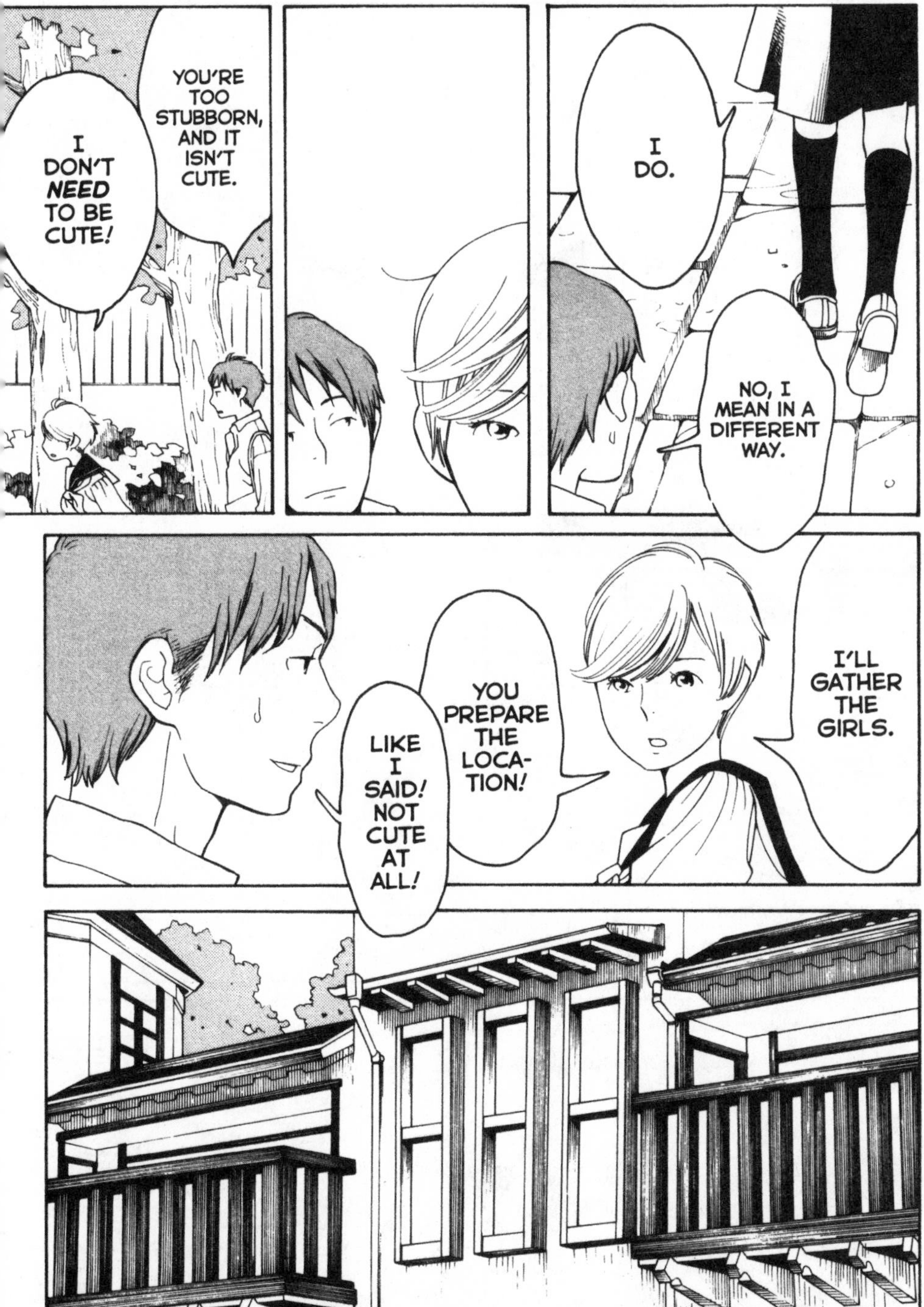
I DO.
NO, I MEAN IN A DIFFERENT WAY.
YOU'RE TOO STUBBORN, AND IT ISN'T CUTE.
I DON'T *NEED* TO BE CUTE!
I'LL GATHER THE GIRLS.
YOU PREPARE THE LOCA- TION!
LIKE I SAID! NOT CUTE AT ALL!

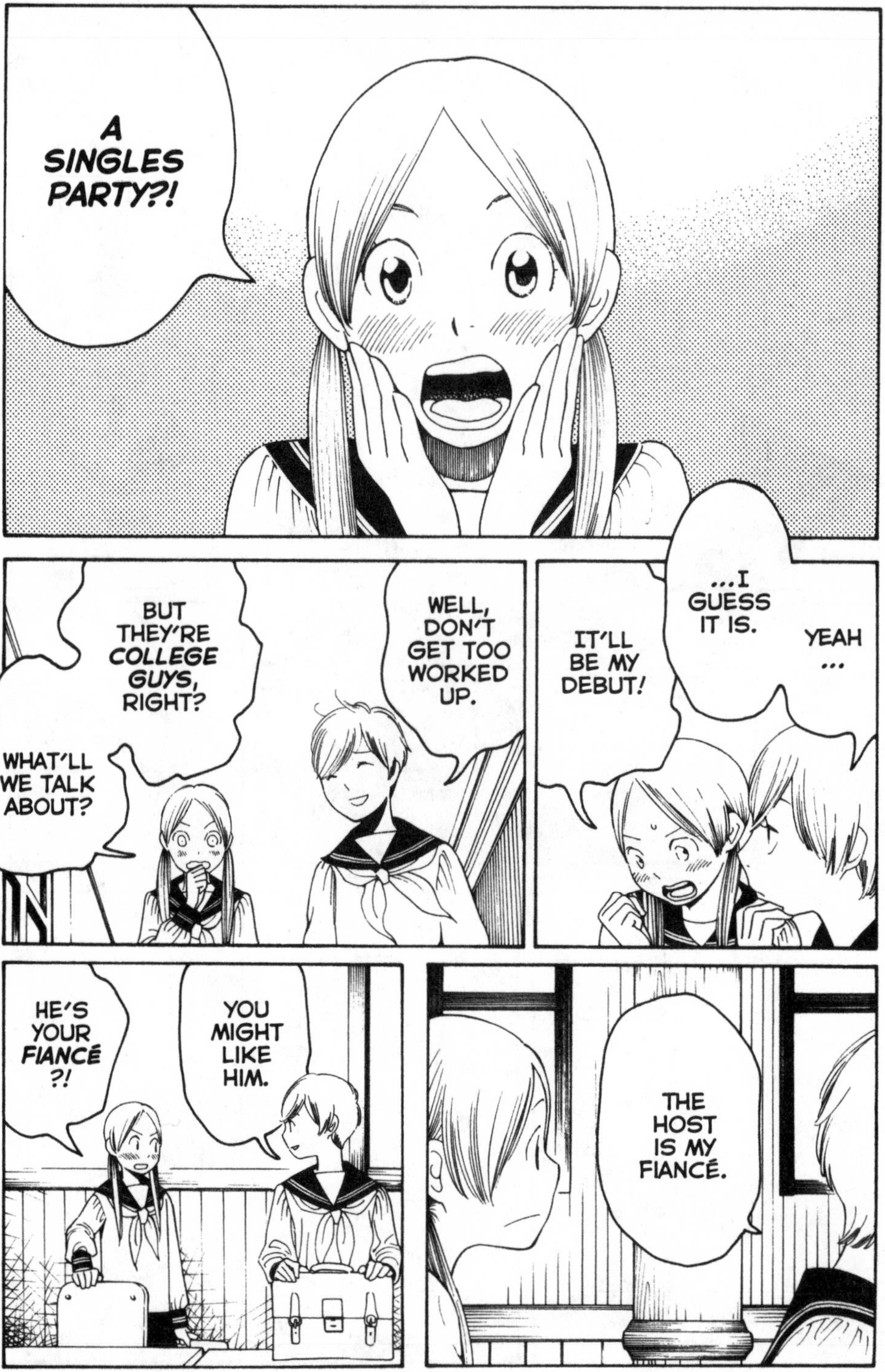
A SINGLES PARTY?!
YEAH ...
...I GUESS IT IS.
IT'LL BE MY DEBUT!
WELL, DON'T GET TOO WORKED UP.
BUT THEY'RE *COLLEGE GUYS*, RIGHT?
WHAT'LL WE TALK ABOUT?
THE HOST IS MY FIANCÉ.
YOU MIGHT LIKE HIM.
HE'S YOUR *FIANCÉ*?!

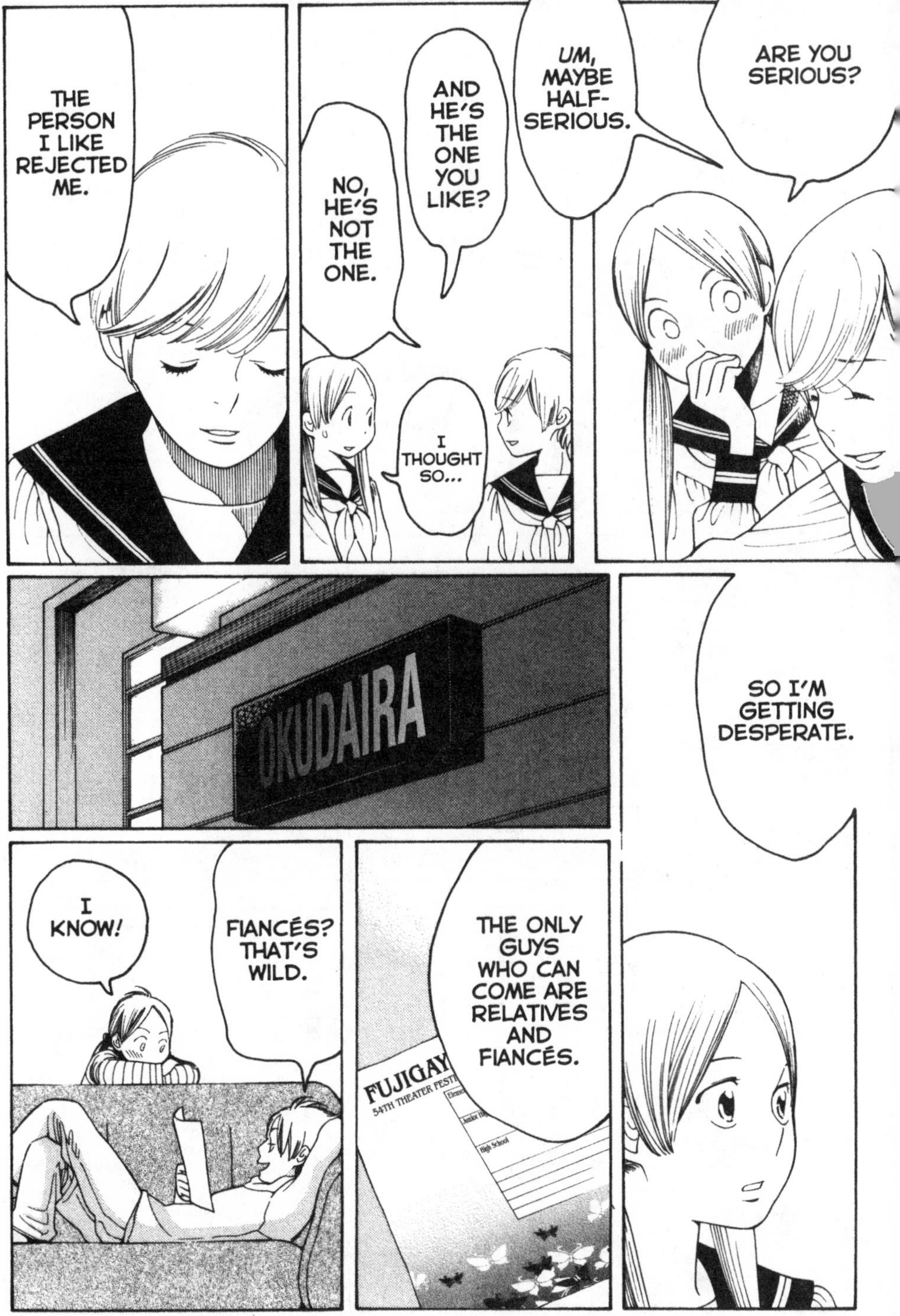
ARE YOU SERIOUS?
UM, MAYBE HALF-SERIOUS.
AND HE'S THE ONE YOU LIKE?
NO, HE'S NOT THE ONE.
I THOUGHT SO...
THE PERSON I LIKE REJECTED ME.
SO I'M GETTING DESPERATE.
OKUDAIRA
THE ONLY GUYS WHO CAN COME ARE RELATIVES AND FIANCÉS.
FIANCÉS? THAT'S WILD.
I KNOW!

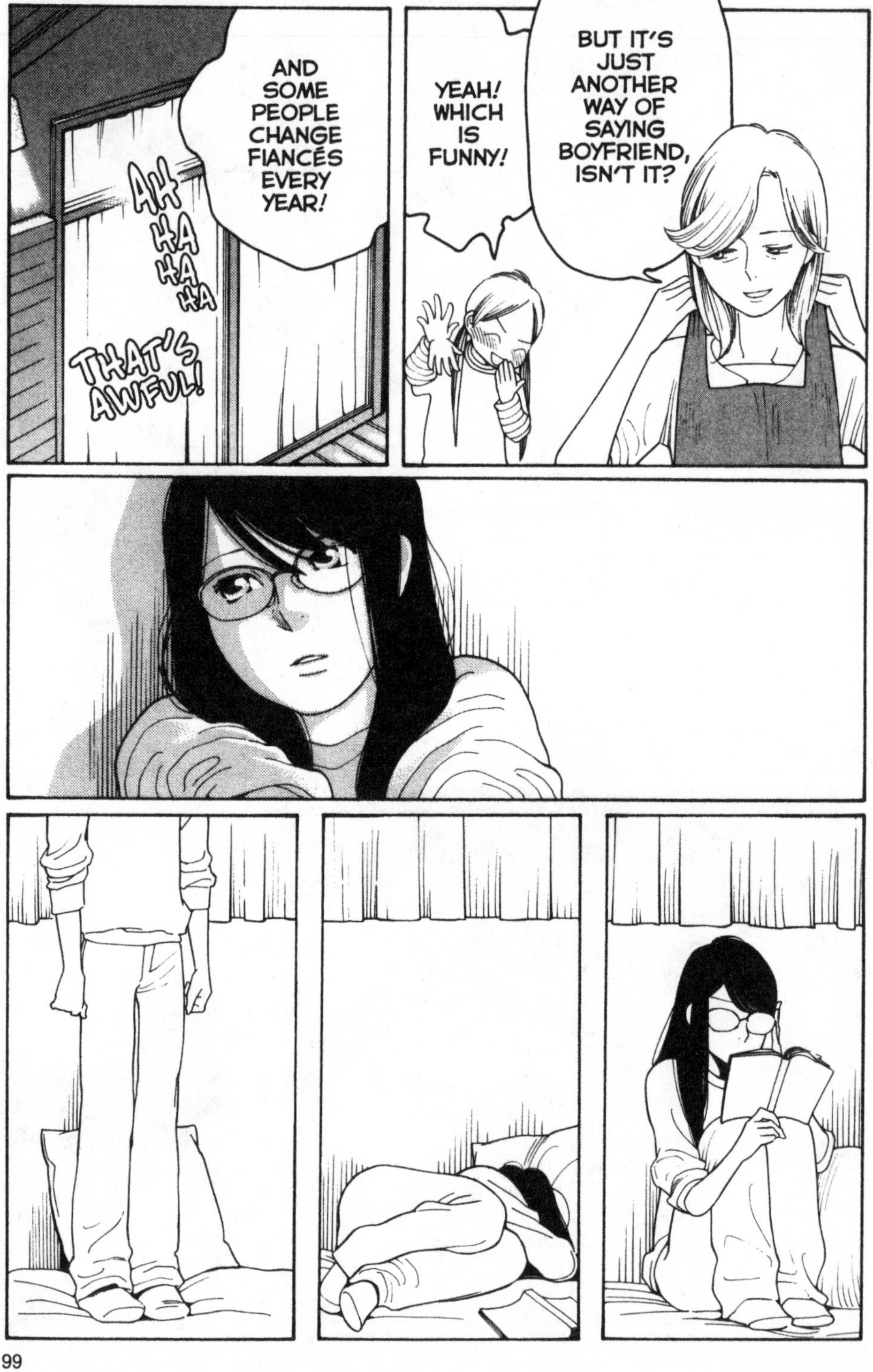
BUT IT'S JUST ANOTHER WAY OF SAYING BOYFRIEND, ISN'T IT?
YEAH! WHICH IS FUNNY!
AND SOME PEOPLE CHANGE FIANCÉS EVERY YEAR!
AH HA HA HA
THAT'S AWFUL!

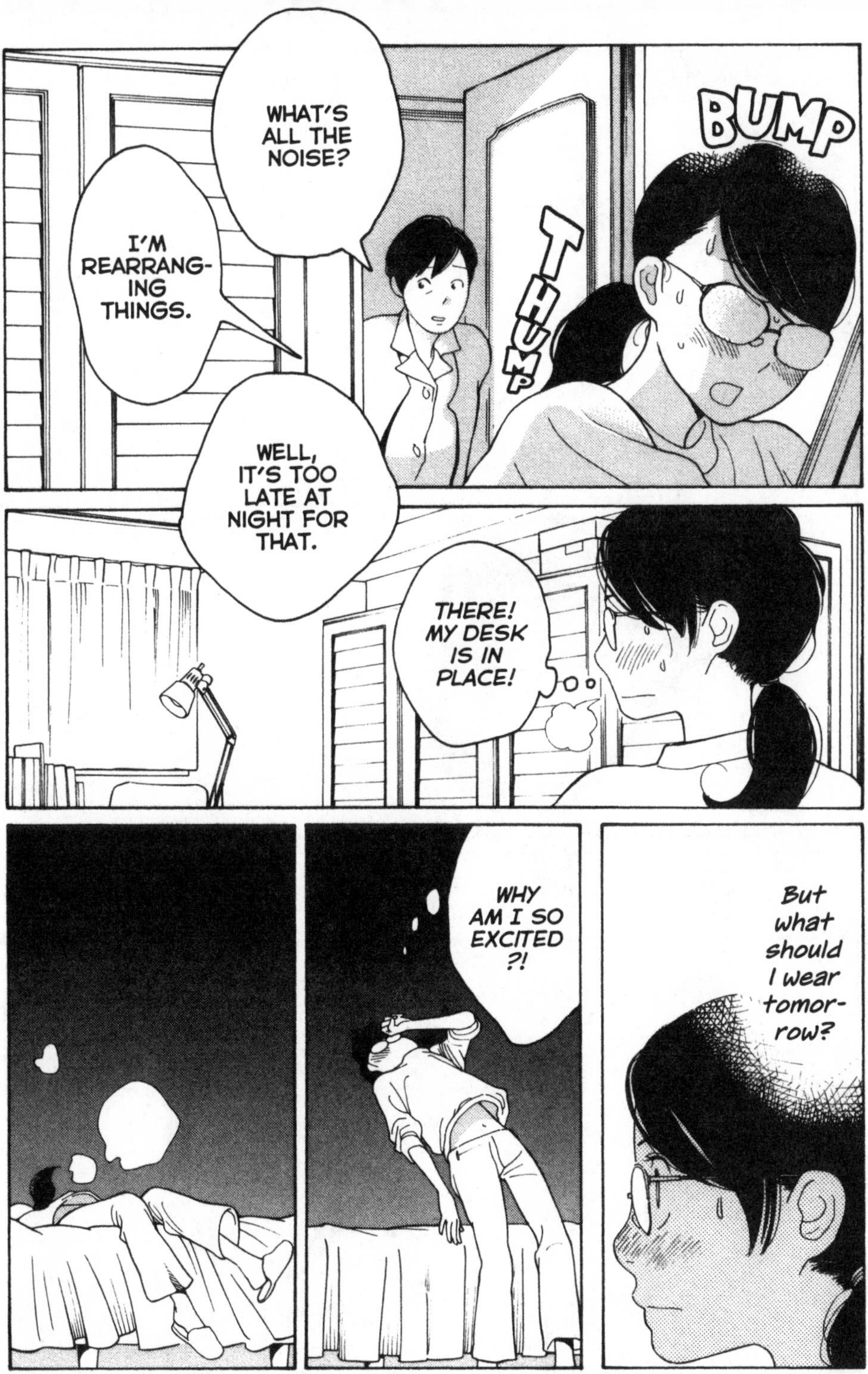
BUMP
THUMP
WHAT'S ALL THE NOISE?
I'M REARRANG-ING THINGS.
WELL, IT'S TOO LATE AT NIGHT FOR THAT.
THERE! MY DESK IS IN PLACE!
But what should I wear tomor-row?
WHY AM I SO EXCITED ?!

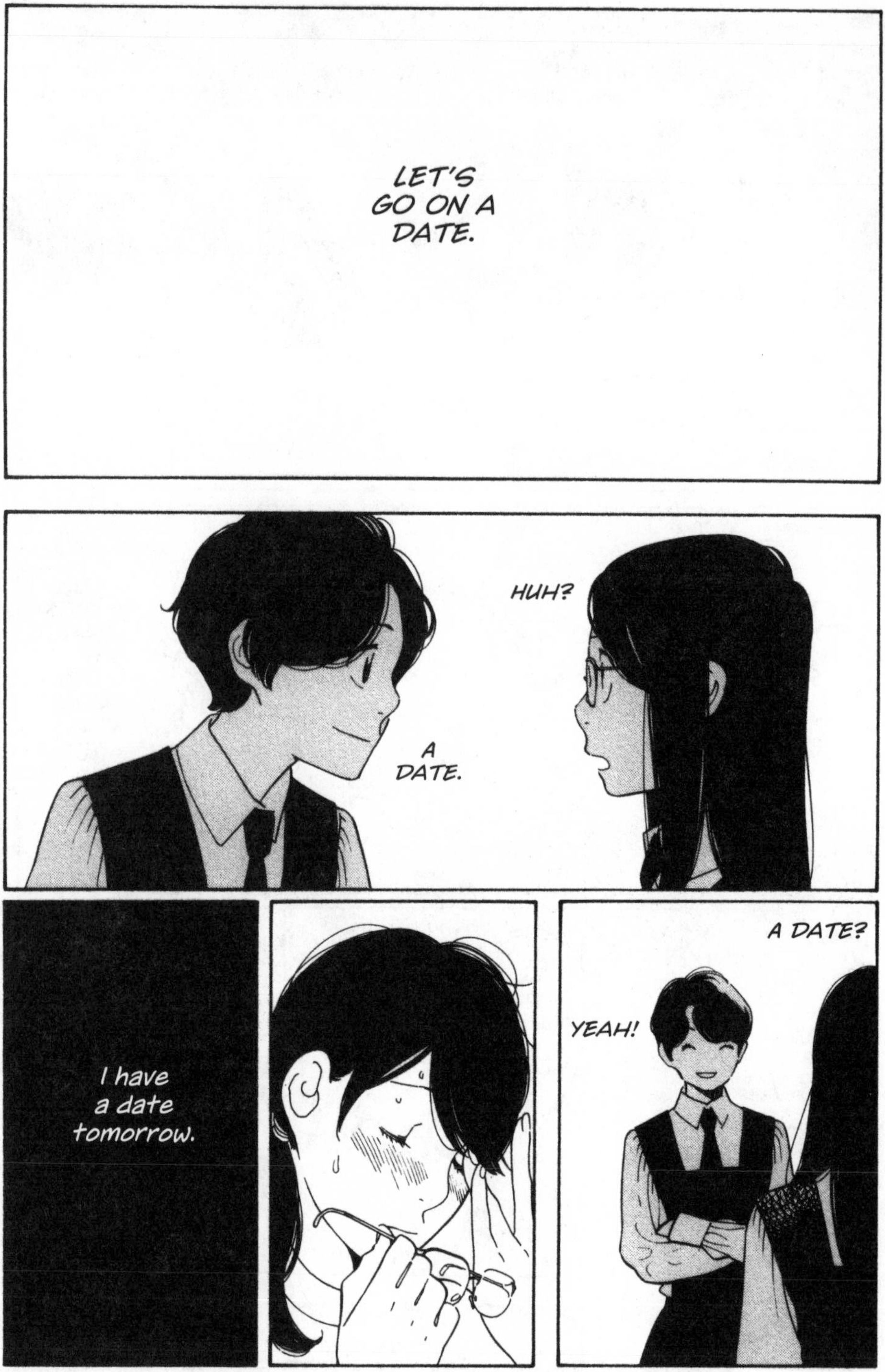
LET'S GO ON A DATE.
HUH?
A DATE.
A DATE?
YEAH!
I have a date tomorrow.

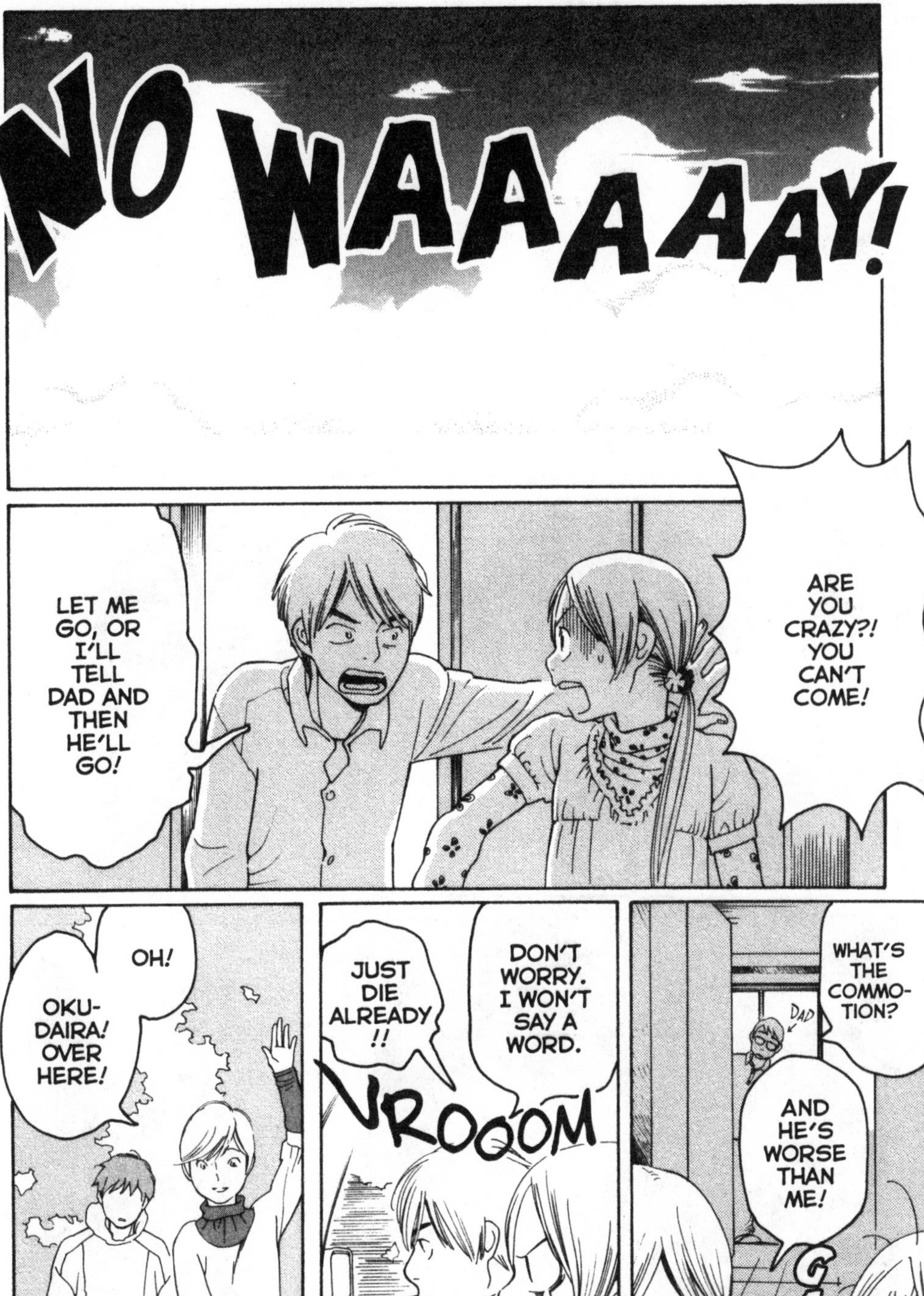
NO WAAAAAY!
ARE YOU CRAZY?! YOU CAN'T COME!
LET ME GO, OR I'LL TELL DAD AND THEN HE'LL GO!
WHAT'S THE COMMO-TION?
DAD
AND HE'S WORSE THAN ME!
GAH!
DON'T WORRY. I WON'T SAY A WORD.
JUST DIE ALREADY!!
VROOOM
OH!
OKU-DAIRA! OVER HERE!

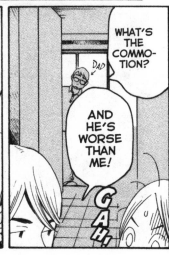

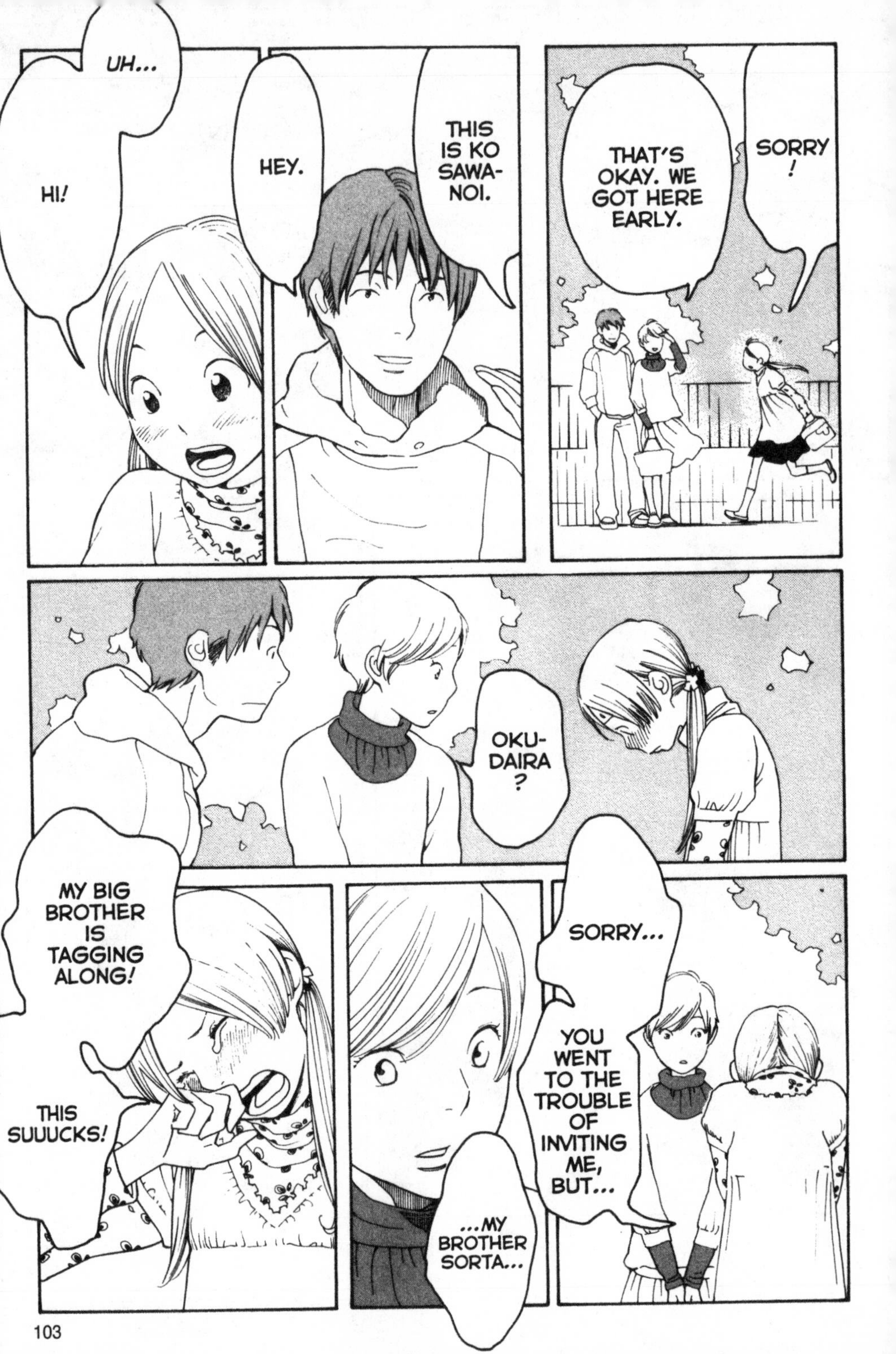
SORRY!
THAT'S OKAY. WE GOT HERE EARLY.
THIS IS KO SAWANOI.
HEY.
UH...
HI!
OKUDAIRA?
SORRY...
YOU WENT TO THE TROUBLE OF INVITING ME, BUT...
...MY BROTHER SORTA...
MY BIG BROTHER IS TAGGING ALONG!
THIS SUUUCKS!

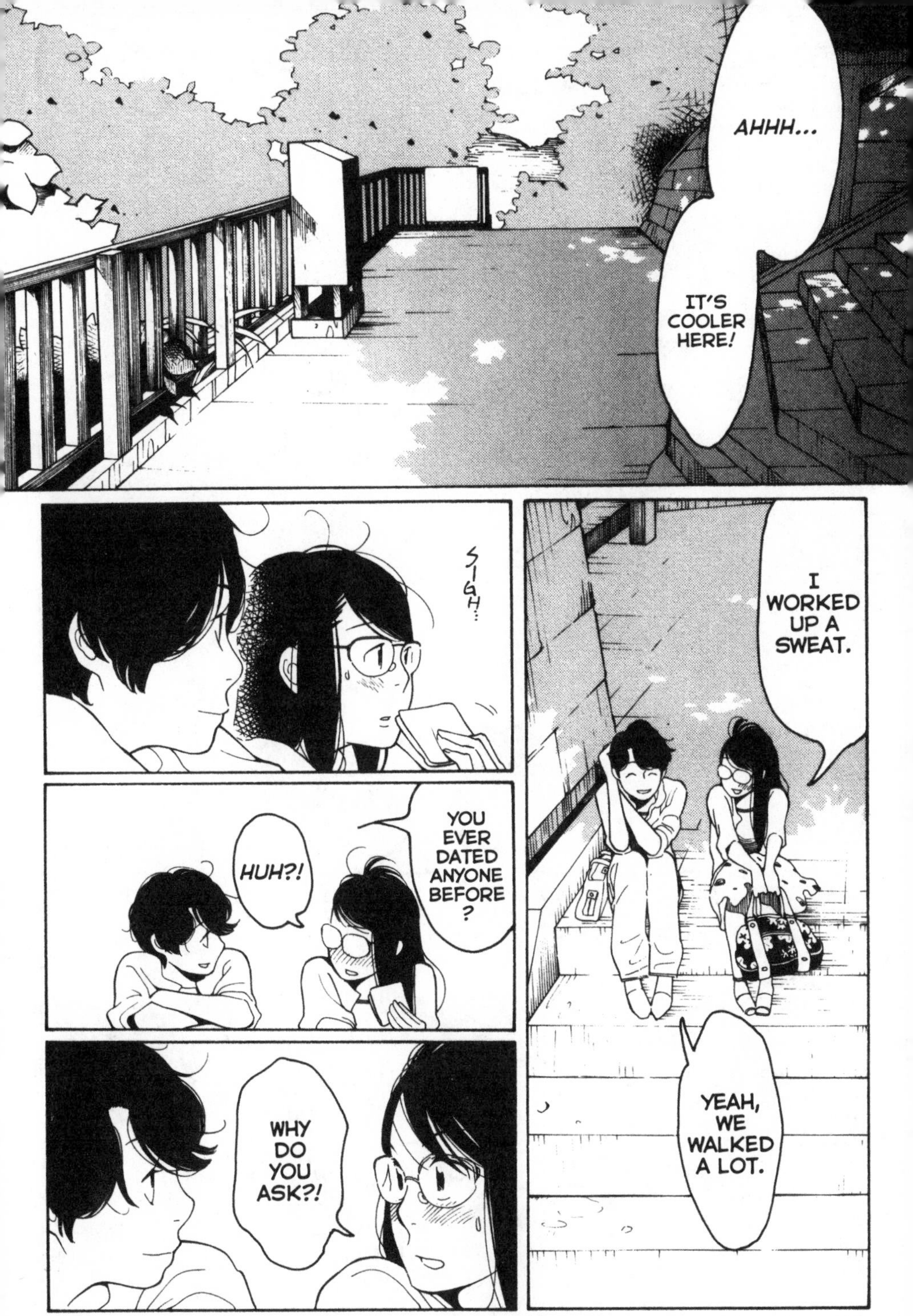
AHHH...
IT'S COOLER HERE!
I WORKED UP A SWEAT.
YEAH, WE WALKED A LOT.
SIGH...
YOU EVER DATED ANYONE BEFORE?
HUH?!
WHY DO YOU ASK?!

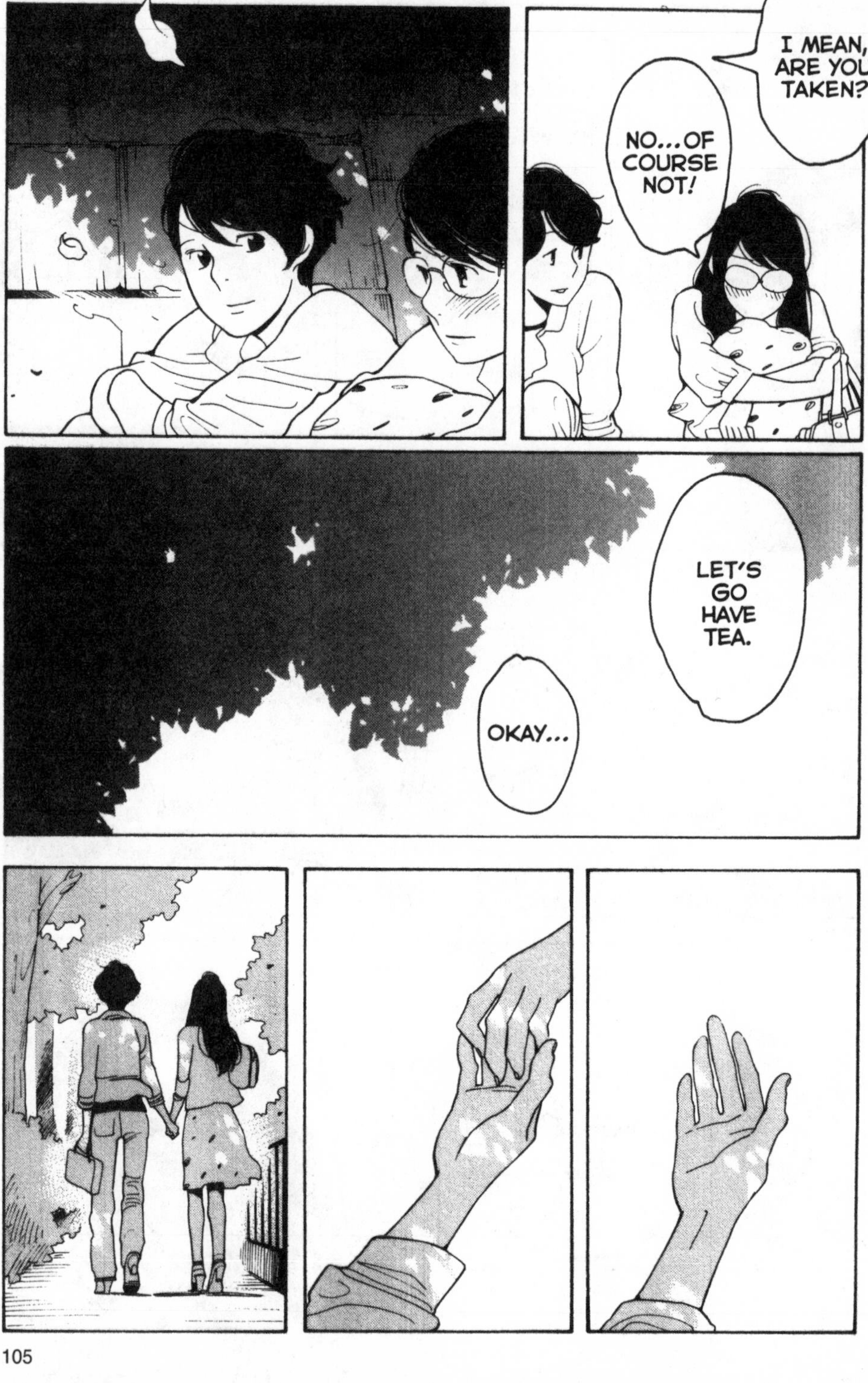
I MEAN, ARE YOU TAKEN?
NO...OF COURSE NOT!
LET'S GO HAVE TEA.
OKAY...

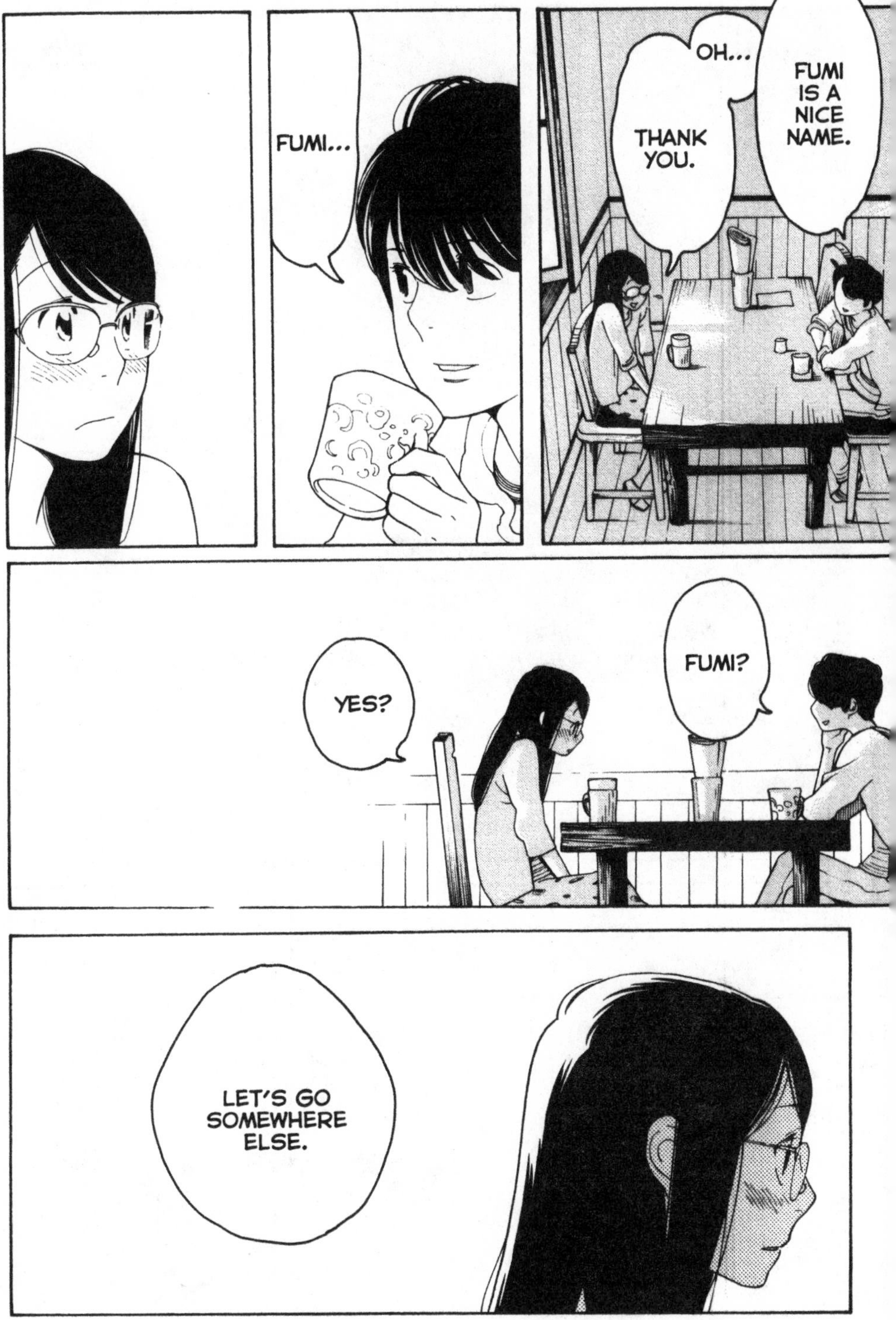
FUMI IS A NICE NAME.
OH...
THANK YOU.
FUMI...
FUMI?
YES?
LET'S GO SOMEWHERE ELSE.

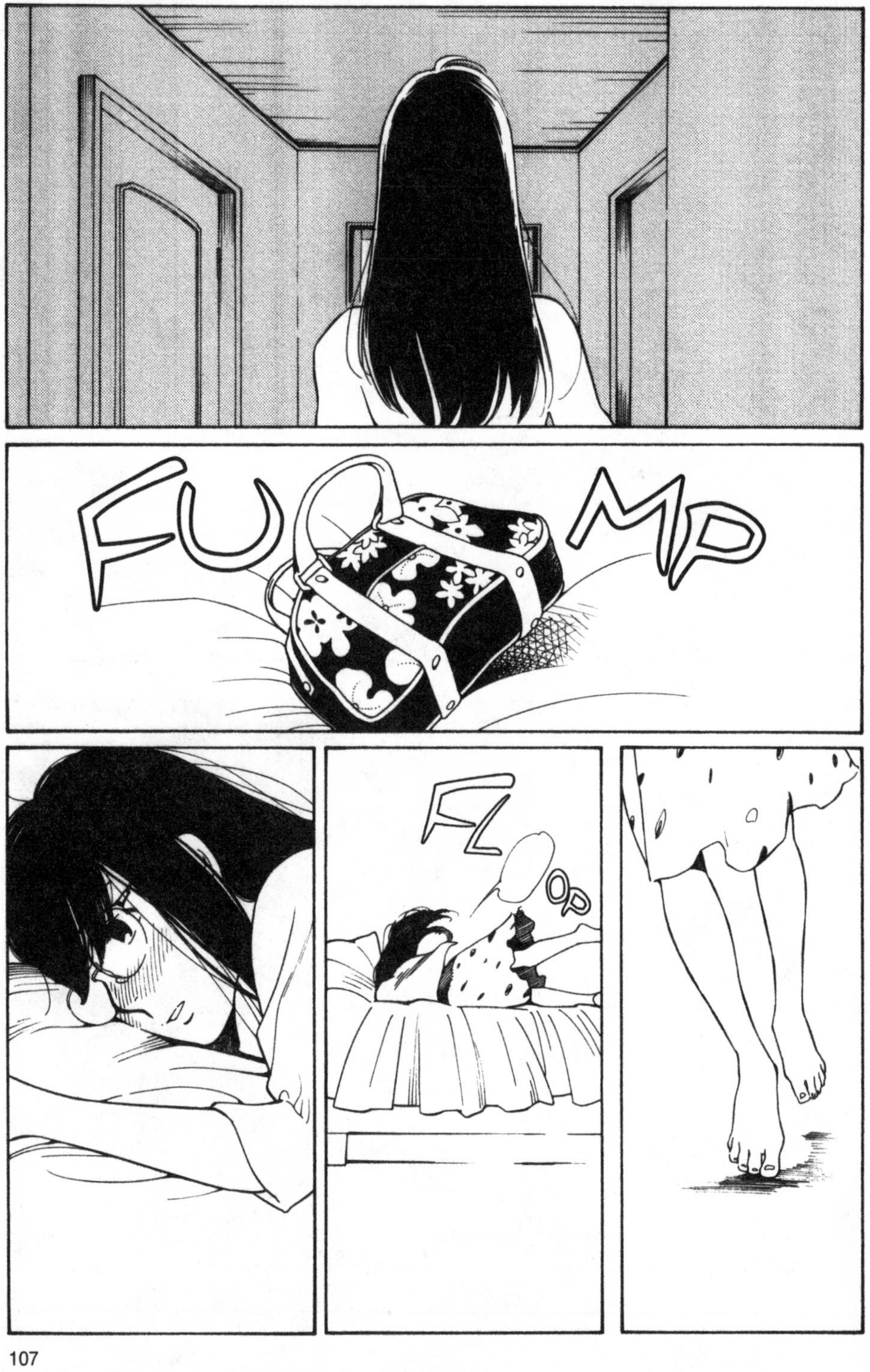
FU MP
FL OP

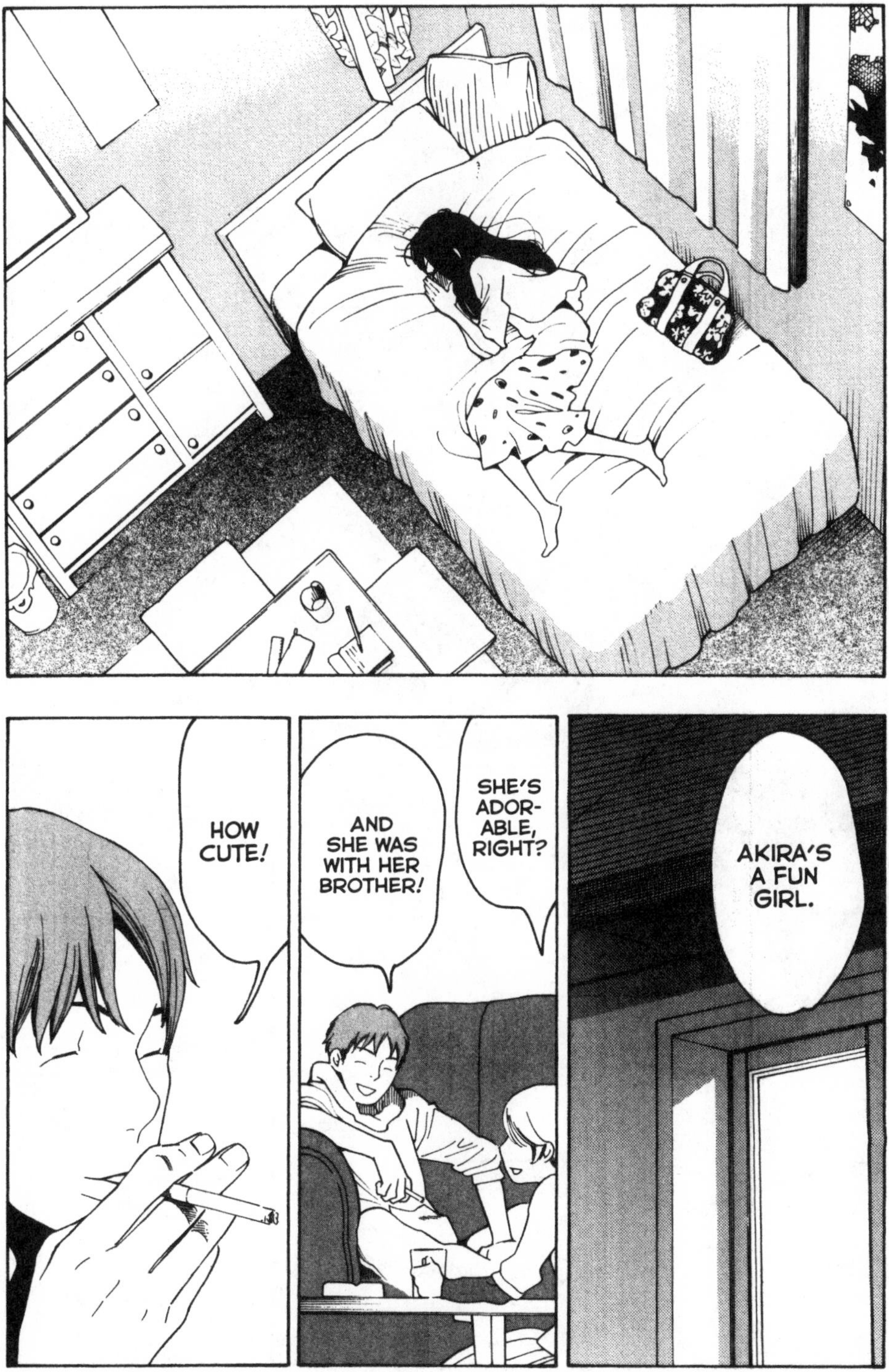
AKIRA'S A FUN GIRL.
SHE'S ADORABLE, RIGHT?
AND SHE WAS WITH HER BROTHER!
HOW CUTE!

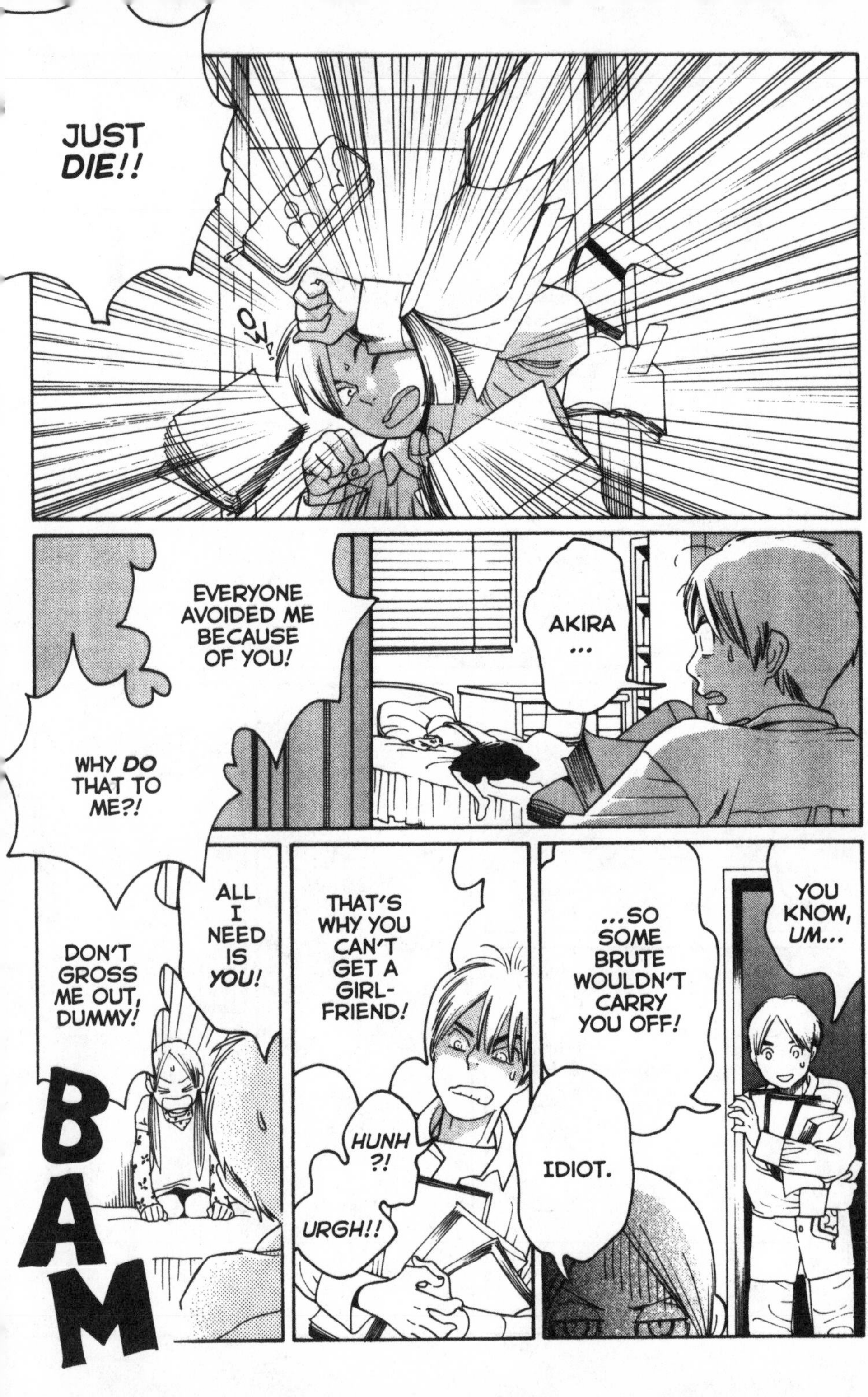
JUST DIE!!
OW!
AKIRA ...
EVERYONE AVOIDED ME BECAUSE OF YOU!
WHY DO THAT TO ME?!
YOU KNOW, UM...
...SO SOME BRUTE WOULDN'T CARRY YOU OFF!
IDIOT.
THAT'S WHY YOU CAN'T GET A GIRL-FRIEND!
HUNH?!
URGH!!
ALL I NEED IS YOU!
DON'T GROSS ME OUT, DUMMY!
BAM

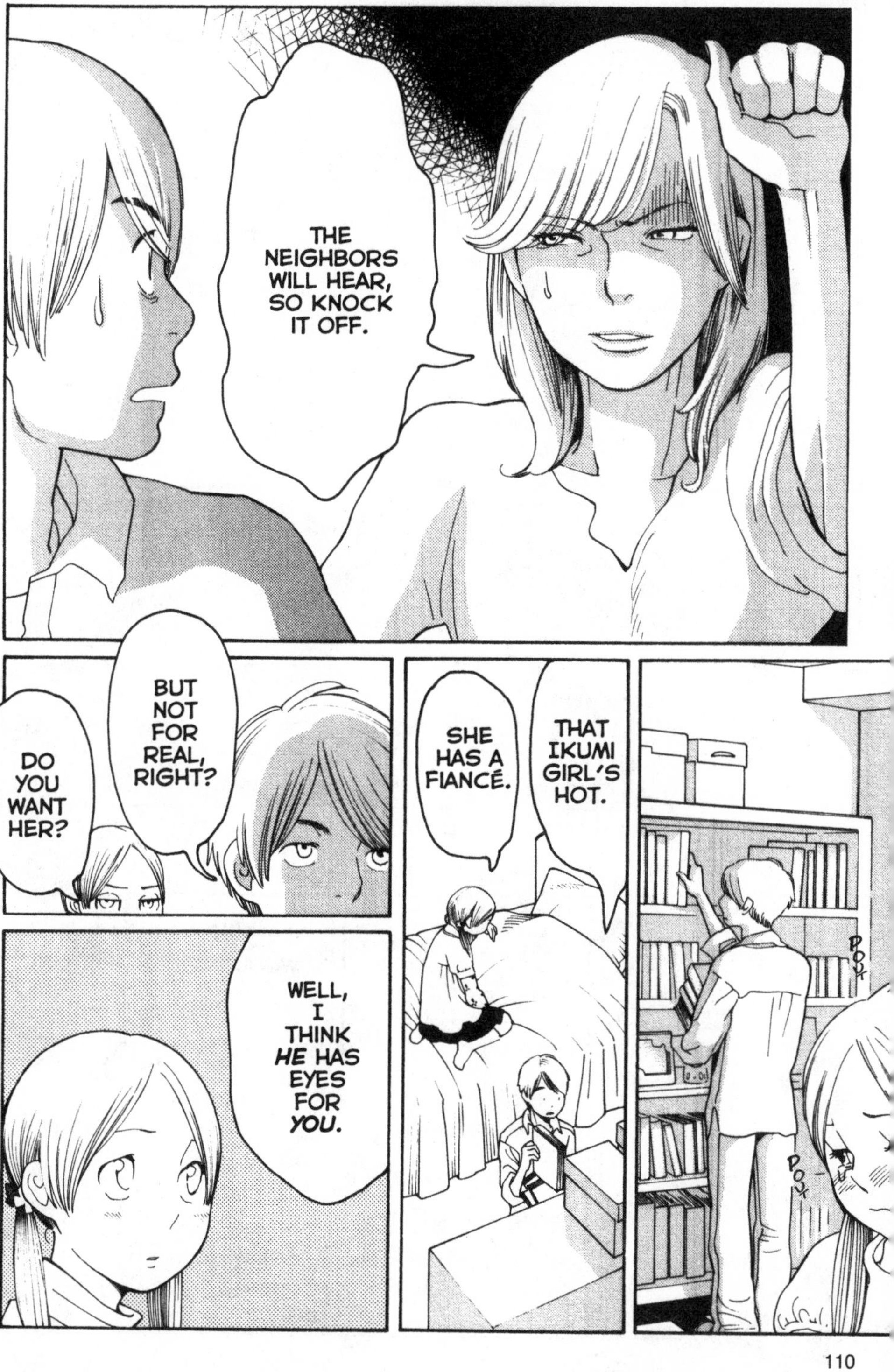
THE NEIGHBORS WILL HEAR, SO KNOCK IT OFF.
POY
POY
THAT IKUMI GIRL'S HOT.
SHE HAS A FIANCÉ.
BUT NOT FOR REAL, RIGHT?
DO YOU WANT HER?
WELL, I THINK *HE* HAS EYES FOR *YOU*.

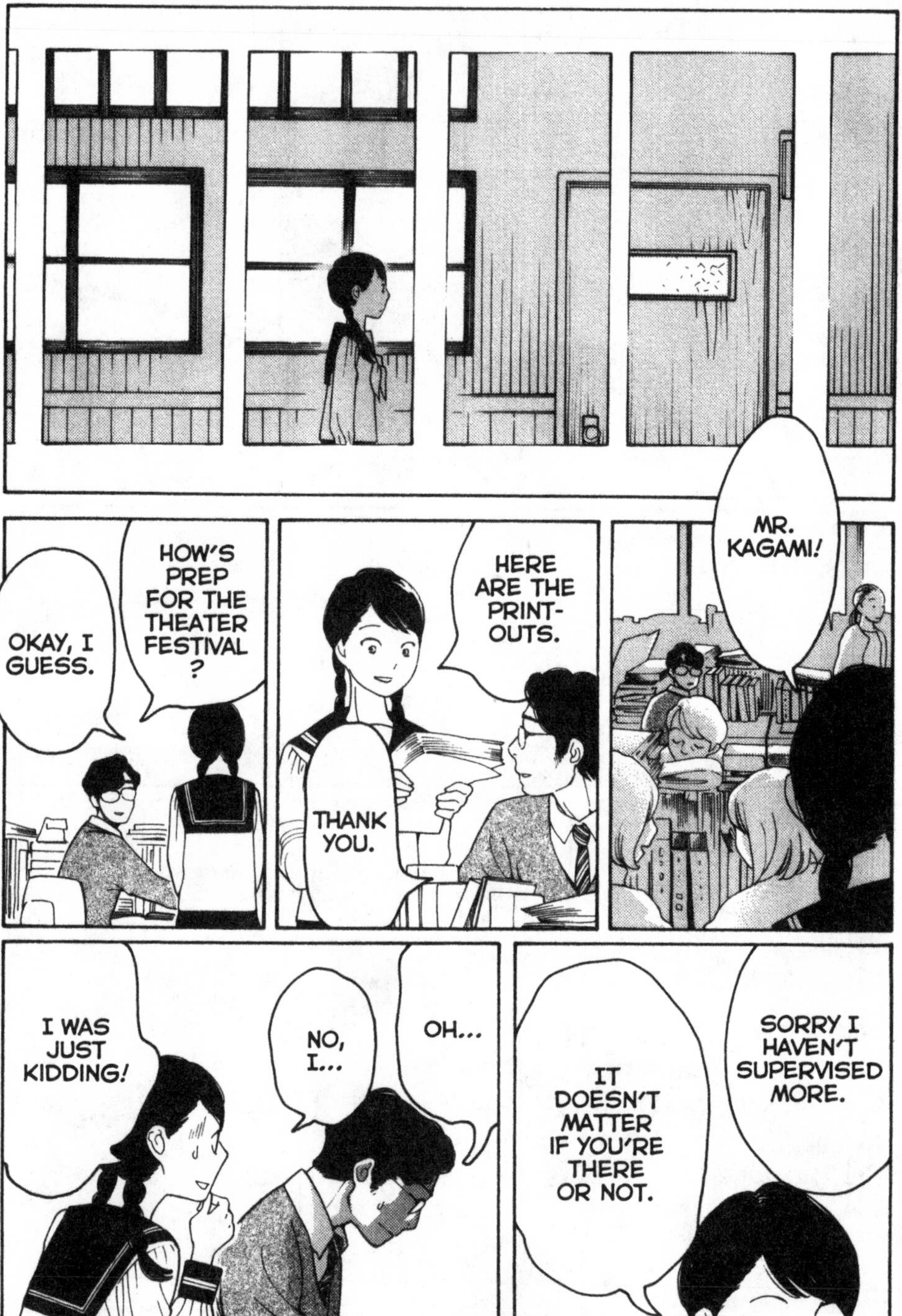
MR. KAGAMI!
HERE ARE THE PRINT-OUTS.
THANK YOU.
HOW'S PREP FOR THE THEATER FESTIVAL?
OKAY, I GUESS.
SORRY I HAVEN'T SUPERVISED MORE.
IT DOESN'T MATTER IF YOU'RE THERE OR NOT.
OH...
NO, I...
I WAS JUST KIDDING!

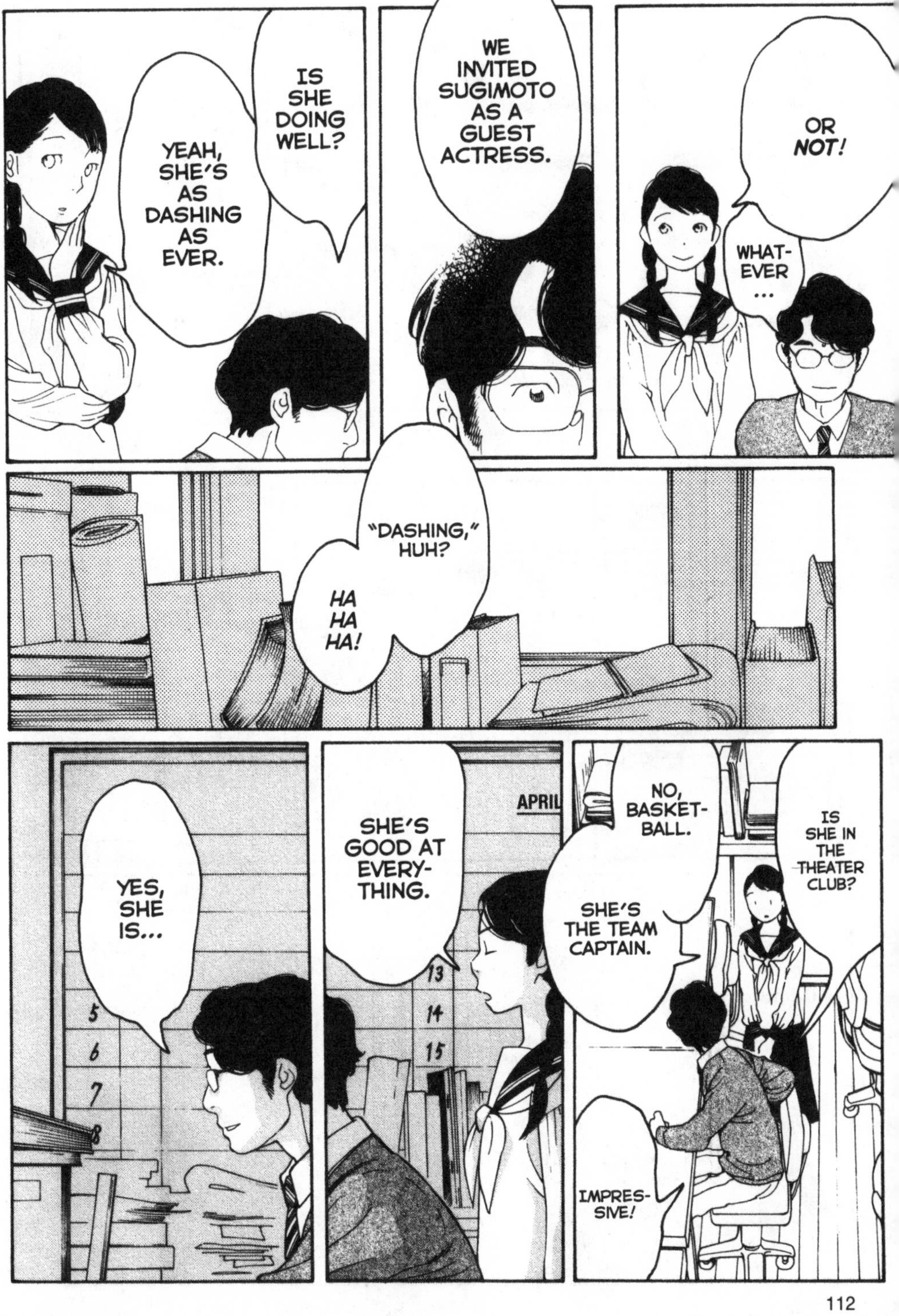
OR NOT!
WHAT-EVER...
WE INVITED SUGIMOTO AS A GUEST ACTRESS.
IS SHE DOING WELL?
YEAH, SHE'S AS DASHING AS EVER.
"DASHING," HUH?
HA HA HA!
IS SHE IN THE THEATER CLUB?
NO, BASKET-BALL.
SHE'S THE TEAM CAPTAIN.
IMPRES-SIVE!
APRIL
SHE'S GOOD AT EVERY-THING.
YES, SHE IS...

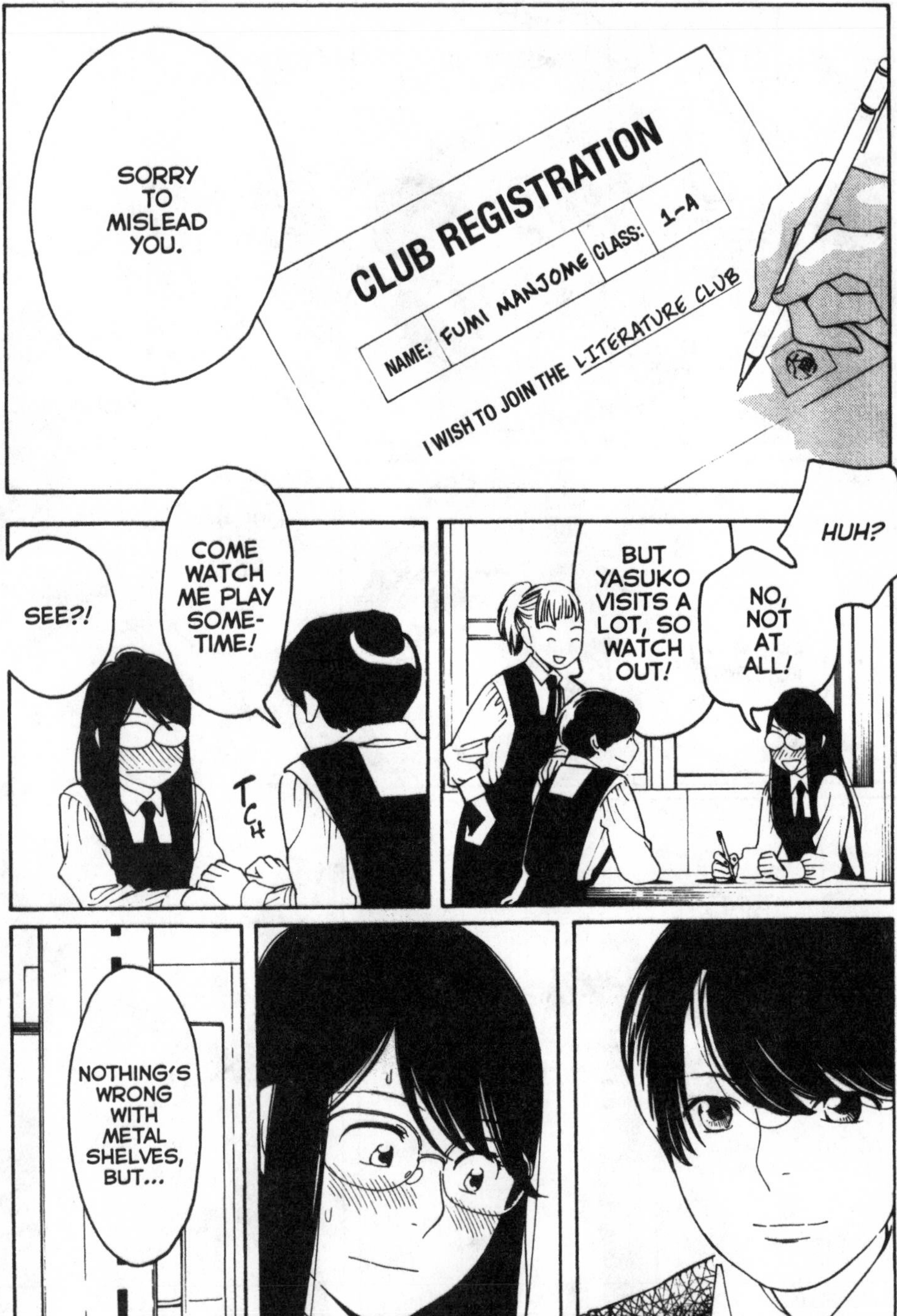
CLUB REGISTRATION
CLASS: 1-A
NAME: FUMI MANJOME
I WISH TO JOIN THE LITERATURE CLUB
SORRY TO MISLEAD YOU.
HUH?
NO, NOT AT ALL!
BUT YASUKO VISITS A LOT, SO WATCH OUT!
COME WATCH ME PLAY SOMETIME!
SEE?!
TCH
NOTHING'S WRONG WITH METAL SHELVES, BUT...

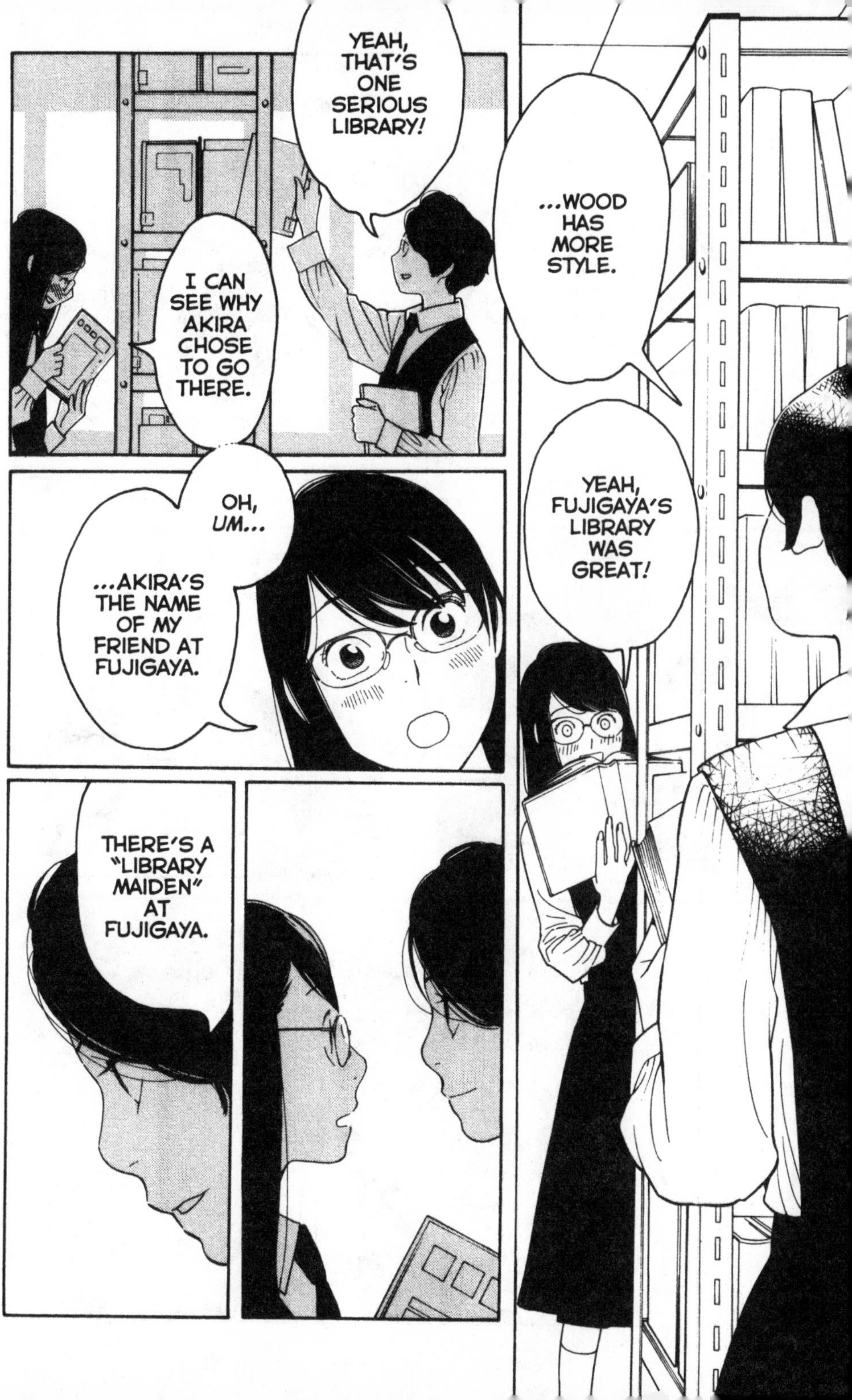
...WOOD HAS MORE STYLE.
YEAH, FUJIGAYA'S LIBRARY WAS GREAT!
YEAH, THAT'S ONE SERIOUS LIBRARY!
I CAN SEE WHY AKIRA CHOSE TO GO THERE.
OH, *UM...*
...AKIRA'S THE NAME OF MY FRIEND AT FUJIGAYA.
THERE'S A "LIBRARY MAIDEN" AT FUJIGAYA.

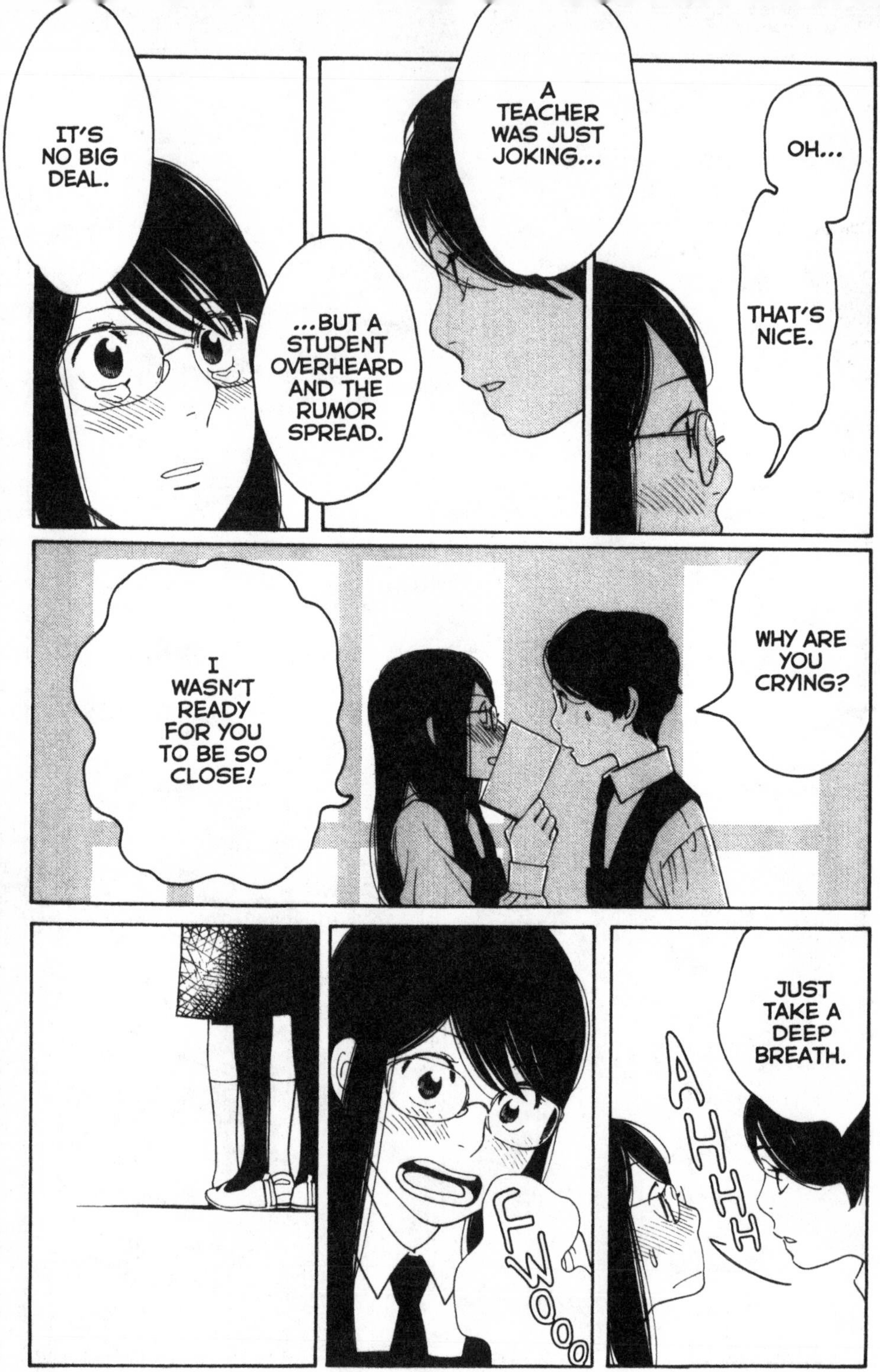
OH...
THAT'S NICE.
A TEACHER WAS JUST JOKING...
...BUT A STUDENT OVERHEARD AND THE RUMOR SPREAD.
IT'S NO BIG DEAL.
WHY ARE YOU CRYING?
I WASN'T READY FOR YOU TO BE SO CLOSE!
JUST TAKE A DEEP BREATH.
AHHHH
FWOOO

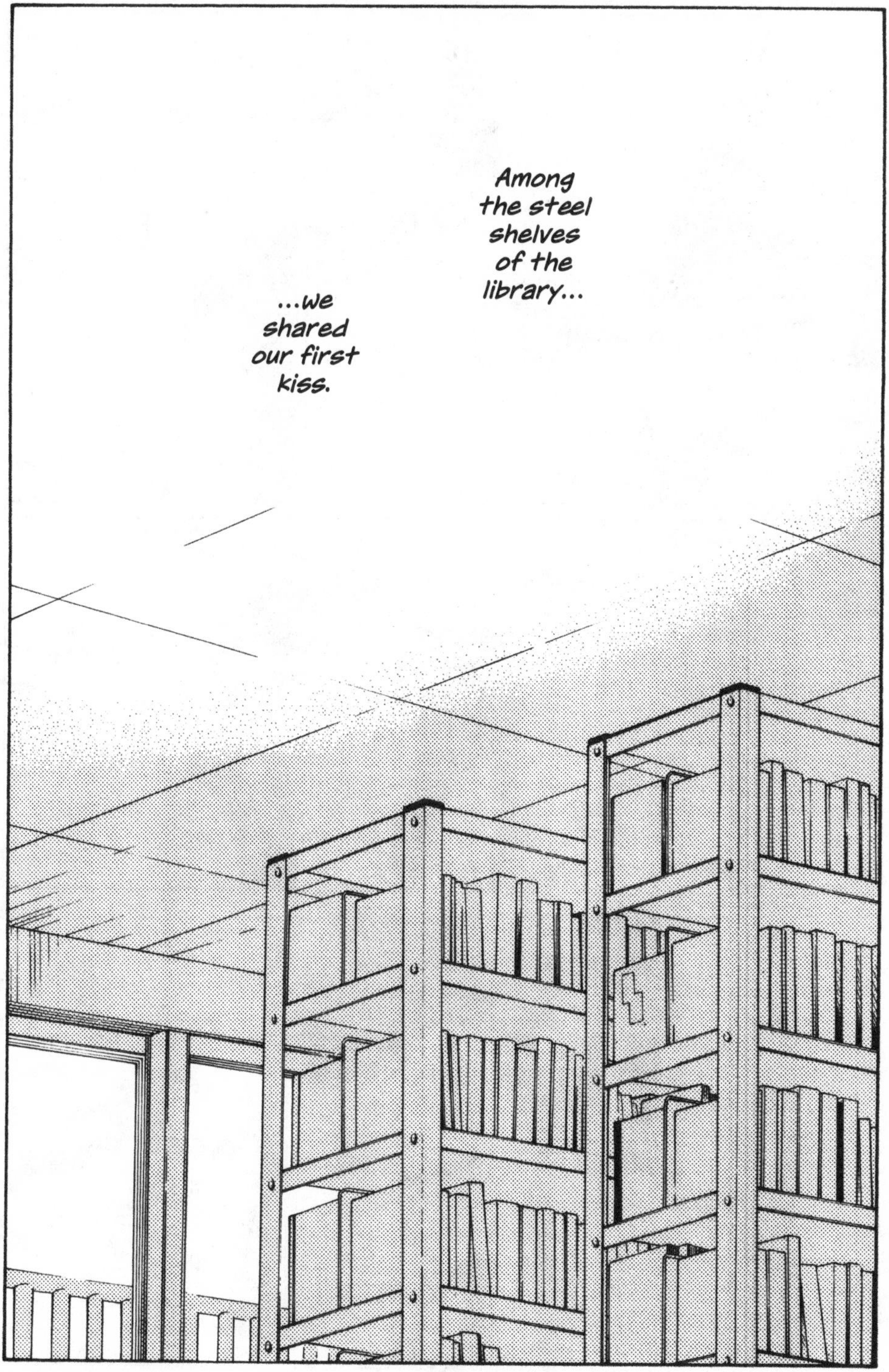
Among the steel shelves of the library...
...we shared our first kiss.

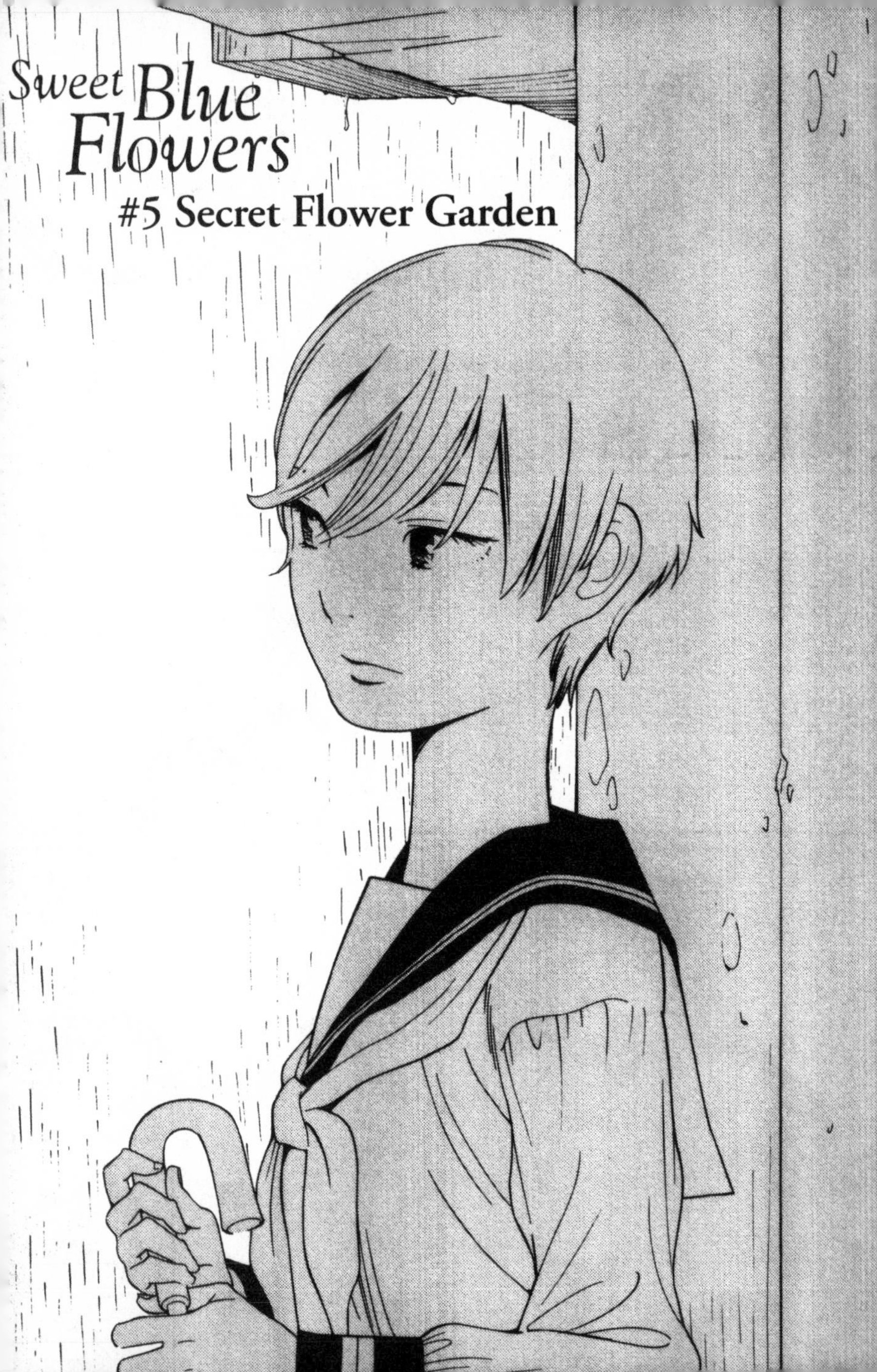
Sweet Blue Flowers
#5 Secret Flower Garden

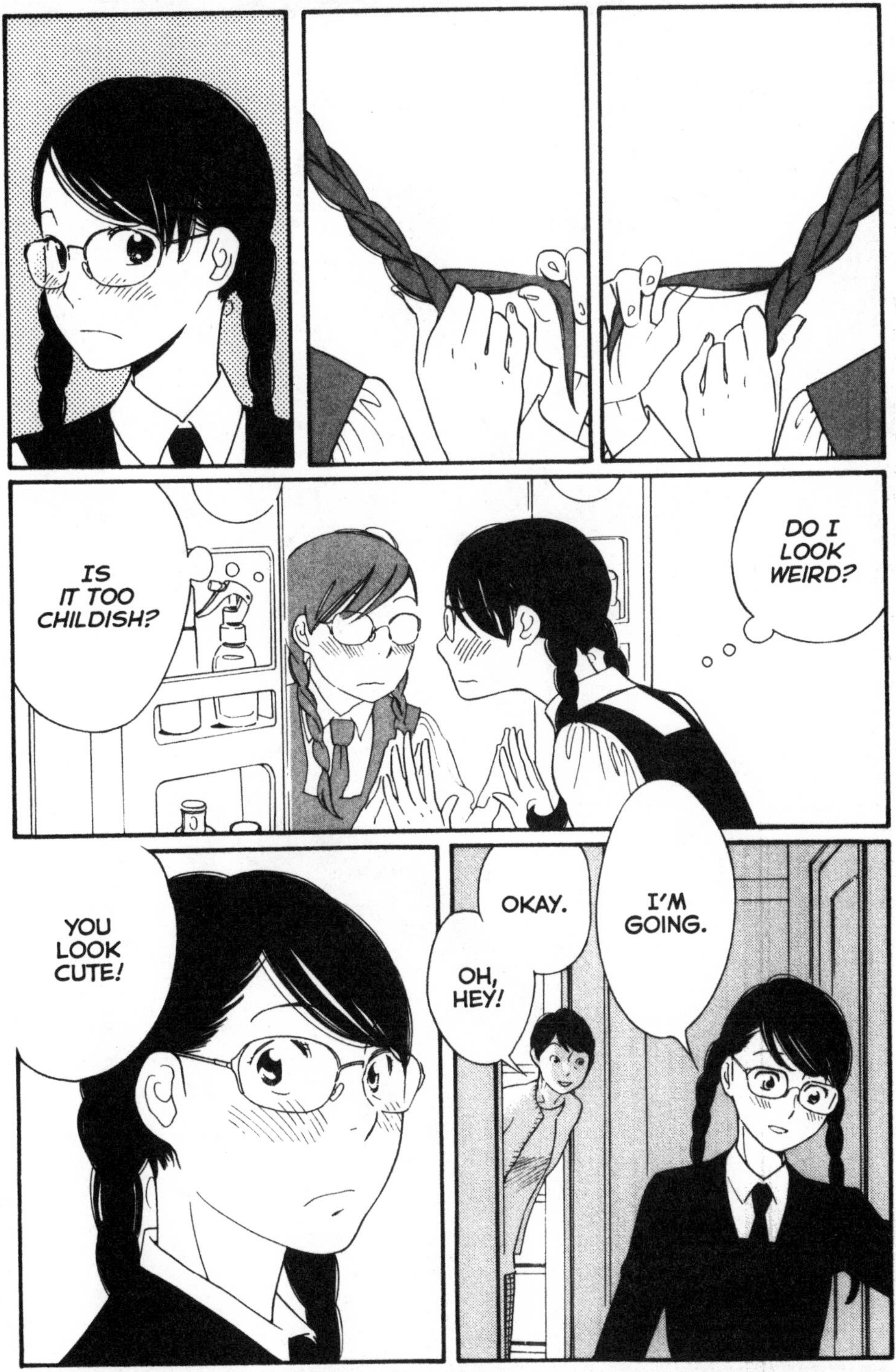
DO I LOOK WEIRD?
IS IT TOO CHILDISH?
I'M GOING.
OKAY.
OH, HEY!
YOU LOOK CUTE!

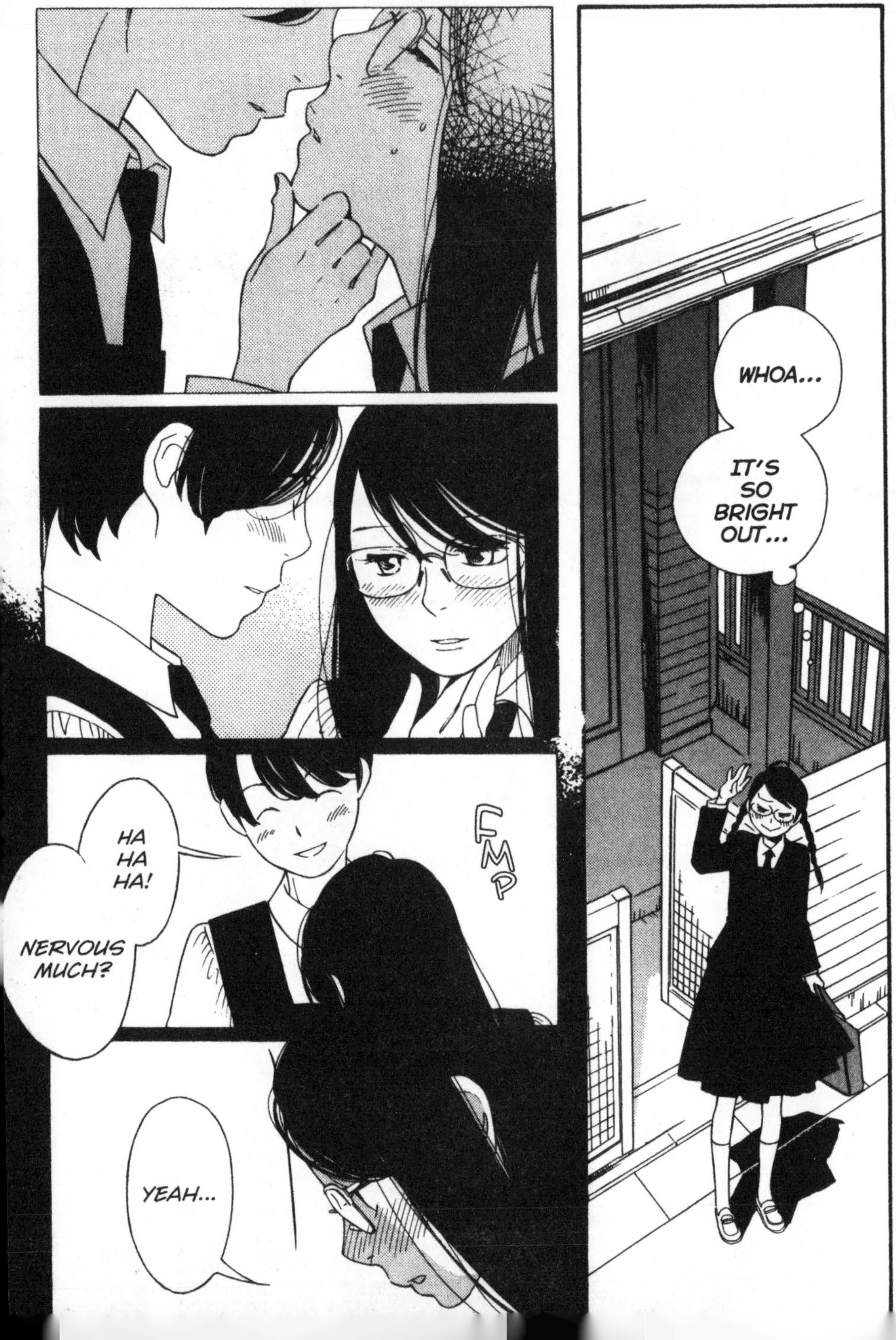
WHOA...
IT'S SO BRIGHT OUT...
FMP
HA HA HA!
NERVOUS MUCH?
YEAH...

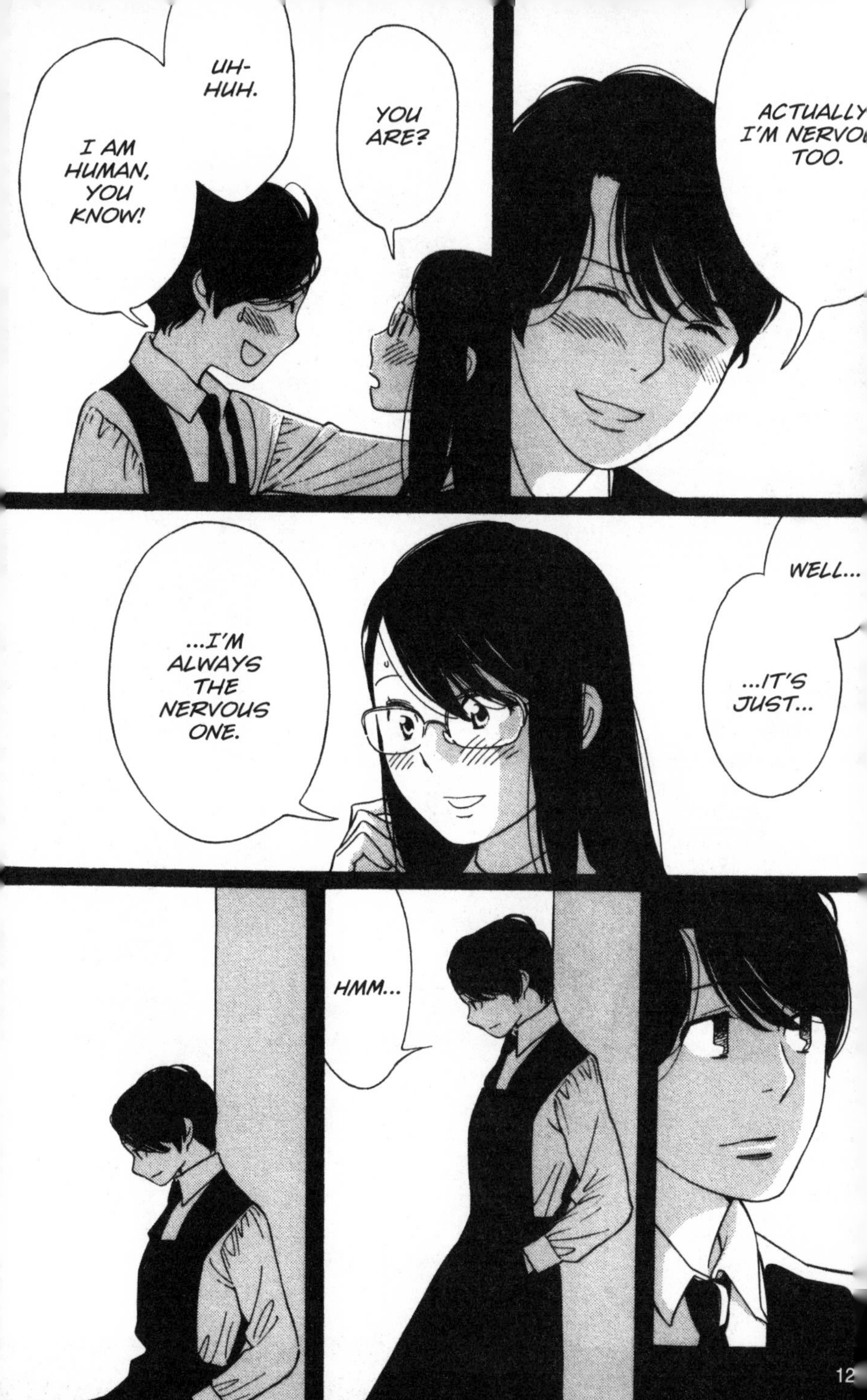
ACTUALLY I'M NERVOU TOO.
YOU ARE?
UH-HUH.
I AM HUMAN, YOU KNOW!
WELL...
...IT'S JUST...
...I'M ALWAYS THE NERVOUS ONE.
HMM...

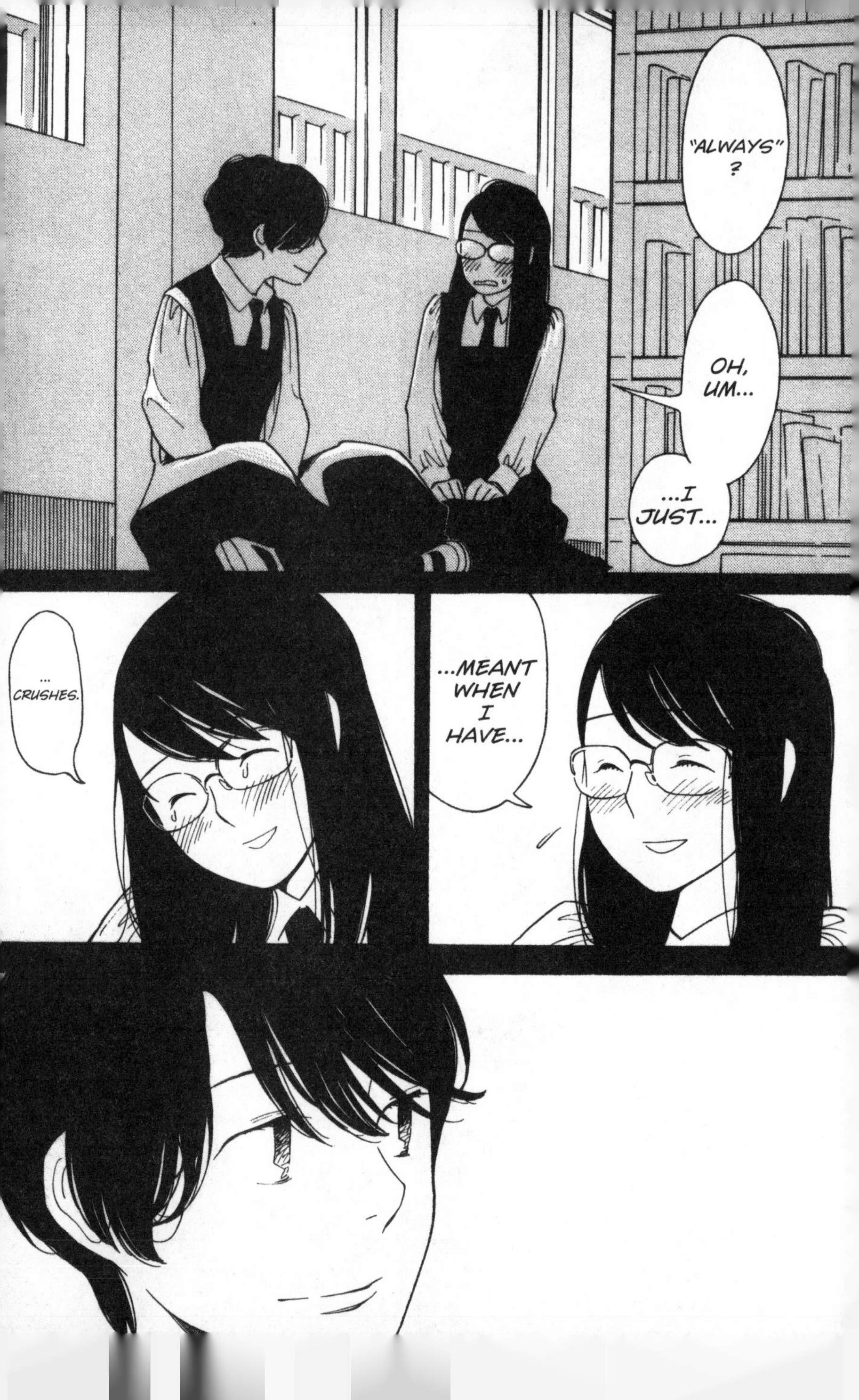
"ALWAYS" ?
OH, UM...
...I JUST...
...MEANT WHEN I HAVE...
... CRUSHES.

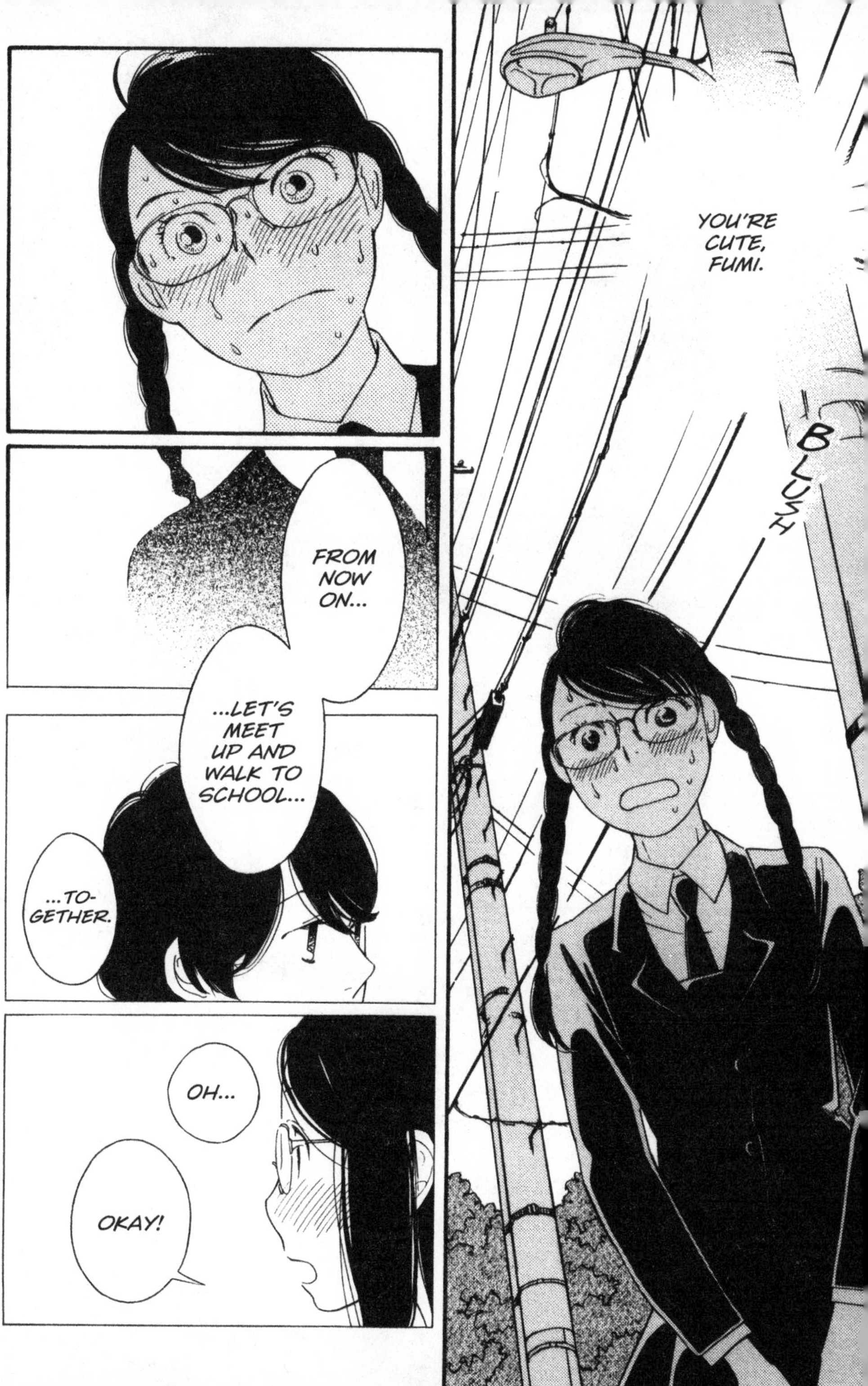
YOU'RE CUTE, FUMI.
BLUSH
FROM NOW ON...
...LET'S MEET UP AND WALK TO SCHOOL...
...TO-GETHER.
OH...
OKAY!

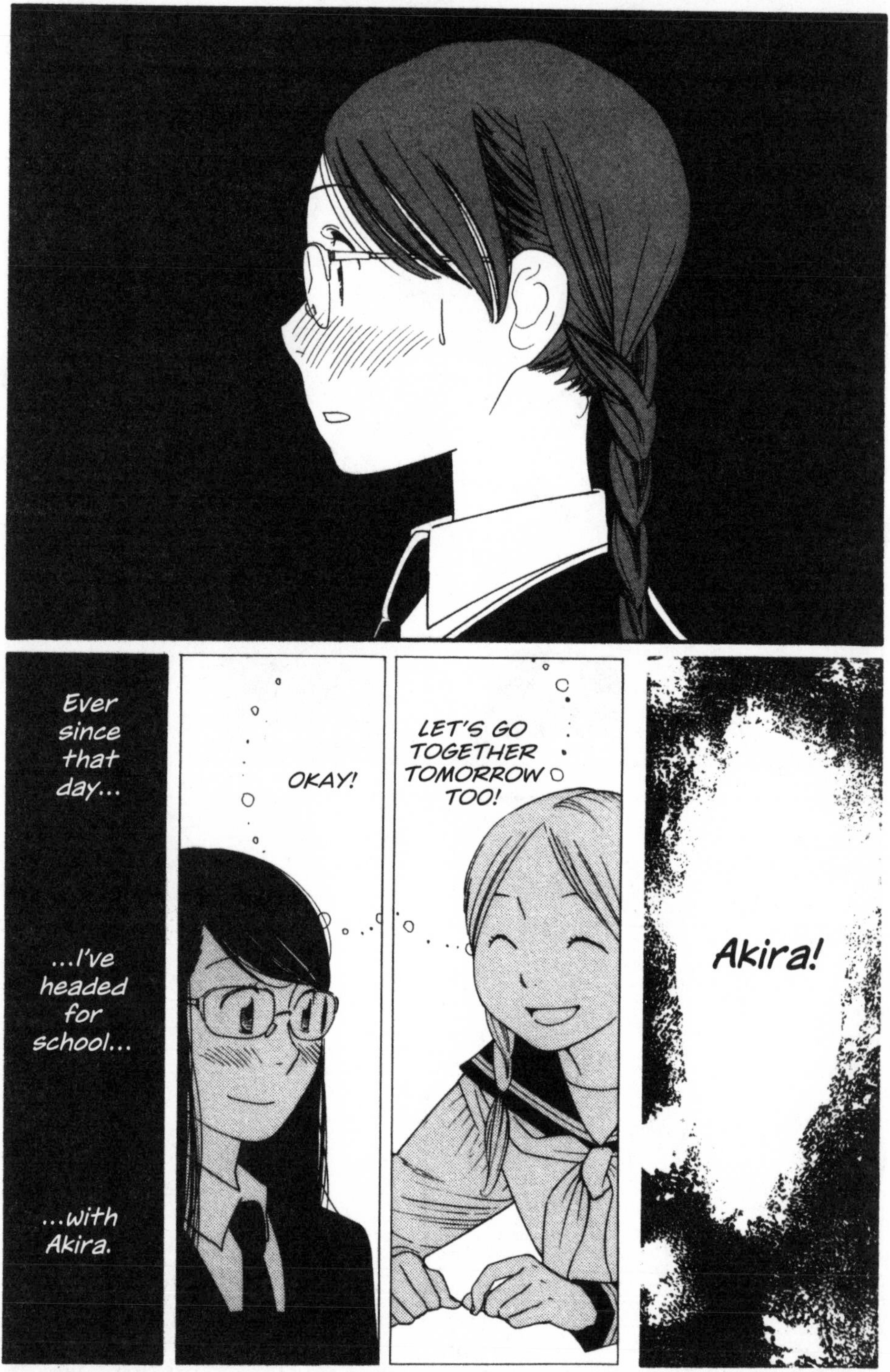
Akira!
LET'S GO TOGETHER TOMORROW TOO!
OKAY!
Ever since that day...
...I've headed for school...
...with Akira.

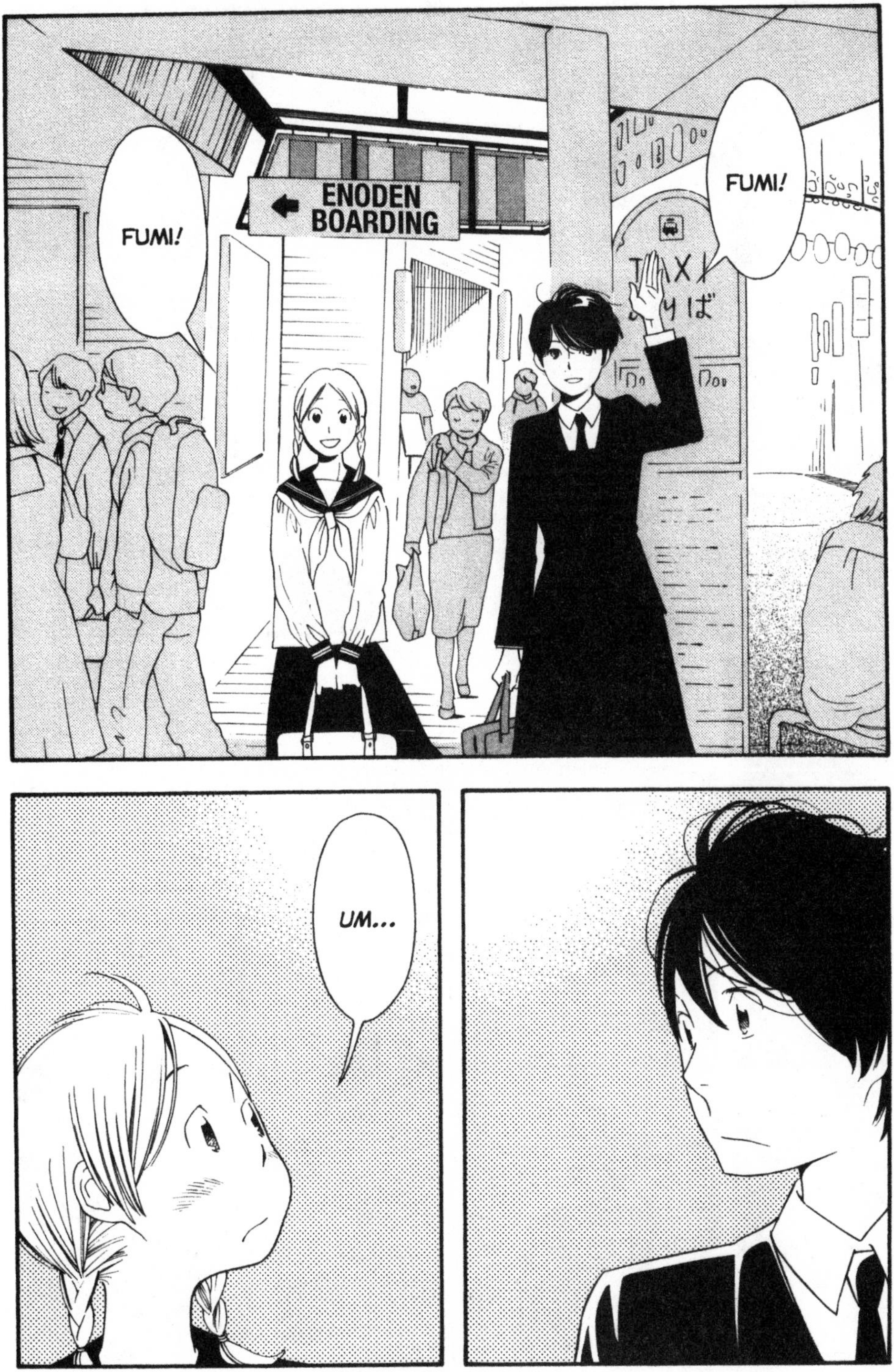
FUMI!
ENODEN
BOARDING
FUMI!
UM...

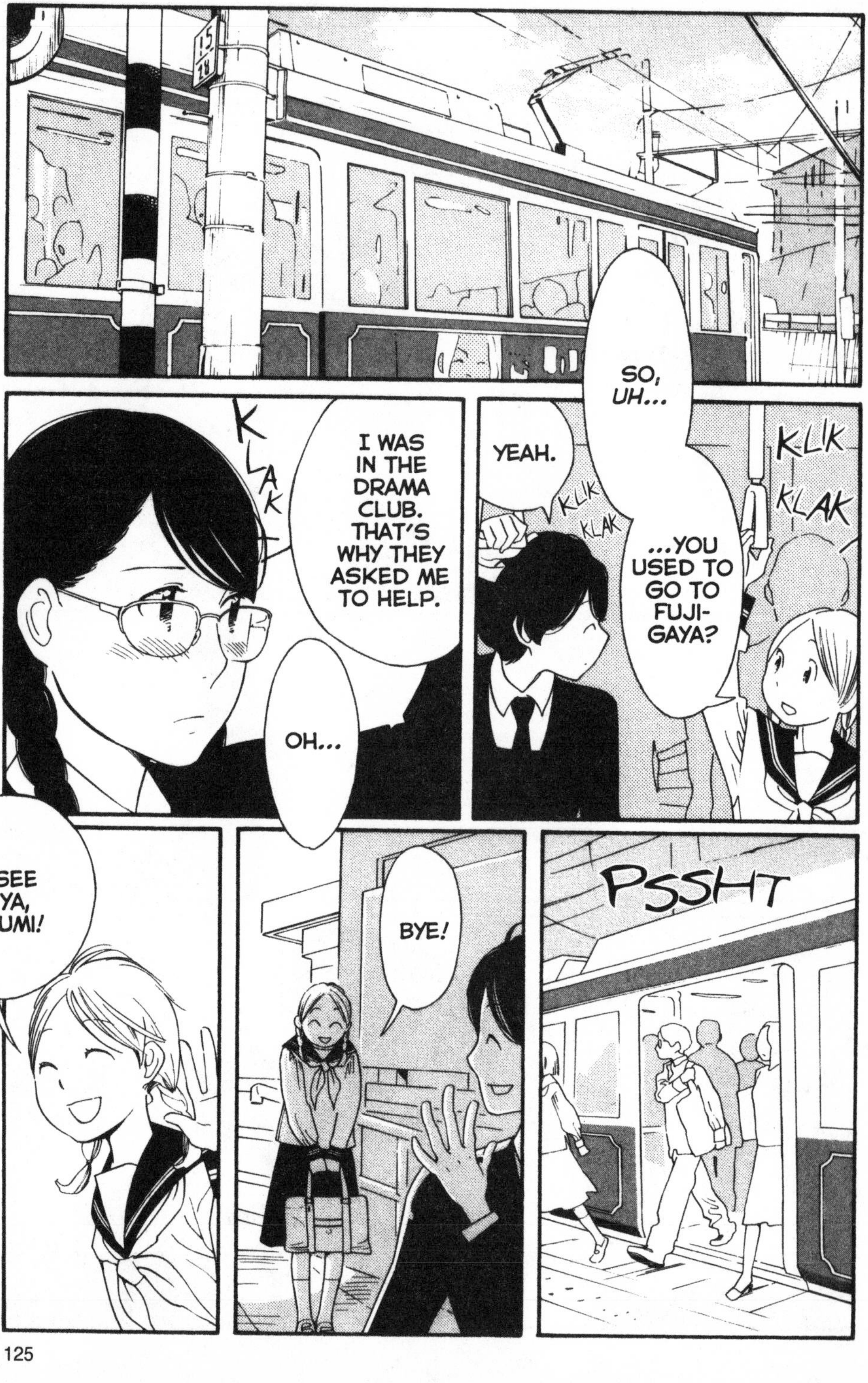
SO, UH...
K-LIK
KLAK
...YOU USED TO GO TO FUJI-GAYA?
YEAH.
K-LIK
KLAK
KLAK
I WAS IN THE DRAMA CLUB. THAT'S WHY THEY ASKED ME TO HELP.
OH...
PSSHT
BYE!
SEE YA, FUMI!

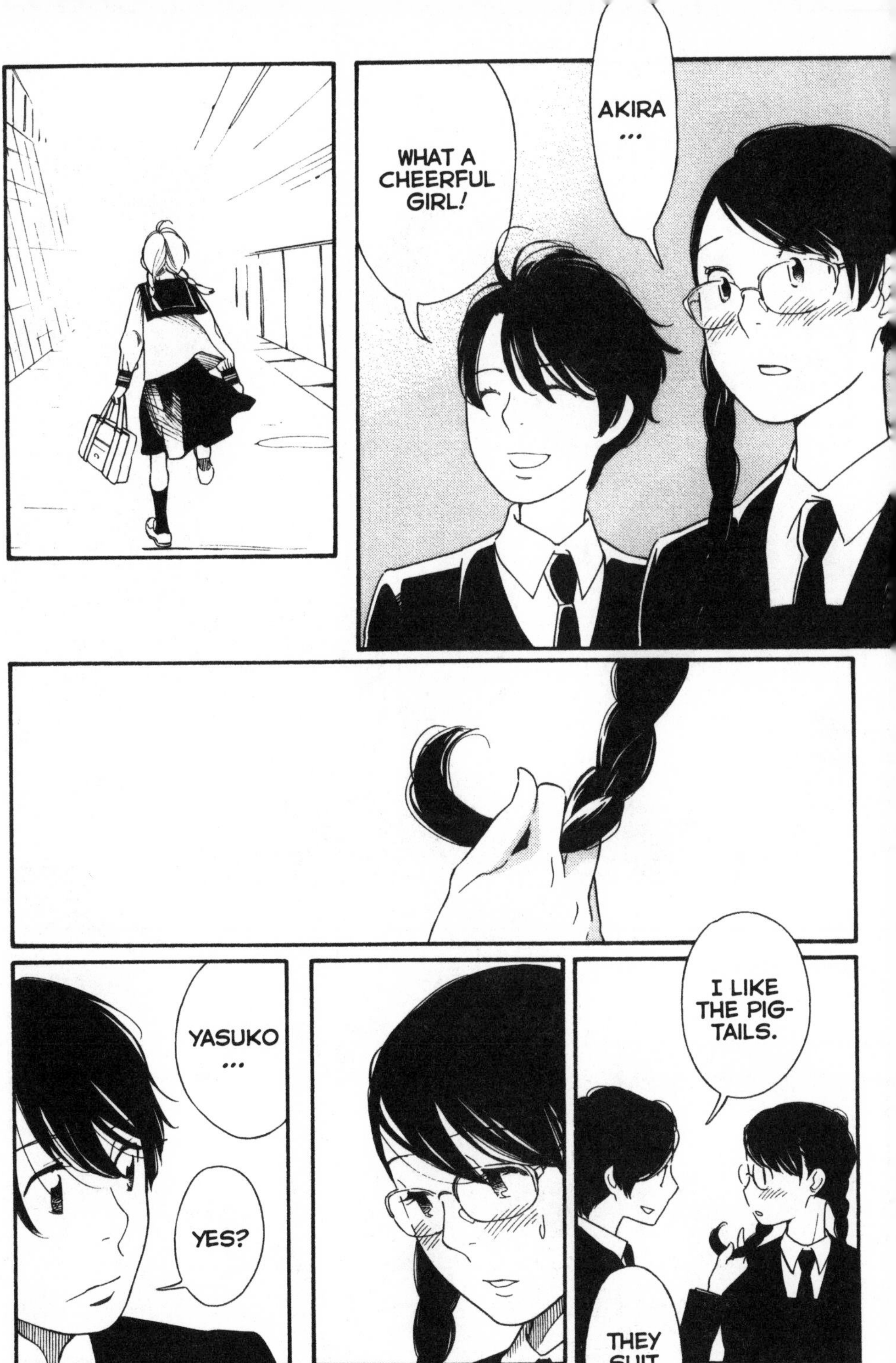
AKIRA ...
WHAT A CHEERFUL GIRL!
I LIKE THE PIG-TAILS.
THEY SUIT YOU.
YASUKO ...
YES?

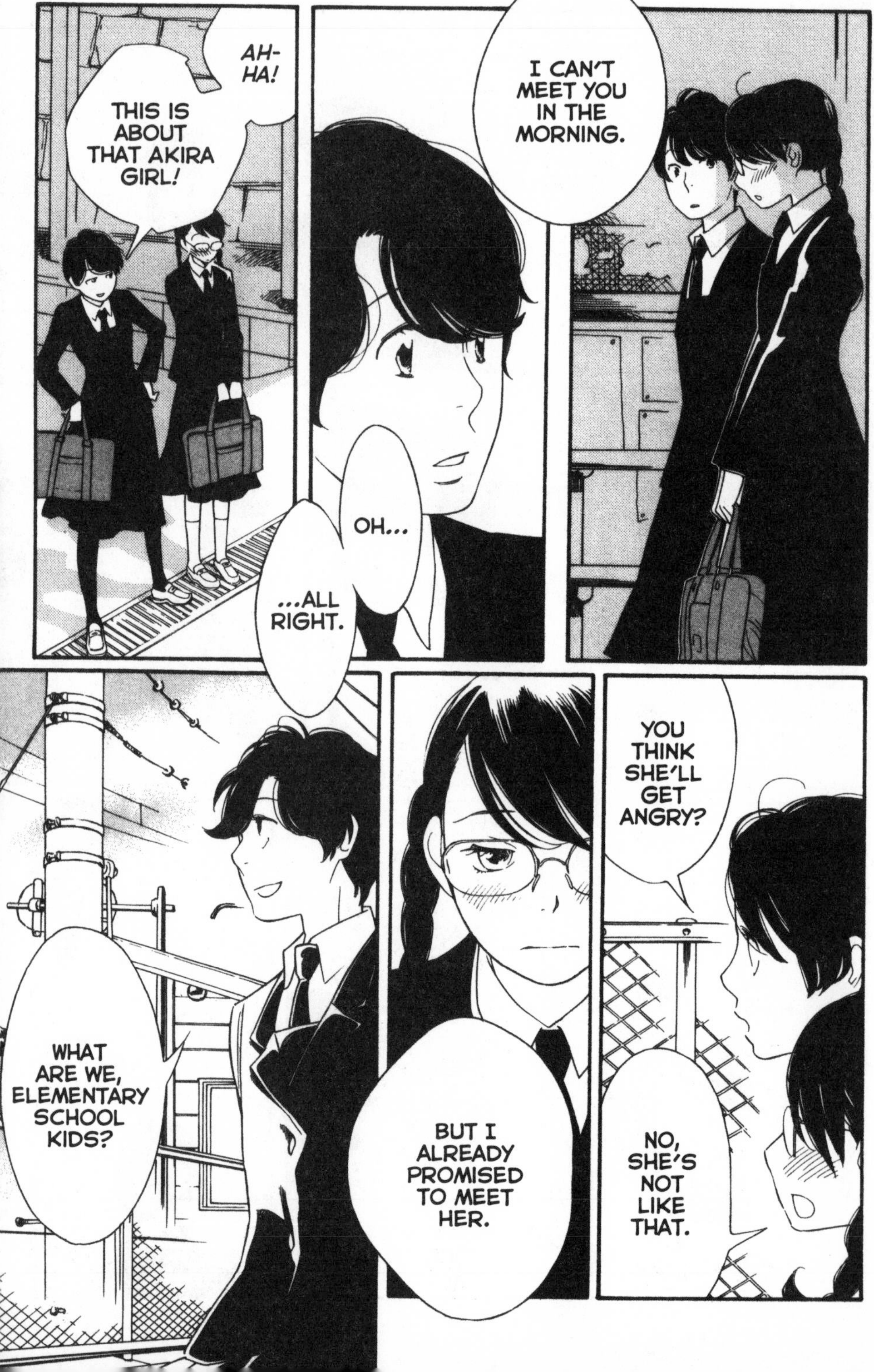
I CAN'T MEET YOU IN THE MORNING.
OH...
...ALL RIGHT.
AH-HA!
THIS IS ABOUT THAT AKIRA GIRL!
YOU THINK SHE'LL GET ANGRY?
NO, SHE'S NOT LIKE THAT.
BUT I ALREADY PROMISED TO MEET HER.
WHAT ARE WE, ELEMENTARY SCHOOL KIDS?

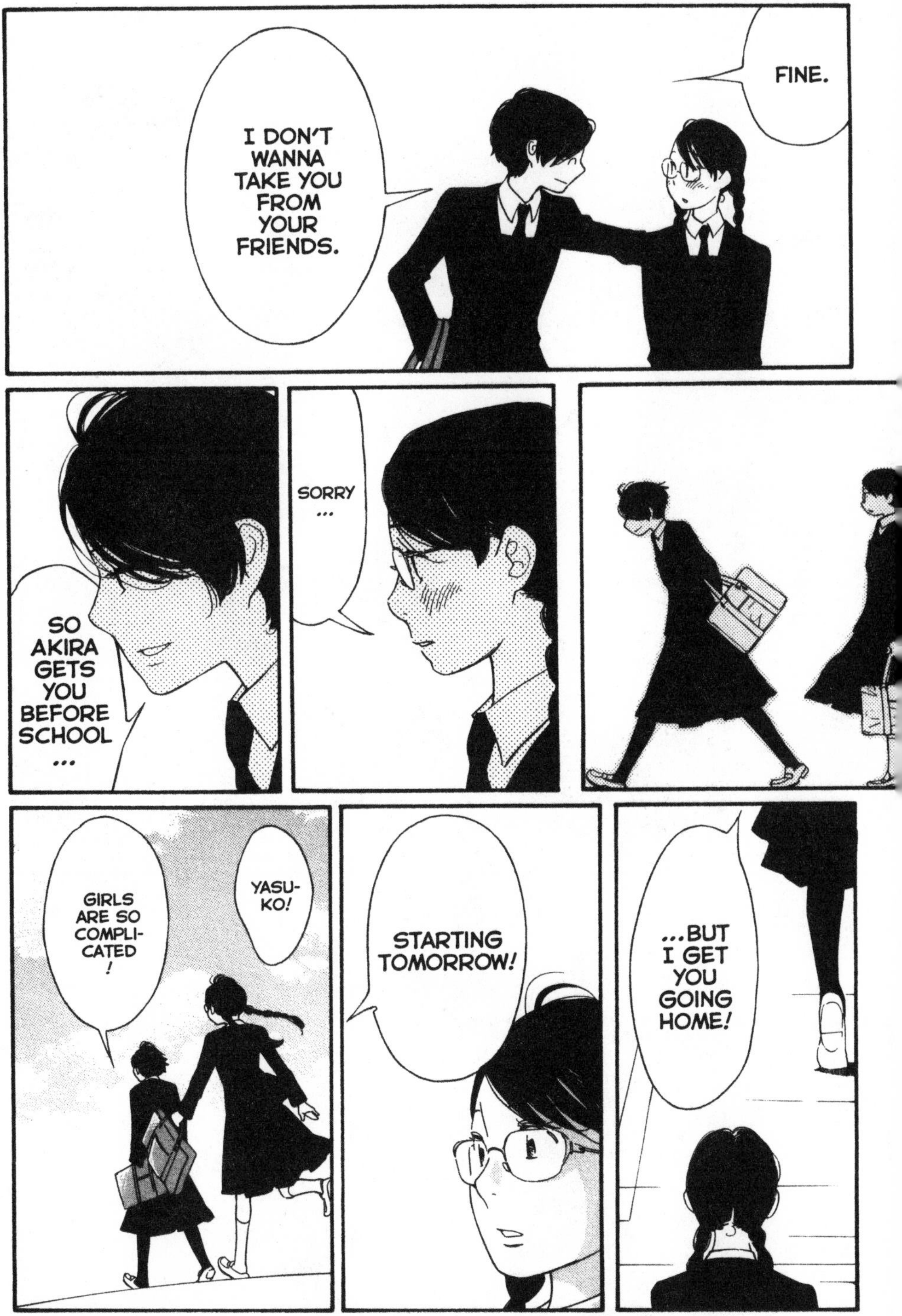
FINE.
I DON'T WANNA TAKE YOU FROM YOUR FRIENDS.
SORRY ...
SO AKIRA GETS YOU BEFORE SCHOOL ...
...BUT I GET YOU GOING HOME!
STARTING TOMORROW!
YASUKO!
GIRLS ARE SO COMPLICATED!

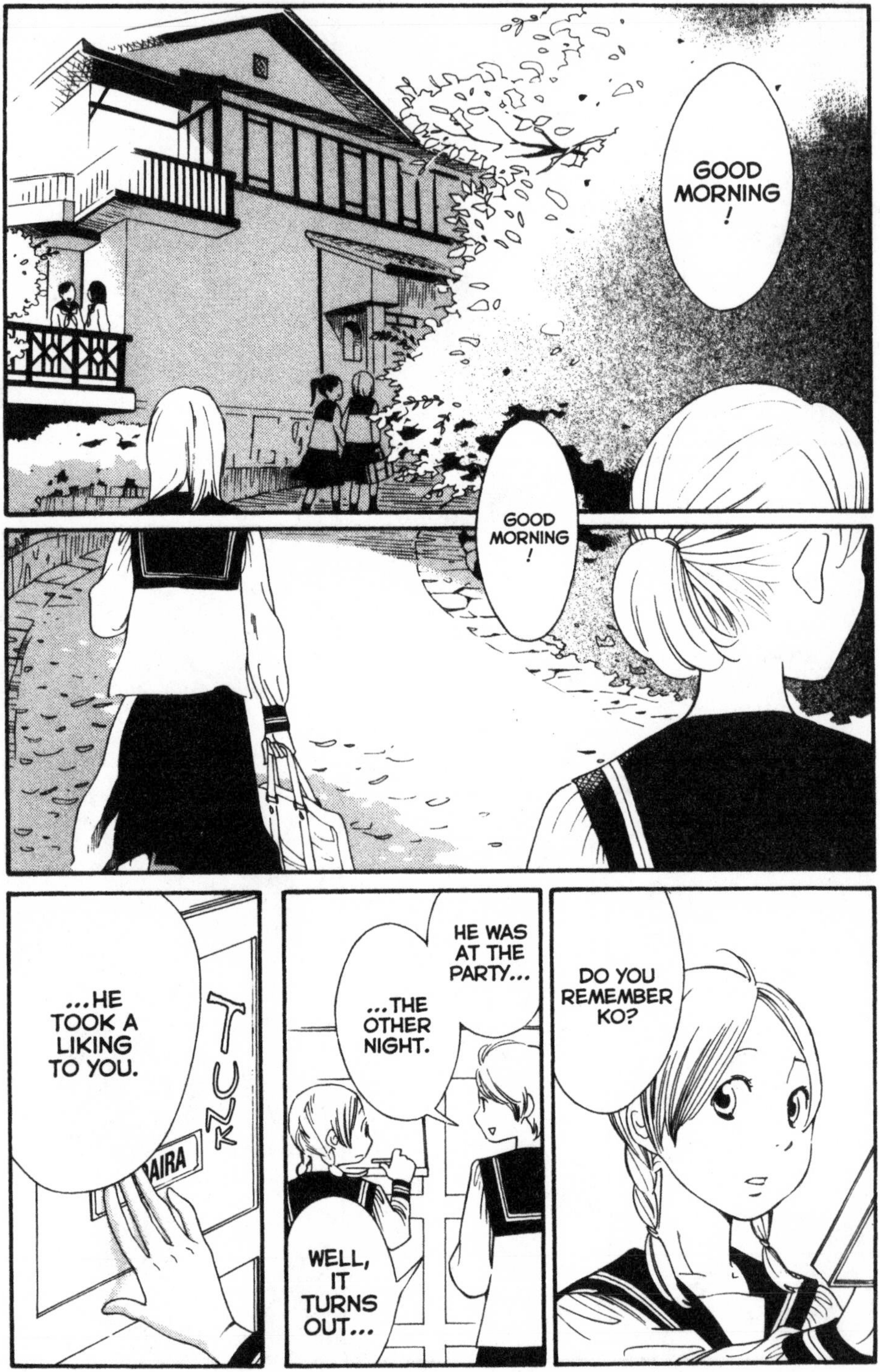
GOOD MORNING!
GOOD MORNING!
DO YOU REMEMBER KO?
HE WAS AT THE PARTY...
...THE OTHER NIGHT.
WELL, IT TURNS OUT...
...HE TOOK A LIKING TO YOU.
TUNK

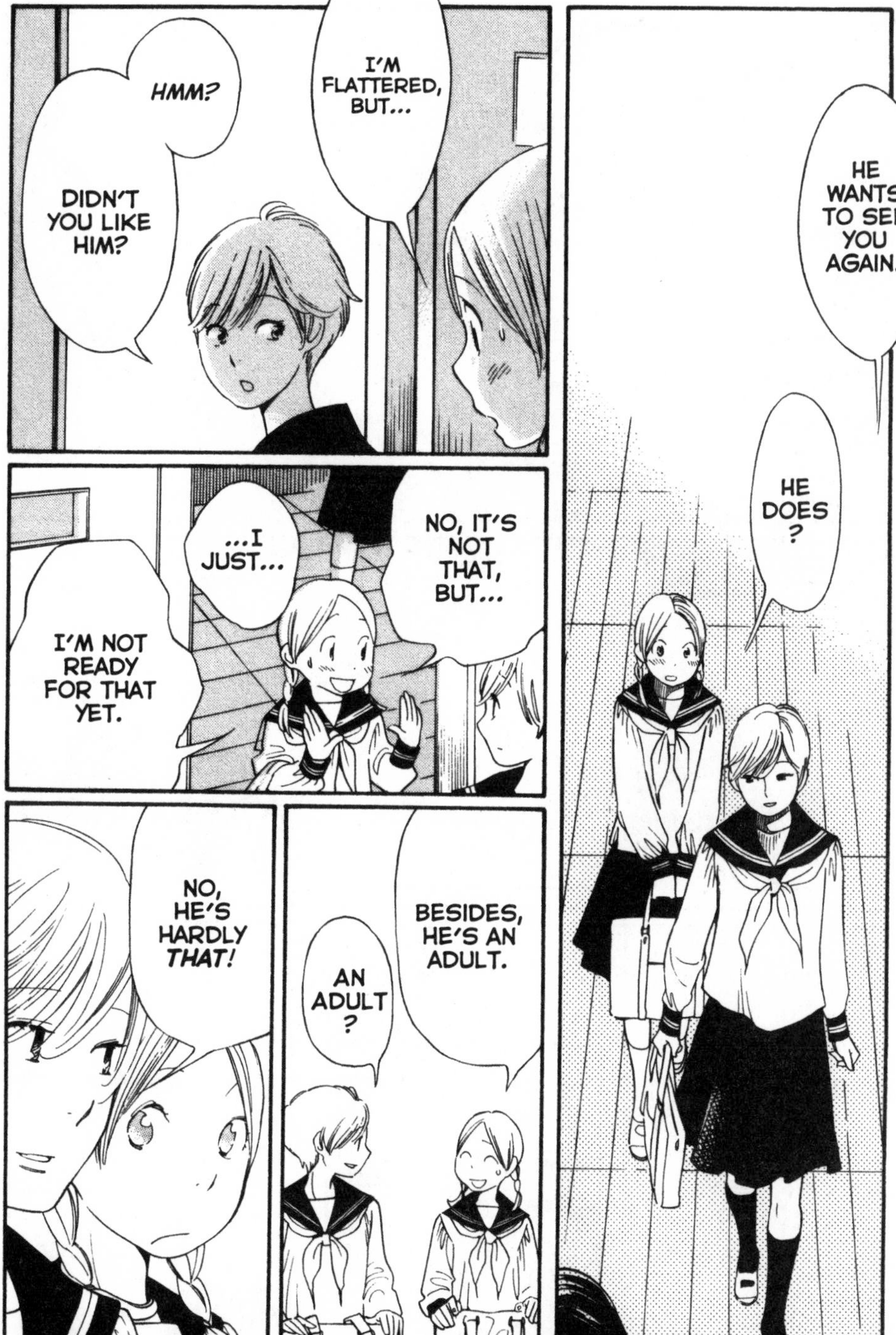
HE WANTS TO SEE YOU AGAIN.
HE DOES?
I'M FLATTERED, BUT...
HMM?
DIDN'T YOU LIKE HIM?
NO, IT'S NOT THAT, BUT...
...I JUST...
I'M NOT READY FOR THAT YET.
BESIDES, HE'S AN ADULT.
AN ADULT?
NO, HE'S HARDLY *THAT!*

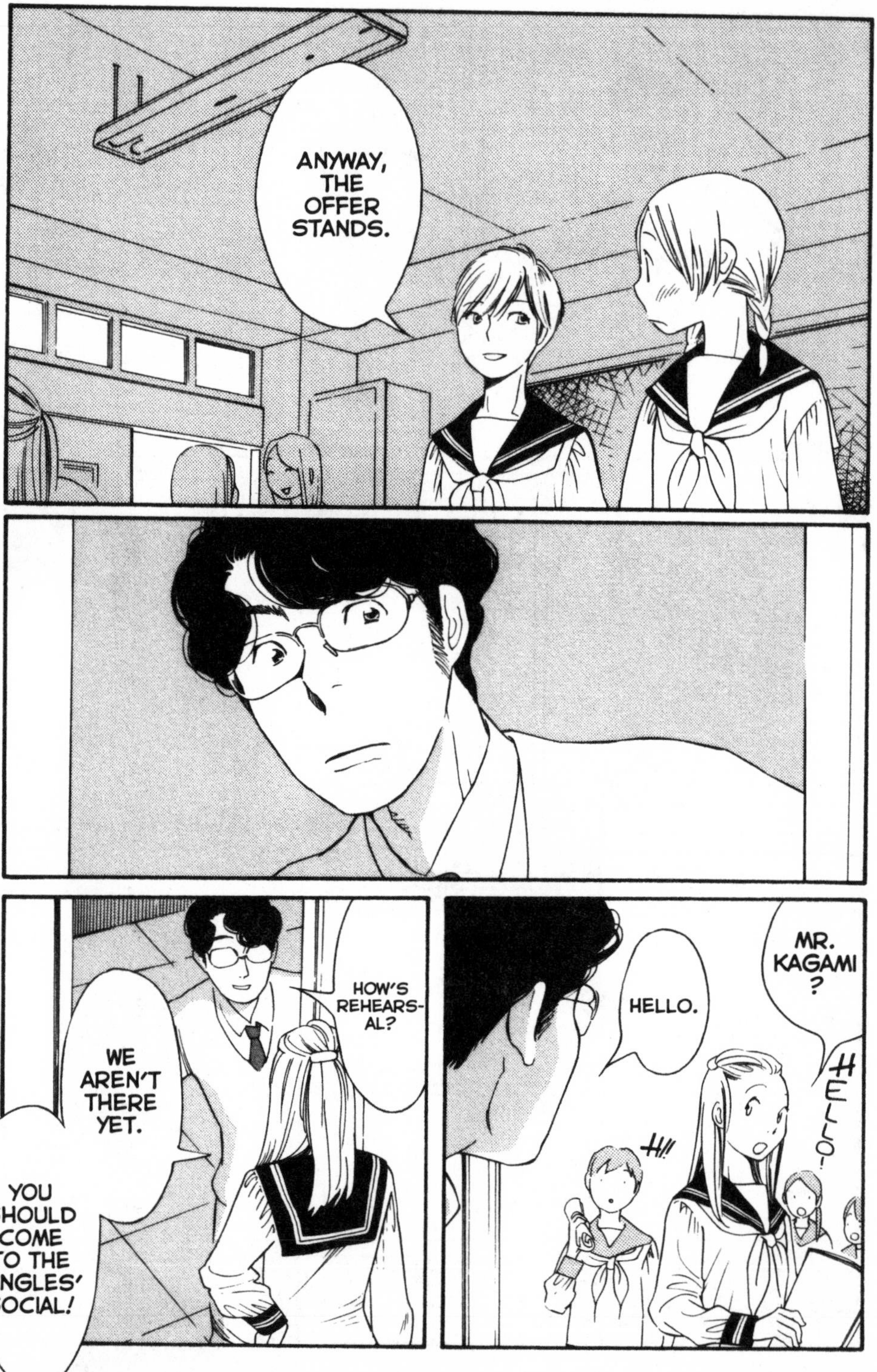
ANYWAY, THE OFFER STANDS.
MR. KAGAMI?
HELLO!
HELLO.
H!!
HOW'S REHEARS-AL?
WE AREN'T THERE YET.
YOU SHOULD COME TO THE SINGLES' SOCIAL!

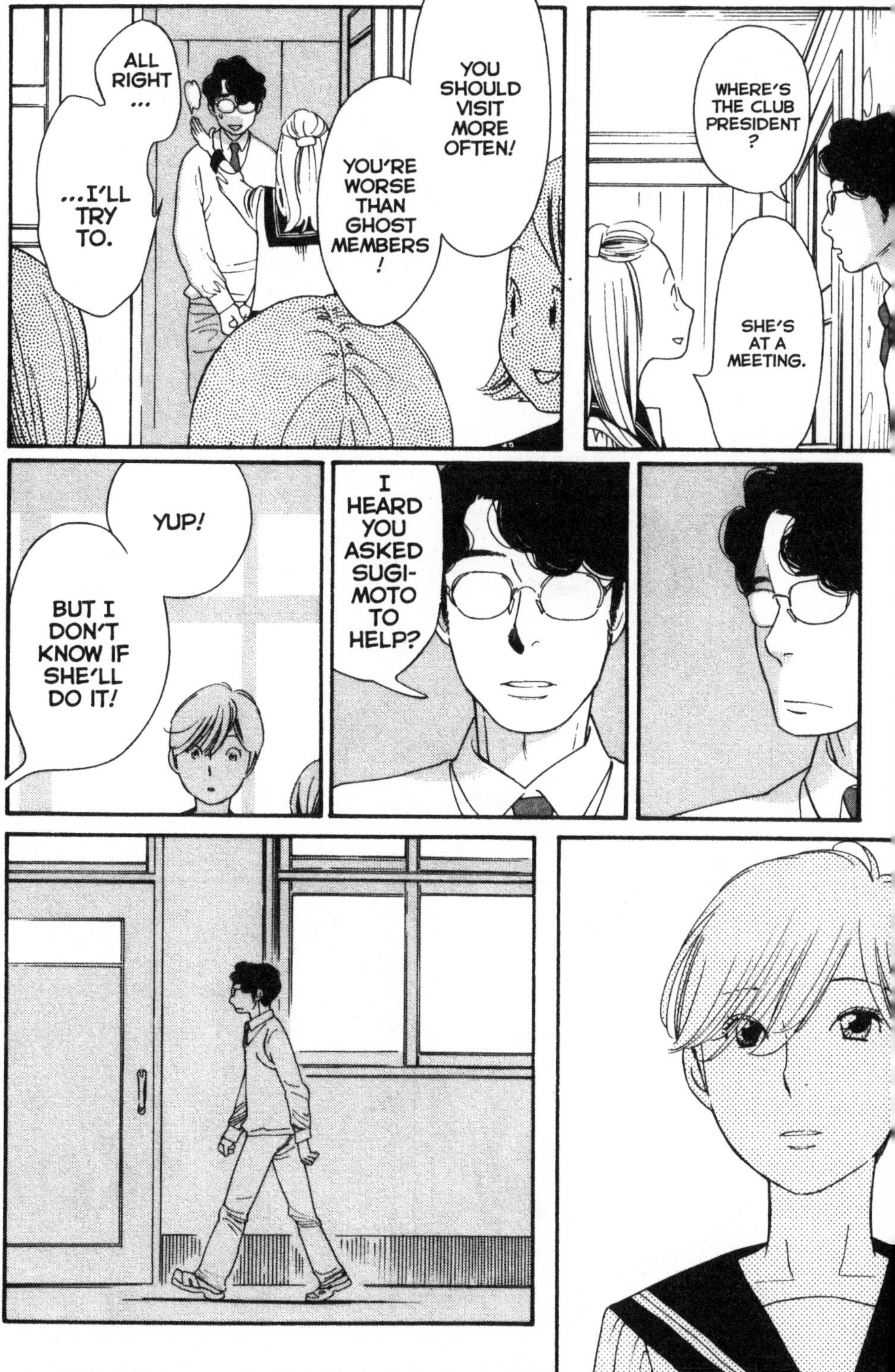
WHERE'S THE CLUB PRESIDENT?
SHE'S AT A MEETING.
YOU SHOULD VISIT MORE OFTEN!
YOU'RE WORSE THAN GHOST MEMBERS!
ALL RIGHT...
...I'LL TRY TO.
I HEARD YOU ASKED SUGIMOTO TO HELP?
YUP!
BUT I DON'T KNOW IF SHE'LL DO IT!

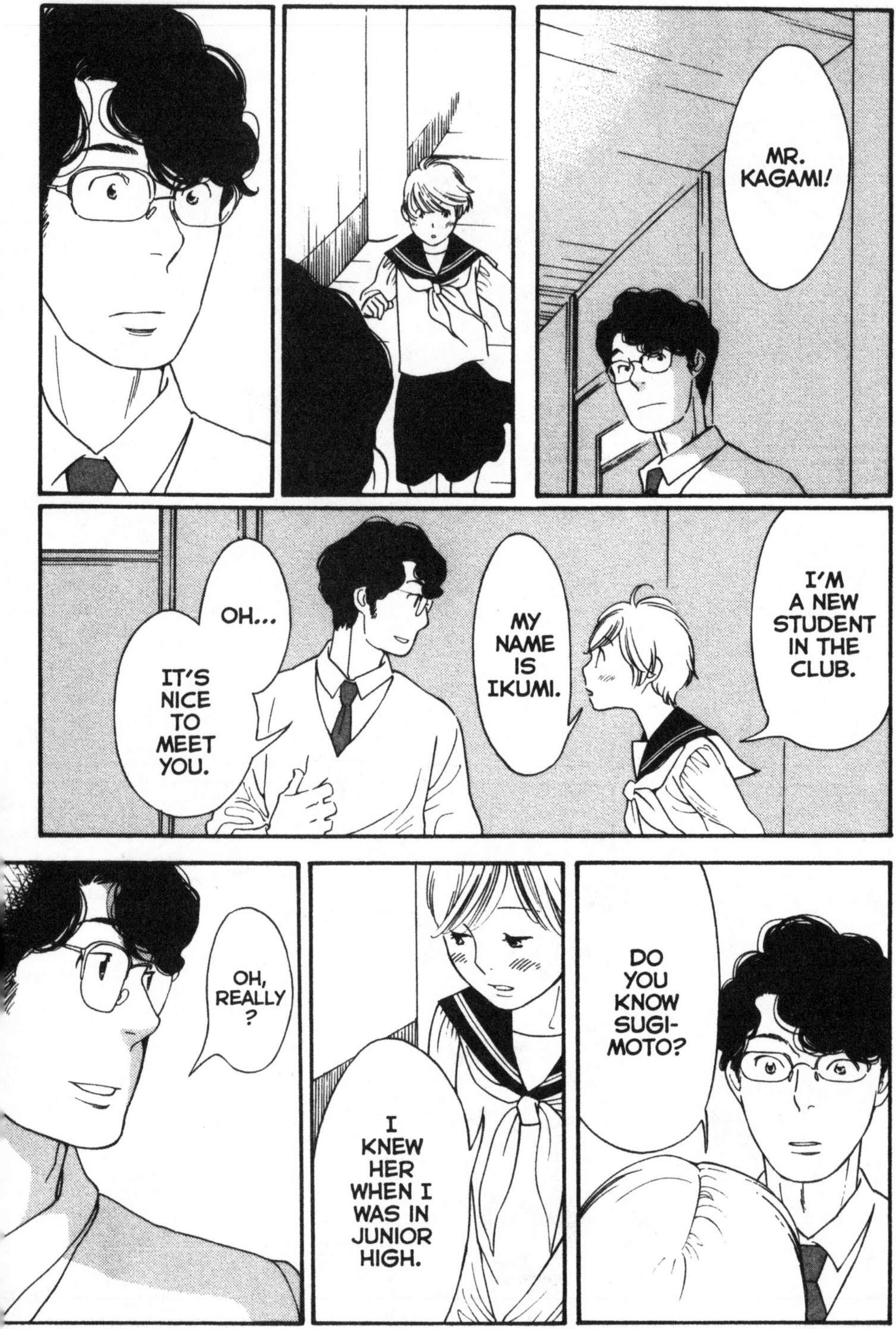
MR. KAGAMI!
I'M A NEW STUDENT IN THE CLUB.
MY NAME IS IKUMI.
OH...
IT'S NICE TO MEET YOU.
DO YOU KNOW SUGI-MOTO?
I KNEW HER WHEN I WAS IN JUNIOR HIGH.
OH, REALLY?

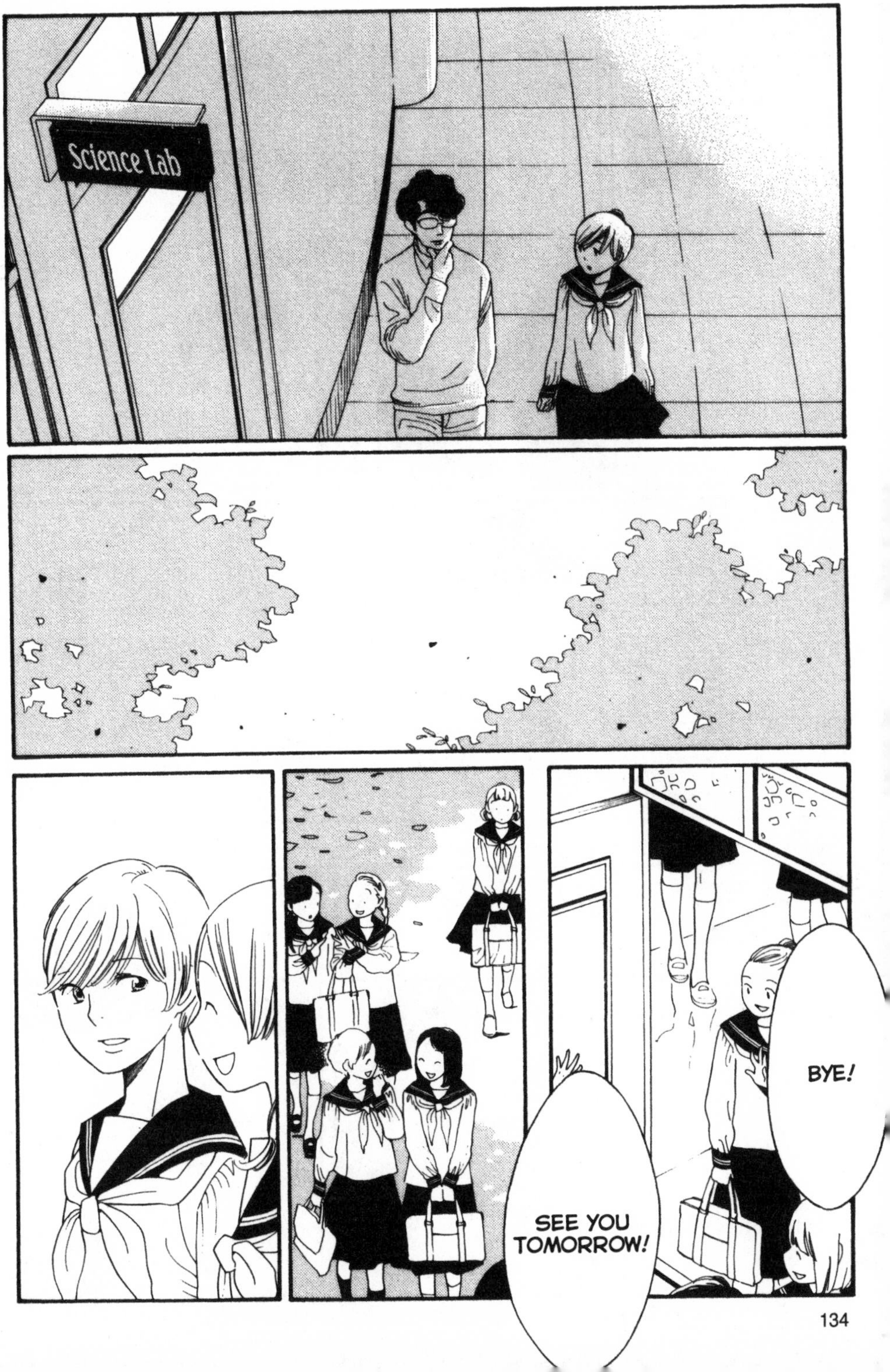
Science Lab
BYE!
SEE YOU TOMORROW!

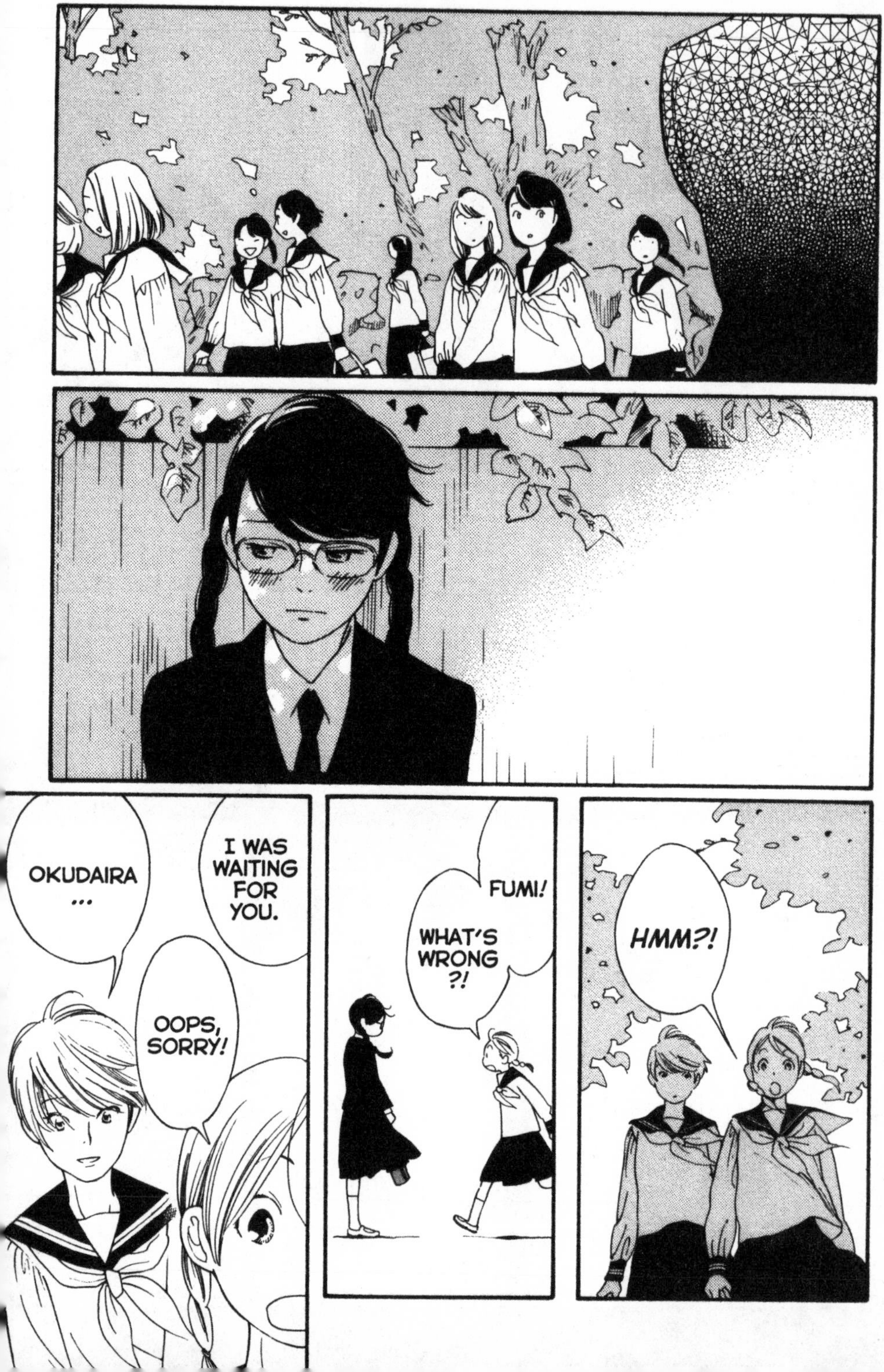
HMM?!
FUMI!
WHAT'S WRONG ?!
I WAS WAITING FOR YOU.
OKUDAIRA ...
OOPS, SORRY!

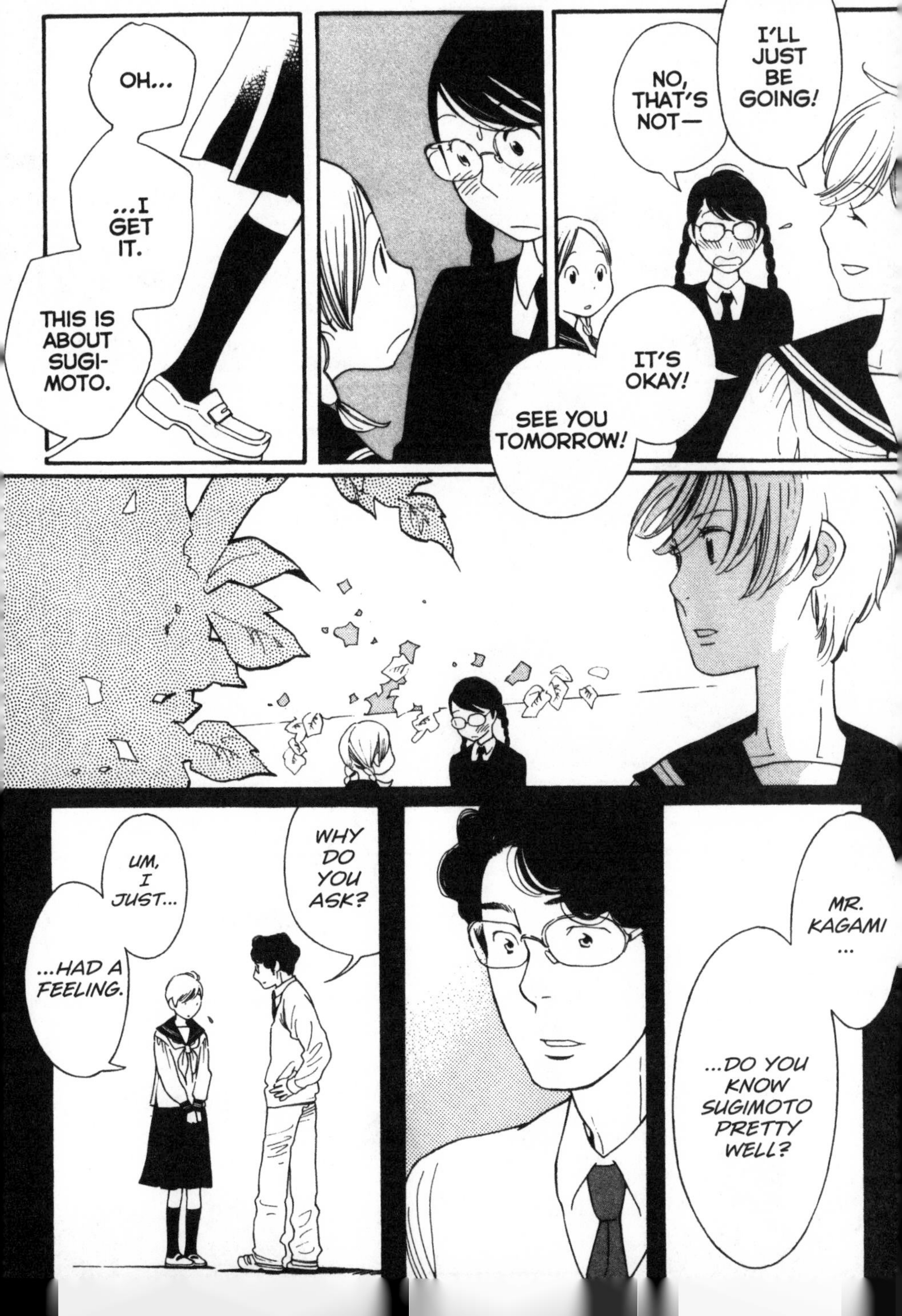
I'LL JUST BE GOING!
NO, THAT'S NOT—
IT'S OKAY! SEE YOU TOMORROW!
OH... ...I GET IT. THIS IS ABOUT SUGIMOTO.
MR. KAGAMI ...
...DO YOU KNOW SUGIMOTO PRETTY WELL?
WHY DO YOU ASK?
UM, I JUST... ...HAD A FEELING.

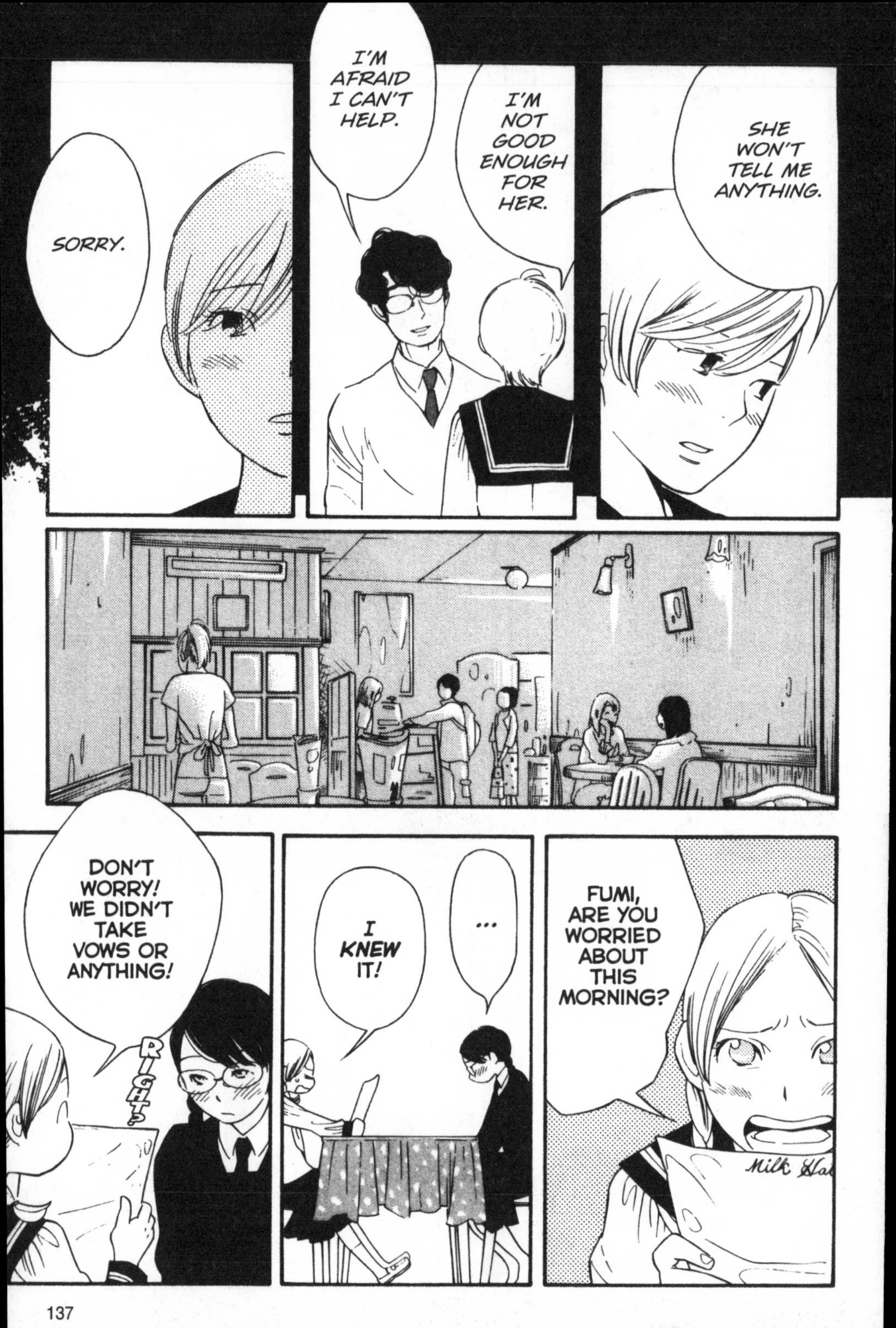
SHE WON'T TELL ME ANYTHING.
I'M NOT GOOD ENOUGH FOR HER.
I'M AFRAID I CAN'T HELP.
SORRY.
FUMI, ARE YOU WORRIED ABOUT THIS MORNING?
...
I KNEW IT!
DON'T WORRY! WE DIDN'T TAKE VOWS OR ANYTHING!
RIGHT?

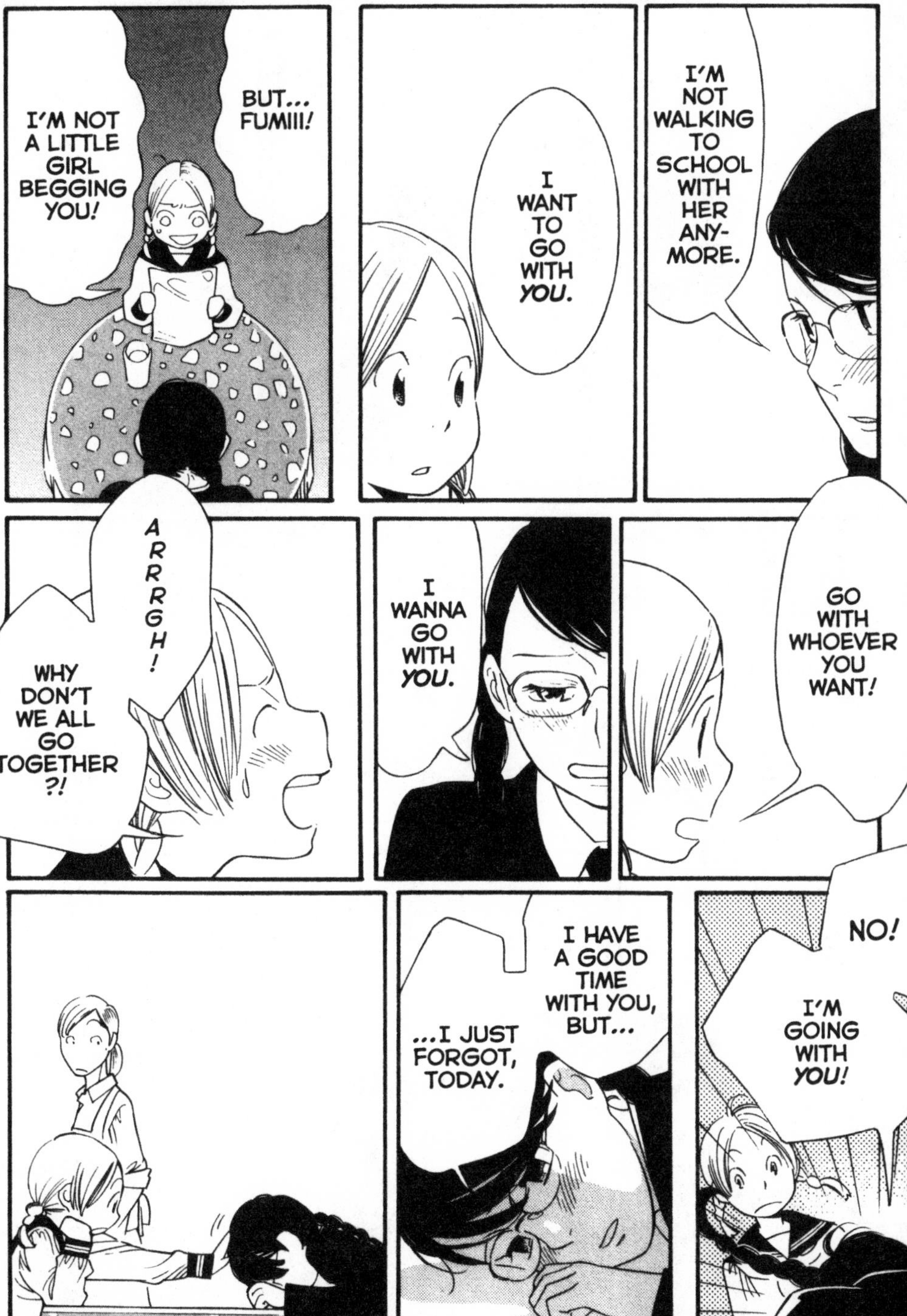
I'M NOT WALKING TO SCHOOL WITH HER ANYMORE.
I WANT TO GO WITH *YOU*.
BUT... FUMIII!
I'M NOT A LITTLE GIRL BEGGING YOU!
GO WITH WHOEVER YOU WANT!
I WANNA GO WITH *YOU*.
ARRRGH!
WHY DON'T WE ALL GO TOGETHER?!
NO!
I'M GOING WITH *YOU*!
I HAVE A GOOD TIME WITH YOU, BUT...
...I JUST FORGOT, TODAY.

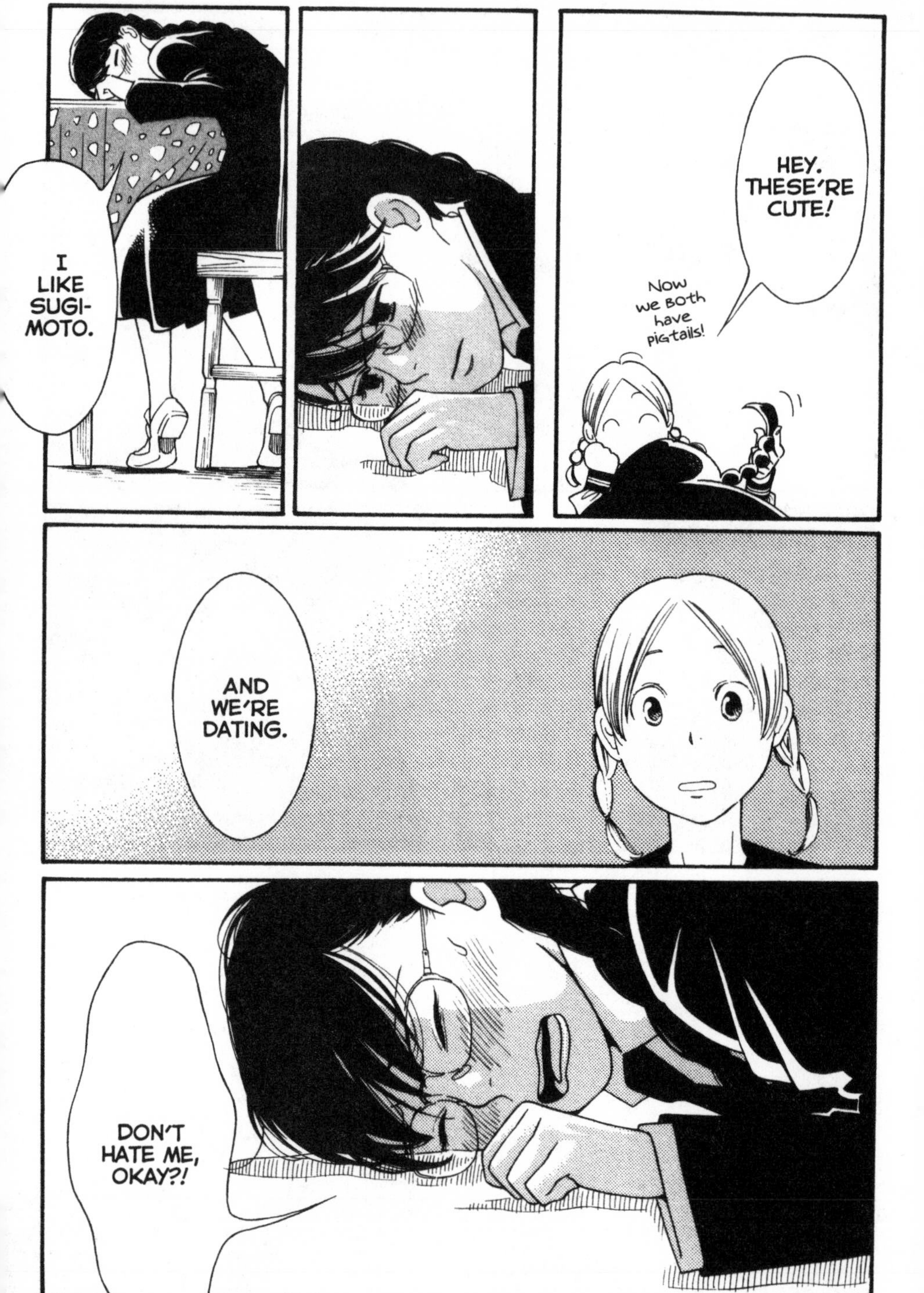
HEY. THESE'RE CUTE!
Now we both have pigtails!
I LIKE SUGI-MOTO.
AND WE'RE DATING.
DON'T HATE ME, OKAY?!

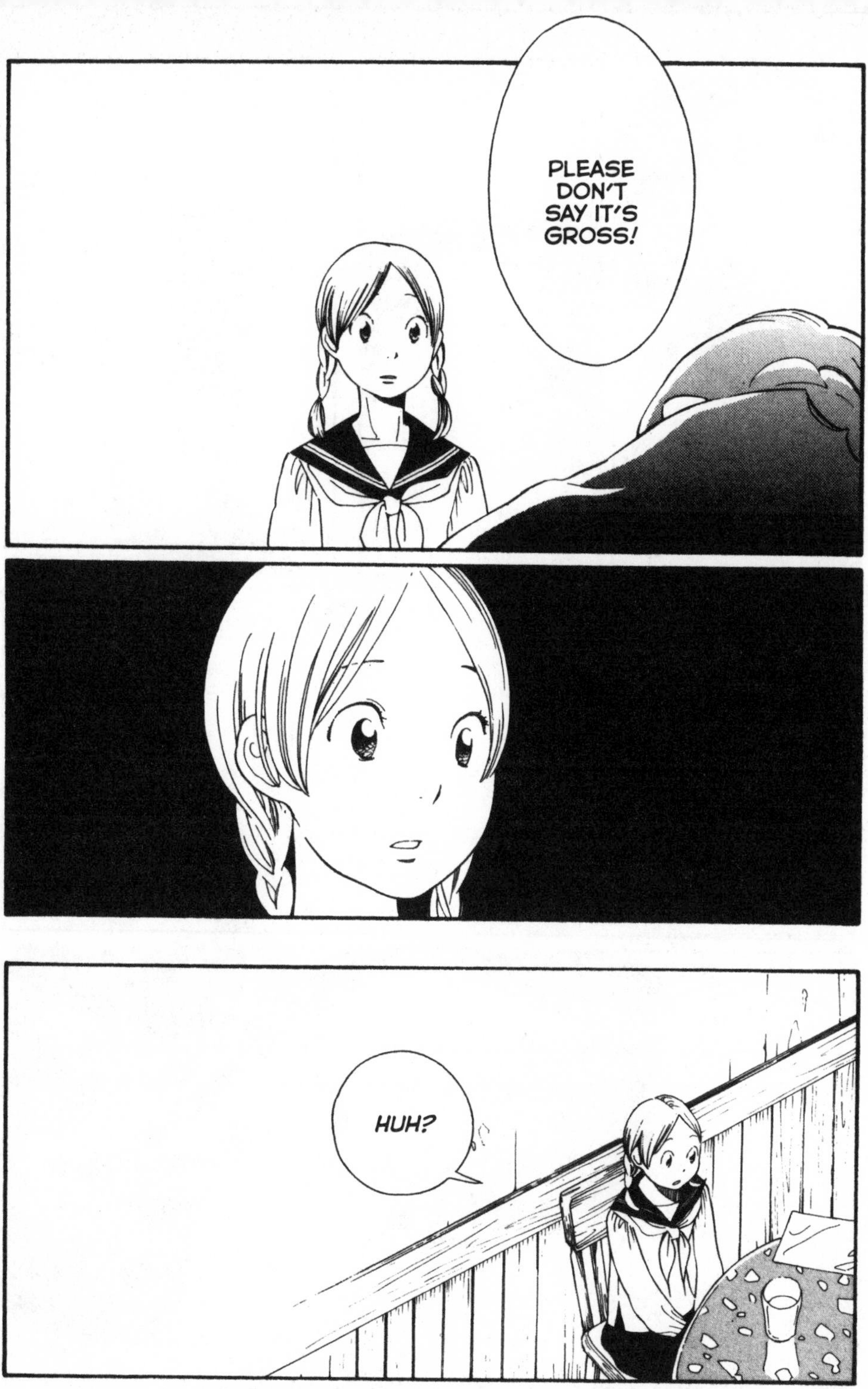
PLEASE DON'T SAY IT'S GROSS!
HUH?

*Fumi*
*wasn't*
*in her*
*usual*
*spot.*

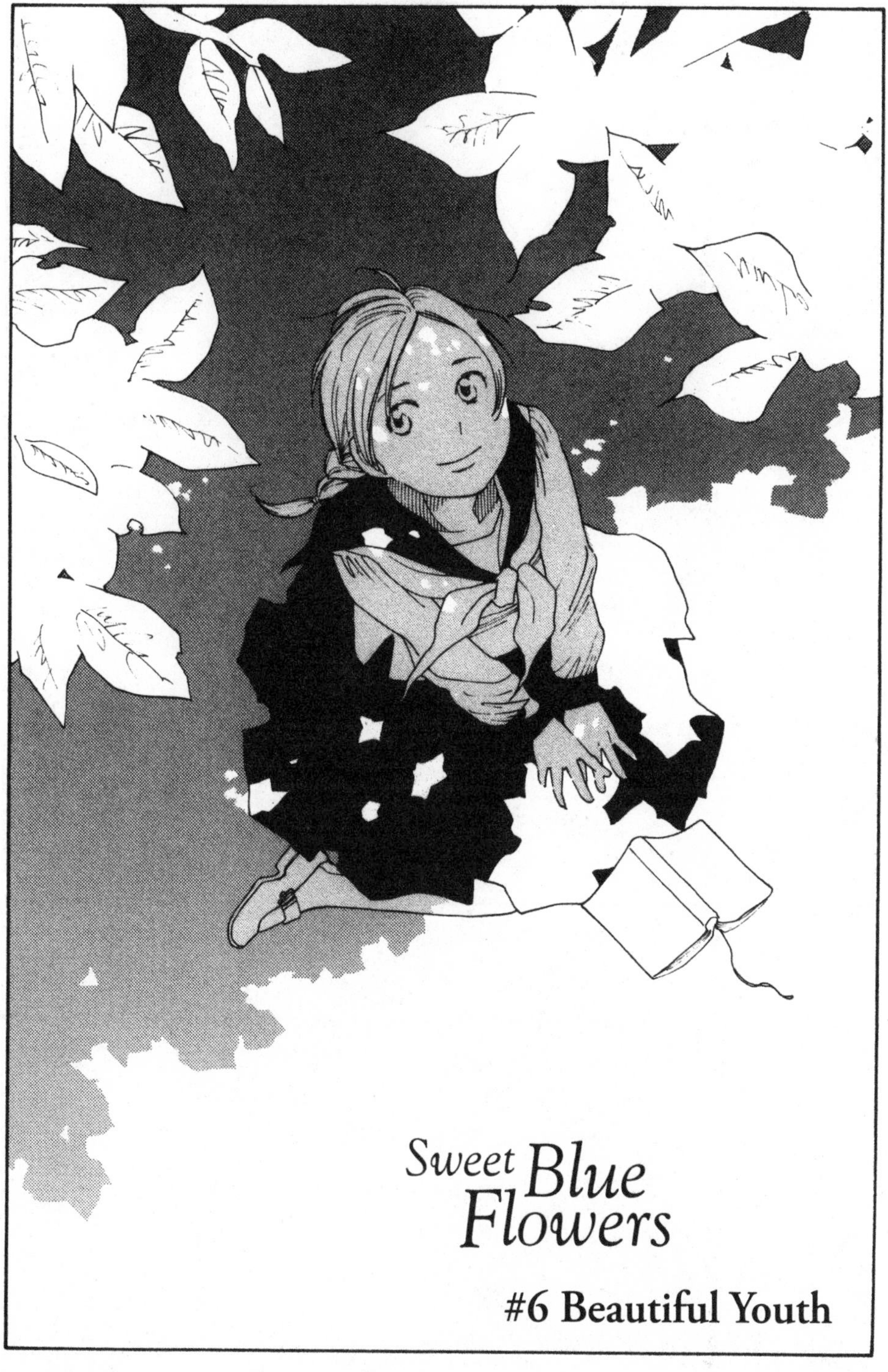

# Sweet Blue Flowers

## #6 Beautiful Youth

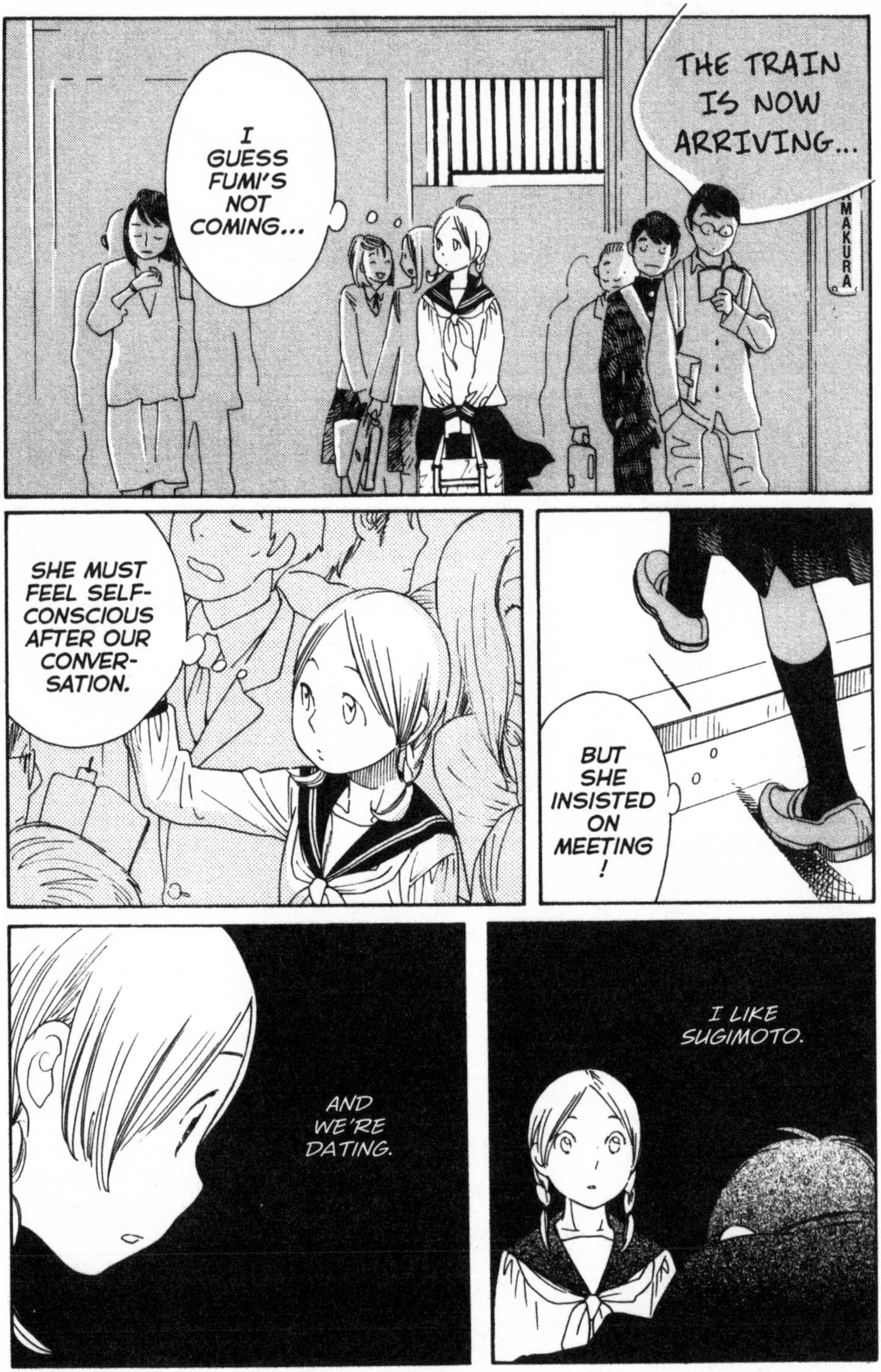
THE TRAIN IS NOW ARRIVING...
I GUESS FUMI'S NOT COMING...
BUT SHE INSISTED ON MEETING!
SHE MUST FEEL SELF-CONSCIOUS AFTER OUR CONVERSATION.
I LIKE SUGIMOTO.
AND WE'RE DATING.

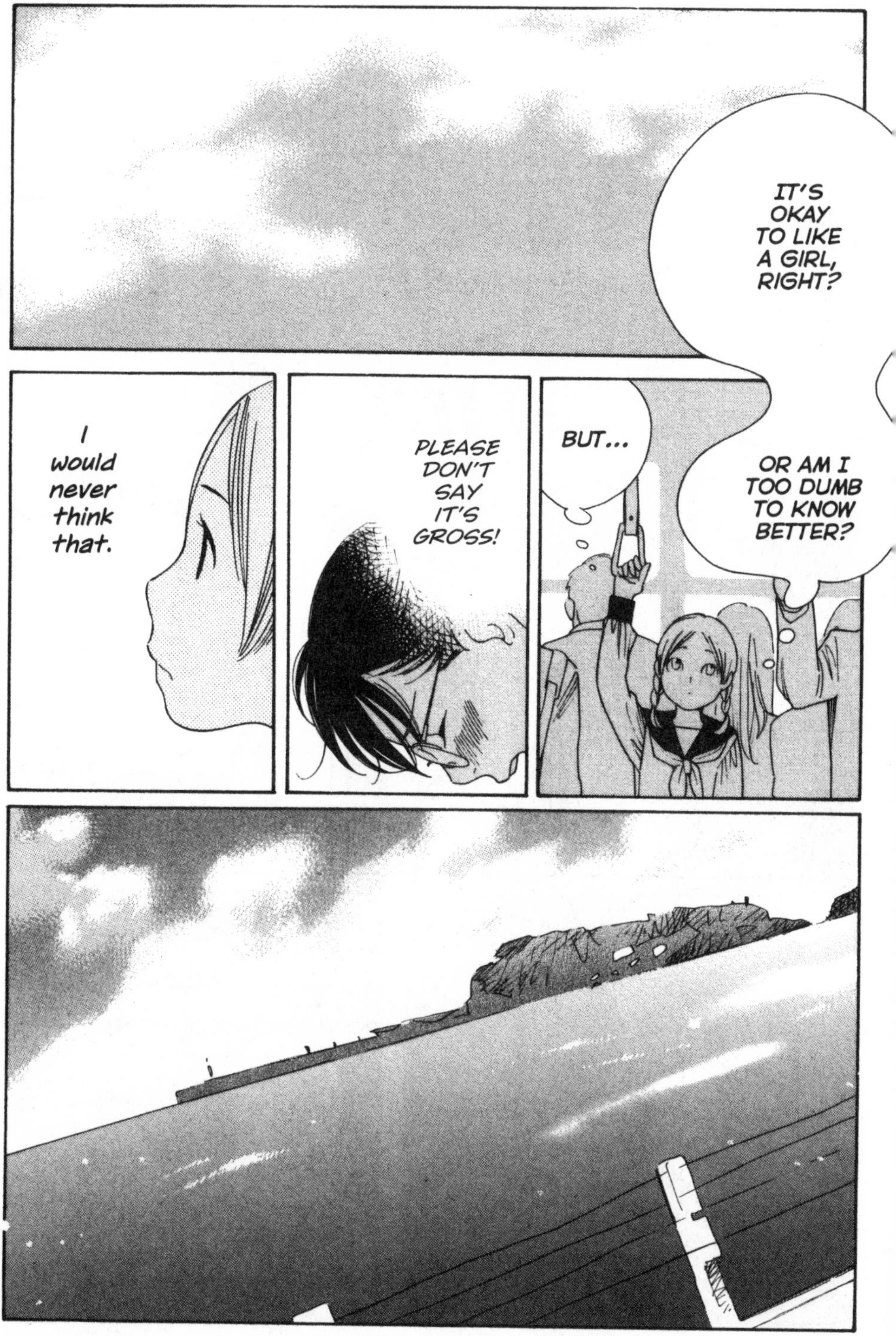
IT'S OKAY TO LIKE A GIRL, RIGHT?
OR AM I TOO DUMB TO KNOW BETTER?
BUT...
PLEASE DON'T SAY IT'S GROSS!
I would never think that.

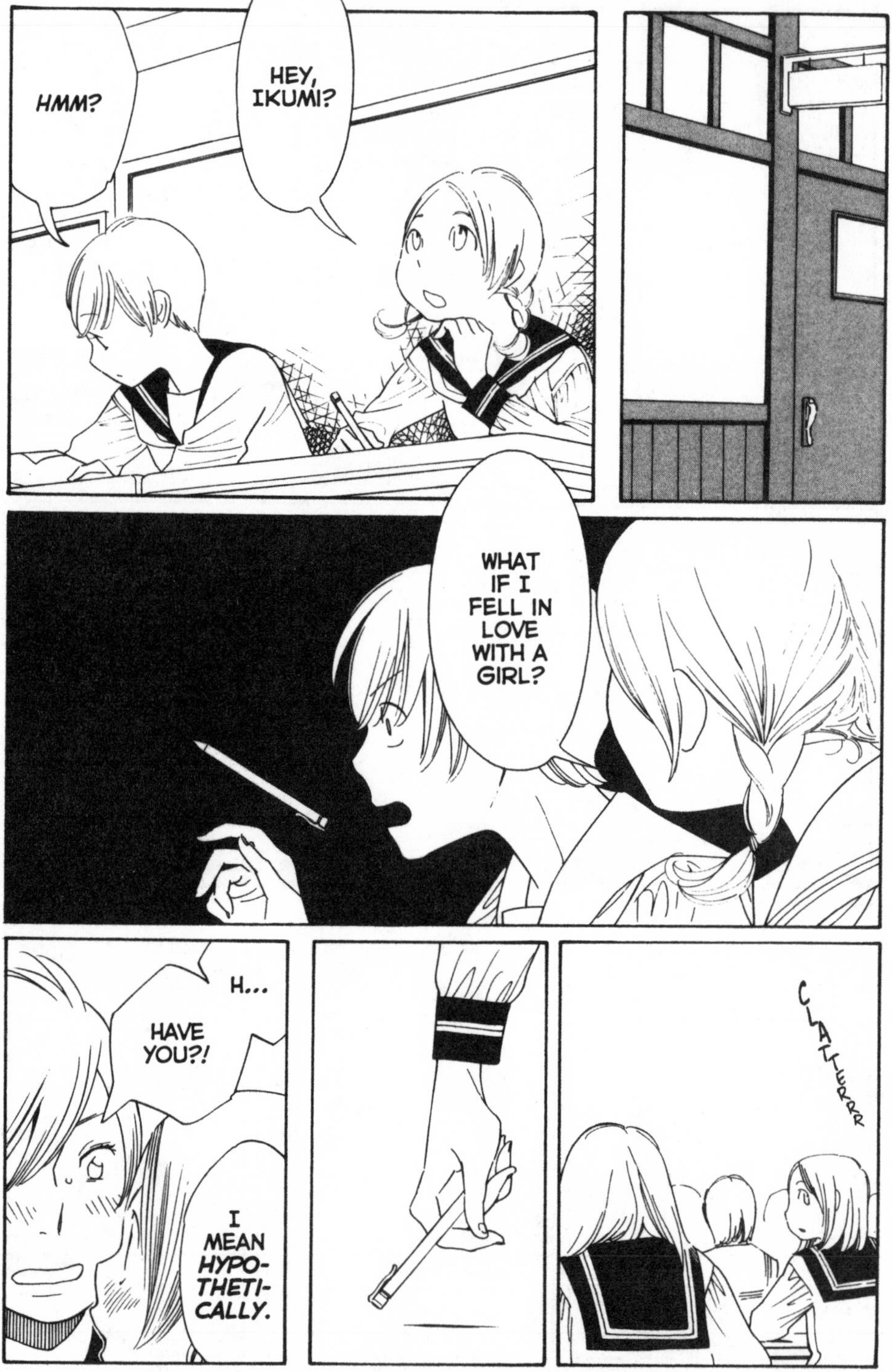
HEY, IKUMI?
HMM?
WHAT IF I FELL IN LOVE WITH A GIRL?
CLATTERRR
H...
HAVE YOU?!
I MEAN *HYPOTHETICALLY*.

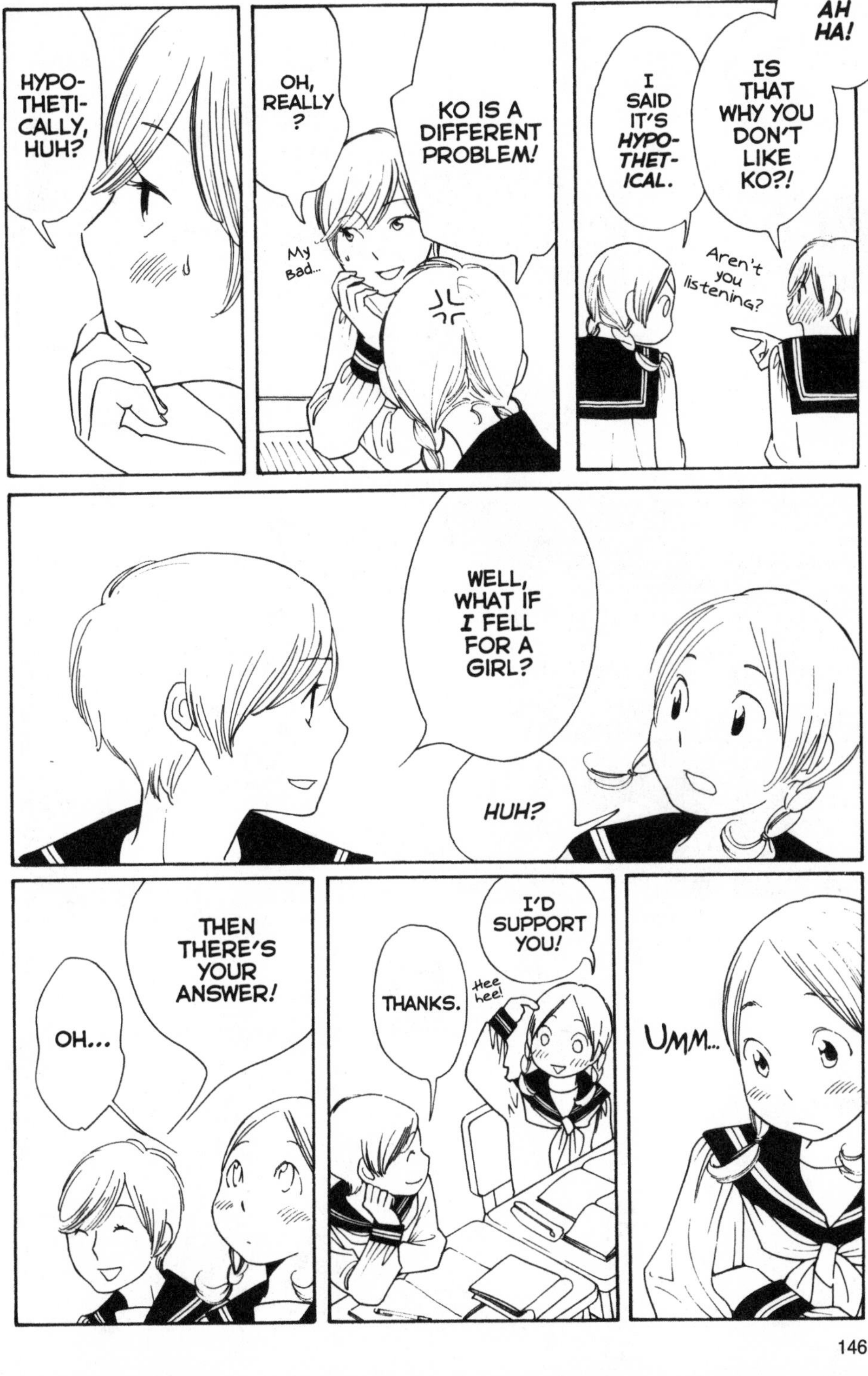
AH HA!
IS THAT WHY YOU DON'T LIKE KO?!
I SAID IT'S HYPOTHETICAL.
Aren't you listening?
KO IS A DIFFERENT PROBLEM!
OH, REALLY?
My bad...
HYPOTHETICALLY, HUH?
WELL, WHAT IF I FELL FOR A GIRL?
HUH?
UMM...
I'D SUPPORT YOU!
Hee hee!
THANKS.
THEN THERE'S YOUR ANSWER!
OH...

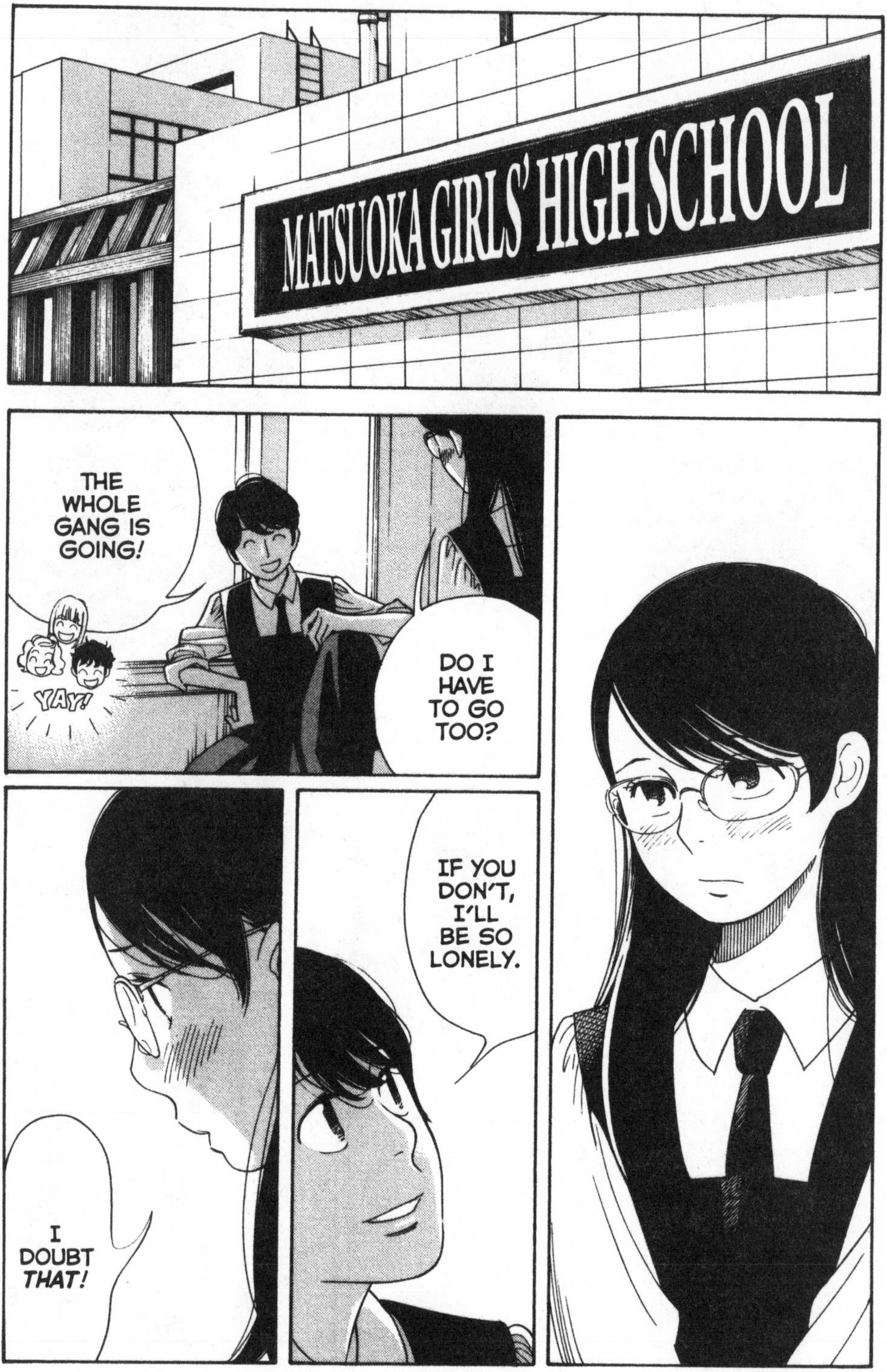
MATSUOKA GIRLS' HIGH SCHOOL
THE WHOLE GANG IS GOING!
YAY!
DO I HAVE TO GO TOO?
IF YOU DON'T, I'LL BE SO LONELY.
I DOUBT THAT!

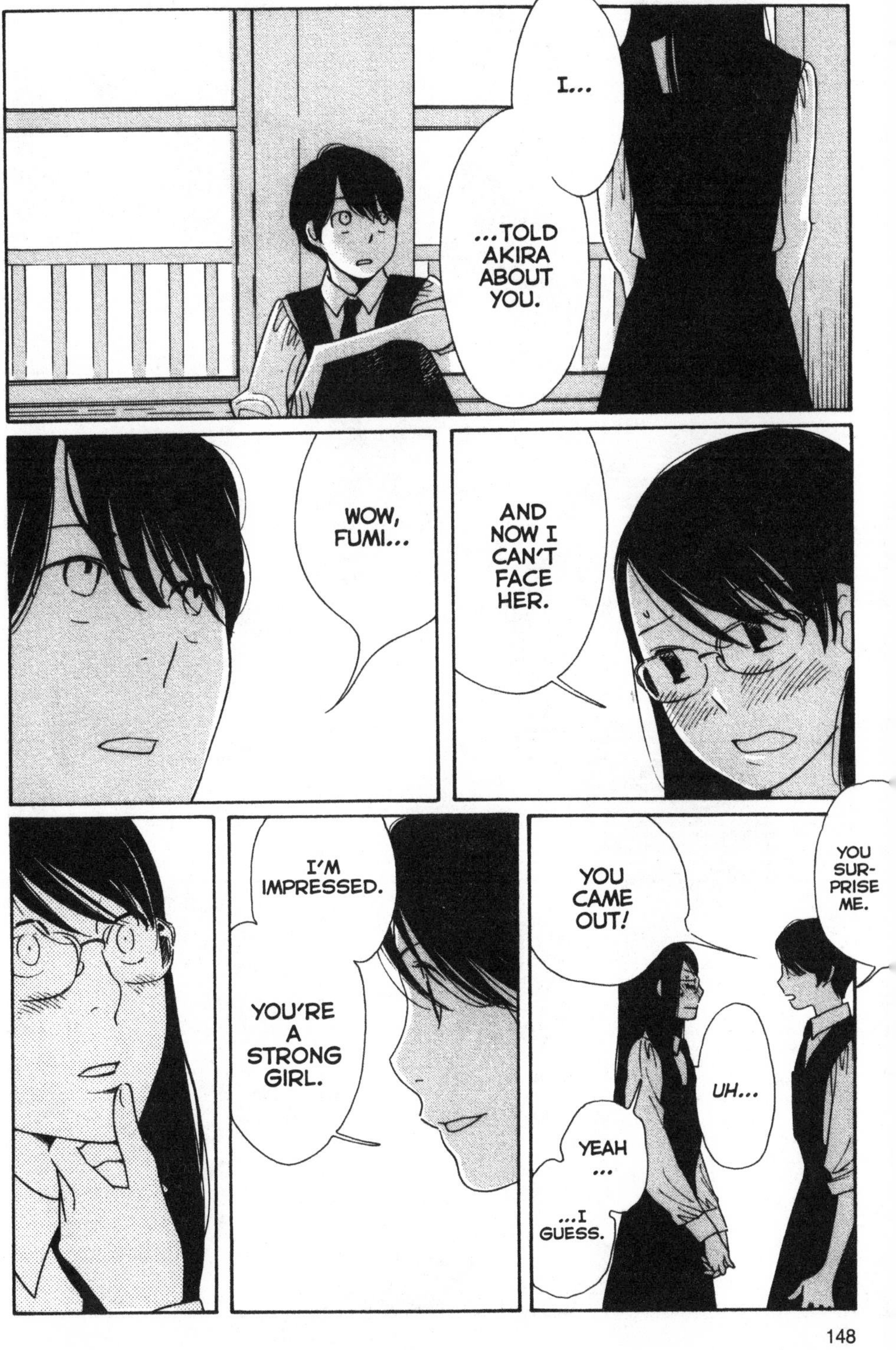
I...
...TOLD AKIRA ABOUT YOU.
AND NOW I CAN'T FACE HER.
WOW, FUMI...
YOU SUR-PRISE ME.
YOU CAME OUT!
UH...
YEAH ...
...I GUESS.
I'M IMPRESSED.
YOU'RE A STRONG GIRL.

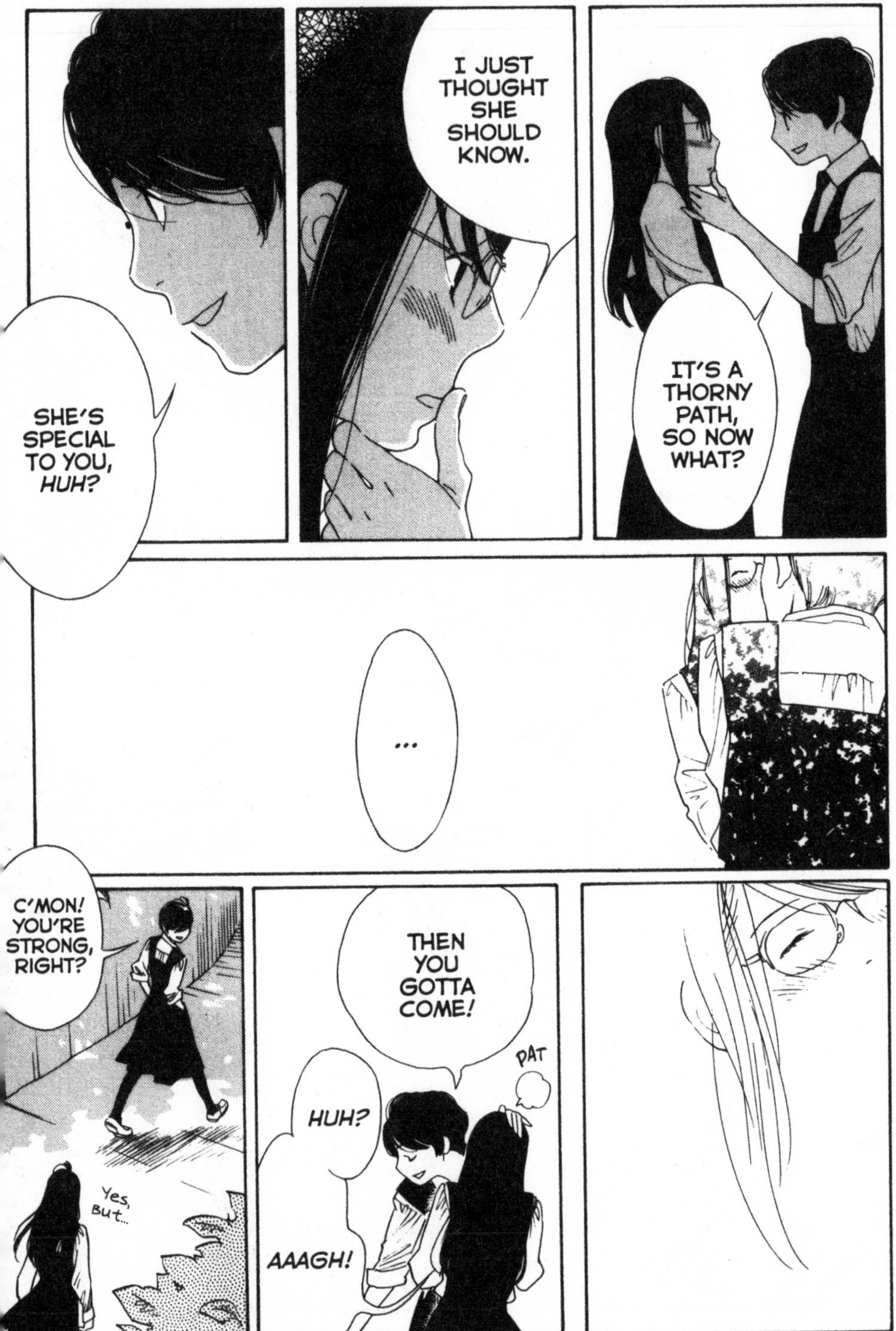
IT'S A THORNY PATH, SO NOW WHAT?
I JUST THOUGHT SHE SHOULD KNOW.
SHE'S SPECIAL TO YOU, *HUH?*
...
THEN YOU GOTTA COME!
PAT
*HUH?*
*AAAGH!*
C'MON! YOU'RE STRONG, RIGHT?
Yes, but...

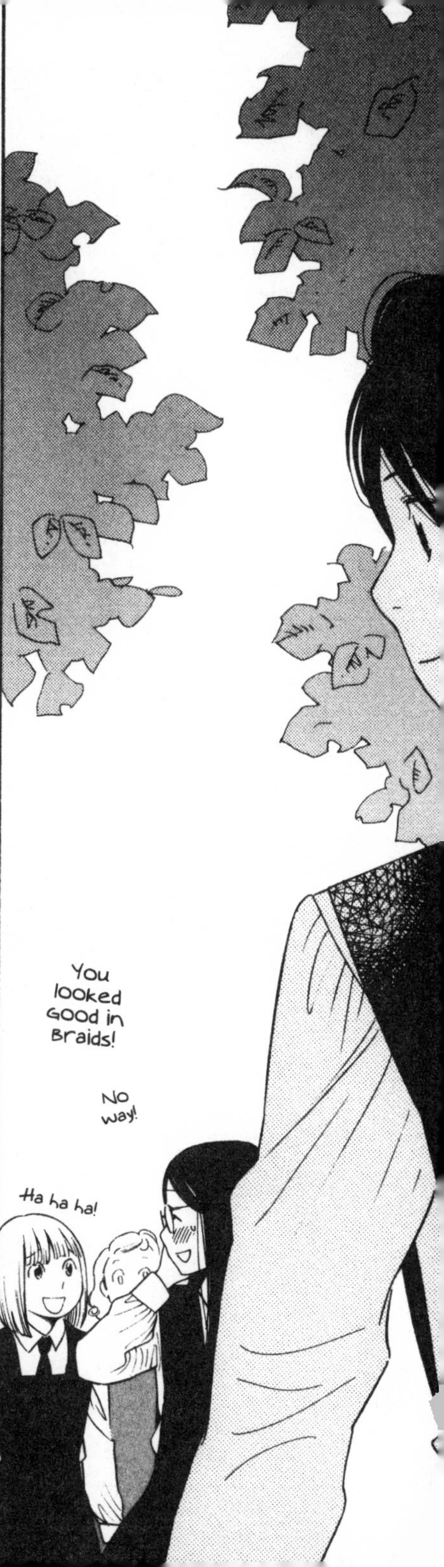
You looked Good in Braids!
No way!
Ha ha ha!
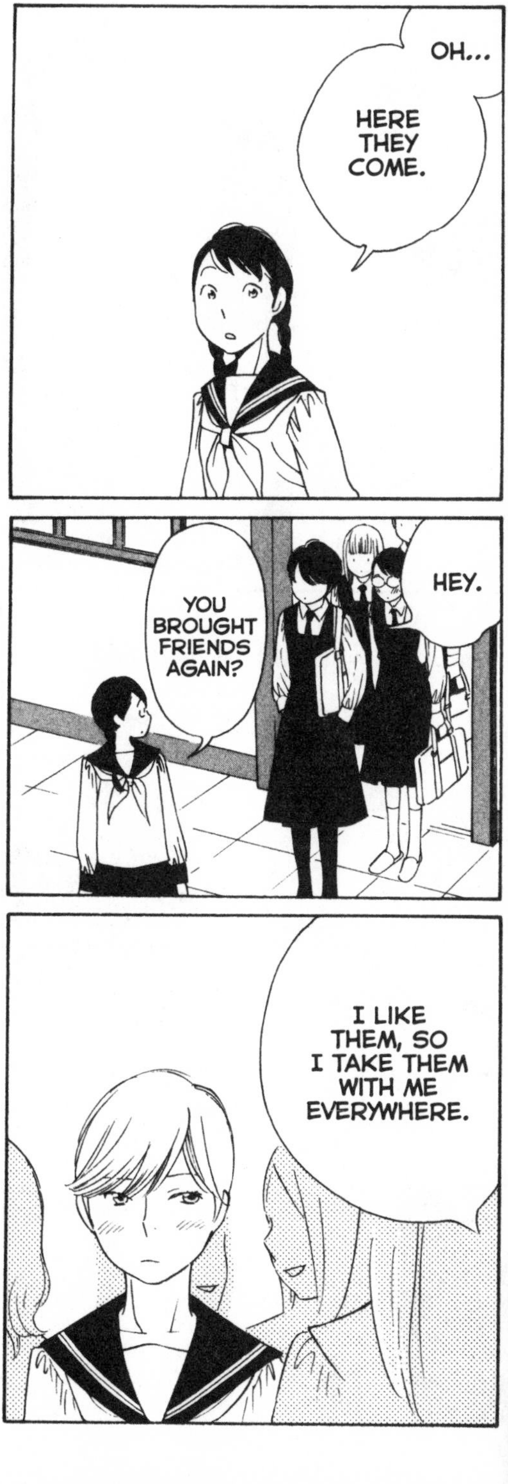
OH...
HERE THEY COME.
HEY.
YOU BROUGHT FRIENDS AGAIN?
I LIKE THEM, SO I TAKE THEM WITH ME EVERYWHERE.

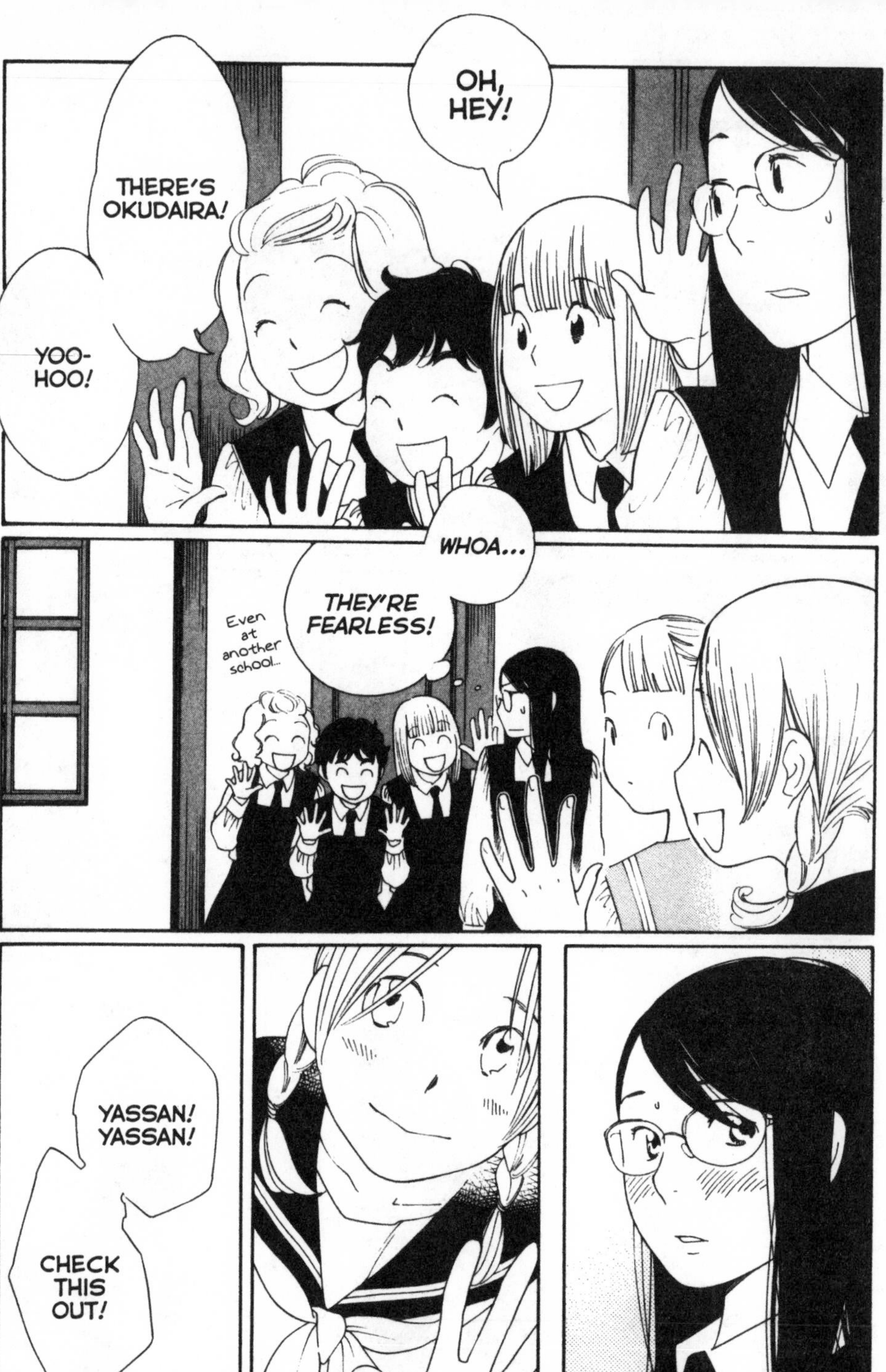
OH, HEY!
THERE'S OKUDAIRA!
YOO-HOO!
WHOA... THEY'RE FEARLESS!
Even at another school...
YASSAN! YASSAN!
CHECK THIS OUT!

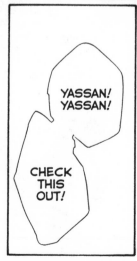

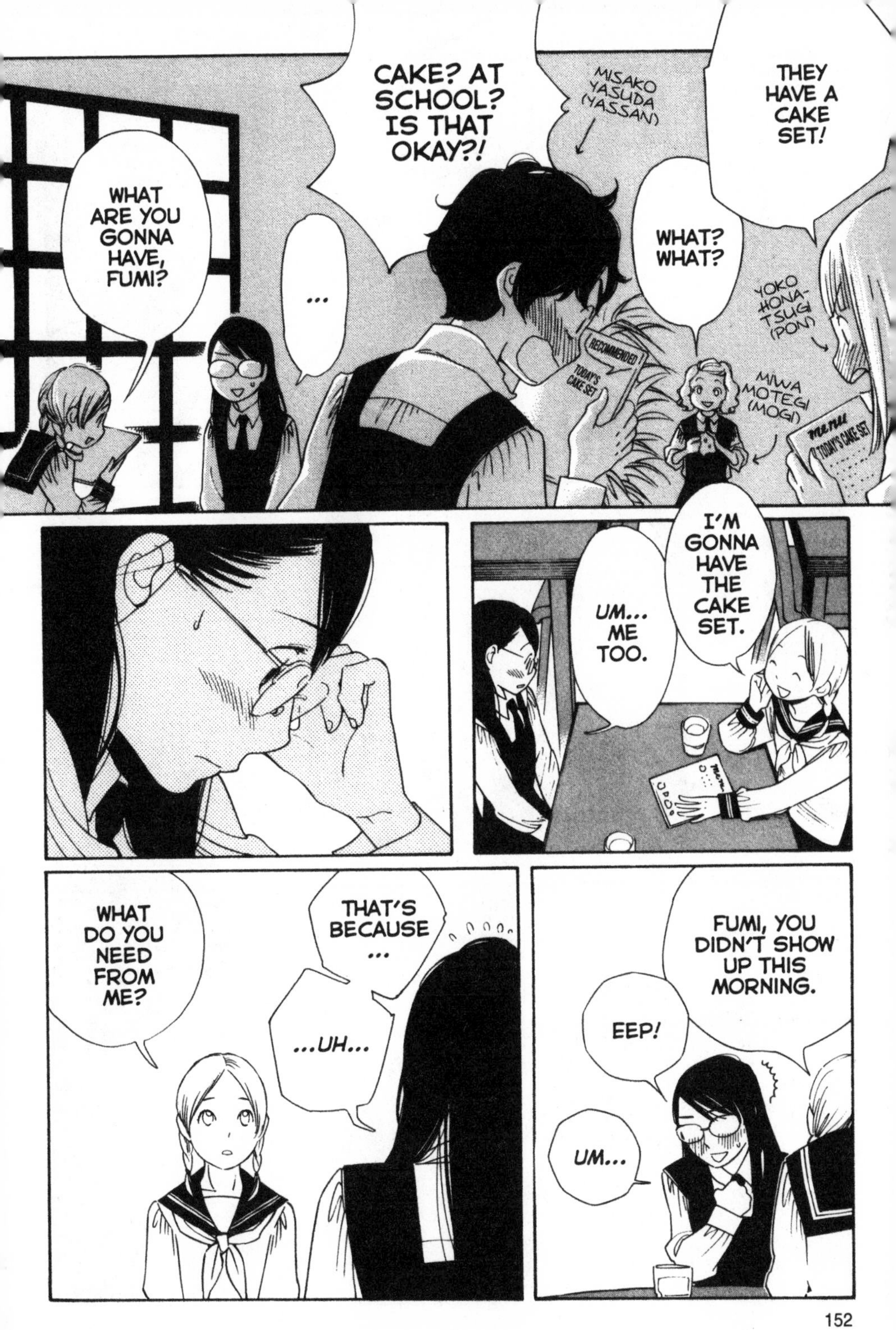
THEY HAVE A CAKE SET!
MISAKO YASUDA (YASSAN)
CAKE? AT SCHOOL? IS THAT OKAY?!
WHAT? WHAT?
YOKO HONATSUGI (PON)
MIWA MOTEGI (MOGI)
menu
TODAY'S CAKE SET
RECOMMENDED
TODAY'S CAKE SET
...
WHAT ARE YOU GONNA HAVE, FUMI?
I'M GONNA HAVE THE CAKE SET.
UM... ME TOO.
FUMI, YOU DIDN'T SHOW UP THIS MORNING.
EEP!
UM...
THAT'S BECAUSE...
...UH...
WHAT DO YOU NEED FROM ME?

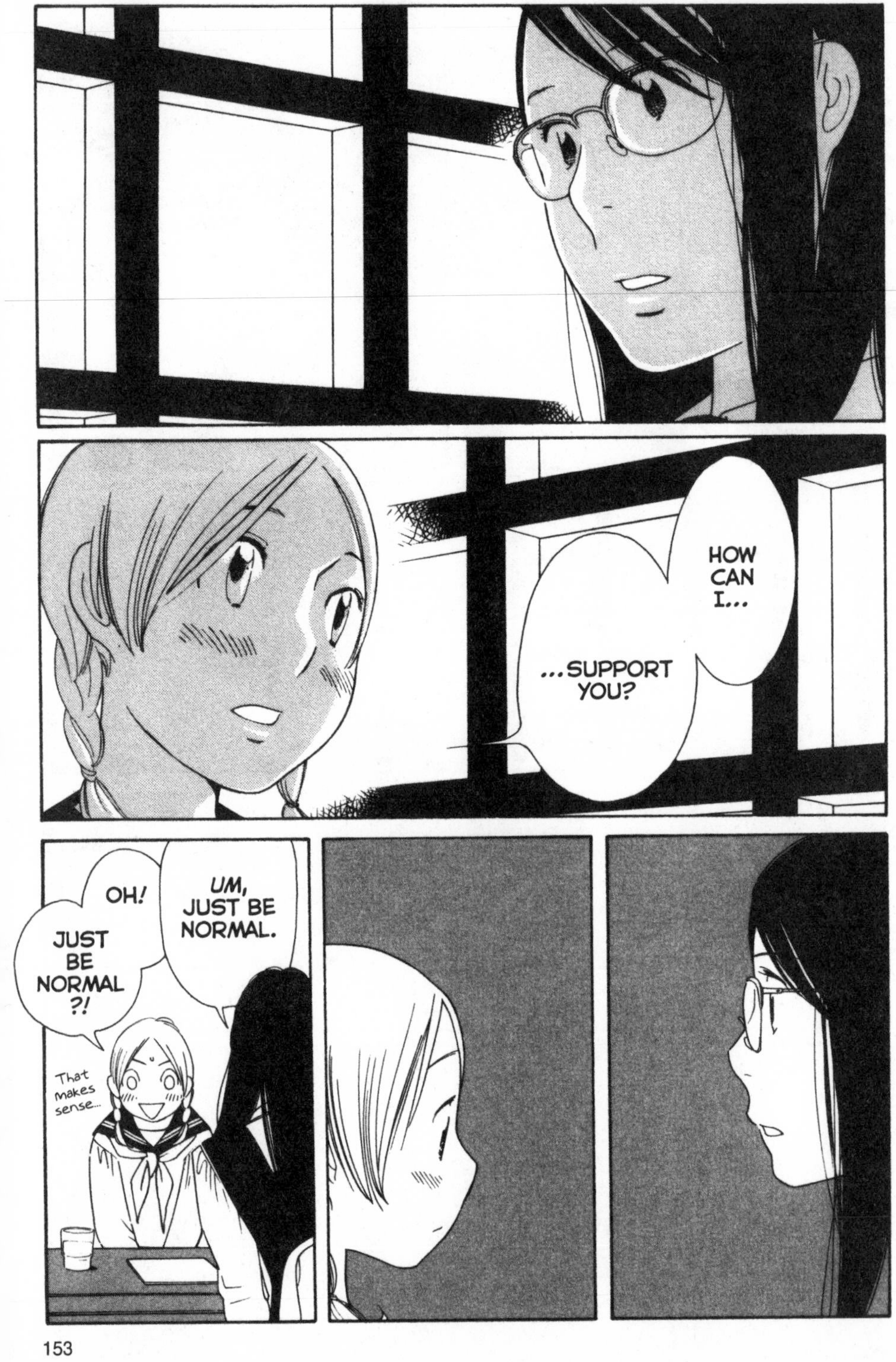
HOW CAN I...
...SUPPORT YOU?
UM, JUST BE NORMAL.
OH!
JUST BE NORMAL?!
That makes sense...

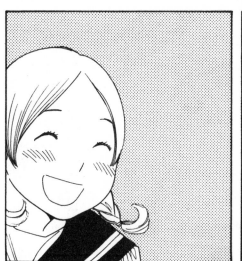

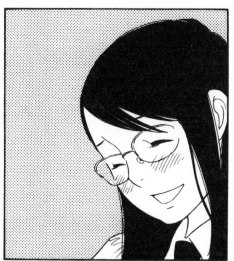

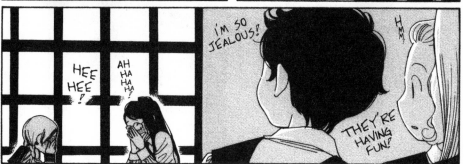

HEE HEE!

AH HA HA HA!

I'M SO JEALOUS!

HMM,

THEY'RE HAVING FUN!

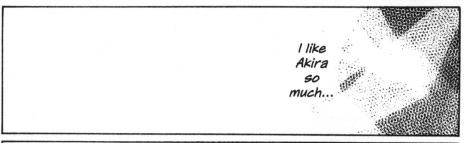

I like Akira so much...

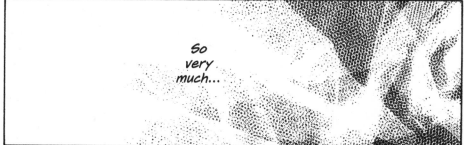

So very much...

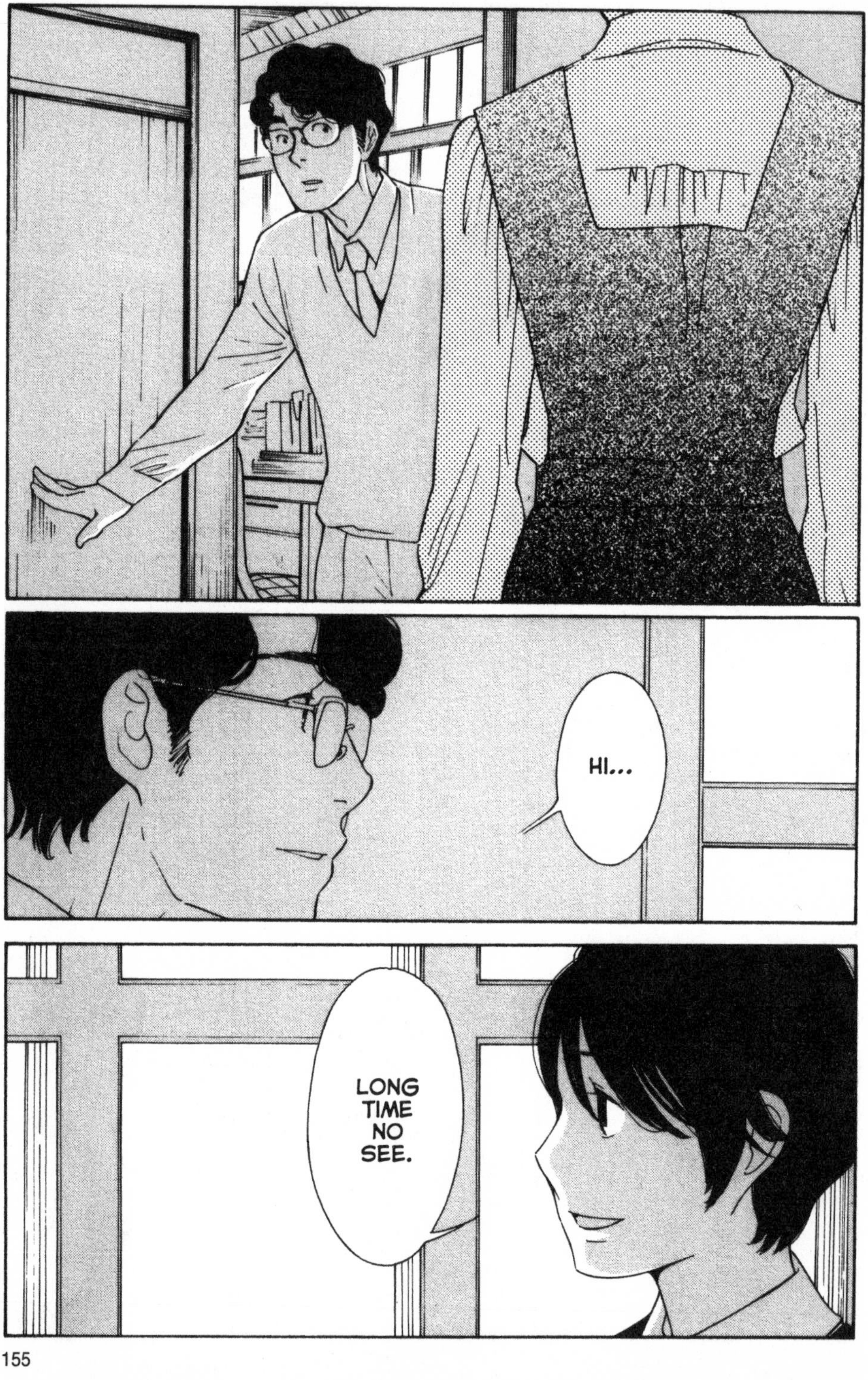
HI...
LONG TIME NO SEE.

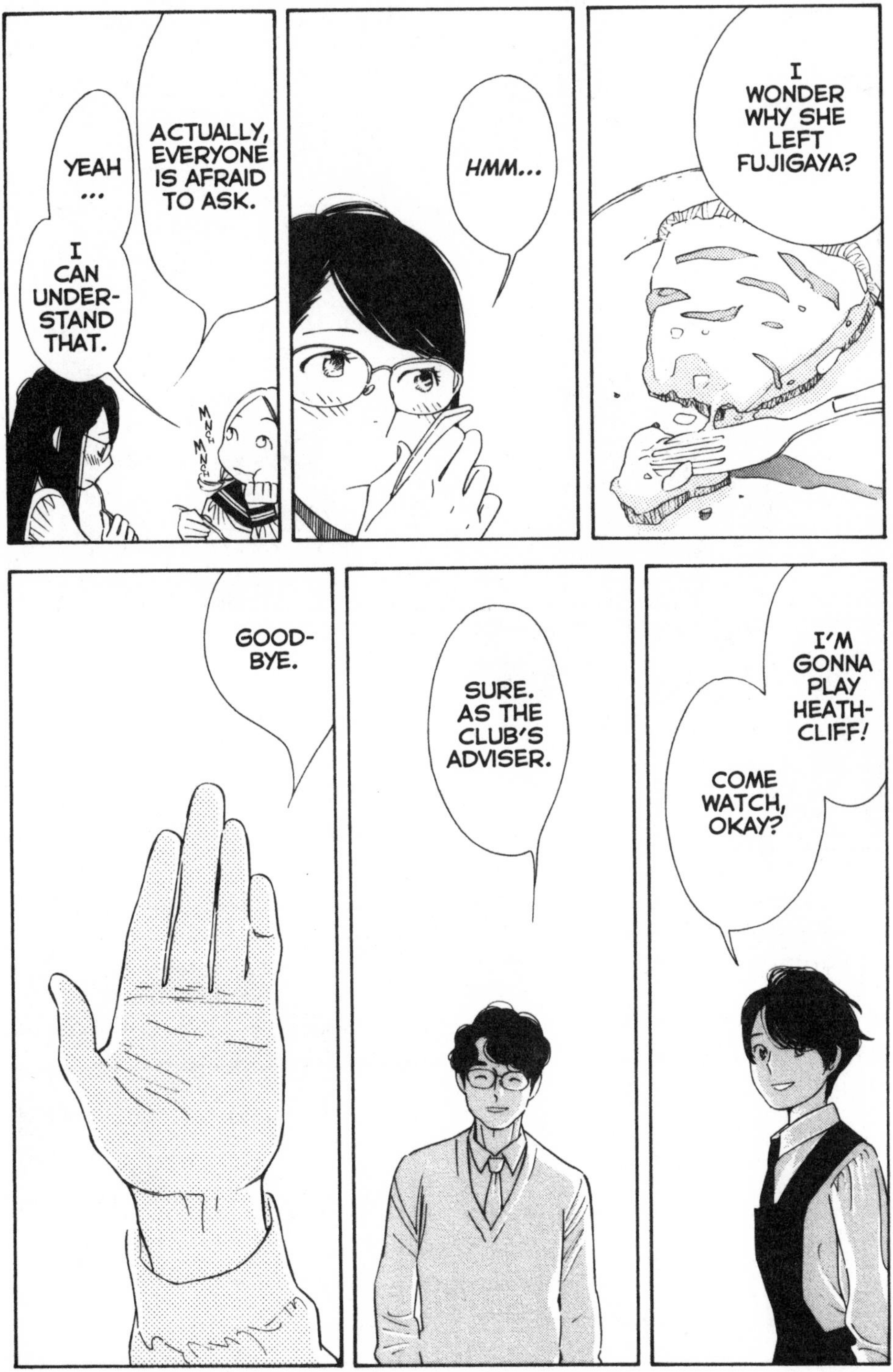
I WONDER WHY SHE LEFT FUJIGAYA?
HMM...
ACTUALLY, EVERYONE IS AFRAID TO ASK.
YEAH ...
I CAN UNDER-STAND THAT.
MNCH MNCH
I'M GONNA PLAY HEATH-CLIFF!
COME WATCH, OKAY?
SURE. AS THE CLUB'S ADVISER.
GOOD-BYE.

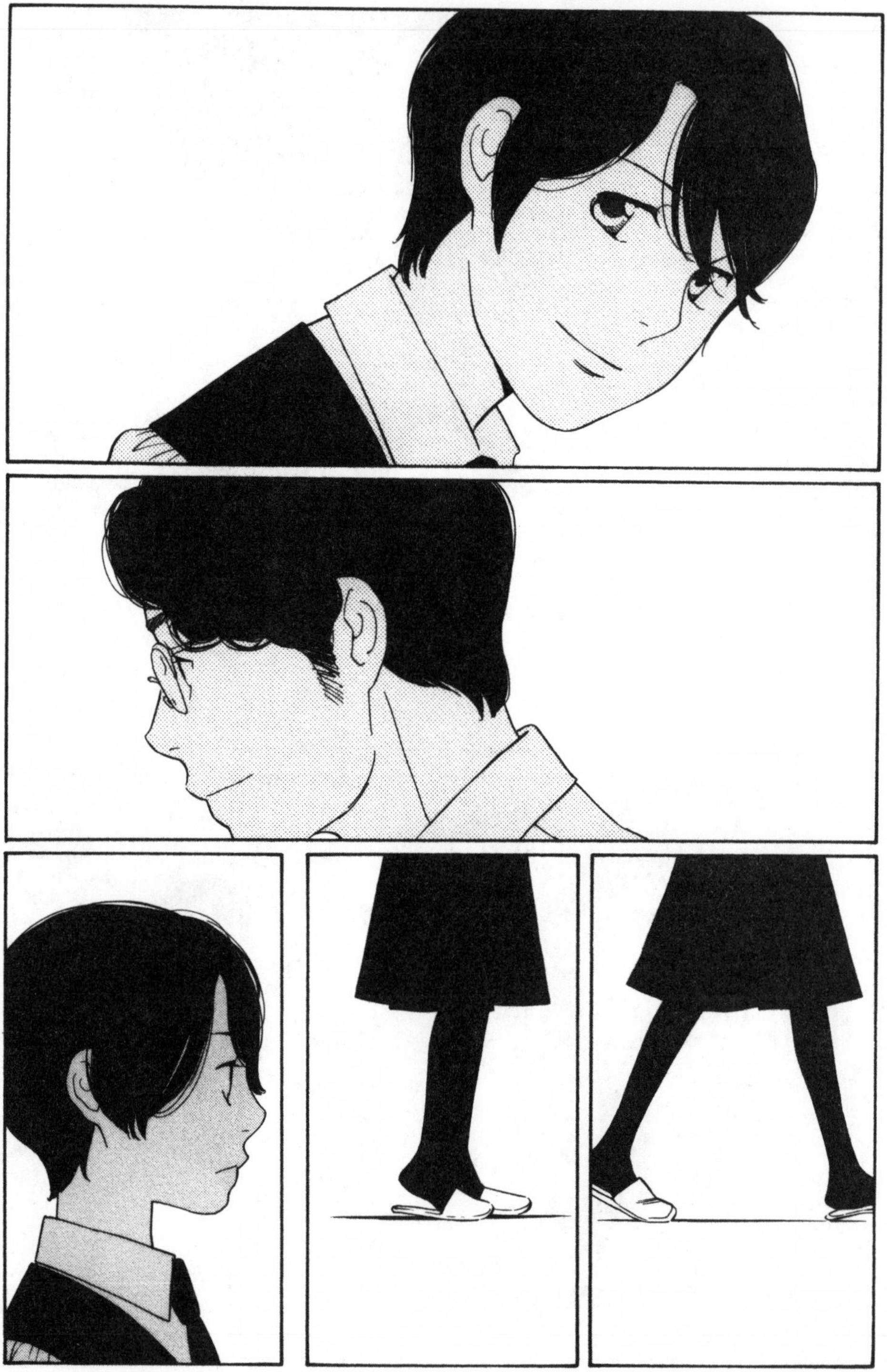

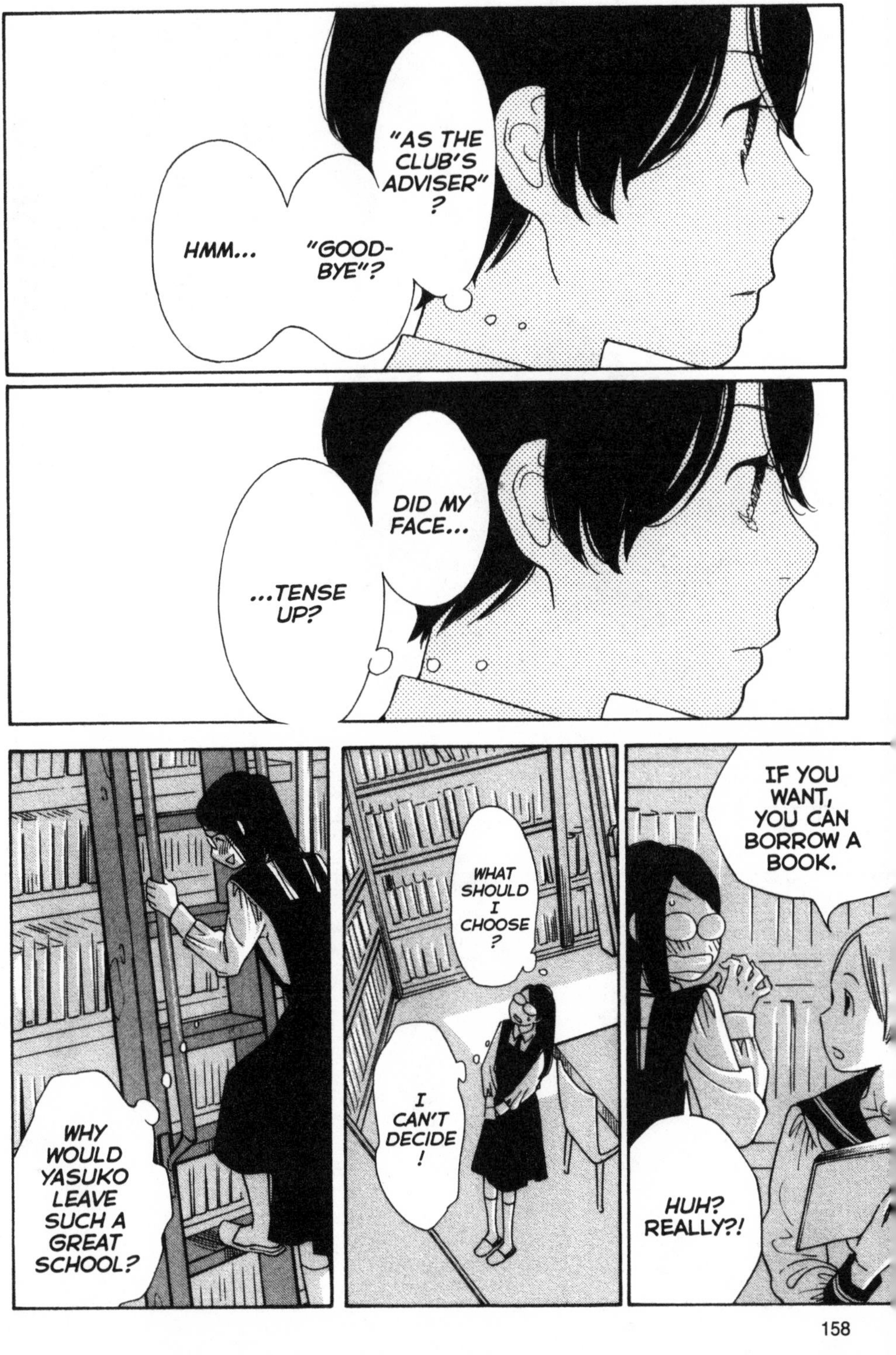
"AS THE CLUB'S ADVISER"?
HMM... "GOOD-BYE"?
DID MY FACE...
...TENSE UP?
IF YOU WANT, YOU CAN BORROW A BOOK.
HUH? REALLY?!
WHAT SHOULD I CHOOSE?
I CAN'T DECIDE!
WHY WOULD YASUKO LEAVE SUCH A GREAT SCHOOL?

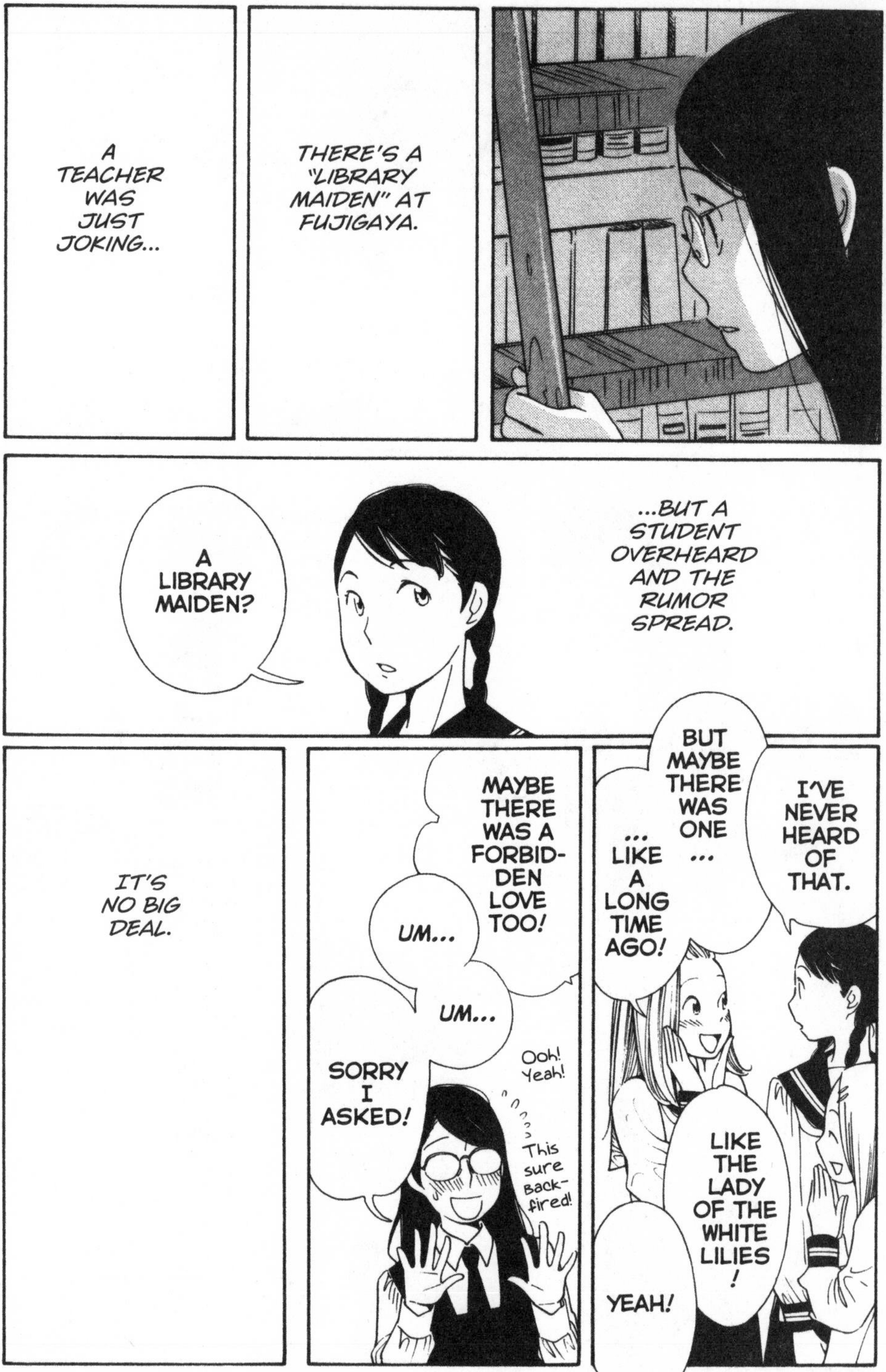

THERE'S A "LIBRARY MAIDEN" AT FUJIGAYA.
A TEACHER WAS JUST JOKING...
...BUT A STUDENT OVERHEARD AND THE RUMOR SPREAD.
A LIBRARY MAIDEN?
I'VE NEVER HEARD OF THAT.
BUT MAYBE THERE WAS ONE ...
... LIKE A LONG TIME AGO!
LIKE THE LADY OF THE WHITE LILIES!
YEAH!
MAYBE THERE WAS A FORBID-DEN LOVE TOO!
UM...
UM...
Ooh! Yeah!
SORRY I ASKED!
This sure back-fired!
IT'S NO BIG DEAL.

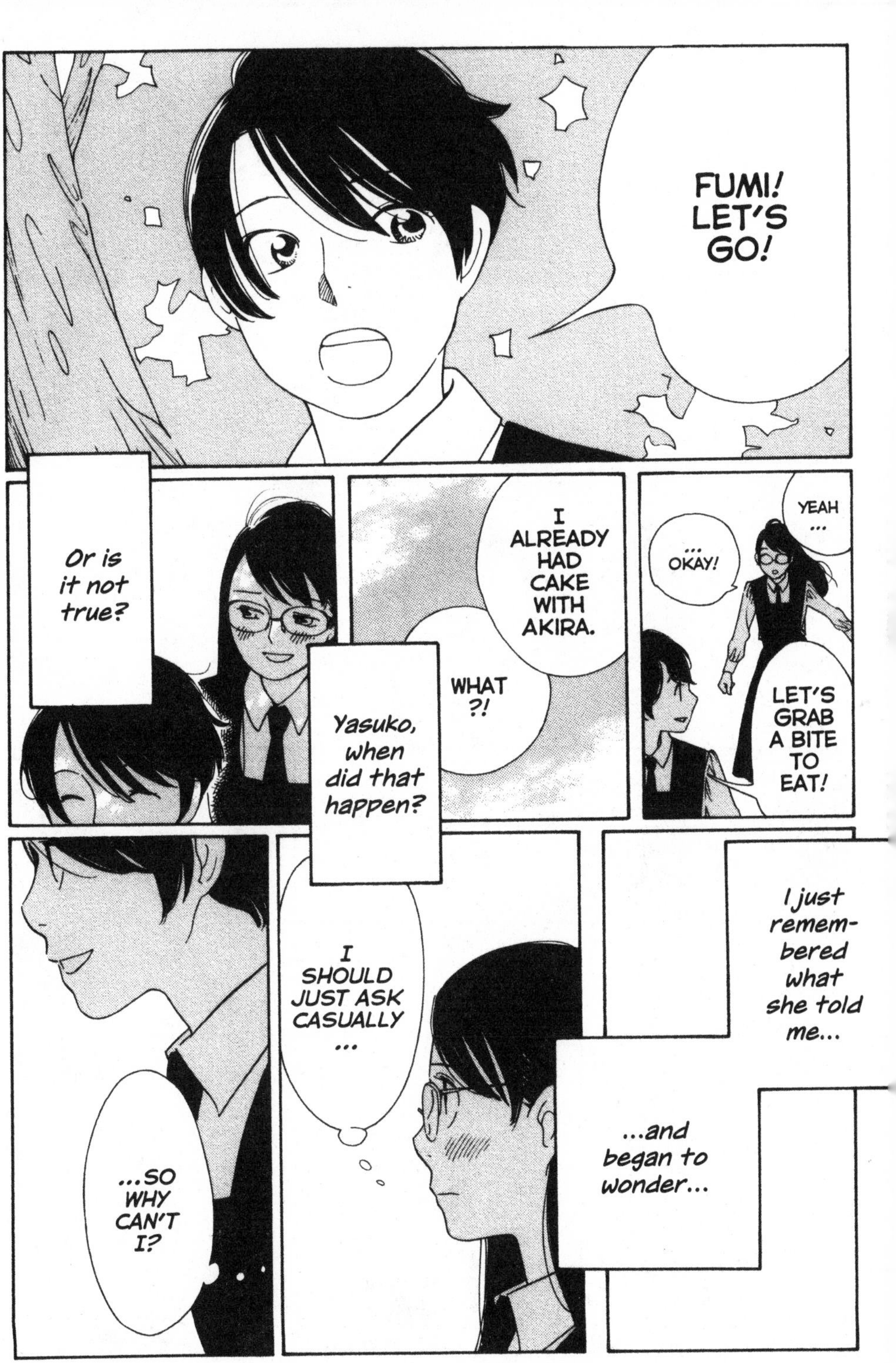
FUMI! LET'S GO!
YEAH...
...OKAY!
LET'S GRAB A BITE TO EAT!
I ALREADY HAD CAKE WITH AKIRA.
WHAT?!
Yasuko, when did that happen?
Or is it not true?
I just remem-bered what she told me...
...and began to wonder...
I SHOULD JUST ASK CASUALLY...
...SO WHY CAN'T I?

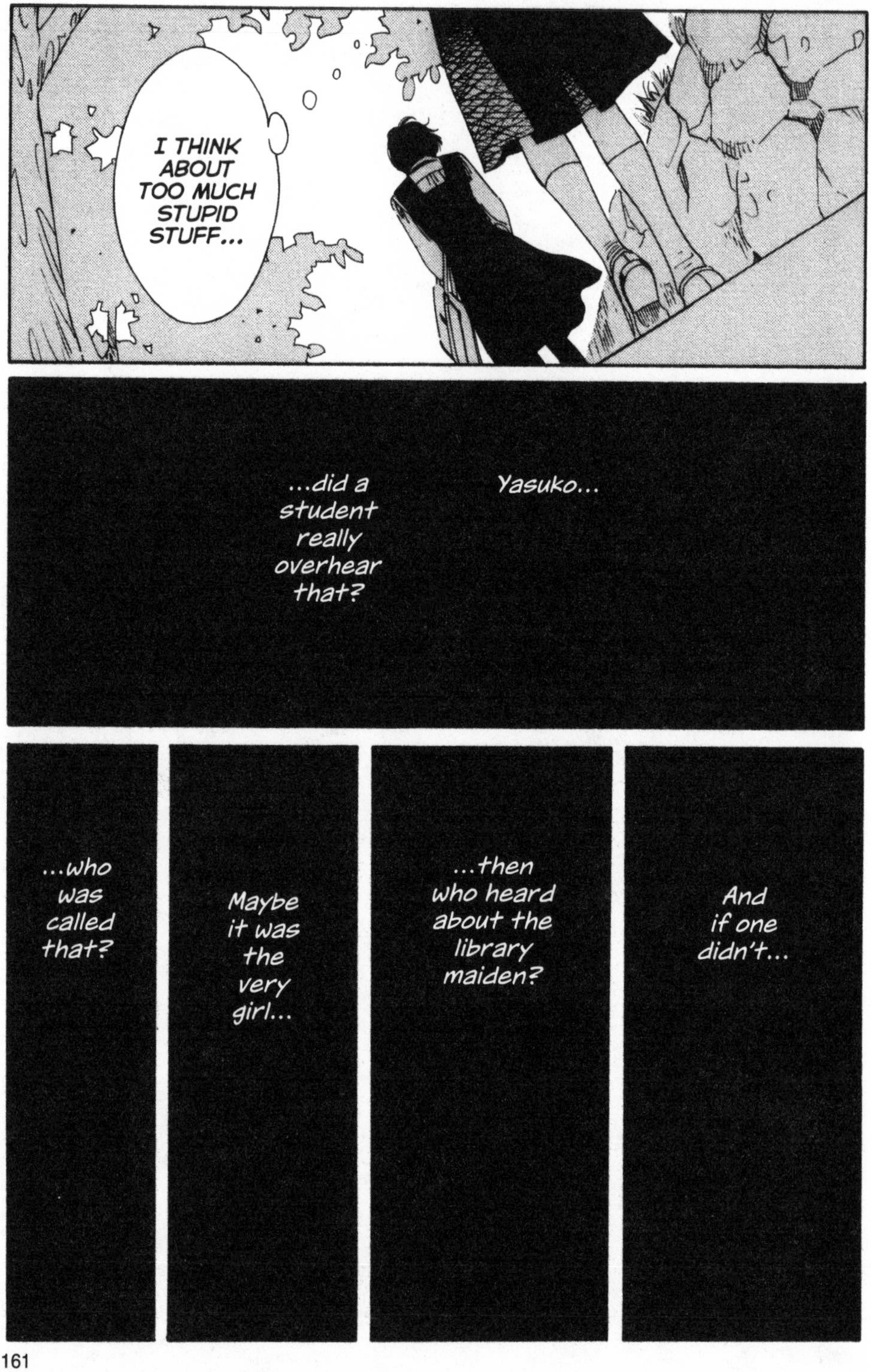
I THINK ABOUT TOO MUCH STUPID STUFF...
Yasuko...
...did a student really overhear that?
And if one didn't...
...then who heard about the library maiden?
Maybe it was the very girl...
...who was called that?

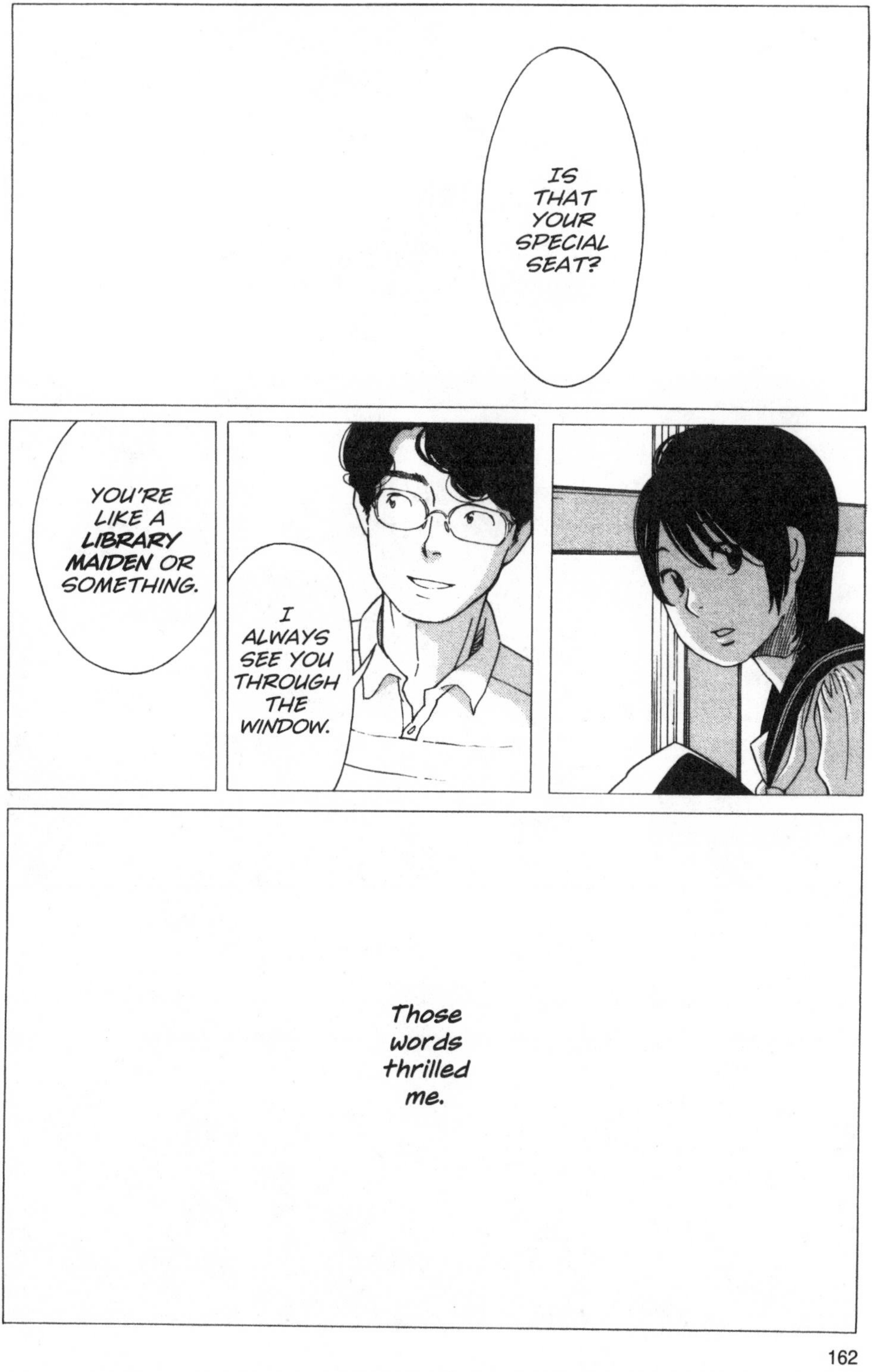
IS THAT YOUR SPECIAL SEAT?
I ALWAYS SEE YOU THROUGH THE WINDOW.
YOU'RE LIKE A LIBRARY MAIDEN OR SOMETHING.
Those words thrilled me.

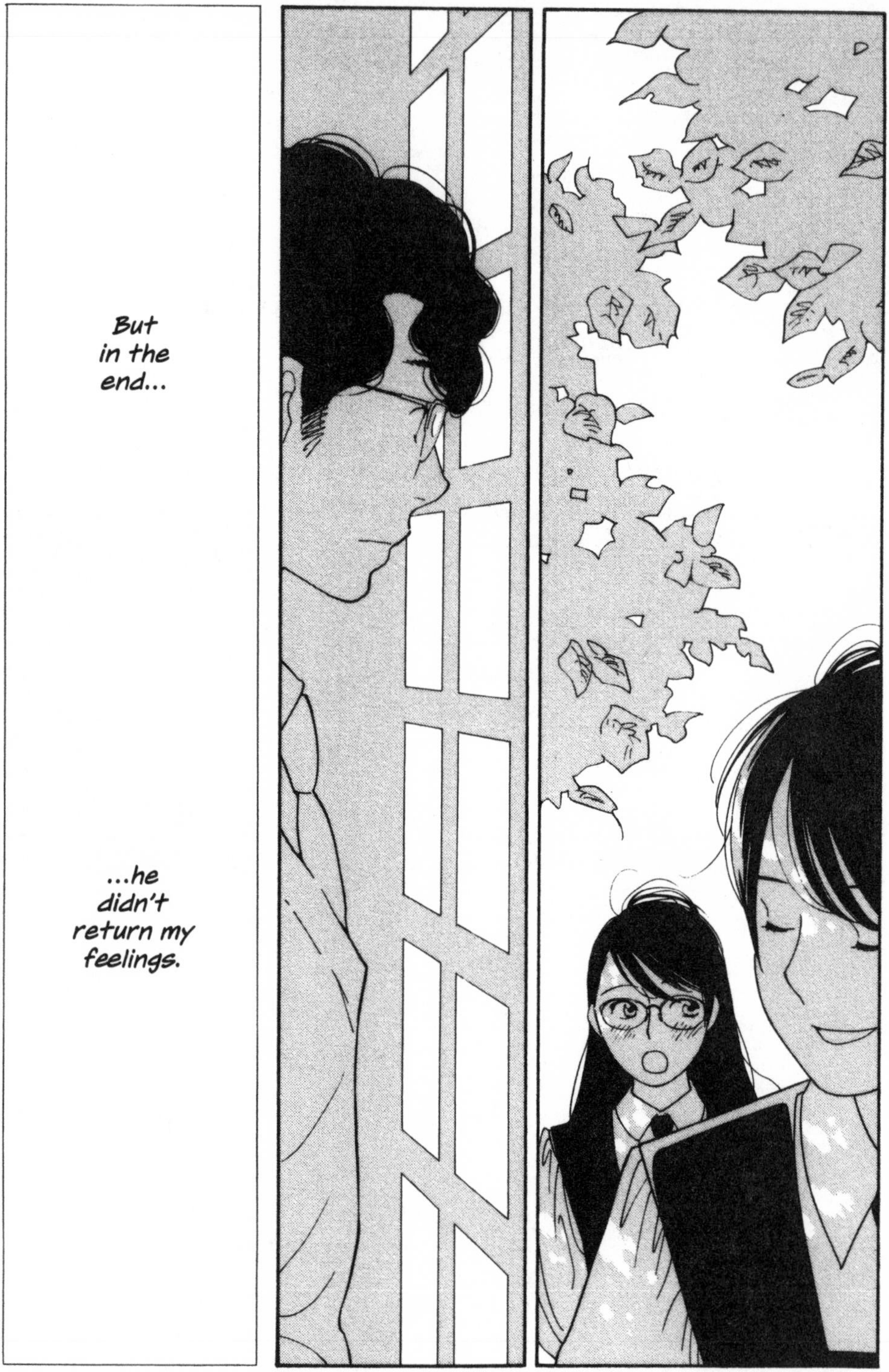
But in the end...
...he didn't return my feelings.

I feel stupid for leaving the school over such a small incident.

But there's a helpless child inside me.

I'll never open myself up to anyone again. But please let me share this one secret with you, Mr. Kagami.


From your selfish Yasuko
            Goodbye.

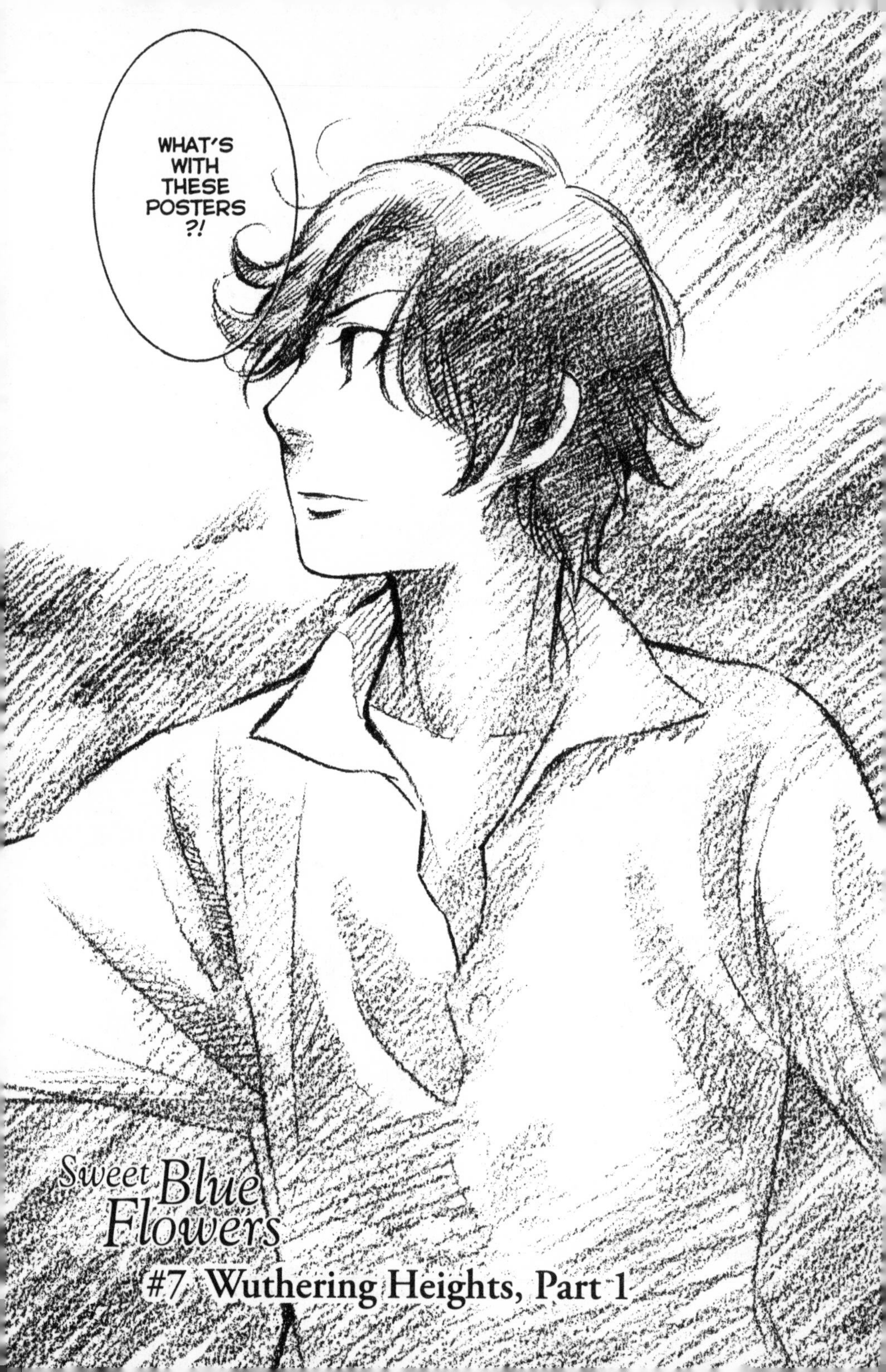
WHAT'S WITH THESE POSTERS ?!

# Sweet Blue Flowers

## #7 Wuthering Heights, Part 1

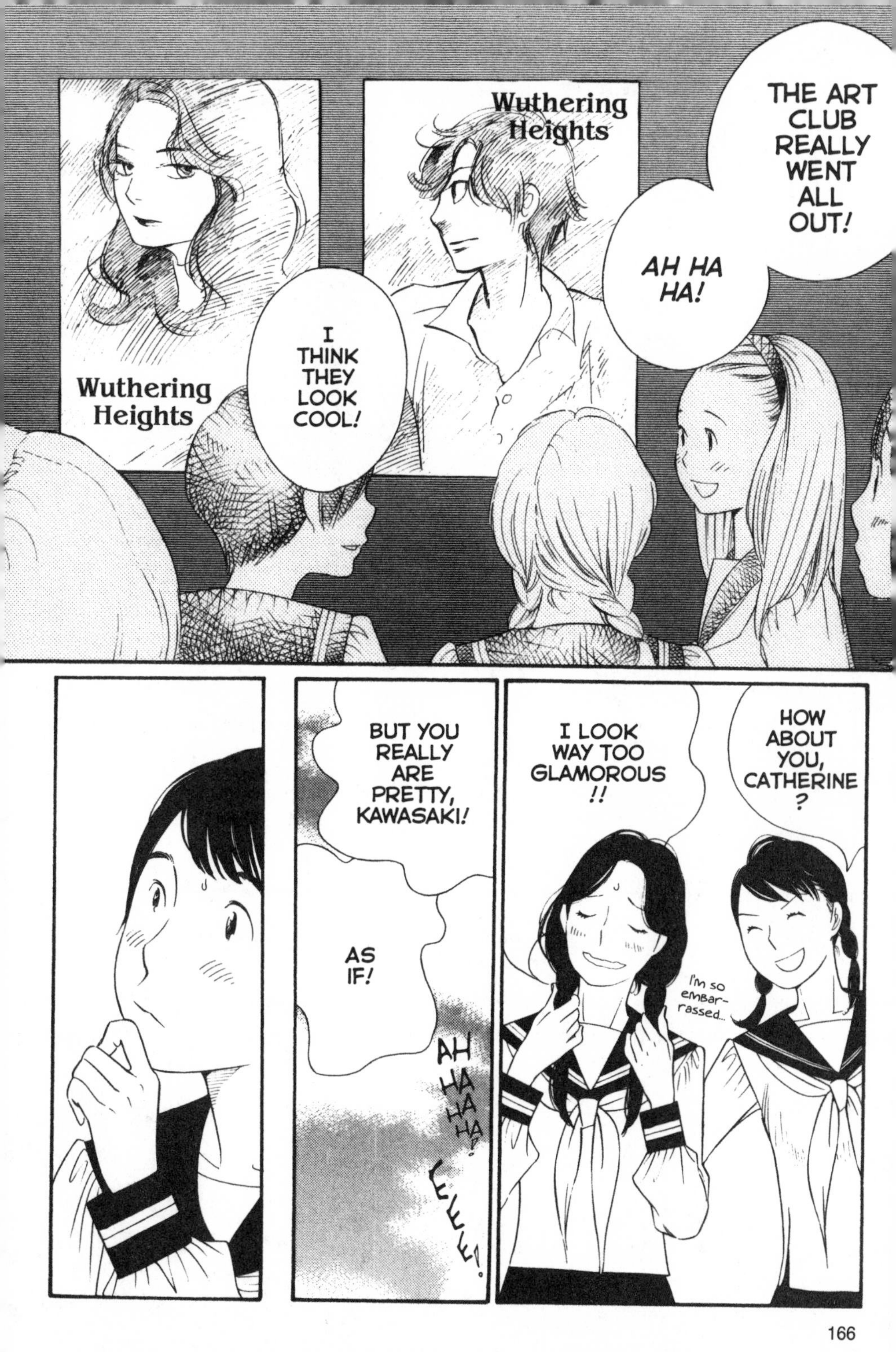
THE ART CLUB REALLY WENT ALL OUT!
AH HA HA!
Wuthering Heights
I THINK THEY LOOK COOL!
Wuthering Heights
HOW ABOUT YOU, CATHERINE?
I LOOK WAY TOO GLAMOROUS!!
I'm so embarrassed...
BUT YOU REALLY ARE PRETTY, KAWASAKI!
AS IF!
AH HA HA HA!
EEEE!

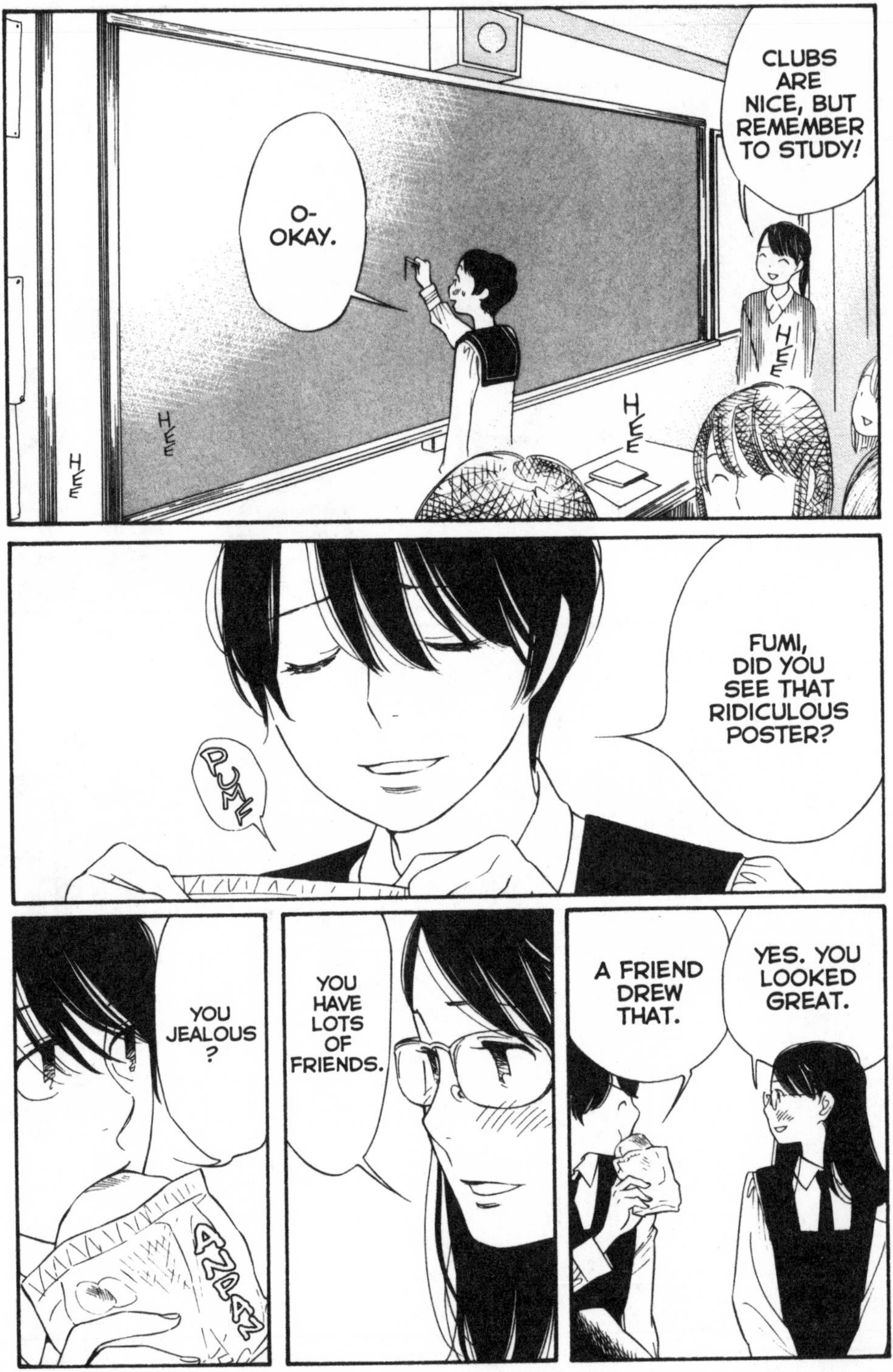
CLUBS ARE NICE, BUT REMEMBER TO STUDY!
O-OKAY.
HEE
HEE
HEE
HEE
FUMI, DID YOU SEE THAT RIDICULOUS POSTER?
PUMF
YES. YOU LOOKED GREAT.
A FRIEND DREW THAT.
YOU HAVE LOTS OF FRIENDS.
YOU JEALOUS?
ANPAN

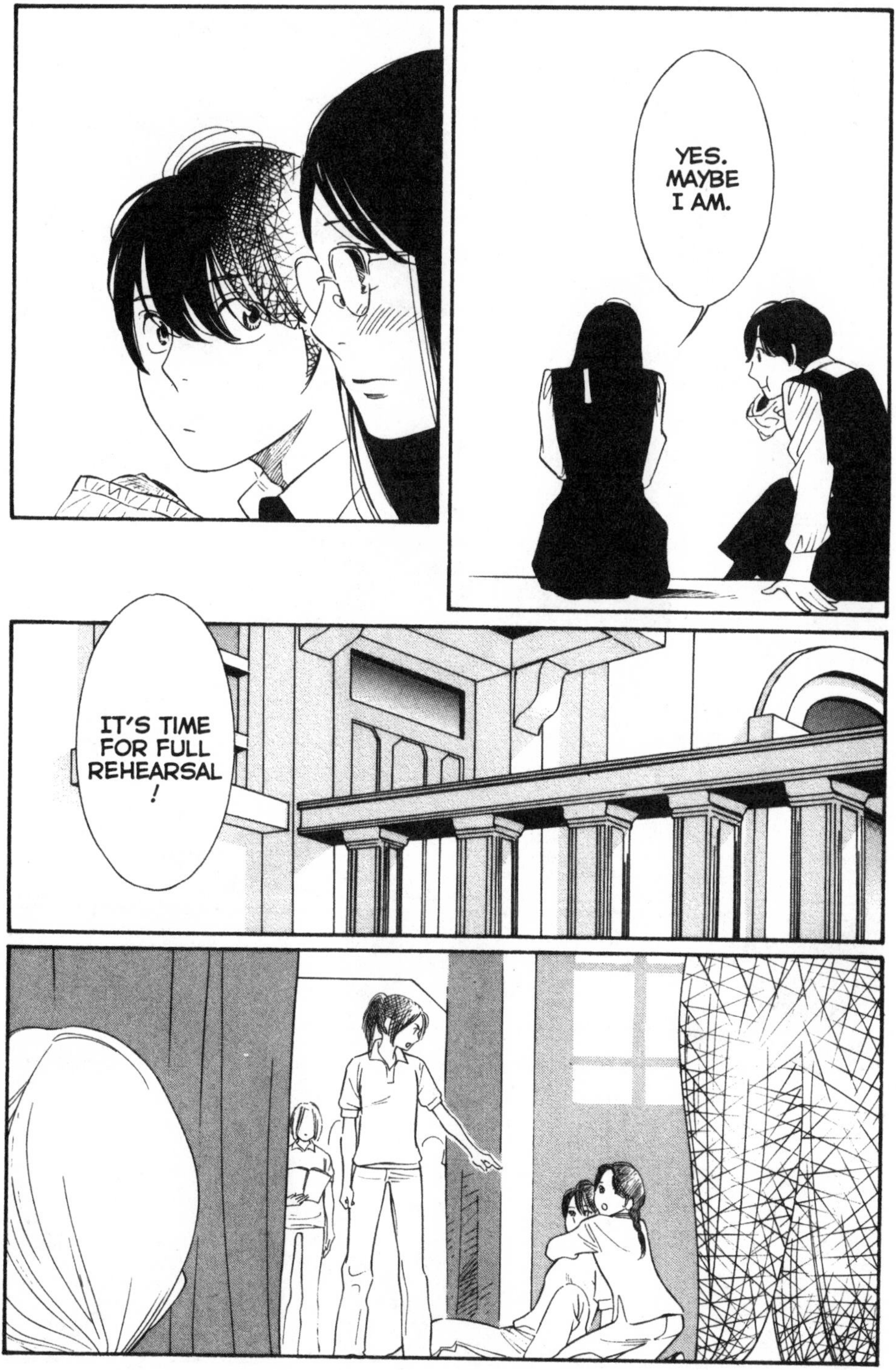
YES. MAYBE I AM.
IT'S TIME FOR FULL REHEARSAL!

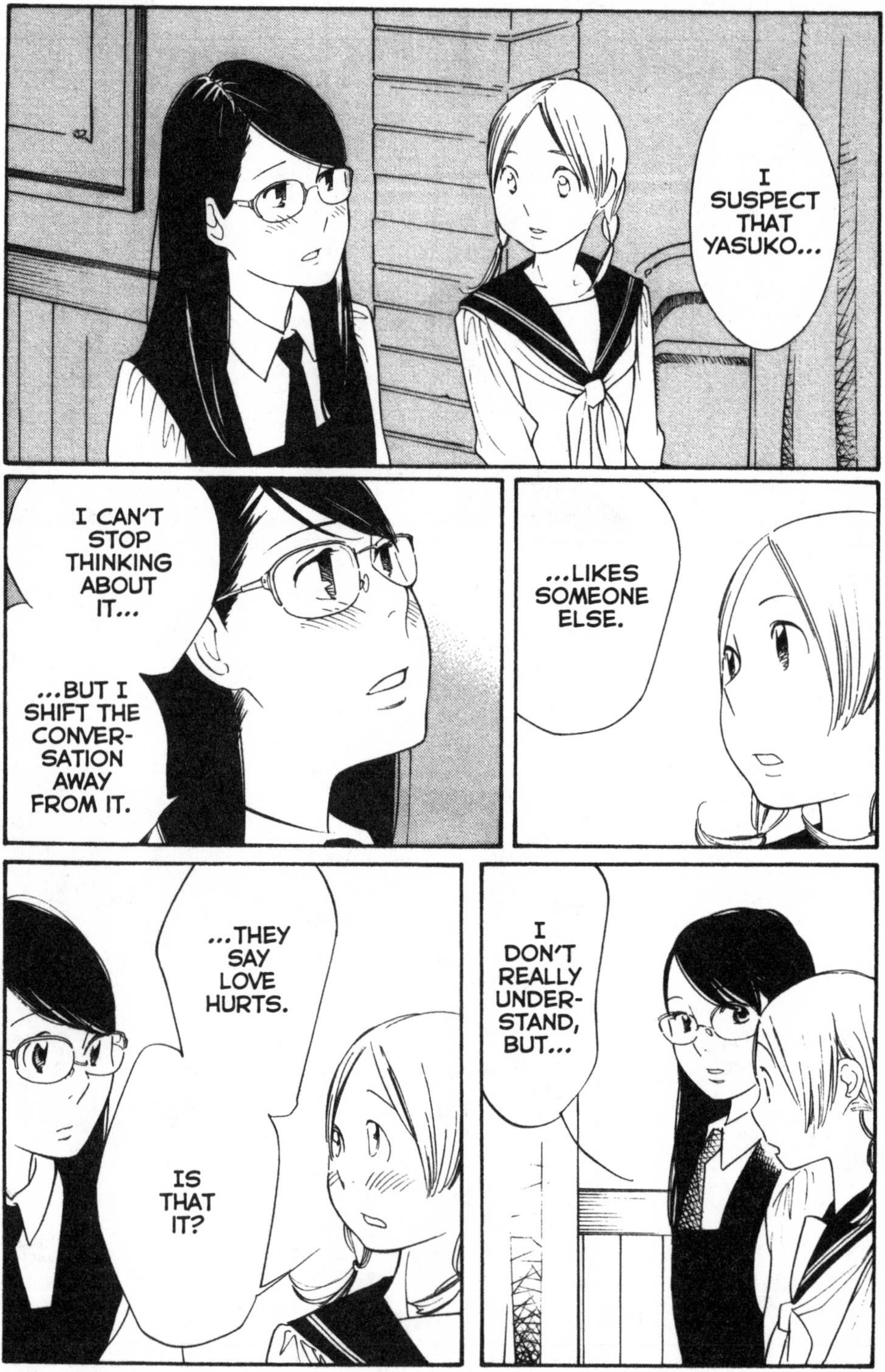
I SUSPECT THAT YASUKO...
...LIKES SOMEONE ELSE.
I CAN'T STOP THINKING ABOUT IT...
...BUT I SHIFT THE CONVERSATION AWAY FROM IT.
I DON'T REALLY UNDERSTAND, BUT...
...THEY SAY LOVE HURTS.
IS THAT IT?

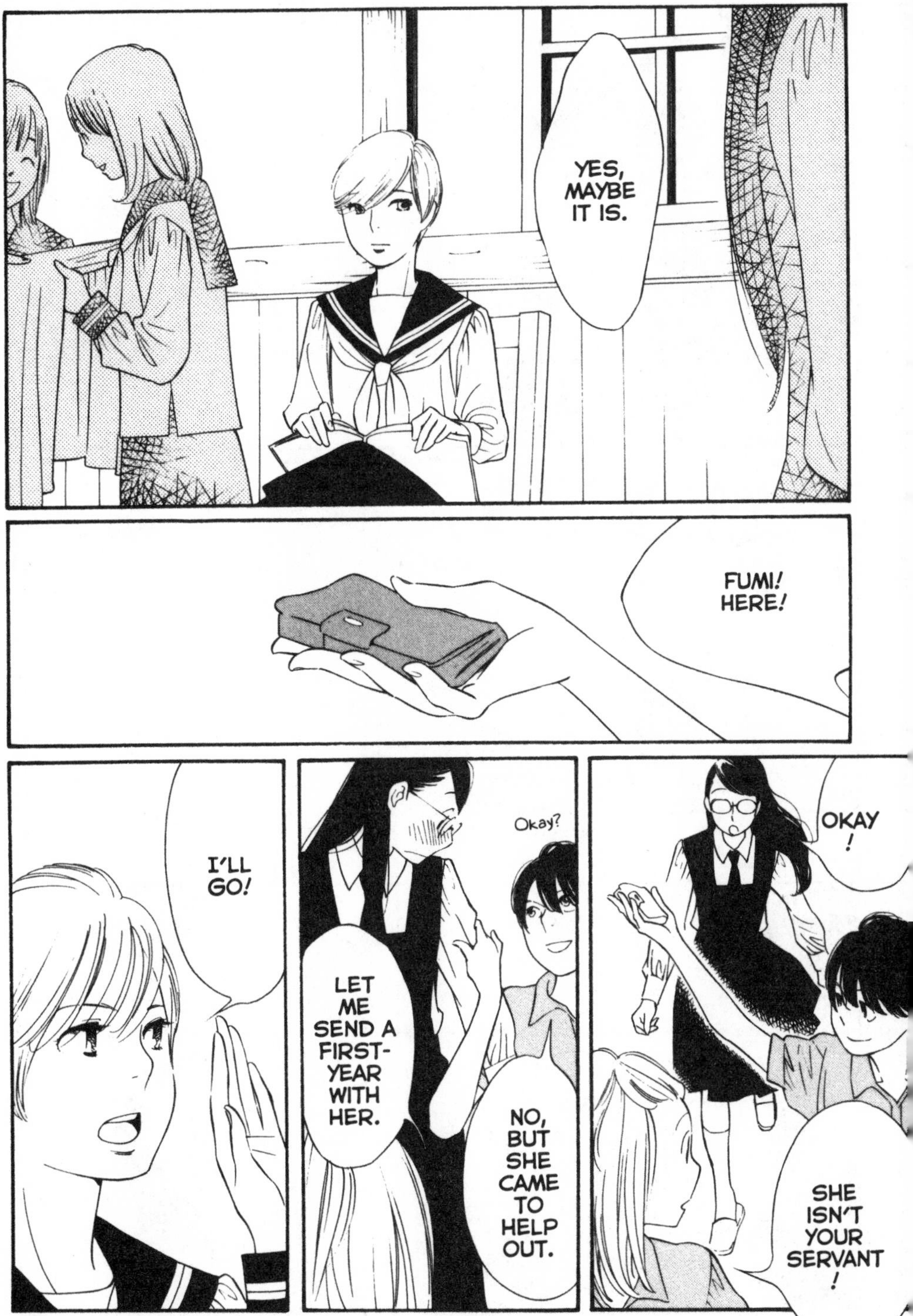
YES, MAYBE IT IS.
FUMI! HERE!
OKAY!
SHE ISN'T YOUR SERVANT!
Okay?
NO, BUT SHE CAME TO HELP OUT.
LET ME SEND A FIRST-YEAR WITH HER.
I'LL GO!

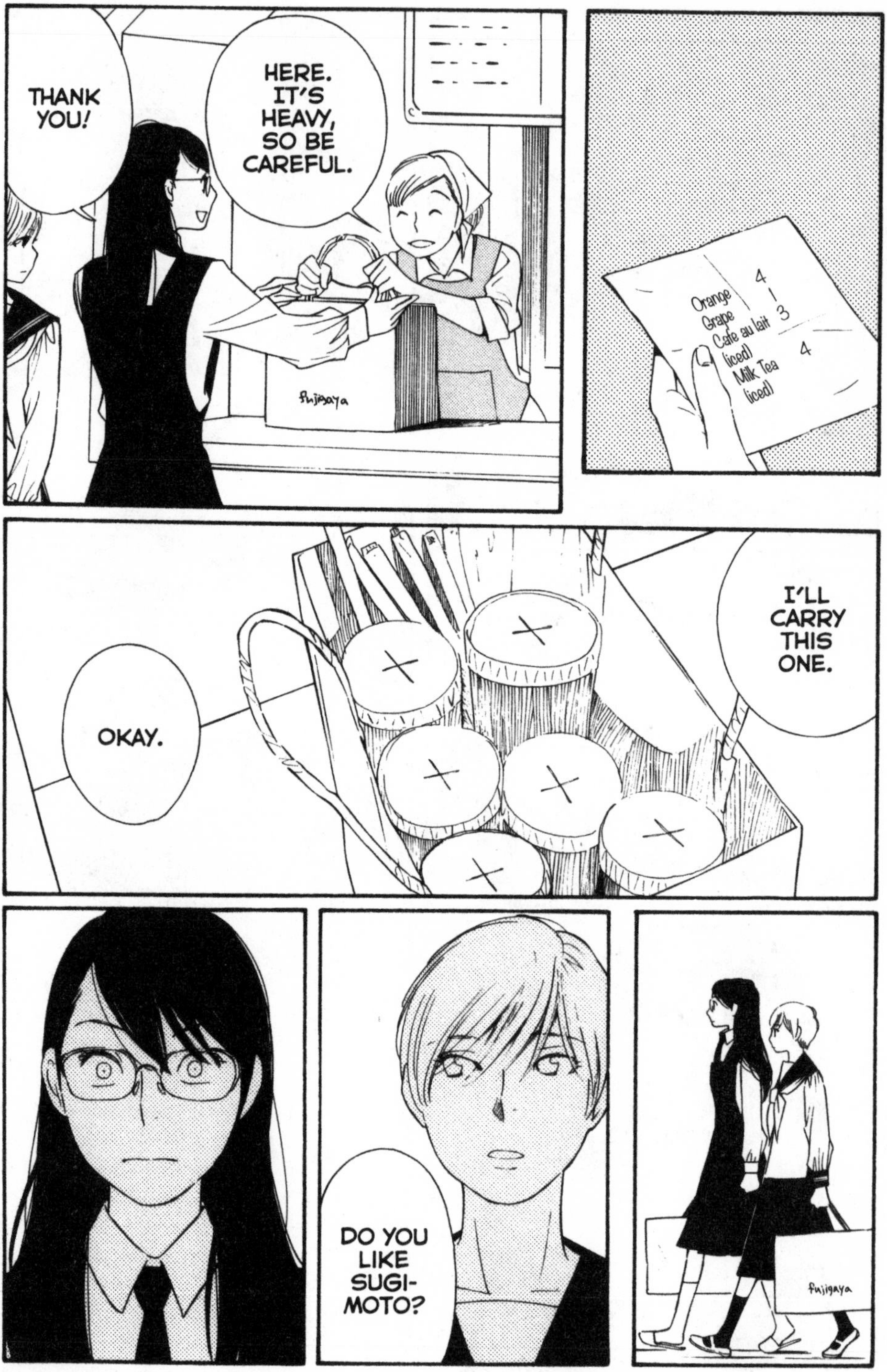
Orange 4
Grape 1
Cafe au lait (iced) 3
Milk Tea (iced) 4
HERE. IT'S HEAVY, SO BE CAREFUL.
THANK YOU!
fujigaya
I'LL CARRY THIS ONE.
OKAY.
fujigaya
DO YOU LIKE SUGI-MOTO?

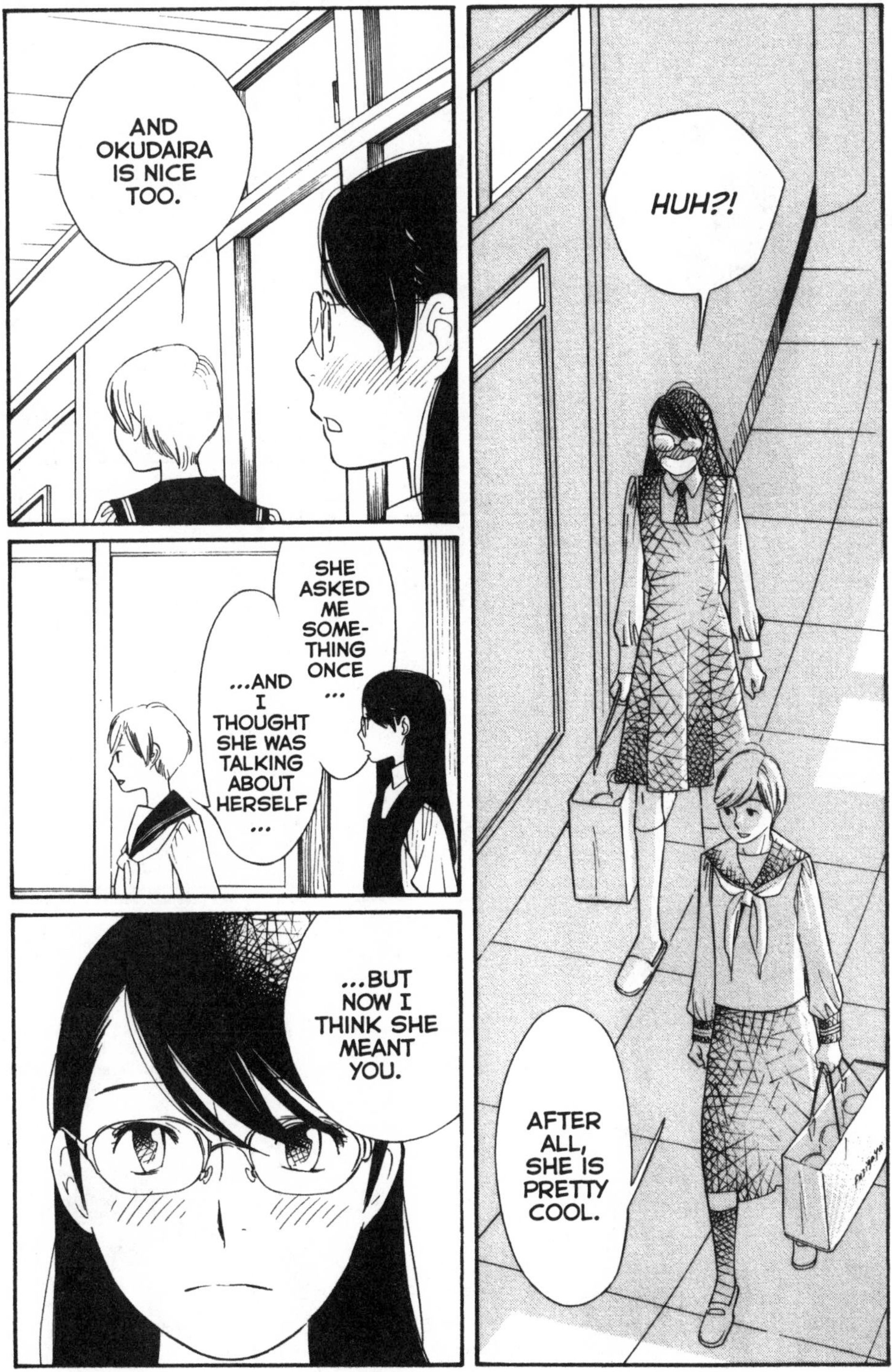
AND OKUDAIRA IS NICE TOO.
SHE ASKED ME SOME-THING ONCE ...
...AND I THOUGHT SHE WAS TALKING ABOUT HERSELF ...
...BUT NOW I THINK SHE MEANT YOU.
HUH?!
AFTER ALL, SHE IS PRETTY COOL.

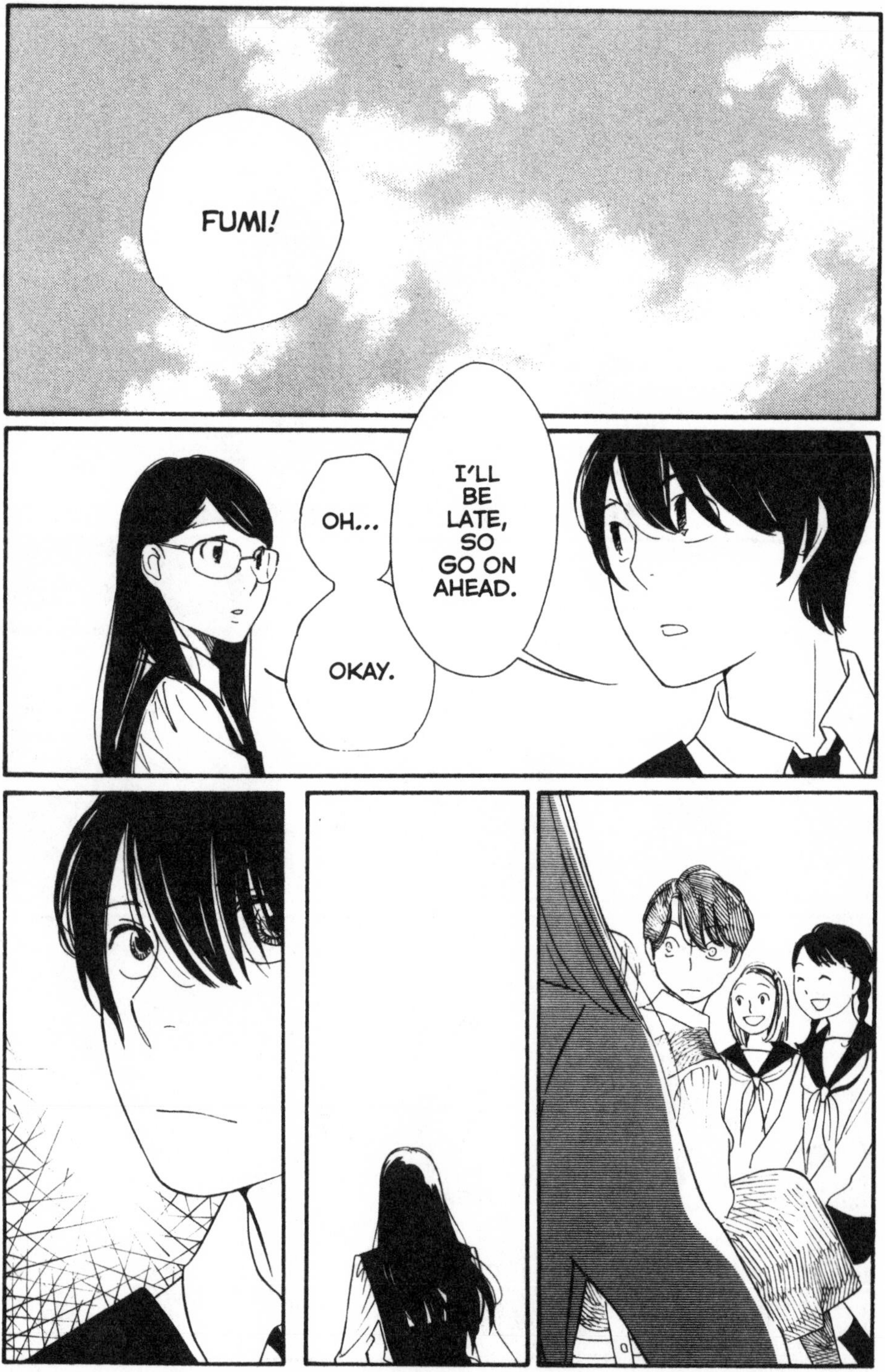
FUMI!
I'LL BE LATE, SO GO ON AHEAD.
OH... OKAY.

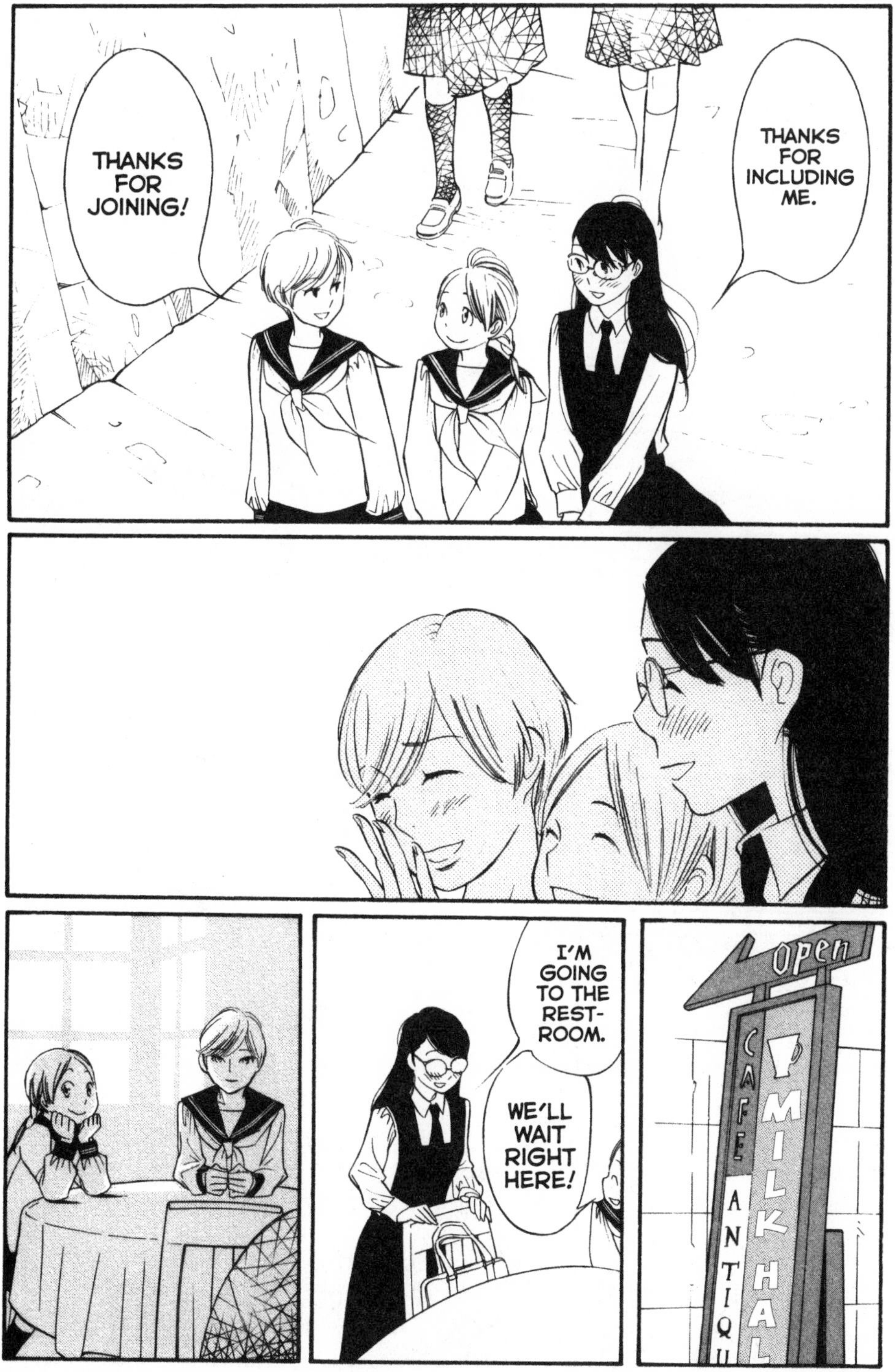
THANKS FOR INCLUDING ME.
THANKS FOR JOINING!
Open
CAFE
MILK HAL
ANTIQU
I'M GOING TO THE REST-ROOM.
WE'LL WAIT RIGHT HERE!

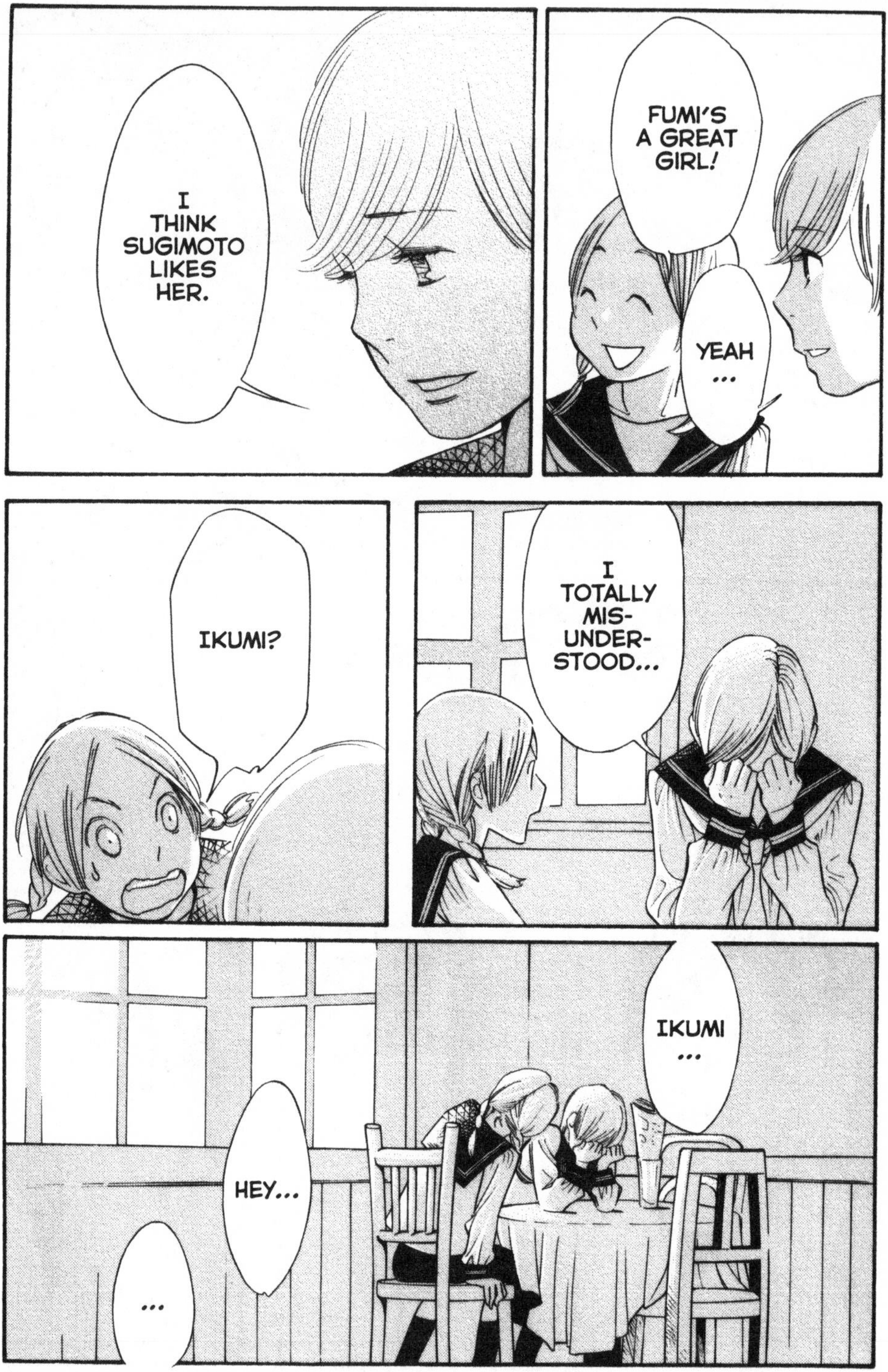
FUMI'S A GREAT GIRL!
YEAH...
I THINK SUGIMOTO LIKES HER.
I TOTALLY MIS-UNDER-STOOD...
IKUMI?
IKUMI...
HEY...
...

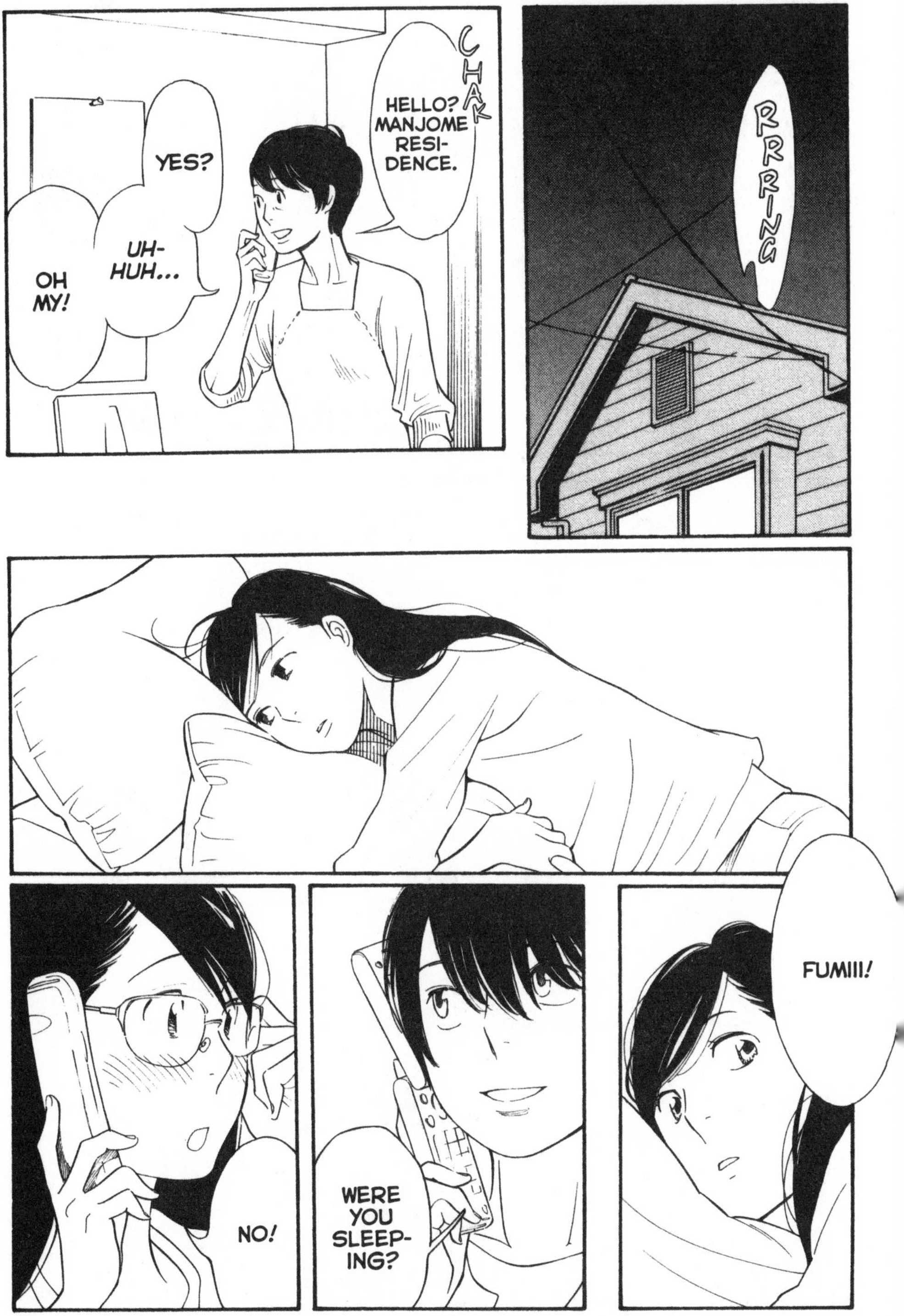
RRRING
CHAK
HELLO? MANJOME RESI-DENCE.
YES?
UH-HUH...
OH MY!
FUMIII!
WERE YOU SLEEP-ING?
NO!

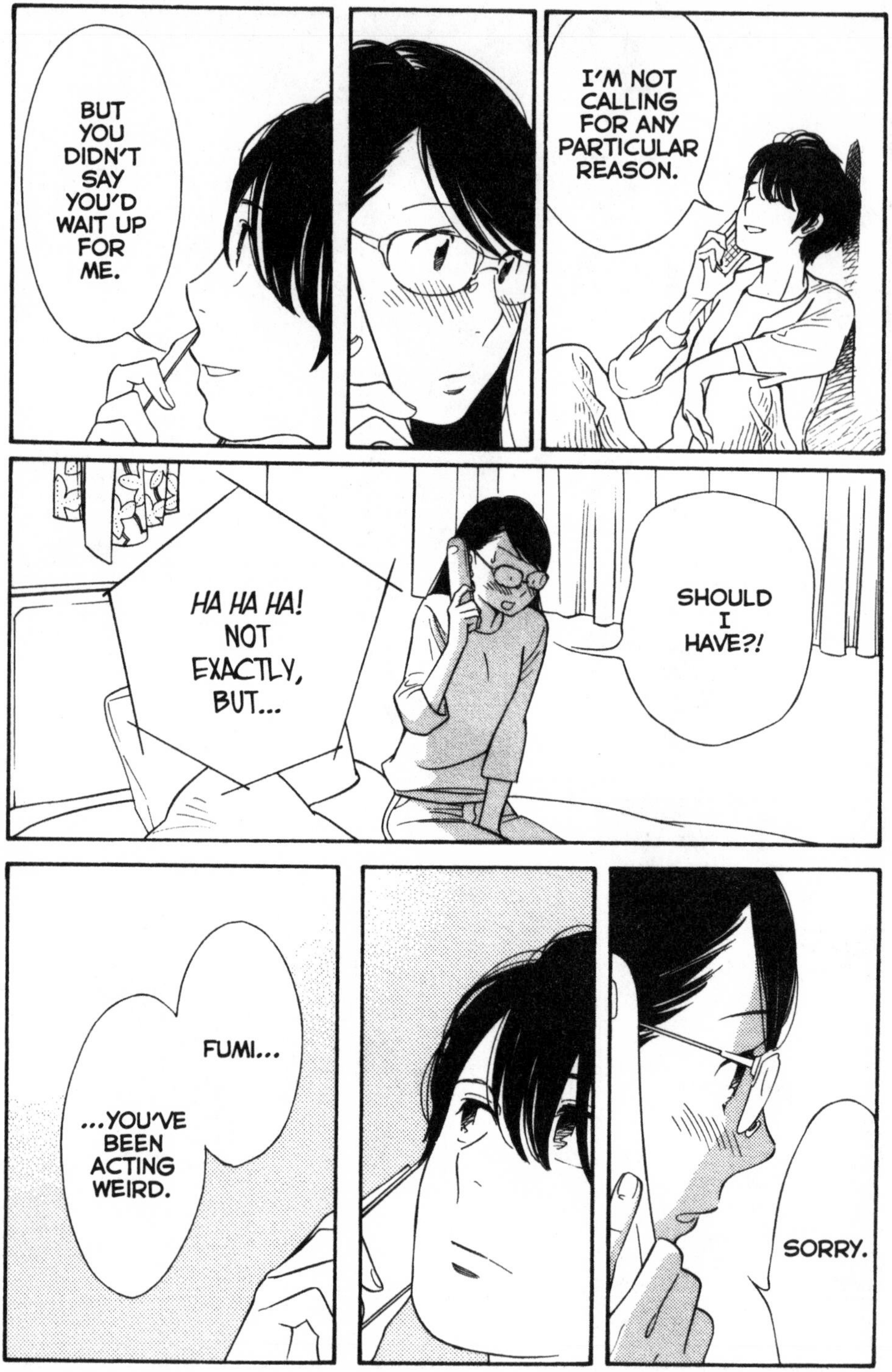
I'M NOT CALLING FOR ANY PARTICULAR REASON.
BUT YOU DIDN'T SAY YOU'D WAIT UP FOR ME.
SHOULD I HAVE?!
*HA HA HA!* NOT EXACTLY, BUT...
SORRY.
FUMI...
...YOU'VE BEEN ACTING WEIRD.

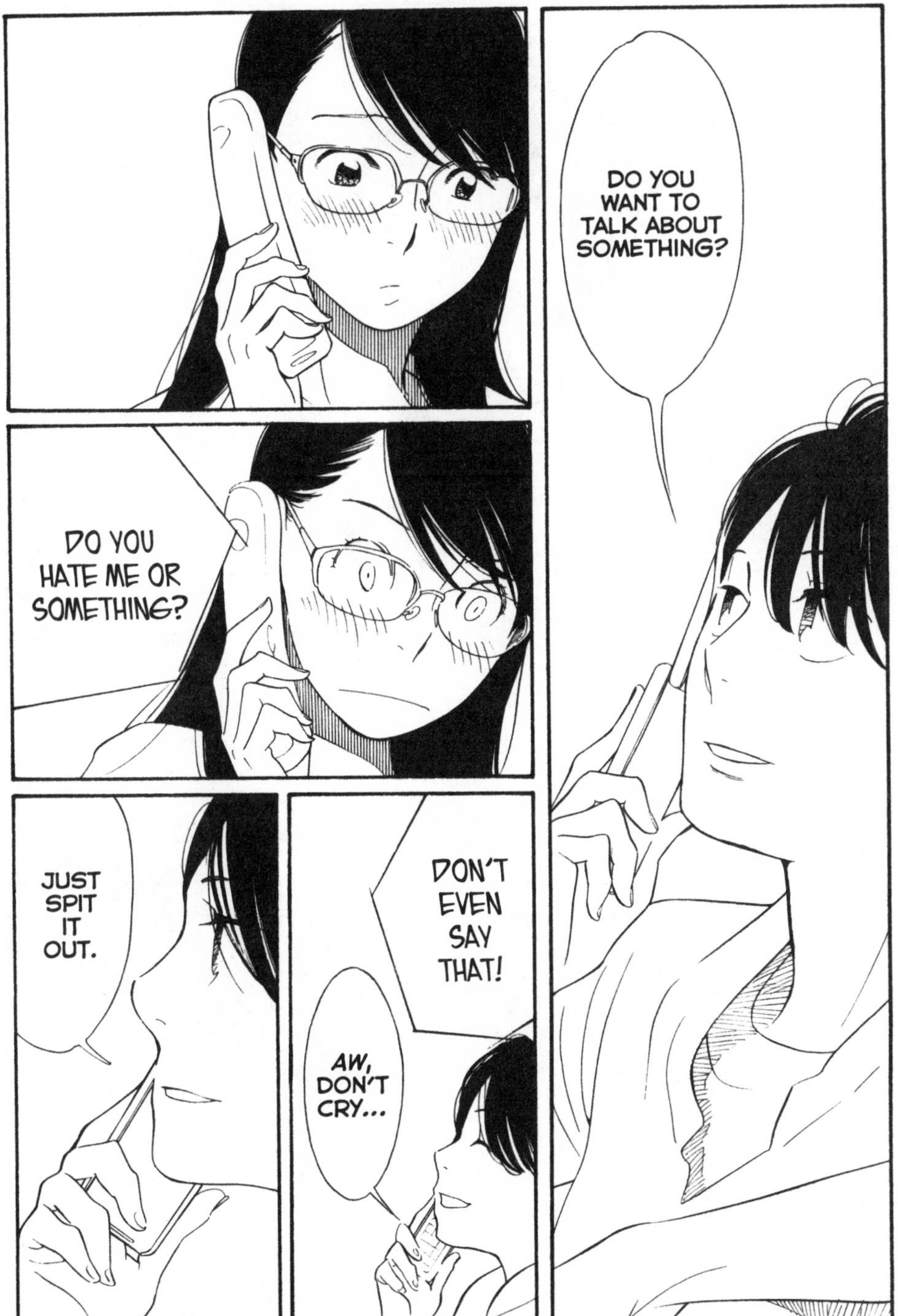
DO YOU WANT TO TALK ABOUT SOMETHING?
DO YOU HATE ME OR SOMETHING?
DON'T EVEN SAY THAT!
AW, DON'T CRY...
JUST SPIT IT OUT.

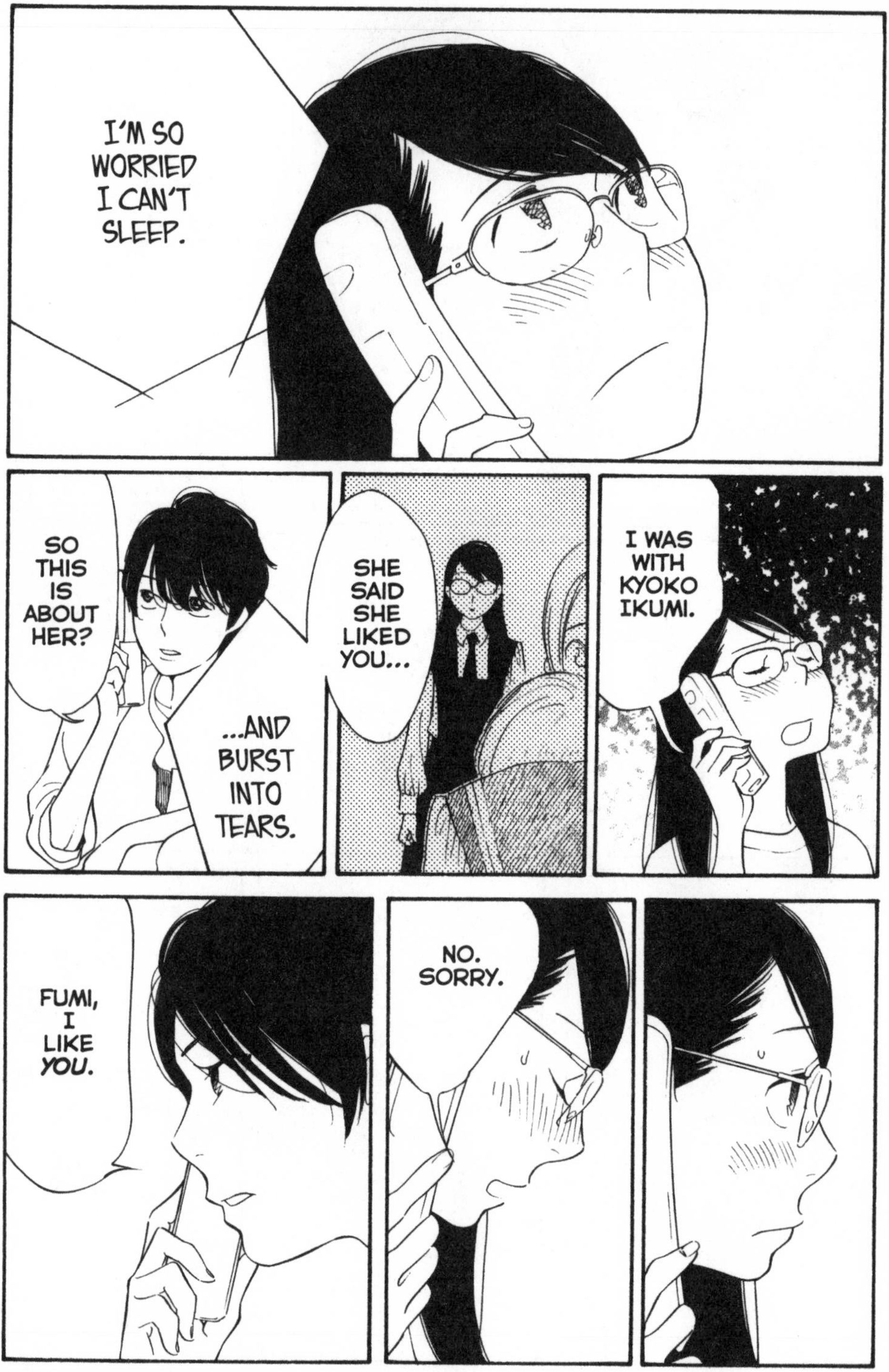
I'M SO WORRIED I CAN'T SLEEP.
I WAS WITH KYOKO IKUMI.
SHE SAID SHE LIKED YOU...
...AND BURST INTO TEARS.
SO THIS IS ABOUT HER?
NO. SORRY.
FUMI, I LIKE *YOU*.

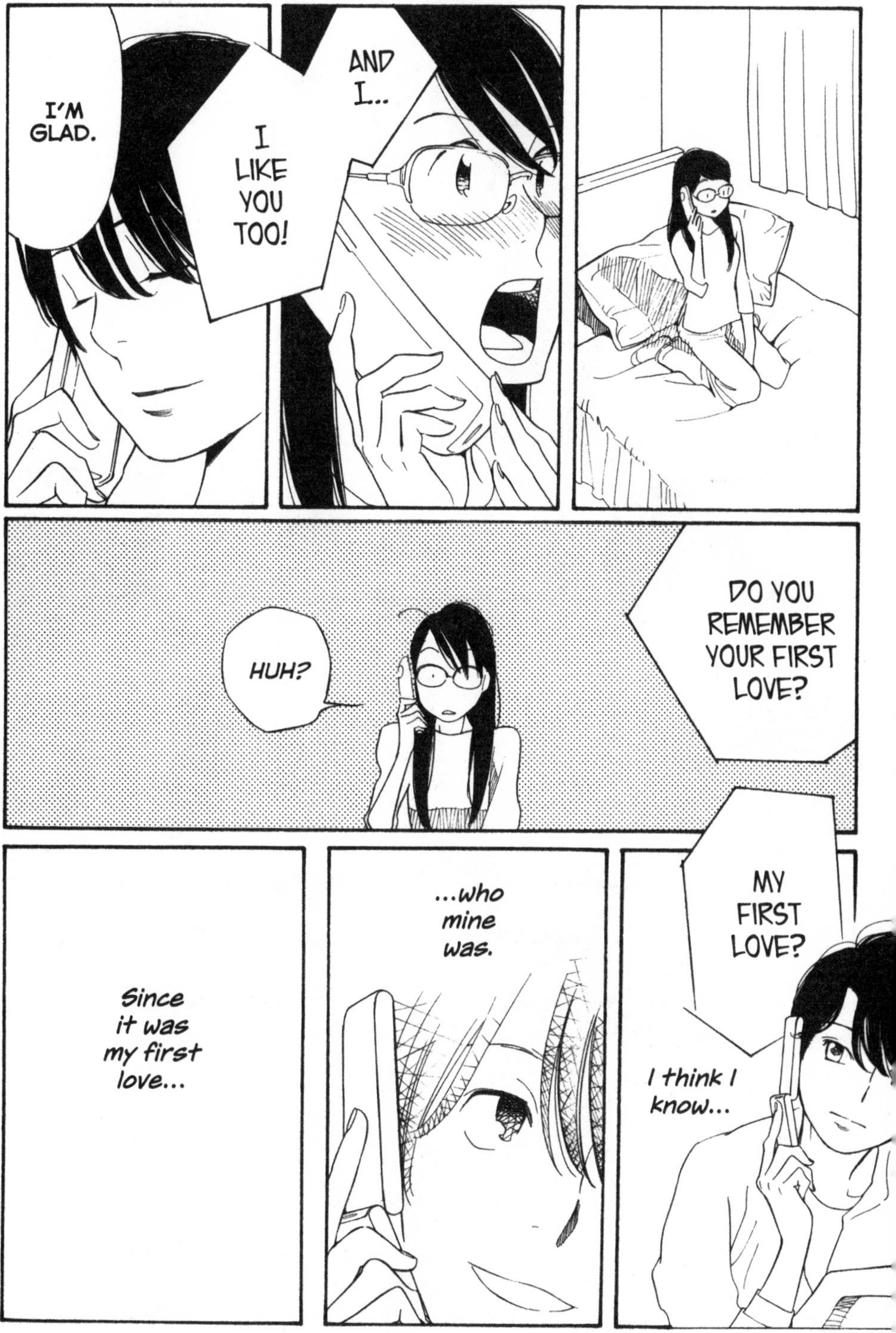
AND I...
I LIKE YOU TOO!
I'M GLAD.
DO YOU REMEMBER YOUR FIRST LOVE?
HUH?
MY FIRST LOVE?
I think I know...
...who mine was.
Since it was my first love...

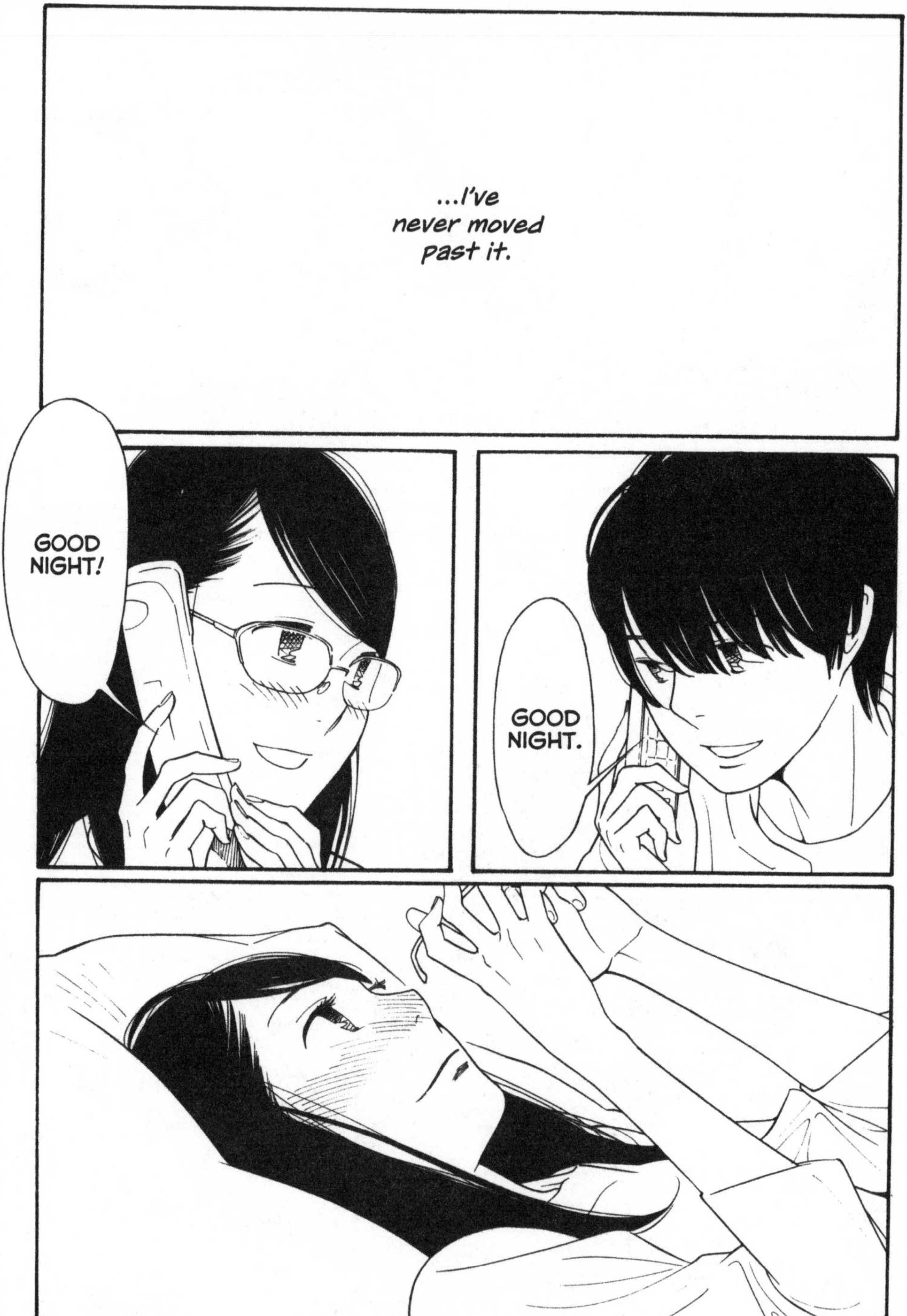
...I've never moved past it.
GOOD NIGHT.
GOOD NIGHT!

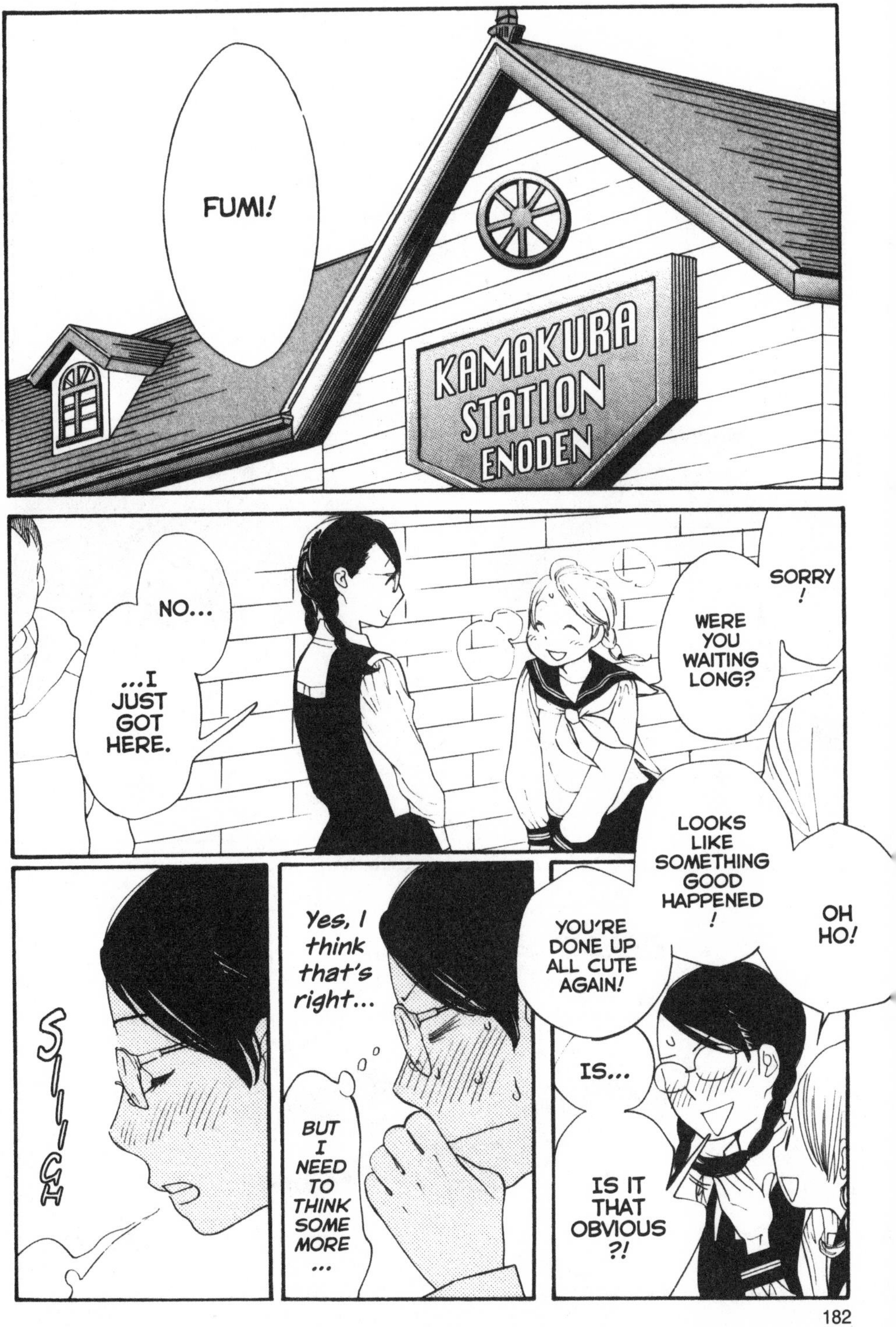
FUMI!
KAMAKURA STATION ENODEN
SORRY!
WERE YOU WAITING LONG?
NO...
...I JUST GOT HERE.
OH HO!
LOOKS LIKE SOMETHING GOOD HAPPENED!
YOU'RE DONE UP ALL CUTE AGAIN!
IS...
IS IT THAT OBVIOUS?!
Yes, I think that's right...
BUT I NEED TO THINK SOME MORE...
SIIIICH

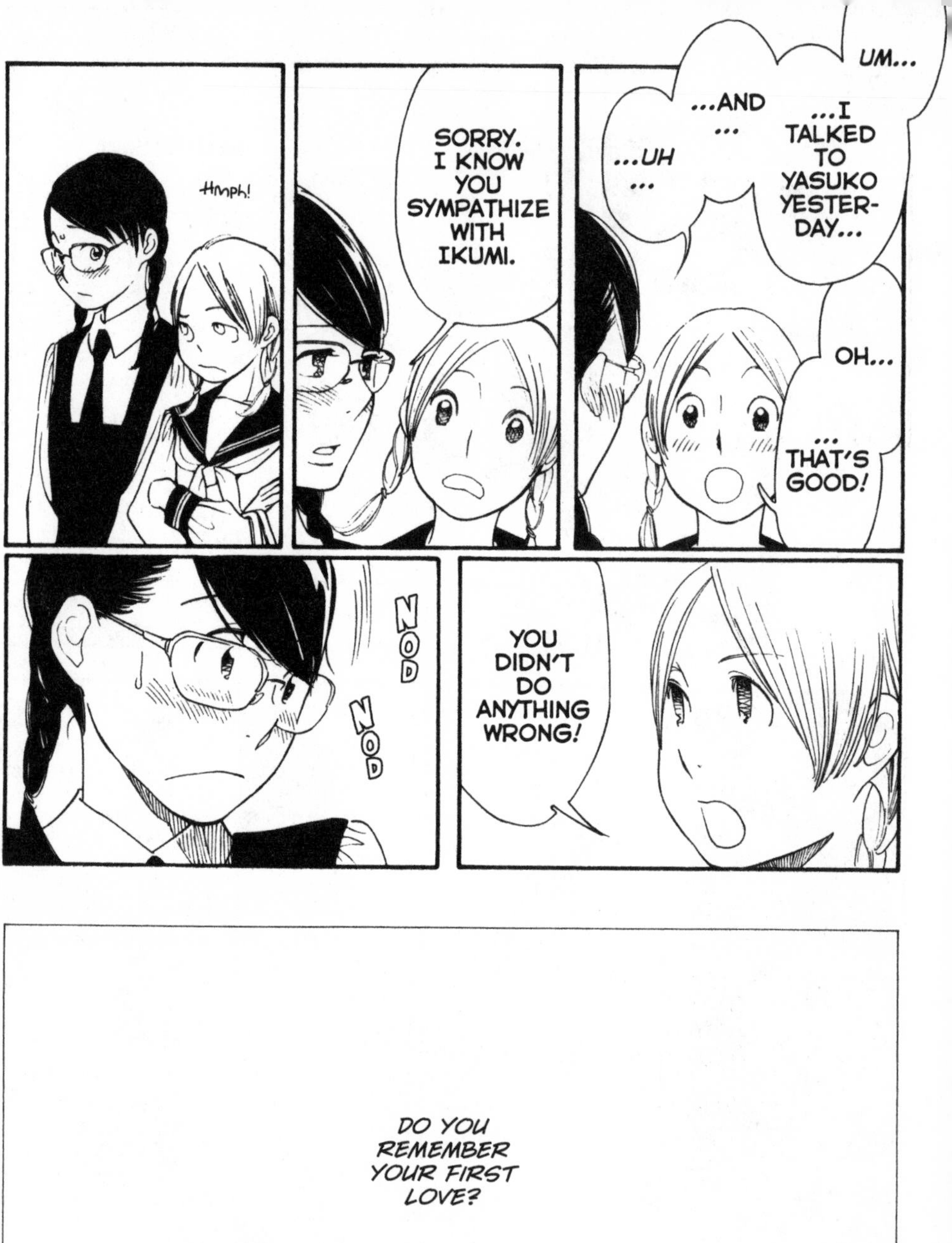
UM...
...I TALKED TO YASUKO YESTER-DAY...
...AND ...
...UH ...
OH...
... THAT'S GOOD!
SORRY. I KNOW YOU SYMPATHIZE WITH IKUMI.
Hmph!
YOU DIDN'T DO ANYTHING WRONG!
NOD
NOD
DO YOU REMEMBER YOUR FIRST LOVE?

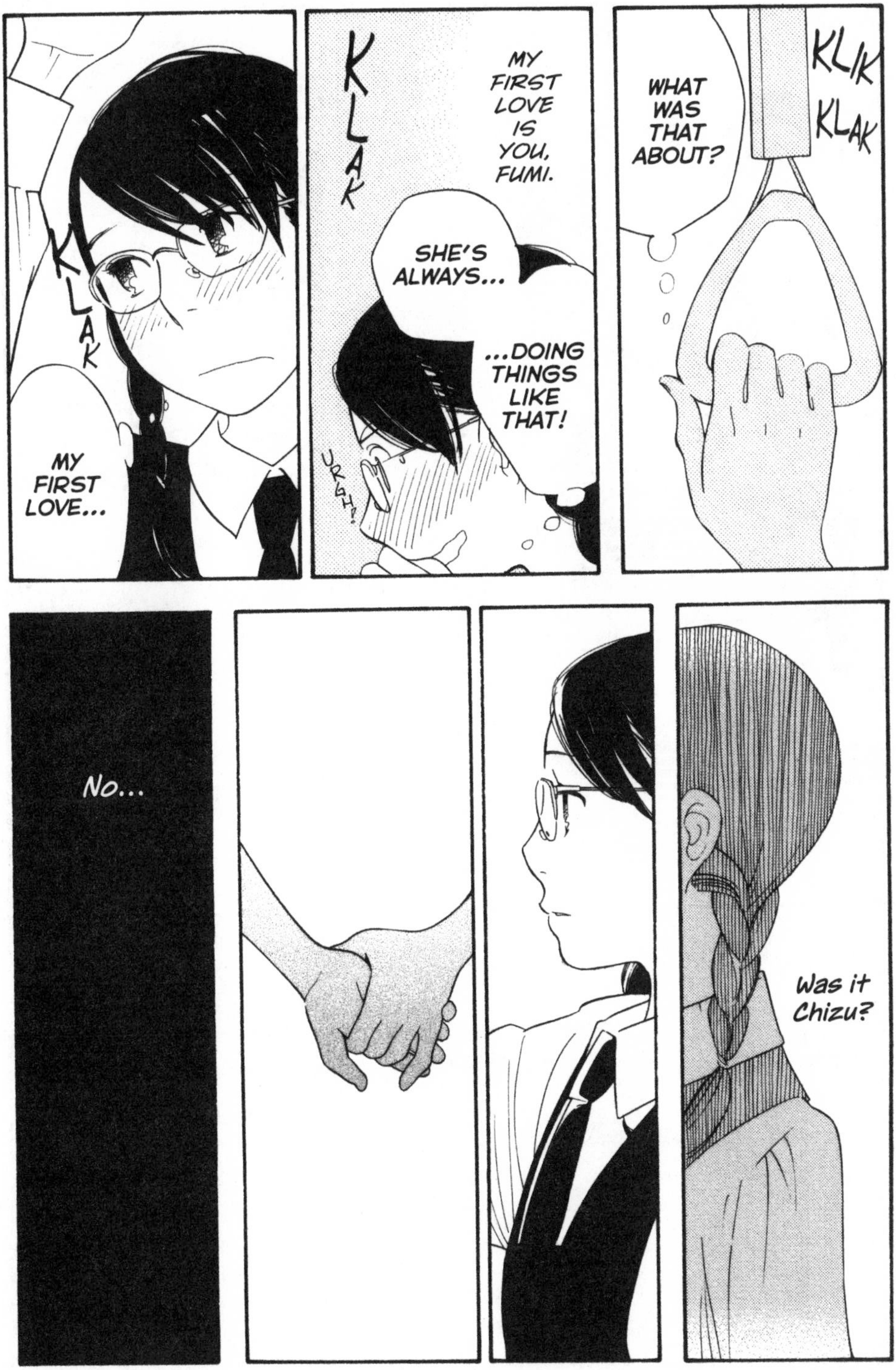
KLIK
KLAK
WHAT WAS THAT ABOUT?
KLAK
MY FIRST LOVE IS YOU, FUMI.
SHE'S ALWAYS...
...DOING THINGS LIKE THAT!
URGH!
KLLAK
MY FIRST LOVE...
Was it Chizu?
No...

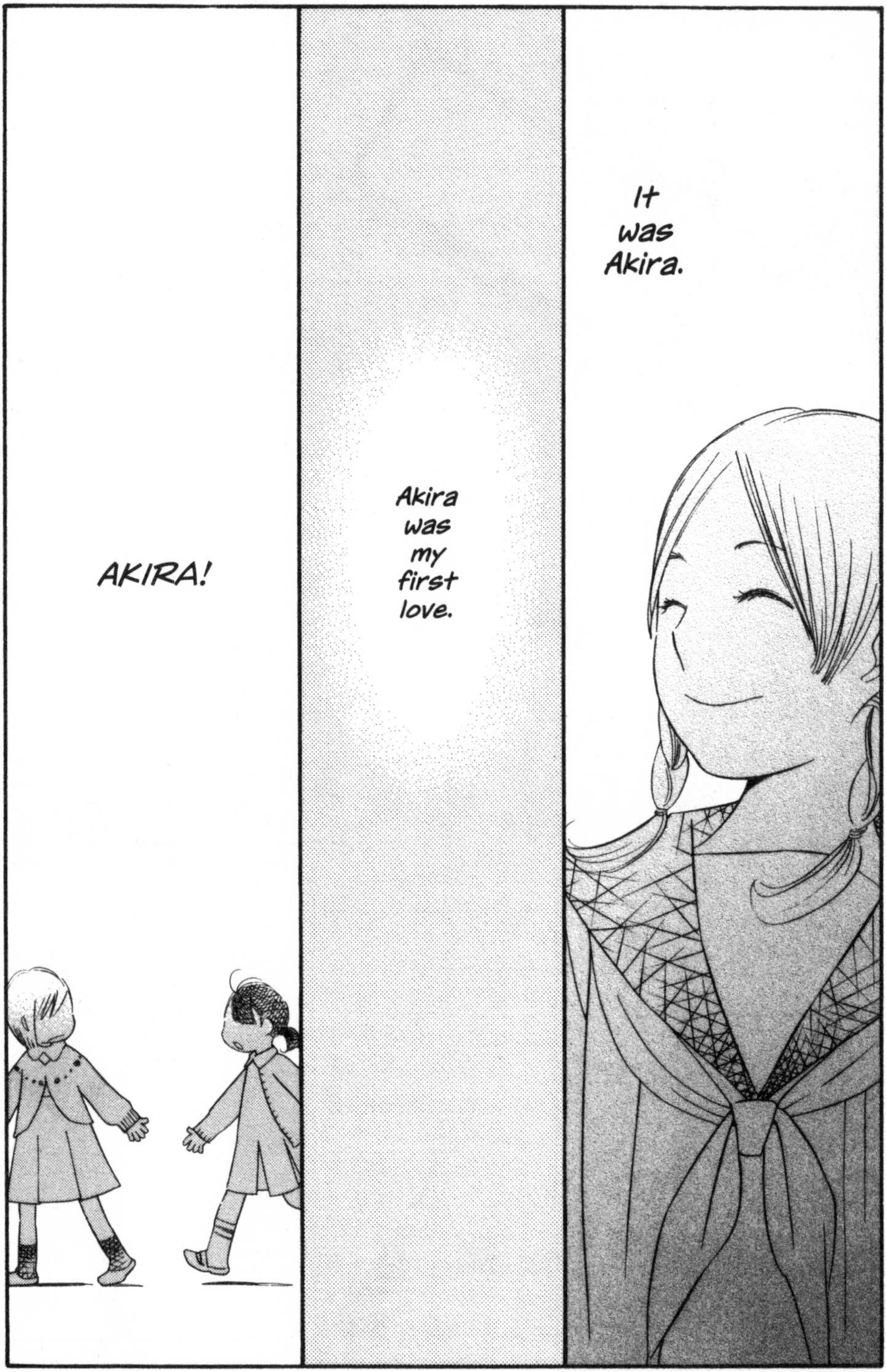
It was Akira.
Akira was my first love.
AKIRA!

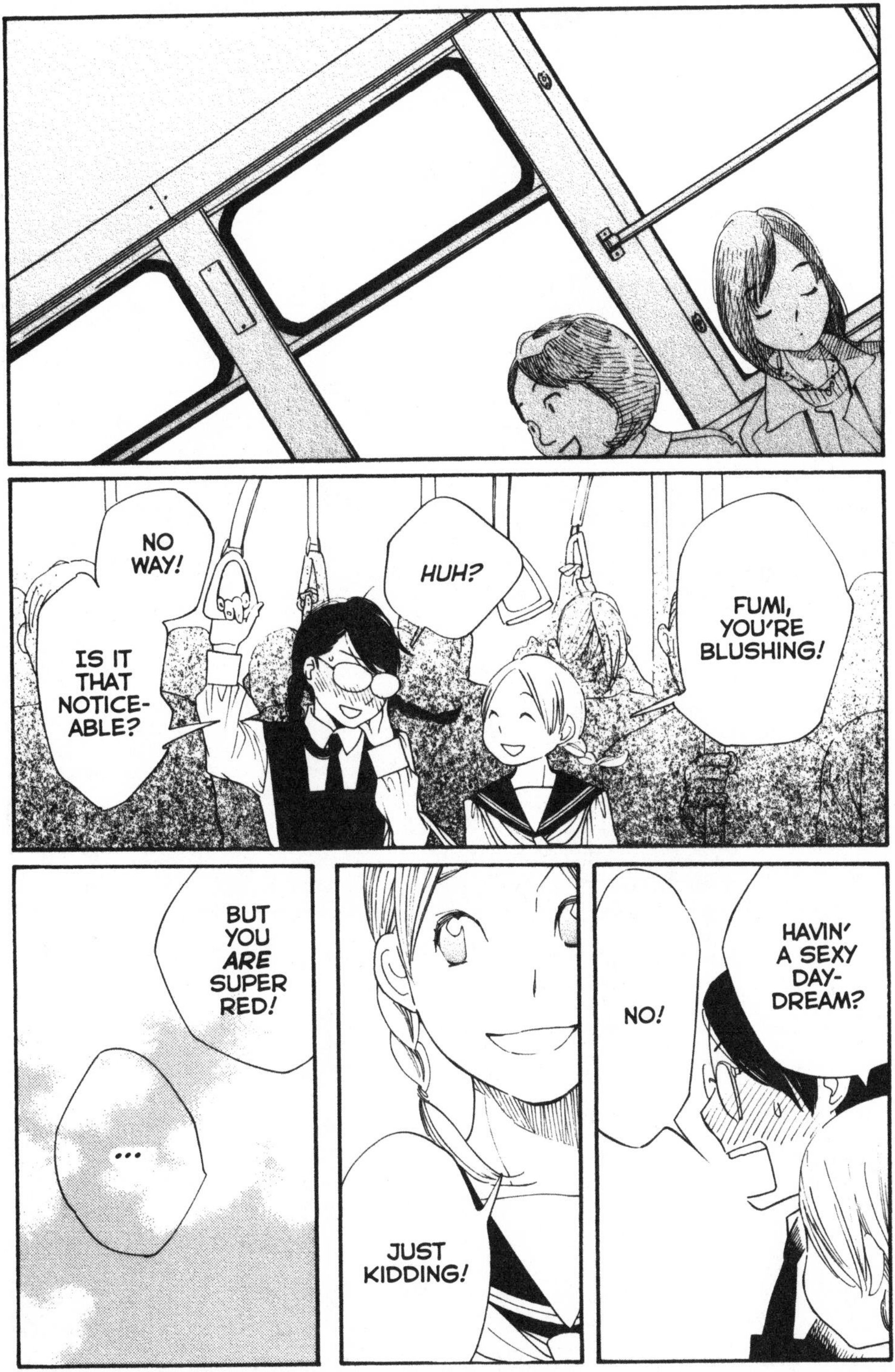
FUMI, YOU'RE BLUSHING!
HUH?
NO WAY!
IS IT THAT NOTICE-ABLE?
HAVIN' A SEXY DAY-DREAM?
NO!
JUST KIDDING!
BUT YOU *ARE* SUPER RED!
...

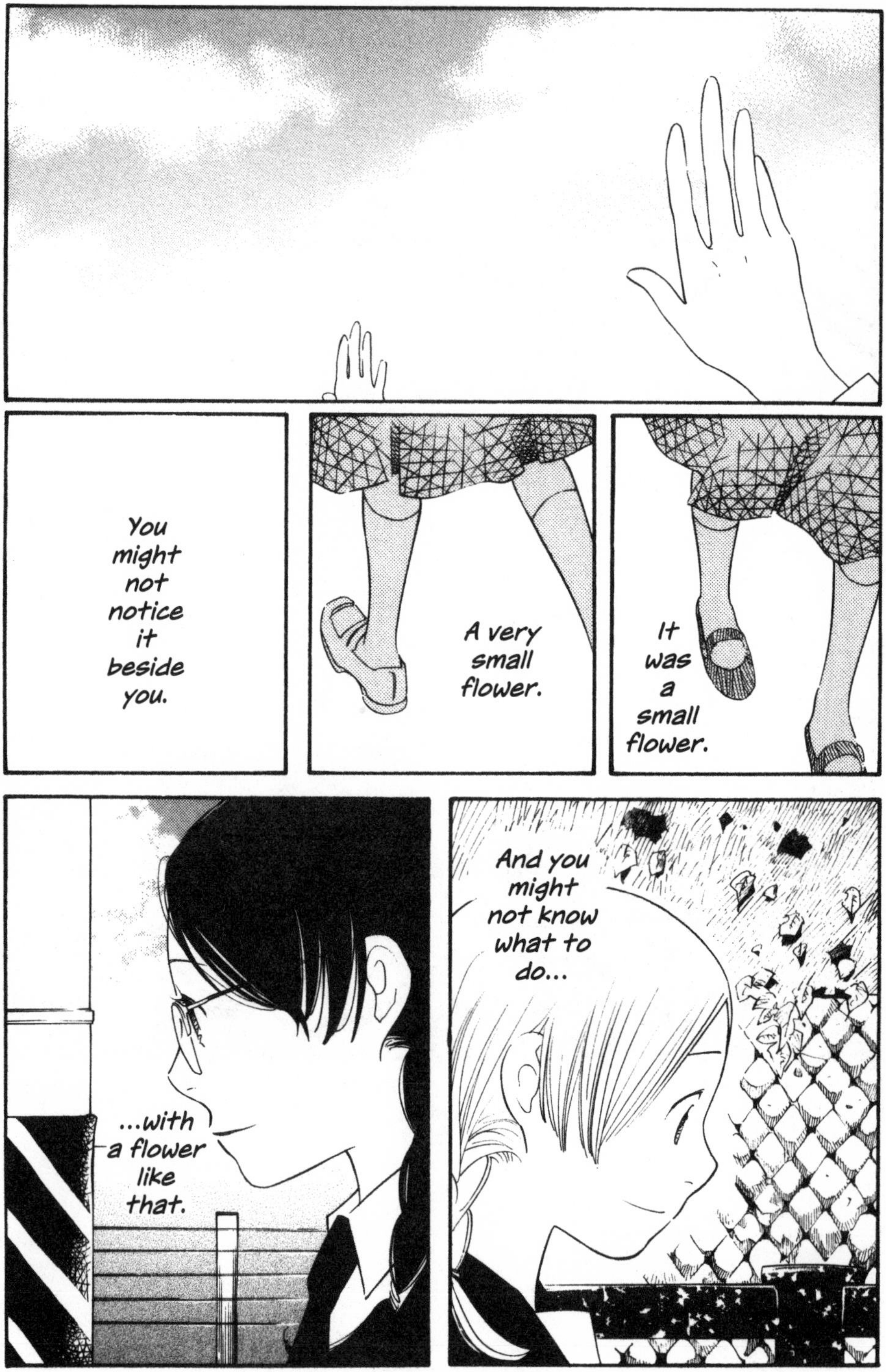
It was a small flower.
A very small flower.
You might not notice it beside you.
And you might not know what to do...
...with a flower like that.

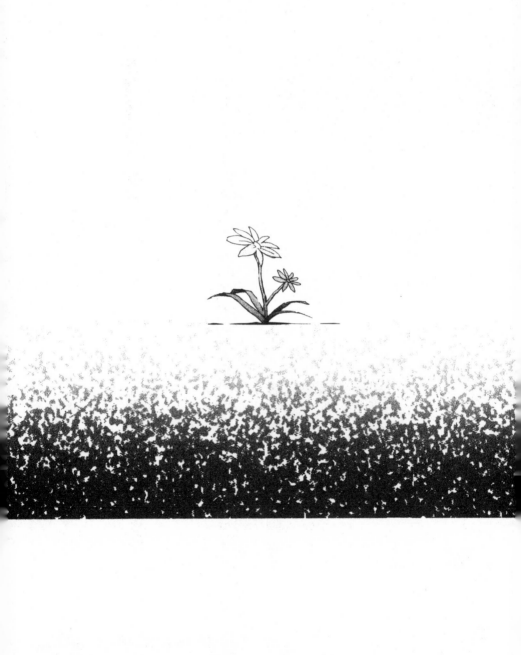

*Sweet* **Blue**
   *Flowers*

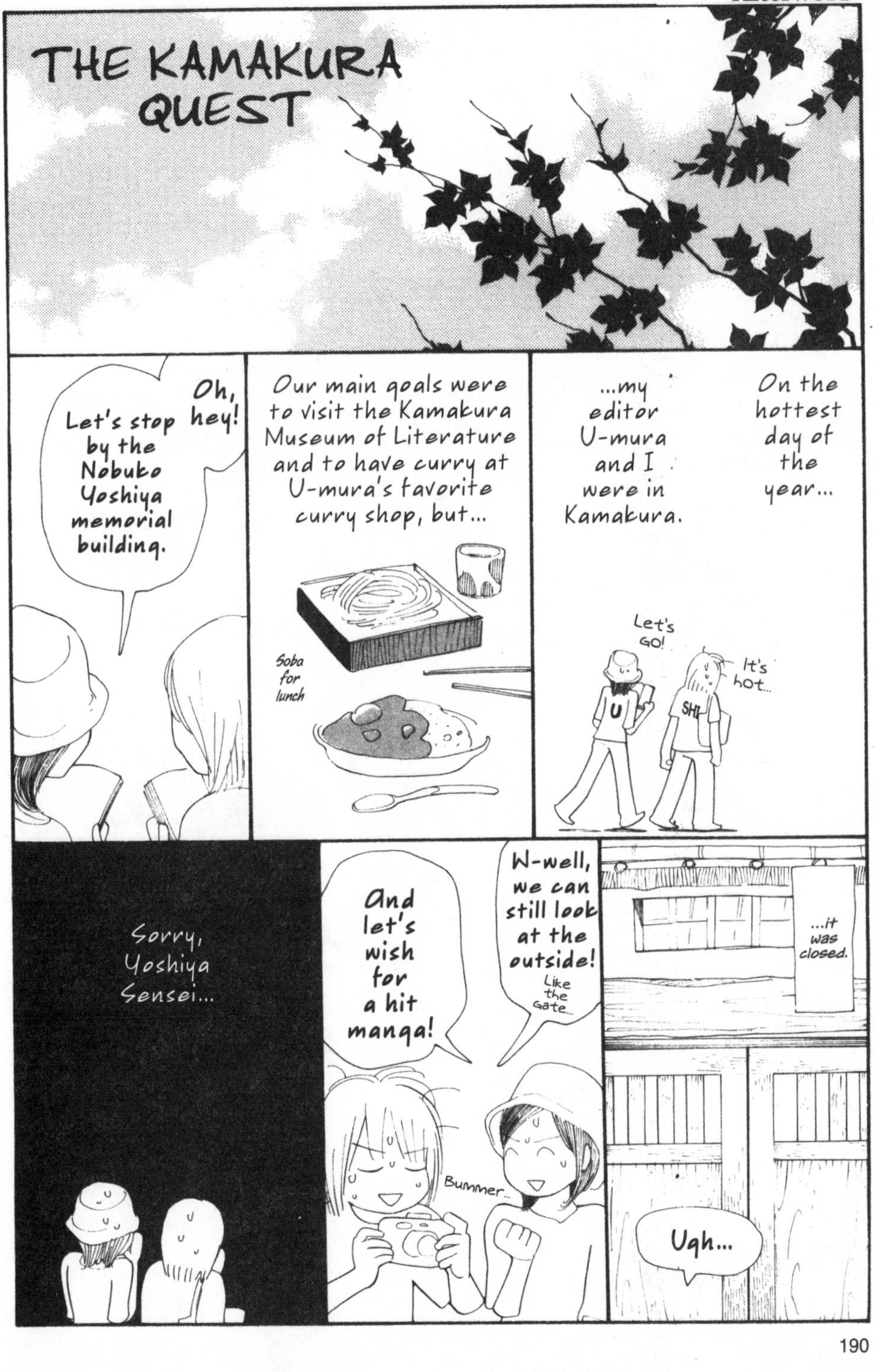
THE KAMAKURA QUEST
On the hottest day of the year...
...my editor U-mura and I were in Kamakura.
Let's GO!
It's hot...
Our main goals were to visit the Kamakura Museum of Literature and to have curry at U-mura's favorite curry shop, but...
Soba for lunch
Oh, hey!
Let's stop by the Nobuko Yoshiya memorial building.
...it was closed.
Ugh...
W-well, we can still look at the outside!
Like the Gate...
And let's wish for a hit manga!
Bummer...
Sorry, Yoshiya Sensei...

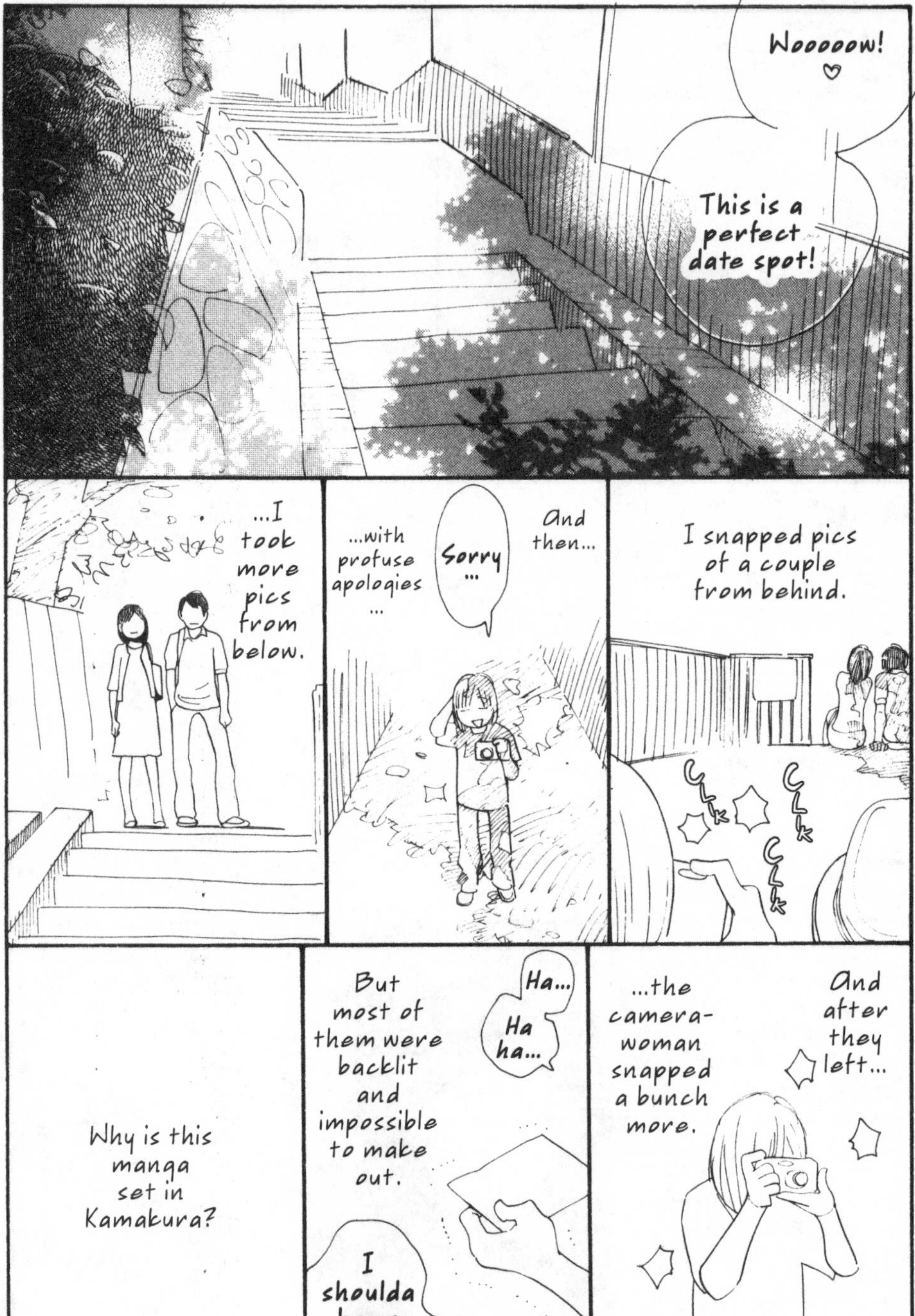
Wooooow! ♡
This is a perfect date spot!
I snapped pics of a couple from behind.
CLK
CLK
CLK
And then...
Sorry...
...with profuse apologies...
...I took more pics from below.
And after they left...
...the camera-woman snapped a bunch more.
Ha... Ha ha...
But most of them were backlit and impossible to make out.
I shoulda been more careful...
Why is this manga set in Kamakura?

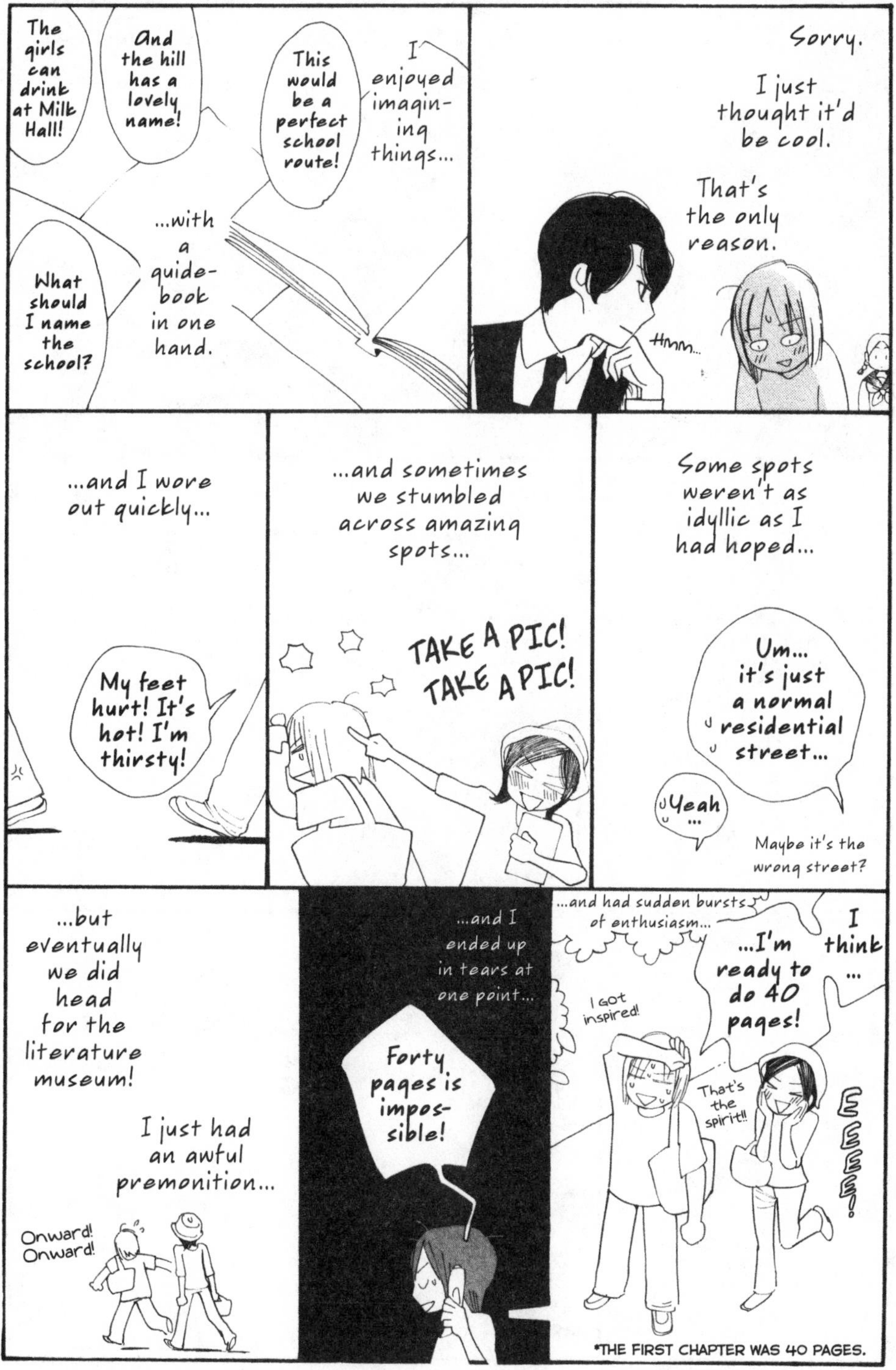
Sorry.
I just thought it'd be cool.
That's the only reason.
Hmm...
I enjoyed imagining things...
This would be a perfect school route!
And the hill has a lovely name!
The girls can drink at Milk Hall!
...with a guidebook in one hand.
What should I name the school?
Some spots weren't as idyllic as I had hoped...
Um... it's just a normal residential street...
Yeah...
Maybe it's the wrong street?
...and sometimes we stumbled across amazing spots...
TAKE A PIC! TAKE A PIC!
...and I wore out quickly...
My feet hurt! It's hot! I'm thirsty!
...and had sudden bursts of enthusiasm...
I think...
...I'm ready to do 40 pages!
I got inspired!
That's the spirit!!
EEEE!
*THE FIRST CHAPTER WAS 40 PAGES.
...and I ended up in tears at one point...
Forty pages is impossible!
...but eventually we did head for the literature museum!
I just had an awful premonition...
Onward! Onward!

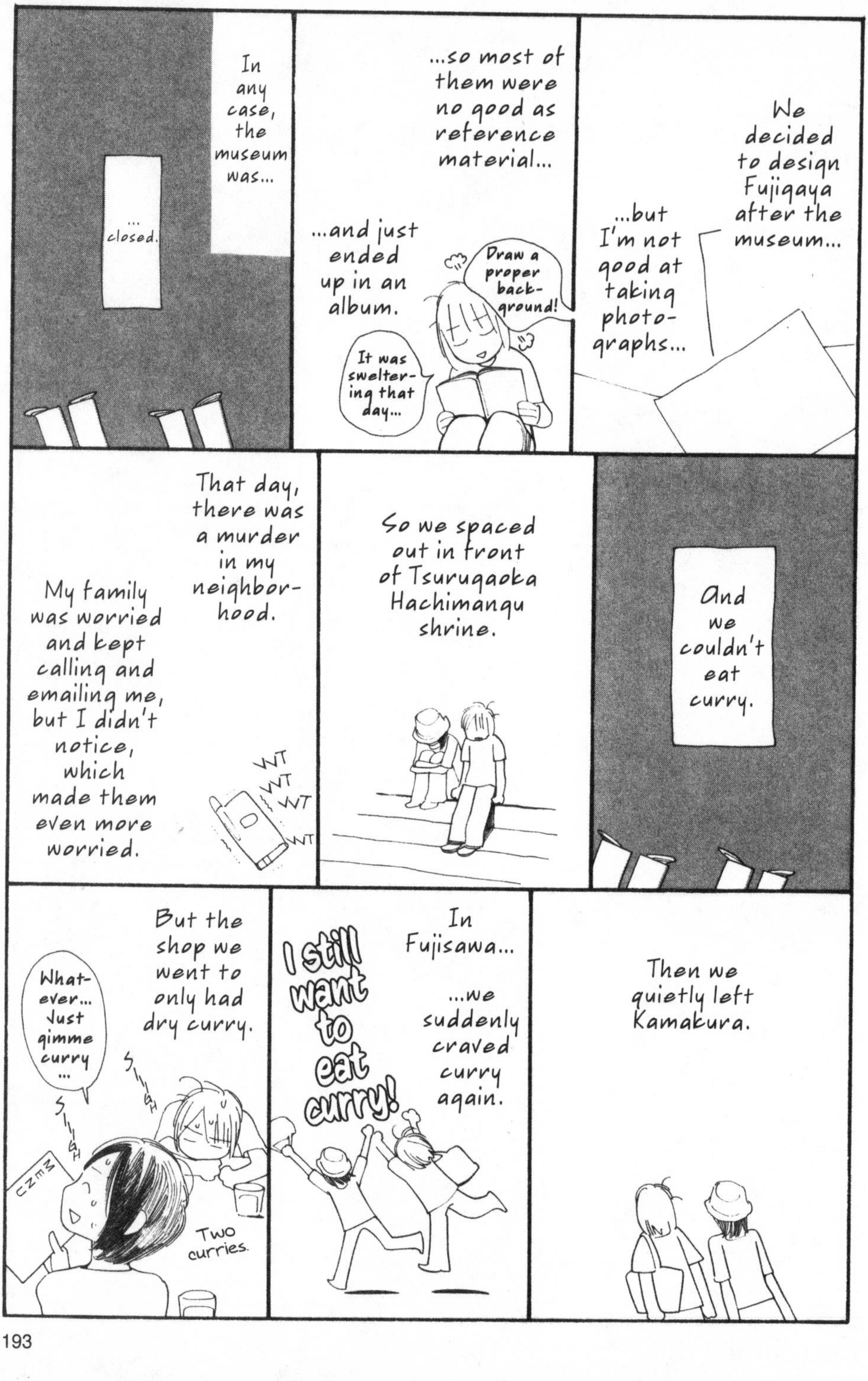
We decided to design Fujigaya after the museum...
...but I'm not good at taking photographs...
...so most of them were no good as reference material...
Draw a proper background!
...and just ended up in an album.
It was sweltering that day...
In any case, the museum was...
...closed.
And we couldn't eat curry.
So we spaced out in front of Tsurugaoka Hachimangu shrine.
That day, there was a murder in my neighborhood.
My family was worried and kept calling and emailing me, but I didn't notice, which made them even more worried.
VVT VVT VVT VVT
Then we quietly left Kamakura.
In Fujisawa...
...we suddenly craved curry again.
I still want to eat curry!
But the shop we went to only had dry curry.
Whatever... Just gimme curry...
SIIGH
SIIGH
Two curries.

*Sweet Blue Flowers*

# Sweet Blue Flowers

## Part Two

Story and Art by
Takako Shimura

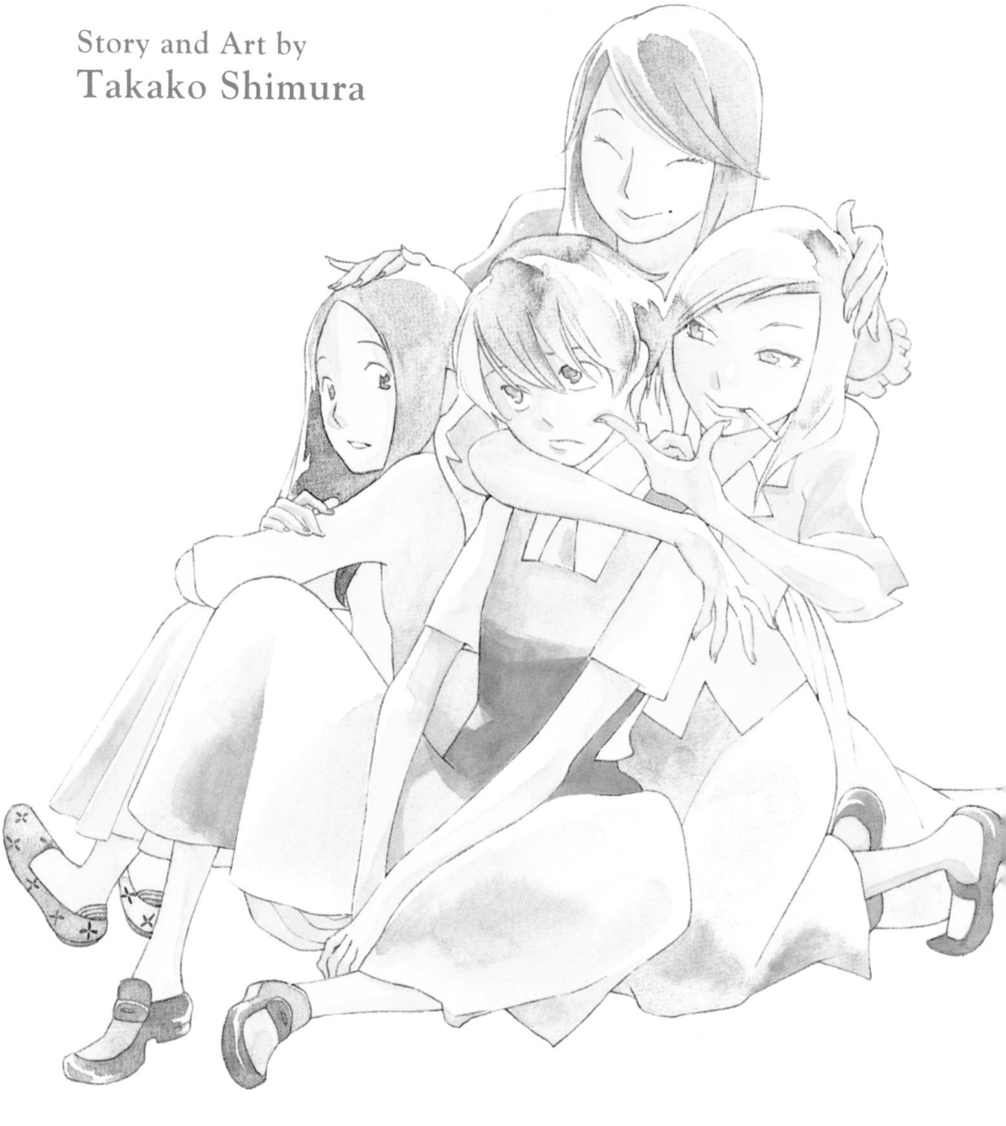

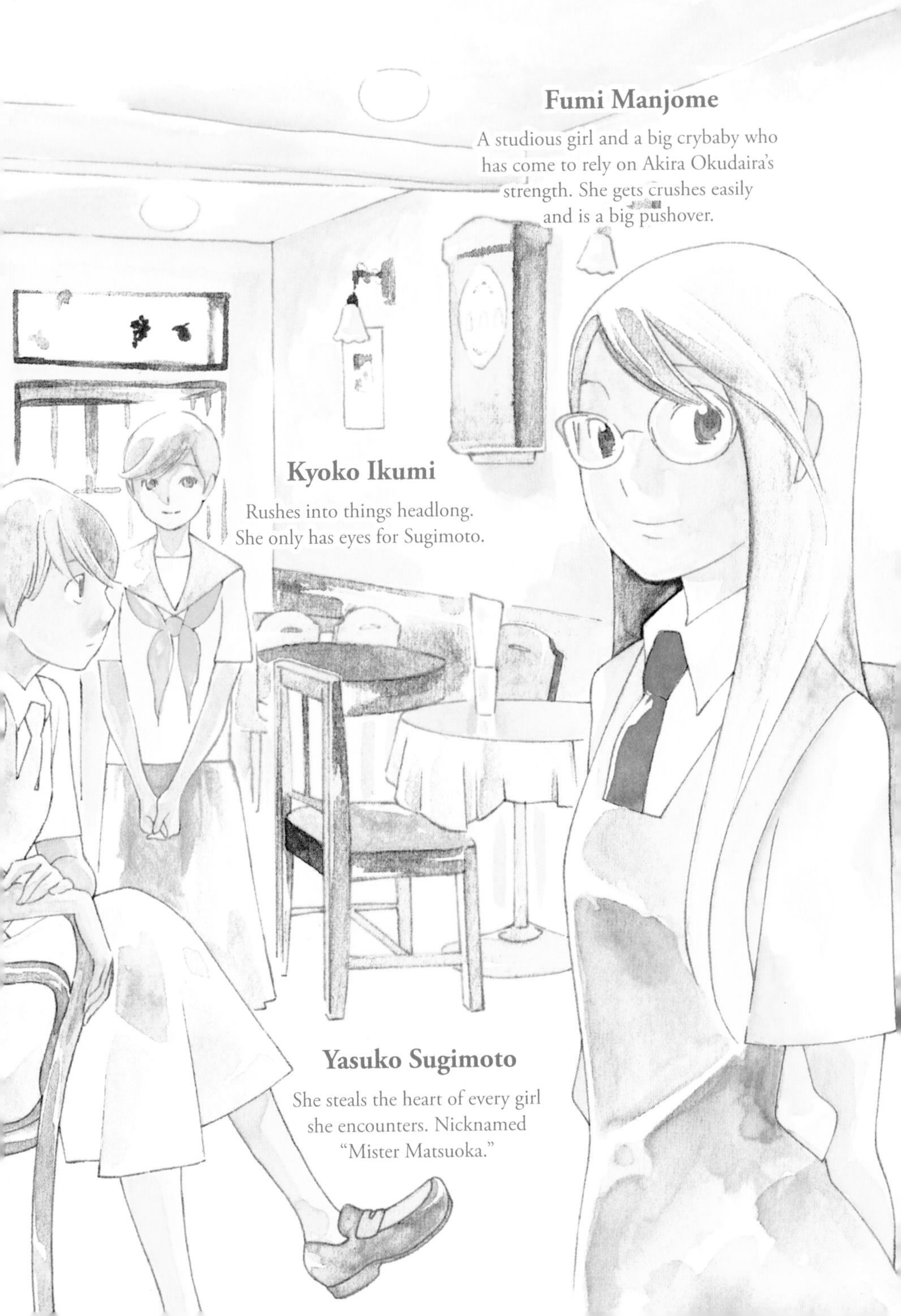
Fumi Manjome
A studious girl and a big crybaby who has come to rely on Akira Okudaira's strength. She gets crushes easily and is a big pushover.
Kyoko Ikumi
Rushes into things headlong. She only has eyes for Sugimoto.
Yasuko Sugimoto
She steals the heart of every girl she encounters. Nicknamed "Mister Matsuoka."

# Characters

## Akira Okudaira

A spirited and straightforward girl. She was a childhood friend of Fumi Manjome, and now they're close again. She is also Manjome's confidant and first love.

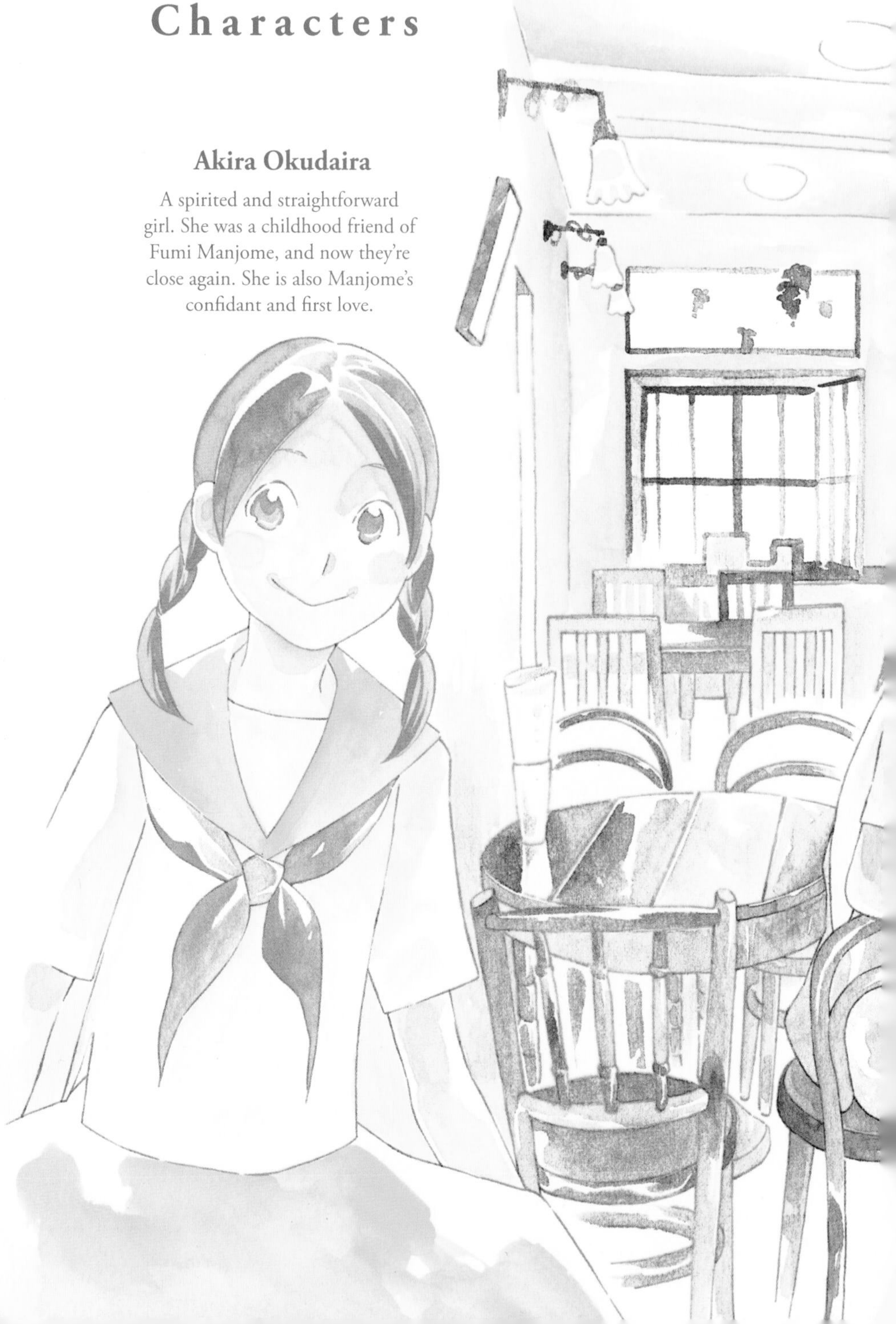

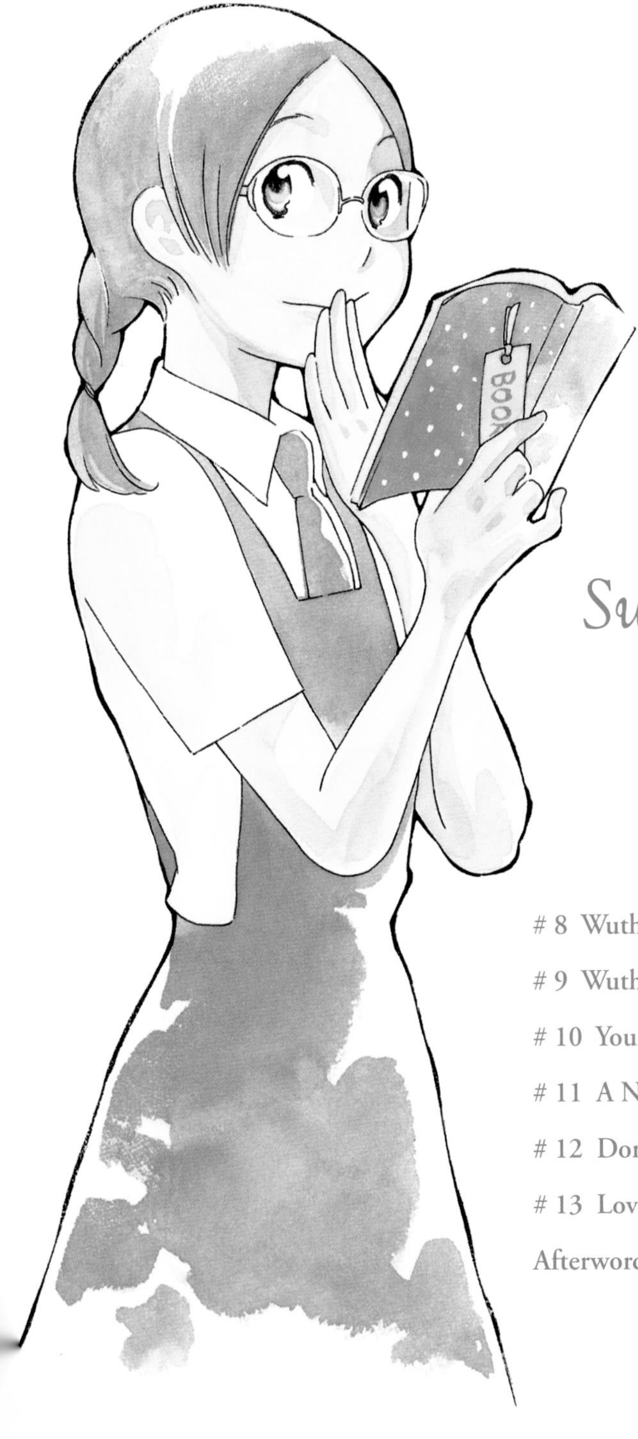

# Sweet Blue Flowers

## Part Two

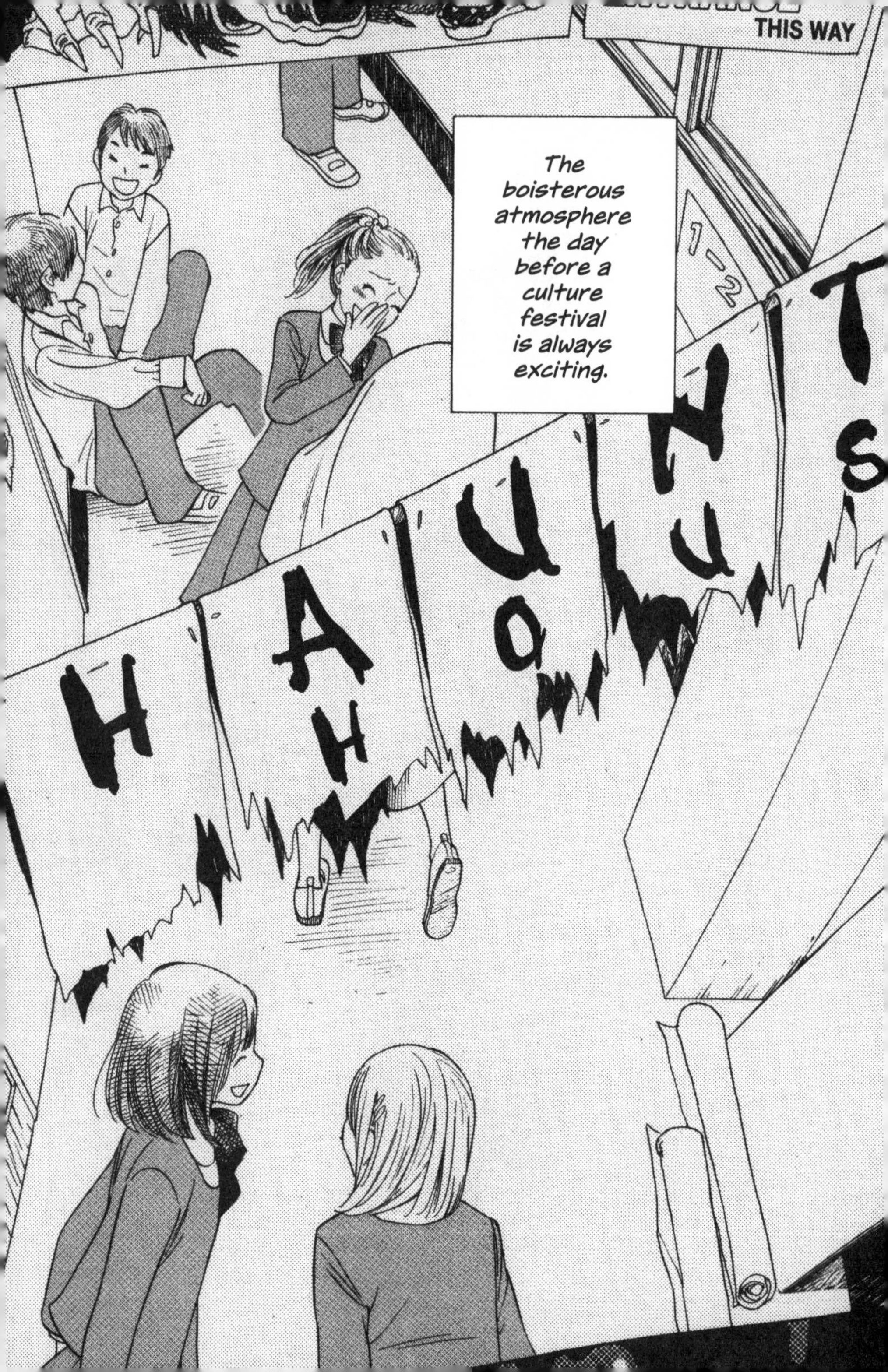

THIS WAY
The boisterous atmosphere the day before a culture festival is always exciting.
1-2
HAUNTS
HAUNTED HOUSE

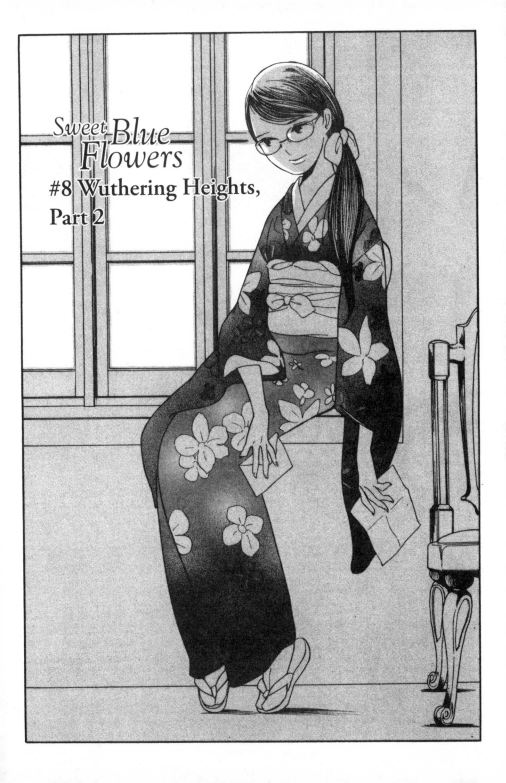

*Sweet* Blue
*Flowers*
#8 Wuthering Heights,
Part 2

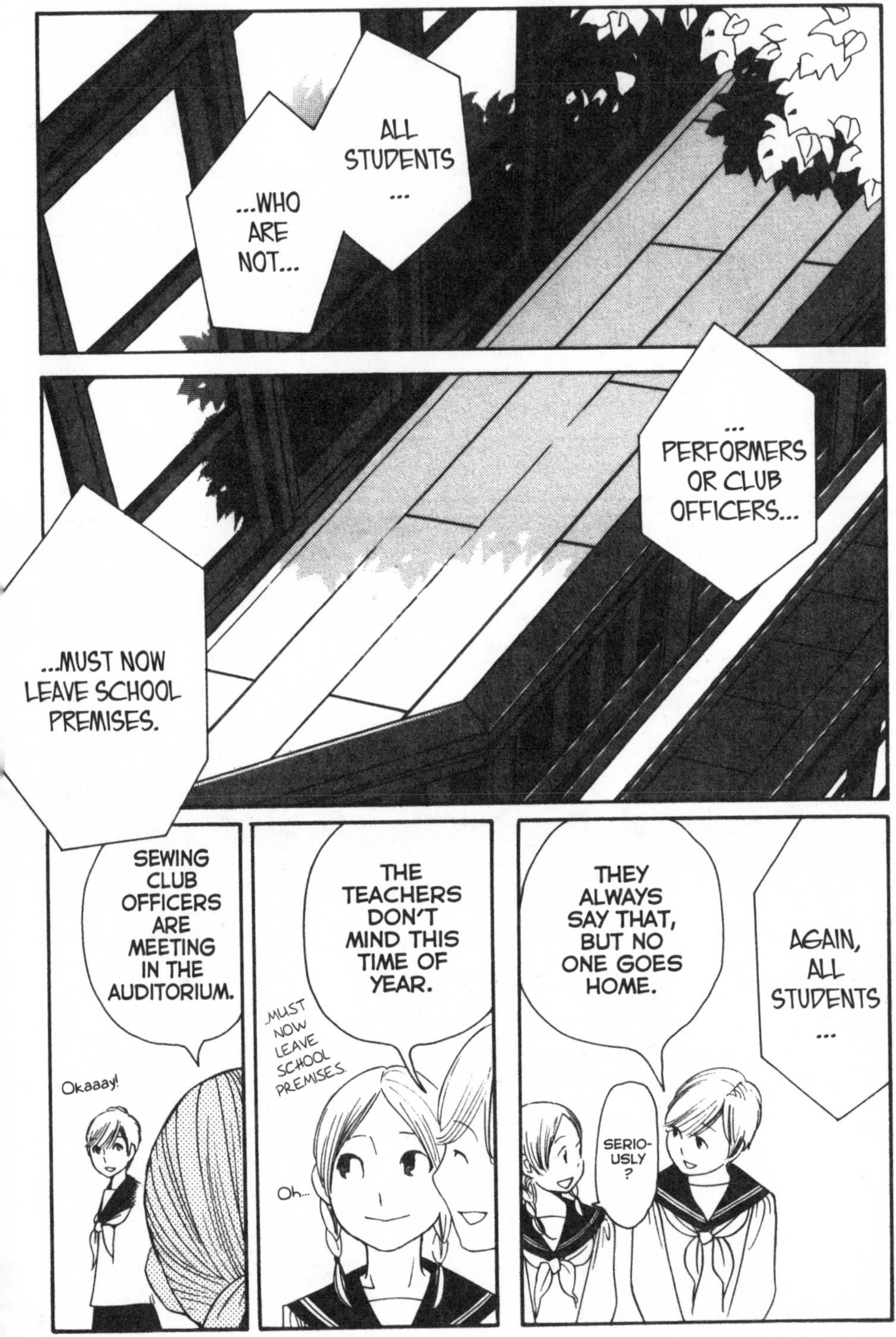
ALL STUDENTS ...
...WHO ARE NOT...
... PERFORMERS OR CLUB OFFICERS...
...MUST NOW LEAVE SCHOOL PREMISES.
AGAIN, ALL STUDENTS ...
THEY ALWAYS SAY THAT, BUT NO ONE GOES HOME.
SERIO-USLY?
...MUST NOW LEAVE SCHOOL PREMISES.
THE TEACHERS DON'T MIND THIS TIME OF YEAR.
Oh...
SEWING CLUB OFFICERS ARE MEETING IN THE AUDITORIUM.
Okaaay!

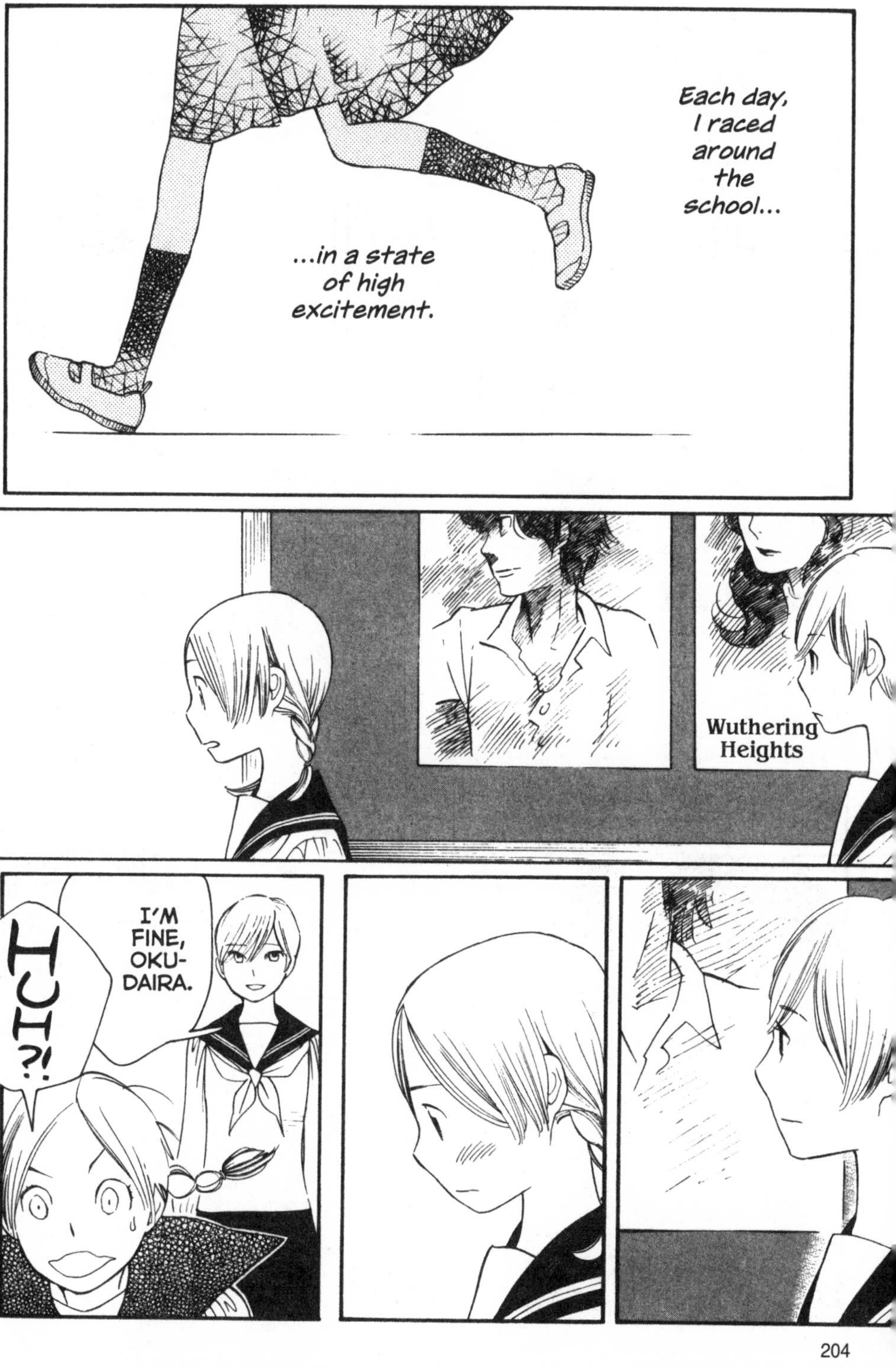
Each day, I raced around the school...
...in a state of high excitement.
Wuthering Heights
I'M FINE, OKU-DAIRA.
HUH?!

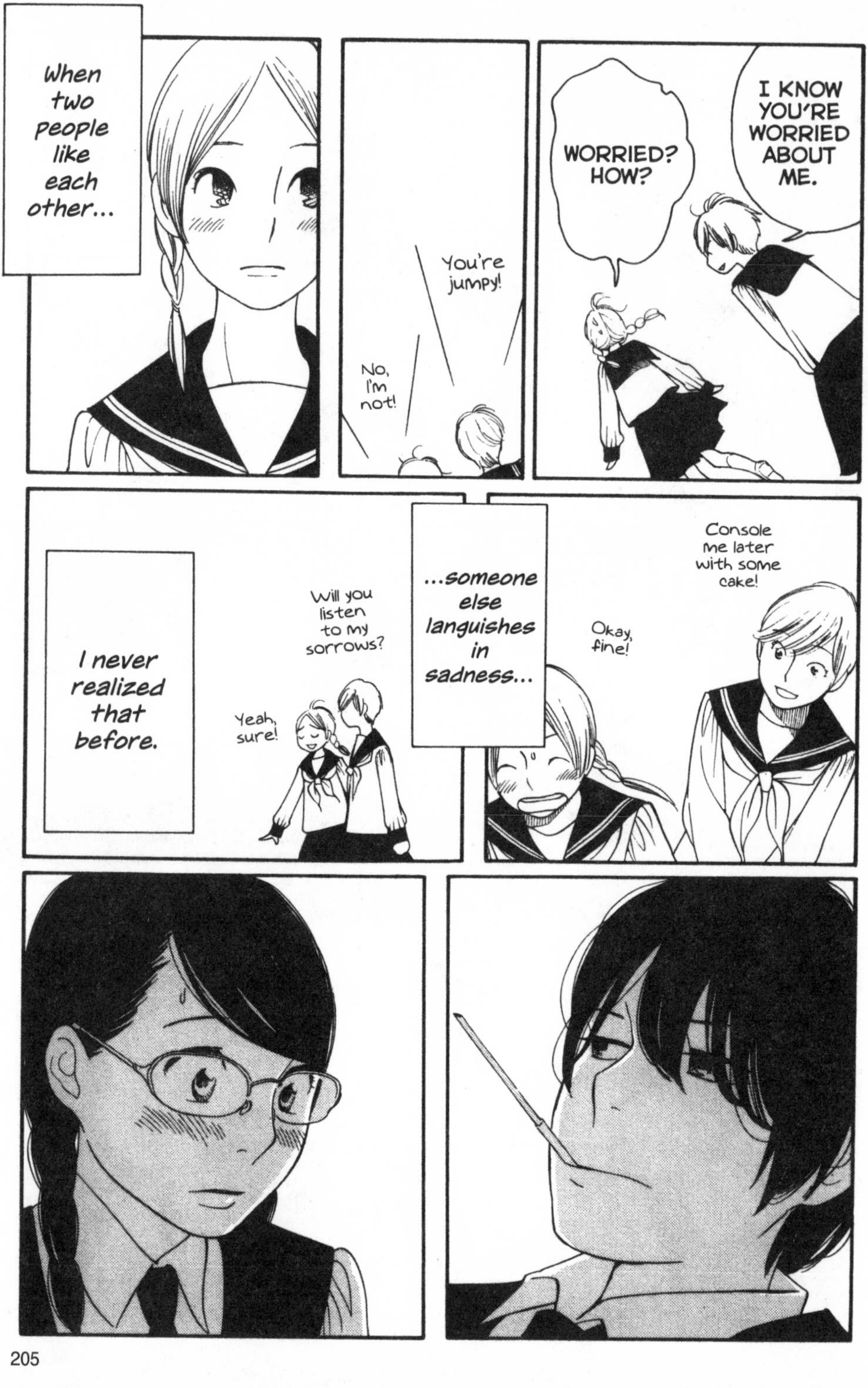
I KNOW YOU'RE WORRIED ABOUT ME.
WORRIED? HOW?
You're jumpy!
No, I'm not!
When two people like each other...
Console me later with some cake!
...someone else languishes in sadness...
Okay, fine!
Will you listen to my sorrows?
Yeah, sure!
I never realized that before.

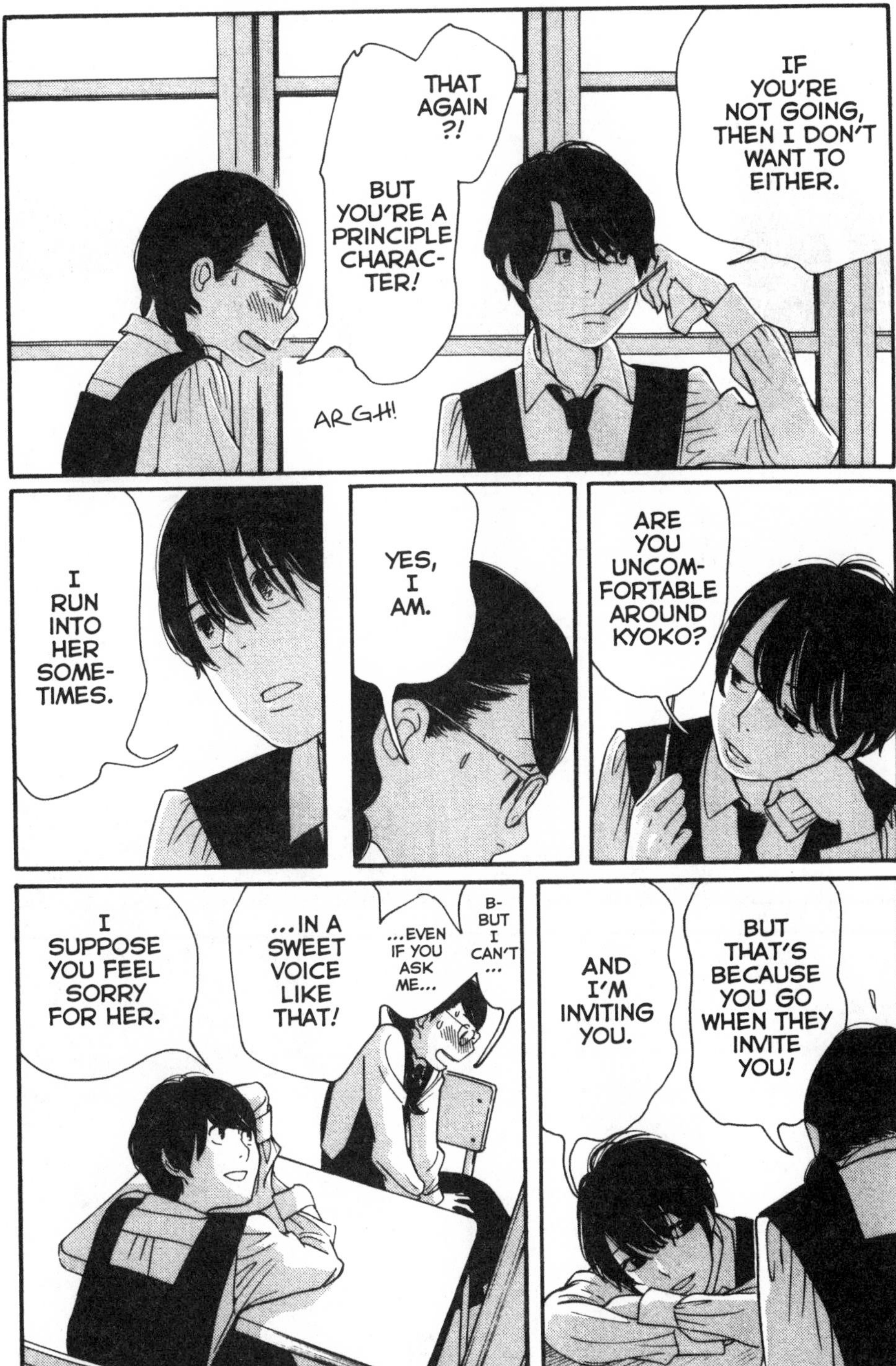
IF YOU'RE NOT GOING, THEN I DON'T WANT TO EITHER.
THAT AGAIN ?!
BUT YOU'RE A PRINCIPLE CHARAC- TER!
ARGH!
ARE YOU UNCOM- FORTABLE AROUND KYOKO?
YES, I AM.
I RUN INTO HER SOME- TIMES.
BUT THAT'S BECAUSE YOU GO WHEN THEY INVITE YOU!
AND I'M INVITING YOU.
B- BUT I CAN'T ...
...EVEN IF YOU ASK ME...
...IN A SWEET VOICE LIKE THAT!
I SUPPOSE YOU FEEL SORRY FOR HER.

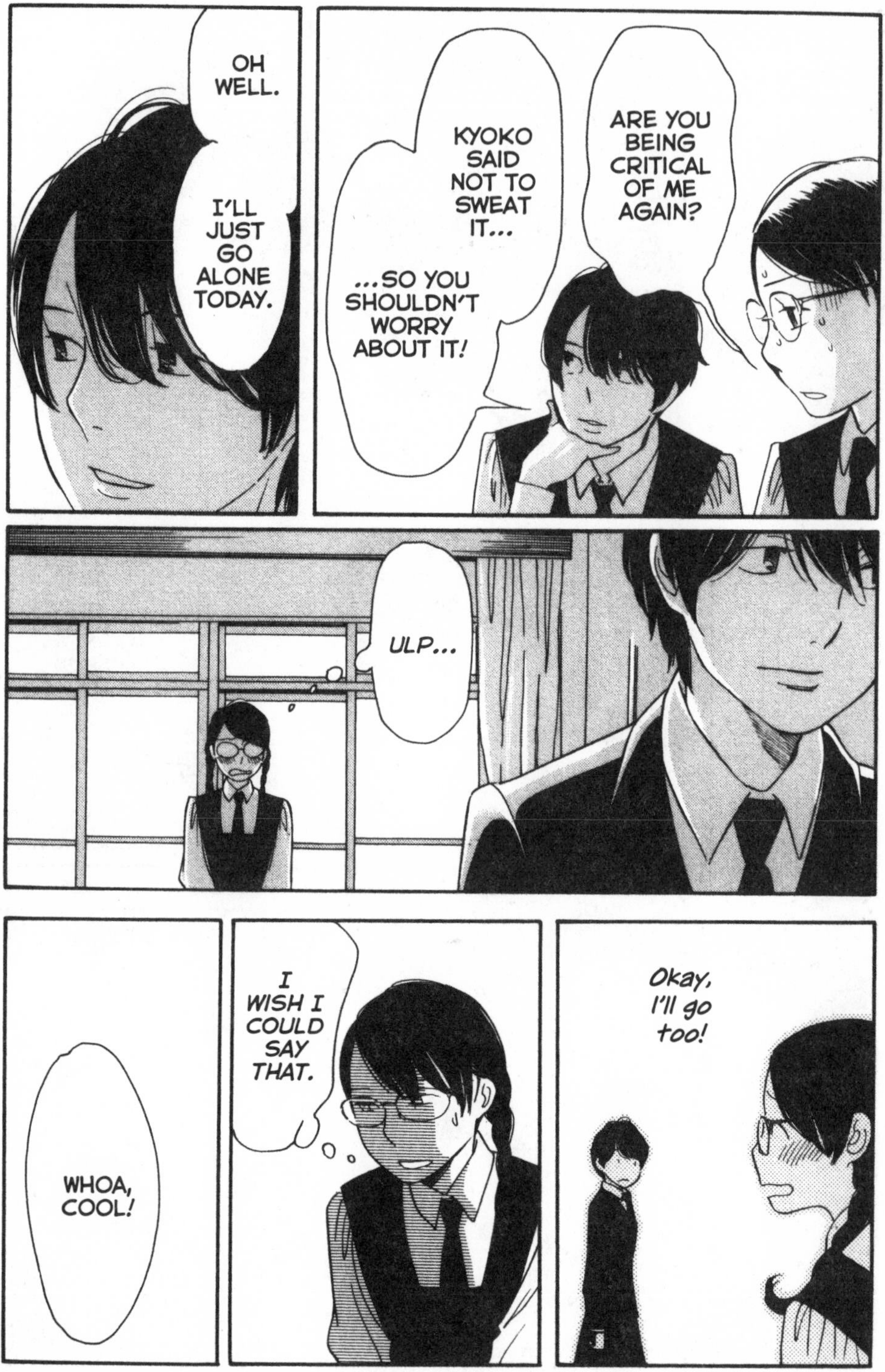
ARE YOU BEING CRITICAL OF ME AGAIN?
KYOKO SAID NOT TO SWEAT IT...
...SO YOU SHOULDN'T WORRY ABOUT IT!
OH WELL.
I'LL JUST GO ALONE TODAY.
ULP...
Okay, I'll go too!
I WISH I COULD SAY THAT.
WHOA, COOL!

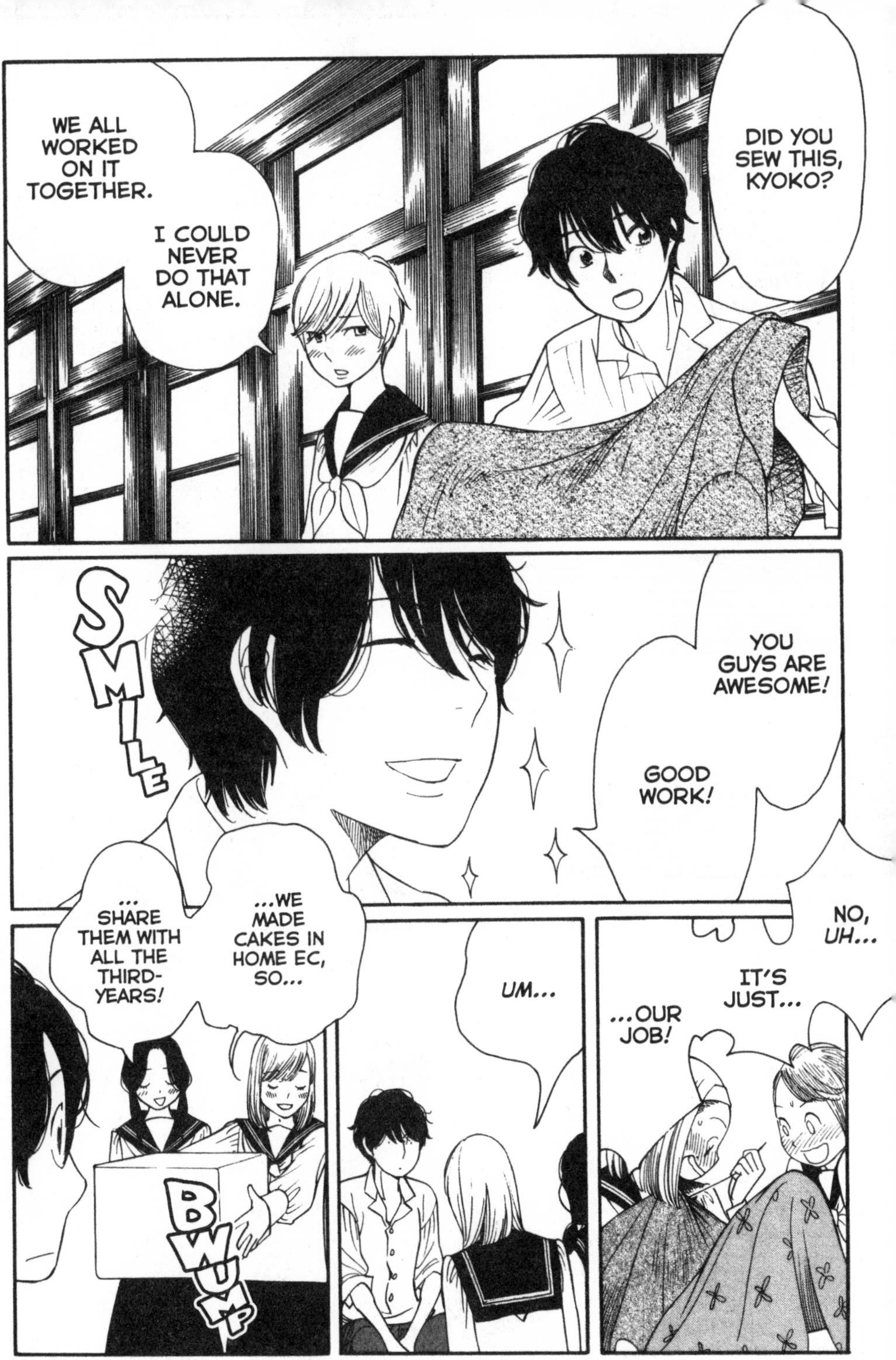
DID YOU SEW THIS, KYOKO?
WE ALL WORKED ON IT TOGETHER.
I COULD NEVER DO THAT ALONE.
YOU GUYS ARE AWESOME!
GOOD WORK!
SMILE
NO, UH...
IT'S JUST...
...OUR JOB!
UM...
...WE MADE CAKES IN HOME EC, SO...
...SHARE THEM WITH ALL THE THIRD-YEARS!
BWUMP

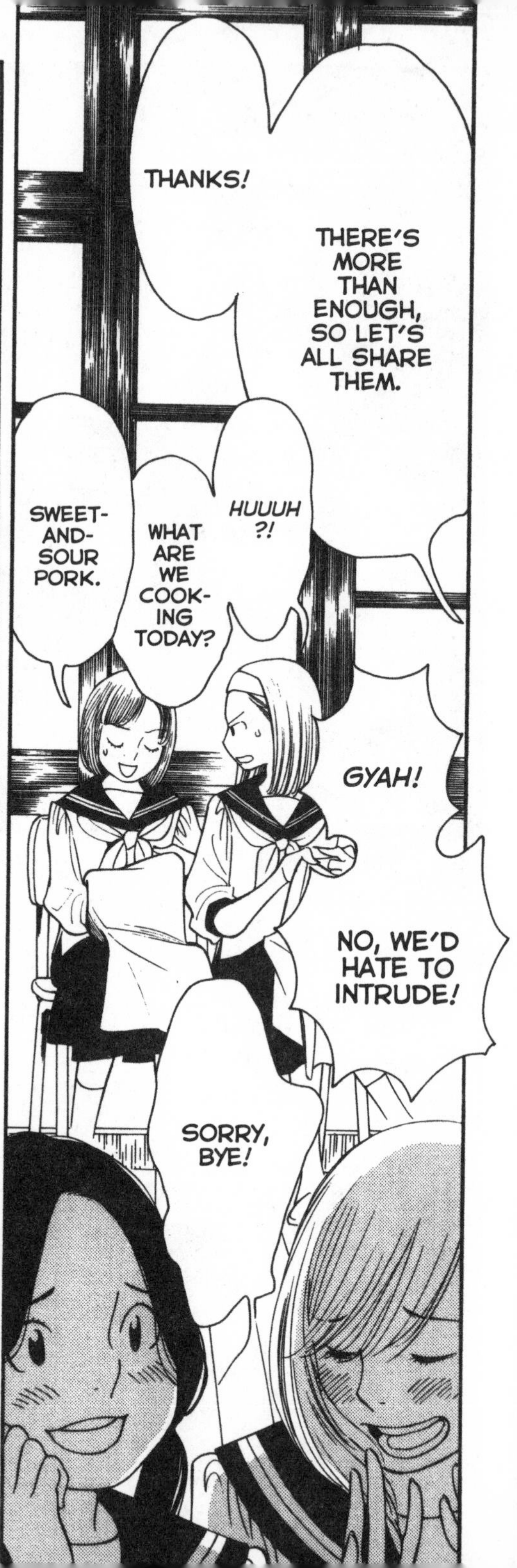
THANKS!
THERE'S MORE THAN ENOUGH, SO LET'S ALL SHARE THEM.
HUUUH?!
WHAT ARE WE COOKING TODAY?
SWEET-AND-SOUR PORK.
GYAH!
NO, WE'D HATE TO INTRUDE!
SORRY, BYE!

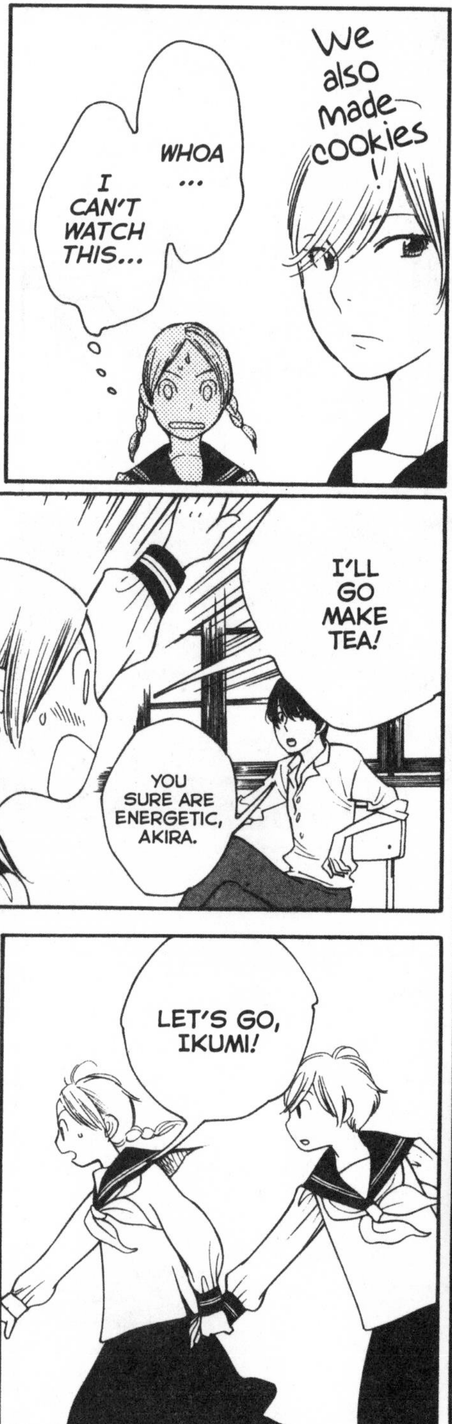
We also made cookies!
WHOA ...
I CAN'T WATCH THIS...
I'LL GO MAKE TEA!
YOU SURE ARE ENERGETIC, AKIRA.
LET'S GO, IKUMI!

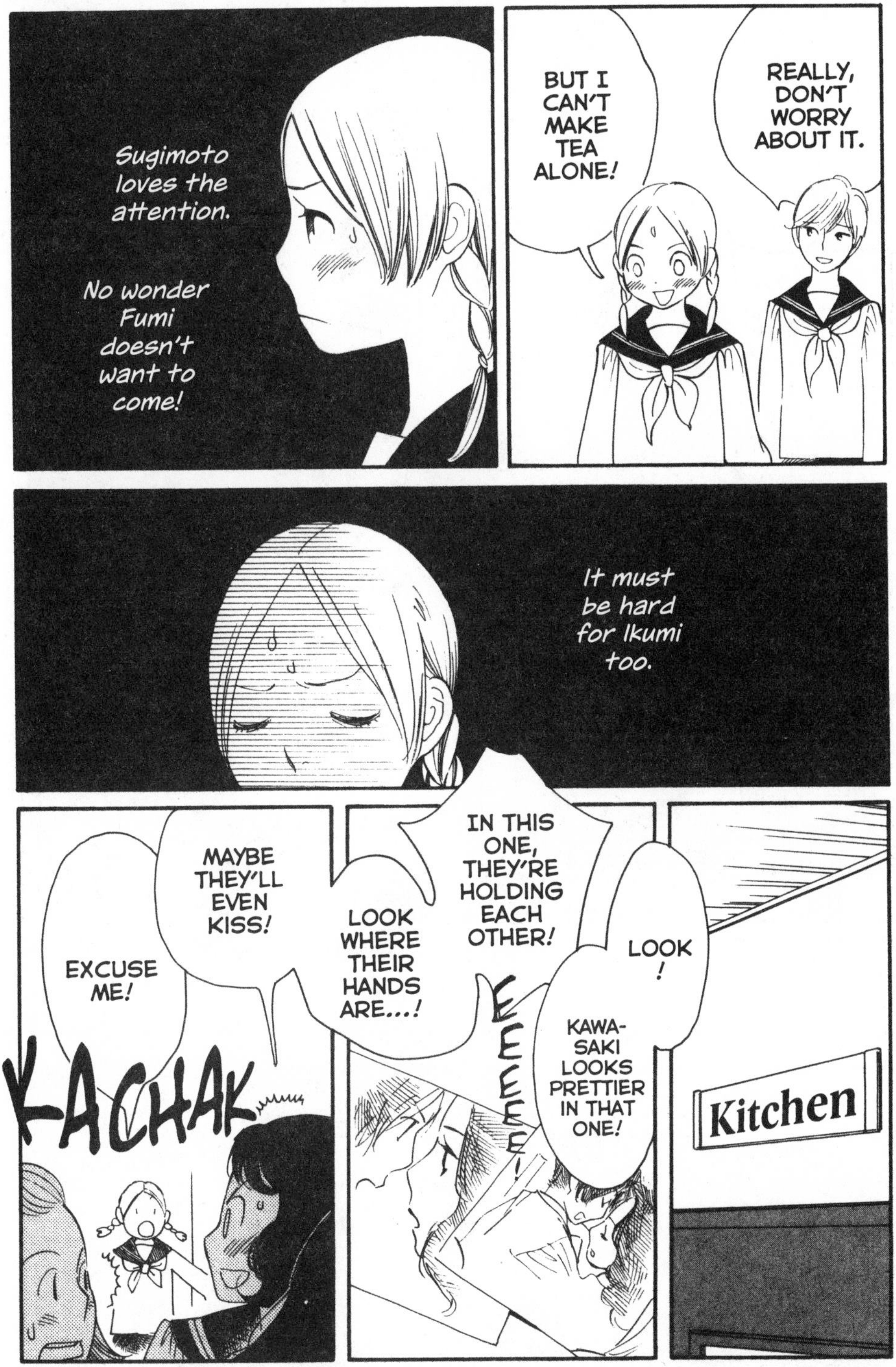
REALLY, DON'T WORRY ABOUT IT.
BUT I CAN'T MAKE TEA ALONE!
Sugimoto loves the attention.
No wonder Fumi doesn't want to come!
It must be hard for Ikumi too.
Kitchen
LOOK!
KAWASAKI LOOKS PRETTIER IN THAT ONE!
IN THIS ONE, THEY'RE HOLDING EACH OTHER!
LOOK WHERE THEIR HANDS ARE...!
EEEEEE!
MAYBE THEY'LL EVEN KISS!
EXCUSE ME!
KACHAK

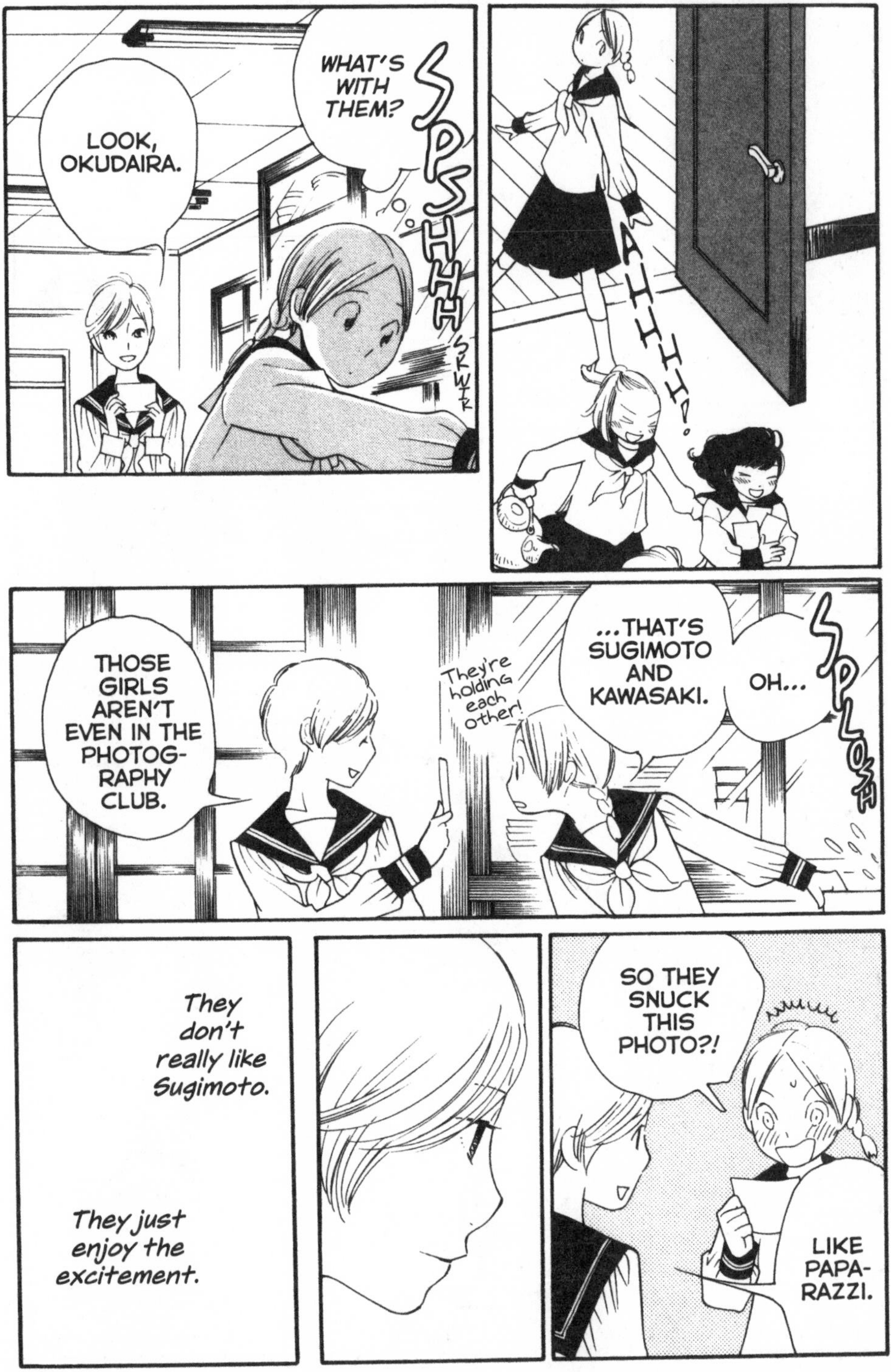
AHHHHHH!
WHAT'S WITH THEM?
SPSHHHH
SKWIK
LOOK, OKUDAIRA.
SPLOOSH
OH...
...THAT'S SUGIMOTO AND KAWASAKI.
They're holding each other!
THOSE GIRLS AREN'T EVEN IN THE PHOTOG-RAPHY CLUB.
SO THEY SNUCK THIS PHOTO?!
LIKE PAPA-RAZZI.
They don't really like Sugimoto.
They just enjoy the excitement.

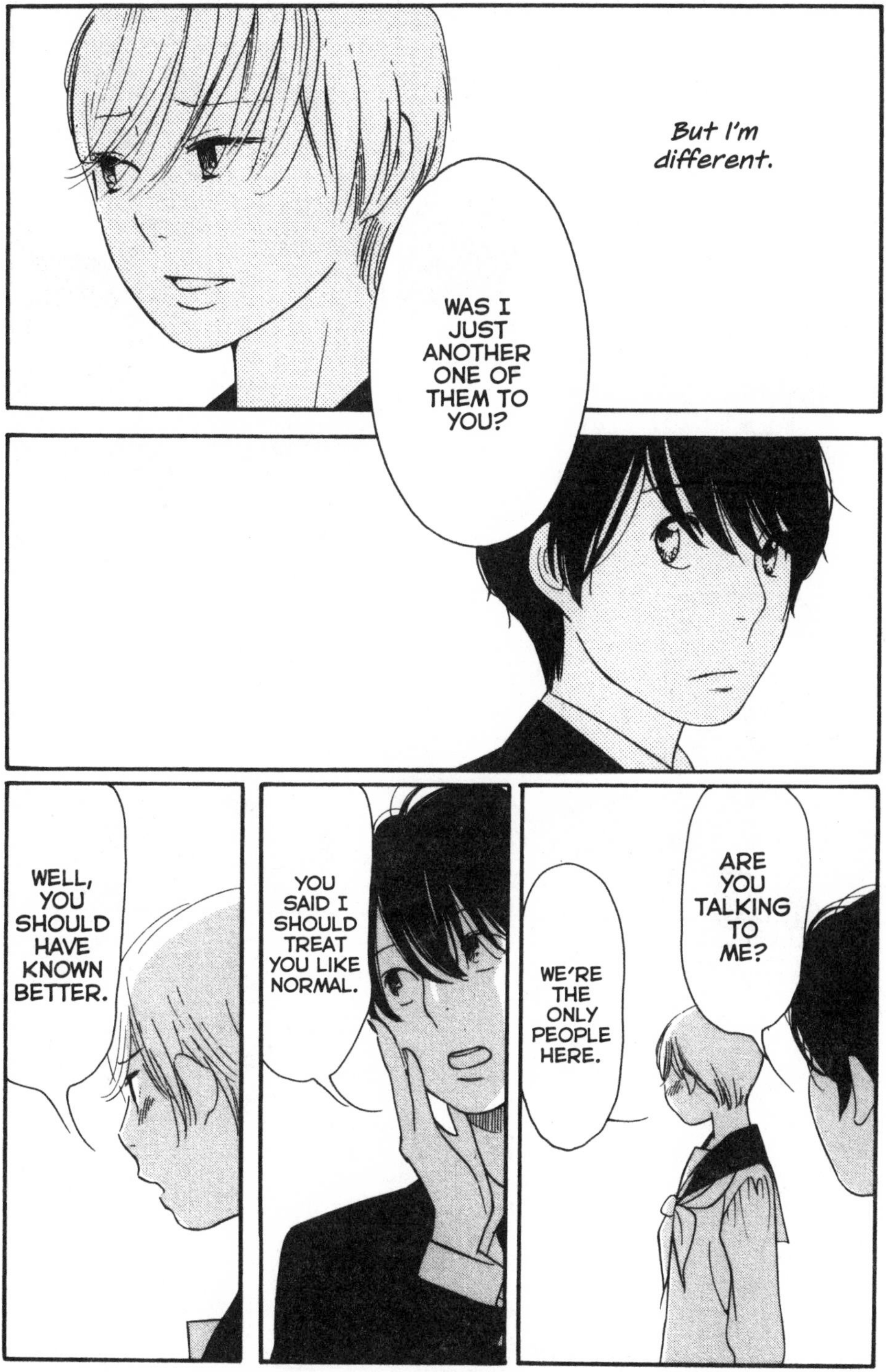
But I'm different.
WAS I JUST ANOTHER ONE OF THEM TO YOU?
ARE YOU TALKING TO ME?
WE'RE THE ONLY PEOPLE HERE.
YOU SAID I SHOULD TREAT YOU LIKE NORMAL.
WELL, YOU SHOULD HAVE KNOWN BETTER.

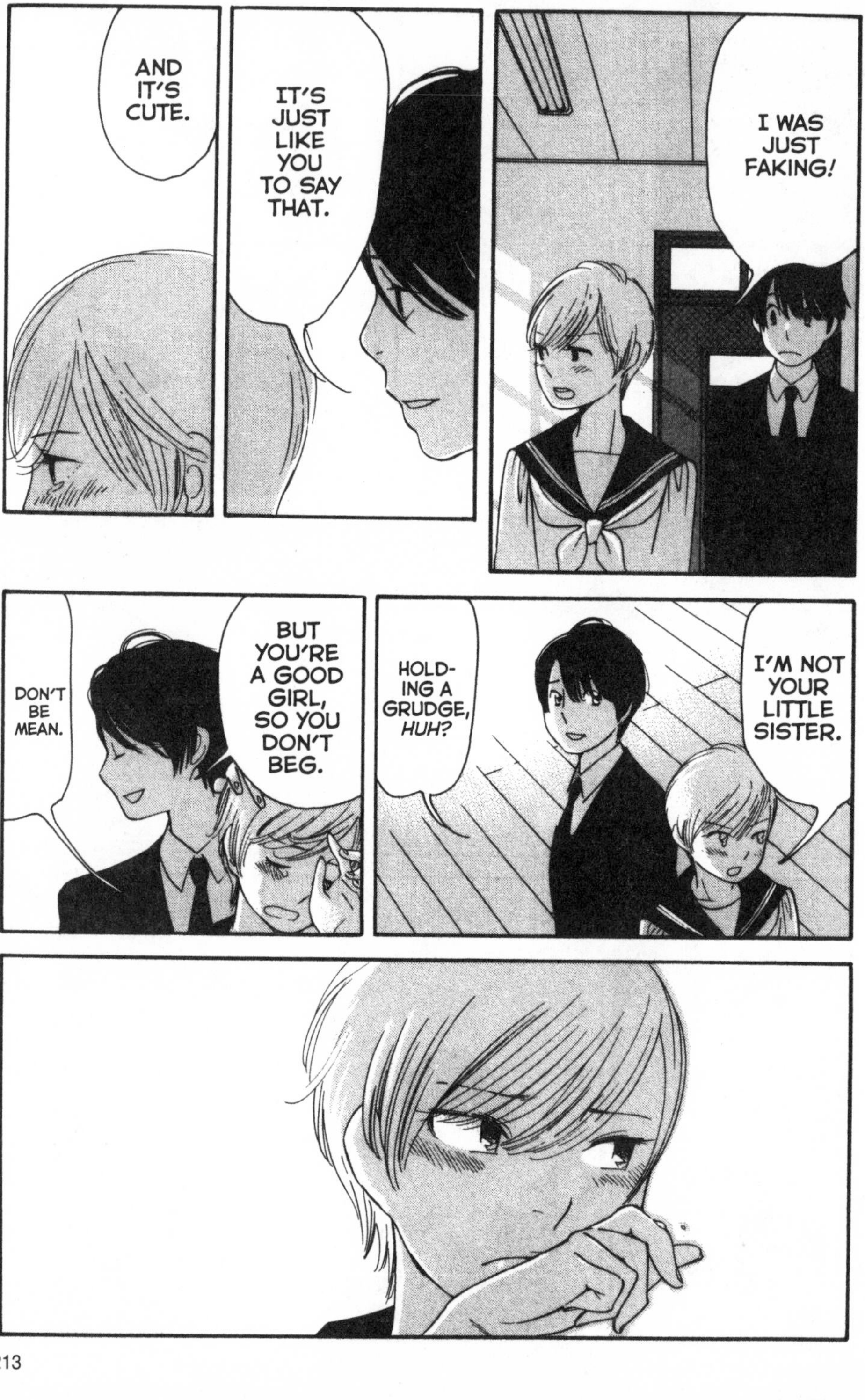
I WAS JUST FAKING!
IT'S JUST LIKE YOU TO SAY THAT.
AND IT'S CUTE.
I'M NOT YOUR LITTLE SISTER.
HOLD-ING A GRUDGE, *HUH?*
BUT YOU'RE A GOOD GIRL, SO YOU DON'T BEG.
DON'T BE MEAN.

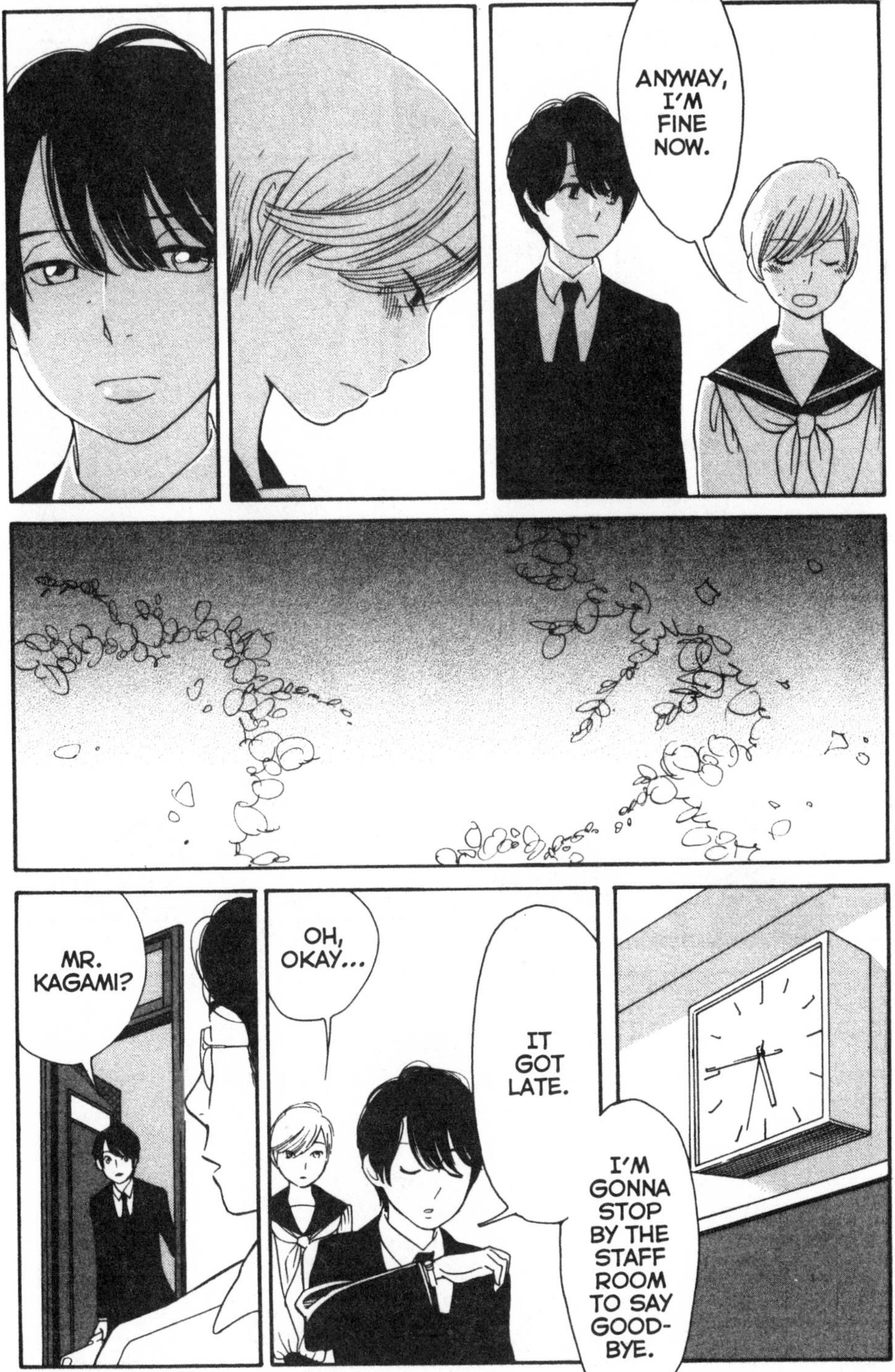
ANYWAY, I'M FINE NOW.
I'M GONNA STOP BY THE STAFF ROOM TO SAY GOOD-BYE.
IT GOT LATE.
OH, OKAY...
MR. KAGAMI?

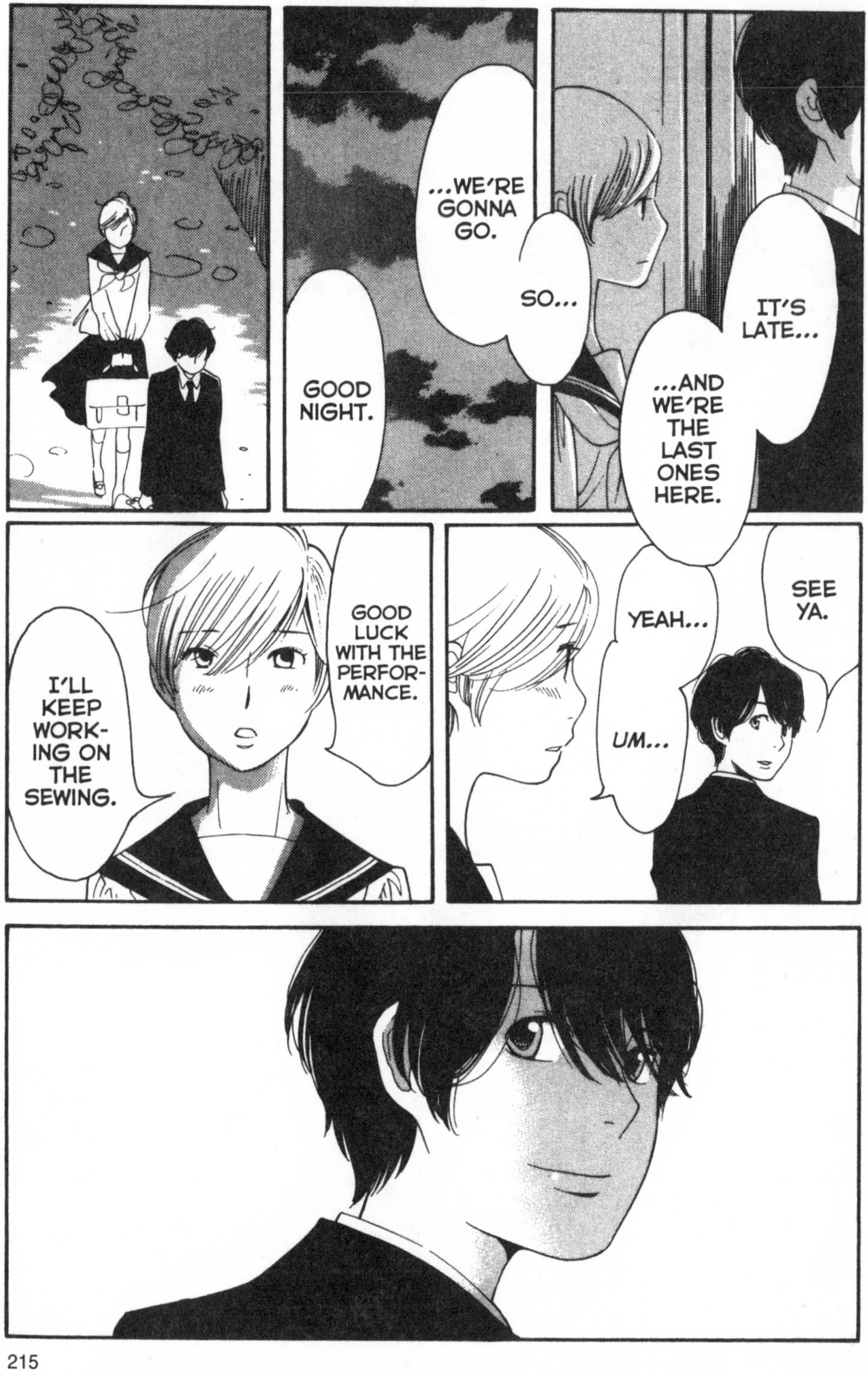
IT'S LATE...
...AND WE'RE THE LAST ONES HERE.
SO...
...WE'RE GONNA GO.
GOOD NIGHT.
SEE YA.
YEAH...
UM...
GOOD LUCK WITH THE PERFORMANCE.
I'LL KEEP WORKING ON THE SEWING.

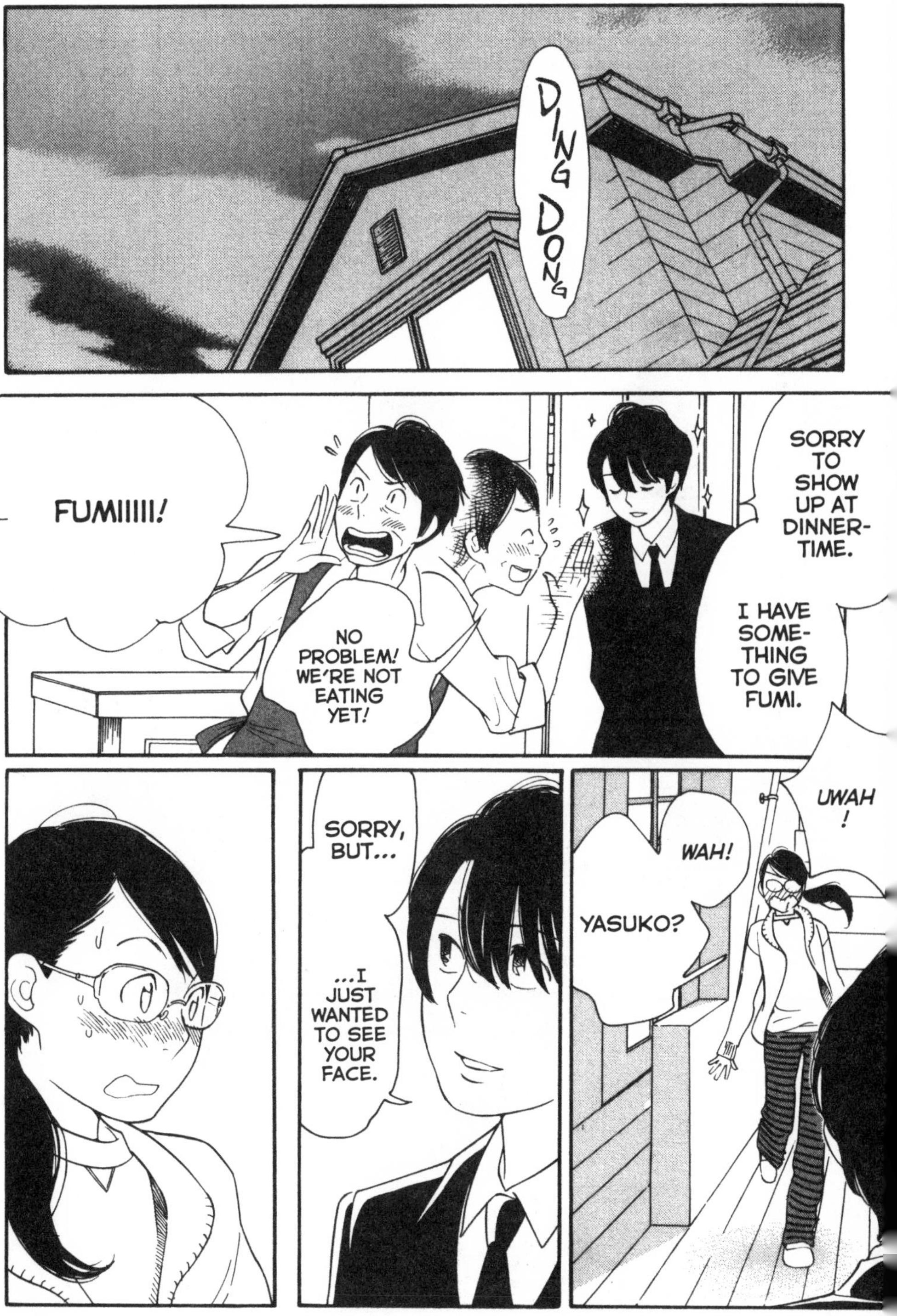
DING DONG
SORRY TO SHOW UP AT DINNER-TIME.
I HAVE SOME-THING TO GIVE FUMI.
NO PROBLEM! WE'RE NOT EATING YET!
FUMIIIIII!
UWAH!
WAH!
YASUKO?
SORRY, BUT...
...I JUST WANTED TO SEE YOUR FACE.

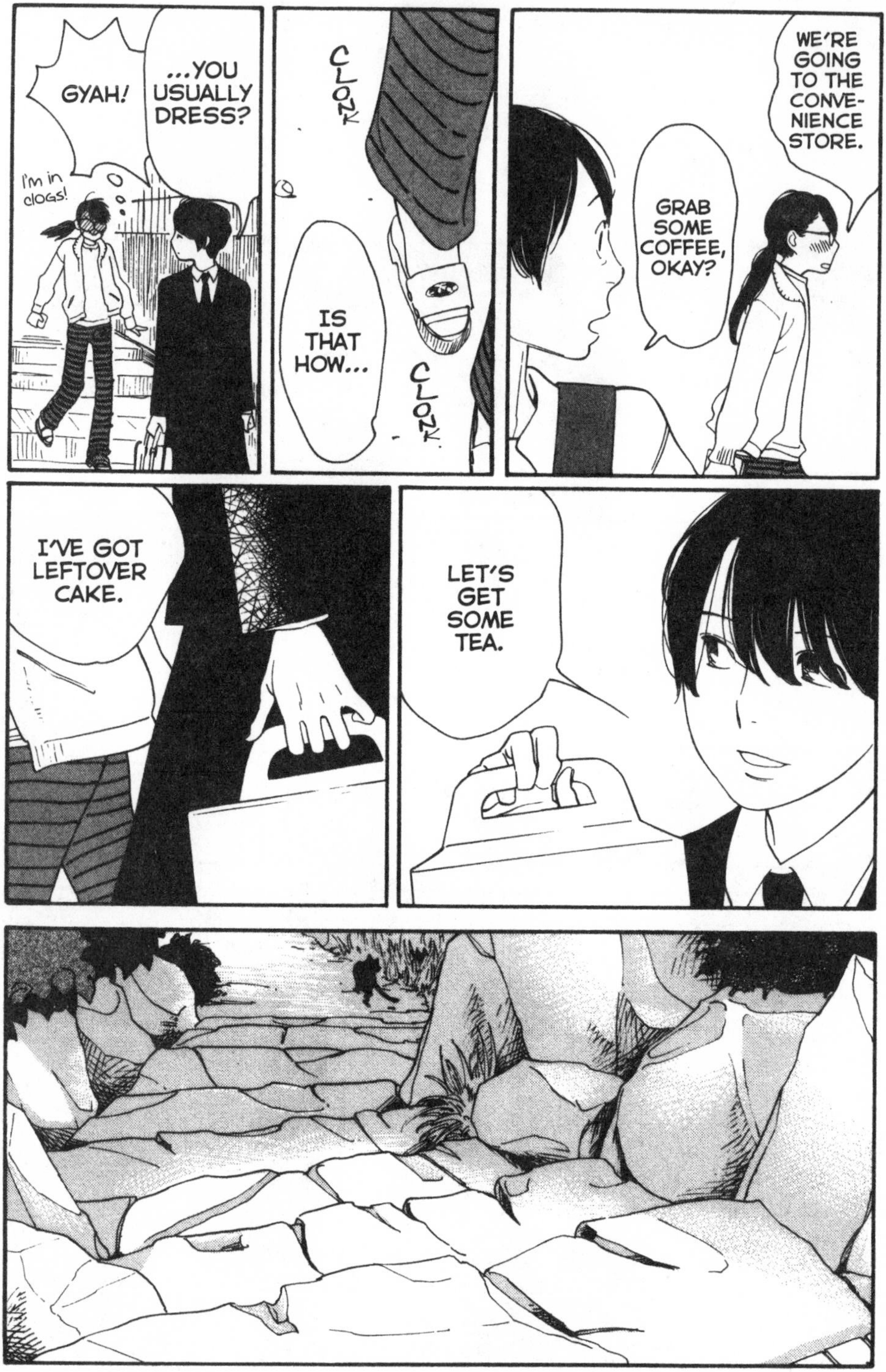
WE'RE GOING TO THE CONVE-NIENCE STORE.
GRAB SOME COFFEE, OKAY?
CLONK
IS THAT HOW...
CLONK
...YOU USUALLY DRESS?
GYAH!
I'm in clogs!
LET'S GET SOME TEA.
I'VE GOT LEFTOVER CAKE.

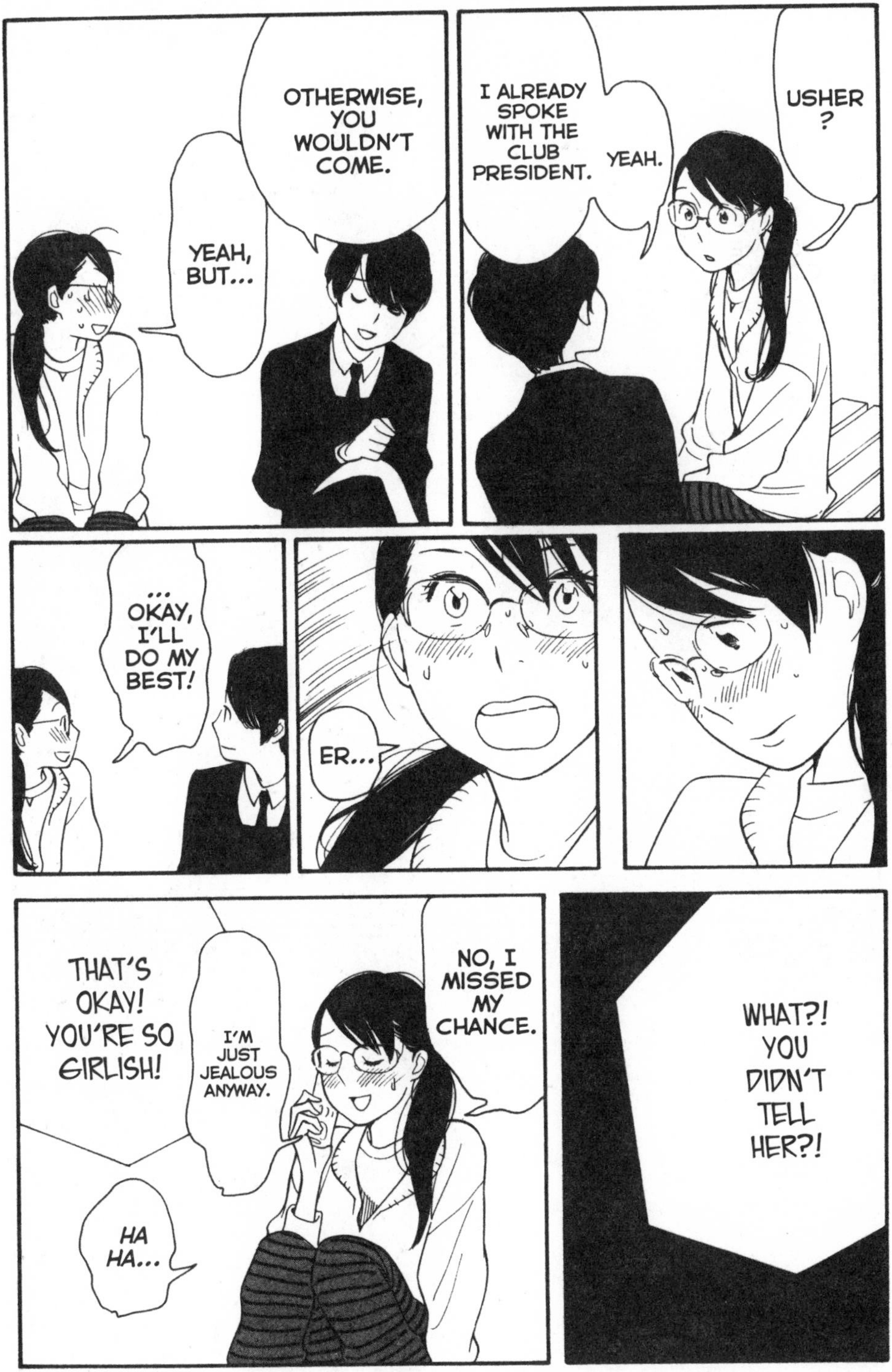
USHER?
YEAH.
I ALREADY SPOKE WITH THE CLUB PRESIDENT.
OTHERWISE, YOU WOULDN'T COME.
YEAH, BUT...
ER...
... OKAY, I'LL DO MY BEST!
WHAT?! YOU DIDN'T TELL HER?!
NO, I MISSED MY CHANCE.
I'M JUST JEALOUS ANYWAY.
THAT'S OKAY! YOU'RE SO GIRLISH!
HA HA...

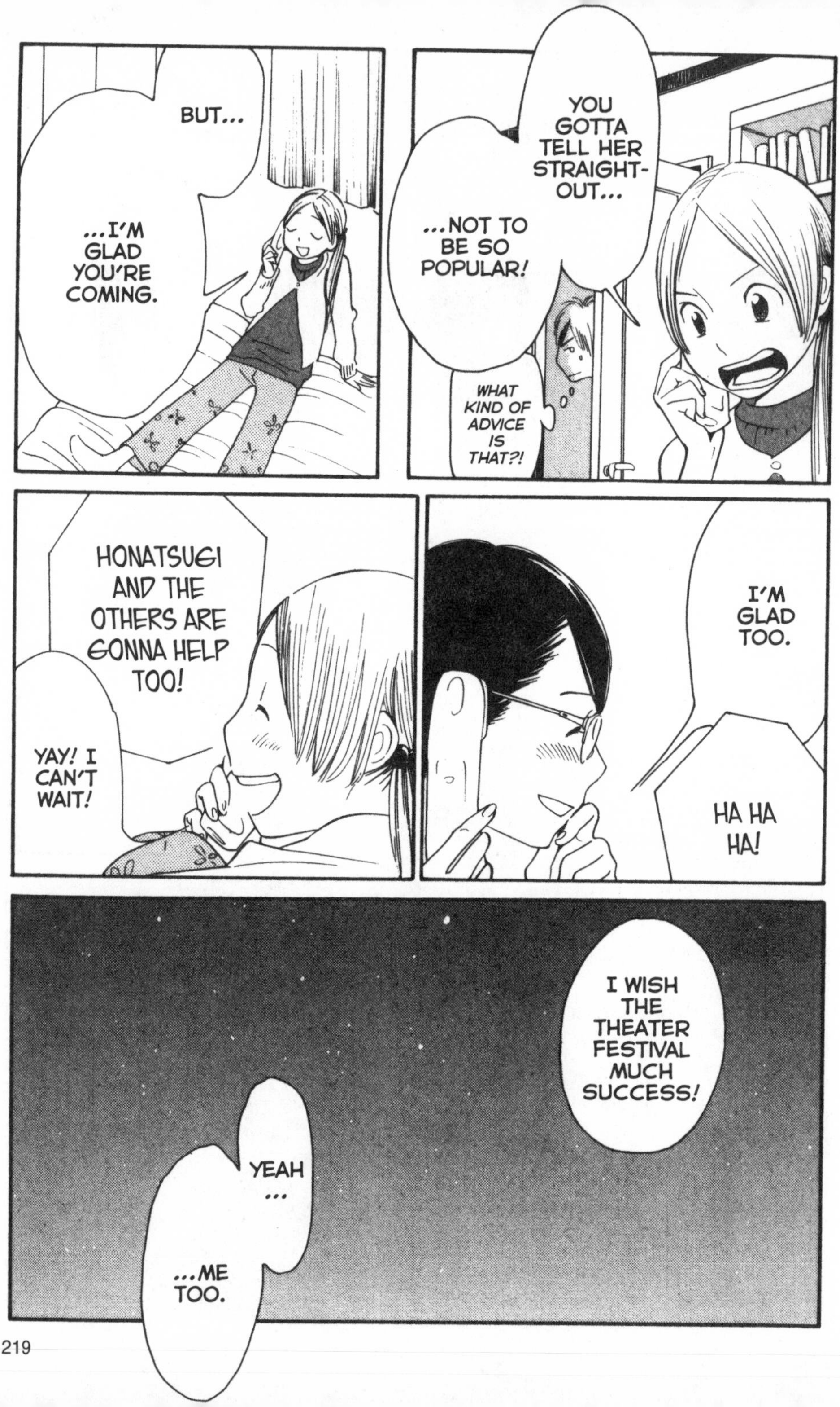
YOU GOTTA TELL HER STRAIGHT-OUT...
...NOT TO BE SO POPULAR!
WHAT KIND OF ADVICE IS THAT?!
BUT...
...I'M GLAD YOU'RE COMING.
I'M GLAD TOO.
HA HA HA!
HONATSUGI AND THE OTHERS ARE GONNA HELP TOO!
YAY! I CAN'T WAIT!
I WISH THE THEATER FESTIVAL MUCH SUCCESS!
YEAH...
...ME TOO.

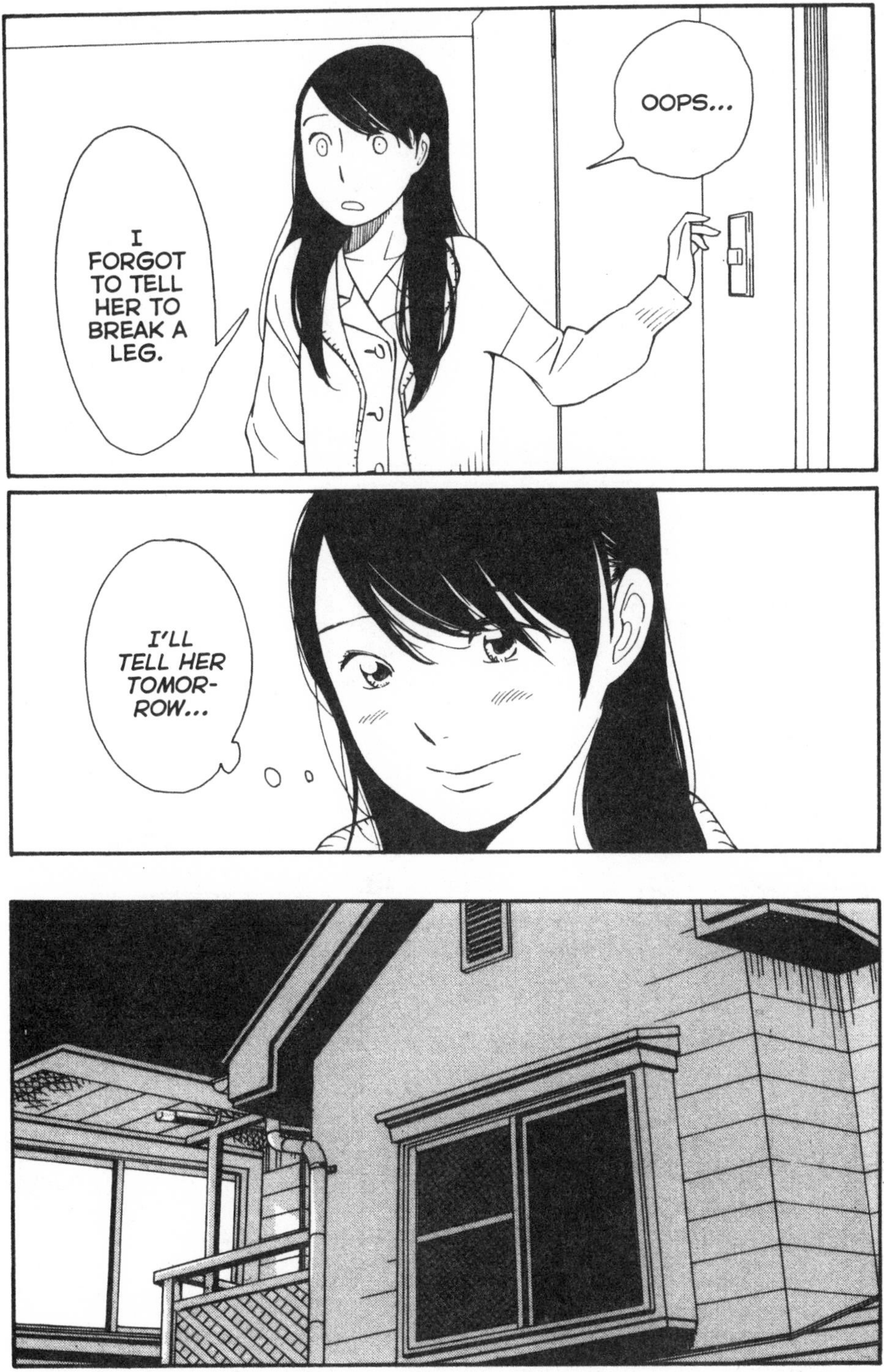
OOPS...
I FORGOT TO TELL HER TO BREAK A LEG.
I'LL TELL HER TOMOR-ROW...

Sweet Blue Flowers

# #9 Wuthering Heights, Part 3

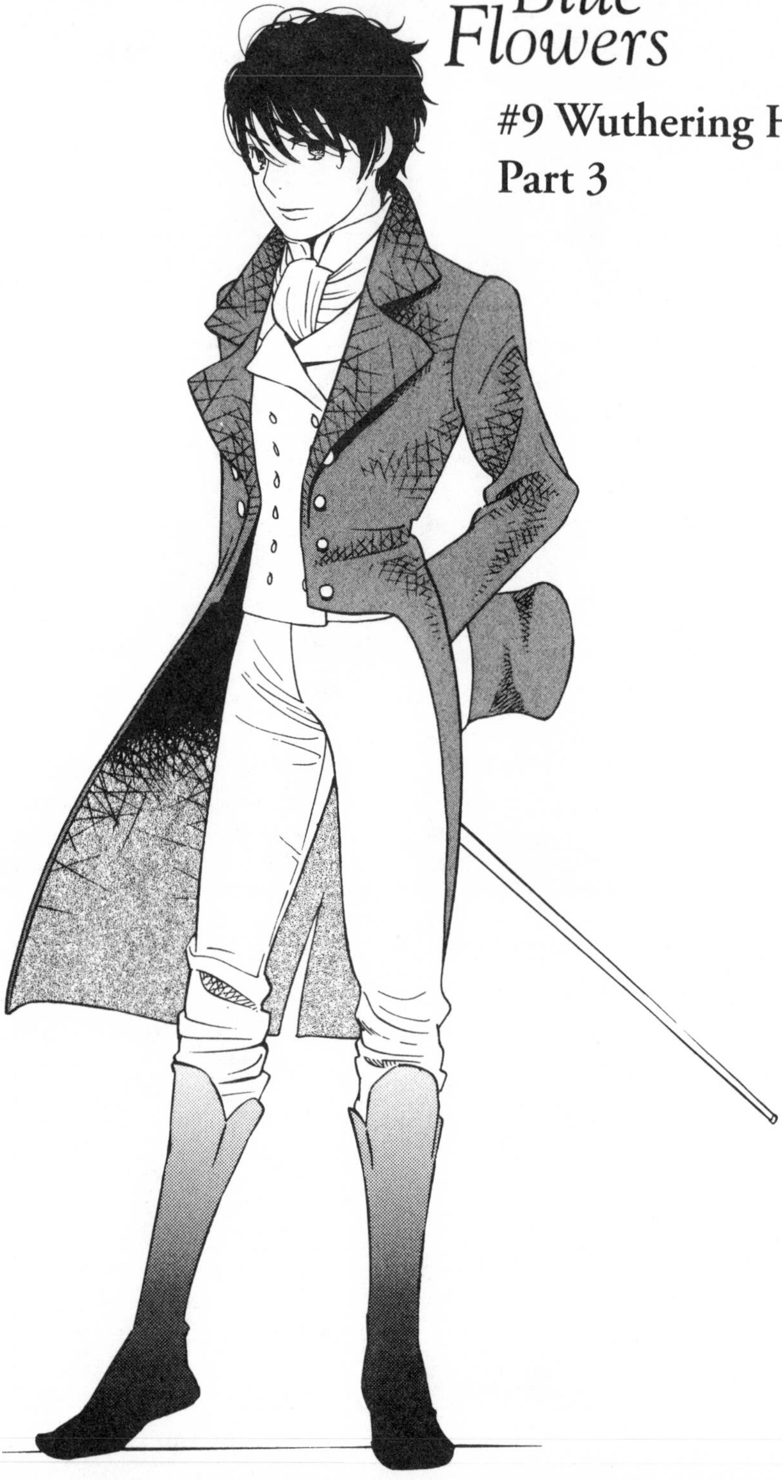

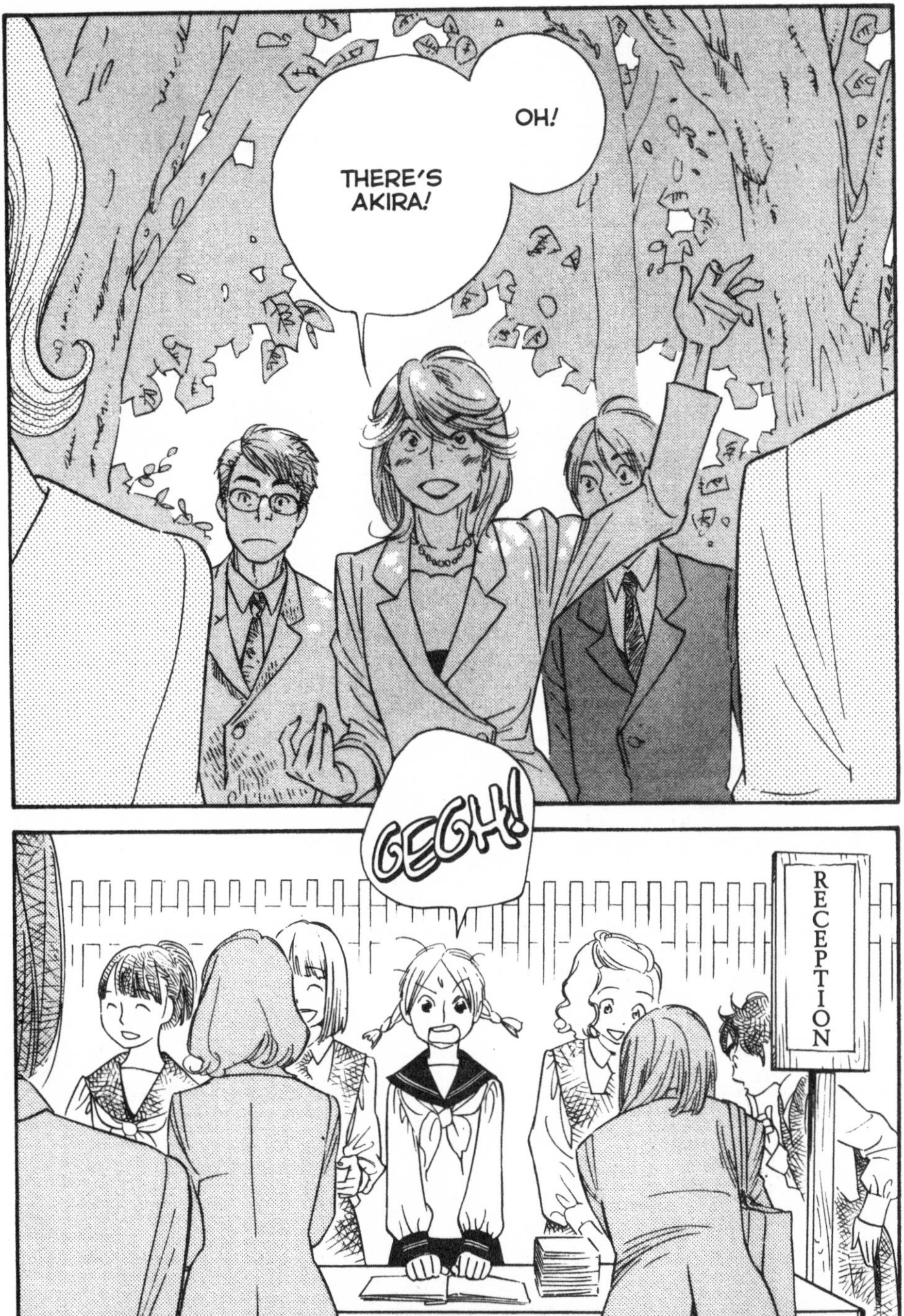
OH!
THERE'S AKIRA!
GEGH!
RECEPTION

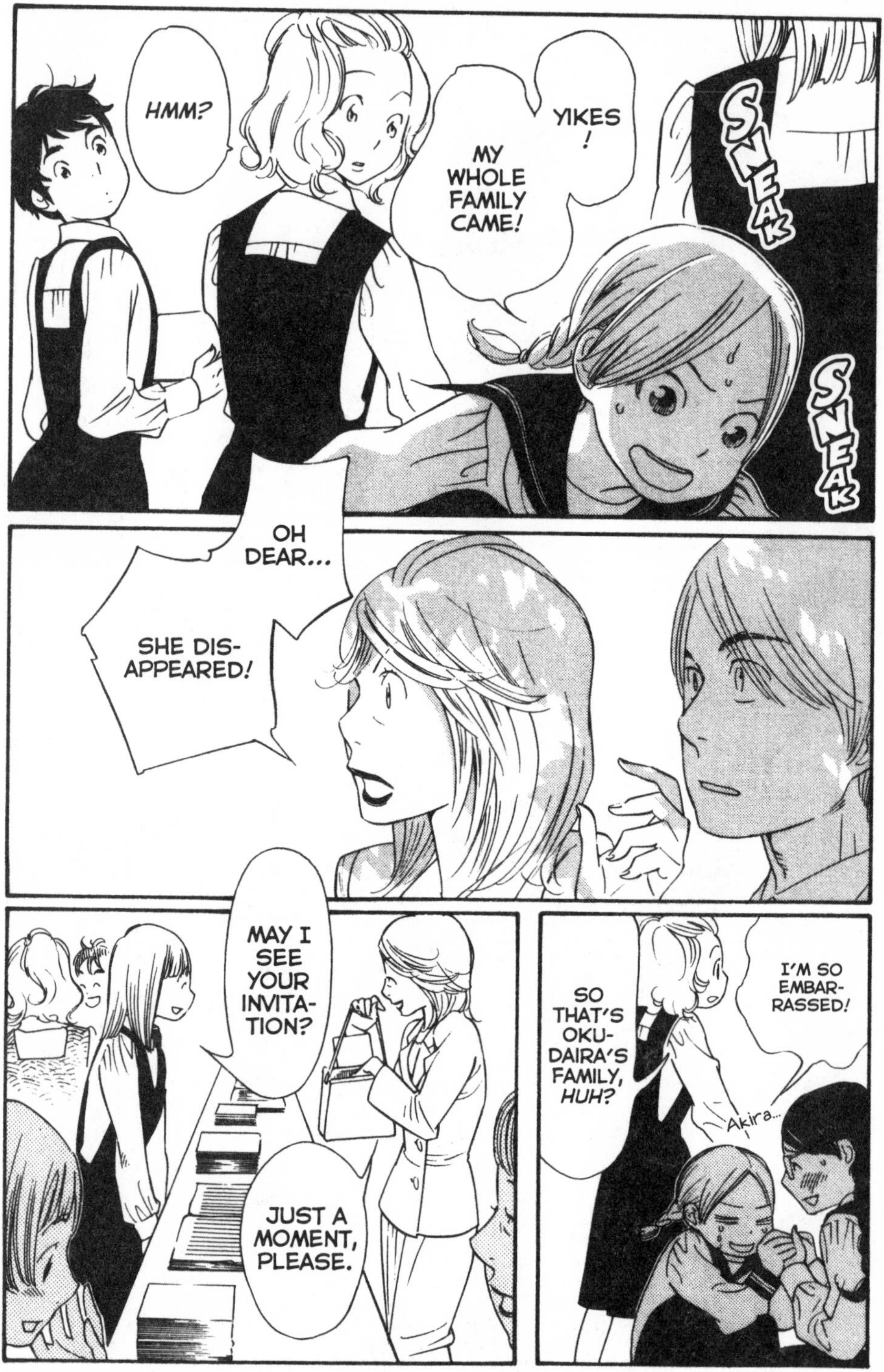
SNEAK
YIKES! MY WHOLE FAMILY CAME!
HMM?
SNEAK
OH DEAR...
SHE DISAPPEARED!
I'M SO EMBARRASSED!
SO THAT'S OKUDAIRA'S FAMILY, HUH?
Akira...
MAY I SEE YOUR INVITATION?
JUST A MOMENT, PLEASE.

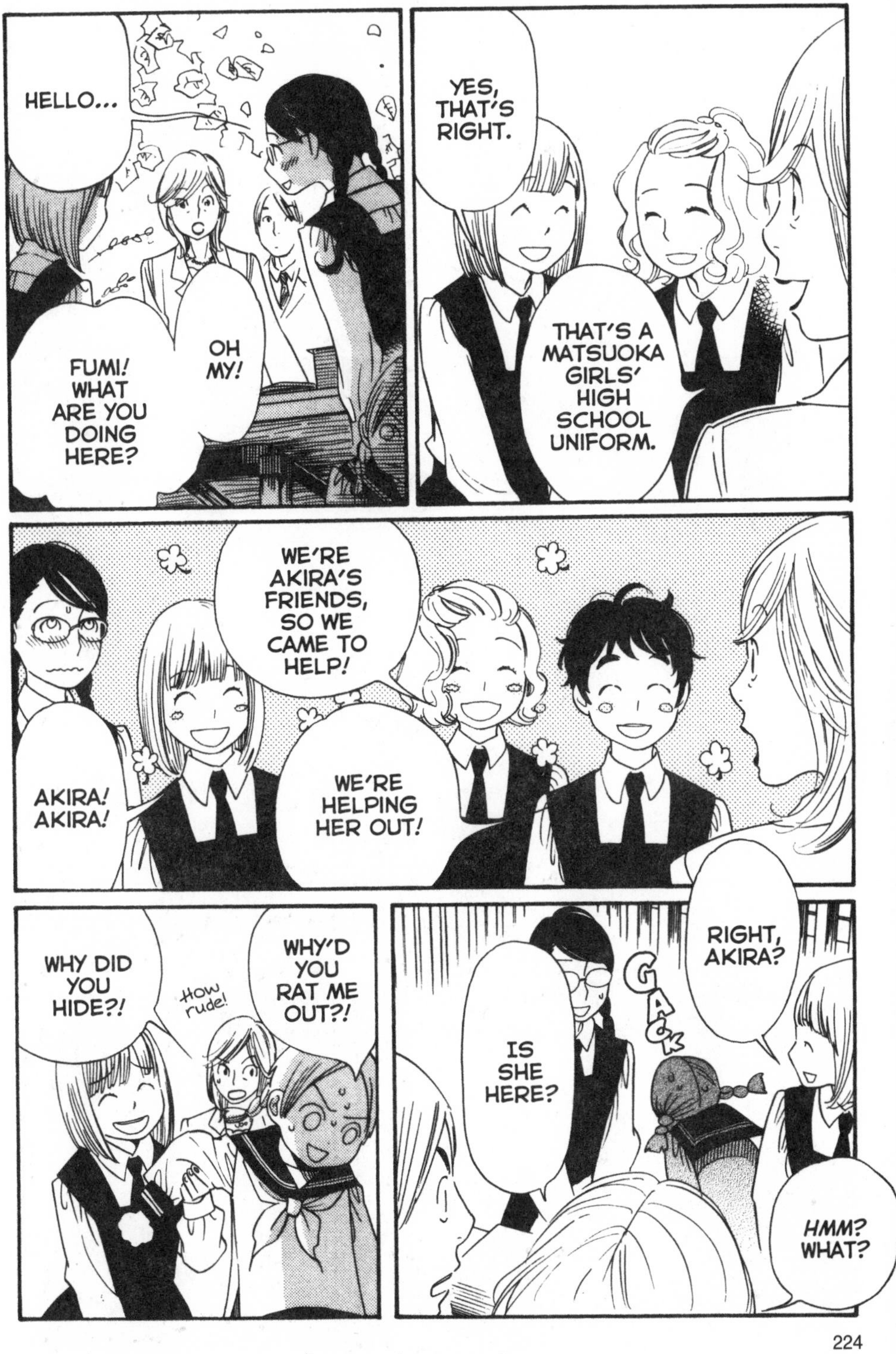
YES, THAT'S RIGHT.
THAT'S A MATSUOKA GIRLS' HIGH SCHOOL UNIFORM.
HELLO...
OH MY!
FUMI! WHAT ARE YOU DOING HERE?
WE'RE AKIRA'S FRIENDS, SO WE CAME TO HELP!
WE'RE HELPING HER OUT!
AKIRA! AKIRA!
RIGHT, AKIRA?
GACK
IS SHE HERE?
HMM? WHAT?
WHY'D YOU RAT ME OUT?!
How rude!
WHY DID YOU HIDE?!

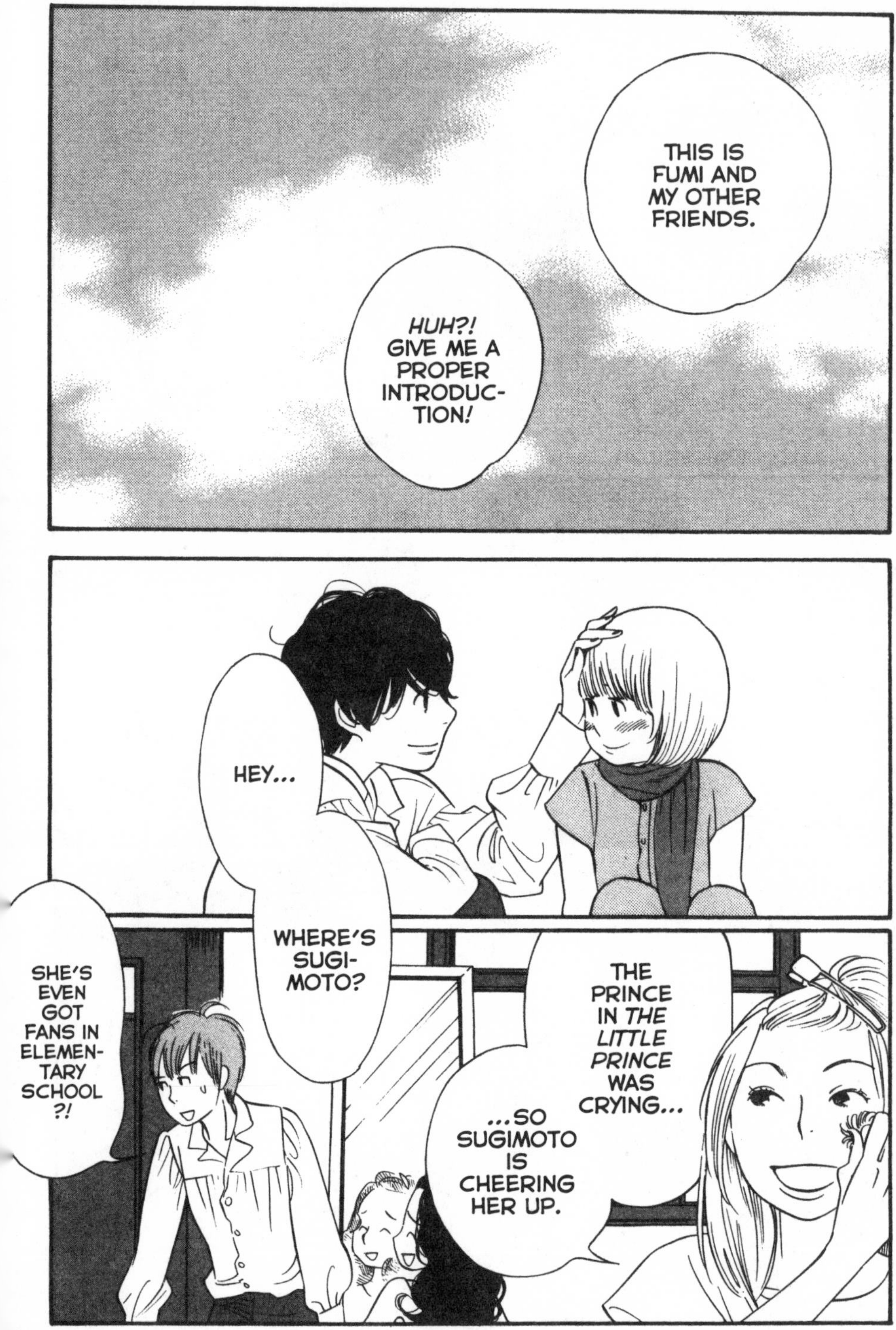
THIS IS FUMI AND MY OTHER FRIENDS.
*HUH?!* GIVE ME A PROPER INTRODUCTION!
HEY... WHERE'S SUGIMOTO?
THE PRINCE IN *THE LITTLE PRINCE* WAS CRYING...
...SO SUGIMOTO IS CHEERING HER UP.
SHE'S EVEN GOT FANS IN ELEMENTARY SCHOOL?!

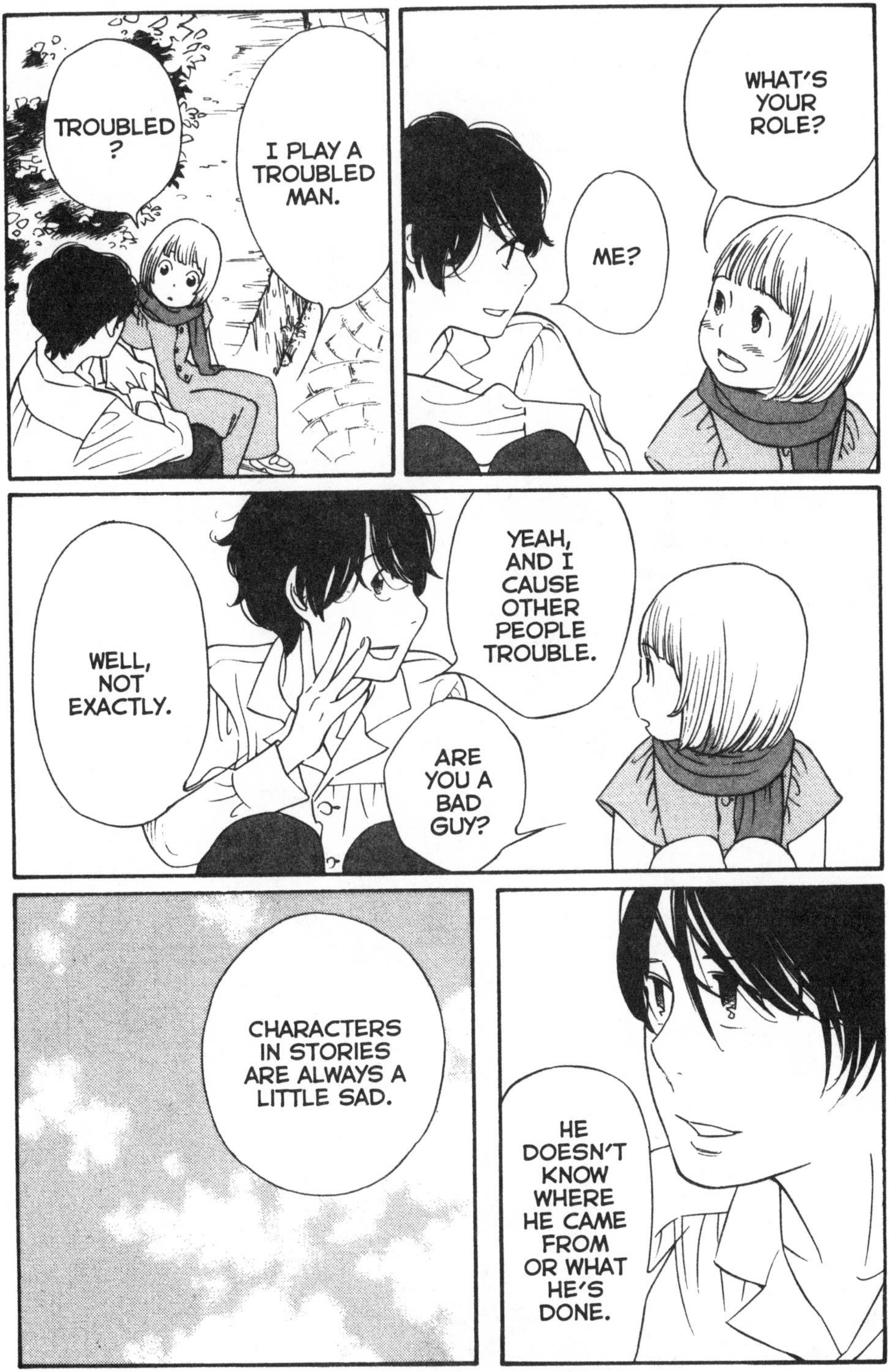
WHAT'S YOUR ROLE?
ME?
I PLAY A TROUBLED MAN.
TROUBLED?
YEAH, AND I CAUSE OTHER PEOPLE TROUBLE.
ARE YOU A BAD GUY?
WELL, NOT EXACTLY.
HE DOESN'T KNOW WHERE HE CAME FROM OR WHAT HE'S DONE.
CHARACTERS IN STORIES ARE ALWAYS A LITTLE SAD.

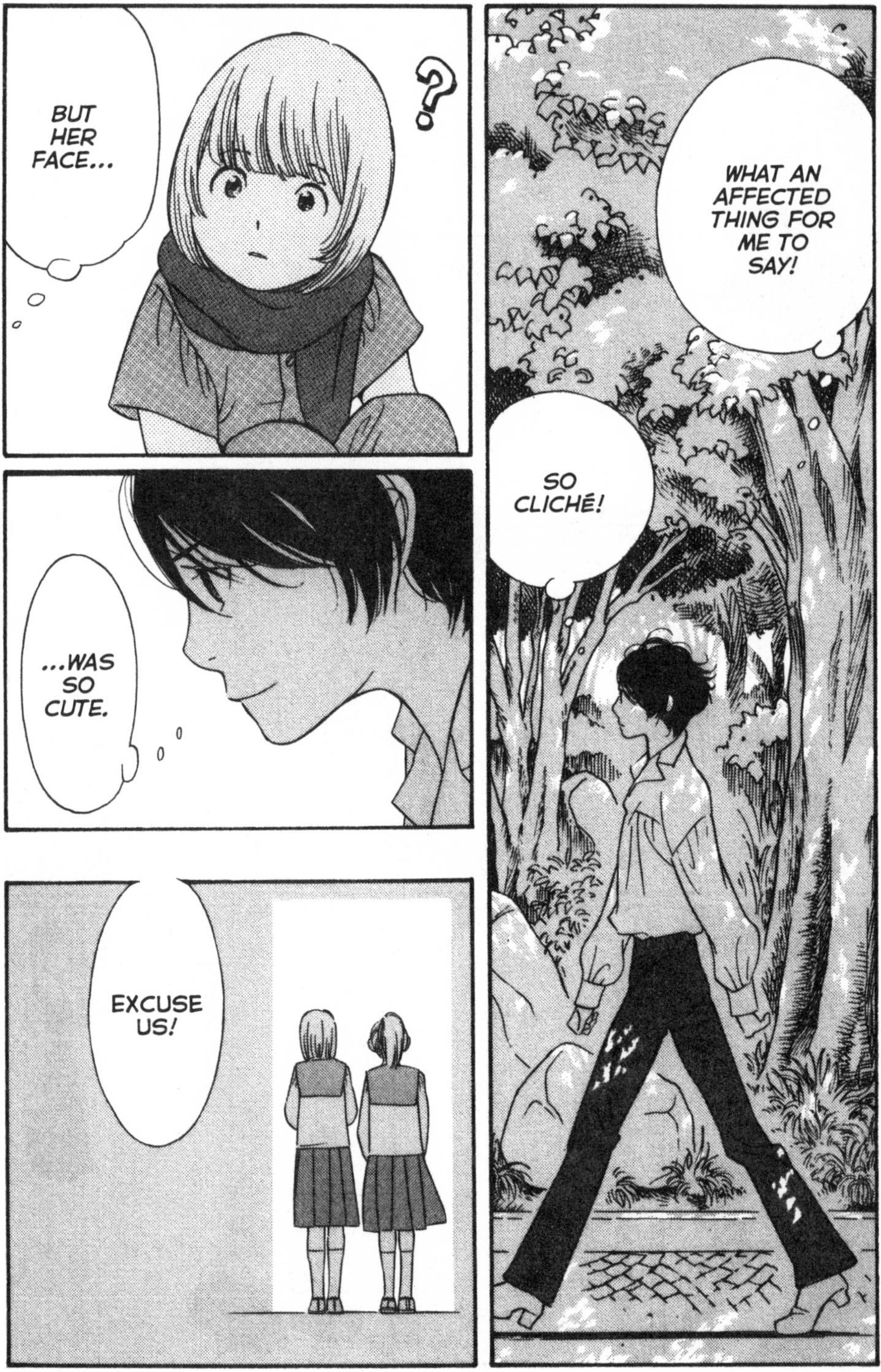
WHAT AN AFFECTED THING FOR ME TO SAY!
SO CLICHÉ!
?
BUT HER FACE...
...WAS SO CUTE.
EXCUSE US!

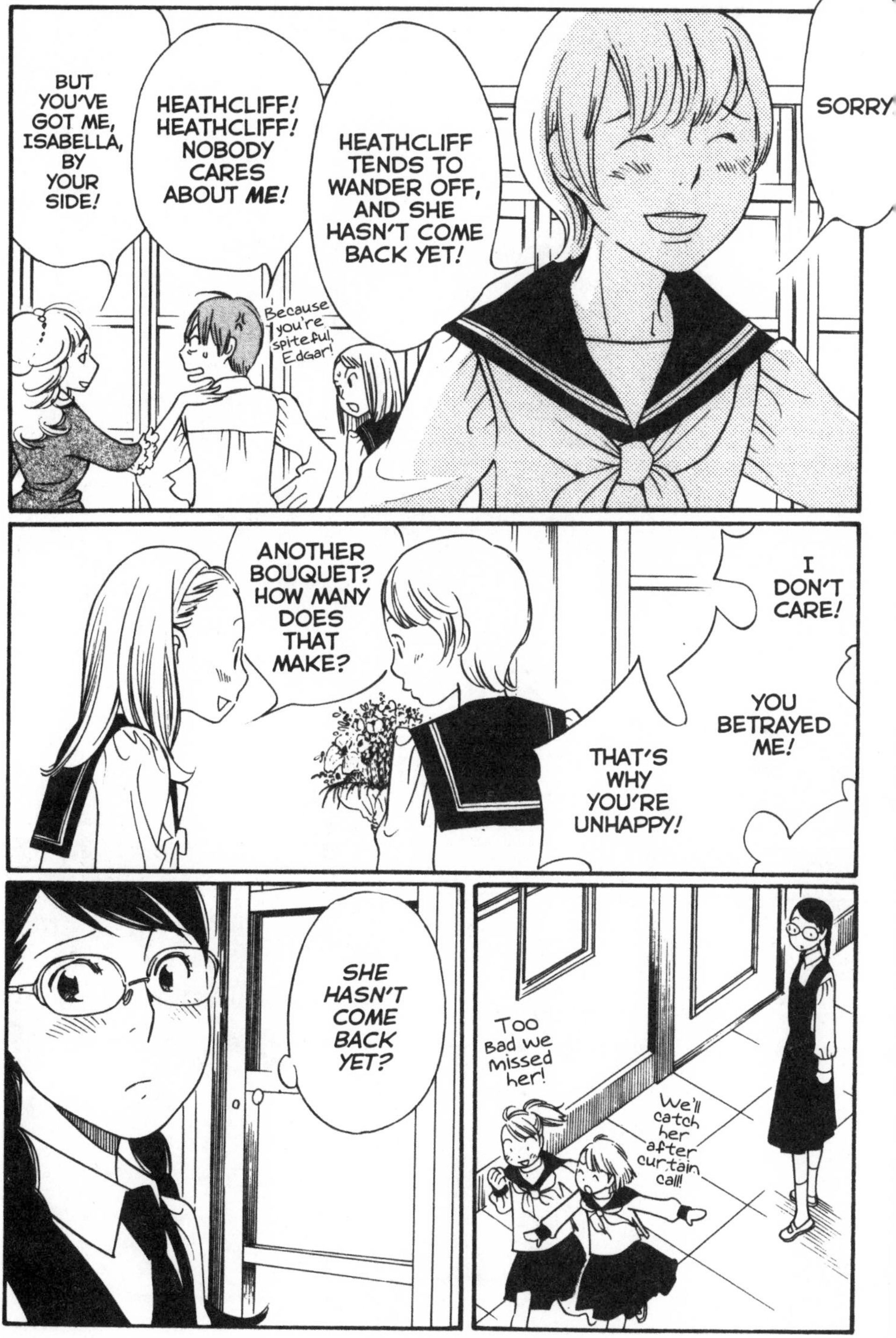
SORRY.
HEATHCLIFF TENDS TO WANDER OFF, AND SHE HASN'T COME BACK YET!
HEATHCLIFF! HEATHCLIFF! NOBODY CARES ABOUT *ME*!
BUT YOU'VE GOT ME, ISABELLA, BY YOUR SIDE!
Because you're spiteful, Edgar!
I DON'T CARE!
YOU BETRAYED ME!
THAT'S WHY YOU'RE UNHAPPY!
ANOTHER BOUQUET? HOW MANY DOES THAT MAKE?
Too bad we missed her!
We'll catch her after curtain call!
*SHE HASN'T COME BACK YET?*

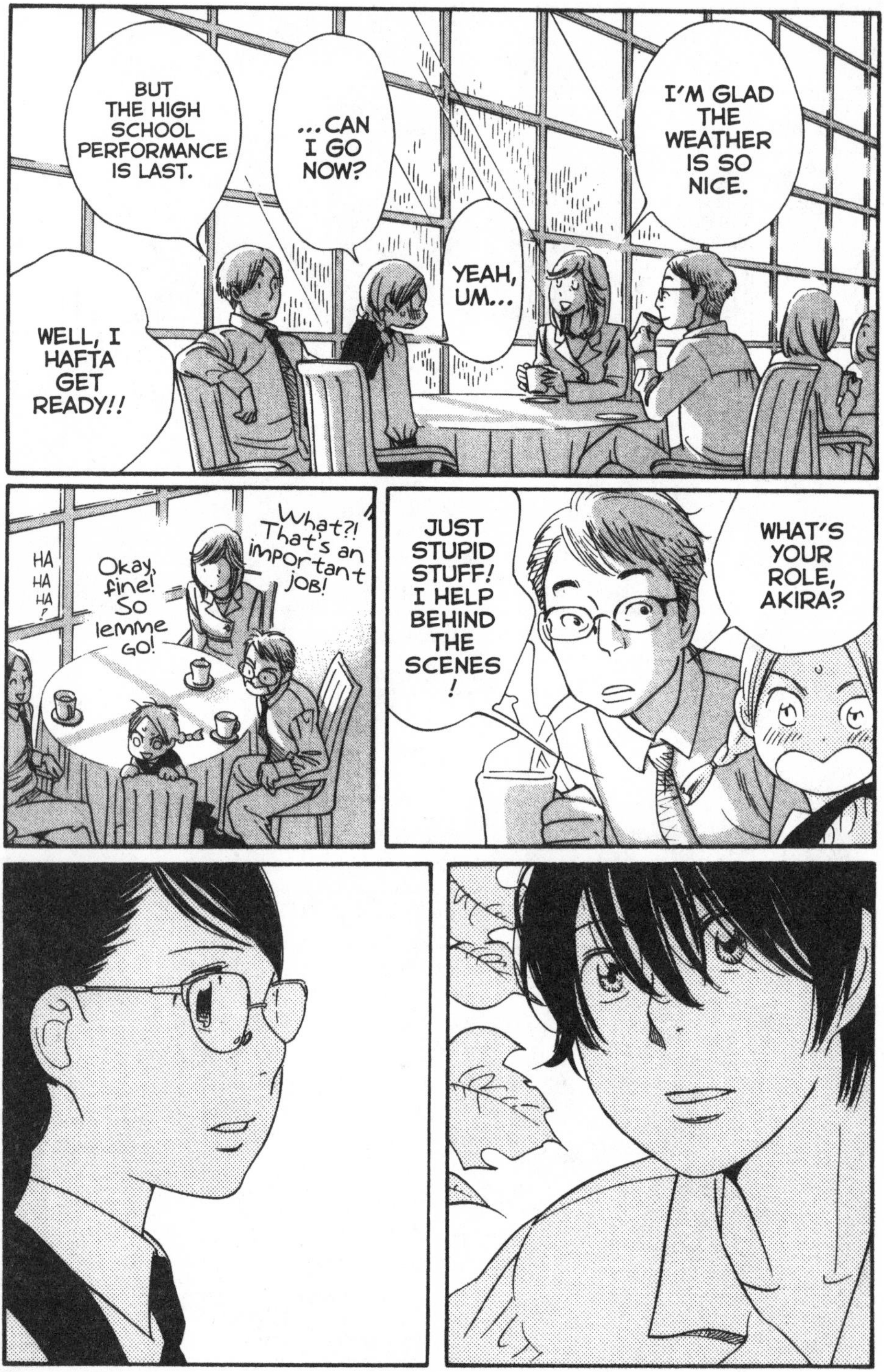
I'M GLAD THE WEATHER IS SO NICE.
YEAH, UM...
...CAN I GO NOW?
BUT THE HIGH SCHOOL PERFORMANCE IS LAST.
WELL, I HAFTA GET READY!!
WHAT'S YOUR ROLE, AKIRA?
JUST STUPID STUFF! I HELP BEHIND THE SCENES!
What?! That's an important job!
Okay, fine! So lemme go!
HA HA HA?

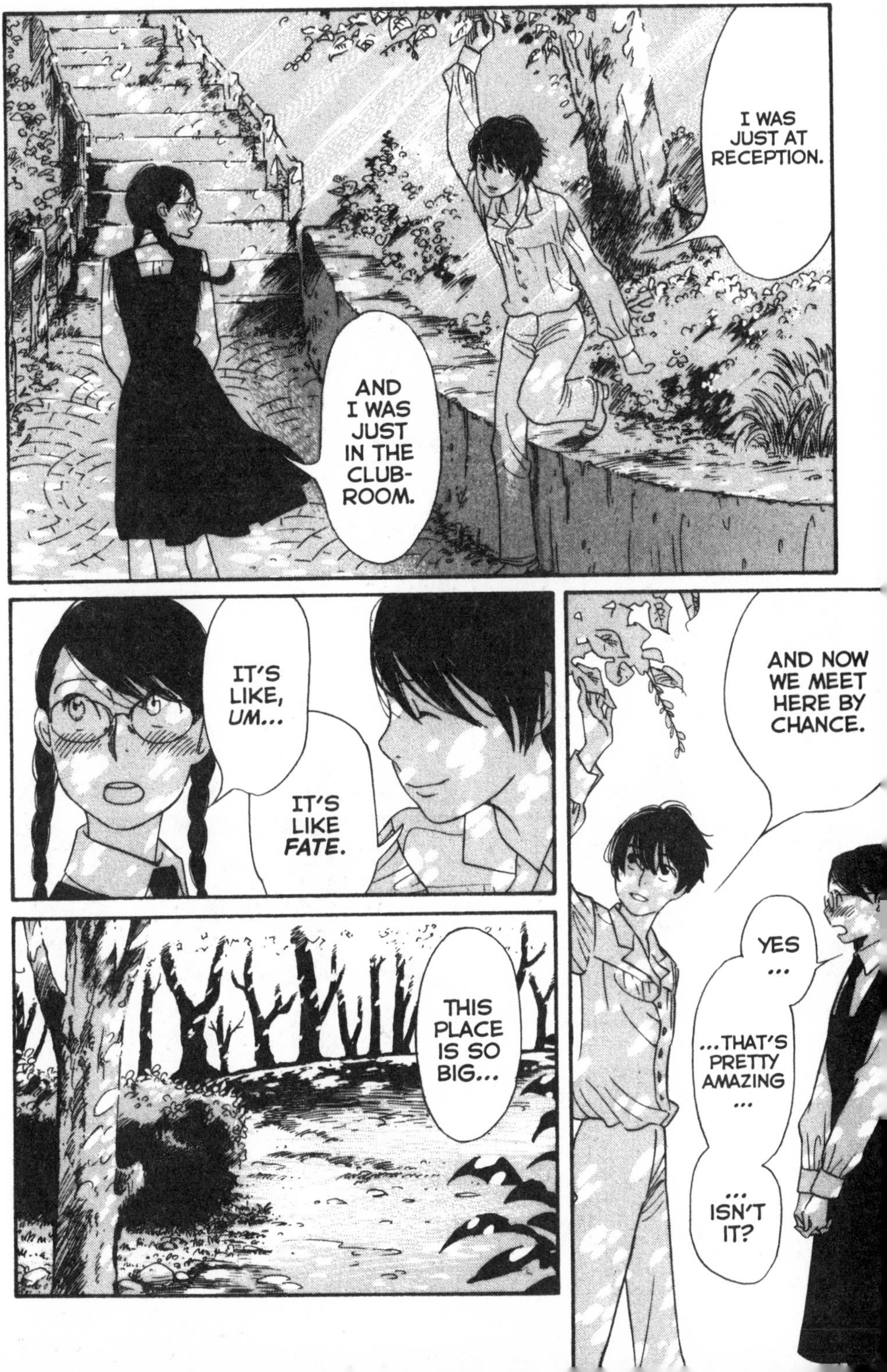
I WAS JUST AT RECEPTION.
AND I WAS JUST IN THE CLUB-ROOM.
AND NOW WE MEET HERE BY CHANCE.
YES ...
...THAT'S PRETTY AMAZING ...
... ISN'T IT?
IT'S LIKE, *UM...*
IT'S LIKE *FATE*.
THIS PLACE IS SO BIG...

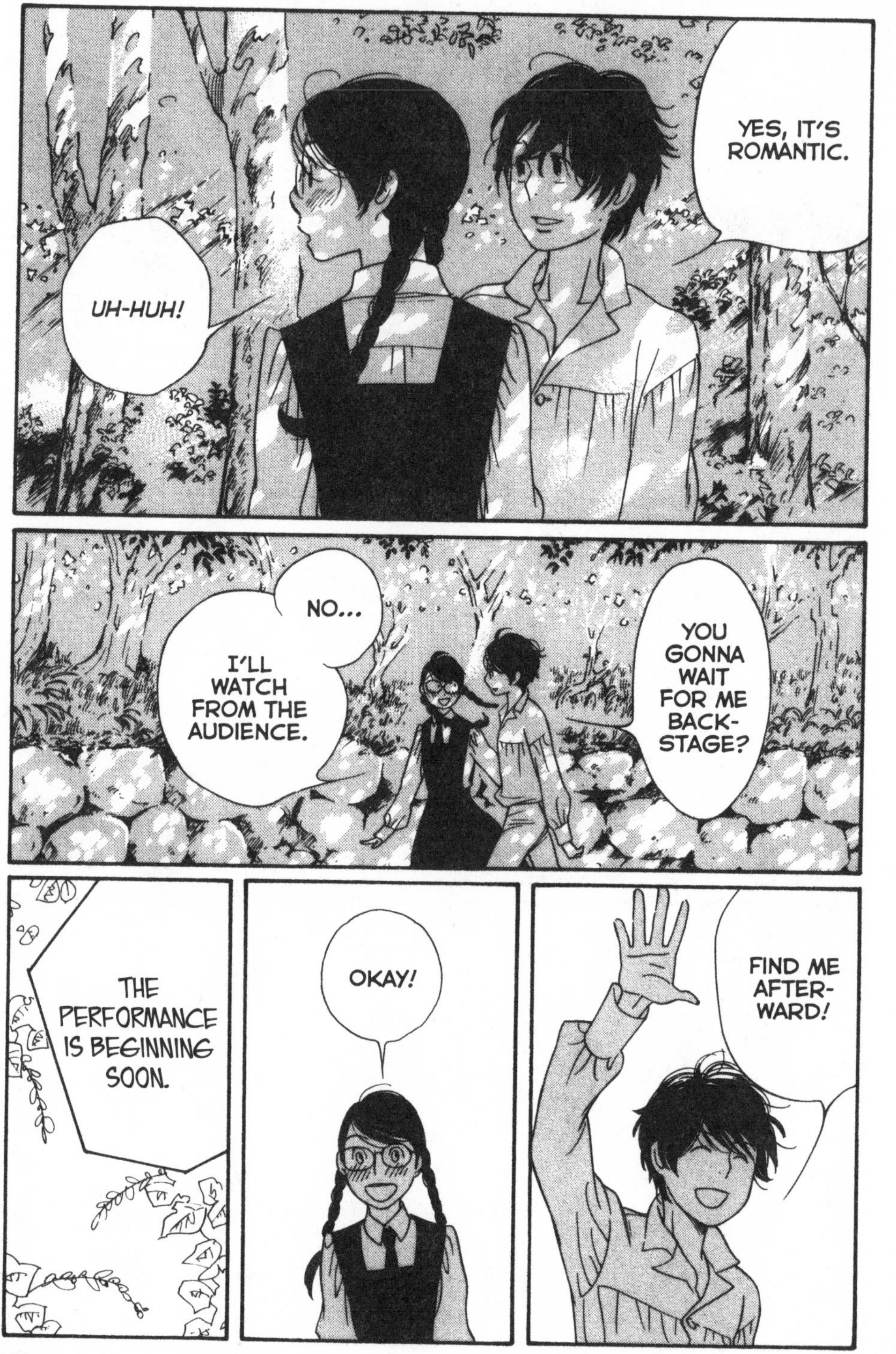
YES, IT'S ROMANTIC.
UH-HUH!
YOU GONNA WAIT FOR ME BACK-STAGE?
NO...
I'LL WATCH FROM THE AUDIENCE.
FIND ME AFTER-WARD!
OKAY!
THE PERFORMANCE IS BEGINNING SOON.

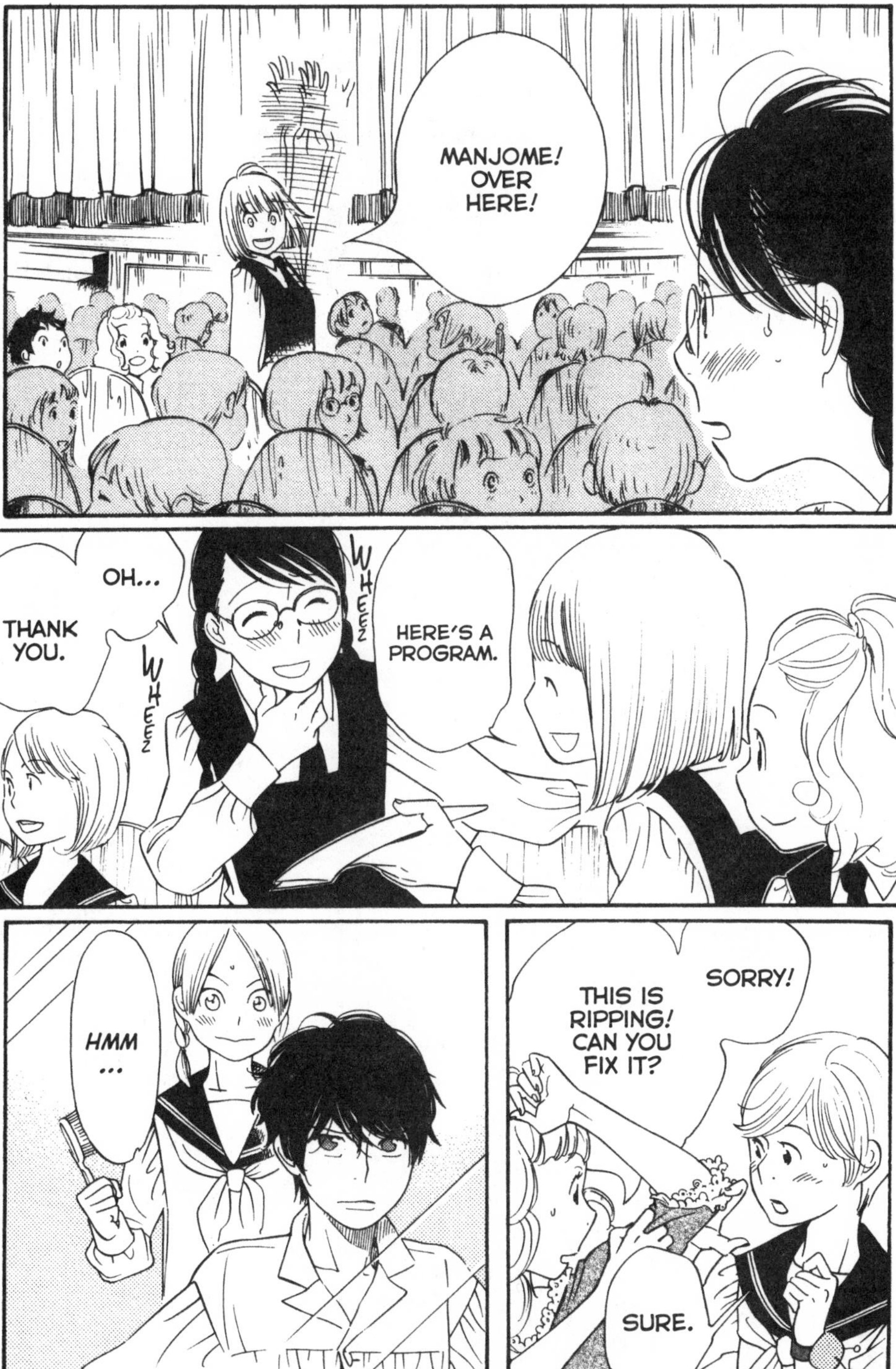
MANJOME! OVER HERE!
HERE'S A PROGRAM.
WHEEZ
WHEEZ
OH... THANK YOU.
SORRY!
THIS IS RIPPING! CAN YOU FIX IT?
SURE.
HMM ...

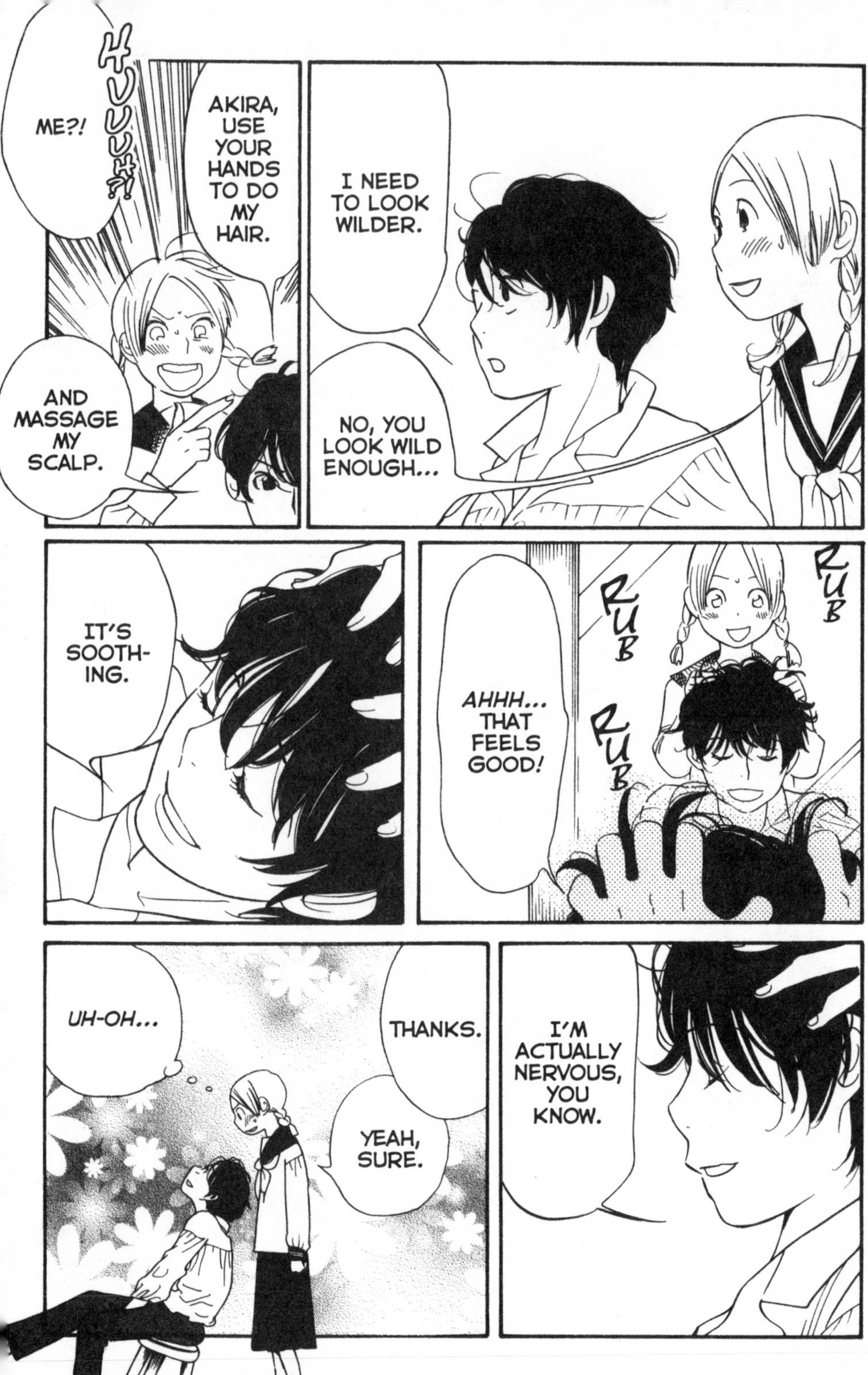
I NEED TO LOOK WILDER.
NO, YOU LOOK WILD ENOUGH...
AKIRA, USE YOUR HANDS TO DO MY HAIR.
HUUUH?!
ME?!
AND MASSAGE MY SCALP.
RUB
RUB
RUB
AHHH... THAT FEELS GOOD!
IT'S SOOTHING.
I'M ACTUALLY NERVOUS, YOU KNOW.
THANKS.
YEAH, SURE.
UH-OH...

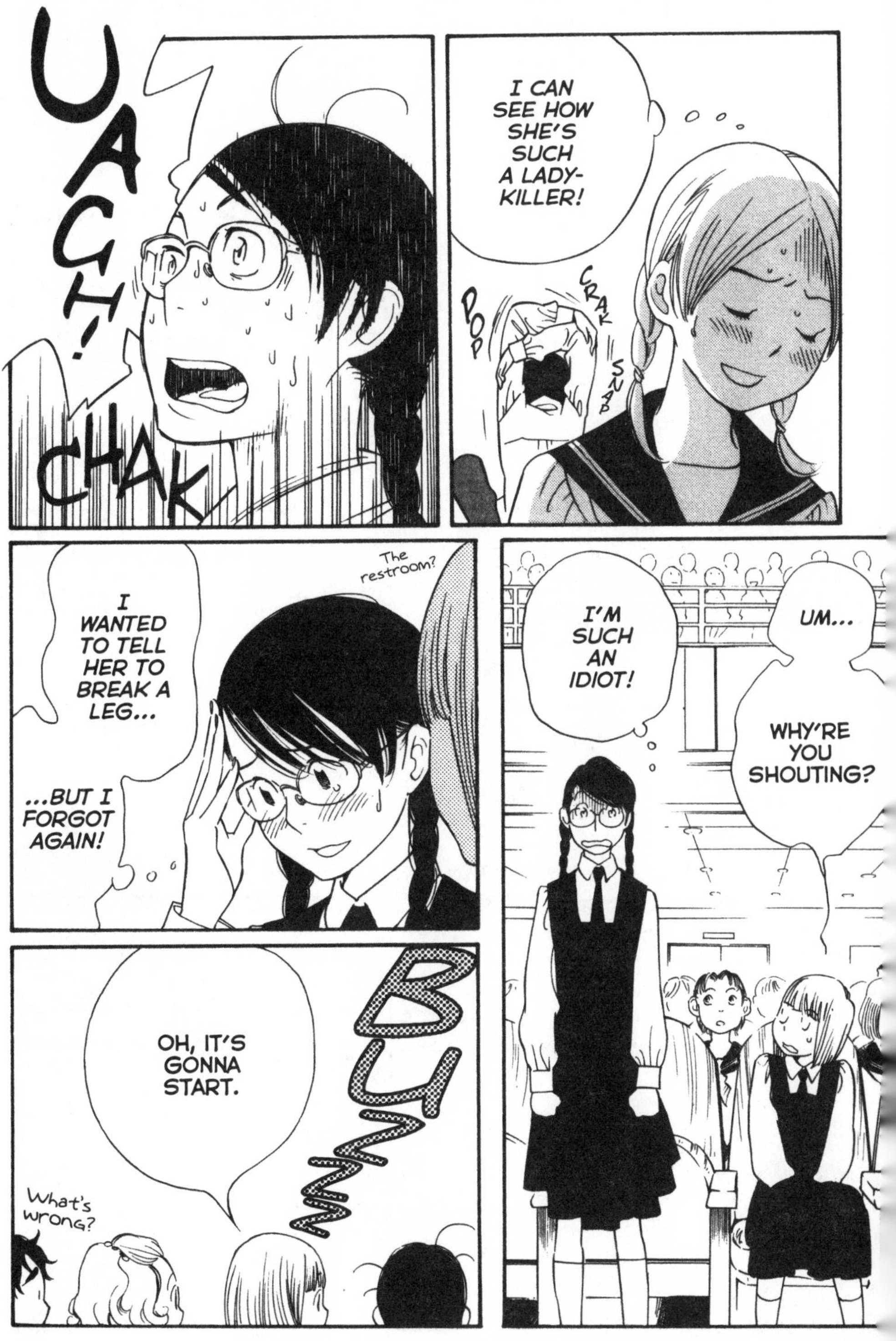
I CAN SEE HOW SHE'S SUCH A LADY-KILLER!
CRAK
POP
SNAP
UACH!
CHAK
UM...
WHY'RE YOU SHOUTING?
I'M SUCH AN IDIOT!
The restroom?
I WANTED TO TELL HER TO BREAK A LEG...
...BUT I FORGOT AGAIN!
BUMMM
OH, IT'S GONNA START.
What's wrong?

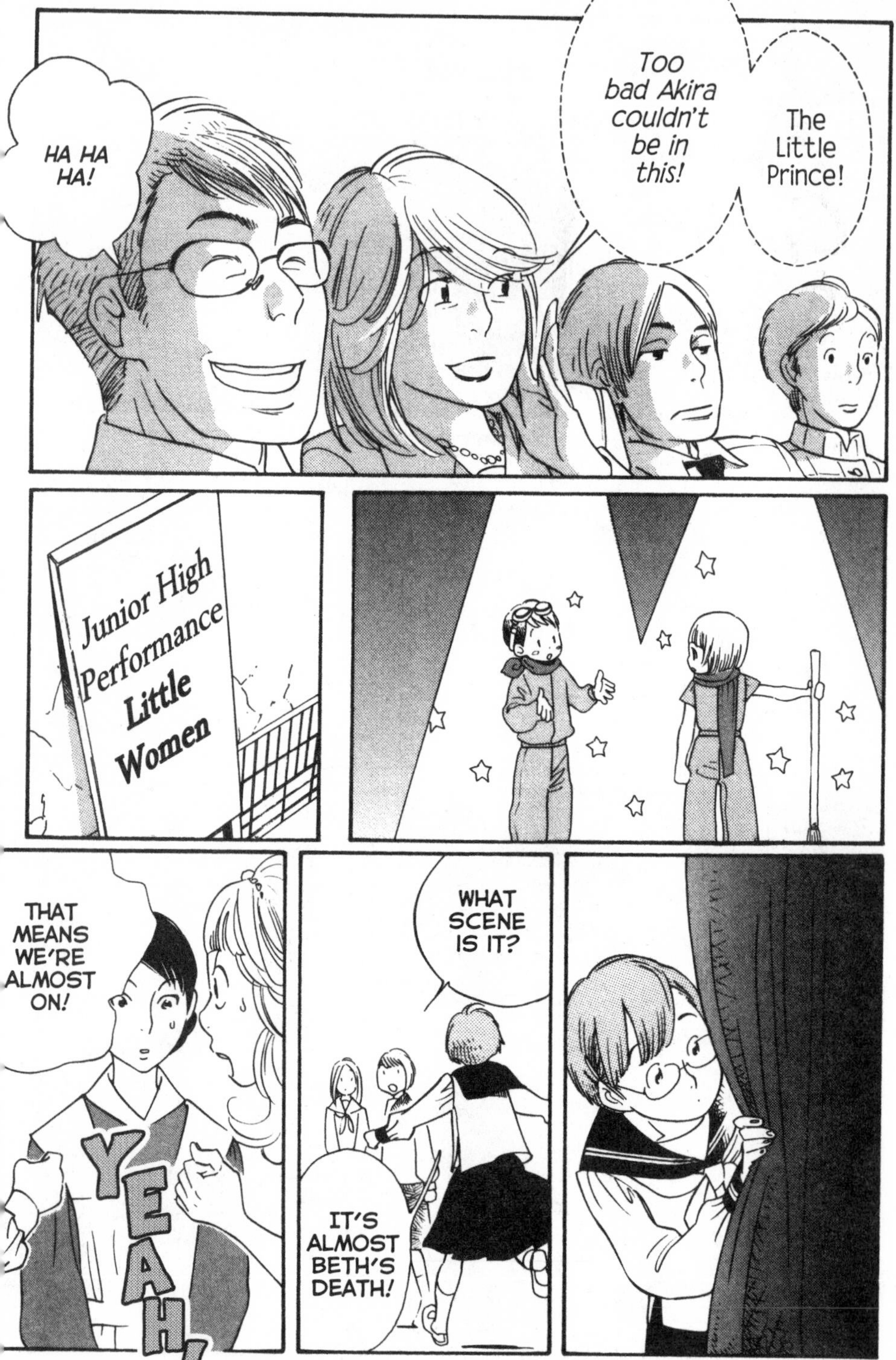
The Little Prince!
Too bad Akira couldn't be in this!
HA HA HA!
Junior High Performance Little Women
WHAT SCENE IS IT?
IT'S ALMOST BETH'S DEATH!
THAT MEANS WE'RE ALMOST ON!
YEAH!

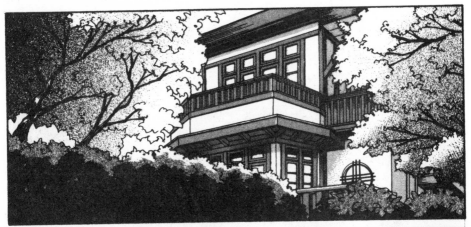

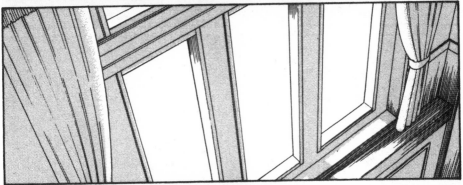

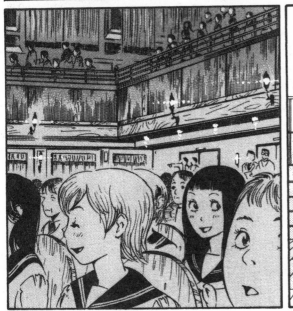

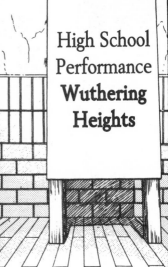

High School
Performance
**Wuthering
Heights**

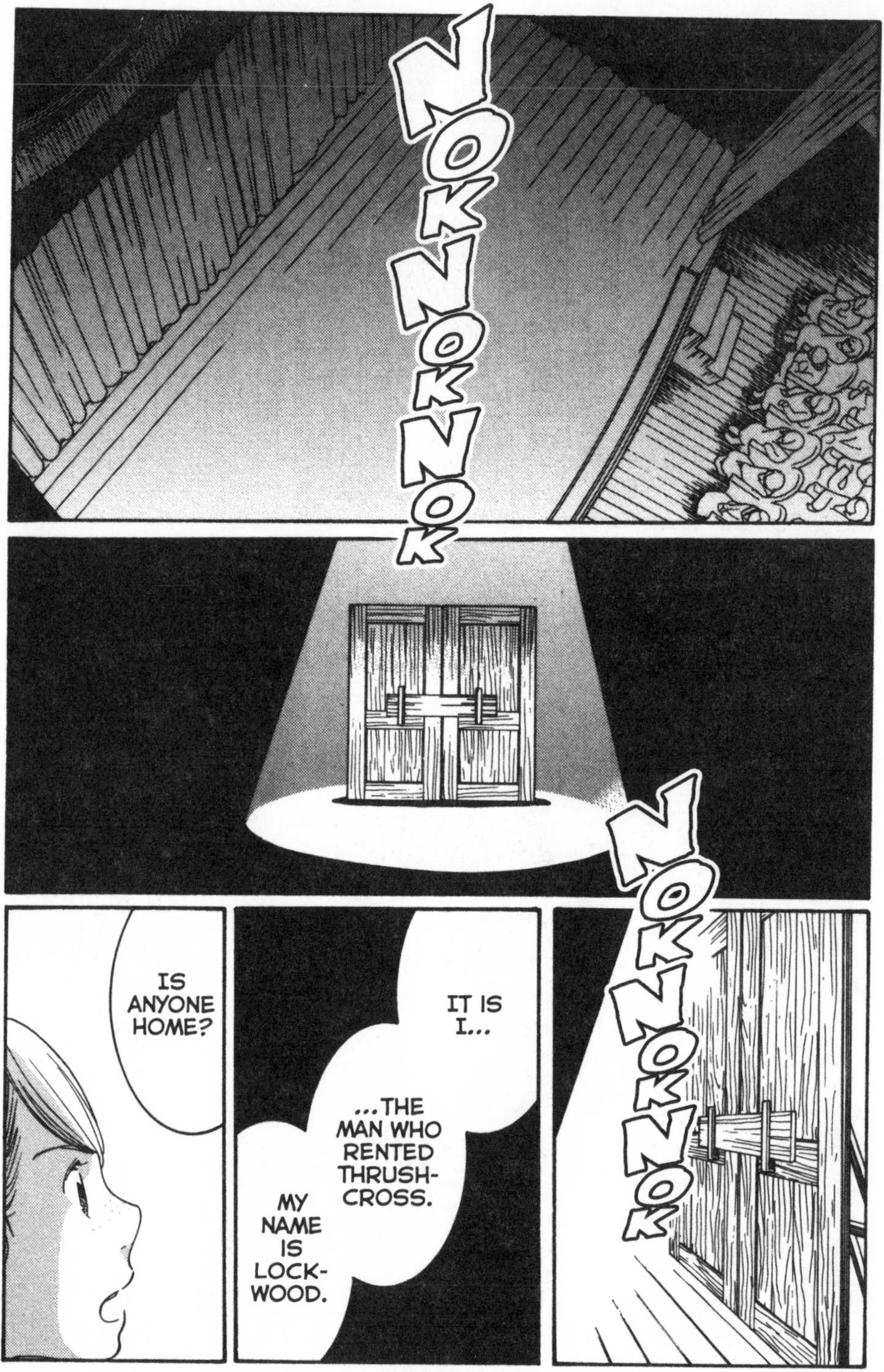
NOKNOKNOK
NOKNOKNOK
IT IS I...
...THE MAN WHO RENTED THRUSH-CROSS.
MY NAME IS LOCK-WOOD.
IS ANYONE HOME?

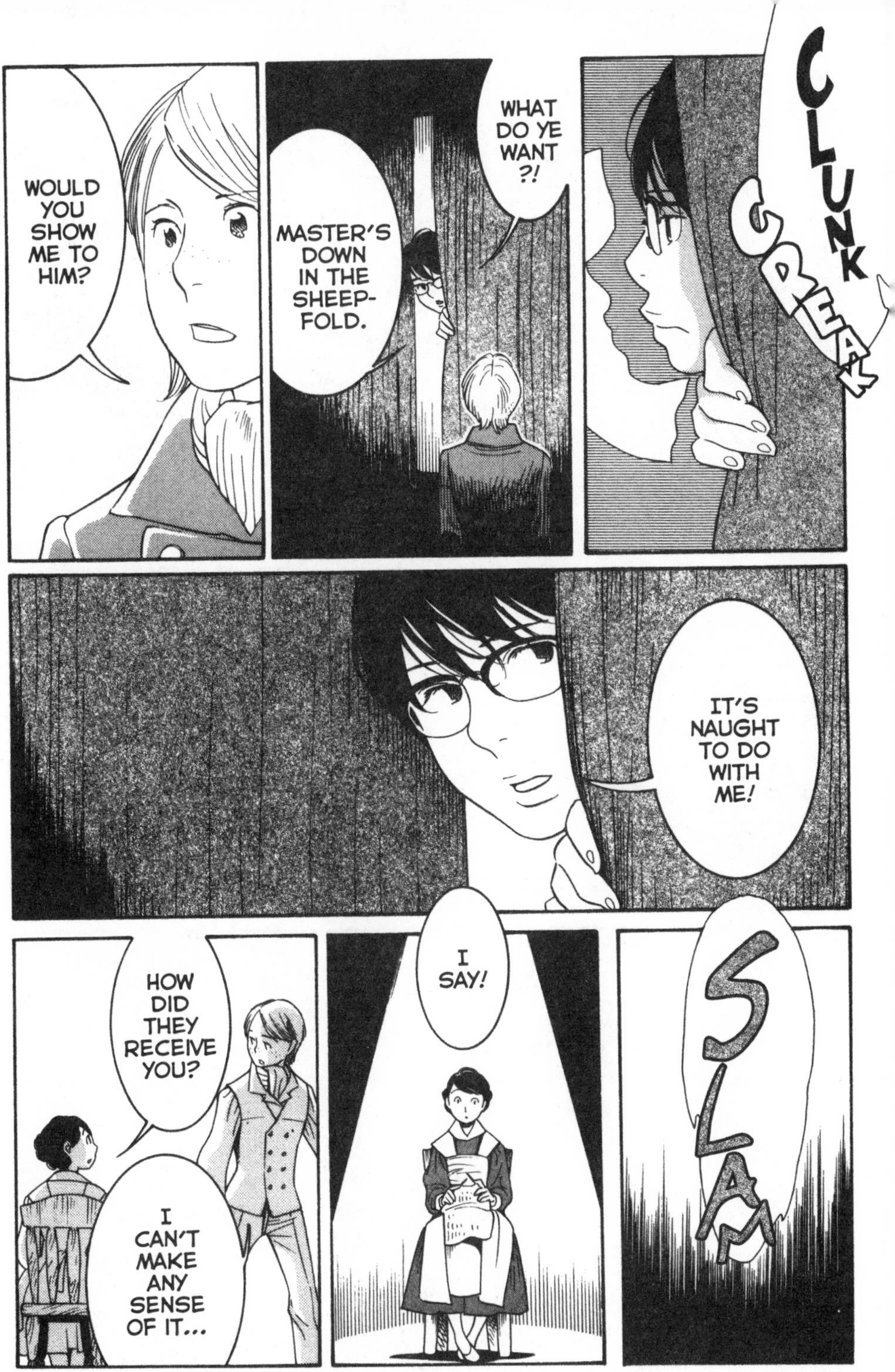
CLUNK
CREAK
WHAT DO YE WANT?!
MASTER'S DOWN IN THE SHEEP-FOLD.
WOULD YOU SHOW ME TO HIM?
IT'S NAUGHT TO DO WITH ME!
SLAM
I SAY!
HOW DID THEY RECEIVE YOU?
I CAN'T MAKE ANY SENSE OF IT...

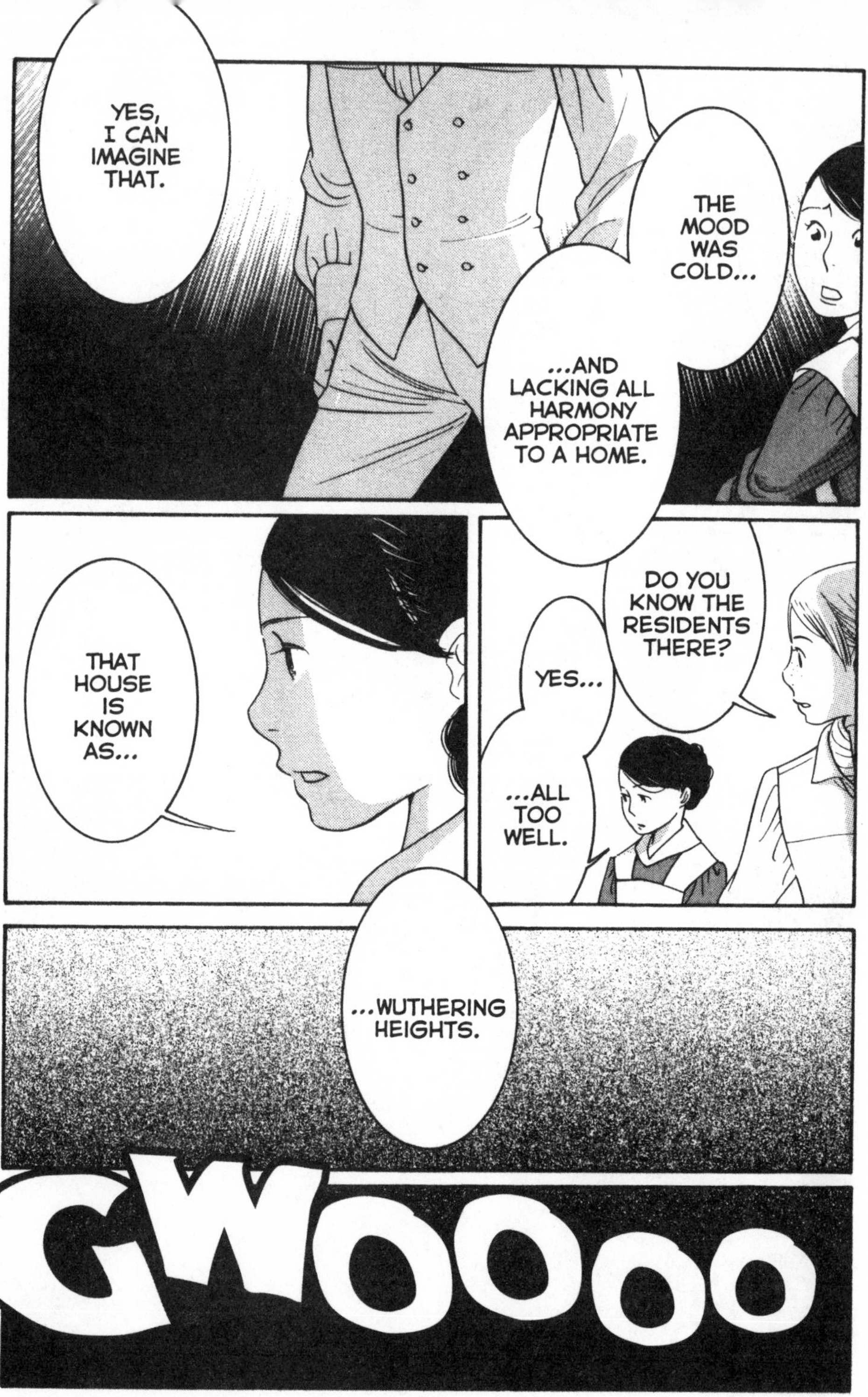
THE MOOD WAS COLD...
...AND LACKING ALL HARMONY APPROPRIATE TO A HOME.
YES, I CAN IMAGINE THAT.
DO YOU KNOW THE RESIDENTS THERE?
YES...
...ALL TOO WELL.
THAT HOUSE IS KNOWN AS...
...WUTHERING HEIGHTS.
GWOOOO

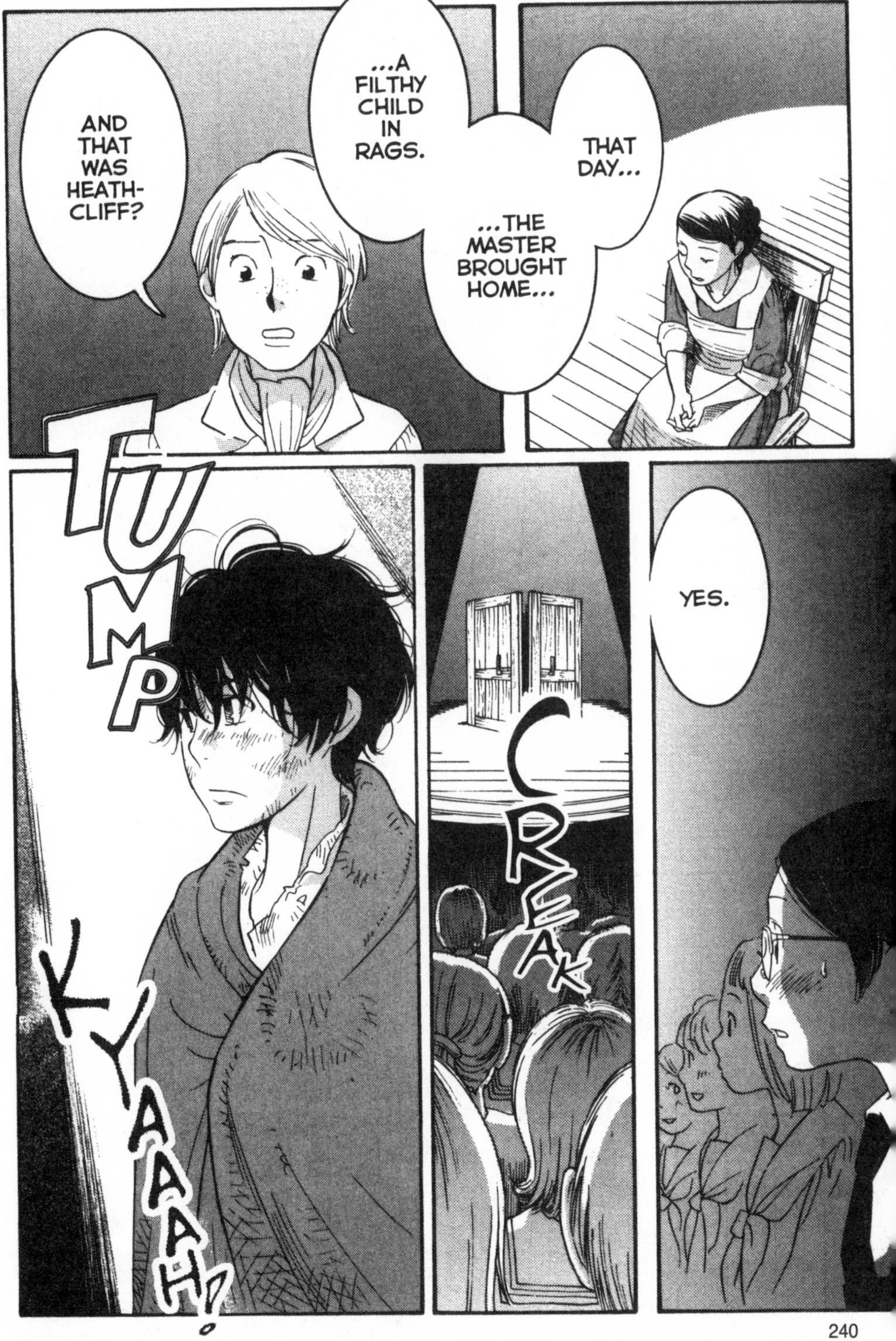
THAT DAY...
...THE MASTER BROUGHT HOME...
...A FILTHY CHILD IN RAGS.
AND THAT WAS HEATHCLIFF?
YES.
CREAK
TUMP
KYAAAAH!

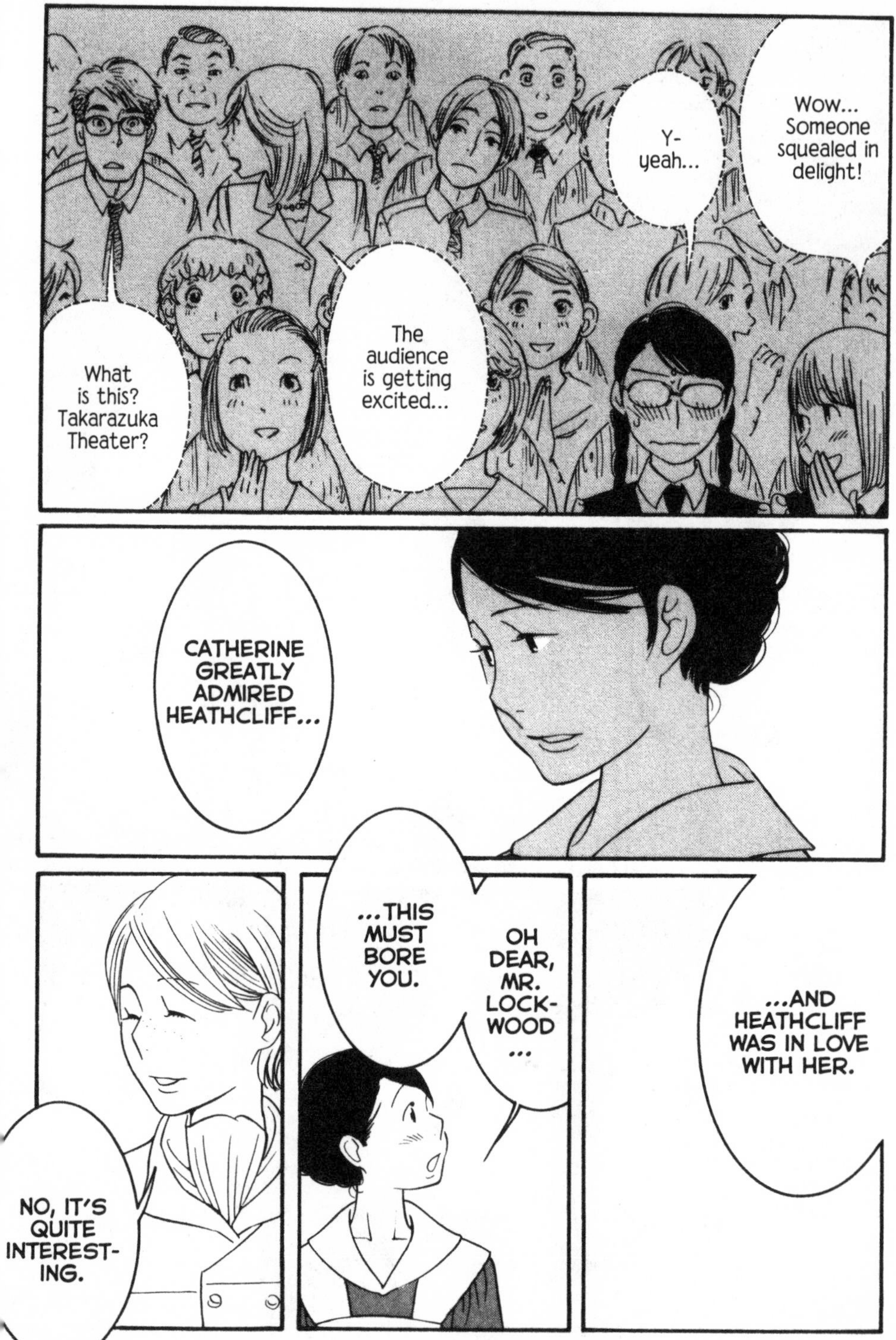
Wow... Someone squealed in delight!
Y-yeah...
The audience is getting excited...
What is this? Takarazuka Theater?
CATHERINE GREATLY ADMIRED HEATHCLIFF...
...AND HEATHCLIFF WAS IN LOVE WITH HER.
OH DEAR, MR. LOCKWOOD...
...THIS MUST BORE YOU.
NO, IT'S QUITE INTERESTING.

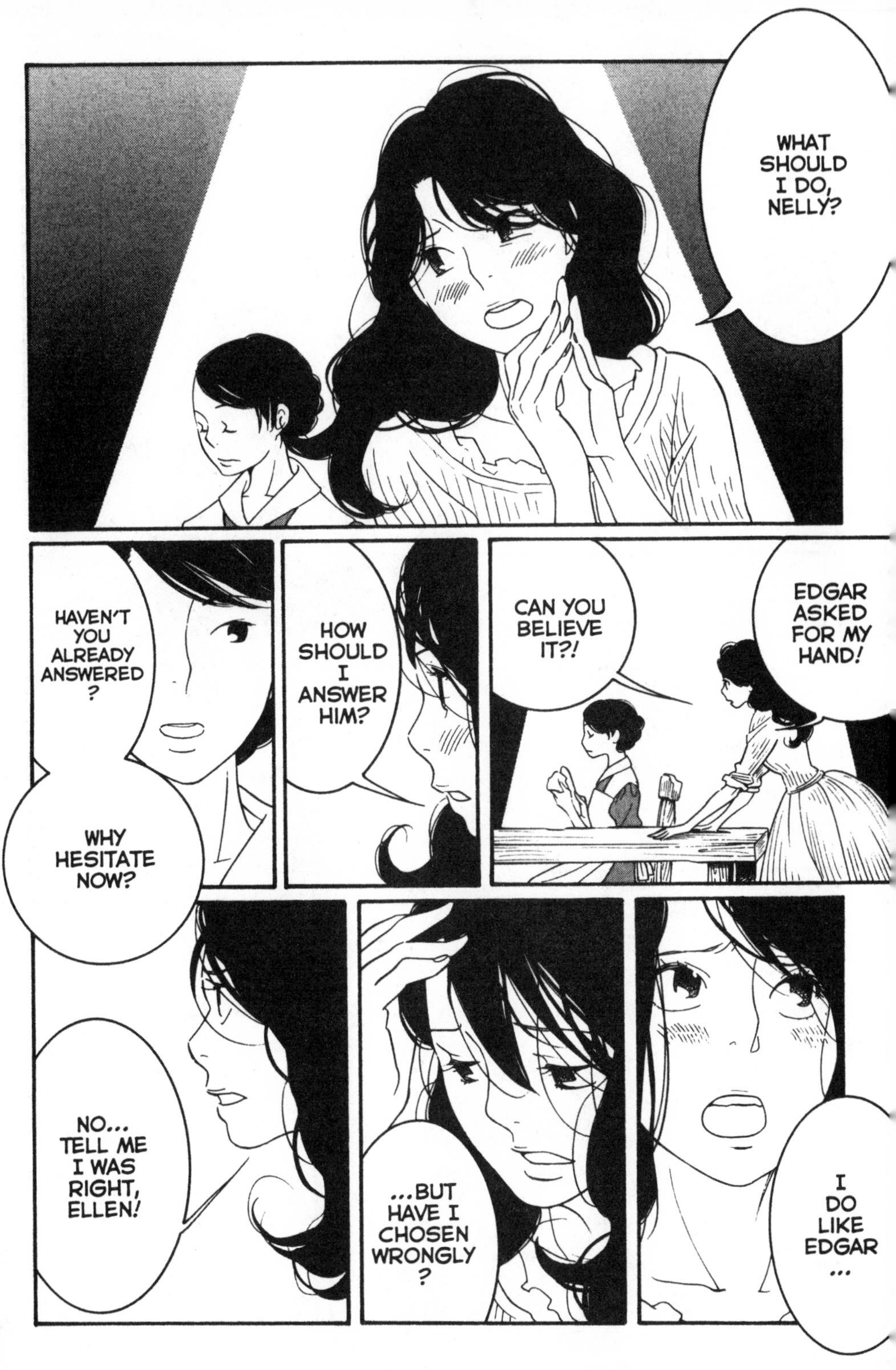
WHAT SHOULD I DO, NELLY?
EDGAR ASKED FOR MY HAND!
CAN YOU BELIEVE IT?!
HOW SHOULD I ANSWER HIM?
HAVEN'T YOU ALREADY ANSWERED?
WHY HESITATE NOW?
I DO LIKE EDGAR...
...BUT HAVE I CHOSEN WRONGLY?
NO... TELL ME I WAS RIGHT, ELLEN!

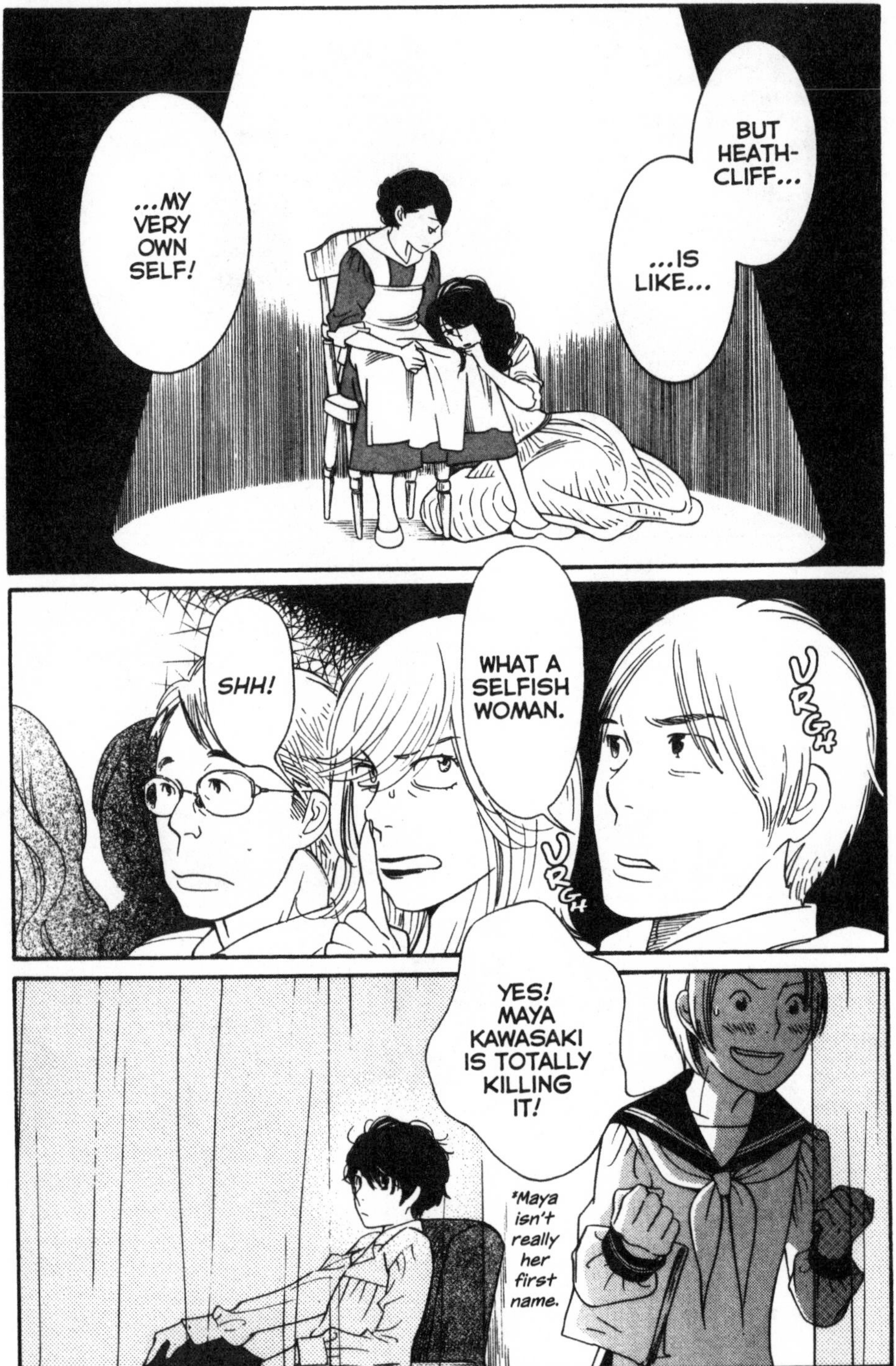
BUT HEATH-CLIFF...
...IS LIKE...
...MY VERY OWN SELF!
URGH
WHAT A SELFISH WOMAN.
URGH
SHH!
YES! MAYA KAWASAKI IS TOTALLY KILLING IT!
*Maya isn't really her first name.

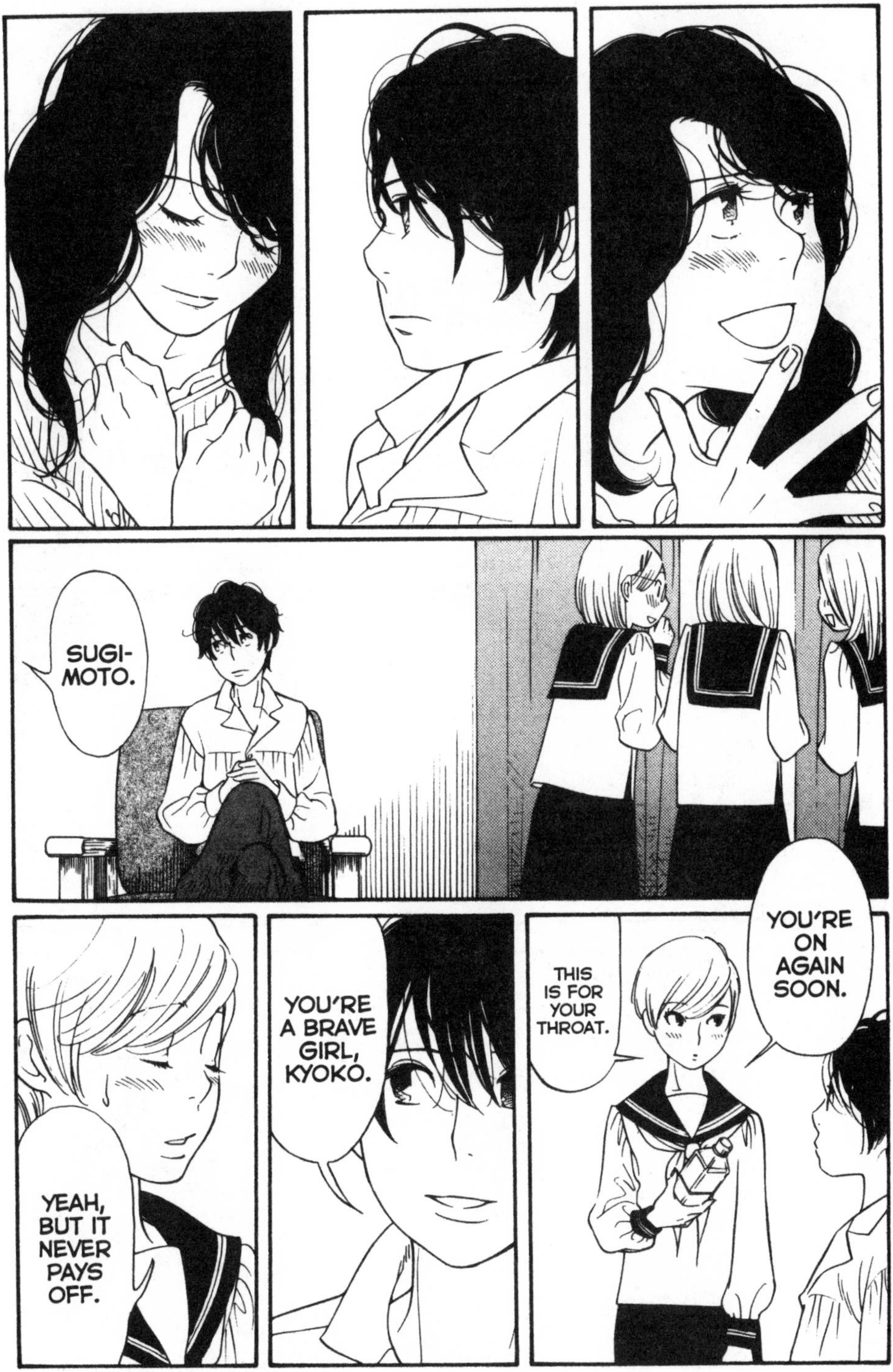
SUGI-MOTO.
YOU'RE ON AGAIN SOON.
THIS IS FOR YOUR THROAT.
YOU'RE A BRAVE GIRL, KYOKO.
YEAH, BUT IT NEVER PAYS OFF.

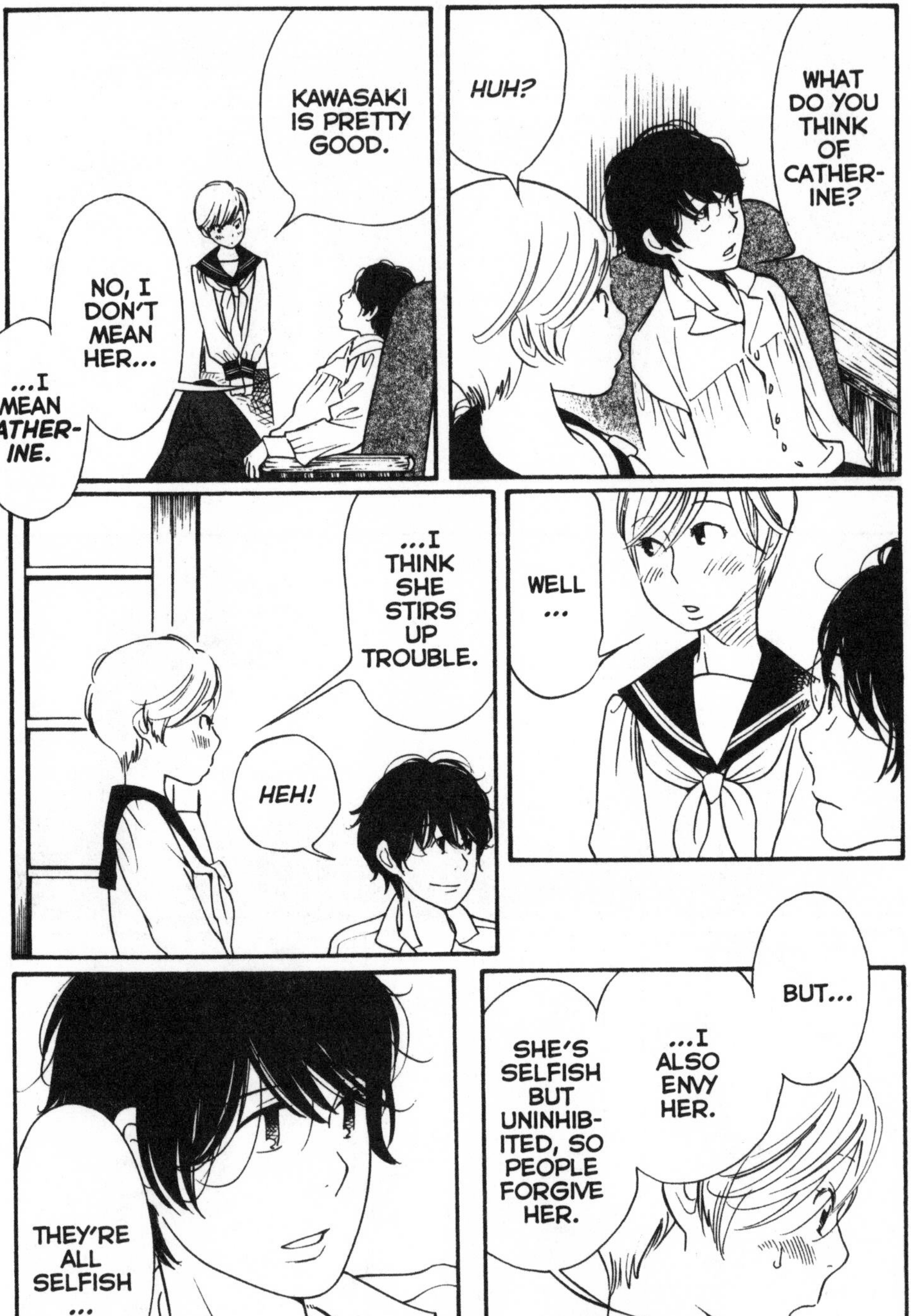
WHAT DO YOU THINK OF CATHER-INE?
HUH?
KAWASAKI IS PRETTY GOOD.
NO, I DON'T MEAN HER...
...I MEAN CATHER-INE.
WELL ...
...I THINK SHE STIRS UP TROUBLE.
HEH!
BUT...
...I ALSO ENVY HER.
SHE'S SELFISH BUT UNINHIB-ITED, SO PEOPLE FORGIVE HER.
THEY'RE ALL SELFISH ...

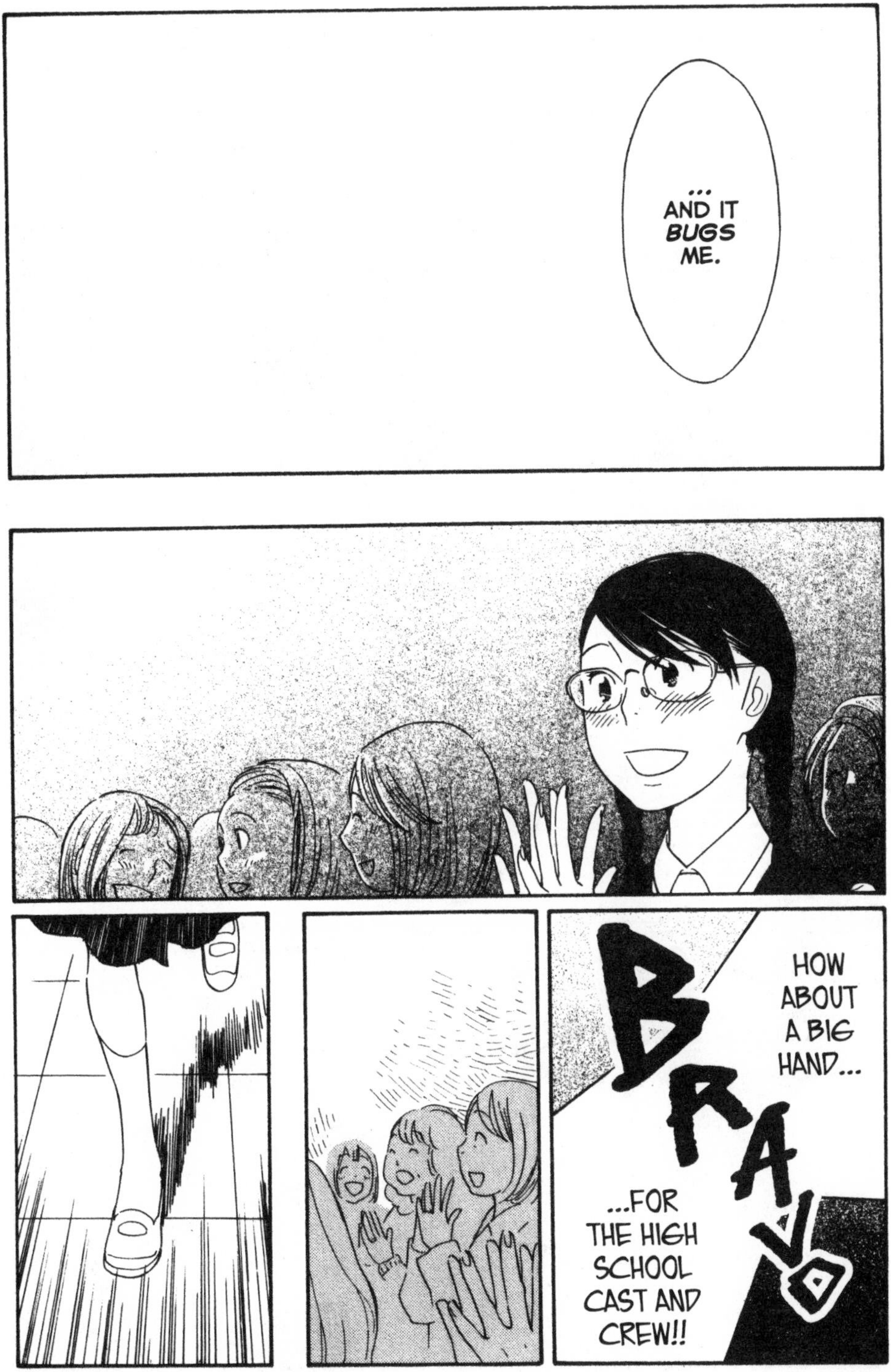
... AND IT BUGS ME.
HOW ABOUT A BIG HAND...
BRAVO
...FOR THE HIGH SCHOOL CAST AND CREW!!

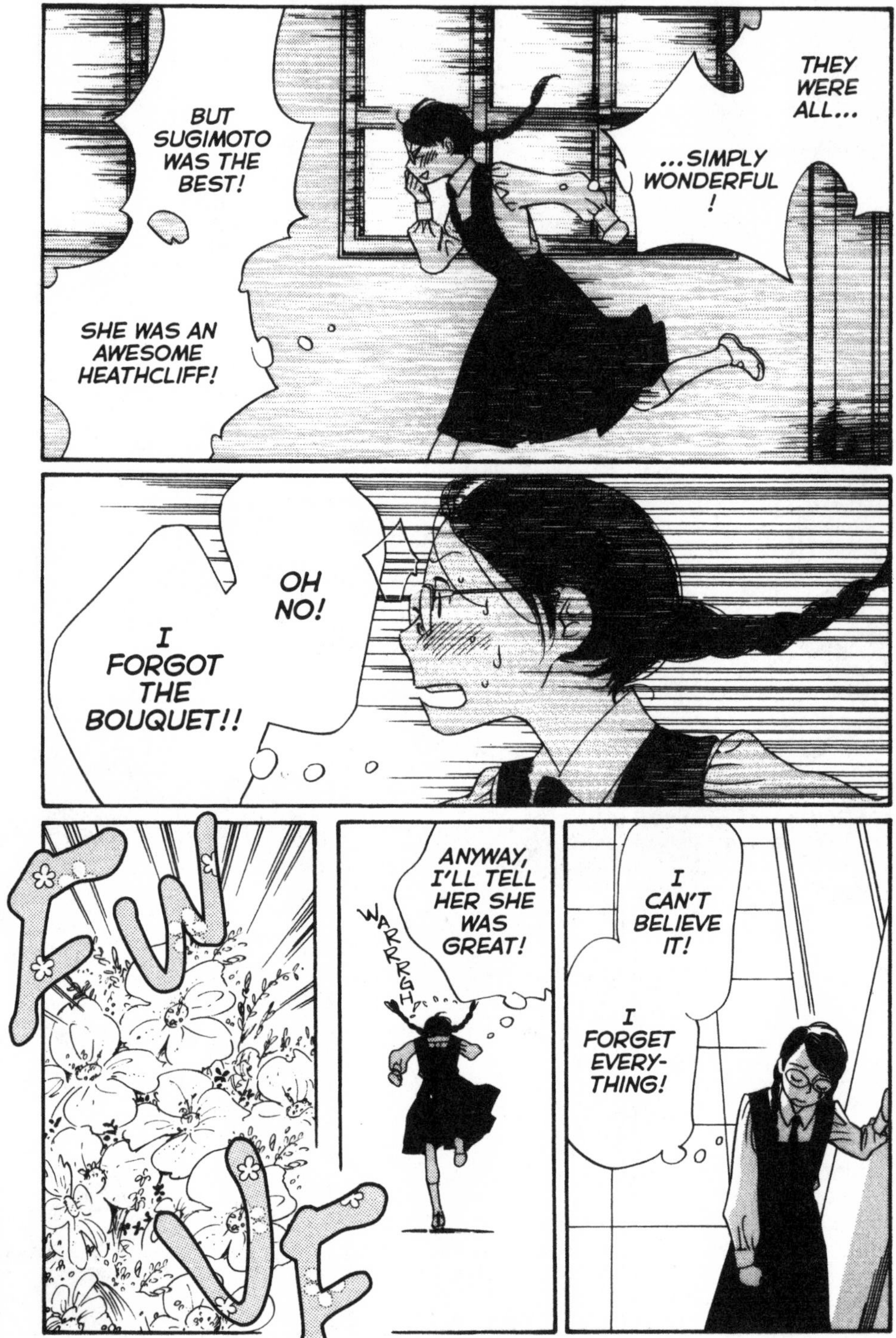
THEY WERE ALL...
...SIMPLY WONDERFUL!
BUT SUGIMOTO WAS THE BEST!
SHE WAS AN AWESOME HEATHCLIFF!
OH NO!
I FORGOT THE BOUQUET!!
I CAN'T BELIEVE IT!
I FORGET EVERY-THING!
ANYWAY, I'LL TELL HER SHE WAS GREAT!
WARRRGH

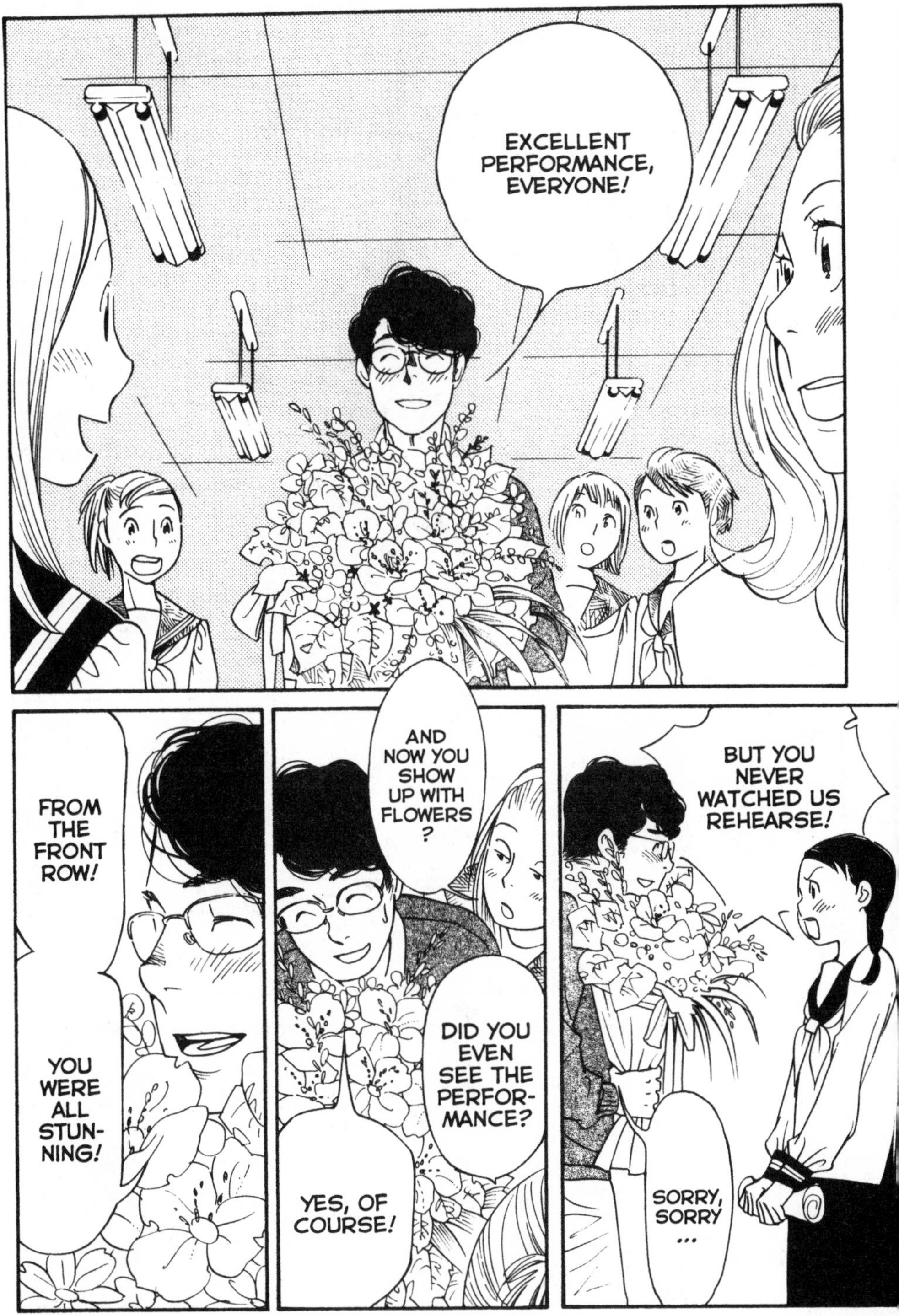
EXCELLENT PERFORMANCE, EVERYONE!
BUT YOU NEVER WATCHED US REHEARSE!
SORRY, SORRY ...
AND NOW YOU SHOW UP WITH FLOWERS?
DID YOU EVEN SEE THE PERFORMANCE?
YES, OF COURSE!
FROM THE FRONT ROW!
YOU WERE ALL STUNNING!

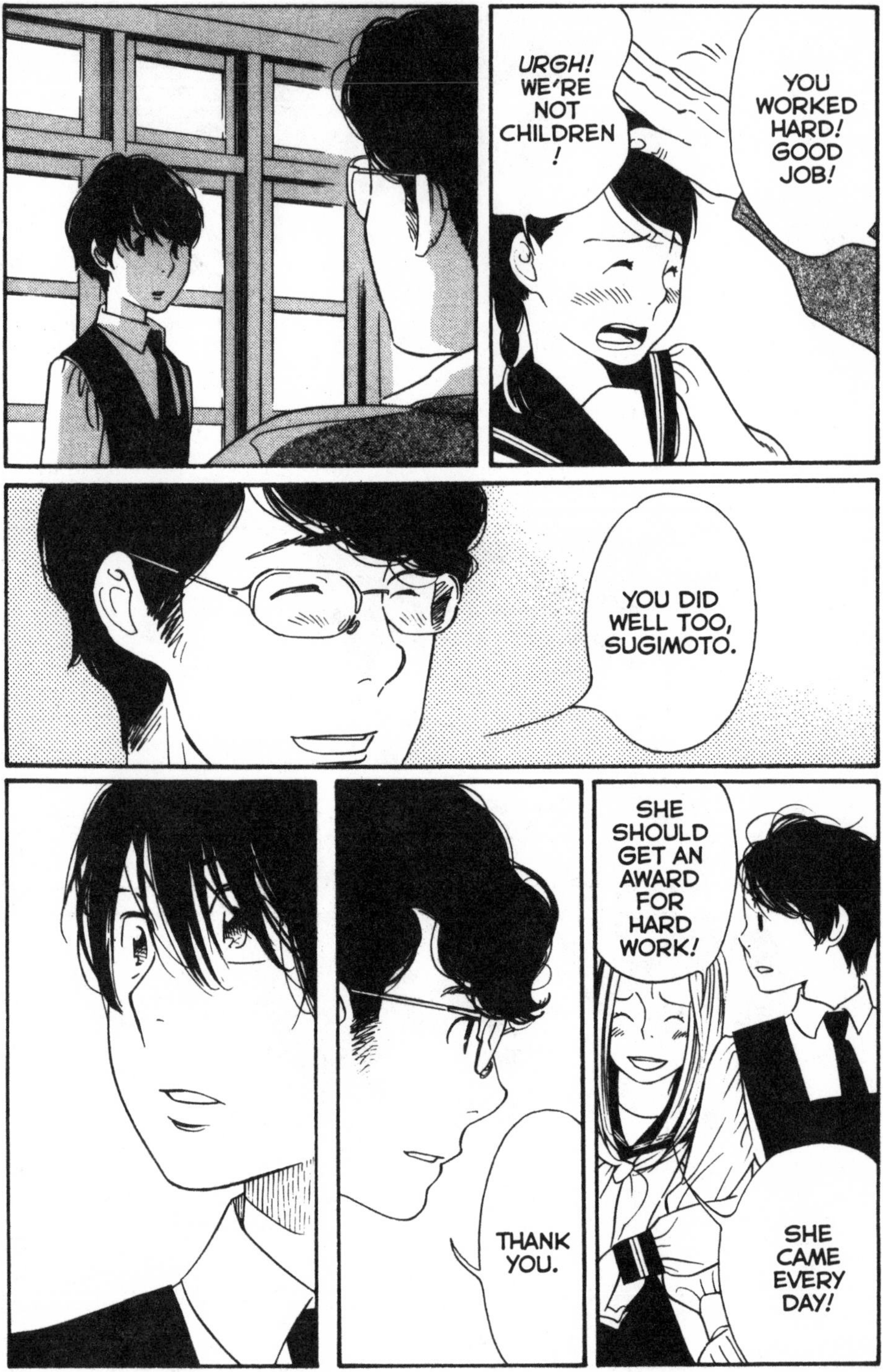
YOU WORKED HARD! GOOD JOB!
URGH! WE'RE NOT CHILDREN!
YOU DID WELL TOO, SUGIMOTO.
SHE SHOULD GET AN AWARD FOR HARD WORK!
SHE CAME EVERY DAY!
THANK YOU.

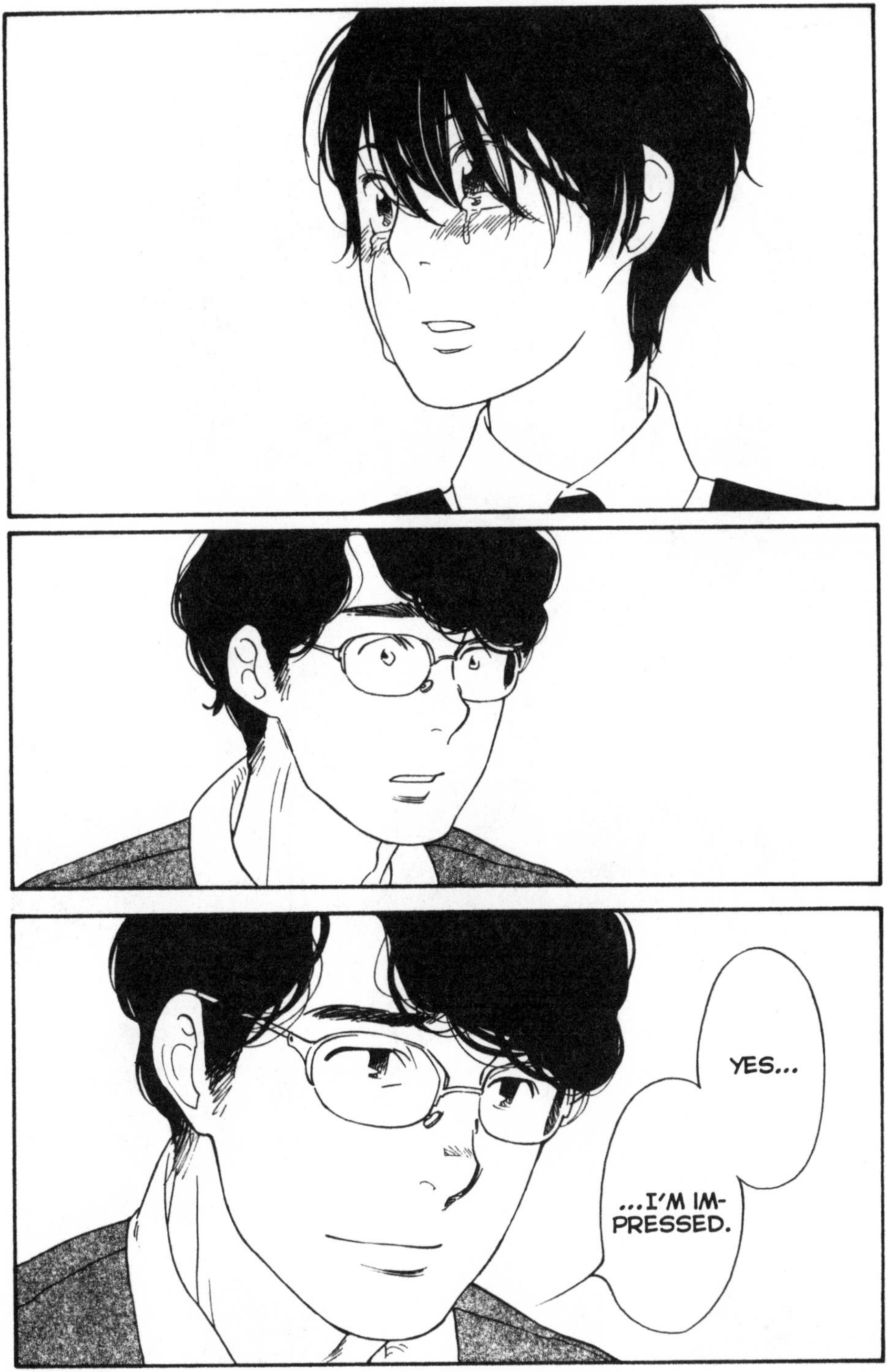
YES...
...I'M IM-
PRESSED.

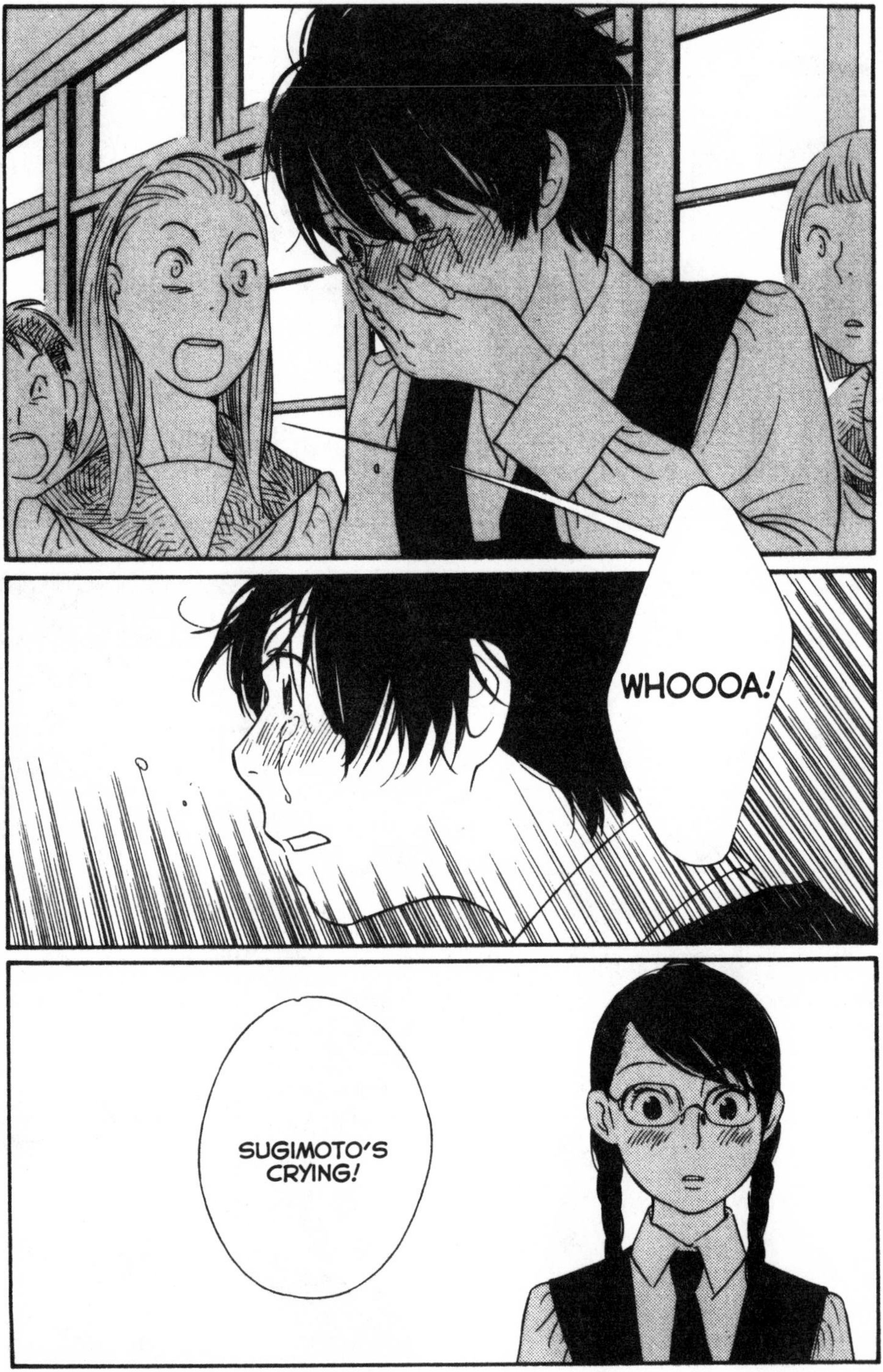
WHOOOA!
SUGIMOTO'S CRYING!

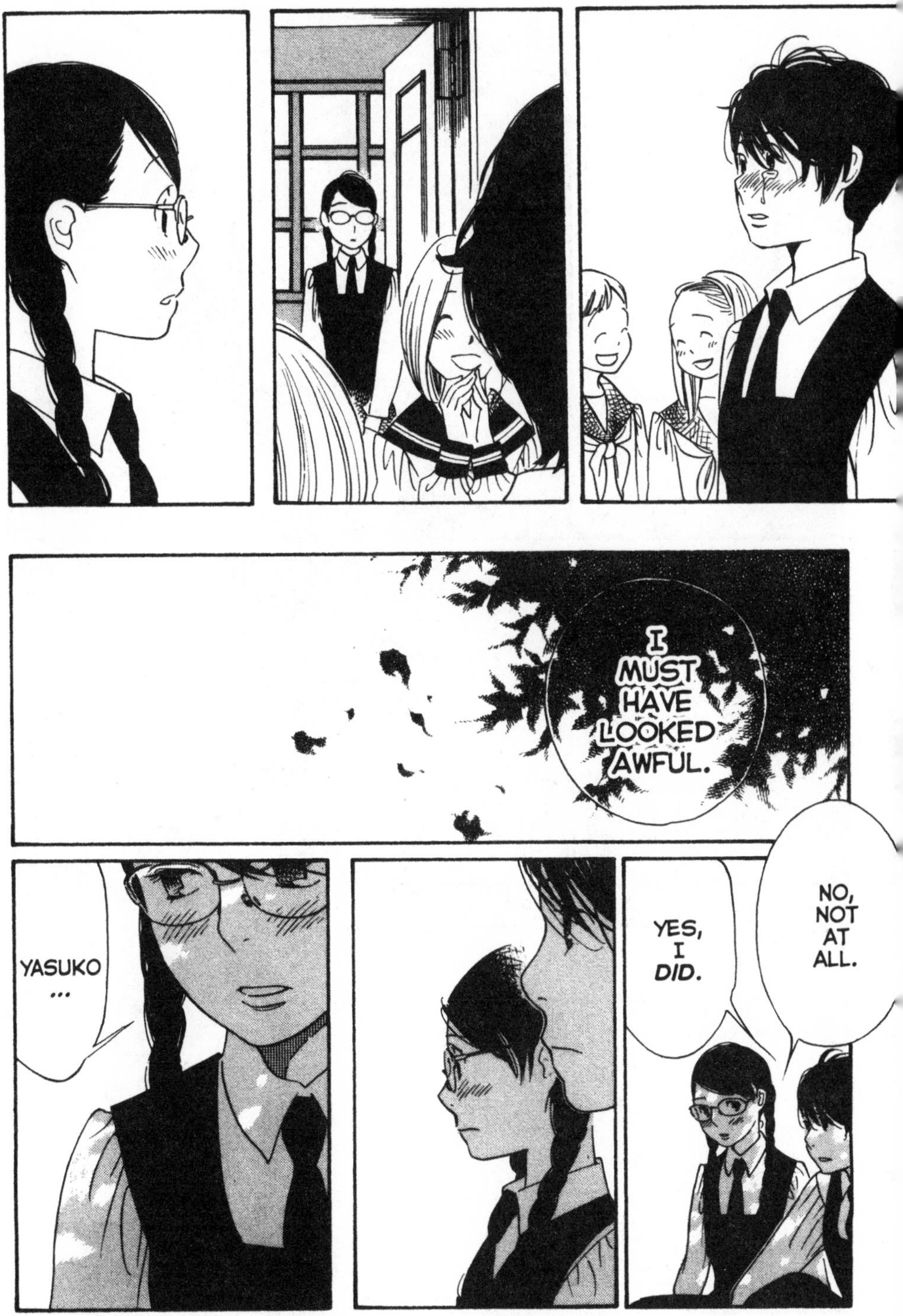
I MUST HAVE LOOKED AWFUL.
NO, NOT AT ALL.
YES, I *DID*.
YASUKO ...

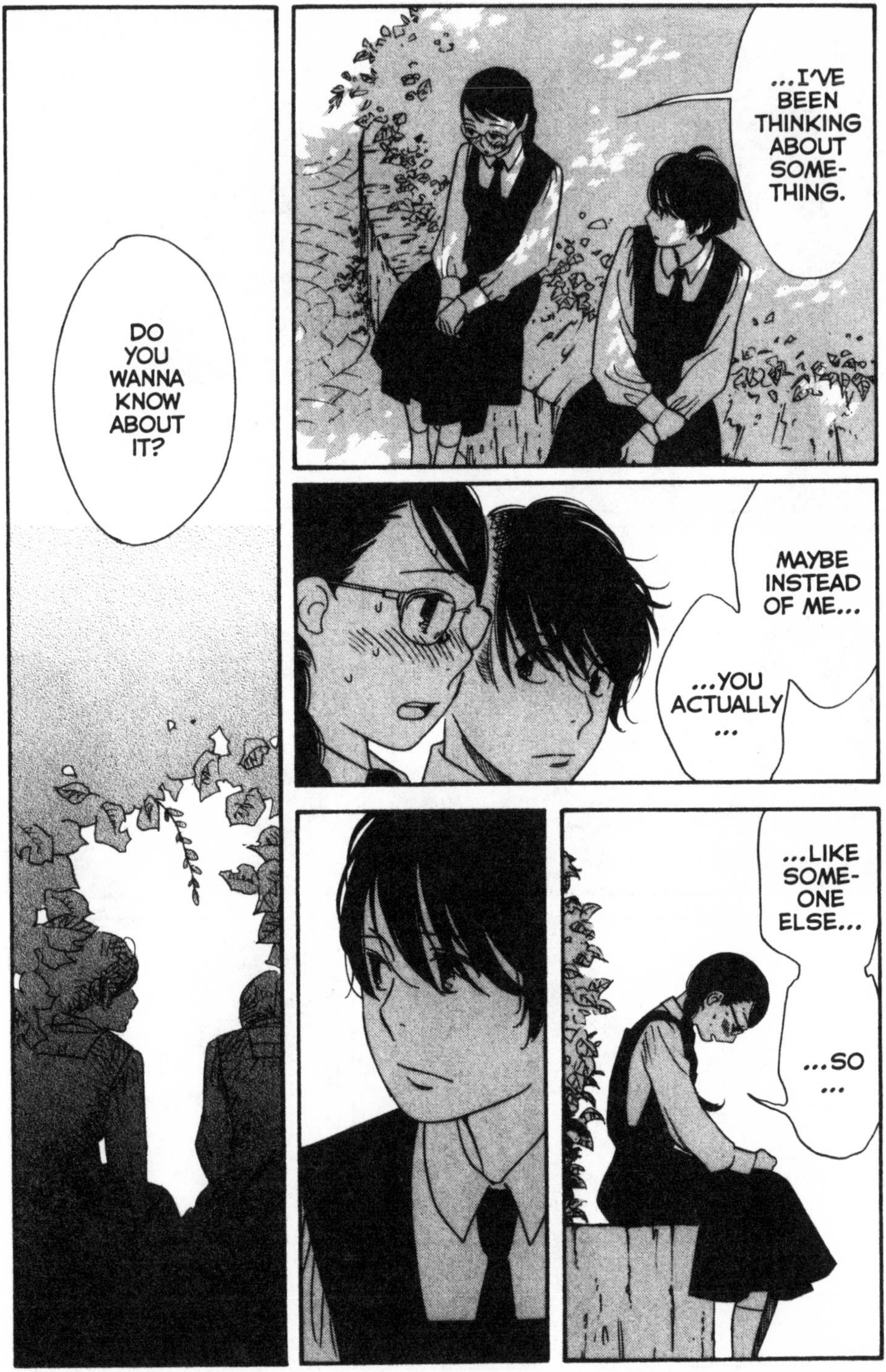
...I'VE BEEN THINKING ABOUT SOME-THING.
MAYBE INSTEAD OF ME...
...YOU ACTUALLY ...
...LIKE SOME-ONE ELSE...
...SO ...
DO YOU WANNA KNOW ABOUT IT?

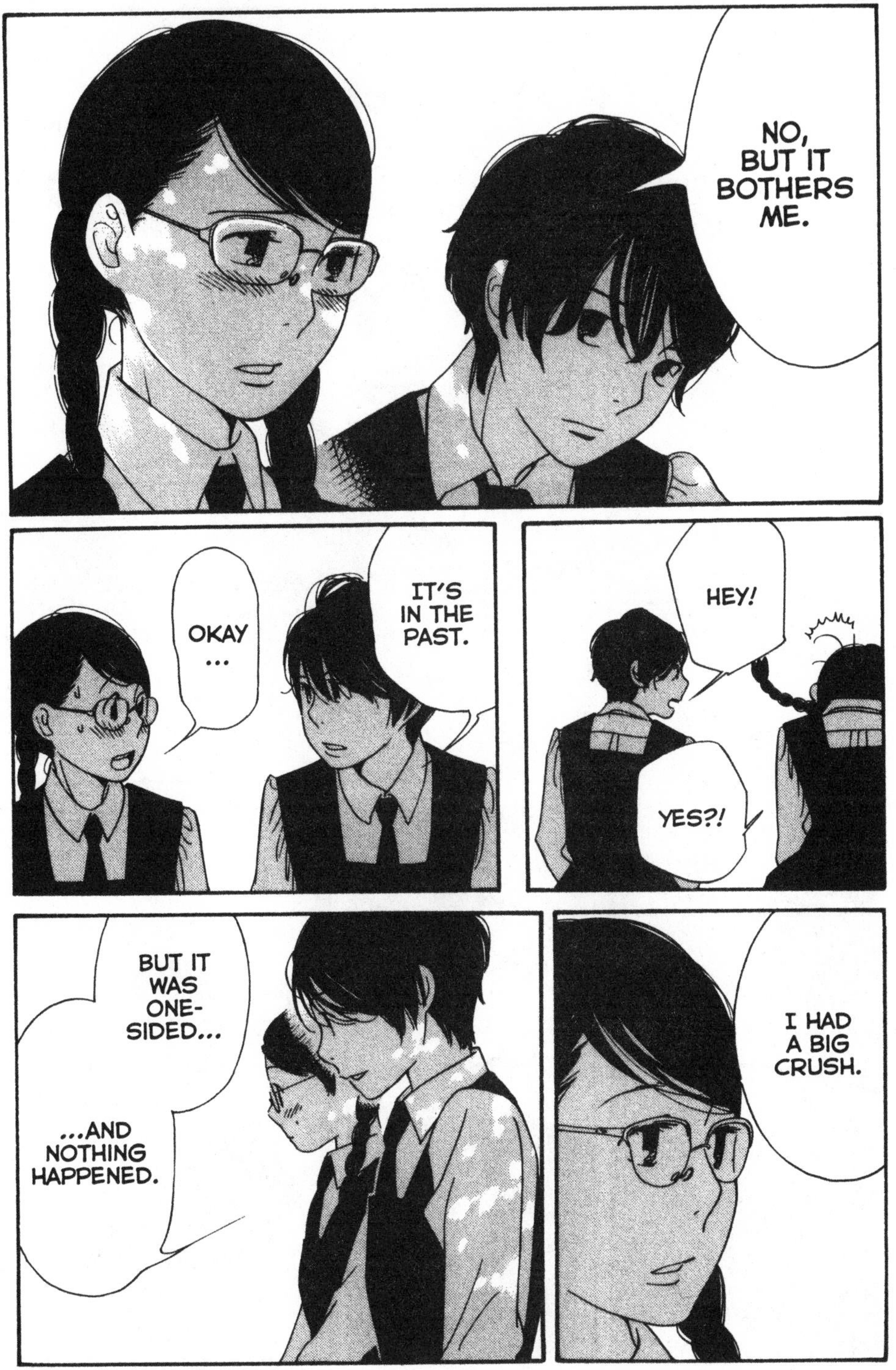
NO, BUT IT BOTHERS ME.
HEY!
YES?!
IT'S IN THE PAST.
OKAY ...
I HAD A BIG CRUSH.
BUT IT WAS ONE-SIDED...
...AND NOTHING HAPPENED.

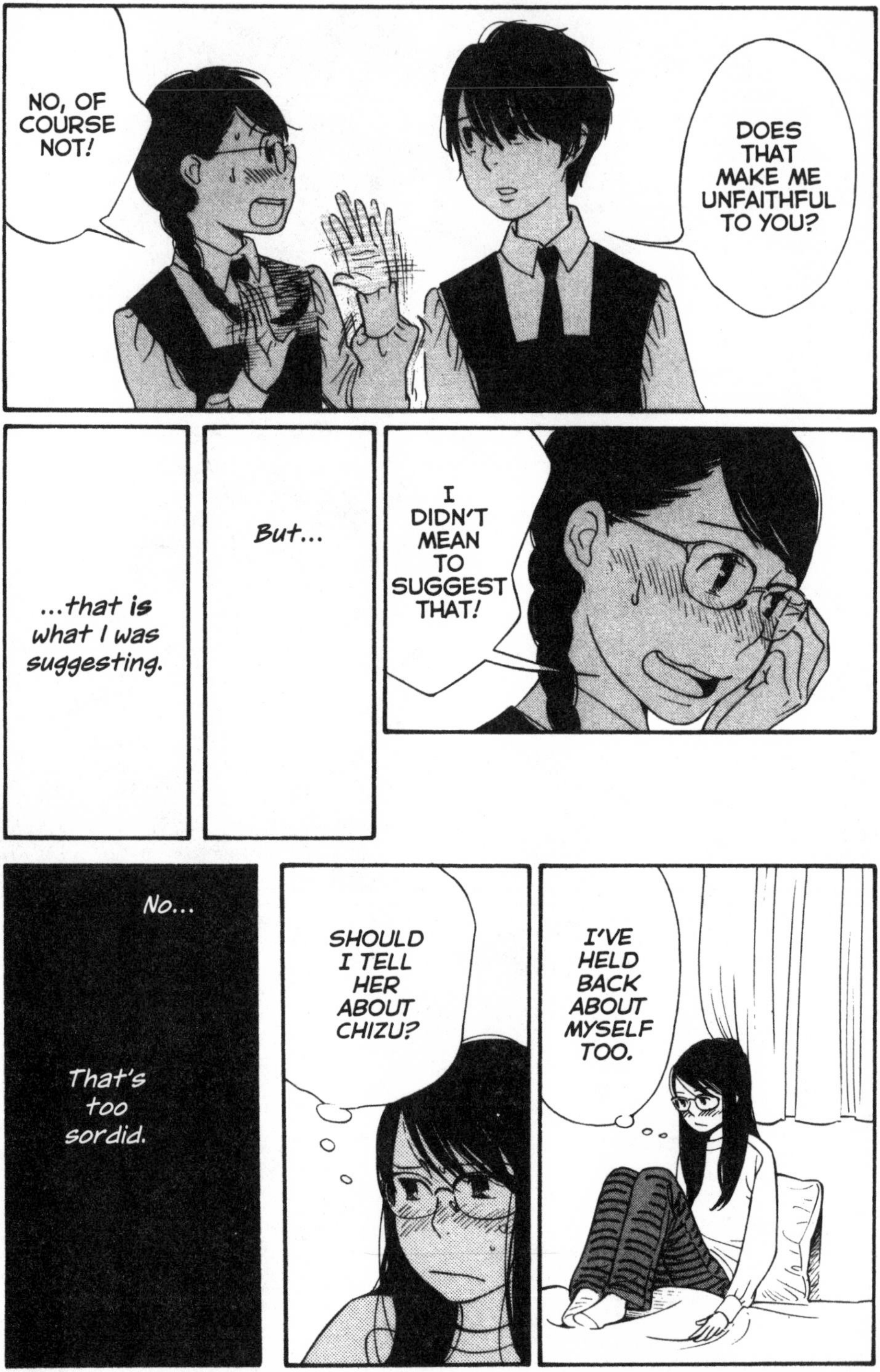
DOES THAT MAKE ME UNFAITHFUL TO YOU?
NO, OF COURSE NOT!
I DIDN'T MEAN TO SUGGEST THAT!
But...
...that is what I was suggesting.
I'VE HELD BACK ABOUT MYSELF TOO.
SHOULD I TELL HER ABOUT CHIZU?
No...
That's too sordid.

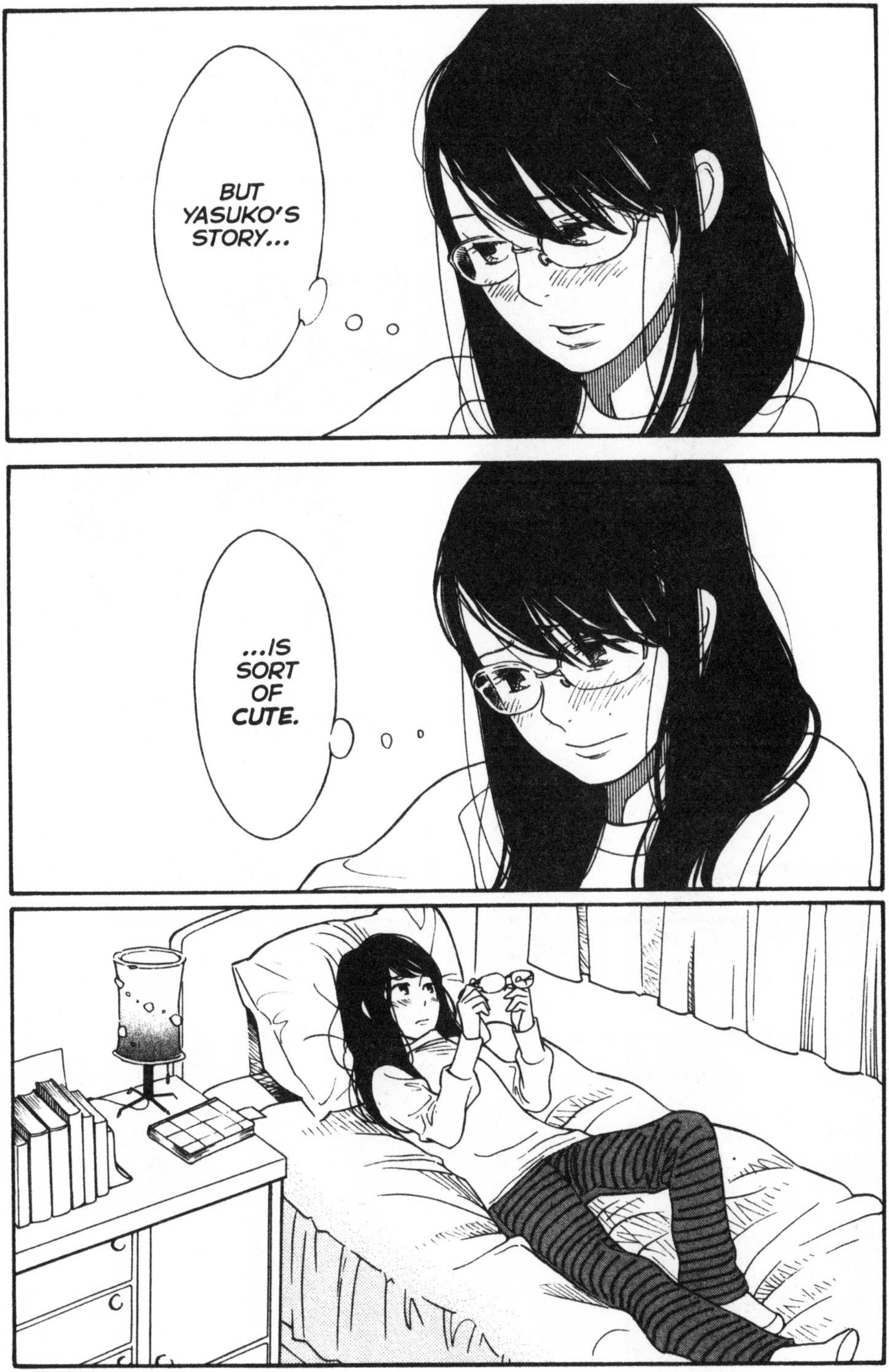
BUT YASUKO'S STORY...
...IS SORT OF CUTE.

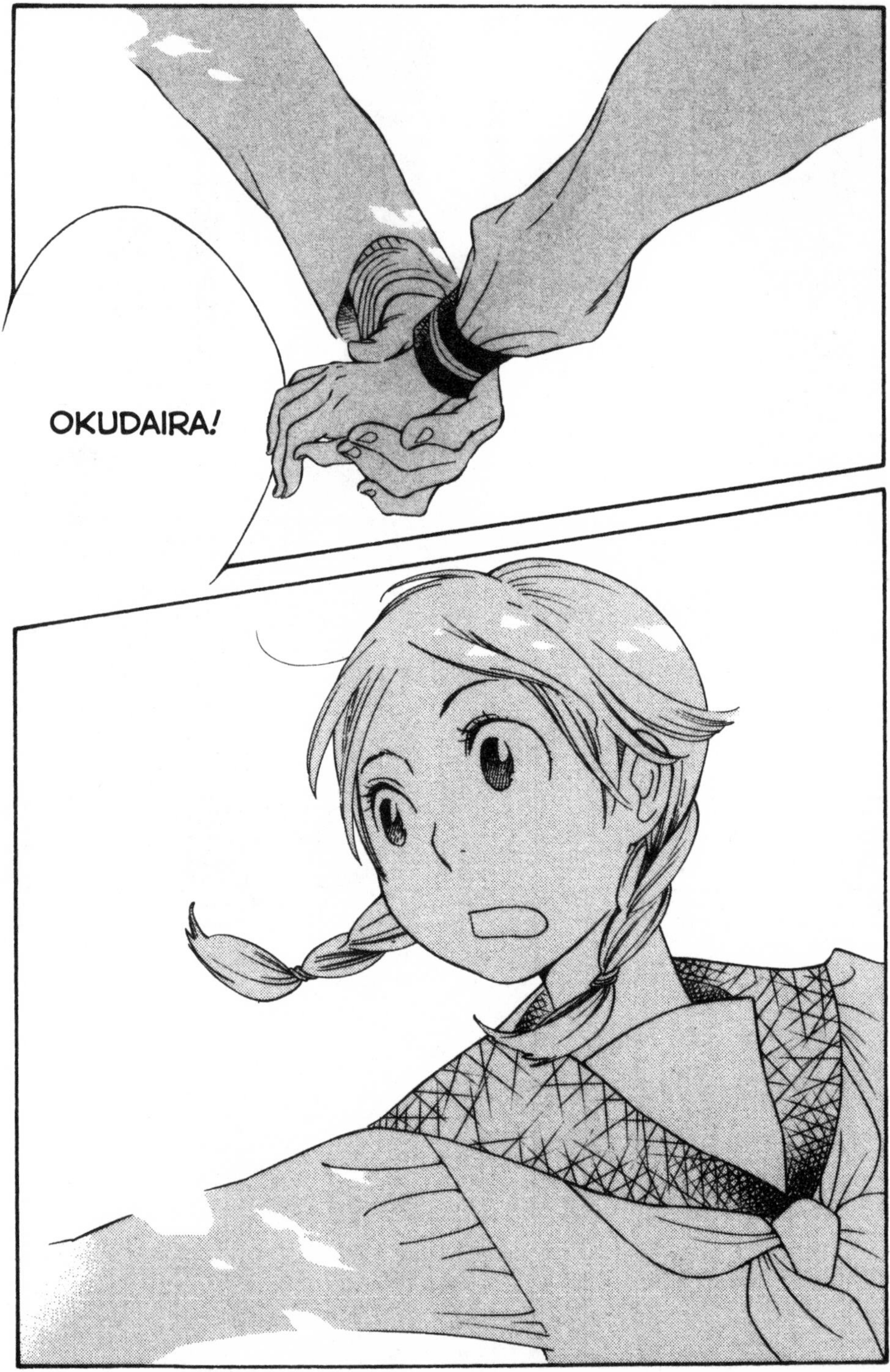
OKUDAIRA!

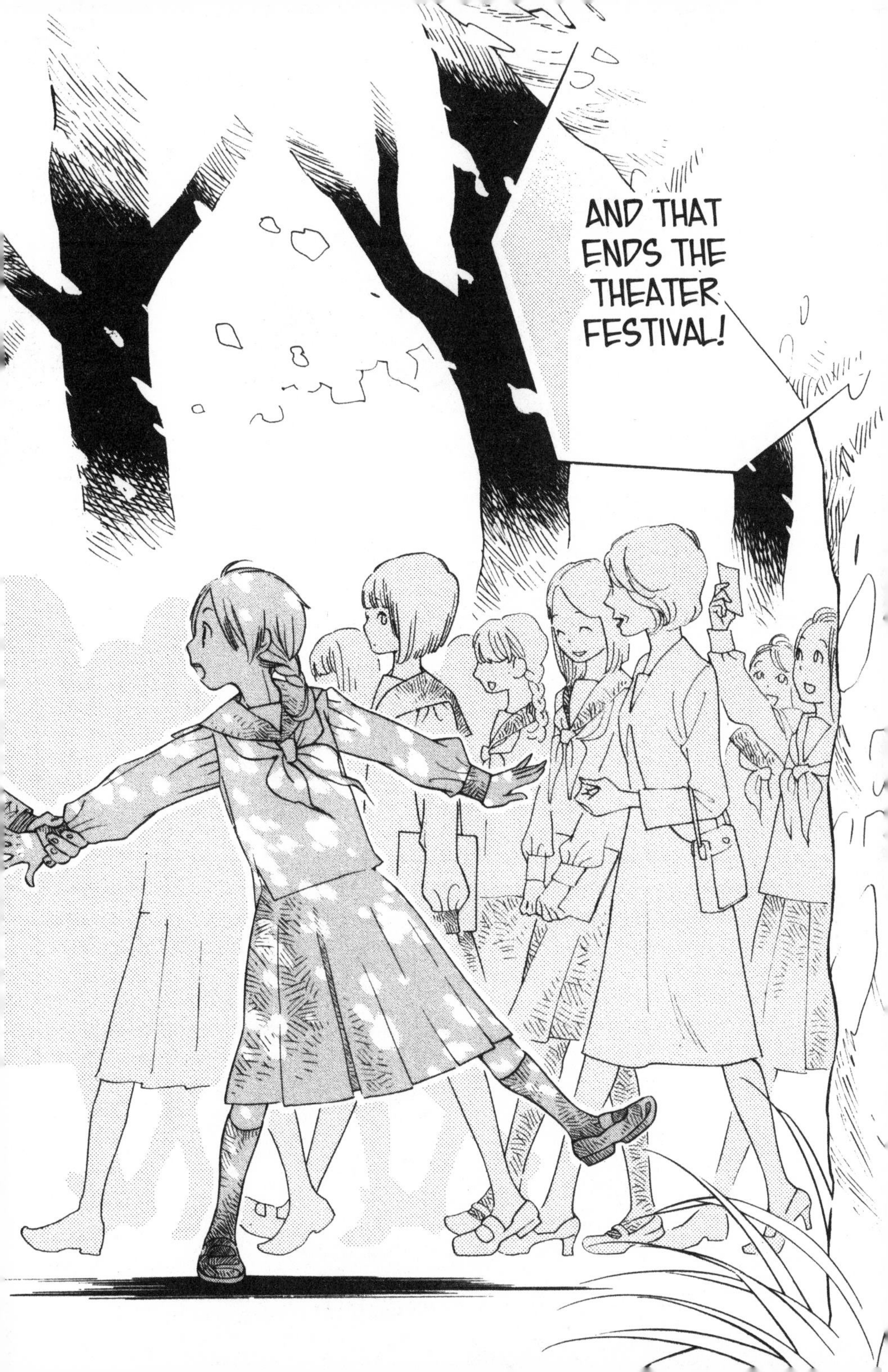
AND THAT ENDS THE THEATER FESTIVAL!

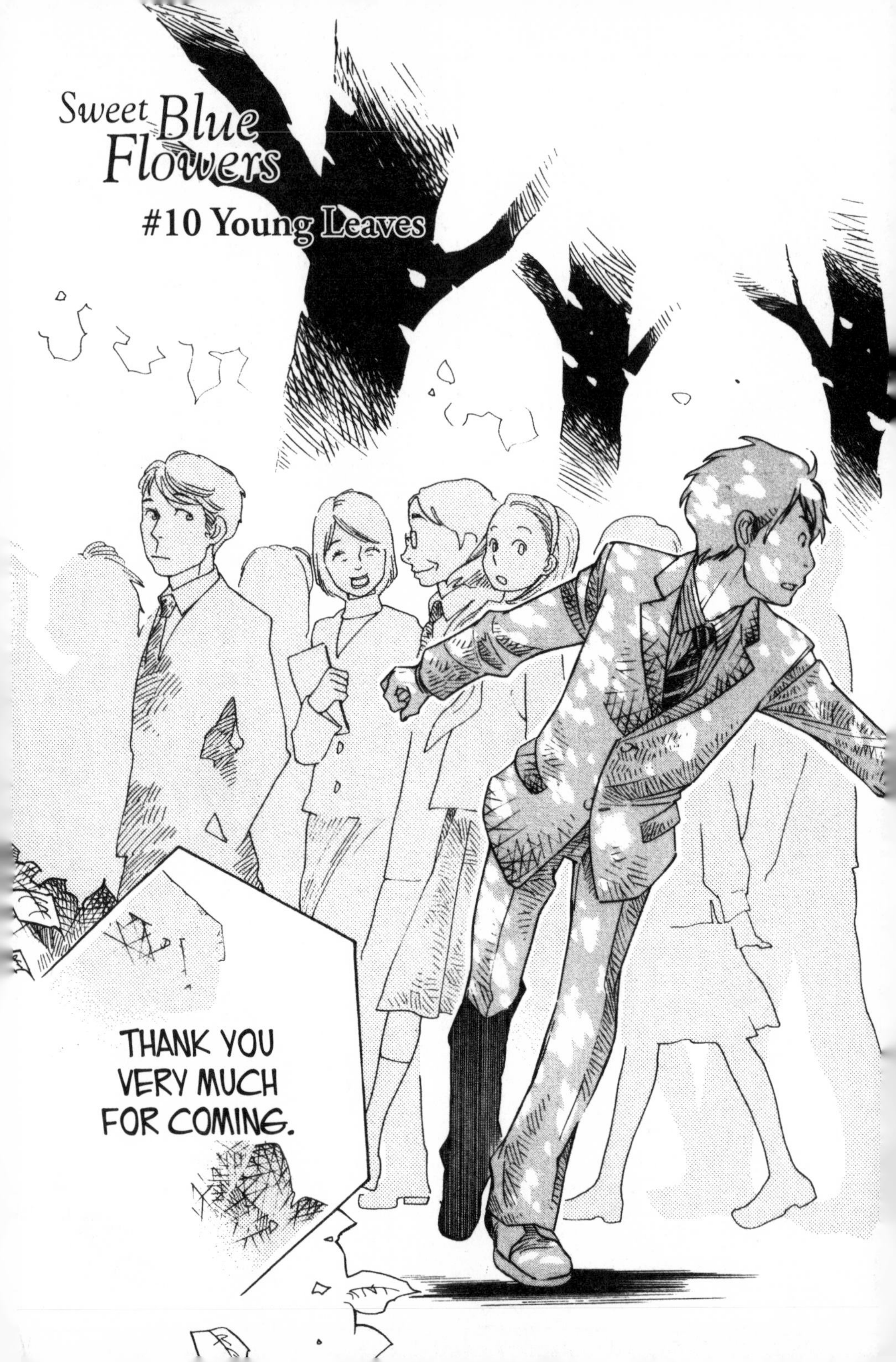
Sweet Blue Flowers
#10 Young Leaves
THANK YOU VERY MUCH FOR COMING.

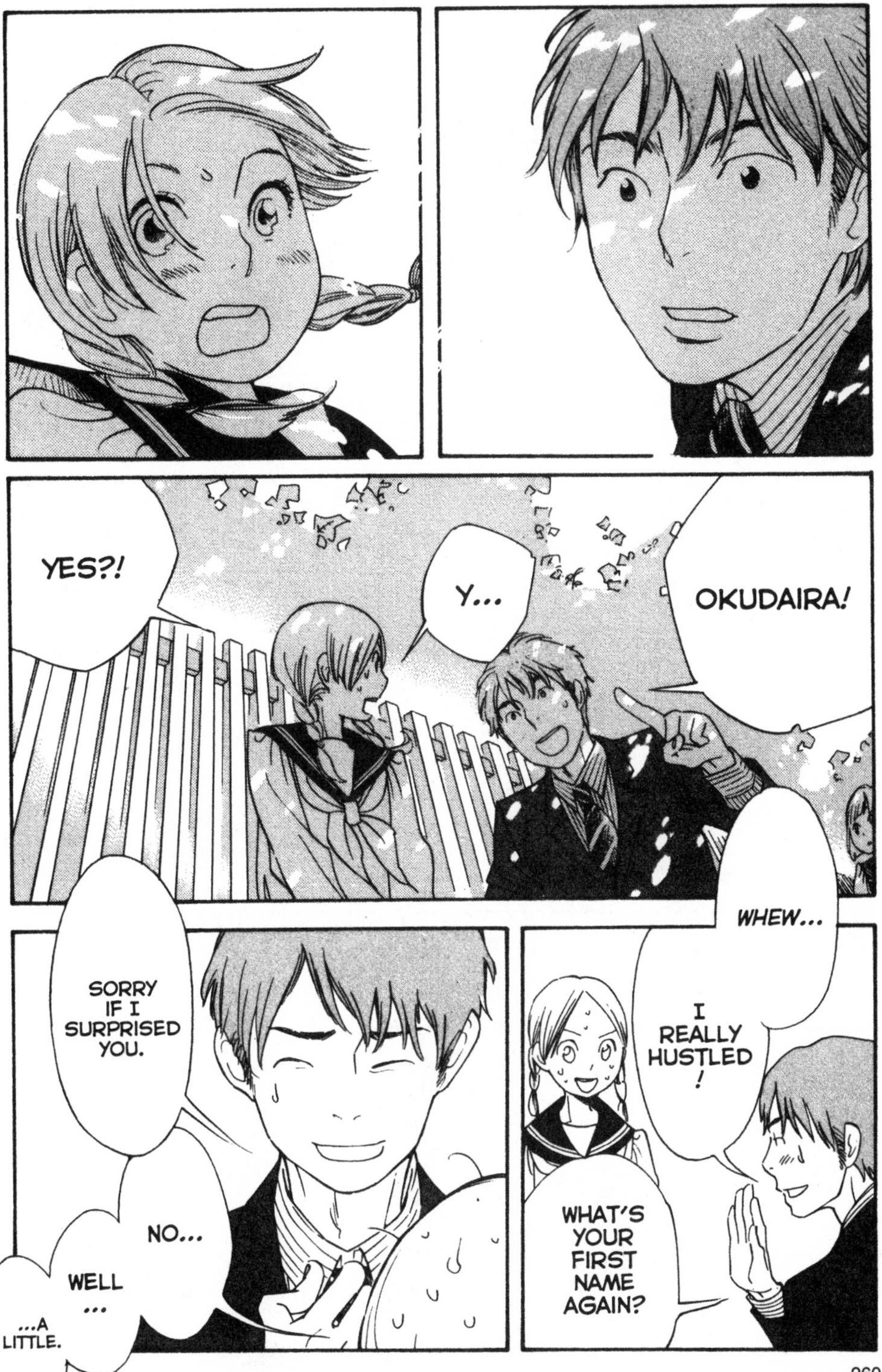
OKUDAIRA!
Y...
YES?!
WHEW...
I REALLY HUSTLED!
WHAT'S YOUR FIRST NAME AGAIN?
SORRY IF I SURPRISED YOU.
NO...
WELL ...
...A LITTLE.

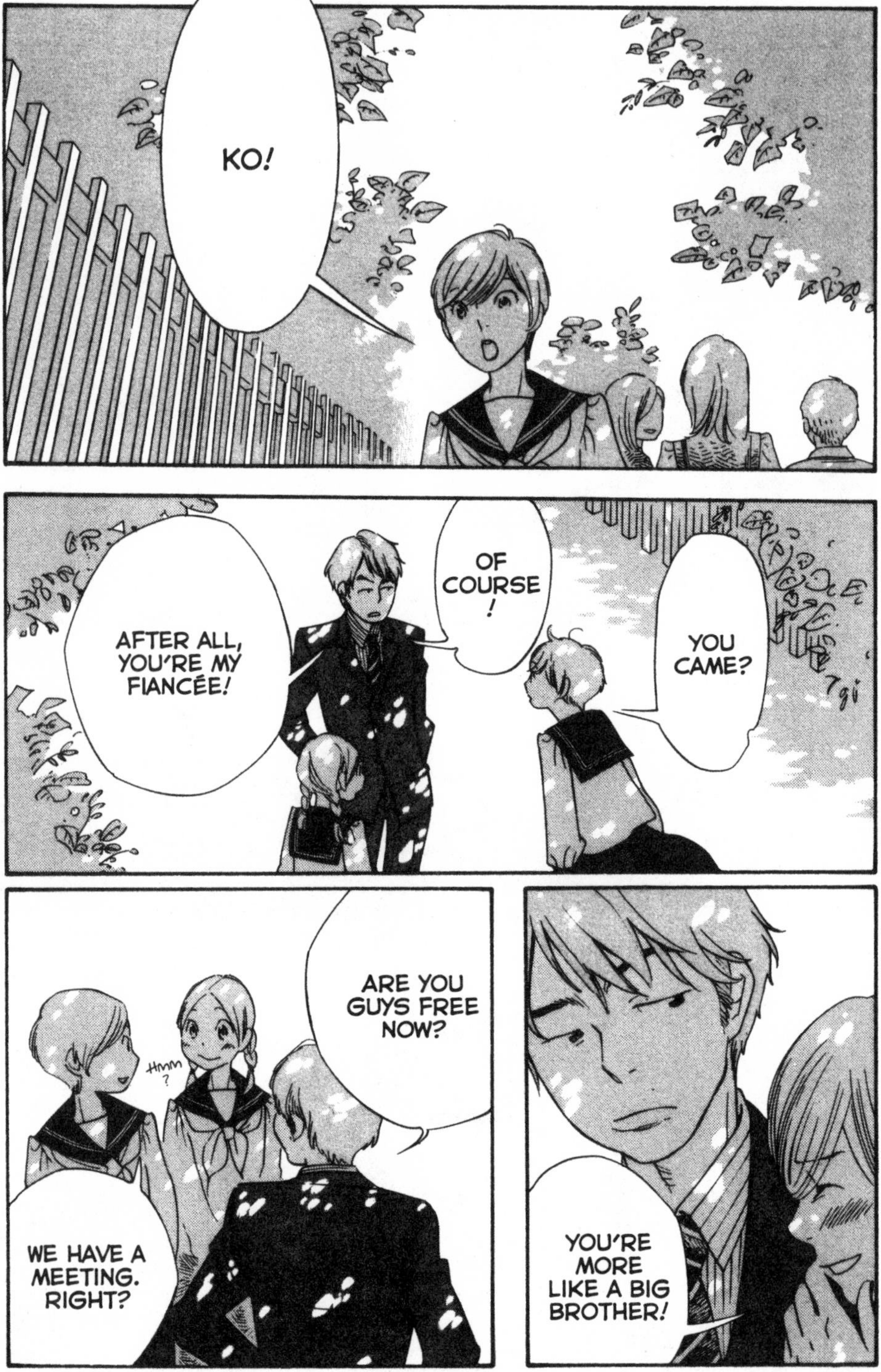
KO!
YOU CAME?
OF COURSE!
AFTER ALL, YOU'RE MY FIANCÉE!
YOU'RE MORE LIKE A BIG BROTHER!
ARE YOU GUYS FREE NOW?
Hmm?
WE HAVE A MEETING. RIGHT?

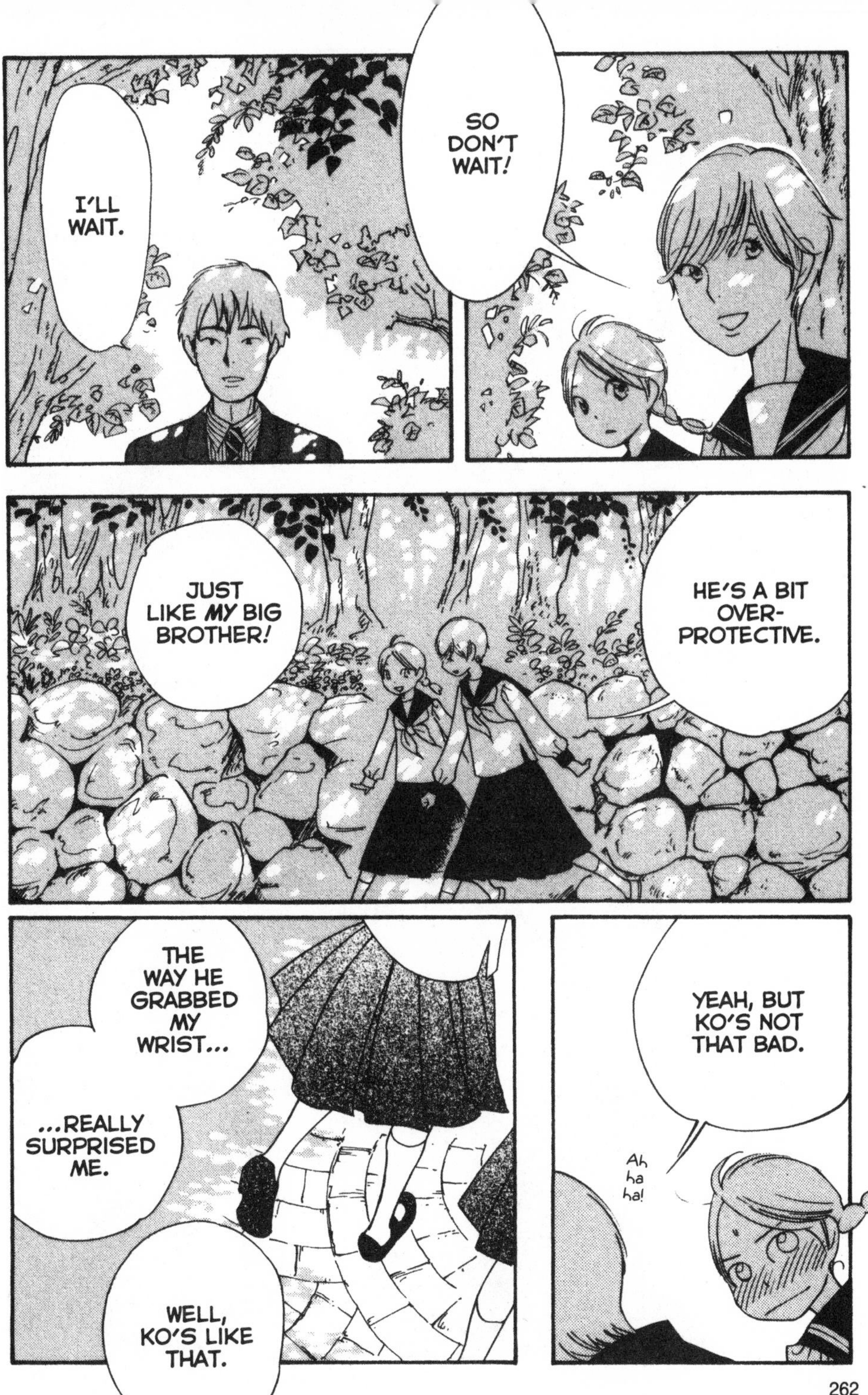
SO DON'T WAIT!
I'LL WAIT.
HE'S A BIT OVER-PROTECTIVE.
JUST LIKE *MY* BIG BROTHER!
YEAH, BUT KO'S NOT THAT BAD.
Ah ha ha!
THE WAY HE GRABBED MY WRIST...
...REALLY SURPRISED ME.
WELL, KO'S LIKE THAT.

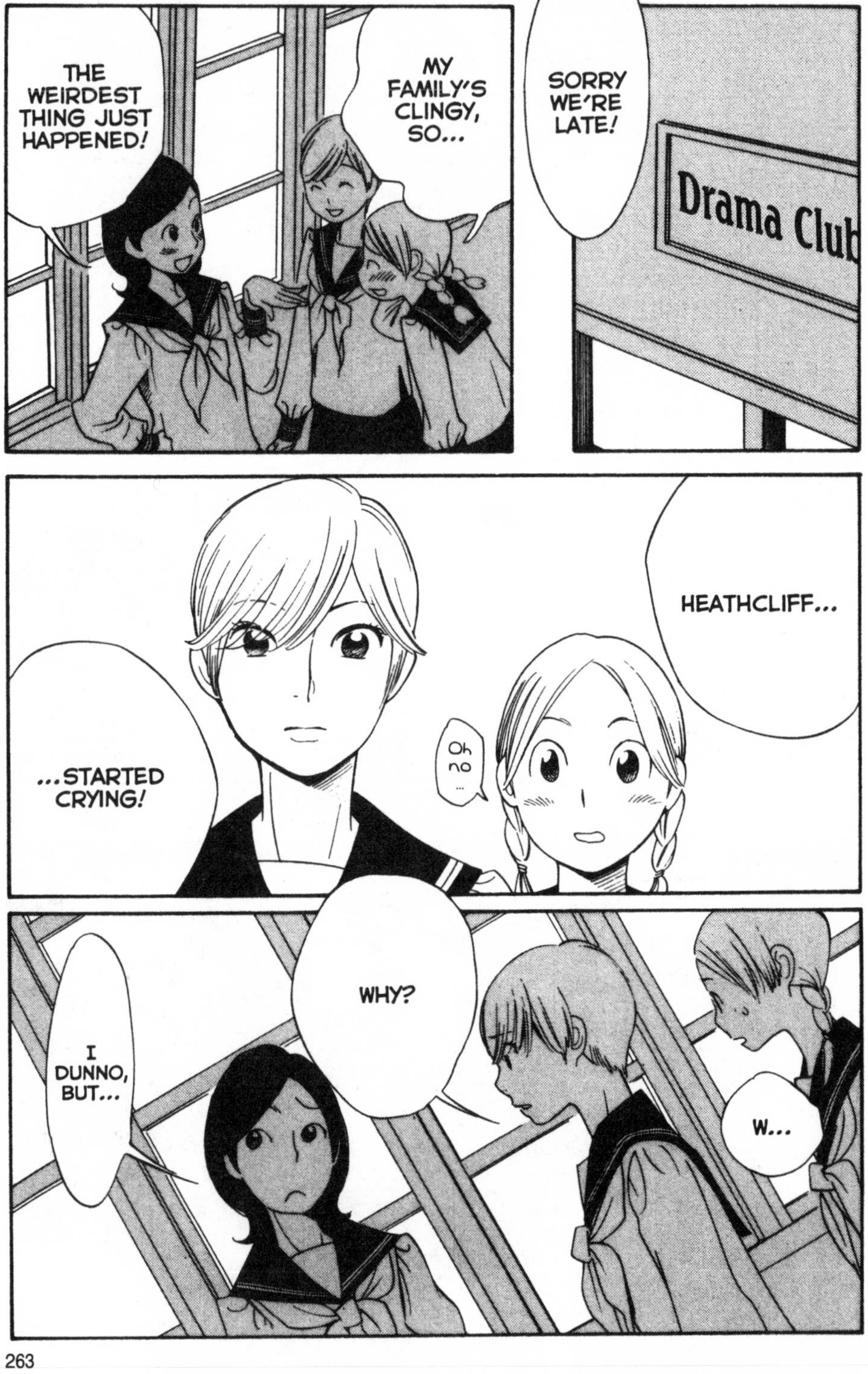
Drama Club
SORRY WE'RE LATE!
MY FAMILY'S CLINGY, SO...
THE WEIRDEST THING JUST HAPPENED!
HEATHCLIFF...
Oh no ...
...STARTED CRYING!
W...
WHY?
I DUNNO, BUT...

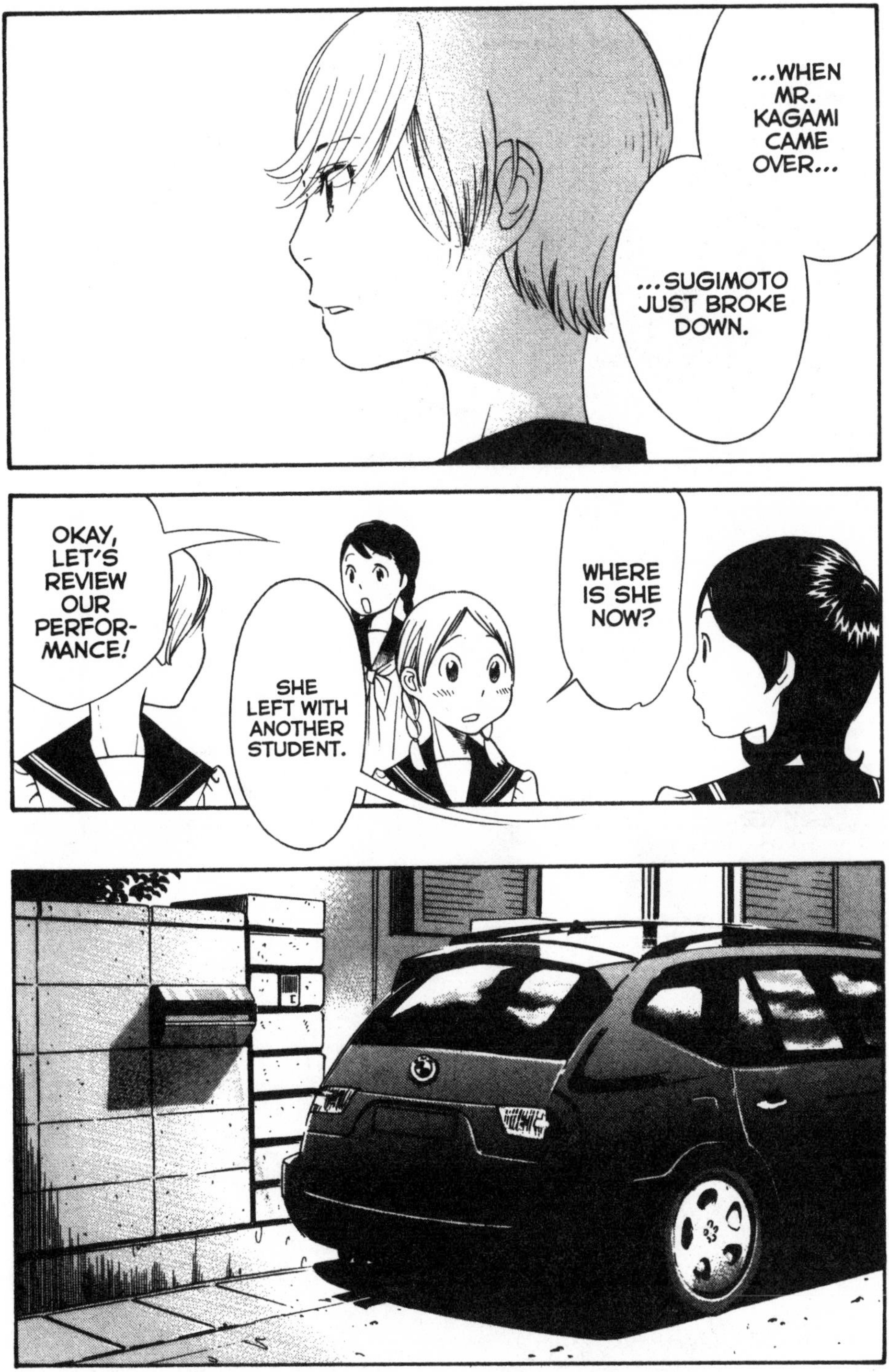
...WHEN MR. KAGAMI CAME OVER...
...SUGIMOTO JUST BROKE DOWN.
WHERE IS SHE NOW?
SHE LEFT WITH ANOTHER STUDENT.
OKAY, LET'S REVIEW OUR PERFORMANCE!

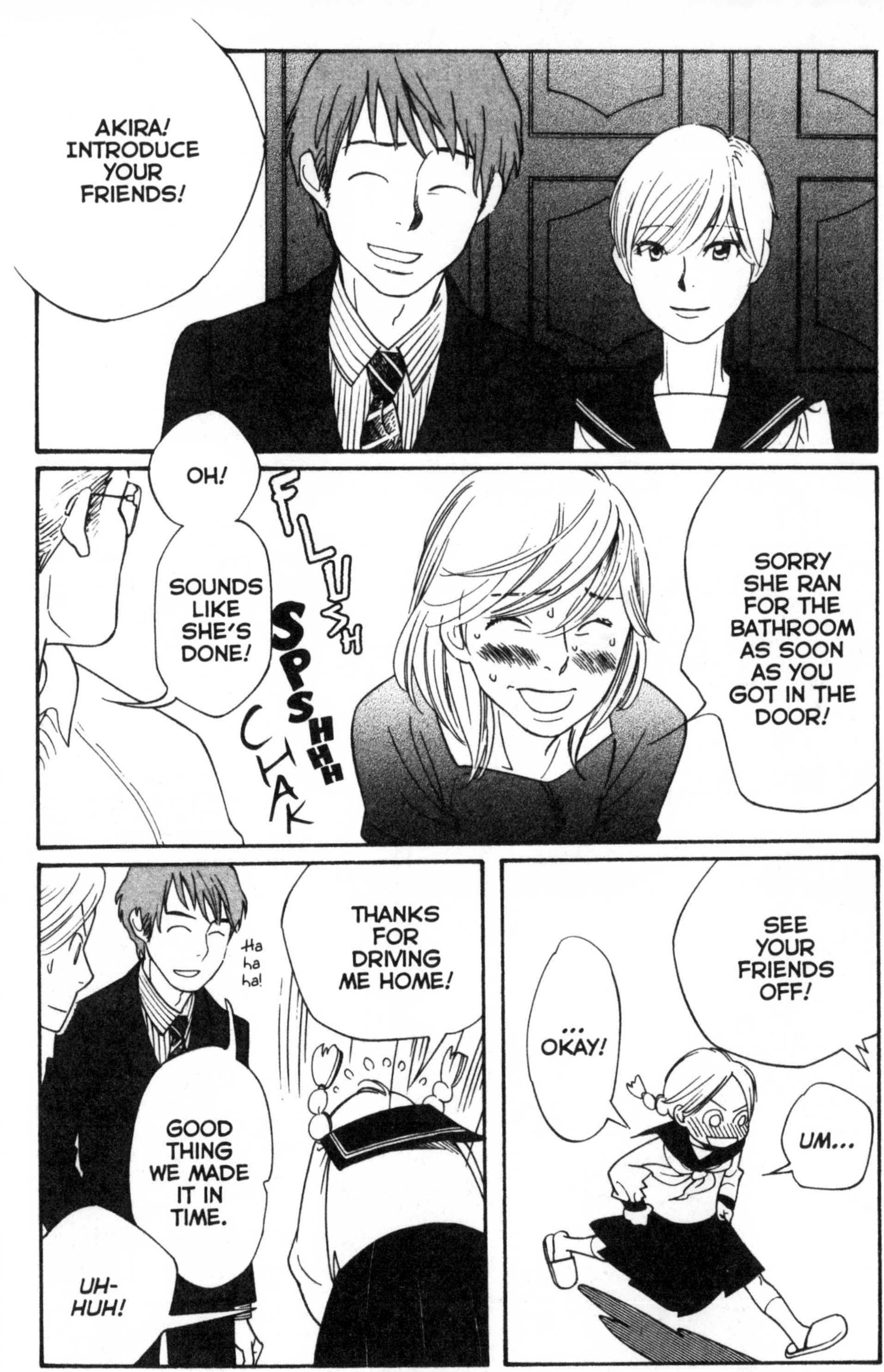
AKIRA! INTRODUCE YOUR FRIENDS!
SORRY SHE RAN FOR THE BATHROOM AS SOON AS YOU GOT IN THE DOOR!
FLUSH
SPSHHH
CHAK
OH!
SOUNDS LIKE SHE'S DONE!
SEE YOUR FRIENDS OFF!
UM...
... OKAY!
THANKS FOR DRIVING ME HOME!
Ha ha ha!
GOOD THING WE MADE IT IN TIME.
UH-HUH!

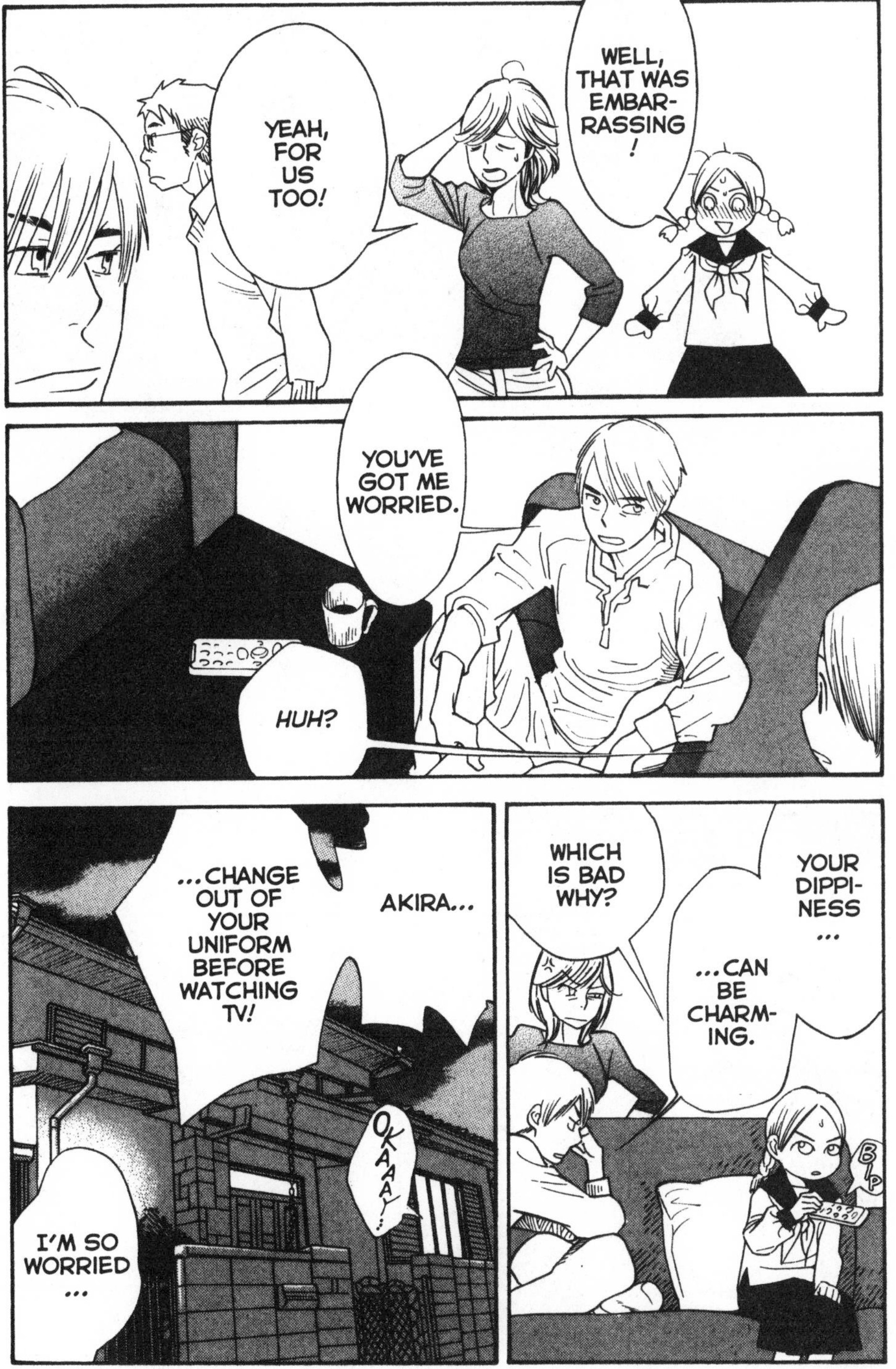
WELL, THAT WAS EMBAR-RASSING!
YEAH, FOR US TOO!
YOU'VE GOT ME WORRIED.
HUH?
YOUR DIPPI-NESS...
...CAN BE CHARM-ING.
WHICH IS BAD WHY?
BIP
AKIRA...
...CHANGE OUT OF YOUR UNIFORM BEFORE WATCHING TV!
OKAAAY...
I'M SO WORRIED...

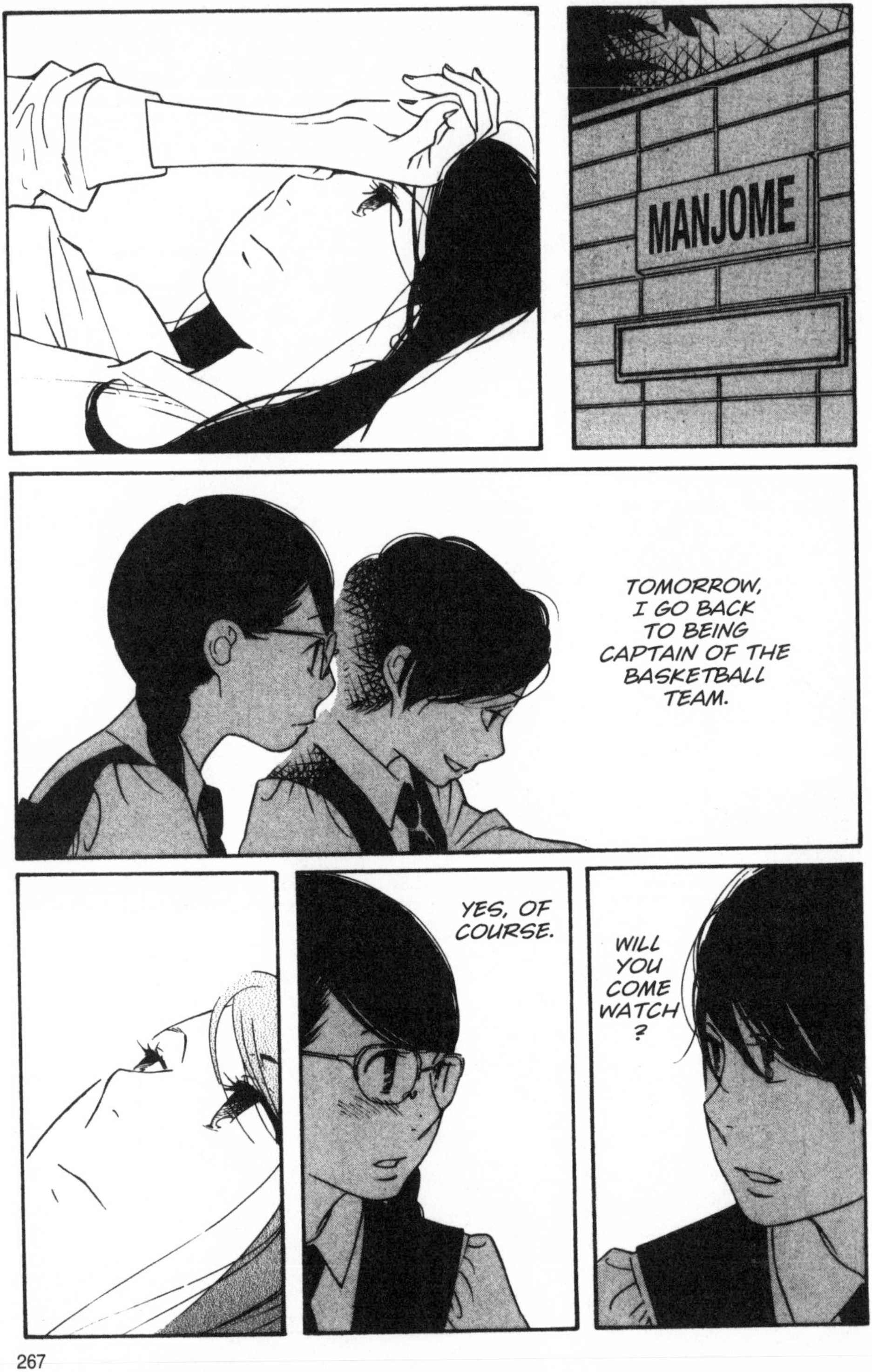
MANJOME
TOMORROW, I GO BACK TO BEING CAPTAIN OF THE BASKETBALL TEAM.
WILL YOU COME WATCH ?
YES, OF COURSE.

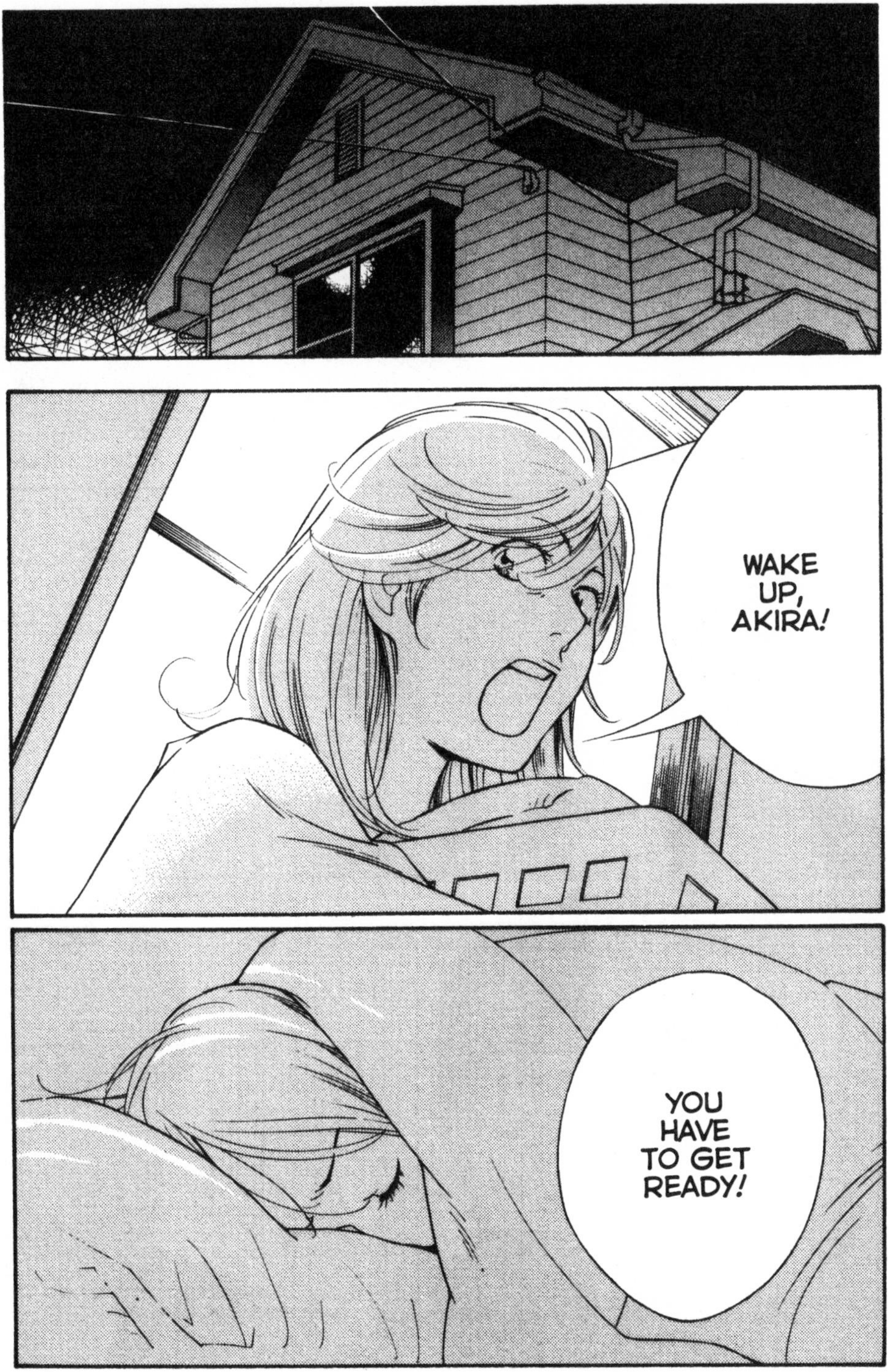
WAKE UP, AKIRA!
YOU HAVE TO GET READY!

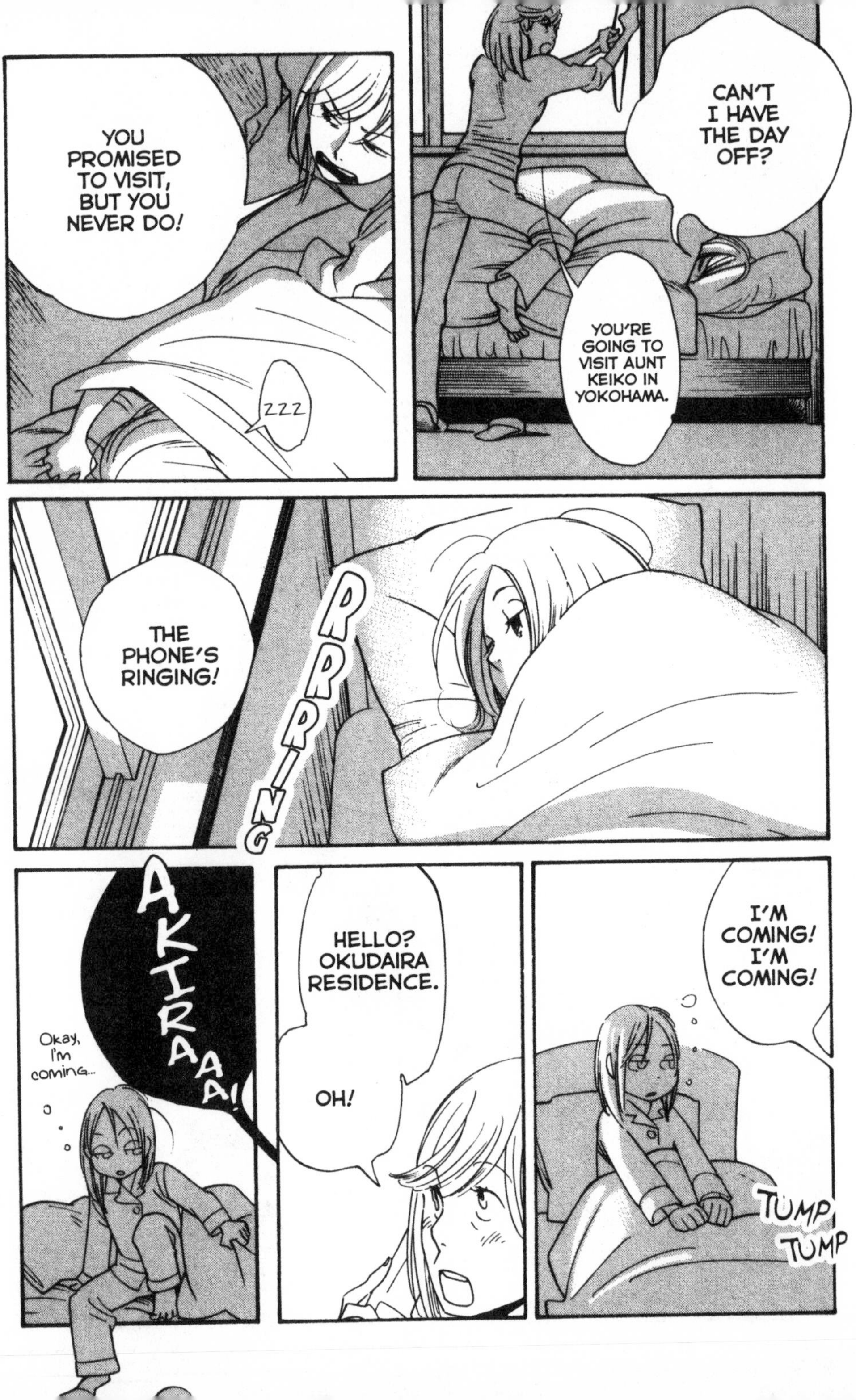
CAN'T I HAVE THE DAY OFF?
YOU'RE GOING TO VISIT AUNT KEIKO IN YOKOHAMA.
YOU PROMISED TO VISIT, BUT YOU NEVER DO!
ZZZ
RRRING
THE PHONE'S RINGING!
I'M COMING! I'M COMING!
TUMP TUMP
HELLO? OKUDAIRA RESIDENCE.
OH!
AKIRAAAA!
Okay, I'm coming...

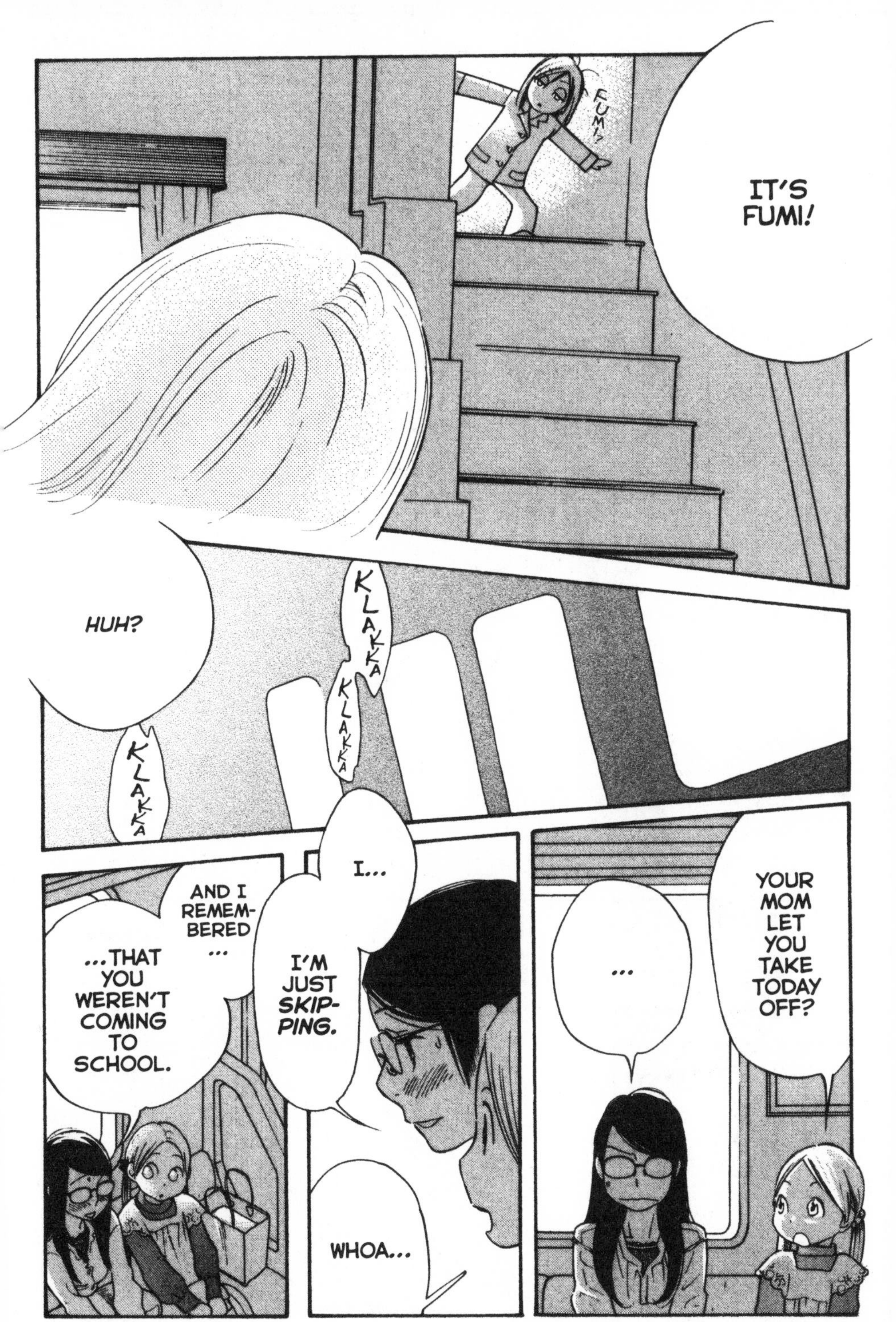
IT'S FUMI!
FUMI?
KLAKKA
KLAKKA
HUH?
KLAKKA
YOUR MOM LET YOU TAKE TODAY OFF?
...
I...
I'M JUST SKIPPING.
WHOA...
AND I REMEMBERED...
...THAT YOU WEREN'T COMING TO SCHOOL.

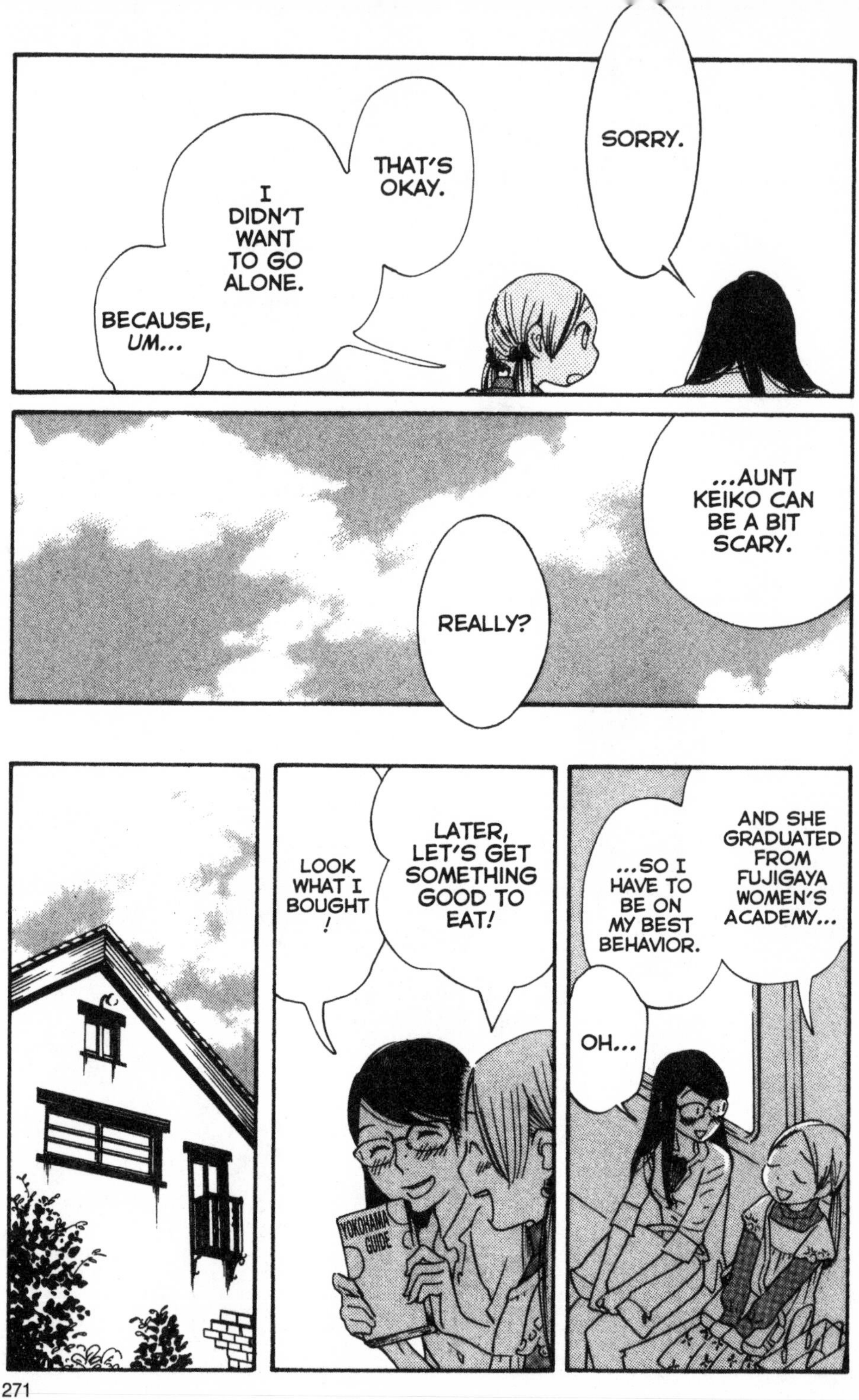
SORRY.
THAT'S OKAY.
I DIDN'T WANT TO GO ALONE.
BECAUSE, UM...
...AUNT KEIKO CAN BE A BIT SCARY.
REALLY?
AND SHE GRADUATED FROM FUJIGAYA WOMEN'S ACADEMY...
...SO I HAVE TO BE ON MY BEST BEHAVIOR.
OH...
LATER, LET'S GET SOMETHING GOOD TO EAT!
LOOK WHAT I BOUGHT!
YOKOHAMA GUIDE

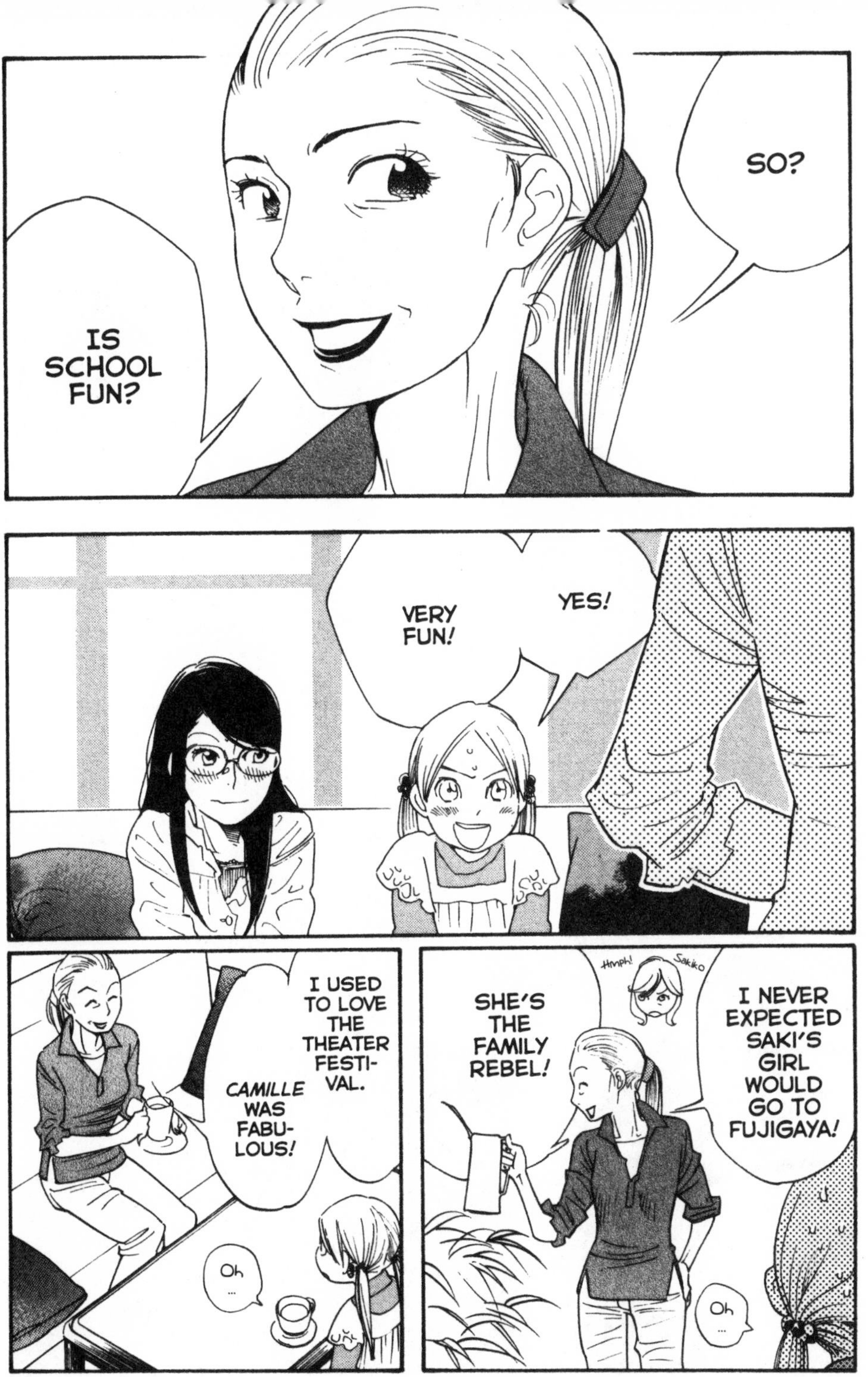
SO?
IS SCHOOL FUN?
YES!
VERY FUN!
I NEVER EXPECTED SAKI'S GIRL WOULD GO TO FUJIGAYA!
Hmph! Sakiko
SHE'S THE FAMILY REBEL!
Oh ...
I USED TO LOVE THE THEATER FESTI-VAL.
CAMILLE WAS FABU-LOUS!
Oh ...

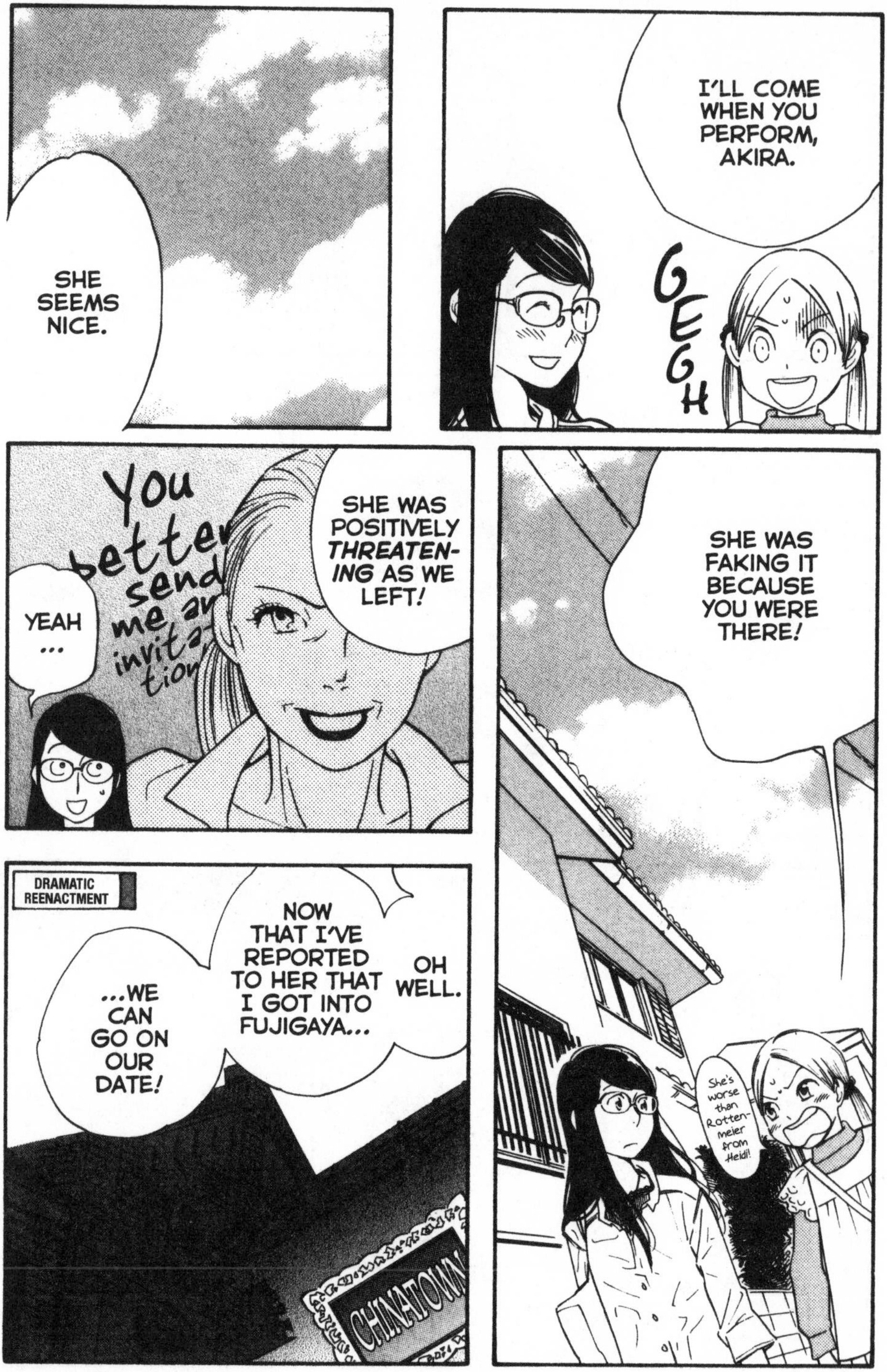
I'LL COME WHEN YOU PERFORM, AKIRA.
GEGH
SHE SEEMS NICE.
SHE WAS FAKING IT BECAUSE YOU WERE THERE!
She's worse than Rotten-meier from Heidi!
SHE WAS POSITIVELY *THREATEN-ING* AS WE LEFT!
You better send me an invita-tion
YEAH...
DRAMATIC REENACTMENT
OH WELL.
NOW THAT I'VE REPORTED TO HER THAT I GOT INTO FUJIGAYA...
...WE CAN GO ON OUR DATE!
CHINATOWN

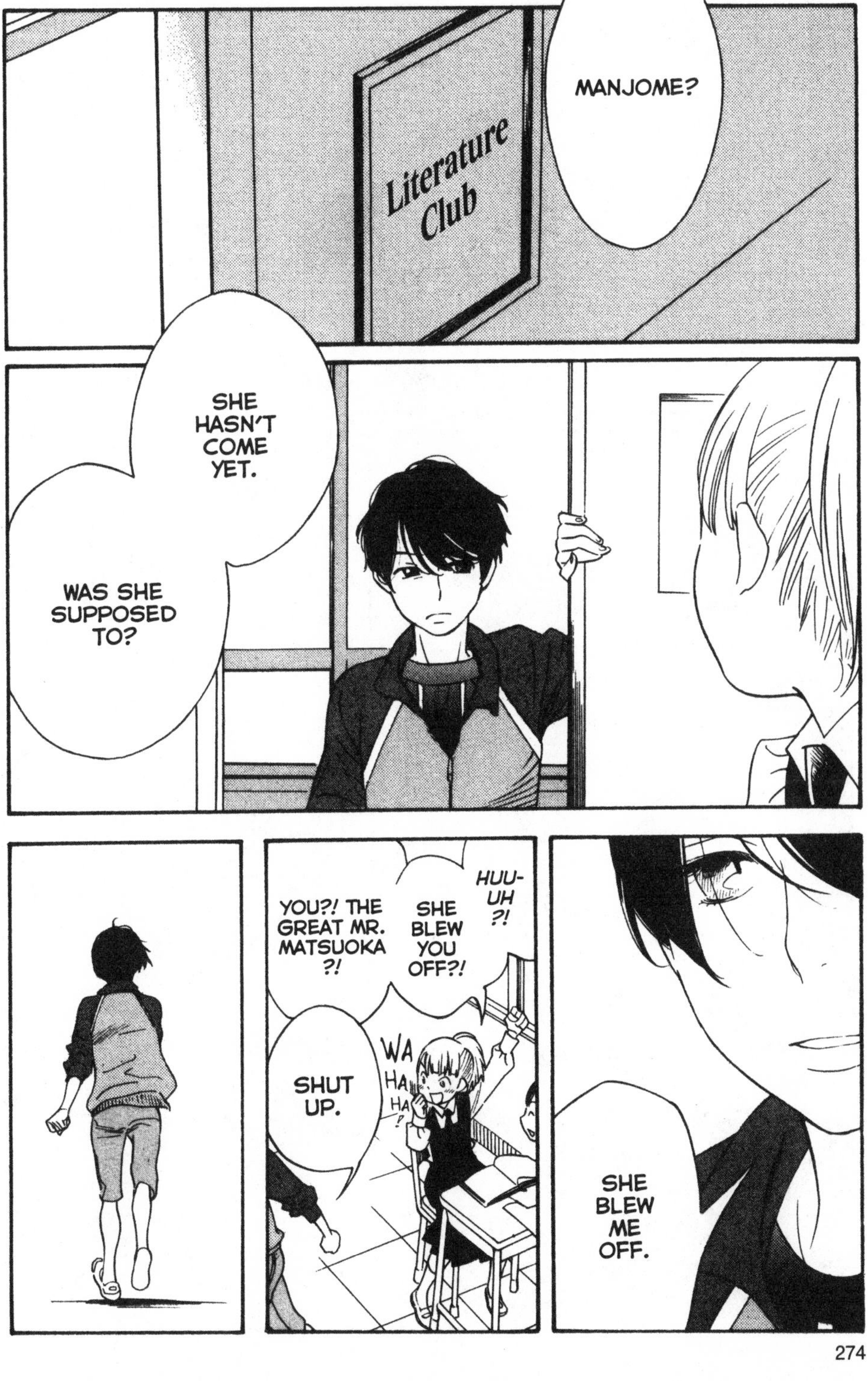
Literature Club
MANJOME?
SHE HASN'T COME YET.
WAS SHE SUPPOSED TO?
SHE BLEW ME OFF.
HUUU-UH ?!
SHE BLEW YOU OFF?!
YOU?! THE GREAT MR. MATSUOKA ?!
WA HA HA ?
SHUT UP.

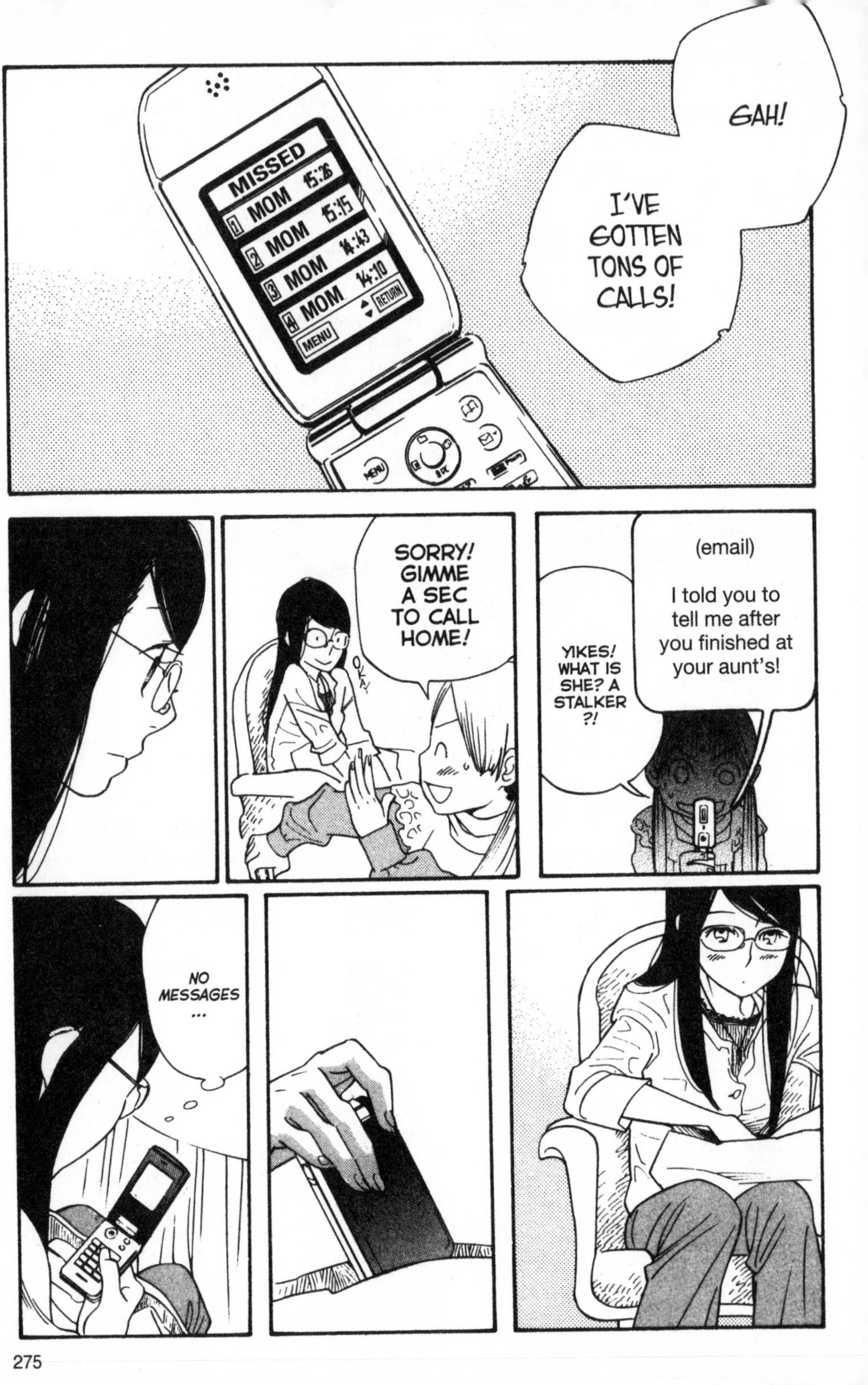
GAH!
I'VE GOTTEN TONS OF CALLS!
MISSED
1 MOM 15:26
2 MOM 15:15
3 MOM 14:43
4 MOM 14:10
MENU
RETURN
(email)
I told you to tell me after you finished at your aunt's!
YIKES! WHAT IS SHE? A STALKER?!
SORRY! GIMME A SEC TO CALL HOME!
OKAY
NO MESSAGES...

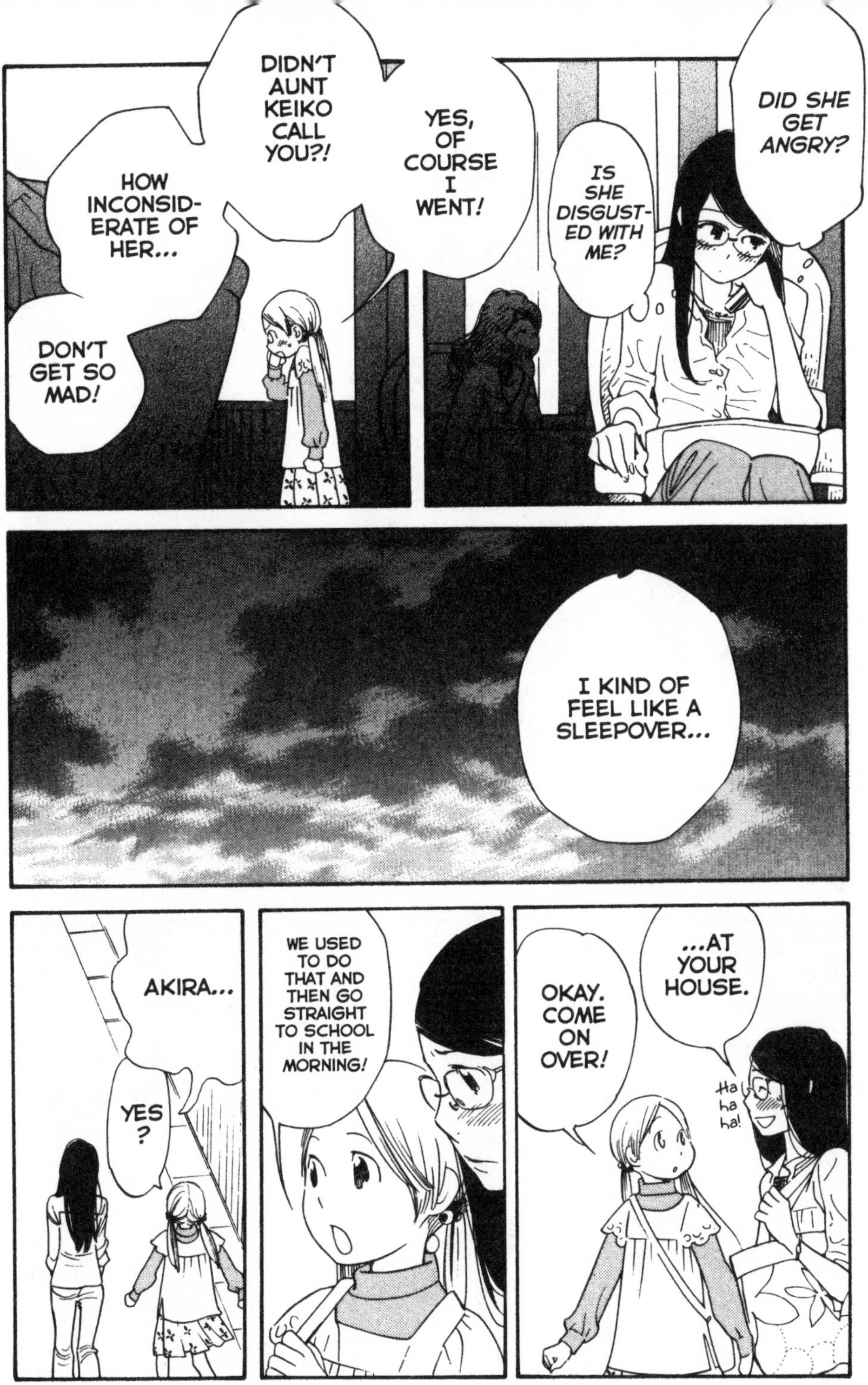
DID SHE GET ANGRY?
IS SHE DISGUST-ED WITH ME?
DIDN'T AUNT KEIKO CALL YOU?!
YES, OF COURSE I WENT!
HOW INCONSID-ERATE OF HER...
DON'T GET SO MAD!
I KIND OF FEEL LIKE A SLEEPOVER...
...AT YOUR HOUSE.
Ha ha ha!
OKAY. COME ON OVER!
WE USED TO DO THAT AND THEN GO STRAIGHT TO SCHOOL IN THE MORNING!
AKIRA...
YES?

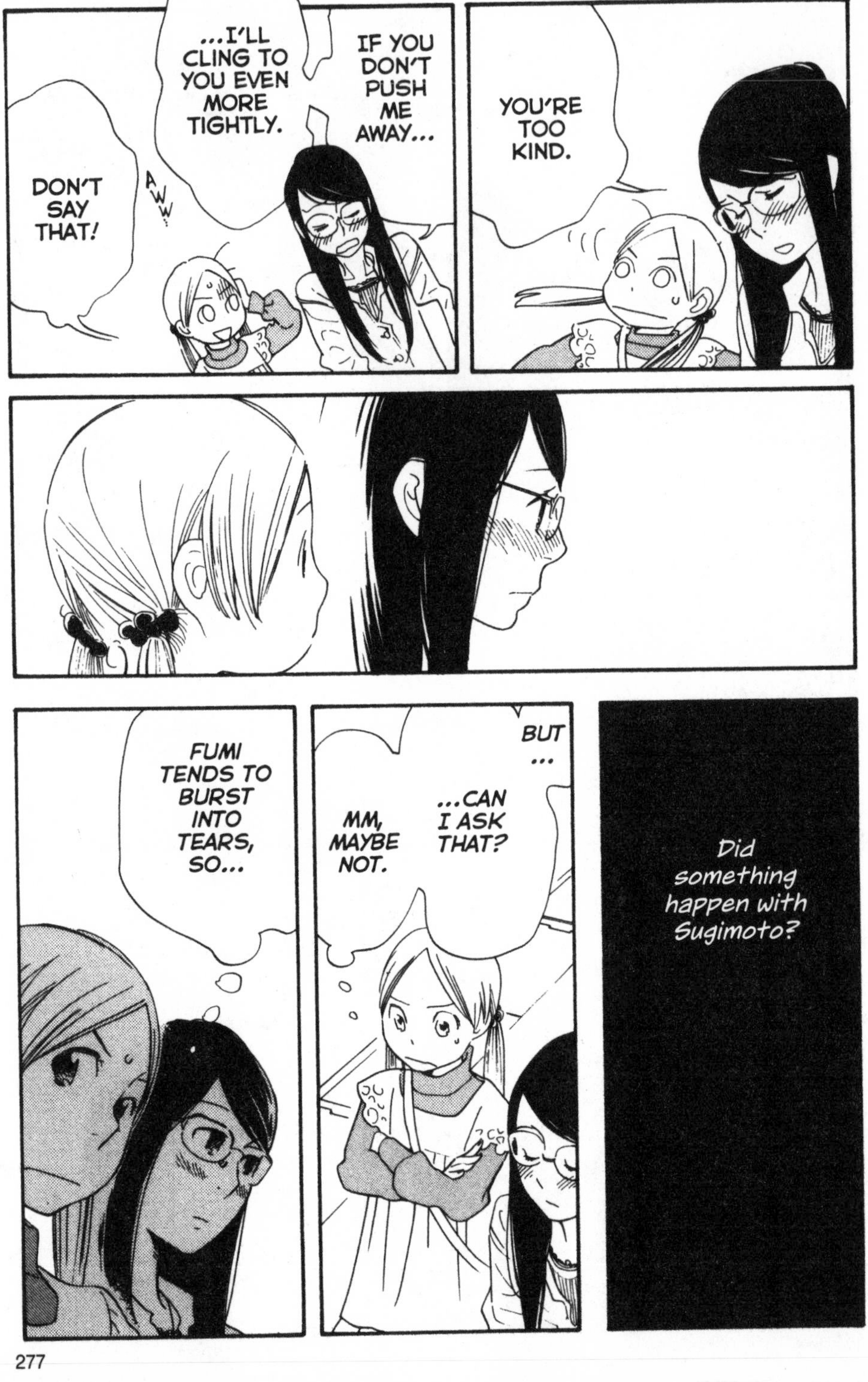
YOU'RE TOO KIND.
IF YOU DON'T PUSH ME AWAY...
...I'LL CLING TO YOU EVEN MORE TIGHTLY.
AWW...
DON'T SAY THAT!
Did something happen with Sugimoto?
BUT ...
...CAN I ASK THAT?
MM, MAYBE NOT.
FUMI TENDS TO BURST INTO TEARS, SO...

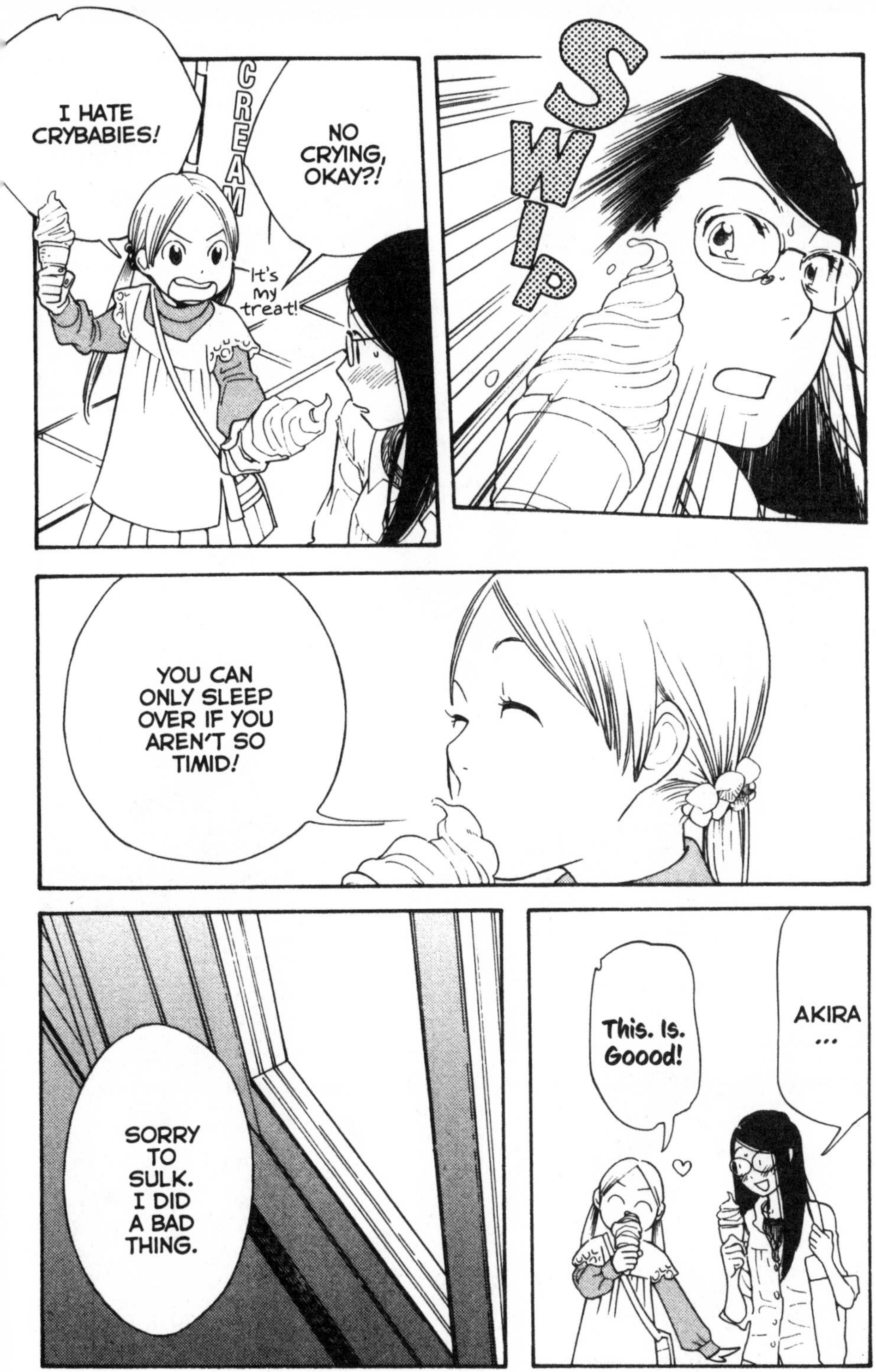
SWIP
NO CRYING, OKAY?!
It's my treat!
CREAM
I HATE CRYBABIES!
YOU CAN ONLY SLEEP OVER IF YOU AREN'T SO TIMID!
AKIRA ...
This. Is. Goood!
SORRY TO SULK. I DID A BAD THING.

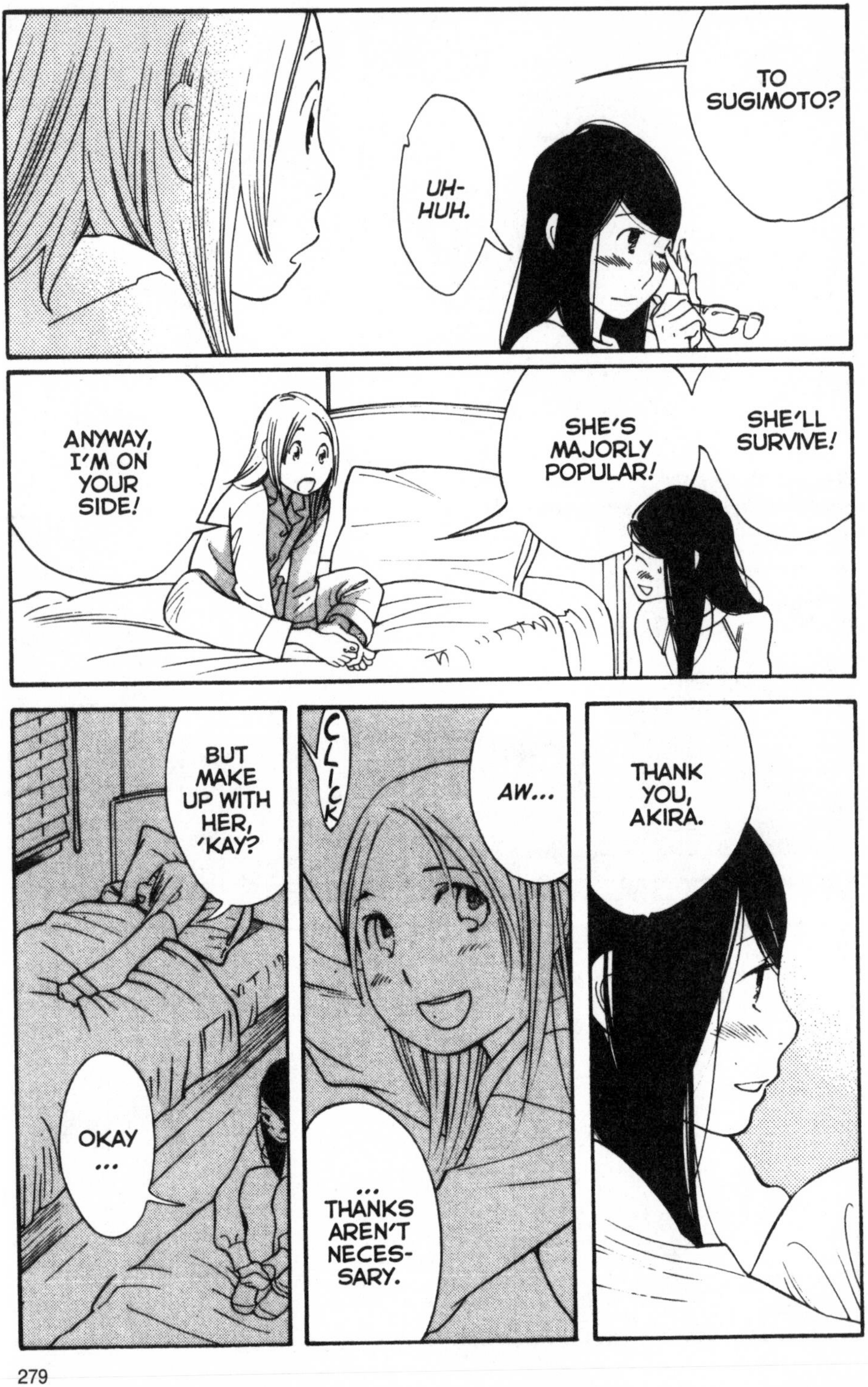
TO SUGIMOTO?
UH-HUH.
SHE'LL SURVIVE!
SHE'S MAJORLY POPULAR!
ANYWAY, I'M ON YOUR SIDE!
THANK YOU, AKIRA.
AW...
CLICK
... THANKS AREN'T NECES-SARY.
BUT MAKE UP WITH HER, 'KAY?
OKAY ...

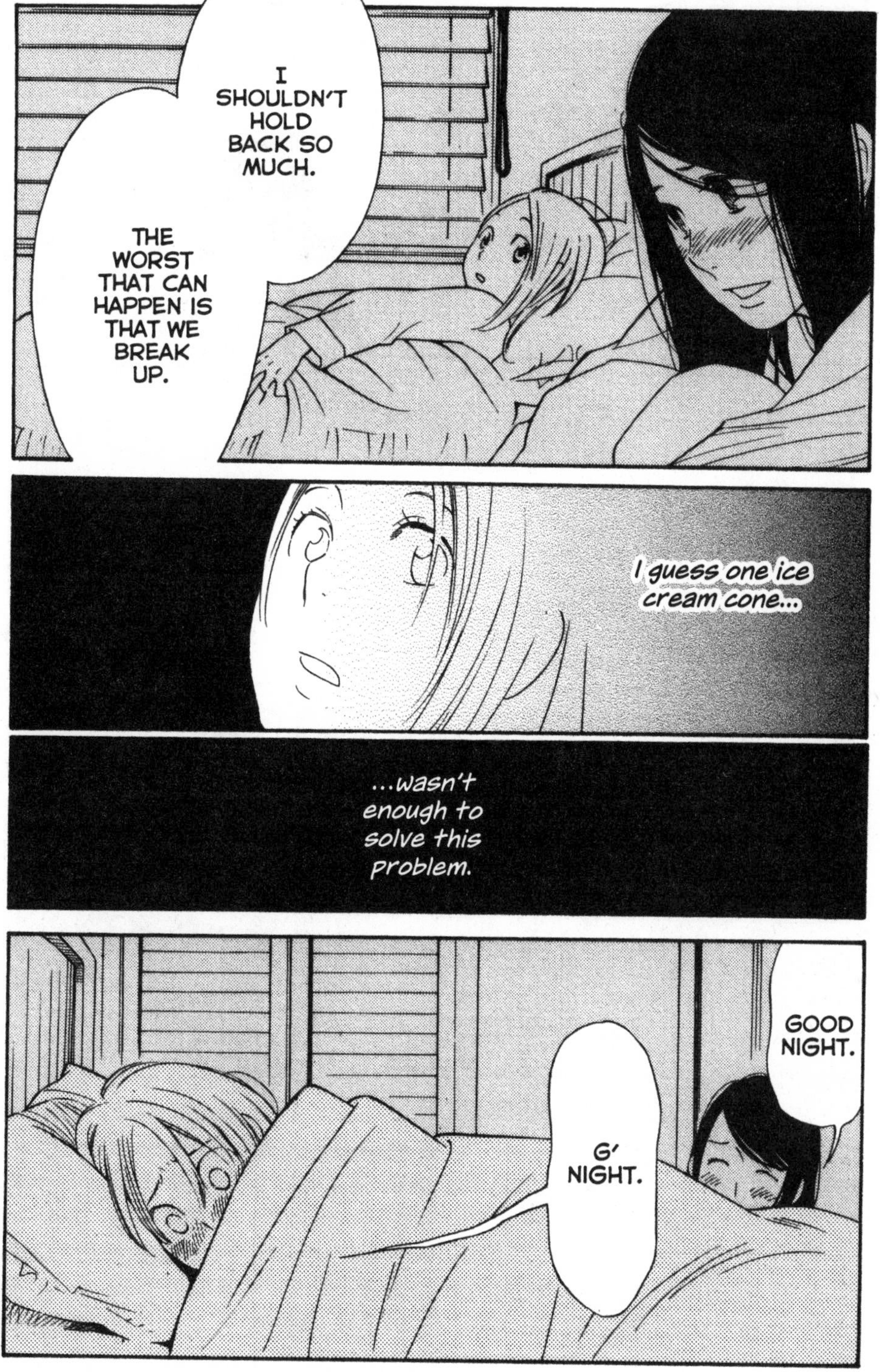
I SHOULDN'T HOLD BACK SO MUCH.
THE WORST THAT CAN HAPPEN IS THAT WE BREAK UP.
I guess one ice cream cone...
...wasn't enough to solve this problem.
GOOD NIGHT.
G' NIGHT.

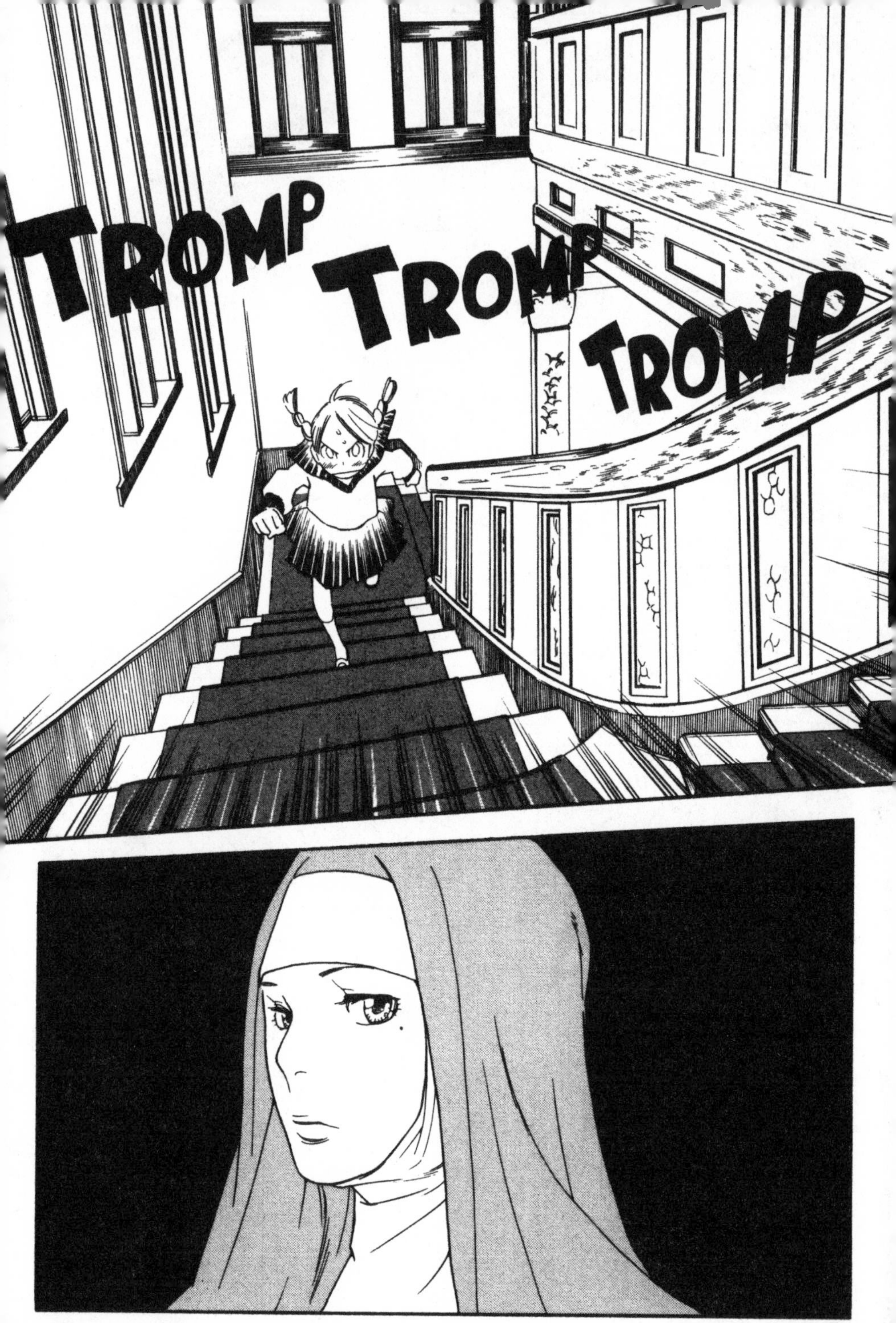
TROMP
TROMP
TROMP

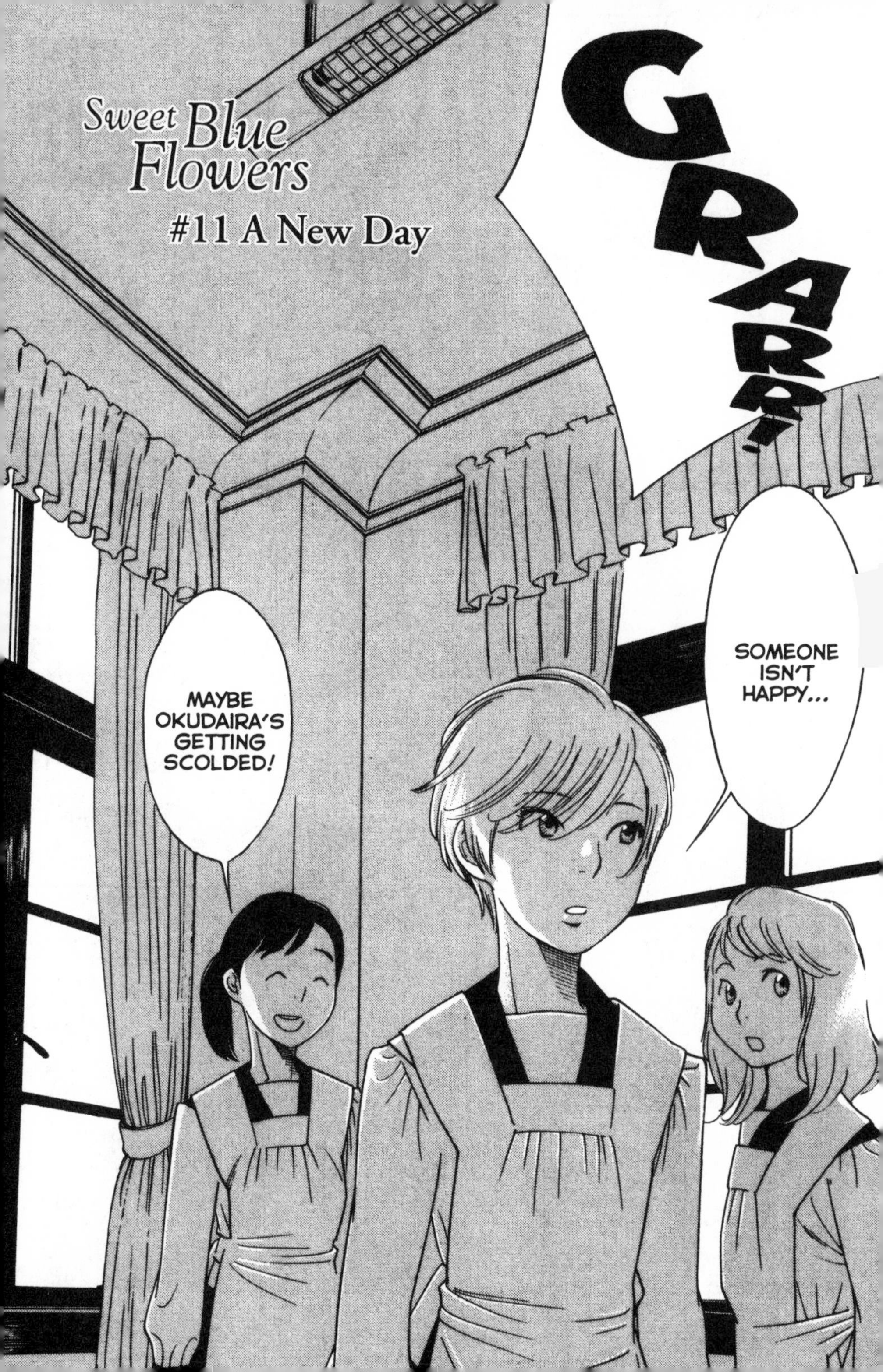
GRARR!
Sweet Blue Flowers
#11 A New Day
SOMEONE ISN'T HAPPY...
MAYBE OKUDAIRA'S GETTING SCOLDED!

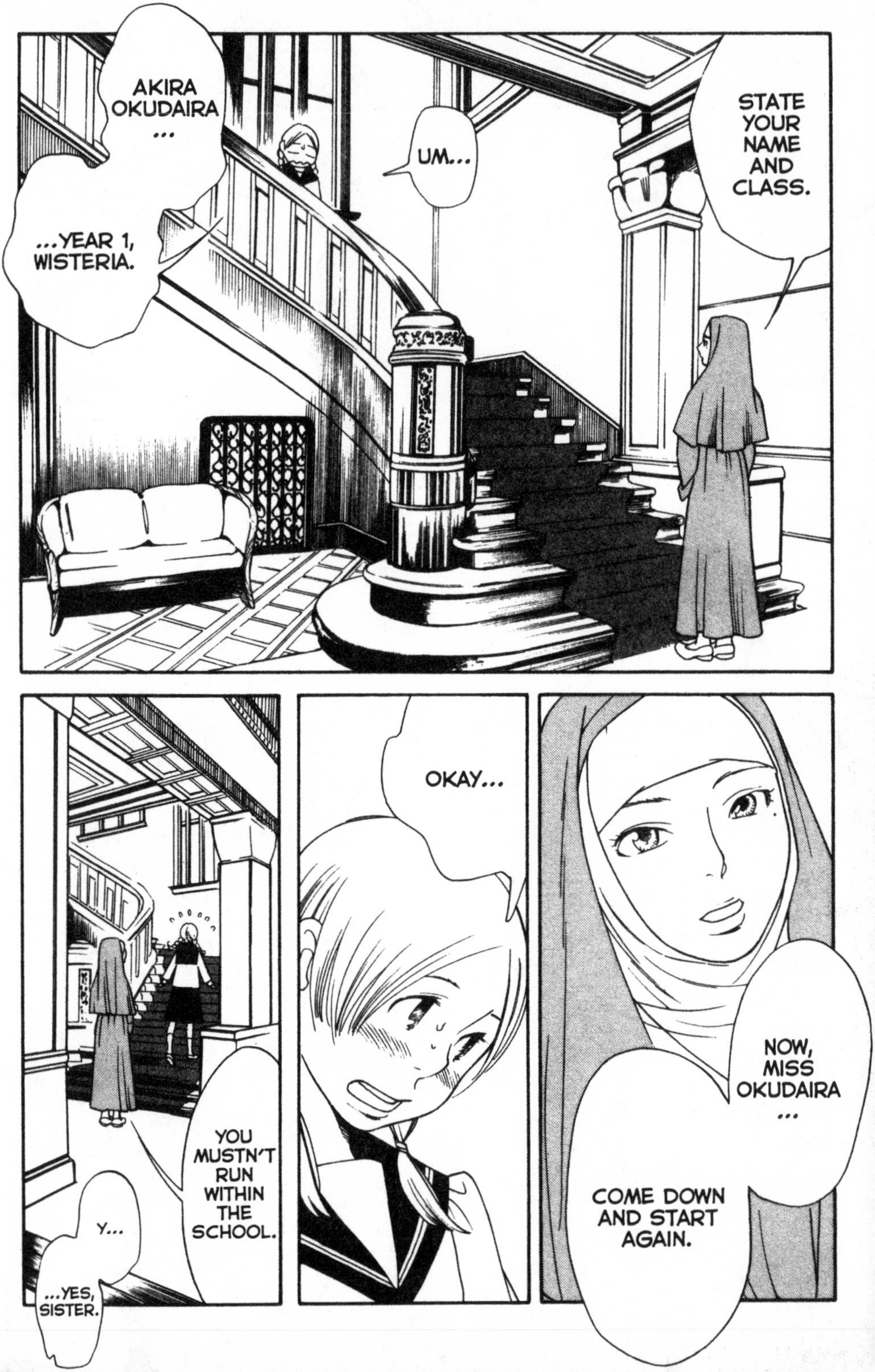
STATE YOUR NAME AND CLASS.
UM...
AKIRA OKUDAIRA...
...YEAR 1, WISTERIA.
NOW, MISS OKUDAIRA...
COME DOWN AND START AGAIN.
OKAY...
YOU MUSTN'T RUN WITHIN THE SCHOOL.
Y...
...YES, SISTER.

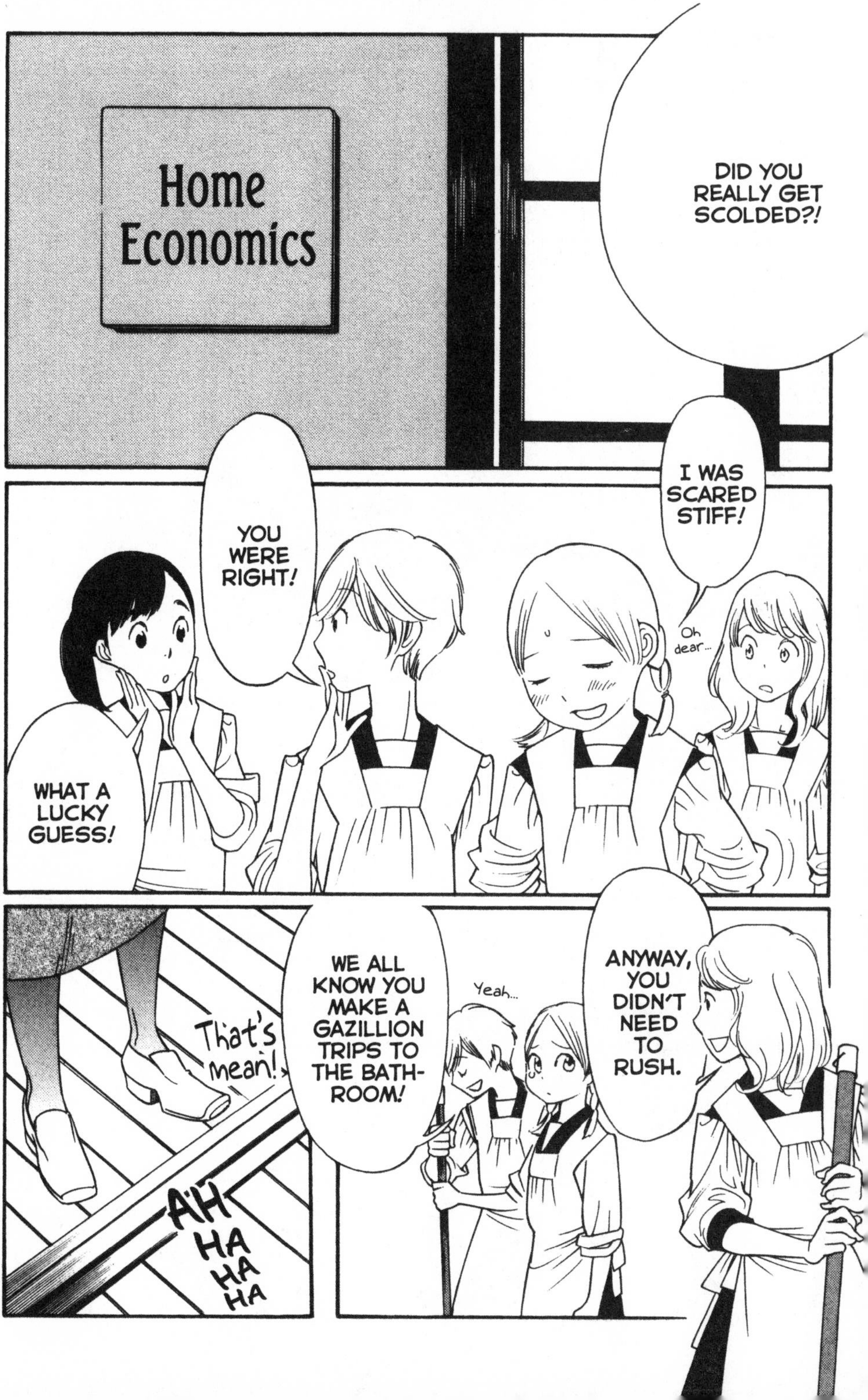
DID YOU REALLY GET SCOLDED?!
Home Economics
I WAS SCARED STIFF!
Oh dear...
YOU WERE RIGHT!
WHAT A LUCKY GUESS!
ANYWAY, YOU DIDN'T NEED TO RUSH.
Yeah...
WE ALL KNOW YOU MAKE A GAZILLION TRIPS TO THE BATH-ROOM!
That's mean!
AH HA HA HA

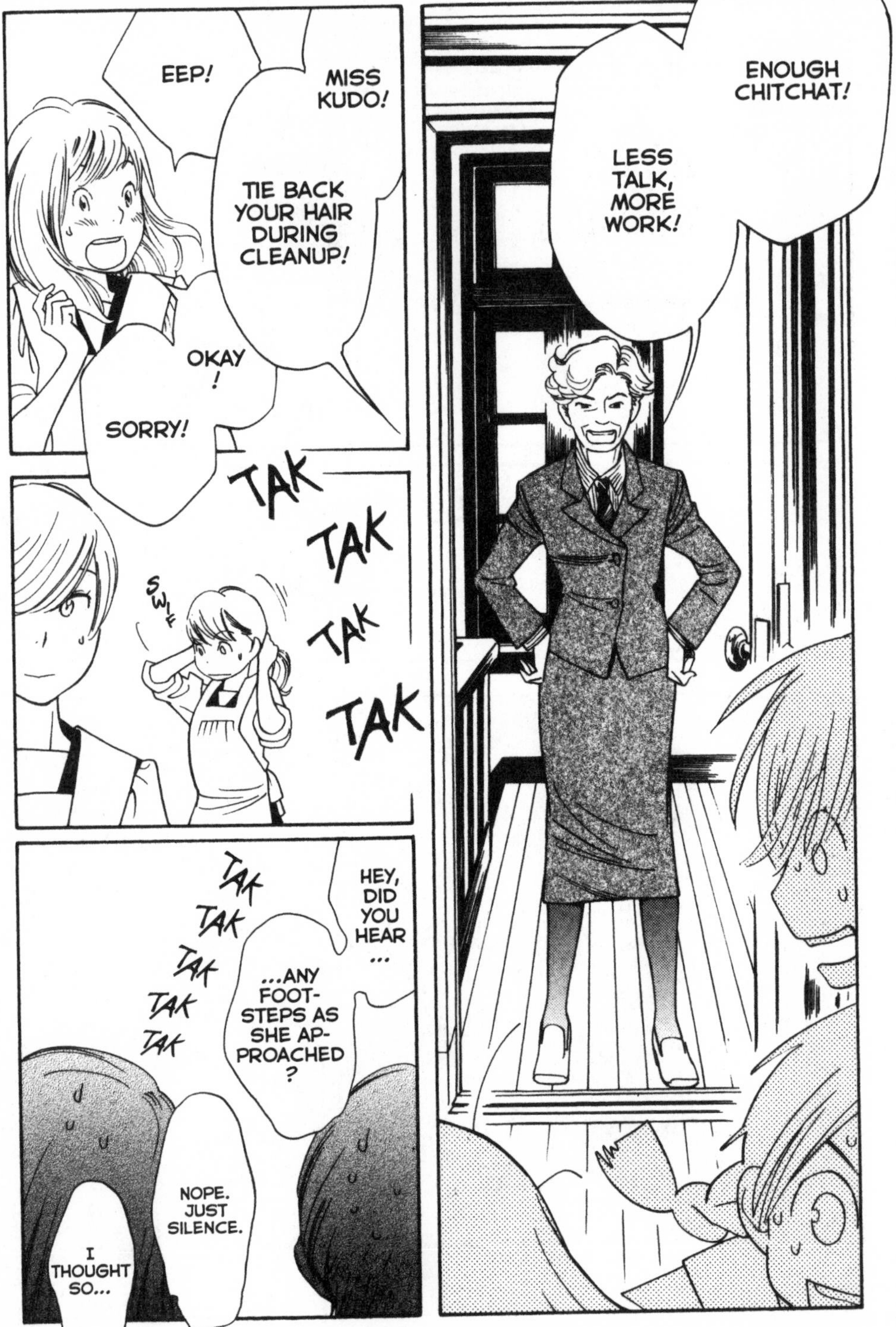
ENOUGH CHITCHAT!
LESS TALK, MORE WORK!
MISS KUDO!
TIE BACK YOUR HAIR DURING CLEANUP!
EEP!
OKAY!
SORRY!
TAK
TAK
TAK
TAK
HEY, DID YOU HEAR...
...ANY FOOT-STEPS AS SHE AP-PROACHED?
TAK
TAK
TAK
TAK
TAK
NOPE. JUST SILENCE.
I THOUGHT SO...

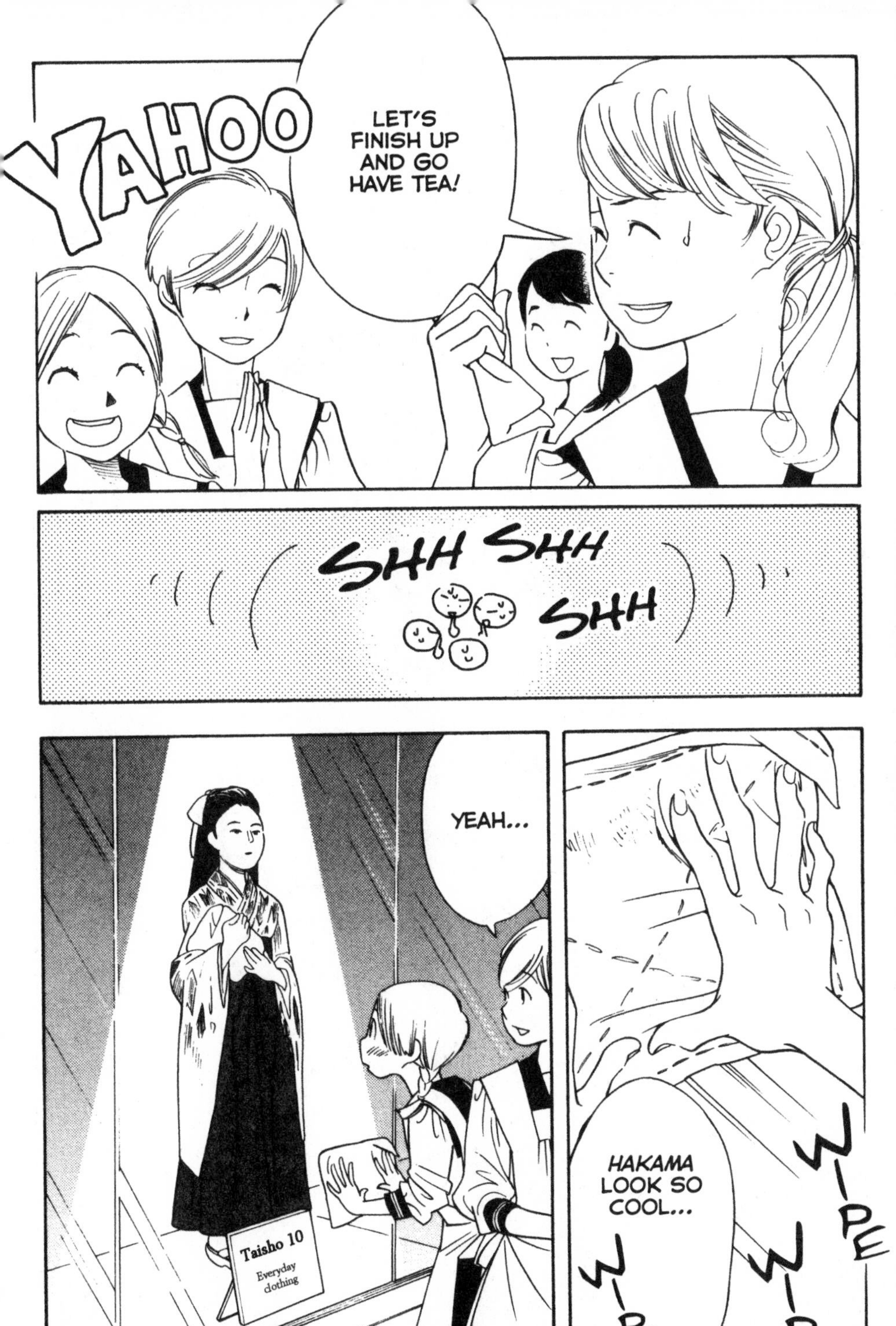
LET'S FINISH UP AND GO HAVE TEA!
YAHOO
SHH SHH
SHH
HAKAMA LOOK SO COOL...
WIPE
WIPE
WIPE
YEAH...
Taisho 10
Everyday clothing

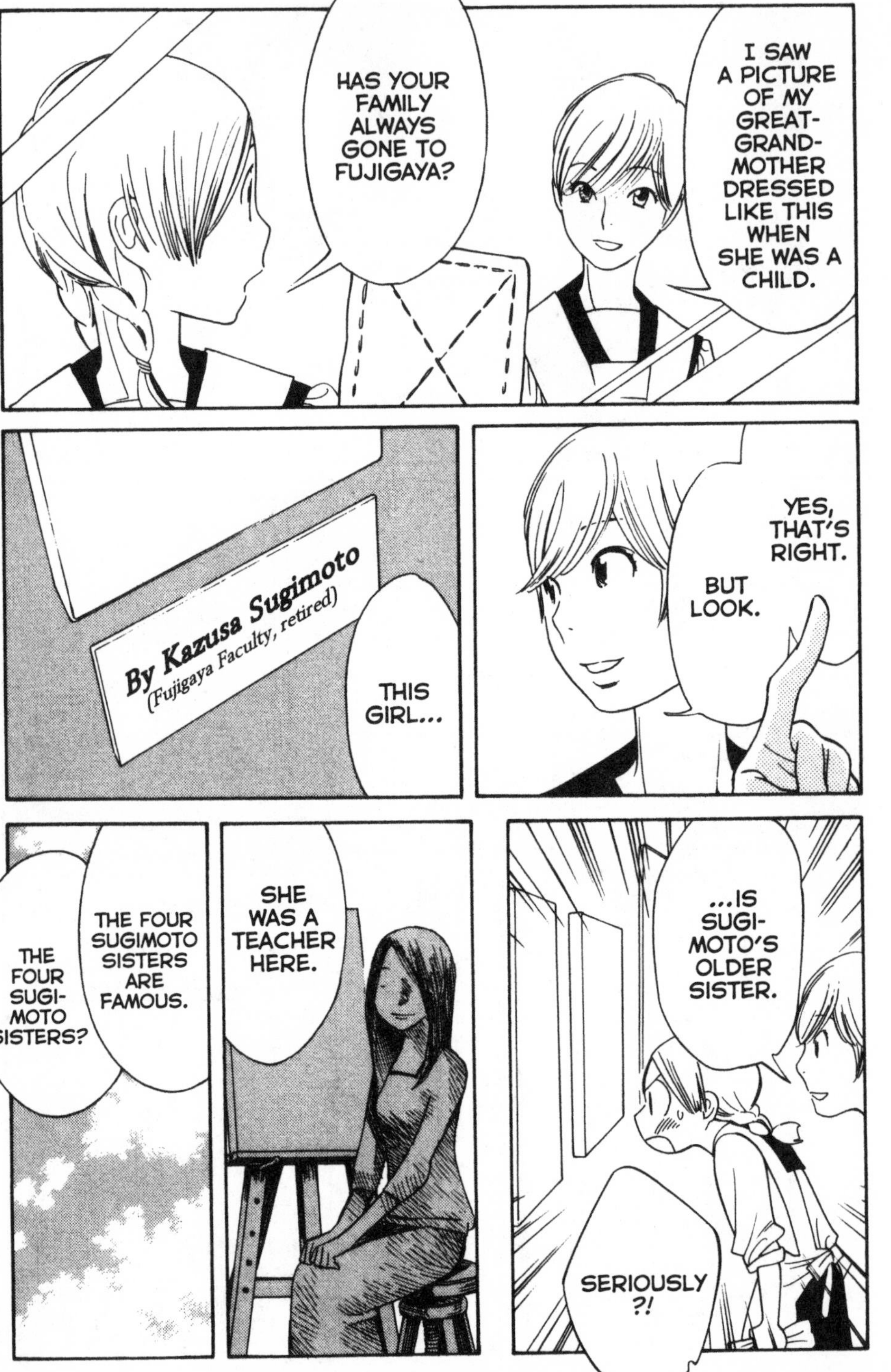
I SAW A PICTURE OF MY GREAT-GRANDMOTHER DRESSED LIKE THIS WHEN SHE WAS A CHILD.
HAS YOUR FAMILY ALWAYS GONE TO FUJIGAYA?
YES, THAT'S RIGHT.
BUT LOOK.
By Kazusa Sugimoto
(Fujigaya Faculty, retired)
THIS GIRL...
...IS SUGIMOTO'S OLDER SISTER.
SERIOUSLY?!
SHE WAS A TEACHER HERE.
THE FOUR SUGIMOTO SISTERS ARE FAMOUS.
THE FOUR SUGIMOTO SISTERS?

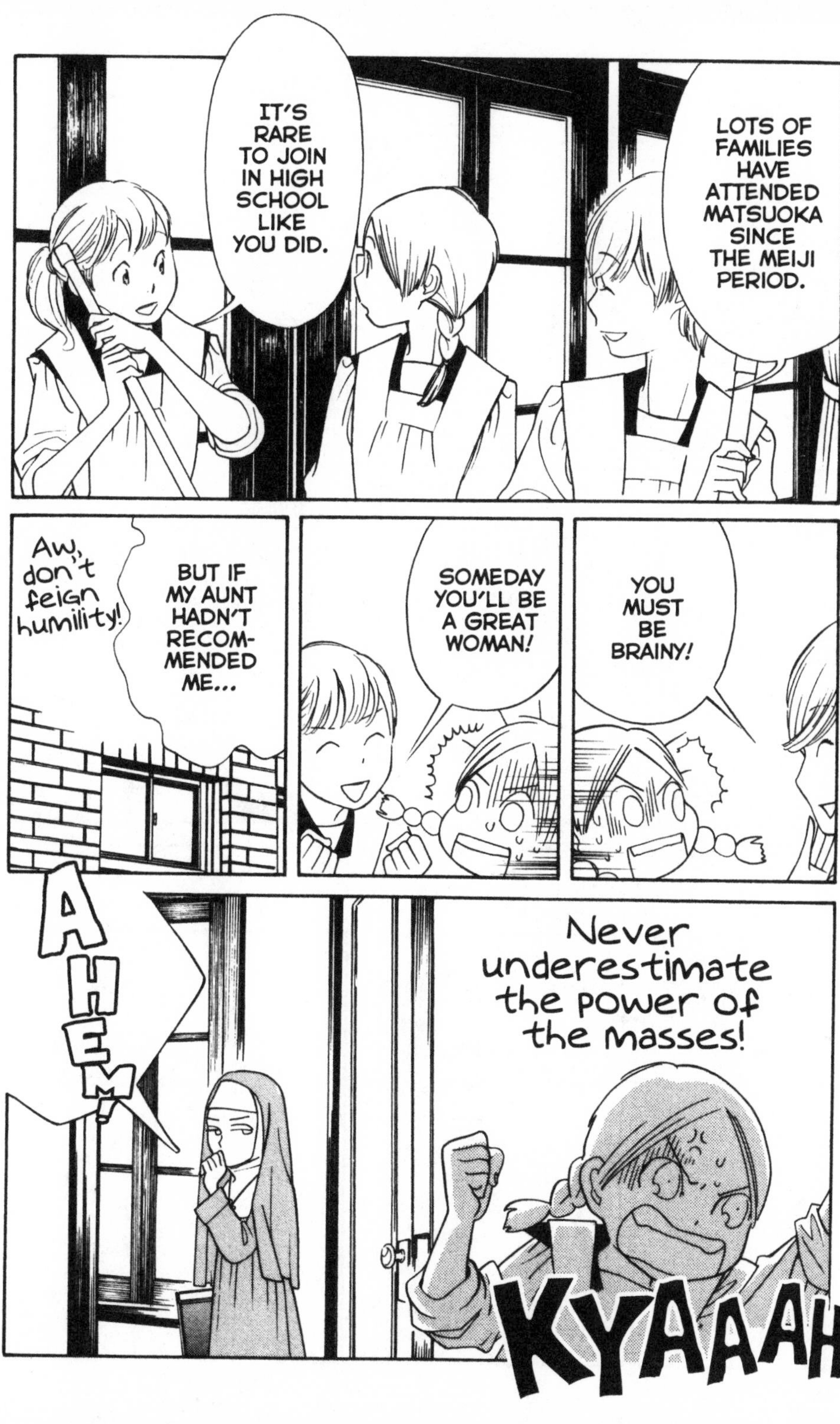
LOTS OF FAMILIES HAVE ATTENDED MATSUOKA SINCE THE MEIJI PERIOD.
IT'S RARE TO JOIN IN HIGH SCHOOL LIKE YOU DID.
YOU MUST BE BRAINY!
SOMEDAY YOU'LL BE A GREAT WOMAN!
BUT IF MY AUNT HADN'T RECOMMENDED ME...
Aw, don't feign humility!
Never underestimate the power of the masses!
KYAAAH
AHEM!

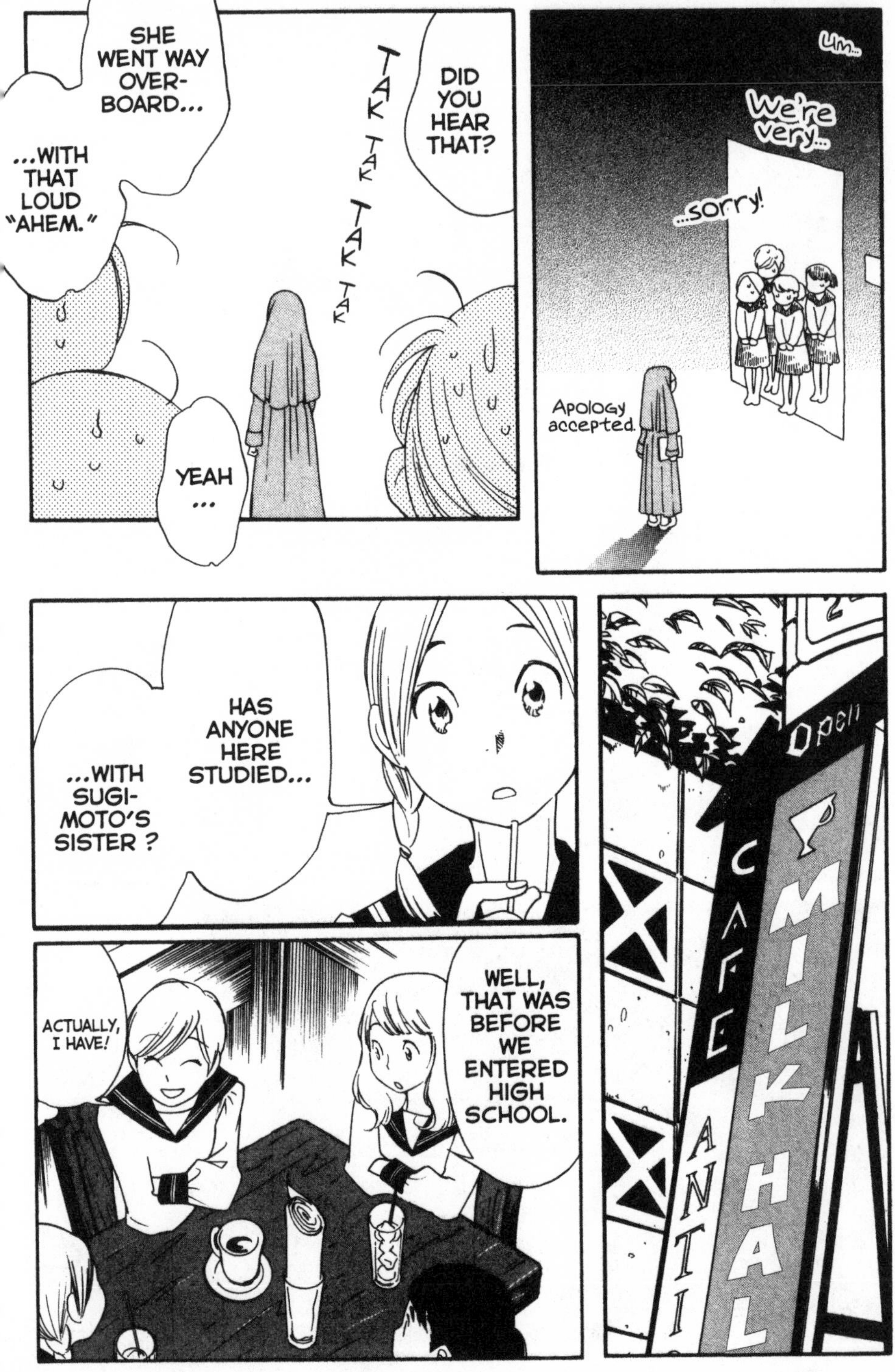
Um...
We're very...
...sorry!
Apology accepted.
DID YOU HEAR THAT?
TAK TAK TAK TAK
SHE WENT WAY OVER-BOARD...
...WITH THAT LOUD "AHEM."
YEAH...
CAFE
MILK HALL
HAS ANYONE HERE STUDIED...
...WITH SUGI-MOTO'S SISTER ?
WELL, THAT WAS BEFORE WE ENTERED HIGH SCHOOL.
ACTUALLY, I HAVE!

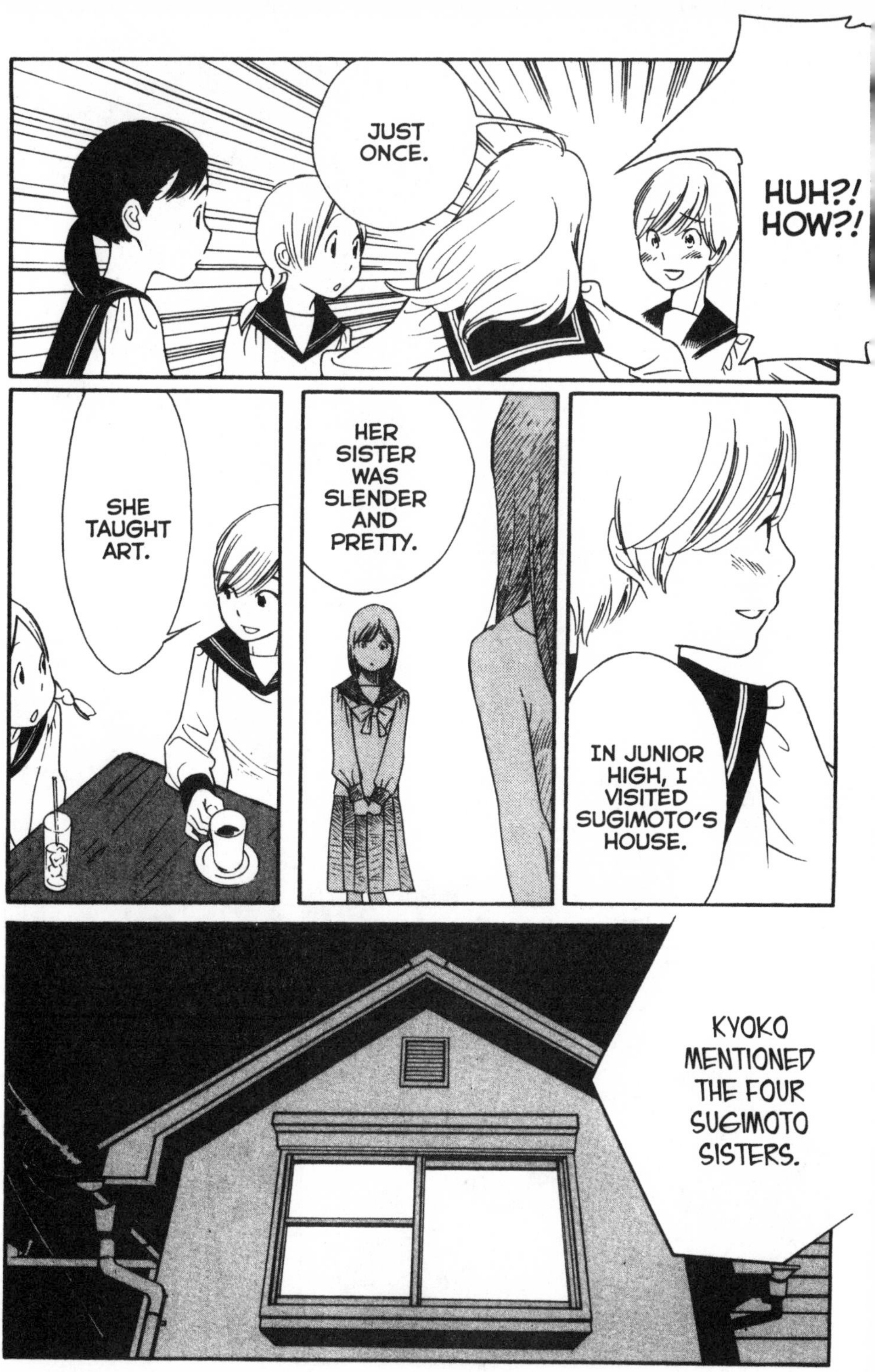
HUH?! HOW?!
JUST ONCE.
IN JUNIOR HIGH, I VISITED SUGIMOTO'S HOUSE.
HER SISTER WAS SLENDER AND PRETTY.
SHE TAUGHT ART.
KYOKO MENTIONED THE FOUR SUGIMOTO SISTERS.

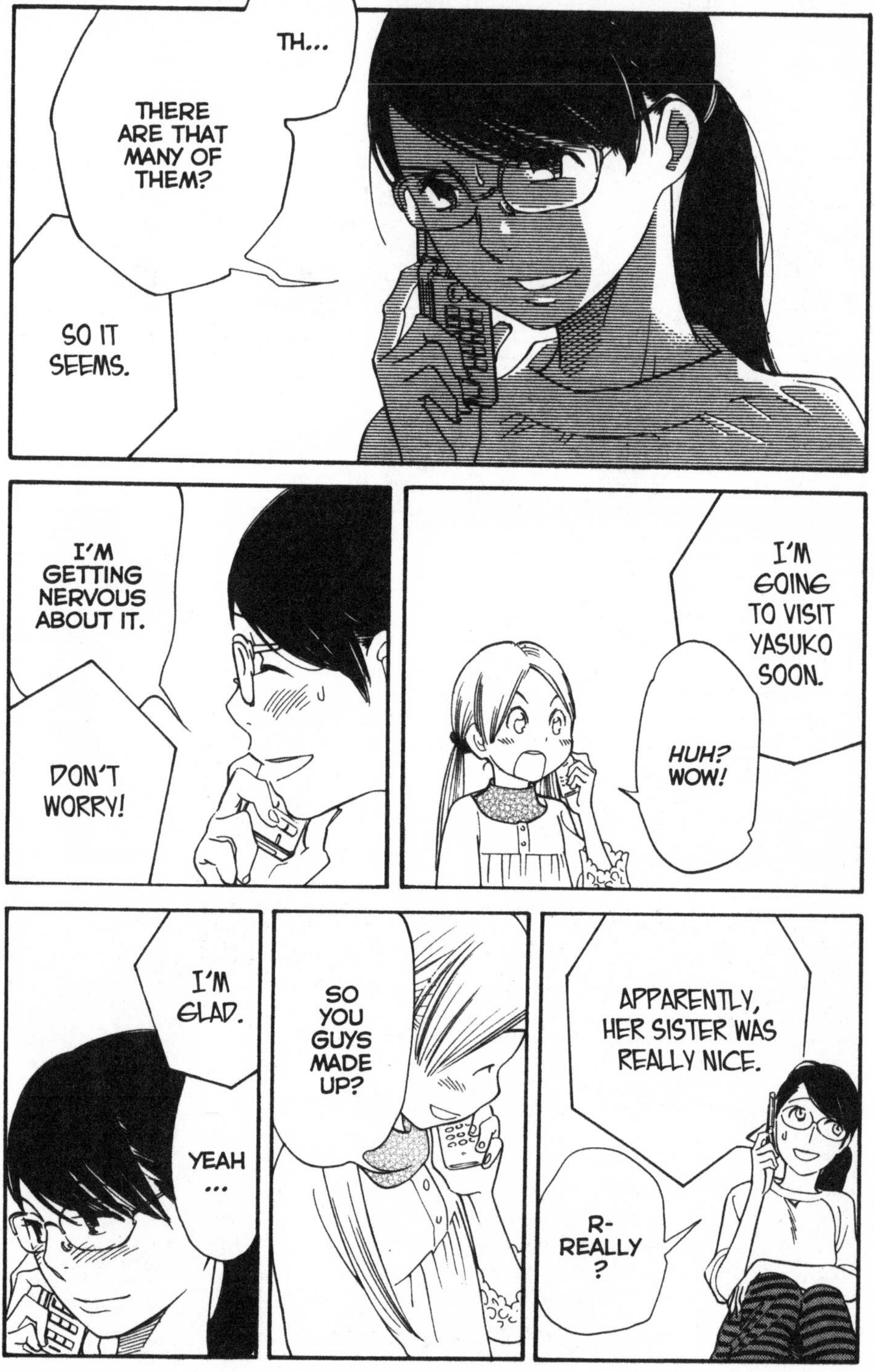
TH...
THERE ARE THAT MANY OF THEM?
SO IT SEEMS.
I'M GOING TO VISIT YASUKO SOON.
HUH? WOW!
I'M GETTING NERVOUS ABOUT IT.
DON'T WORRY!
APPARENTLY, HER SISTER WAS REALLY NICE.
R-REALLY?
SO YOU GUYS MADE UP?
I'M GLAD.
YEAH...

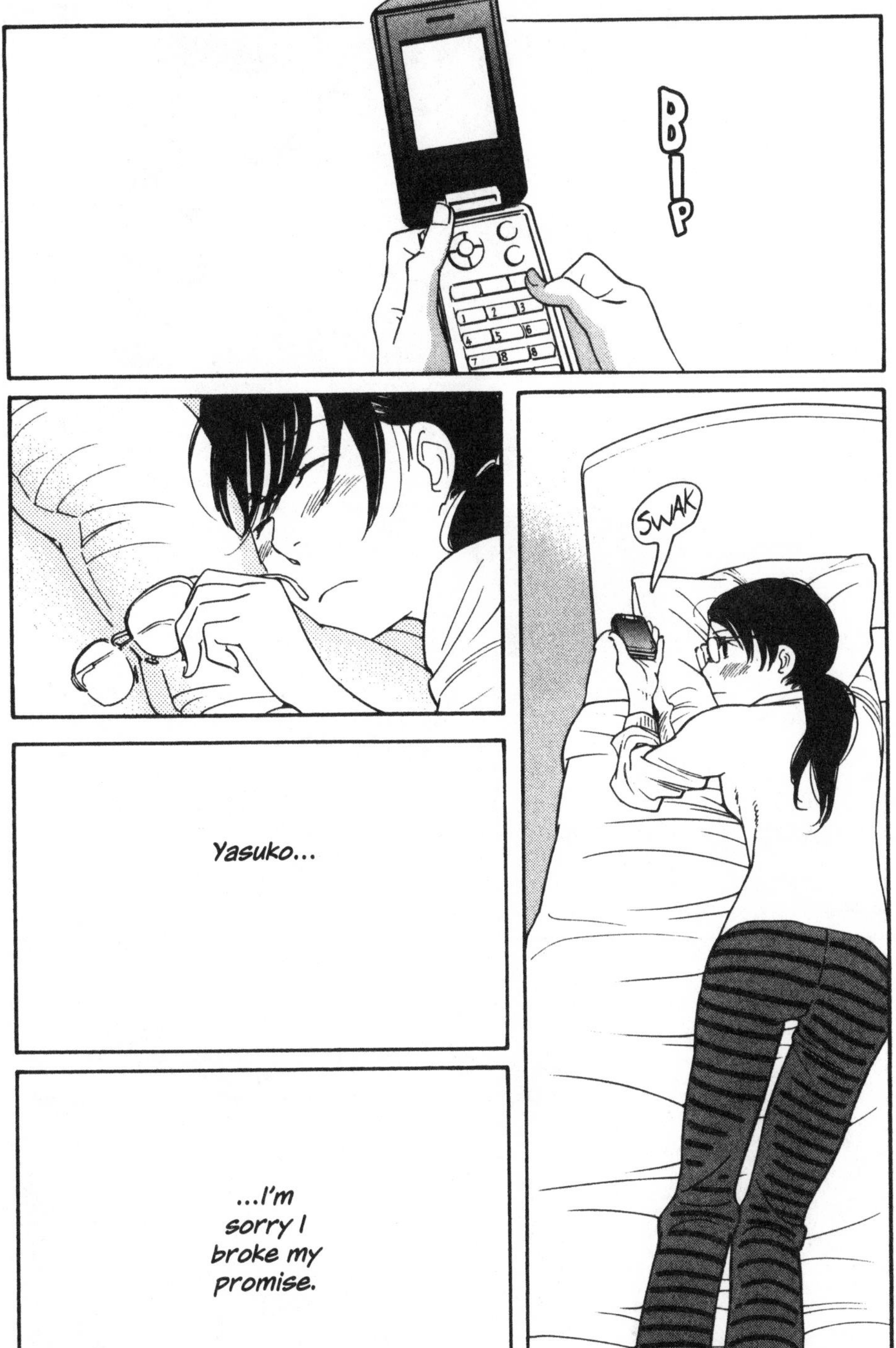
BIP
SWAK
Yasuko...
...I'm sorry I broke my promise.

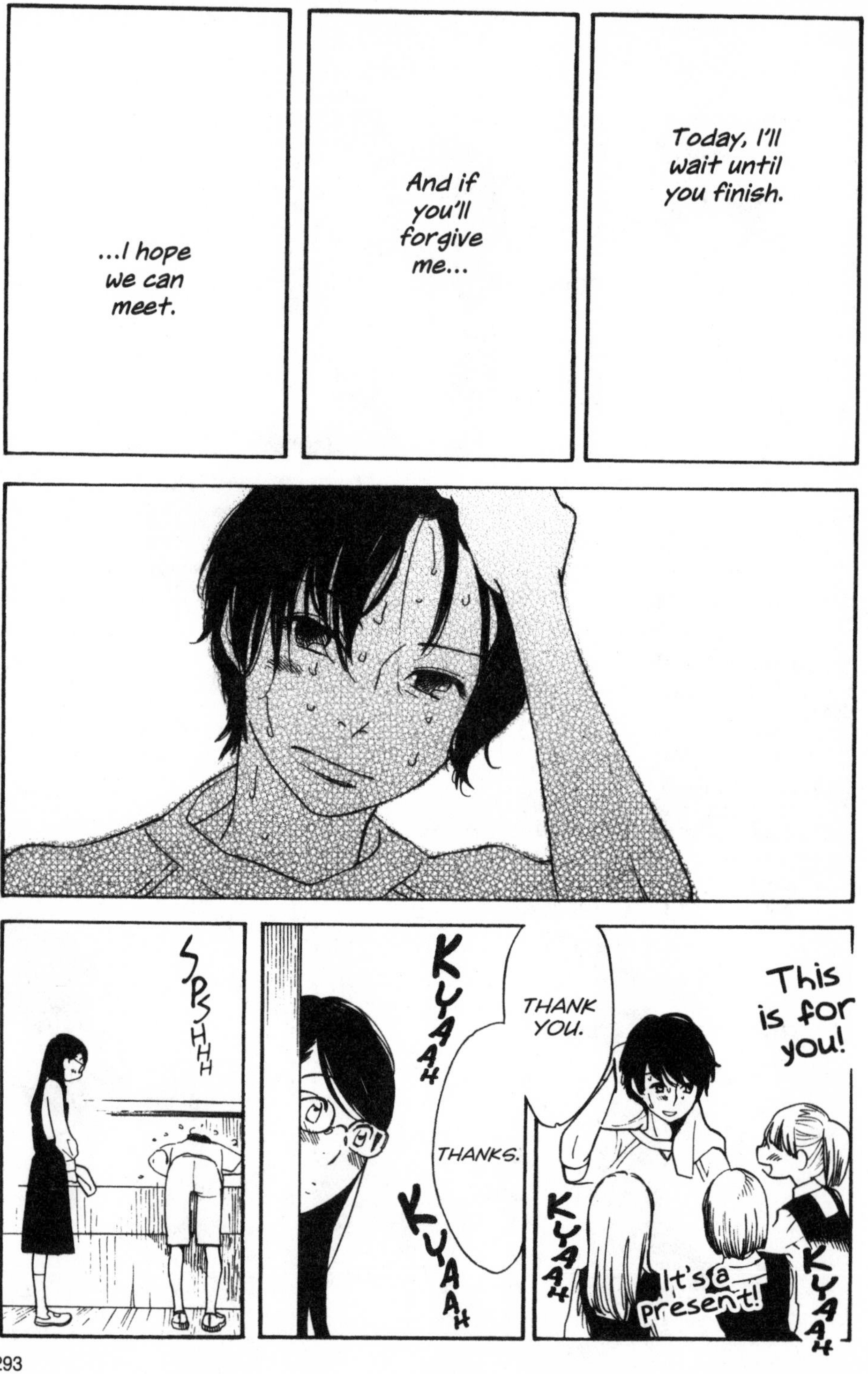
Today, I'll wait until you finish.
And if you'll forgive me...
...I hope we can meet.
This is for you!
KYAAH
It's a present!
KYAAH
THANK YOU.
KYAAH
THANKS.
KYAAH
SPSHHH

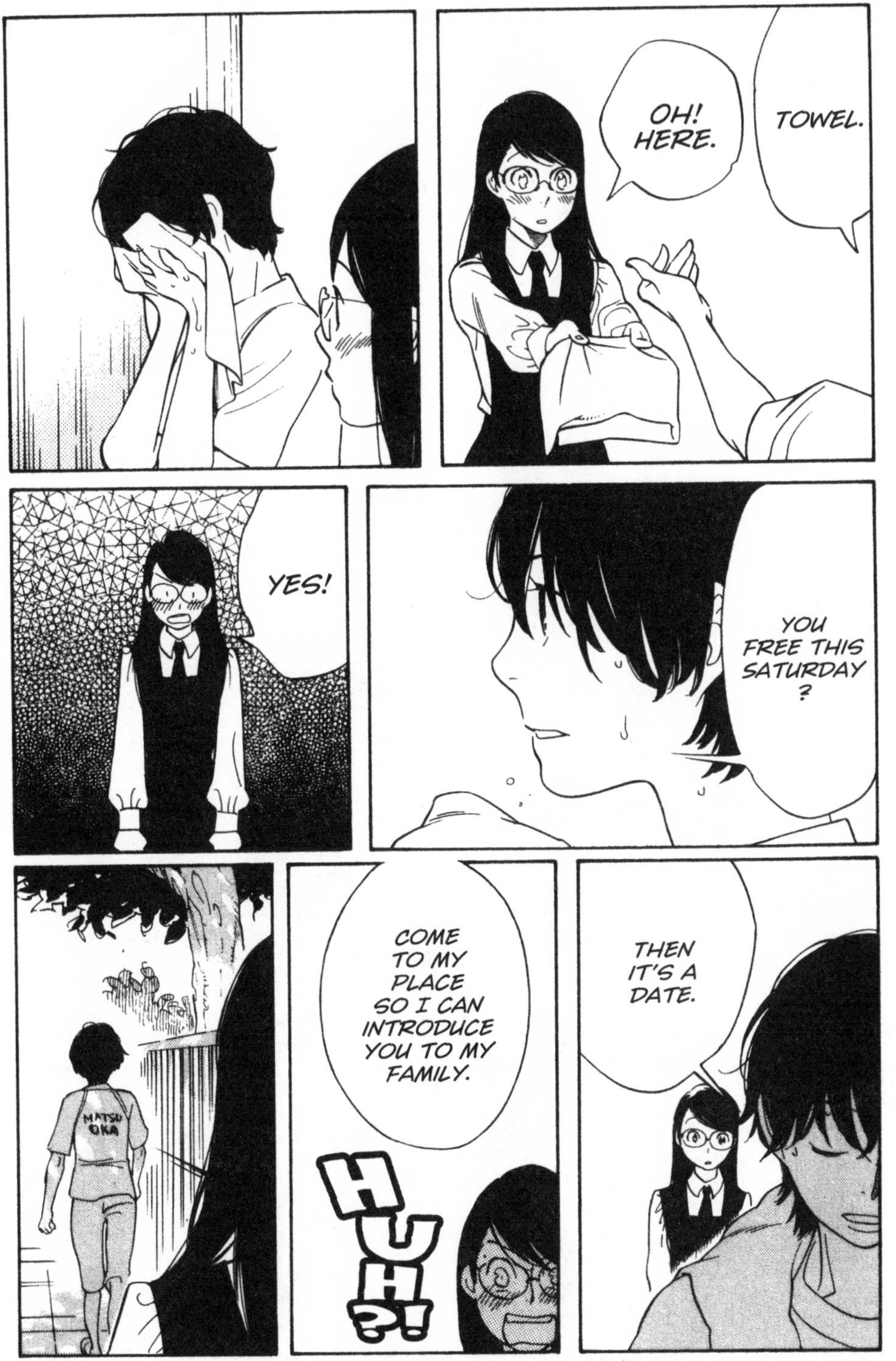
TOWEL.
OH! HERE.
YOU FREE THIS SATURDAY?
YES!
THEN IT'S A DATE.
COME TO MY PLACE SO I CAN INTRODUCE YOU TO MY FAMILY.
HUH?!
MATSU OKA

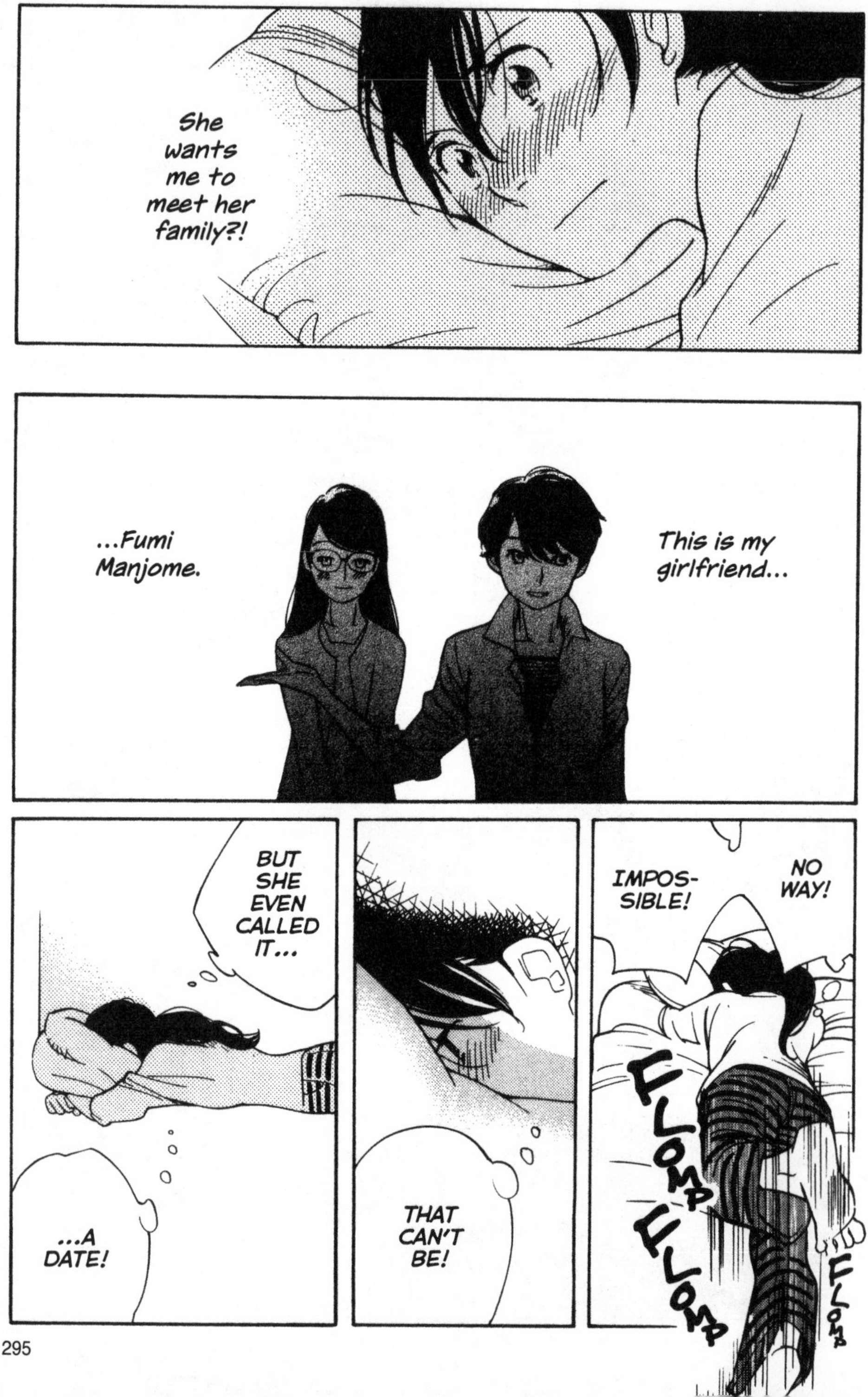
She wants me to meet her family?!
This is my girlfriend...
...Fumi Manjome.
NO WAY!
IMPOS-SIBLE!
FLOMP FLOMP
FLOMP
THAT CAN'T BE!
BUT SHE EVEN CALLED IT...
...A DATE!

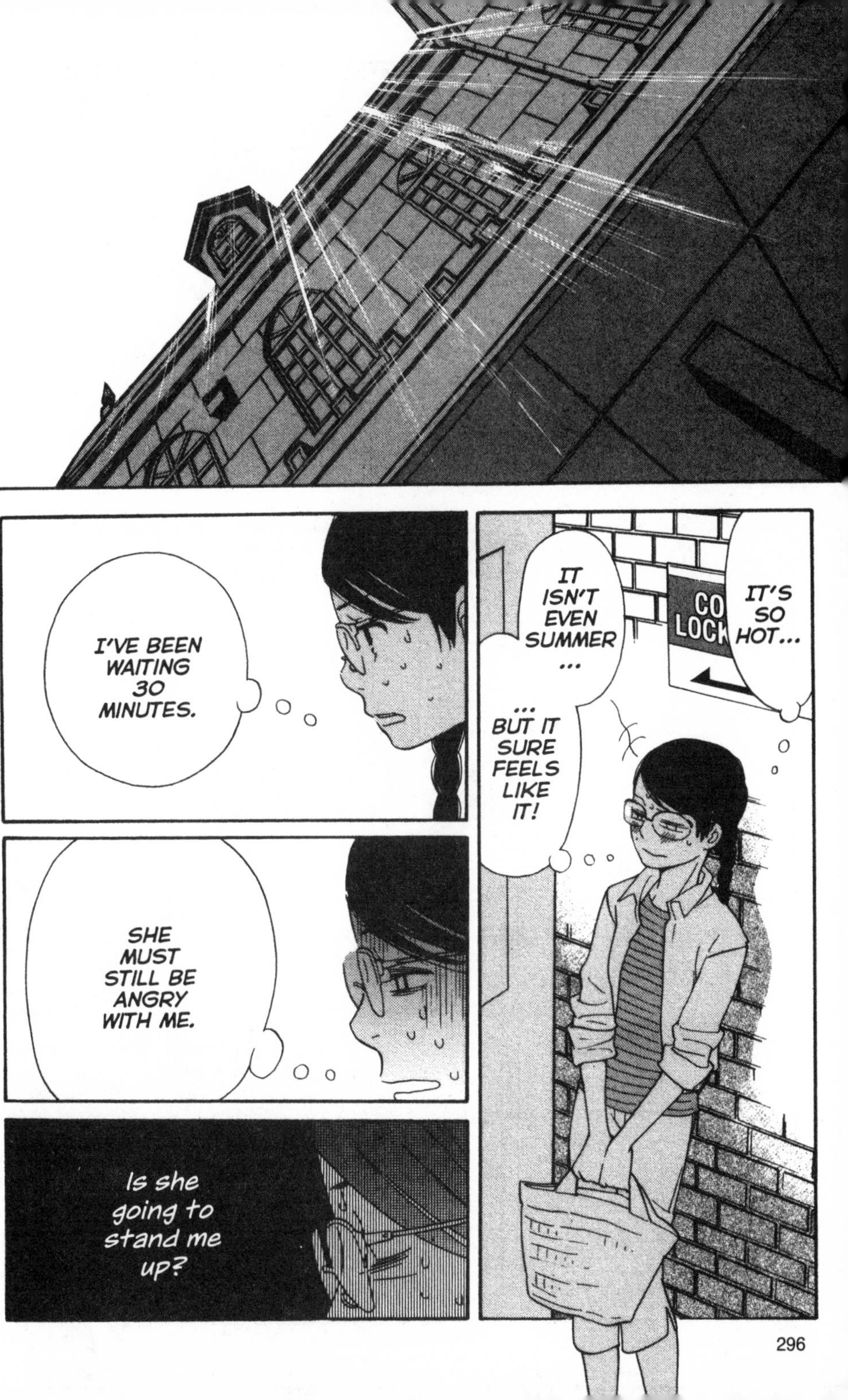
IT'S SO HOT...
IT ISN'T EVEN SUMMER ...
... BUT IT SURE FEELS LIKE IT!
I'VE BEEN WAITING 30 MINUTES.
SHE MUST STILL BE ANGRY WITH ME.
Is she going to stand me up?

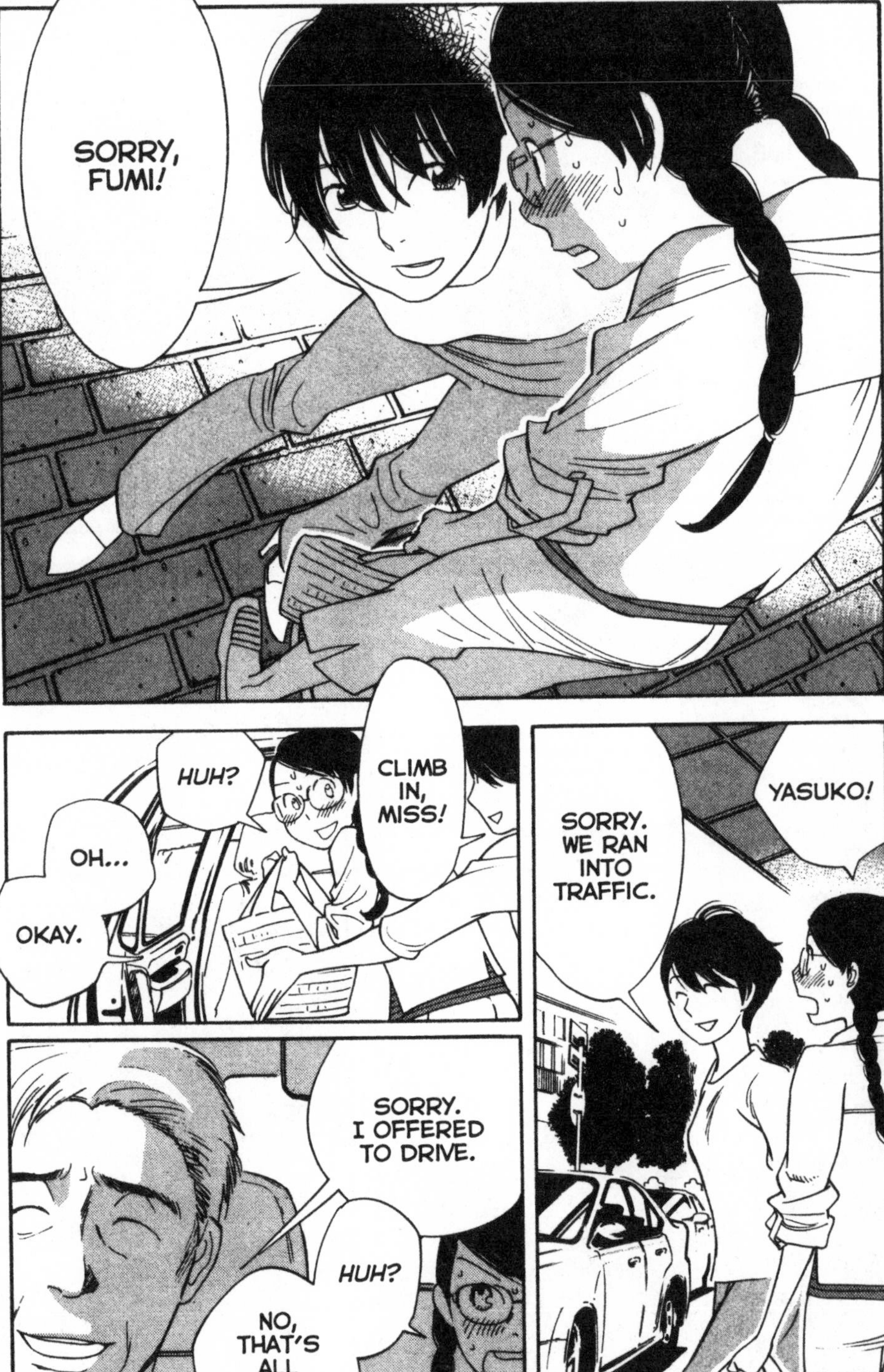
SORRY, FUMI!
YASUKO!
SORRY. WE RAN INTO TRAFFIC.
CLIMB IN, MISS!
HUH?
OH...
OKAY.
SORRY. I OFFERED TO DRIVE.
HUH?
NO, THAT'S ALL RIGHT!

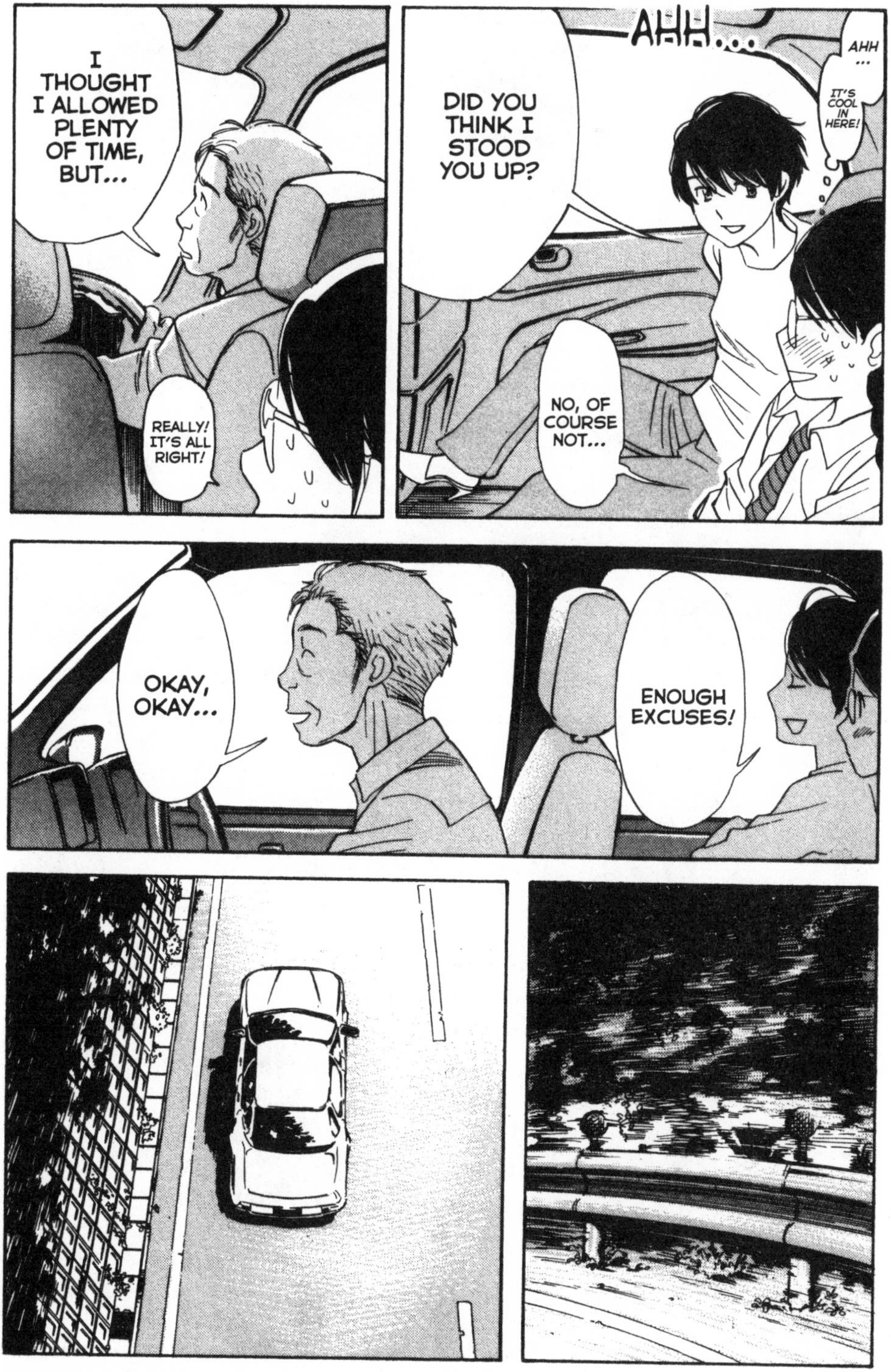
AHH...
AHH... IT'S COOL IN HERE!
DID YOU THINK I STOOD YOU UP?
NO, OF COURSE NOT...
I THOUGHT I ALLOWED PLENTY OF TIME, BUT...
REALLY! IT'S ALL RIGHT!
ENOUGH EXCUSES!
OKAY, OKAY...

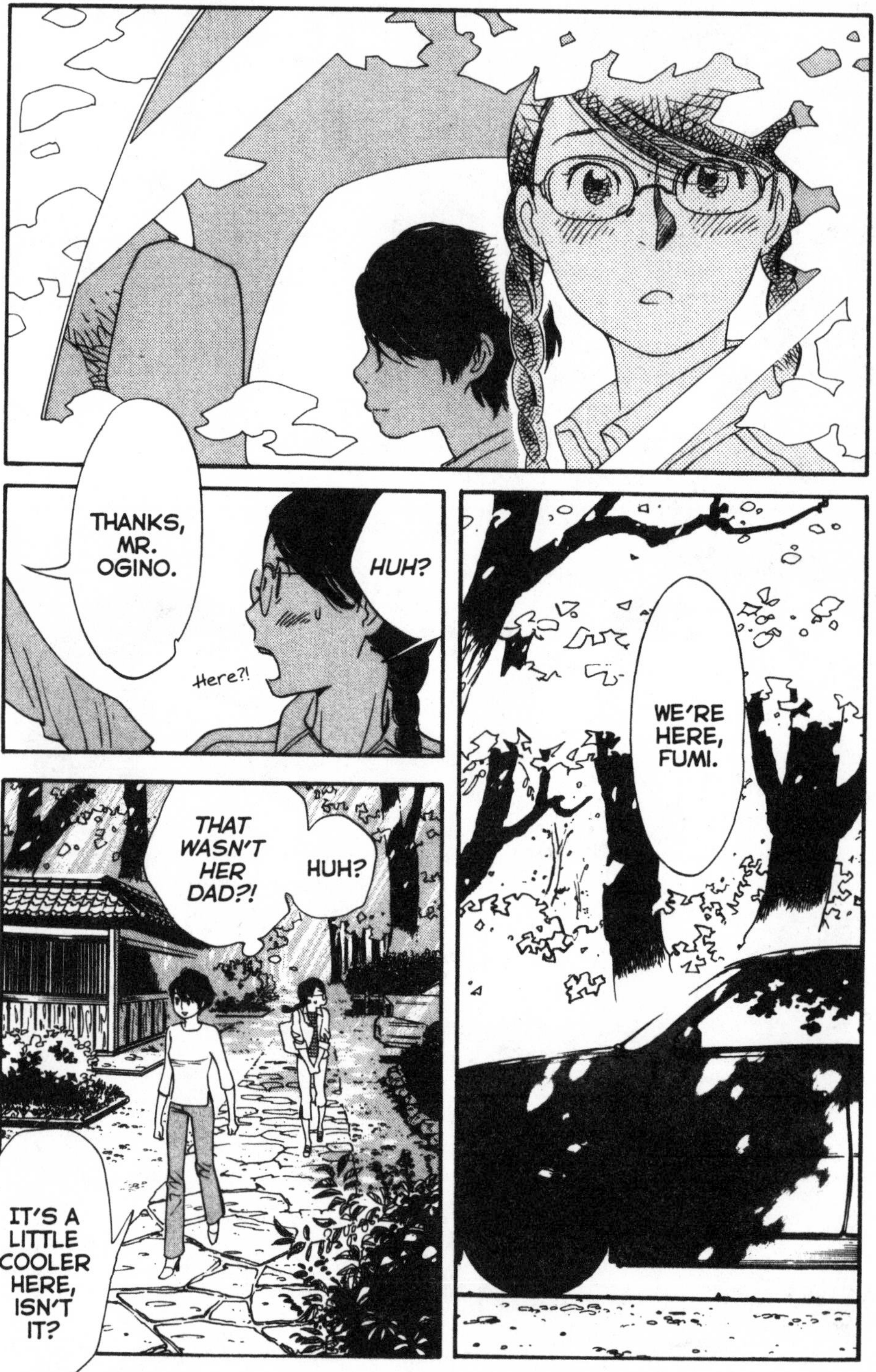
WE'RE HERE, FUMI.
THANKS, MR. OGINO.
HUH?
Here?!
HUH?
THAT WASN'T HER DAD?!
IT'S A LITTLE COOLER HERE, ISN'T IT?

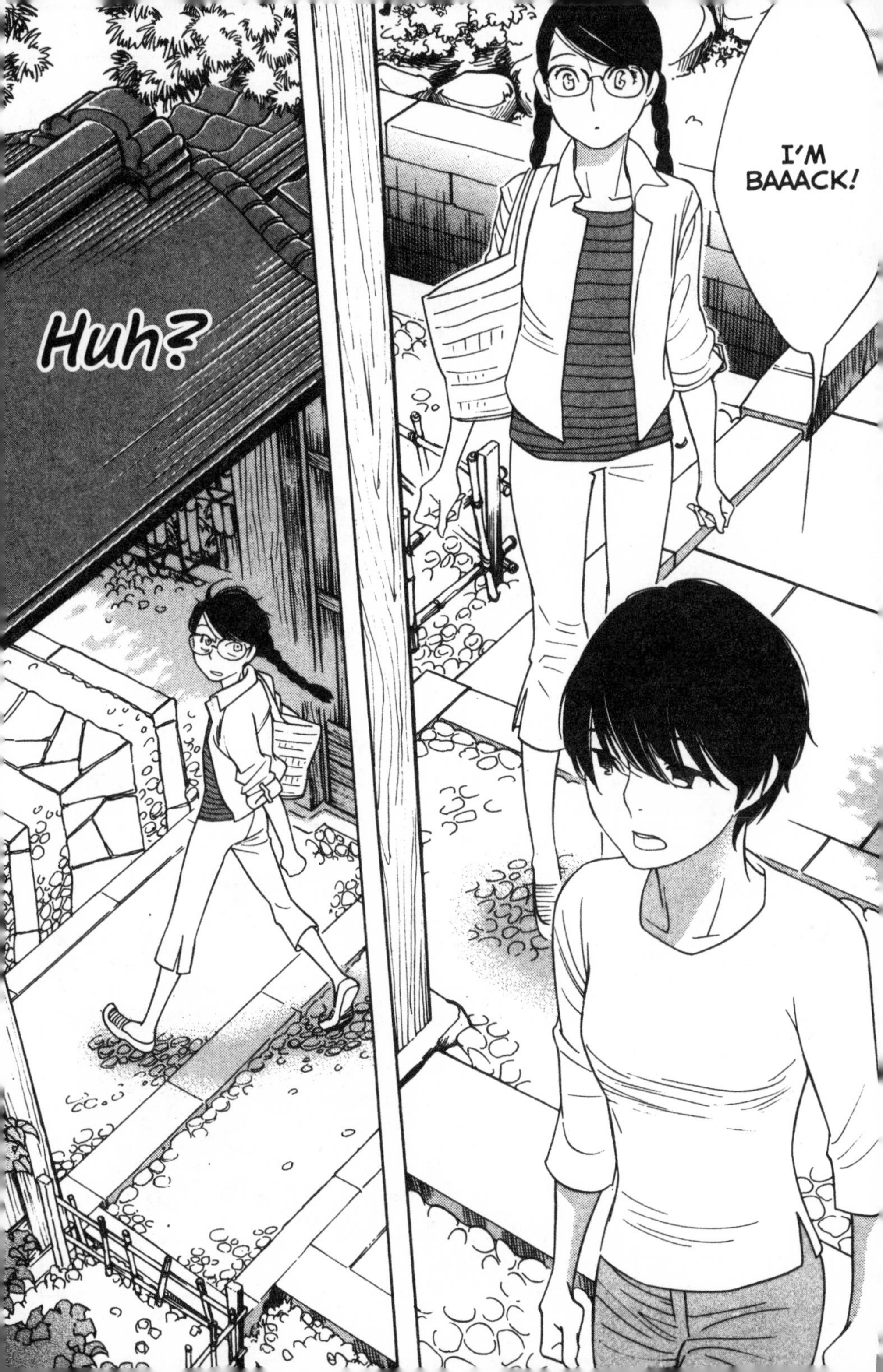
I'M BAAACK!
Huh?

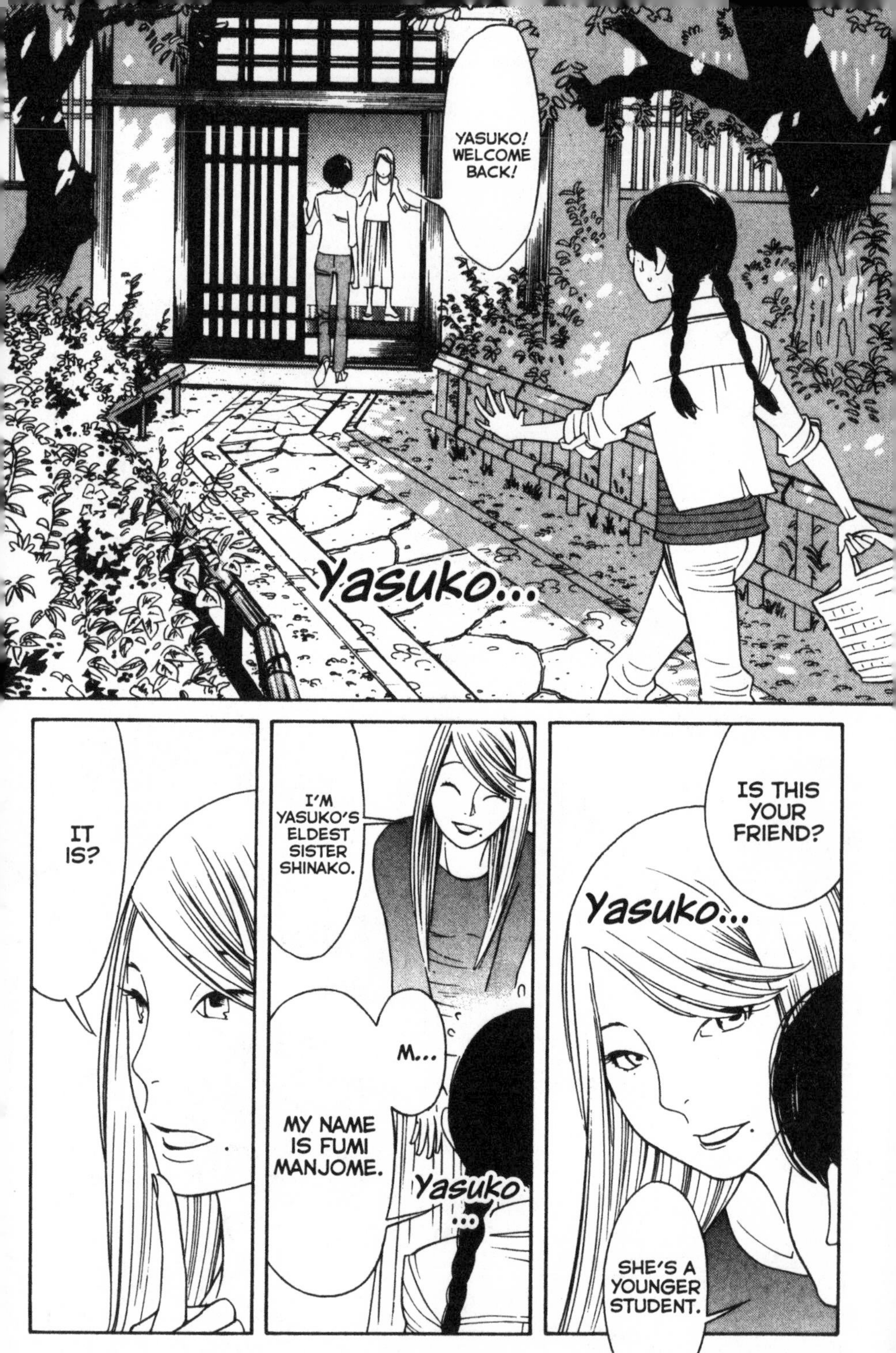
YASUKO! WELCOME BACK!
Yasuko...
IS THIS YOUR FRIEND?
Yasuko...
SHE'S A YOUNGER STUDENT.
I'M YASUKO'S ELDEST SISTER SHINAKO.
M...
MY NAME IS FUMI MANJOME.
Yasuko...
IT IS?

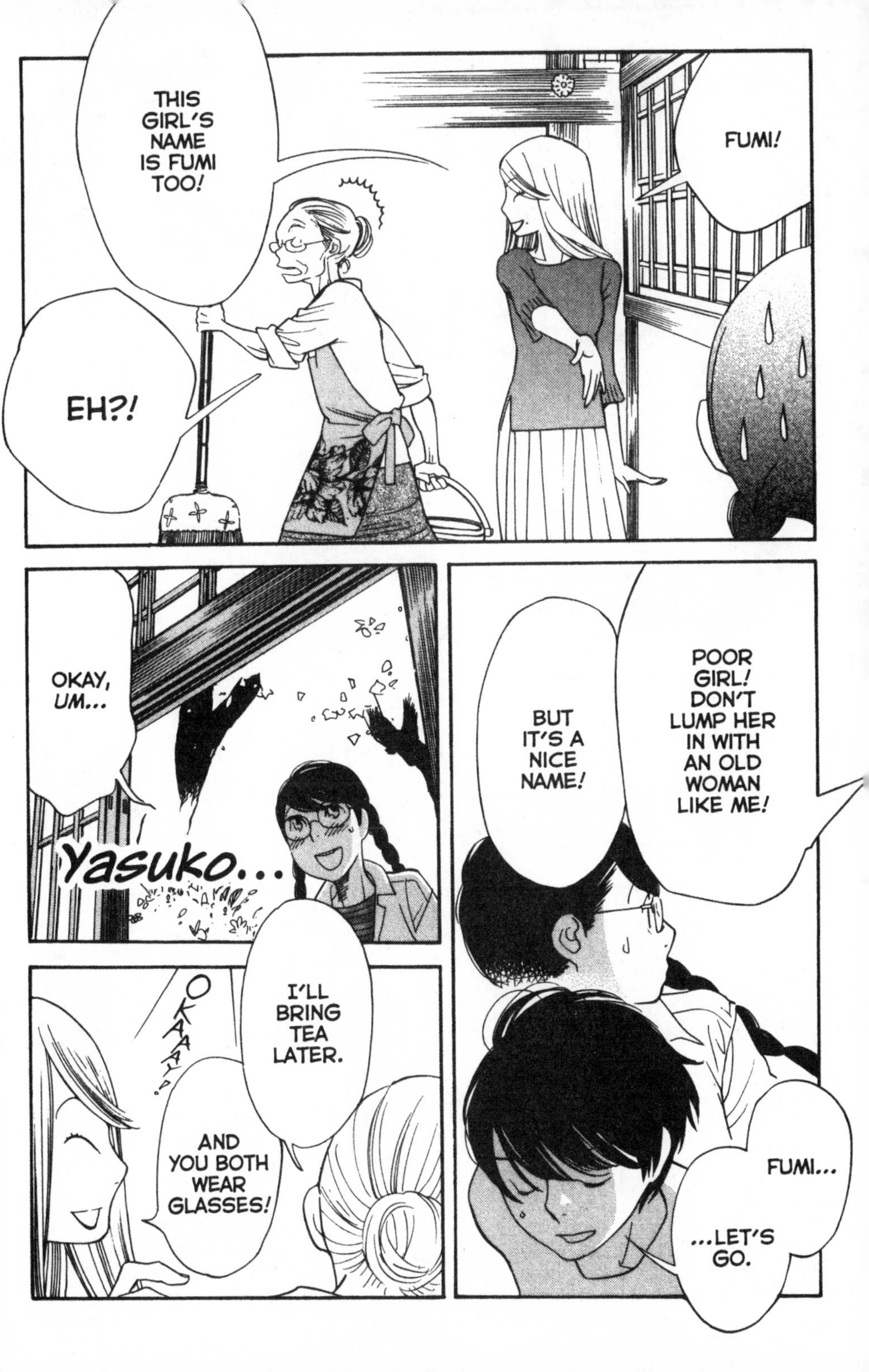

FUMI!
THIS GIRL'S NAME IS FUMI TOO!
EH?!
POOR GIRL! DON'T LUMP HER IN WITH AN OLD WOMAN LIKE ME!
BUT IT'S A NICE NAME!
FUMI...
...LET'S GO.
OKAY, UM...
Yasuko...
I'LL BRING TEA LATER.
OKAAAY!
AND YOU BOTH WEAR GLASSES!

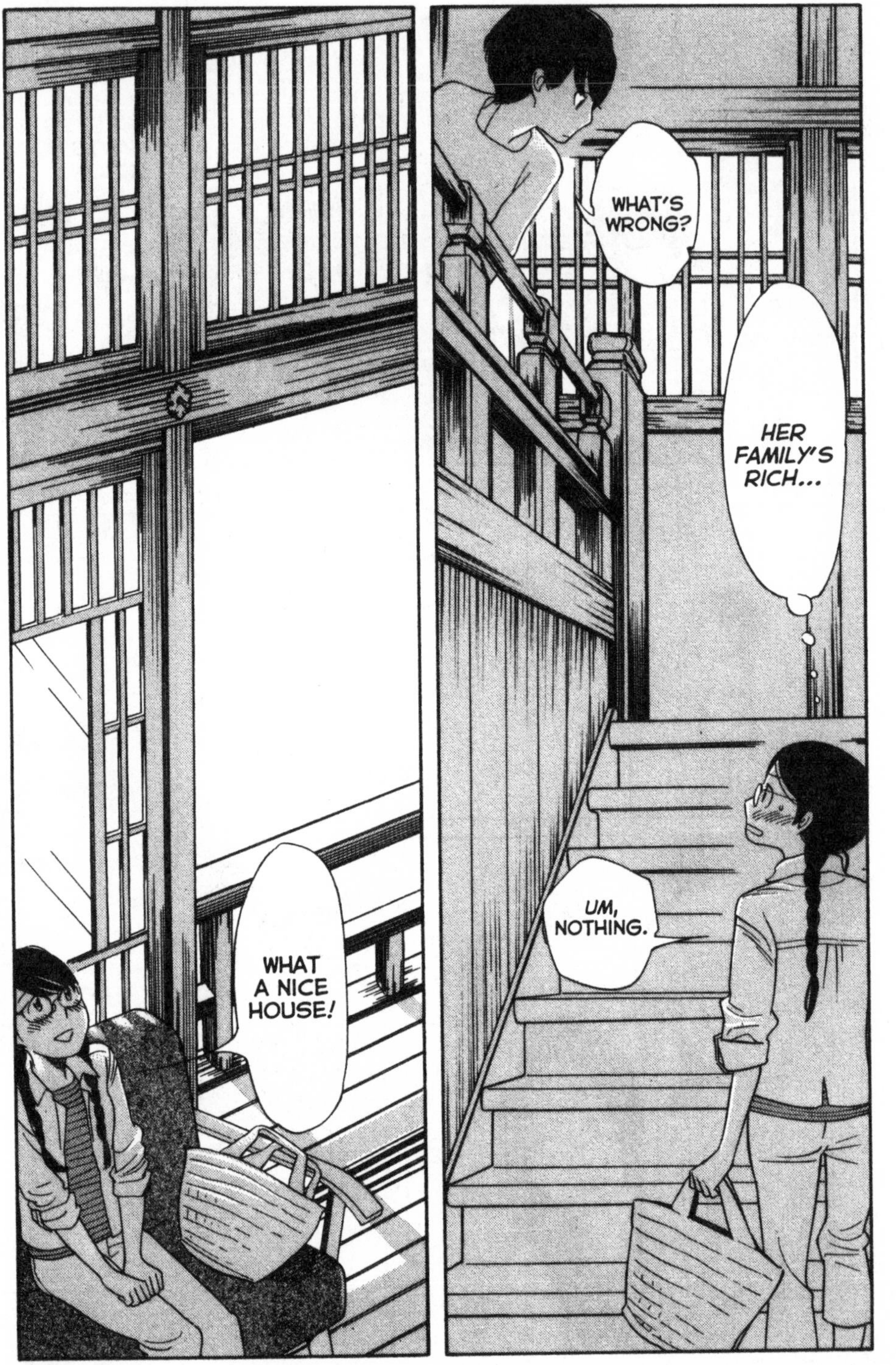
WHAT'S WRONG?
HER FAMILY'S RICH...
UM, NOTHING.
WHAT A NICE HOUSE!

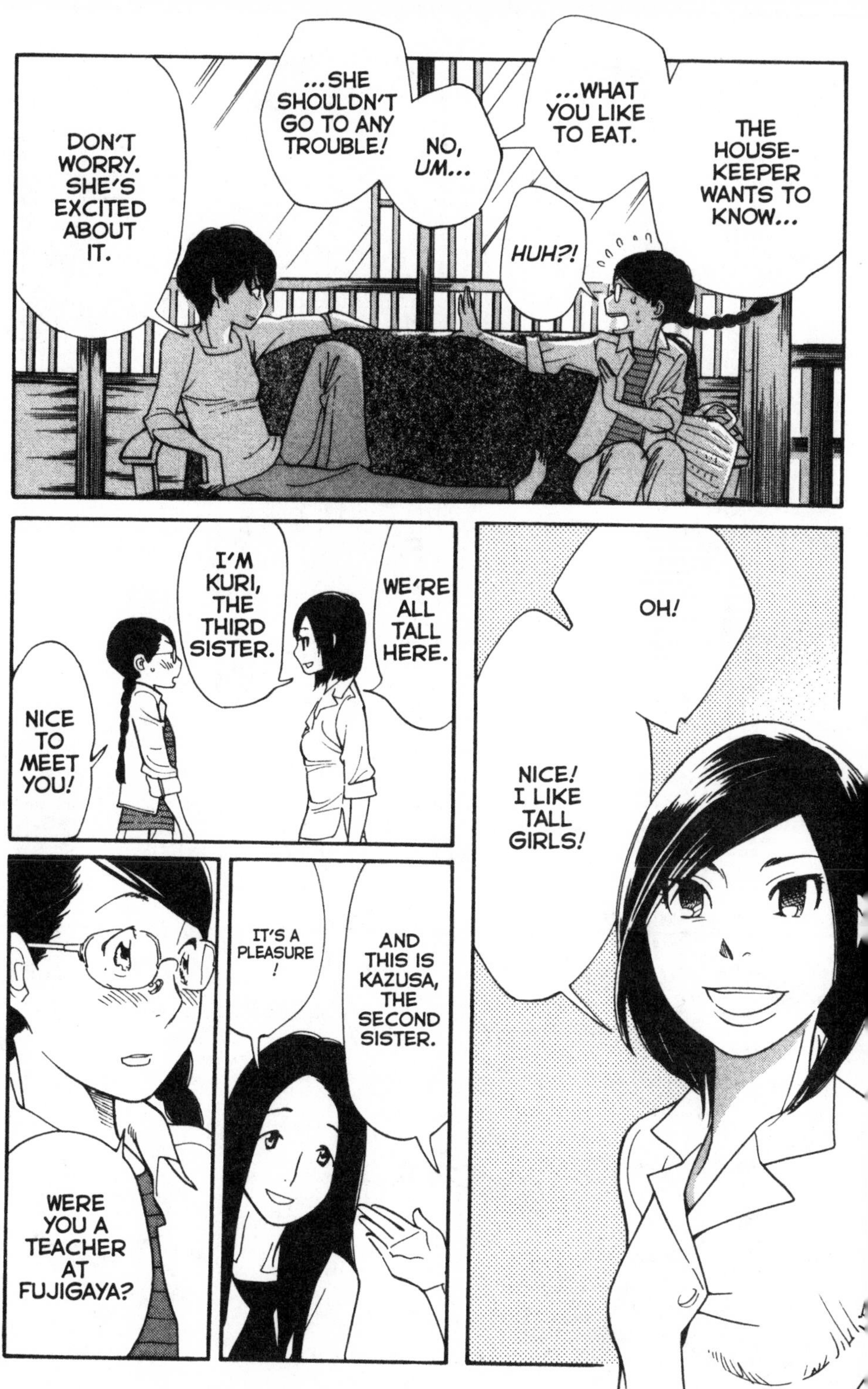
THE HOUSE-KEEPER WANTS TO KNOW...
...WHAT YOU LIKE TO EAT.
HUH?!
NO, UM...
...SHE SHOULDN'T GO TO ANY TROUBLE!
DON'T WORRY. SHE'S EXCITED ABOUT IT.
OH!
NICE! I LIKE TALL GIRLS!
WE'RE ALL TALL HERE.
I'M KURI, THE THIRD SISTER.
NICE TO MEET YOU!
AND THIS IS KAZUSA, THE SECOND SISTER.
IT'S A PLEASURE!
WERE YOU A TEACHER AT FUJIGAYA?

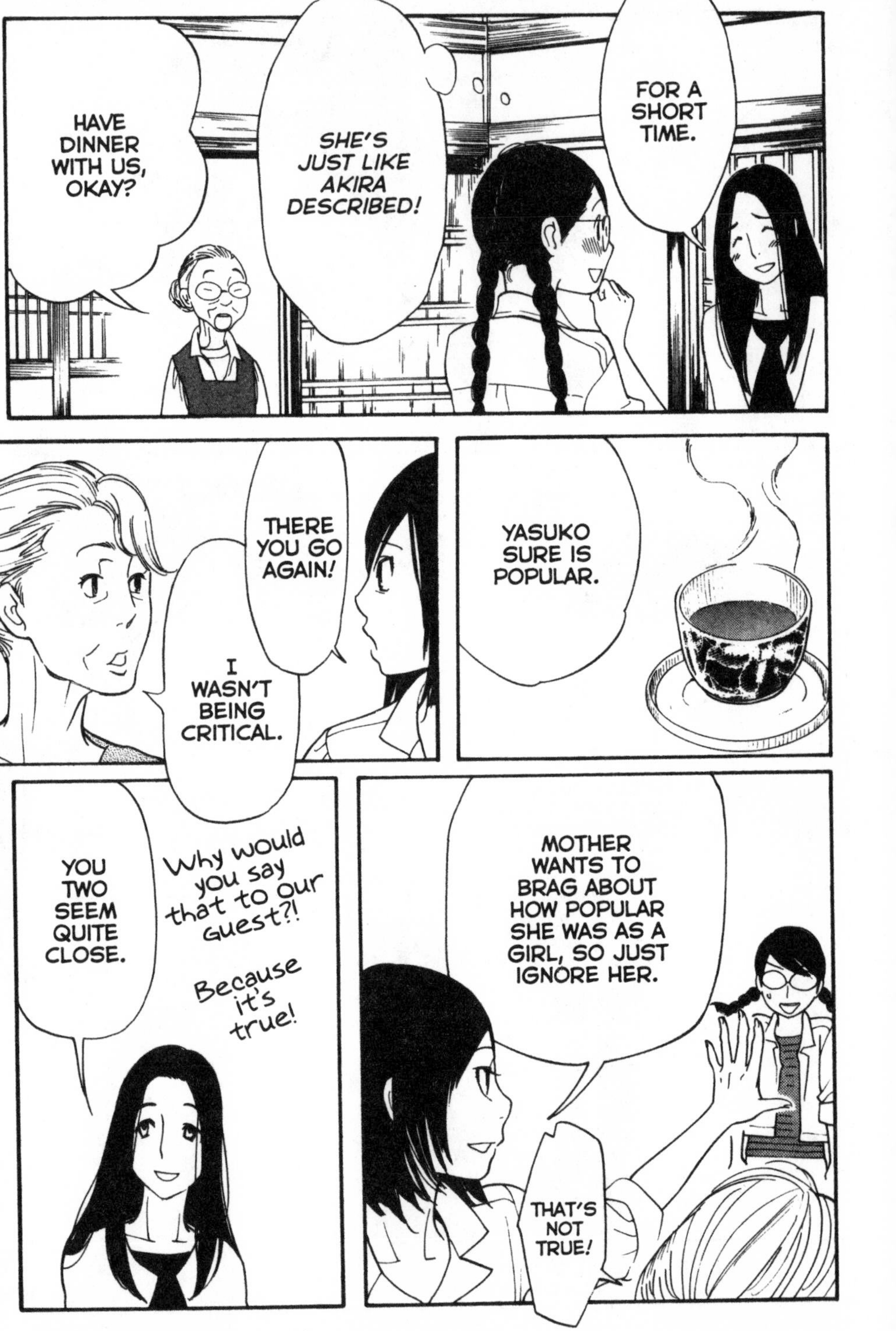
FOR A SHORT TIME.
SHE'S JUST LIKE AKIRA DESCRIBED!
HAVE DINNER WITH US, OKAY?
YASUKO SURE IS POPULAR.
THERE YOU GO AGAIN!
I WASN'T BEING CRITICAL.
MOTHER WANTS TO BRAG ABOUT HOW POPULAR SHE WAS AS A GIRL, SO JUST IGNORE HER.
THAT'S NOT TRUE!
YOU TWO SEEM QUITE CLOSE.
Why would you say that to our guest?!
Because it's true!

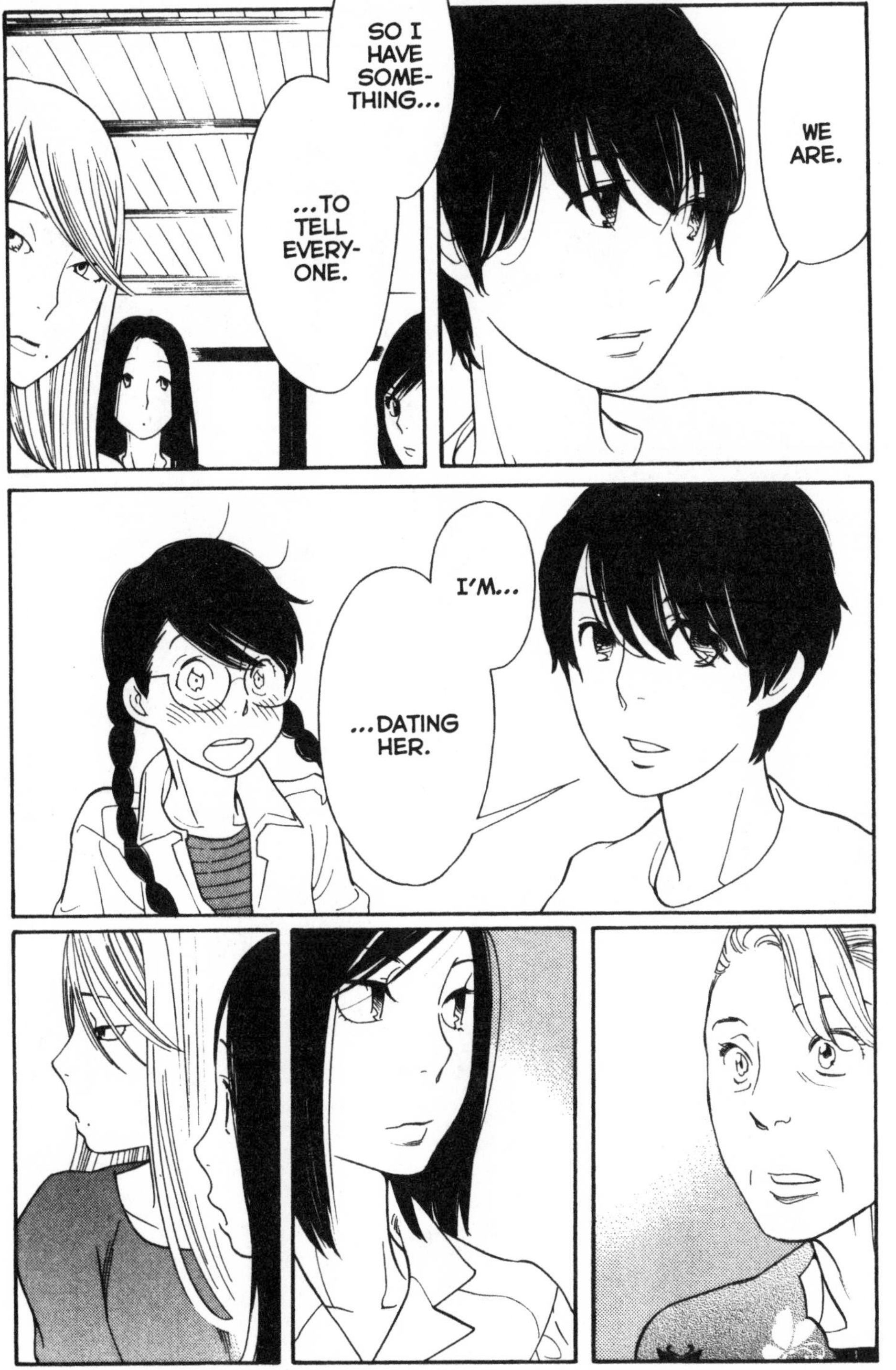
WE ARE.
SO I HAVE SOMETHING...
...TO TELL EVERYONE.
I'M...
...DATING HER.

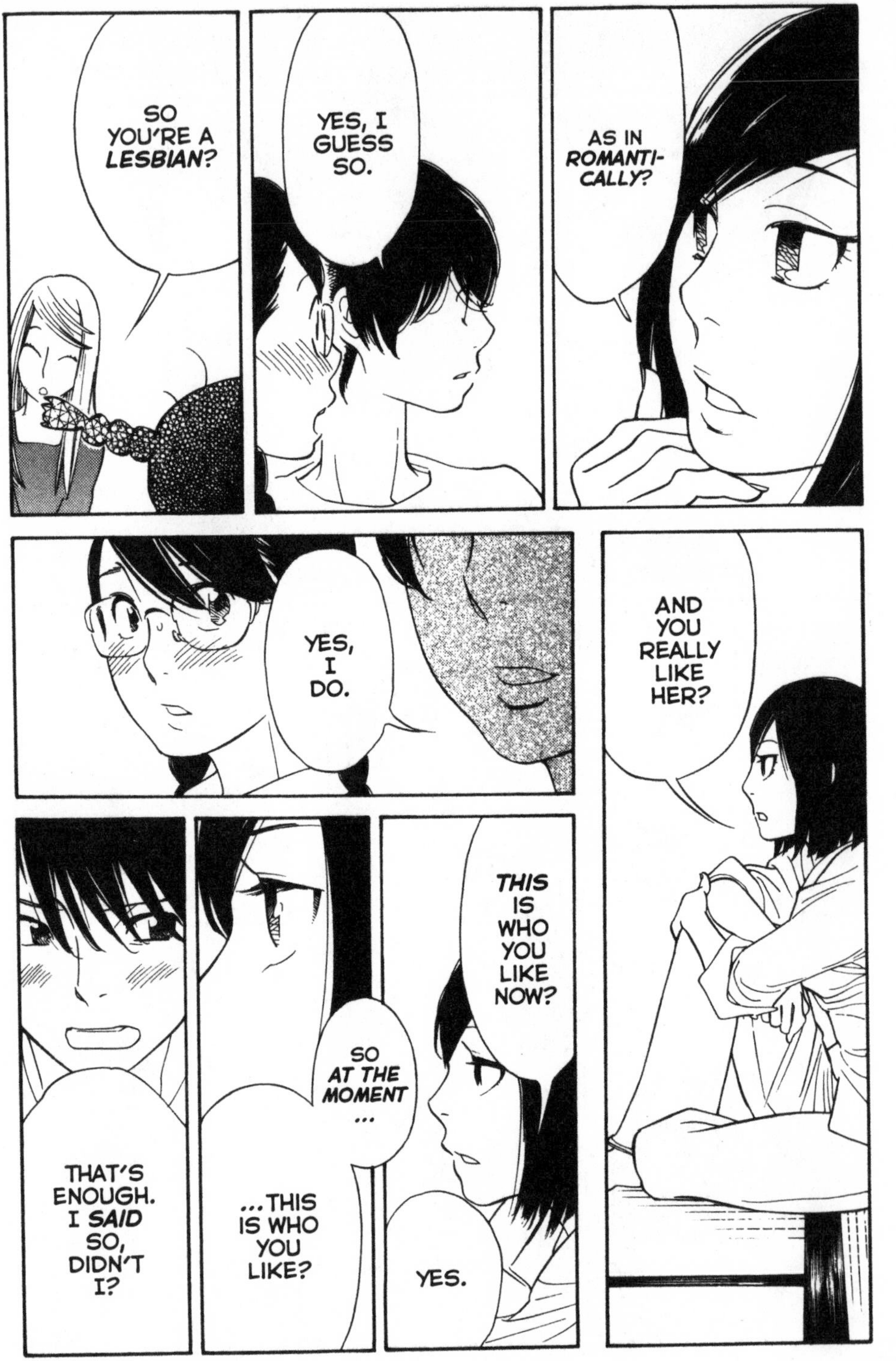
AS IN *ROMANTICALLY?*
YES, I GUESS SO.
SO YOU'RE A *LESBIAN?*
AND YOU REALLY LIKE HER?
YES, I DO.
*THIS* IS WHO YOU LIKE NOW?
SO *AT THE MOMENT* ...
YES.
...THIS IS WHO YOU LIKE?
THAT'S ENOUGH. I *SAID* SO, DIDN'T I?

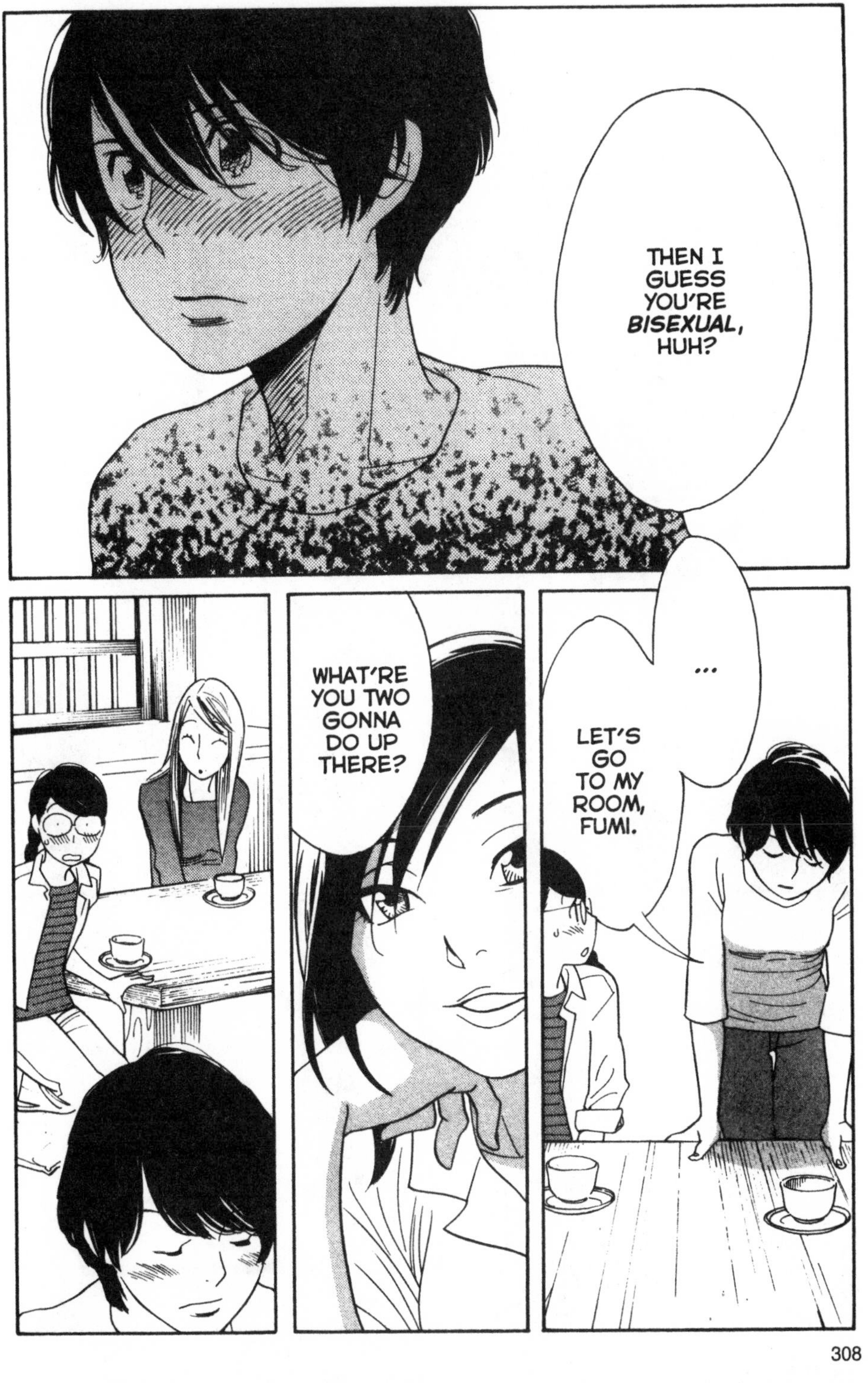
THEN I GUESS YOU'RE ***BISEXUAL***, HUH?
...
LET'S GO TO MY ROOM, FUMI.
WHAT'RE YOU TWO GONNA DO UP THERE?

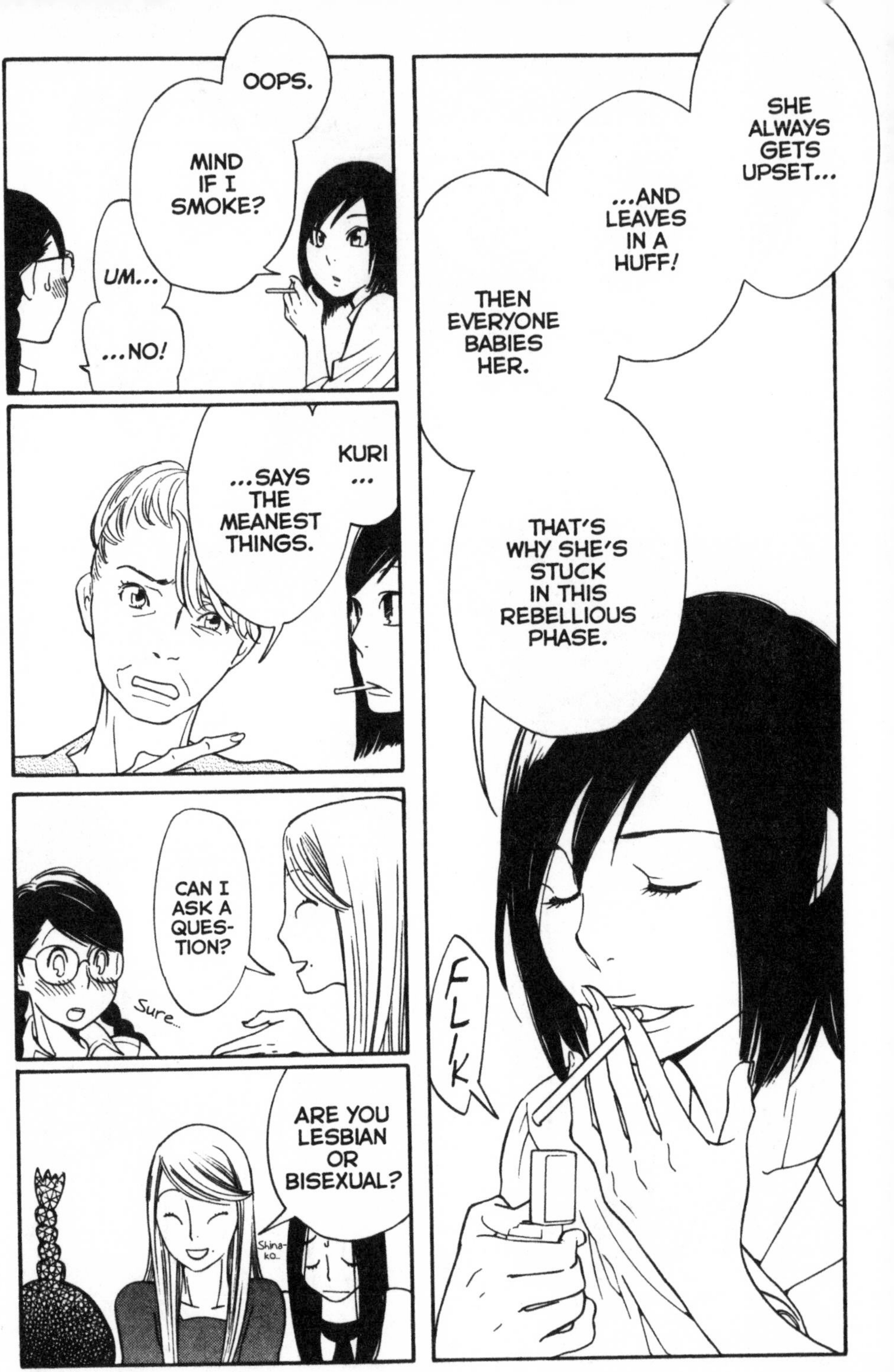
SHE ALWAYS GETS UPSET...
...AND LEAVES IN A HUFF!
THEN EVERYONE BABIES HER.
THAT'S WHY SHE'S STUCK IN THIS REBELLIOUS PHASE.
FLIK
OOPS.
MIND IF I SMOKE?
UM...
...NO!
KURI...
...SAYS THE MEANEST THINGS.
CAN I ASK A QUES-TION?
Sure...
ARE YOU LESBIAN OR BISEXUAL?
Shina-ko...

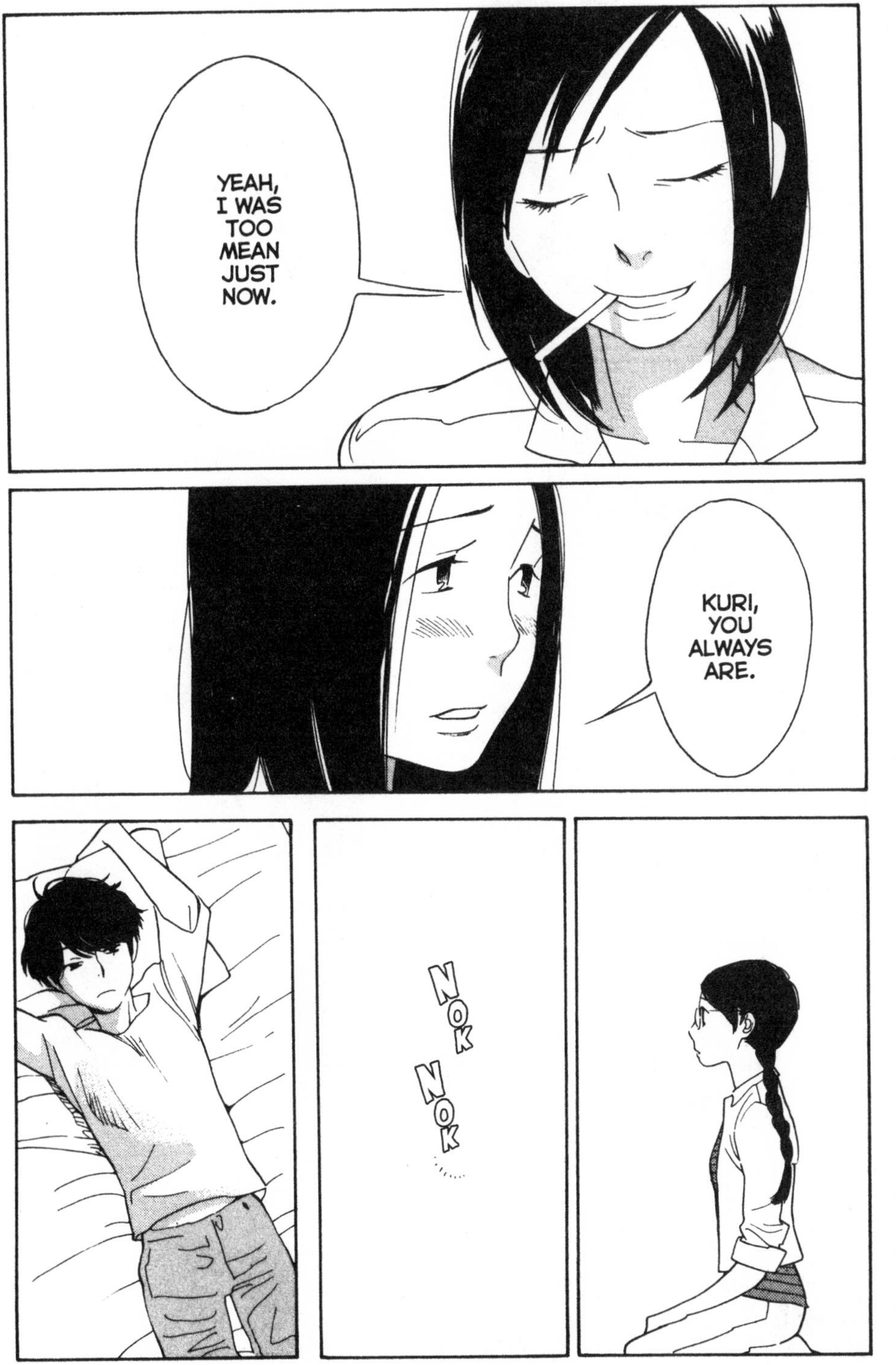
YEAH, I WAS TOO MEAN JUST NOW.
KURI, YOU ALWAYS ARE.
NOK NOK

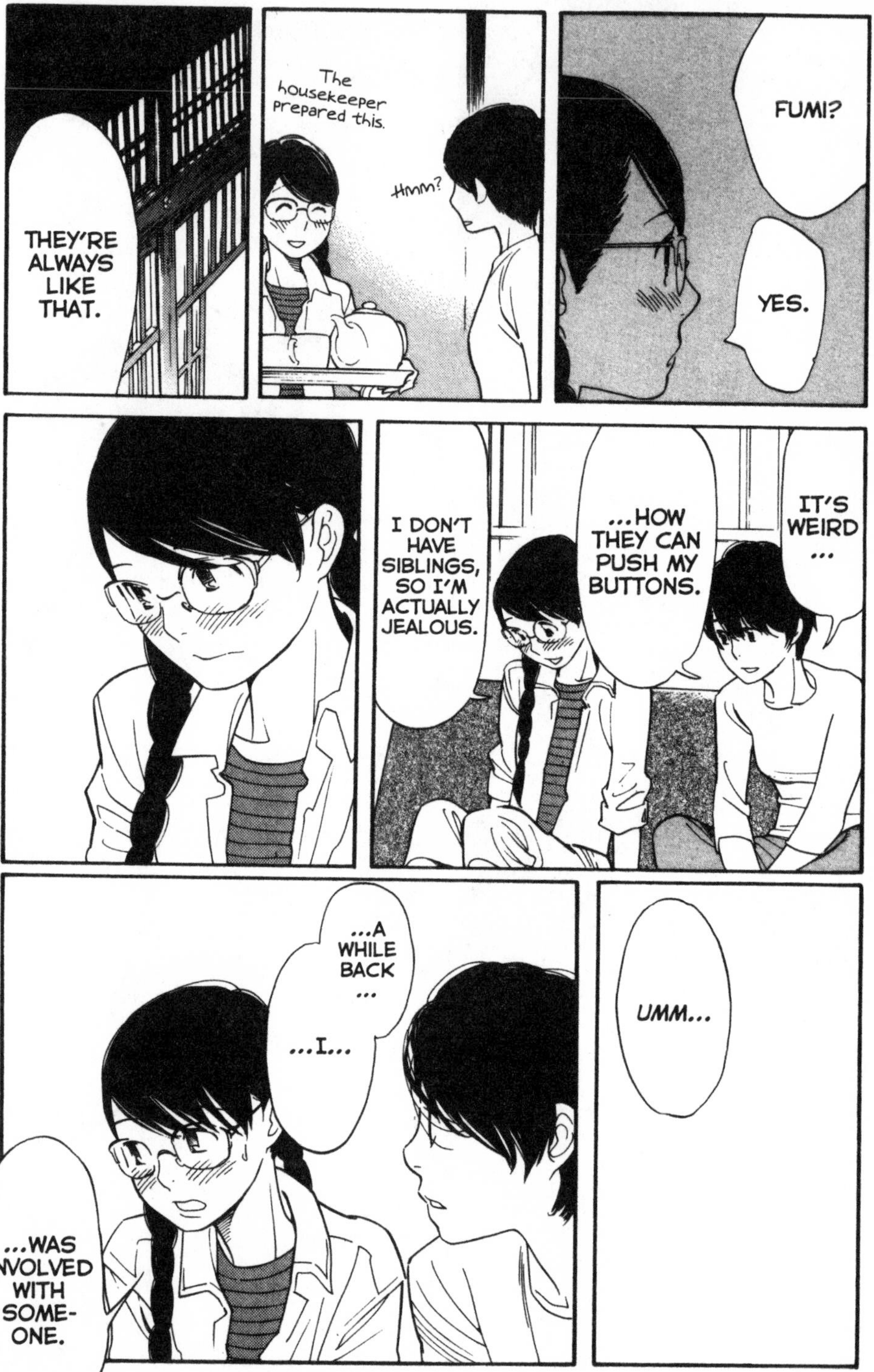
FUMI?
YES.
The housekeeper prepared this.
Hmm?
THEY'RE ALWAYS LIKE THAT.
IT'S WEIRD...
...HOW THEY CAN PUSH MY BUTTONS.
I DON'T HAVE SIBLINGS, SO I'M ACTUALLY JEALOUS.
UMM...
...A WHILE BACK...
...I...
...WAS INVOLVED WITH SOME-ONE.

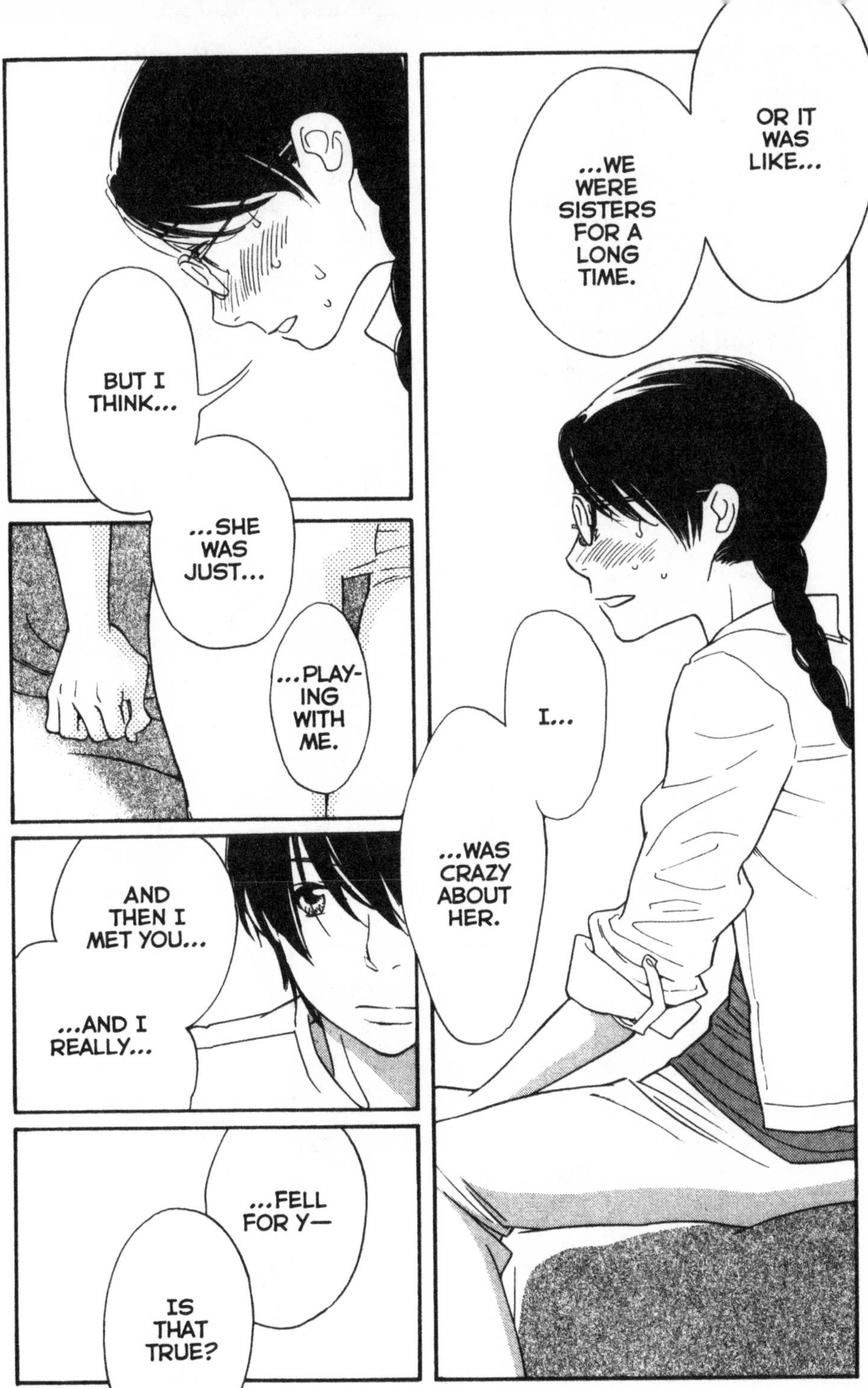
OR IT WAS LIKE...
...WE WERE SISTERS FOR A LONG TIME.
I...
...WAS CRAZY ABOUT HER.
BUT I THINK...
...SHE WAS JUST...
...PLAYING WITH ME.
AND THEN I MET YOU...
...AND I REALLY...
...FELL FOR Y—
IS THAT TRUE?

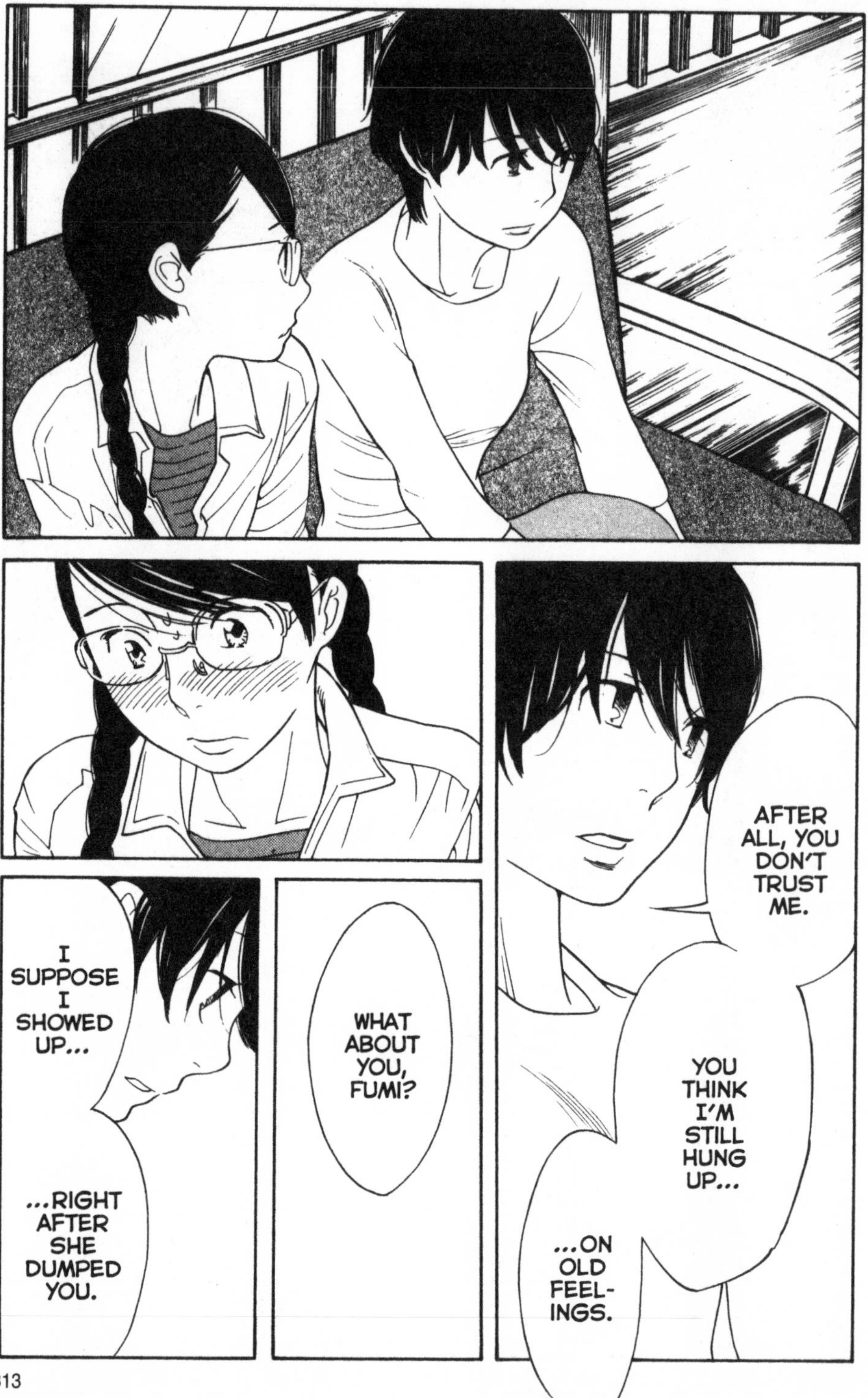
AFTER ALL, YOU DON'T TRUST ME.
YOU THINK I'M STILL HUNG UP...
...ON OLD FEELINGS.
WHAT ABOUT YOU, FUMI?
I SUPPOSE I SHOWED UP...
...RIGHT AFTER SHE DUMPED YOU.

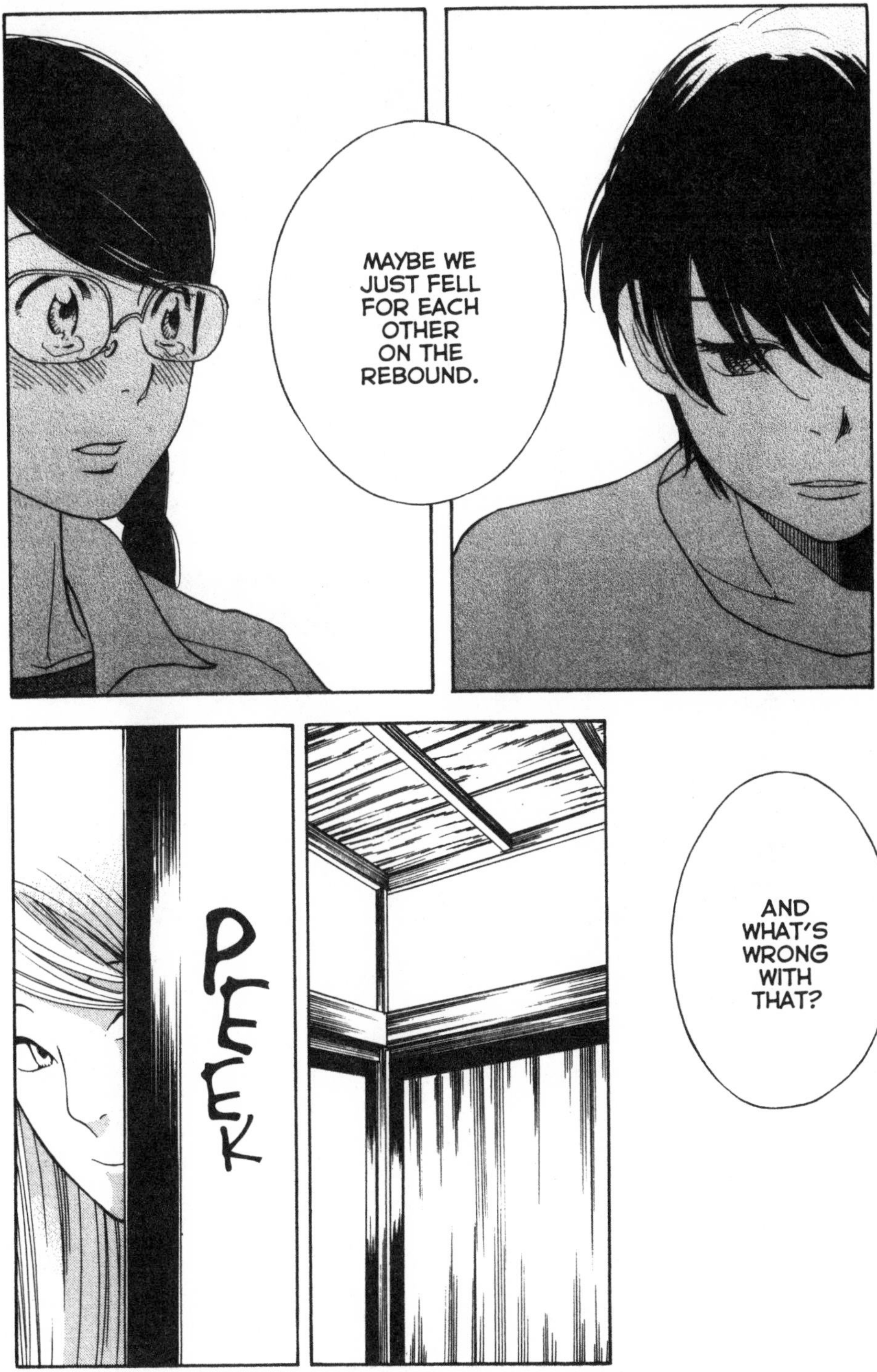
MAYBE WE JUST FELL FOR EACH OTHER ON THE REBOUND.
AND WHAT'S WRONG WITH THAT?
PEEK

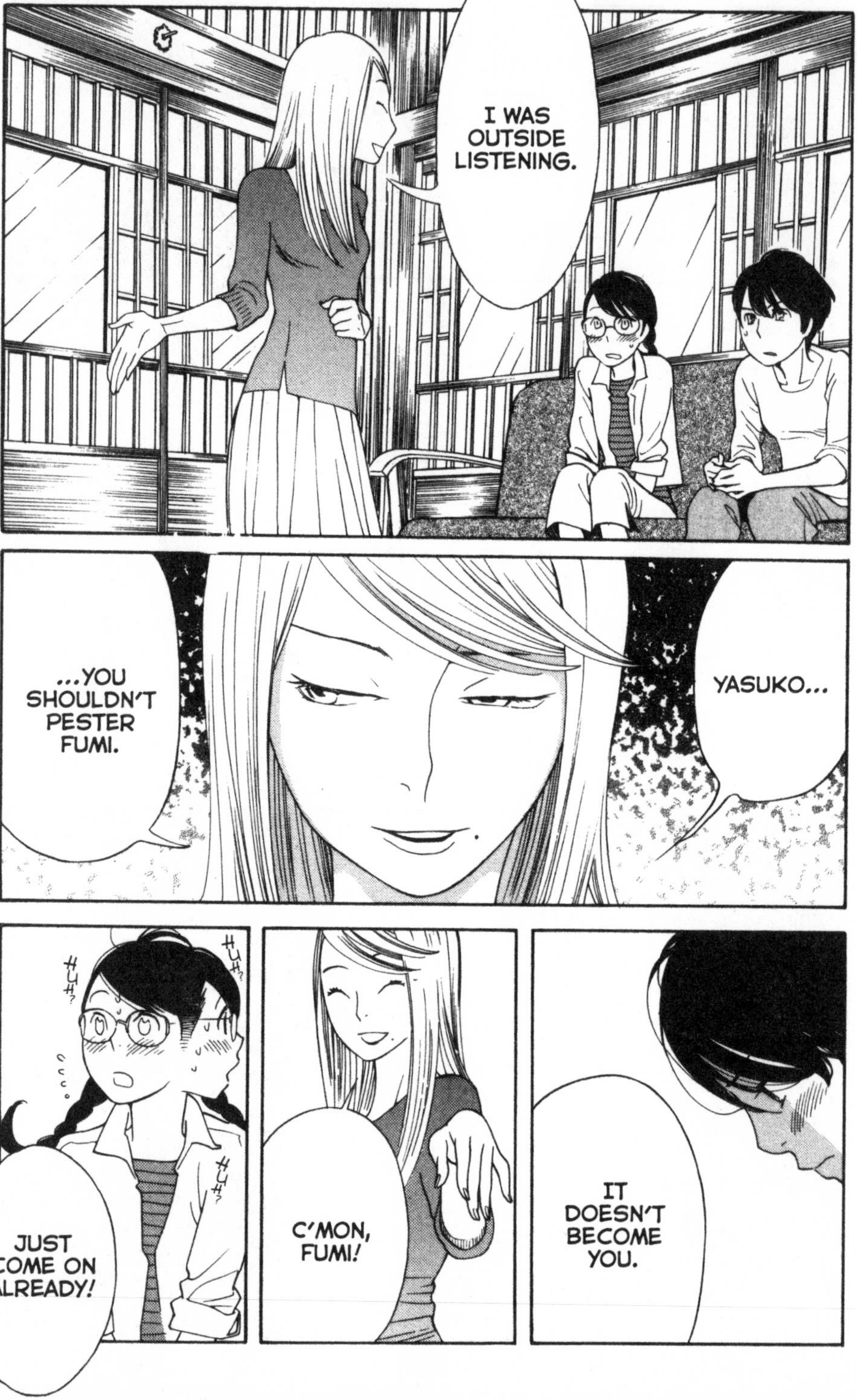
I WAS OUTSIDE LISTENING.
YASUKO...
...YOU SHOULDN'T PESTER FUMI.
IT DOESN'T BECOME YOU.
C'MON, FUMI!
JUST COME ON ALREADY!

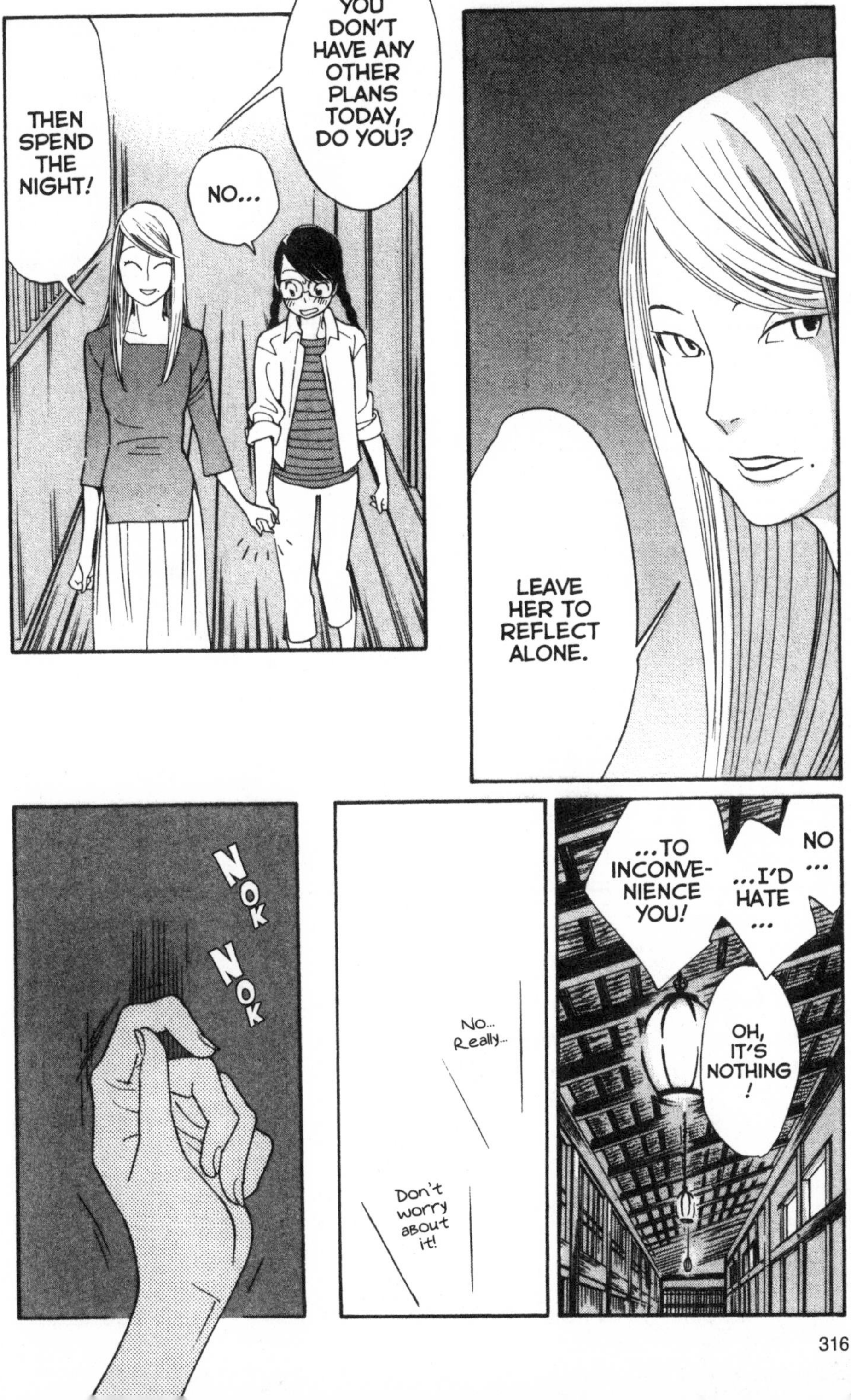
LEAVE HER TO REFLECT ALONE.
YOU DON'T HAVE ANY OTHER PLANS TODAY, DO YOU?
NO...
THEN SPEND THE NIGHT!
NO...
...I'D HATE...
...TO INCONVENIENCE YOU!
OH, IT'S NOTHING!
No... Really...
Don't worry about it!
NOK NOK

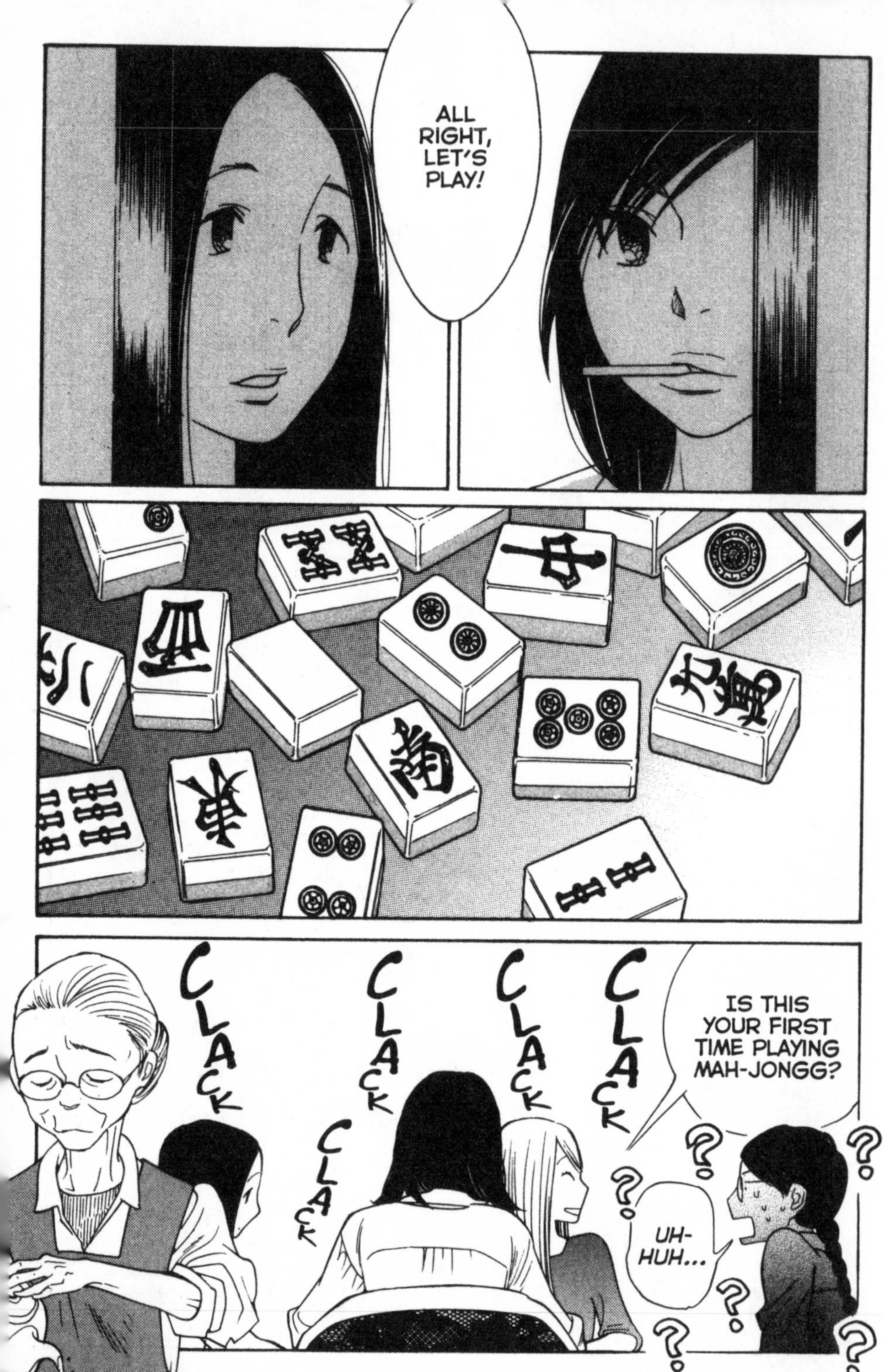
ALL RIGHT, LET'S PLAY!
IS THIS YOUR FIRST TIME PLAYING MAH-JONGG?
UH-HUH...
CLACK
CLACK
CLACK
CLACK
CLACK

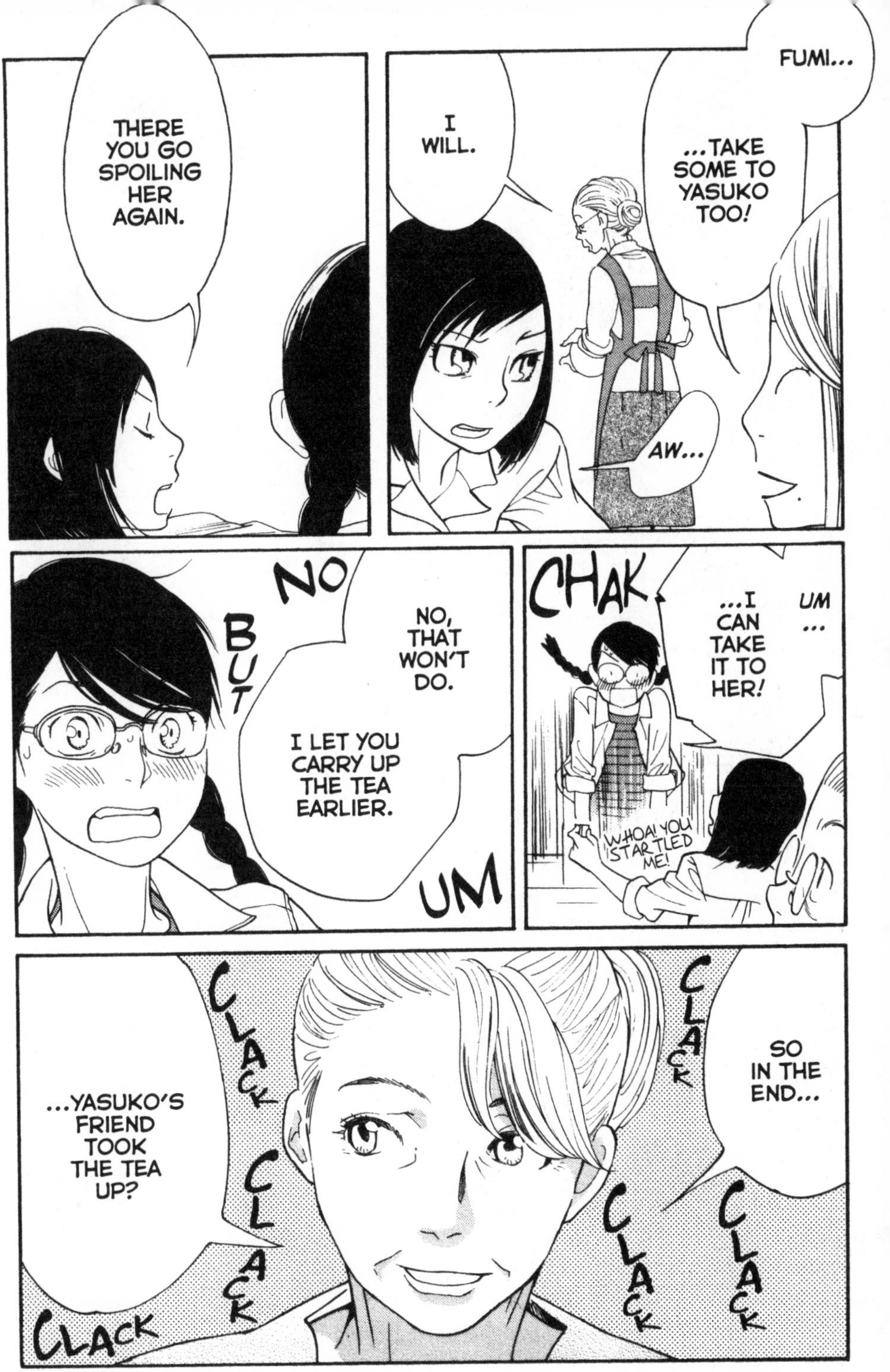
FUMI...
...TAKE SOME TO YASUKO TOO!
I WILL.
AW...
THERE YOU GO SPOILING HER AGAIN.
CHAK
...I CAN TAKE IT TO HER!
UM...
WHOA! YOU STARTLED ME!
NO
NO, THAT WON'T DO.
I LET YOU CARRY UP THE TEA EARLIER.
BUT
UM
SO IN THE END...
CLACK
CLACK
CLACK
...YASUKO'S FRIEND TOOK THE TEA UP?
CLACK
CLACK
CLACK

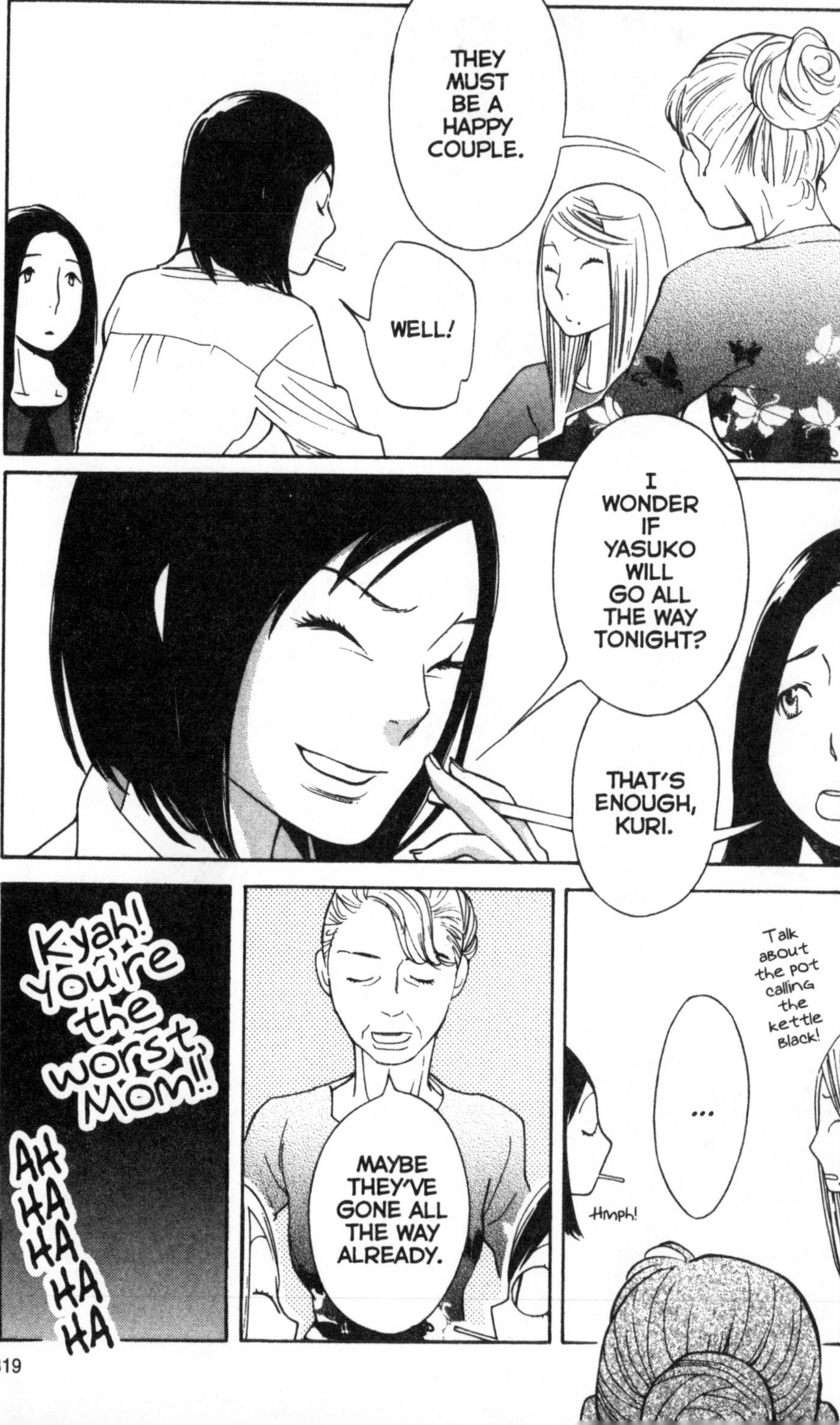
THEY MUST BE A HAPPY COUPLE.
WELL!
I WONDER IF YASUKO WILL GO ALL THE WAY TONIGHT?
THAT'S ENOUGH, KURI.
Talk about the pot calling the kettle Black!
...
Hmph!
MAYBE THEY'VE GONE ALL THE WAY ALREADY.
Kyah! You're the worst, Mom!!
AH HA HA HA HA HA

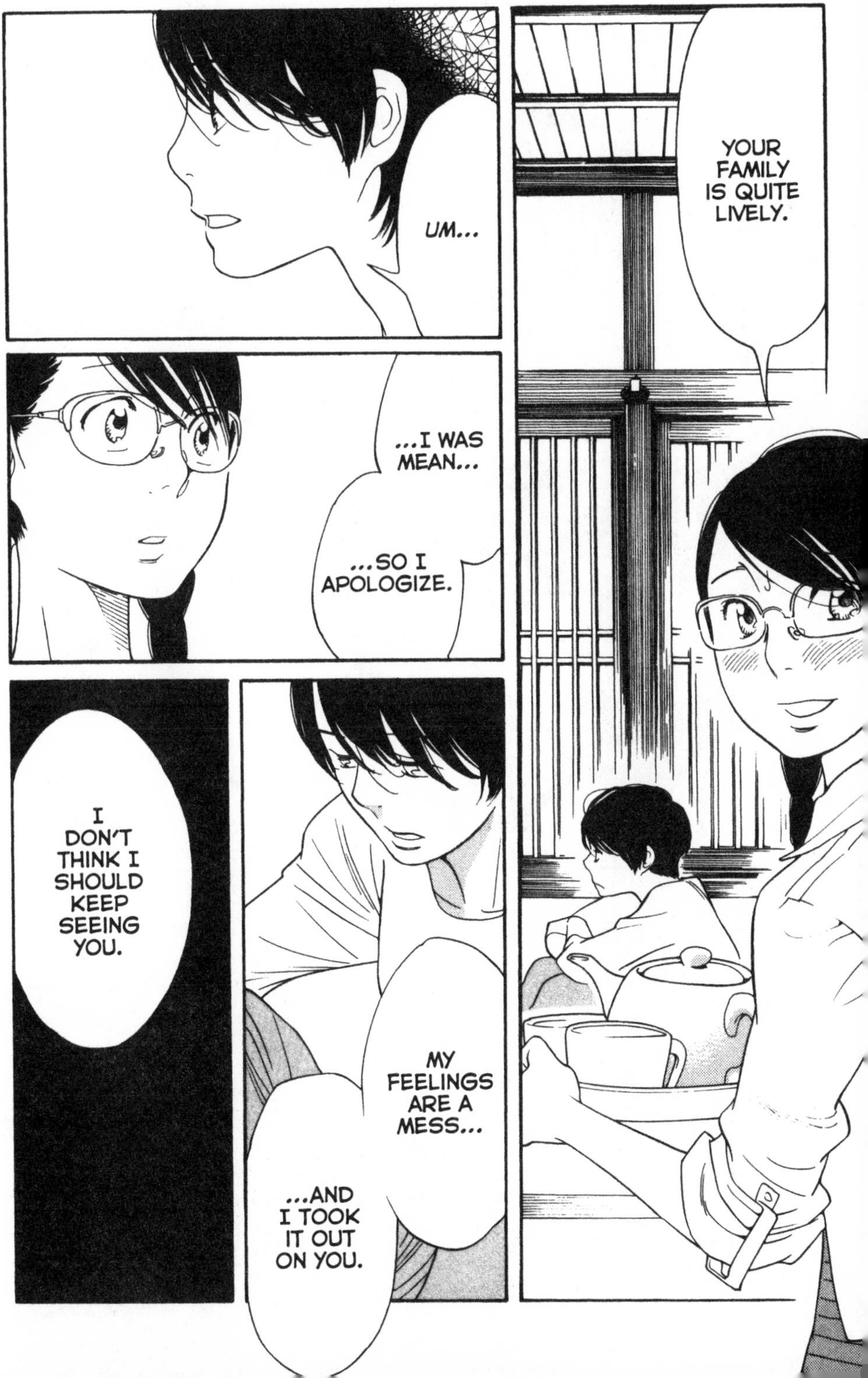
YOUR FAMILY IS QUITE LIVELY.
UM...
...I WAS MEAN...
...SO I APOLOGIZE.
MY FEELINGS ARE A MESS...
...AND I TOOK IT OUT ON YOU.
I DON'T THINK I SHOULD KEEP SEEING YOU.

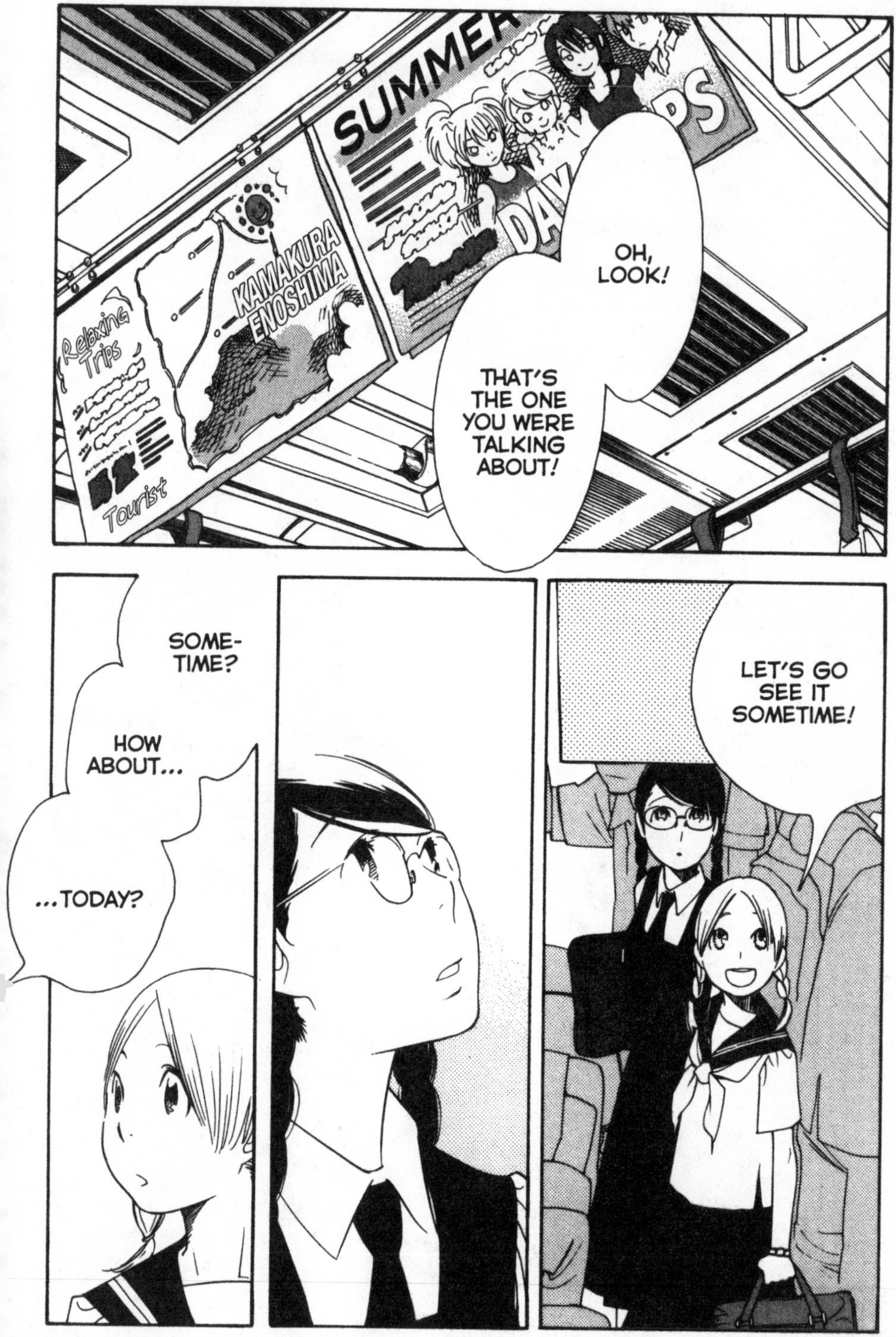
SUMMER
KAMAKURA ENOSHIMA
Relaxing Trips
Tourist
OH, LOOK!
THAT'S THE ONE YOU WERE TALKING ABOUT!
LET'S GO SEE IT SOMETIME!
SOME-TIME?
HOW ABOUT...
...TODAY?

# Sweet Blue Flowers

## #12 Don't Say Goodbye

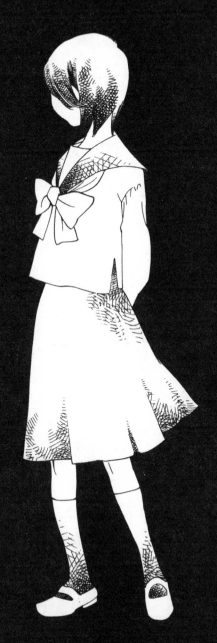

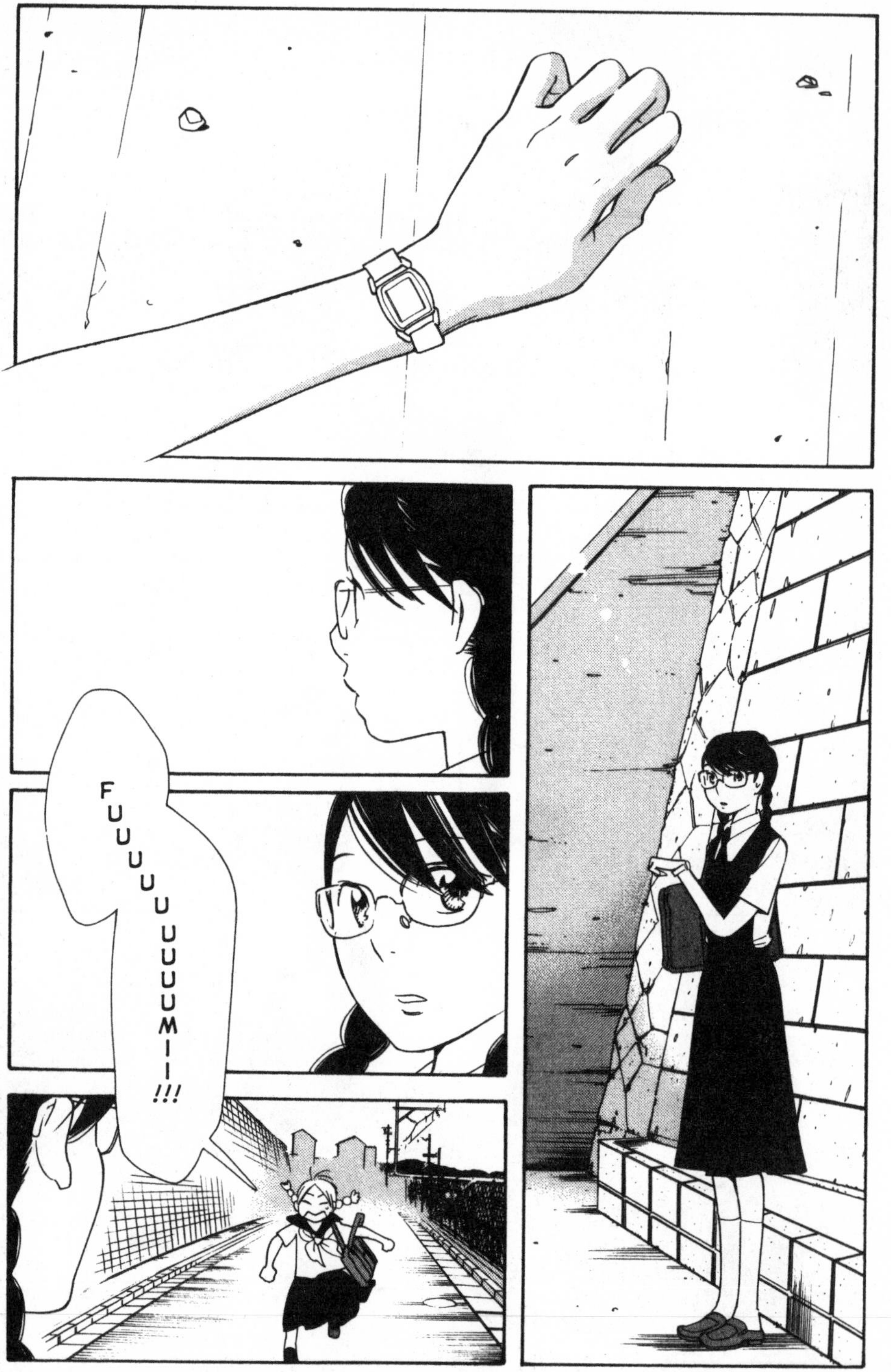
FUUUUUUUUUUMII!!!

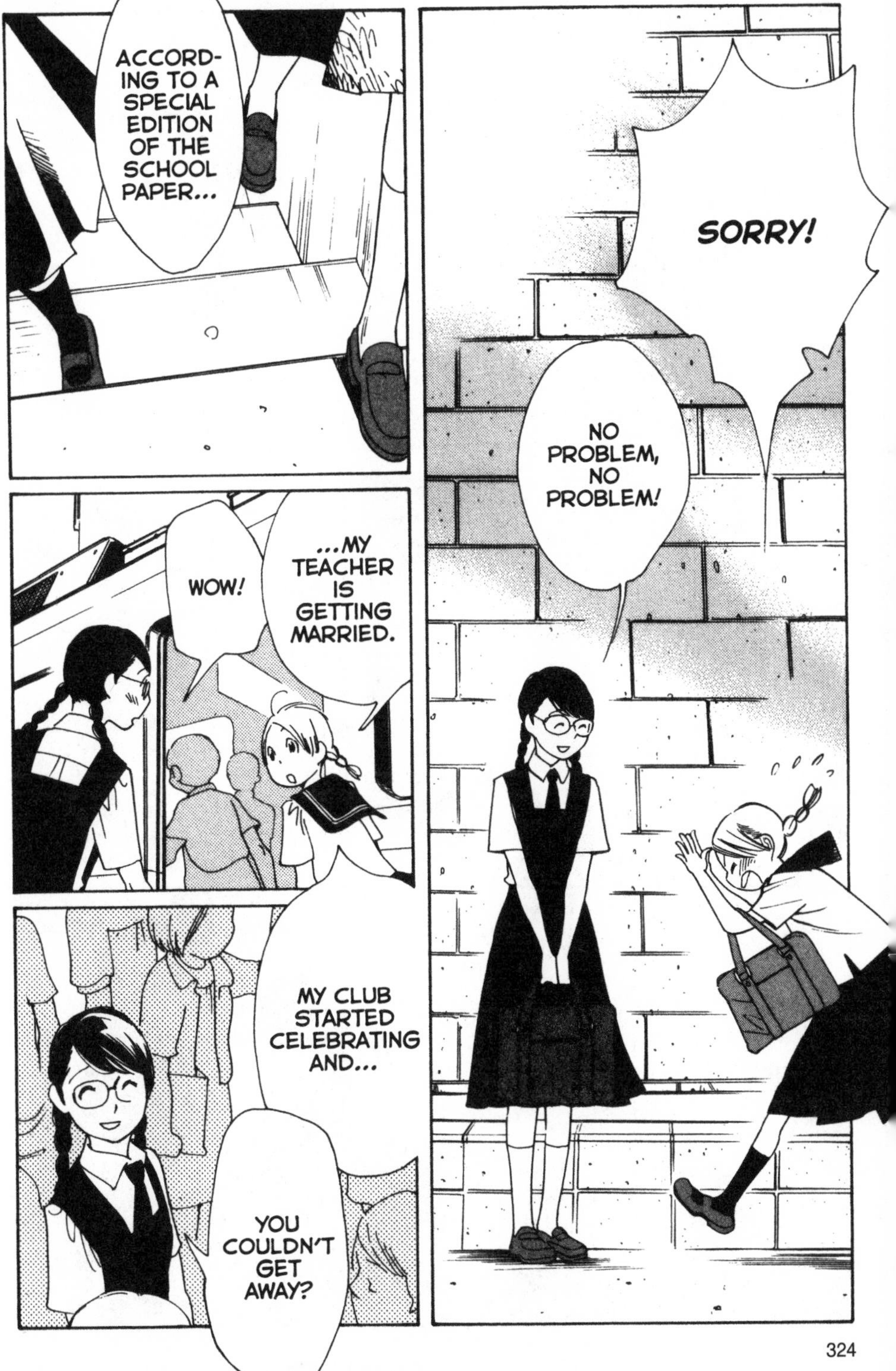
SORRY!
NO PROBLEM, NO PROBLEM!
ACCORDING TO A SPECIAL EDITION OF THE SCHOOL PAPER...
...MY TEACHER IS GETTING MARRIED.
WOW!
MY CLUB STARTED CELEBRATING AND...
YOU COULDN'T GET AWAY?

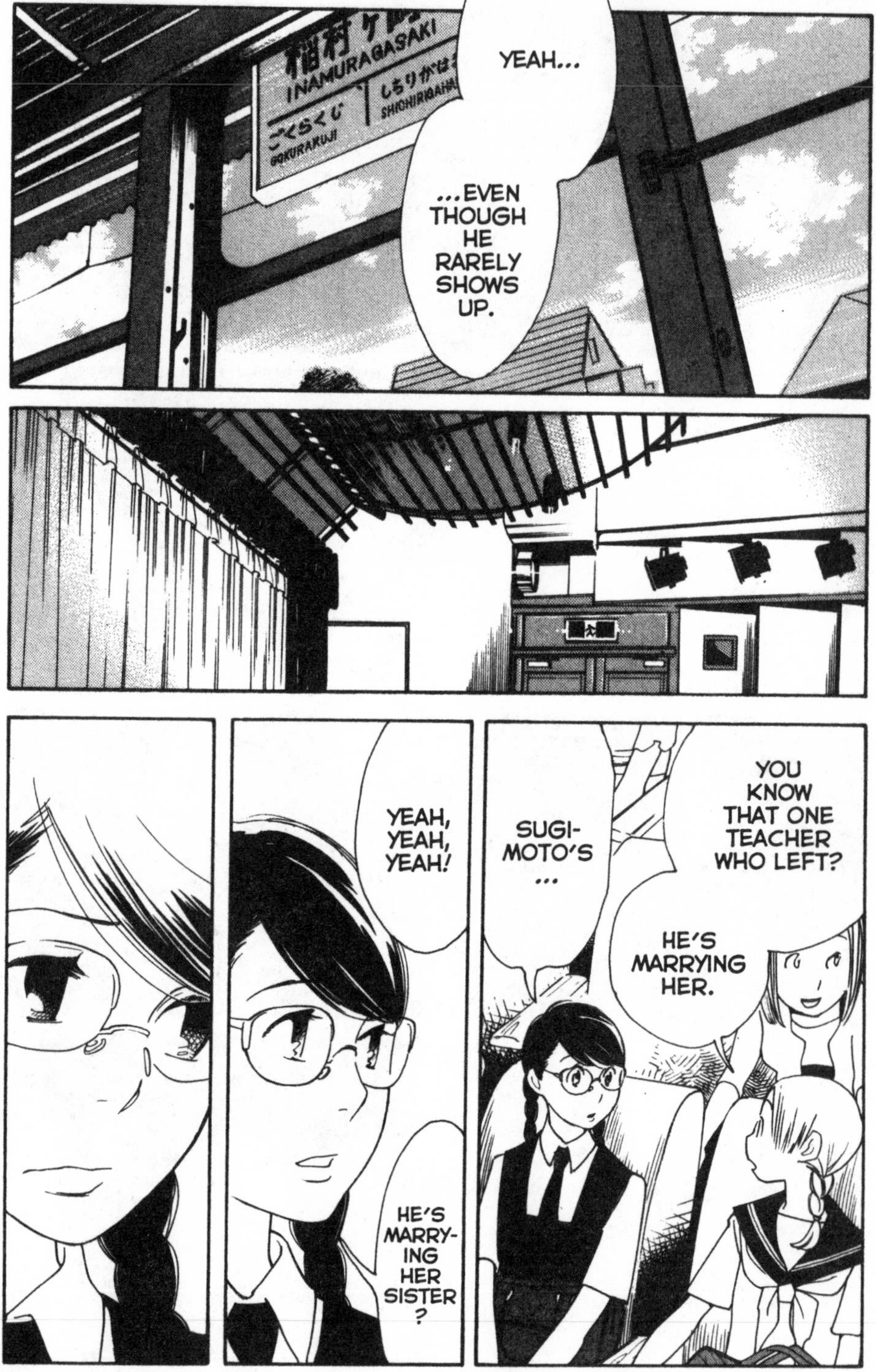

稲村ケ
INAMURAGASAKI
ごくらくじ
GOKURAKUJI
YEAH...
...EVEN THOUGH HE RARELY SHOWS UP.
YOU KNOW THAT ONE TEACHER WHO LEFT?
HE'S MARRYING HER.
SUGI-MOTO'S ...
YEAH, YEAH, YEAH!
HE'S MARRY-ING HER SISTER?

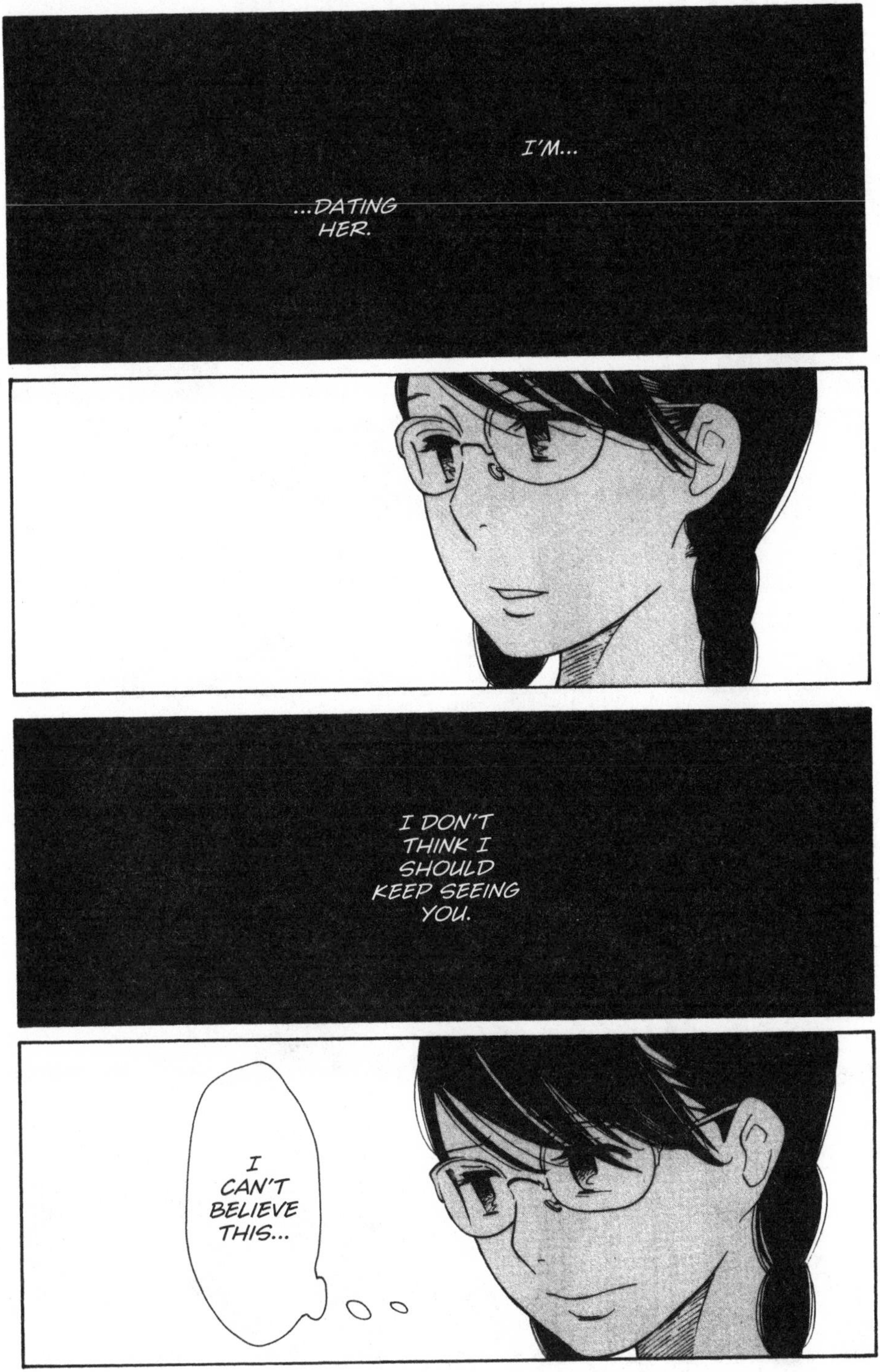
I'M...
...DATING HER.
I DON'T THINK I SHOULD KEEP SEEING YOU.
I CAN'T BELIEVE THIS...

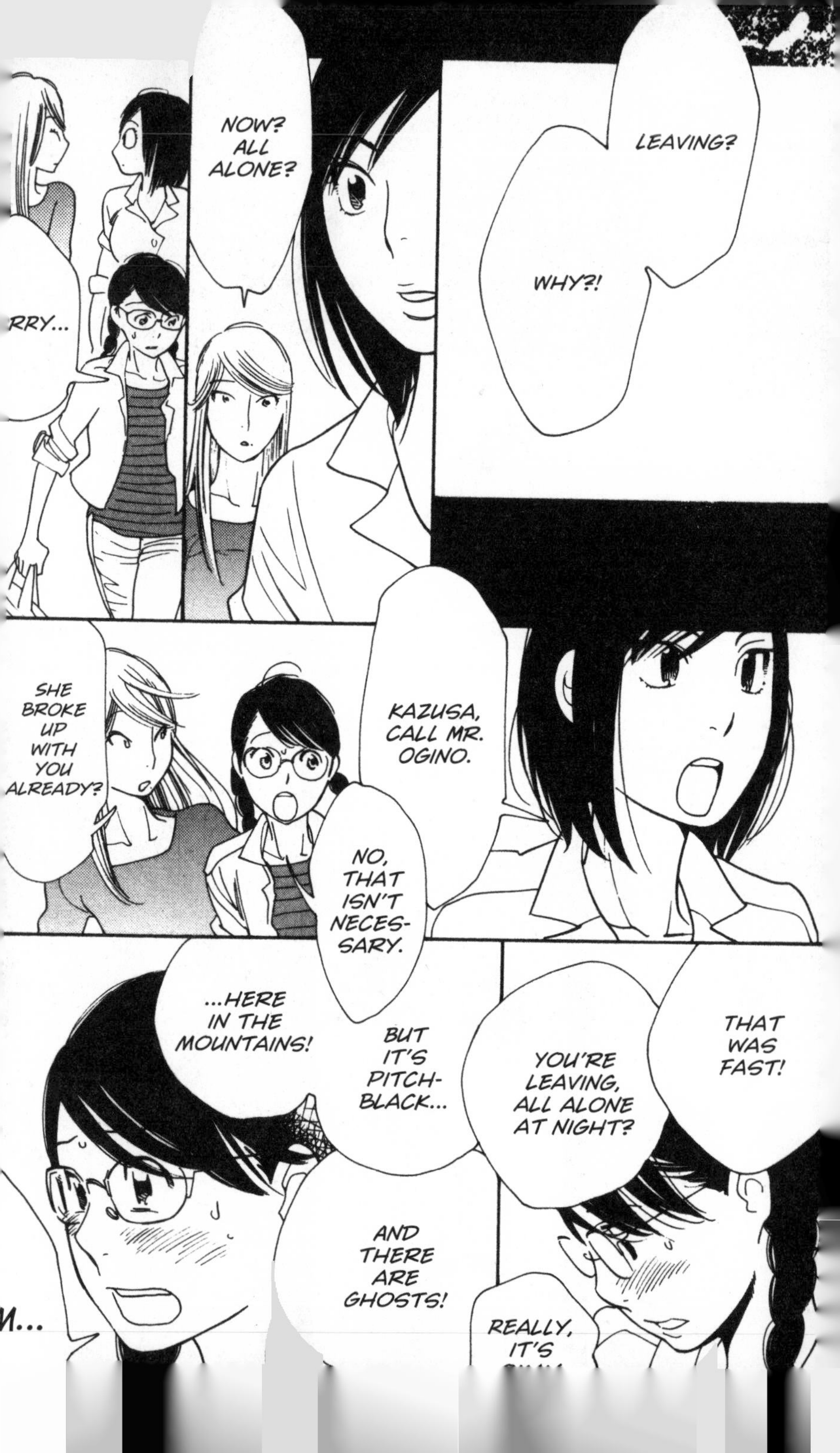
LEAVING?
WHY?!
NOW? ALL ALONE?
RRY...
KAZUSA, CALL MR. OGINO.
SHE BROKE UP WITH YOU ALREADY?
NO, THAT ISN'T NECES-SARY.
THAT WAS FAST!
YOU'RE LEAVING, ALL ALONE AT NIGHT?
REALLY, IT'S
BUT IT'S PITCH-BLACK...
...HERE IN THE MOUNTAINS!
AND THERE ARE GHOSTS!

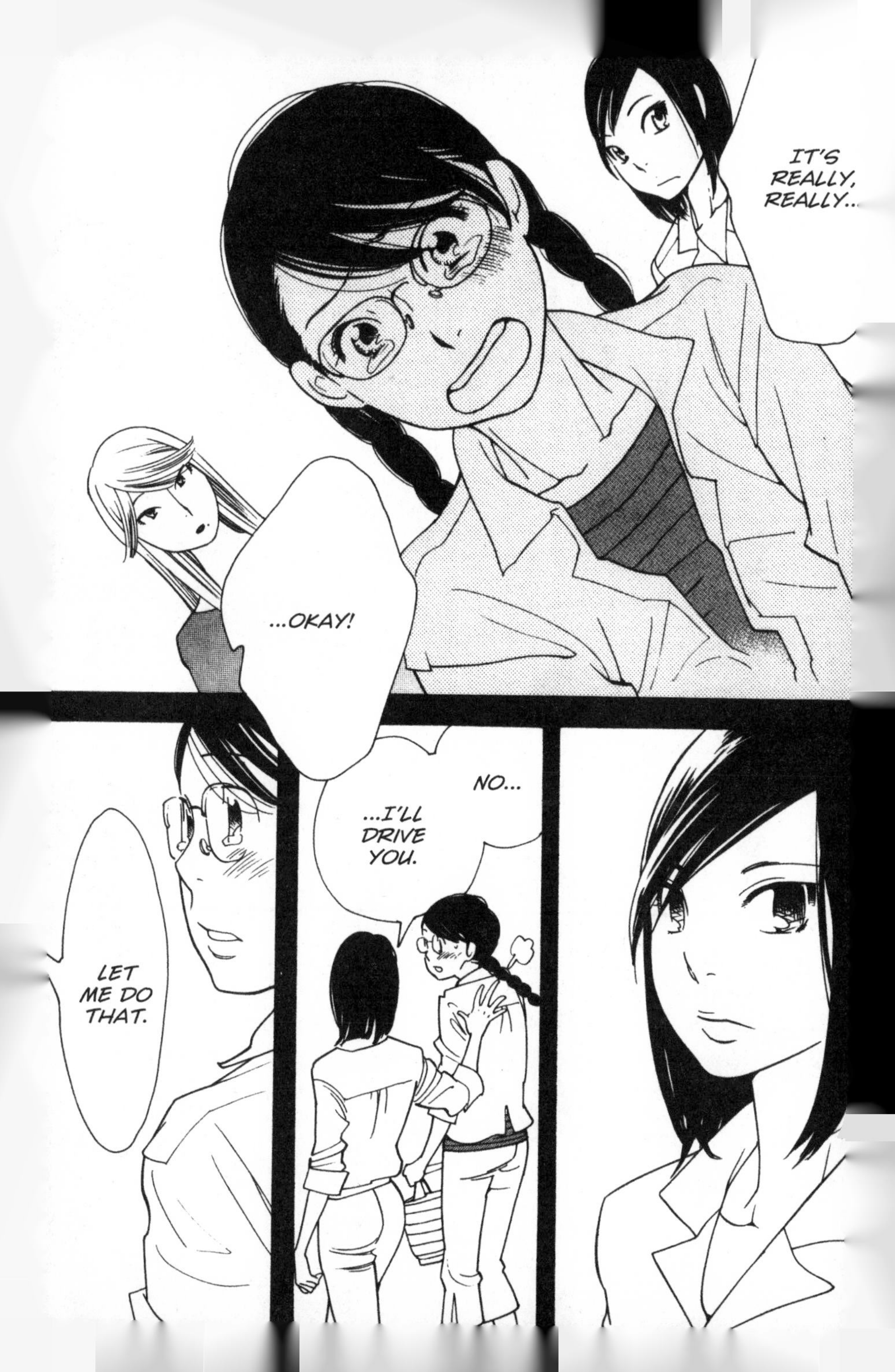
IT'S REALLY, REALLY...
...OKAY!
NO...
...I'LL DRIVE YOU.
LET ME DO THAT.

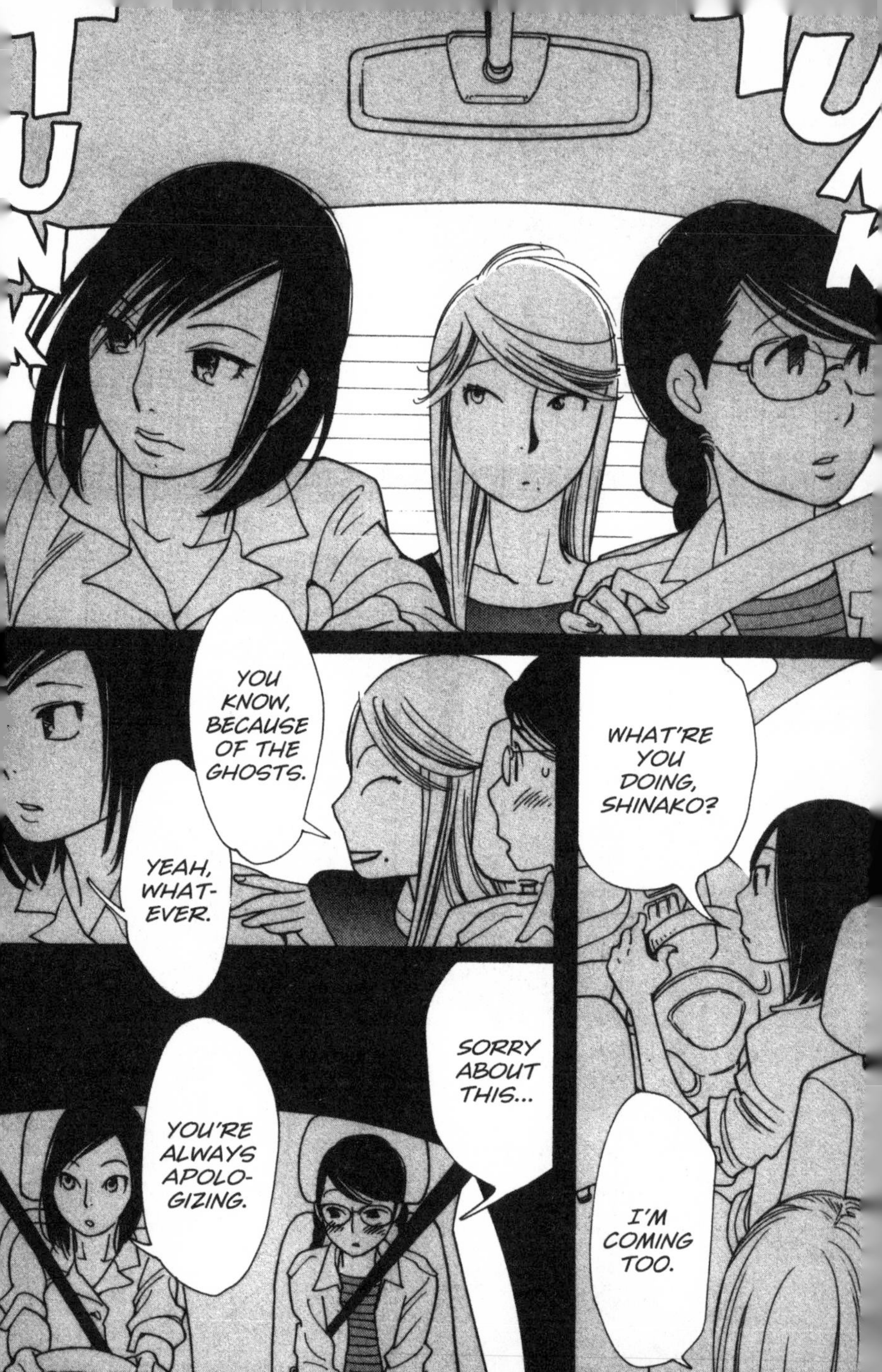
TUNK
TUNK
WHAT'RE YOU DOING, SHINAKO?
I'M COMING TOO.
YOU KNOW, BECAUSE OF THE GHOSTS.
YEAH, WHAT-EVER.
SORRY ABOUT THIS...
YOU'RE ALWAYS APOLO-GIZING.

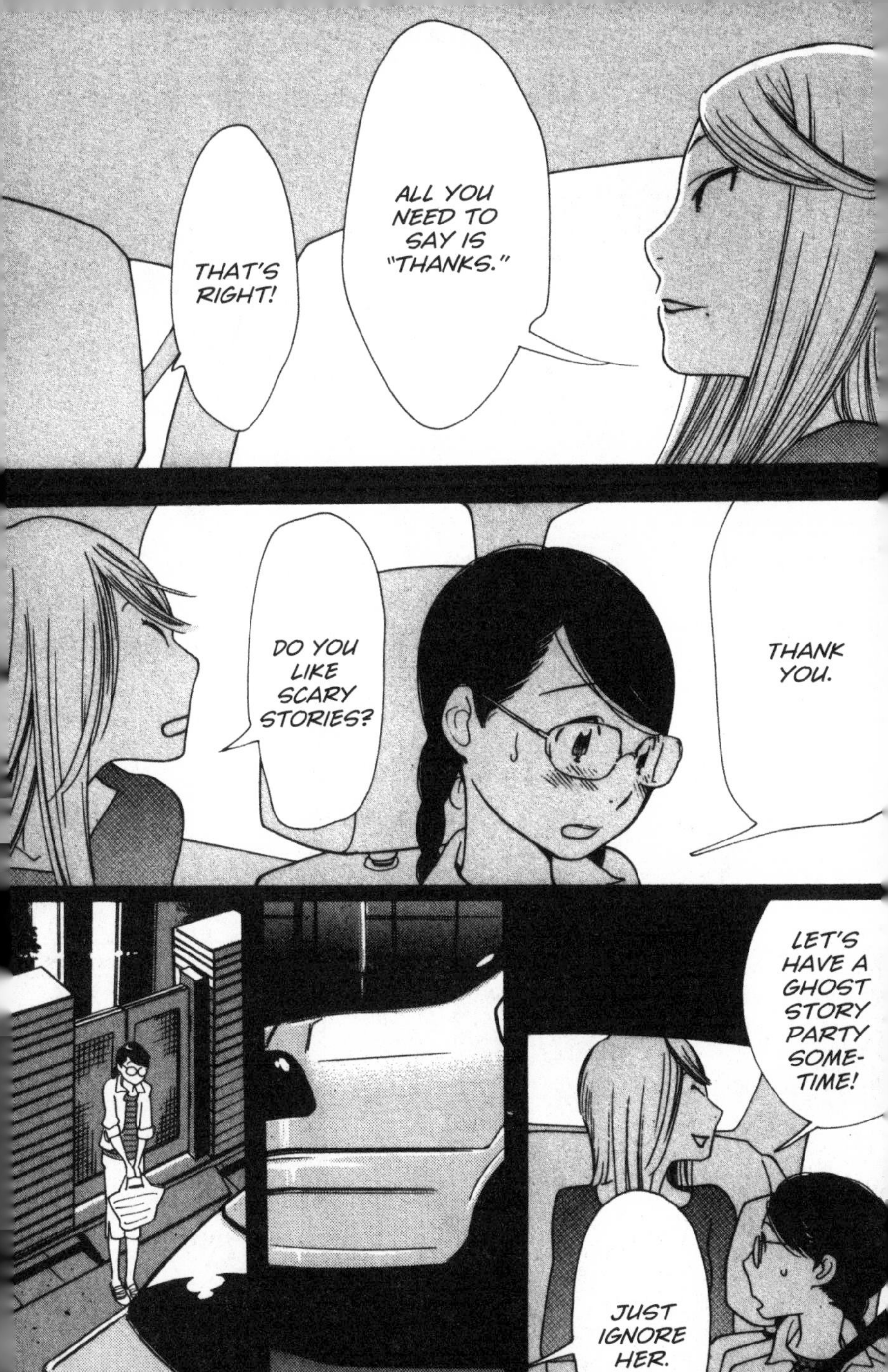
ALL YOU NEED TO SAY IS "THANKS."
THAT'S RIGHT!
THANK YOU.
DO YOU LIKE SCARY STORIES?
LET'S HAVE A GHOST STORY PARTY SOME-TIME!
JUST IGNORE HER.

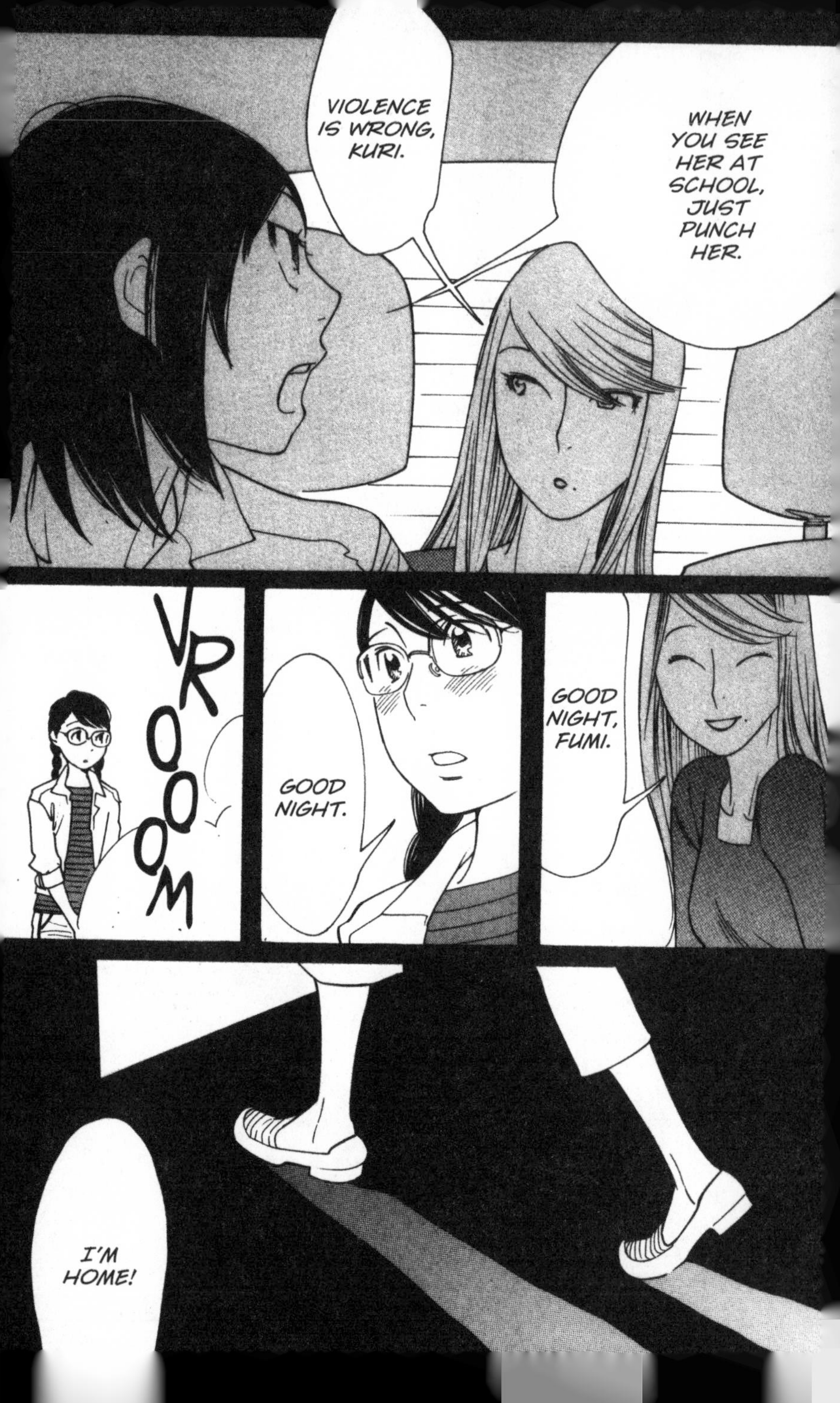
WHEN YOU SEE HER AT SCHOOL, JUST PUNCH HER.
VIOLENCE IS WRONG, KURI.
GOOD NIGHT, FUMI.
GOOD NIGHT.
VROOOM
I'M HOME!

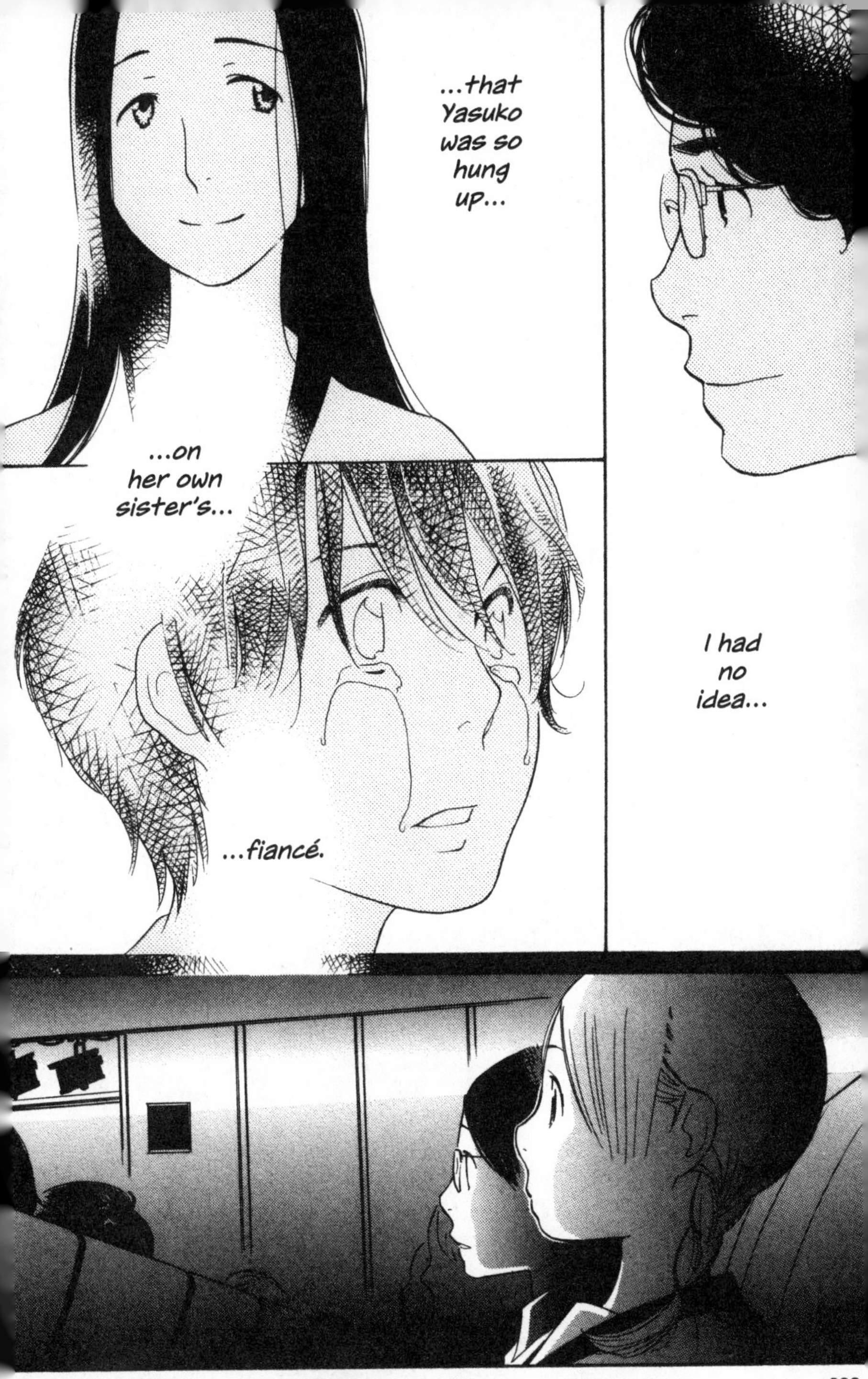
I had no idea...
...that Yasuko was so hung up...
...on her own sister's...
...fiancé.

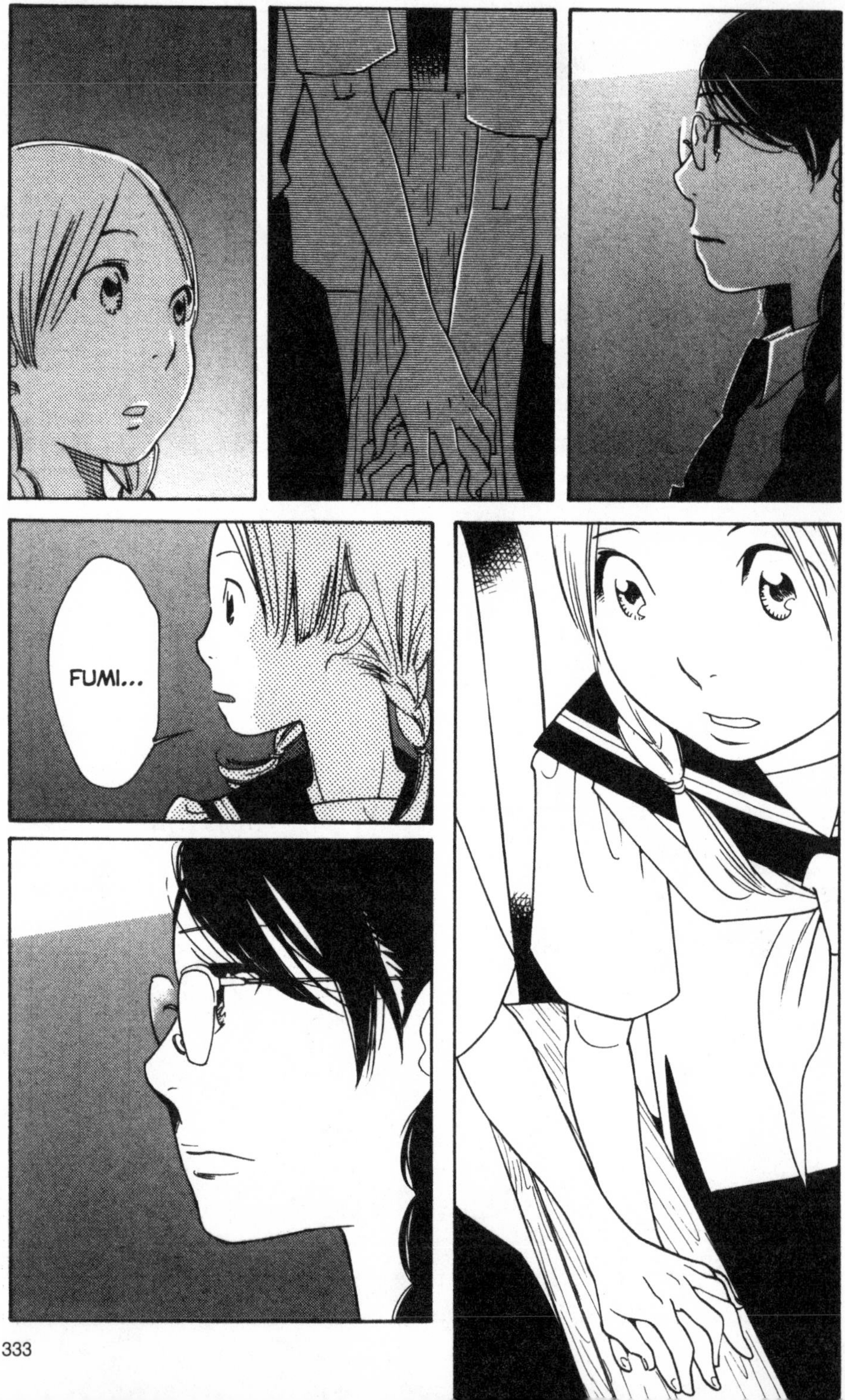
FUMI...

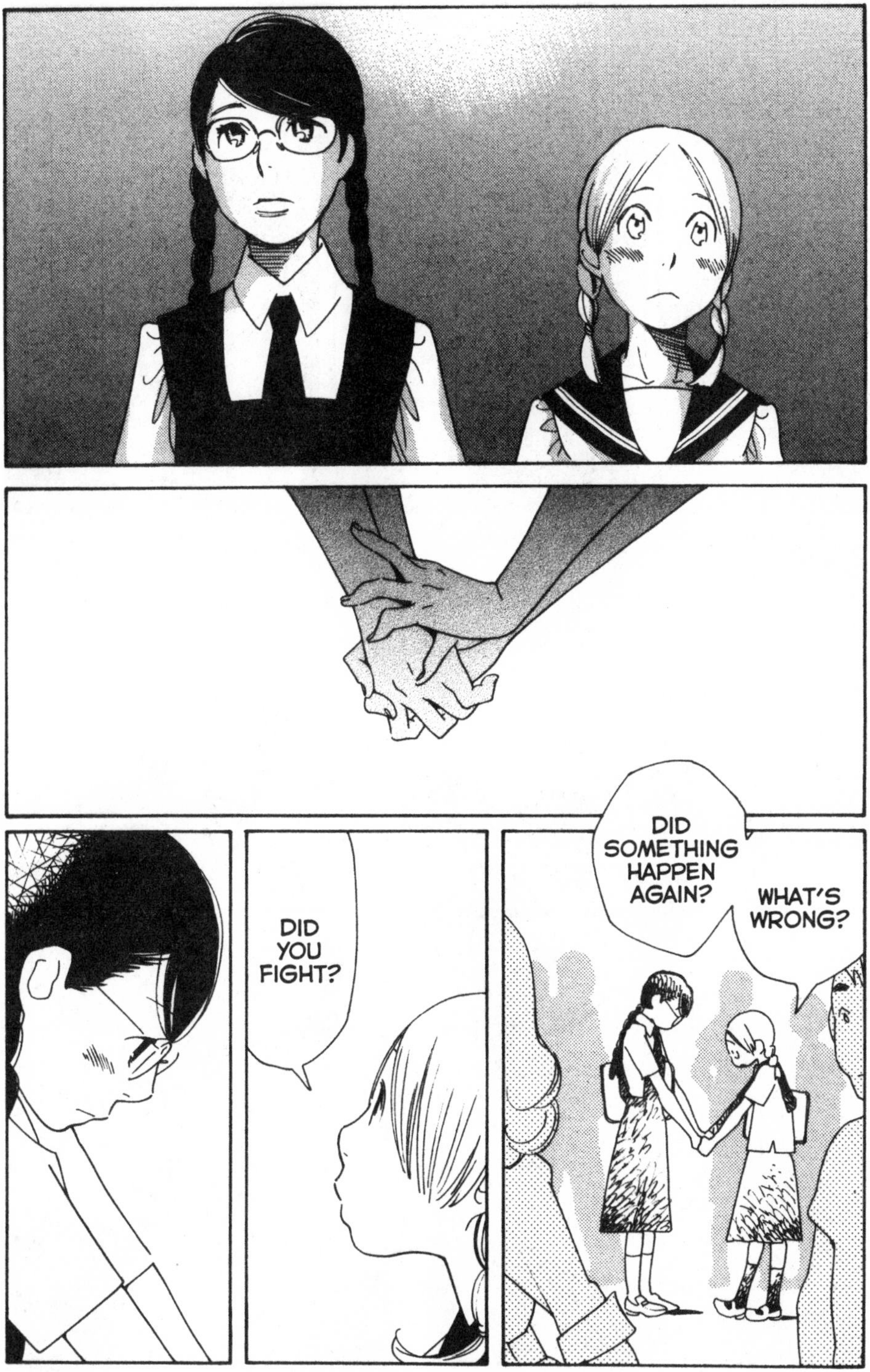
WHAT'S WRONG?
DID SOMETHING HAPPEN AGAIN?
DID YOU FIGHT?

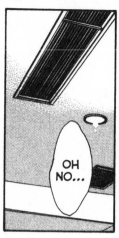

OH NO...

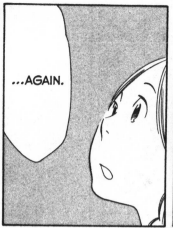

...AGAIN.

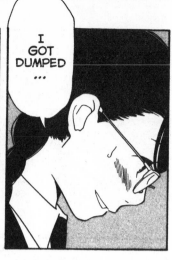

I GOT DUMPED...

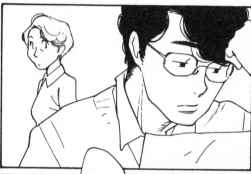

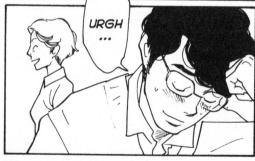

URGH...

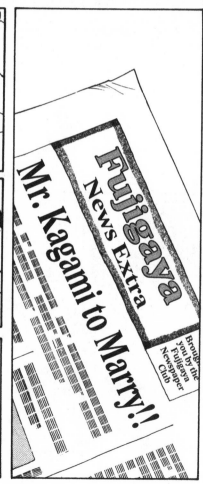

Fujigaya News Extra

Mr. Kagami to Marry!!

Brought to you by the Fujigaya Newspaper Club

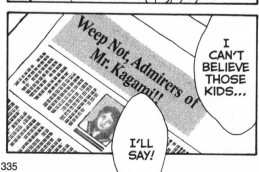

Weep Not, Admirers of Mr. Kagami!!

I CAN'T BELIEVE THOSE KIDS...

I'LL SAY!

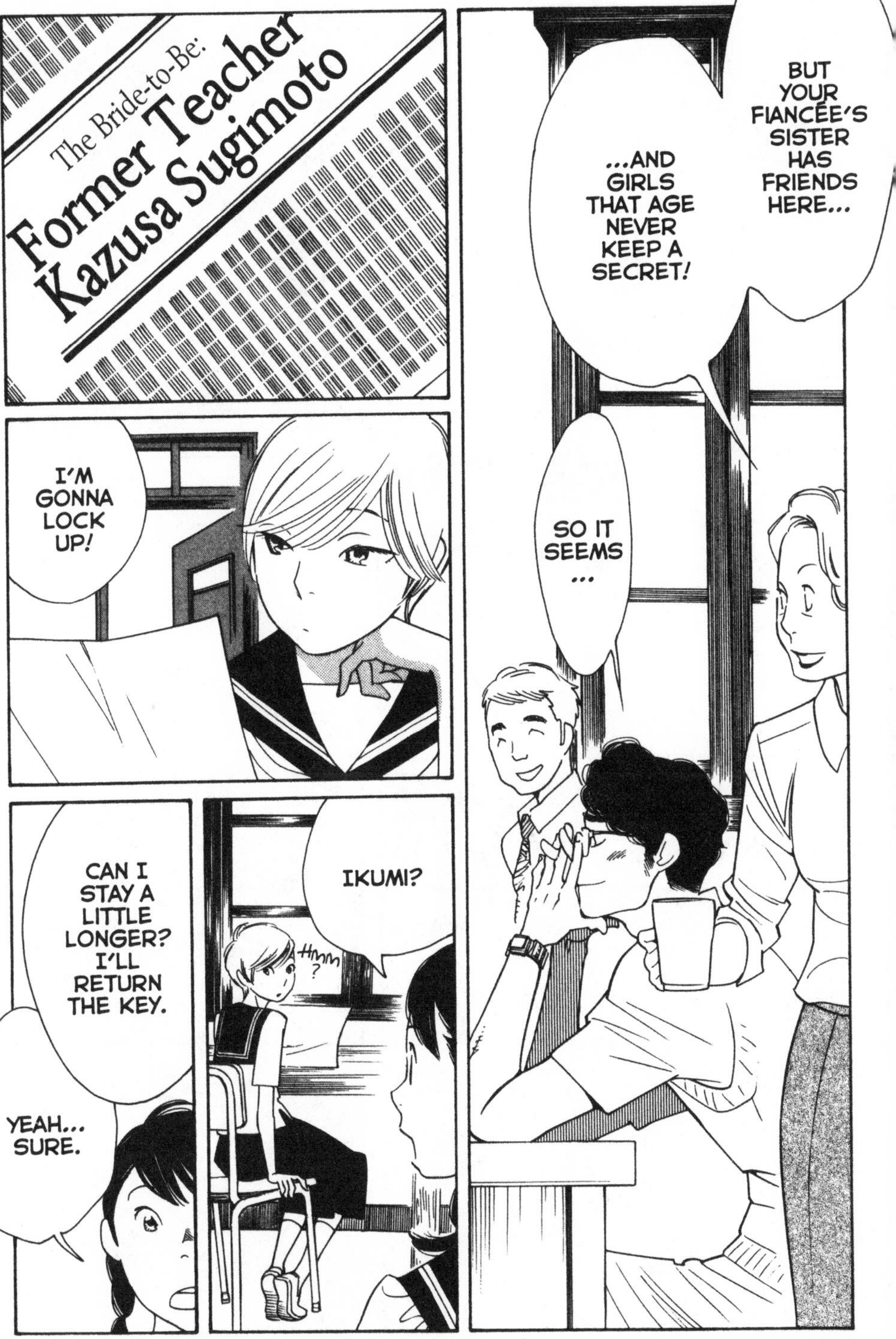
BUT YOUR FIANCÉE'S SISTER HAS FRIENDS HERE...
...AND GIRLS THAT AGE NEVER KEEP A SECRET!
SO IT SEEMS...
The Bride-to-Be: Former Teacher Kazusa Sugimoto
I'M GONNA LOCK UP!
IKUMI?
Hmm?
CAN I STAY A LITTLE LONGER? I'LL RETURN THE KEY.
YEAH... SURE.

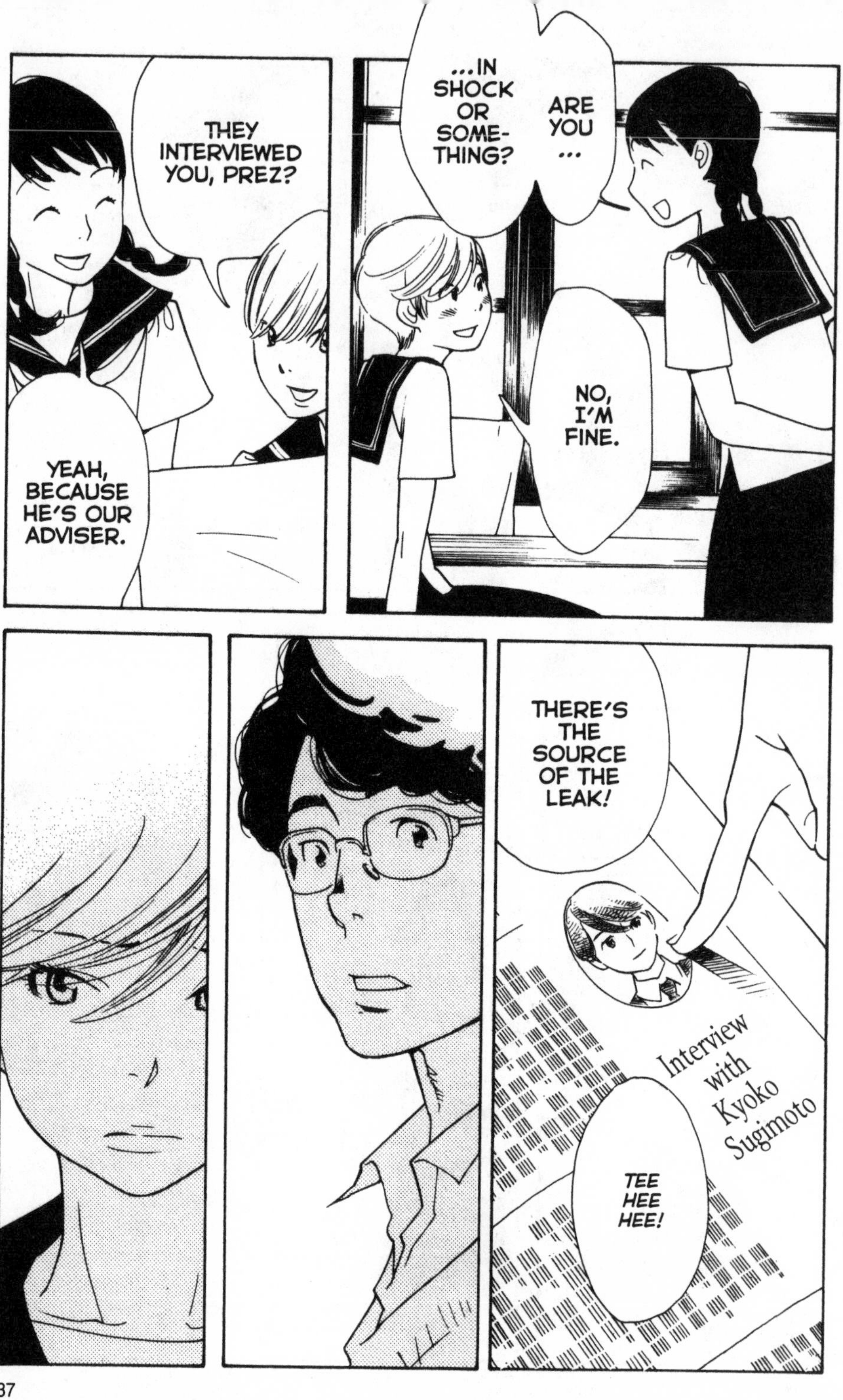
ARE YOU ...
...IN SHOCK OR SOME-THING?
NO, I'M FINE.
THEY INTERVIEWED YOU, PREZ?
YEAH, BECAUSE HE'S OUR ADVISER.
THERE'S THE SOURCE OF THE LEAK!
Interview with Kyoko Sugimoto
TEE HEE HEE!

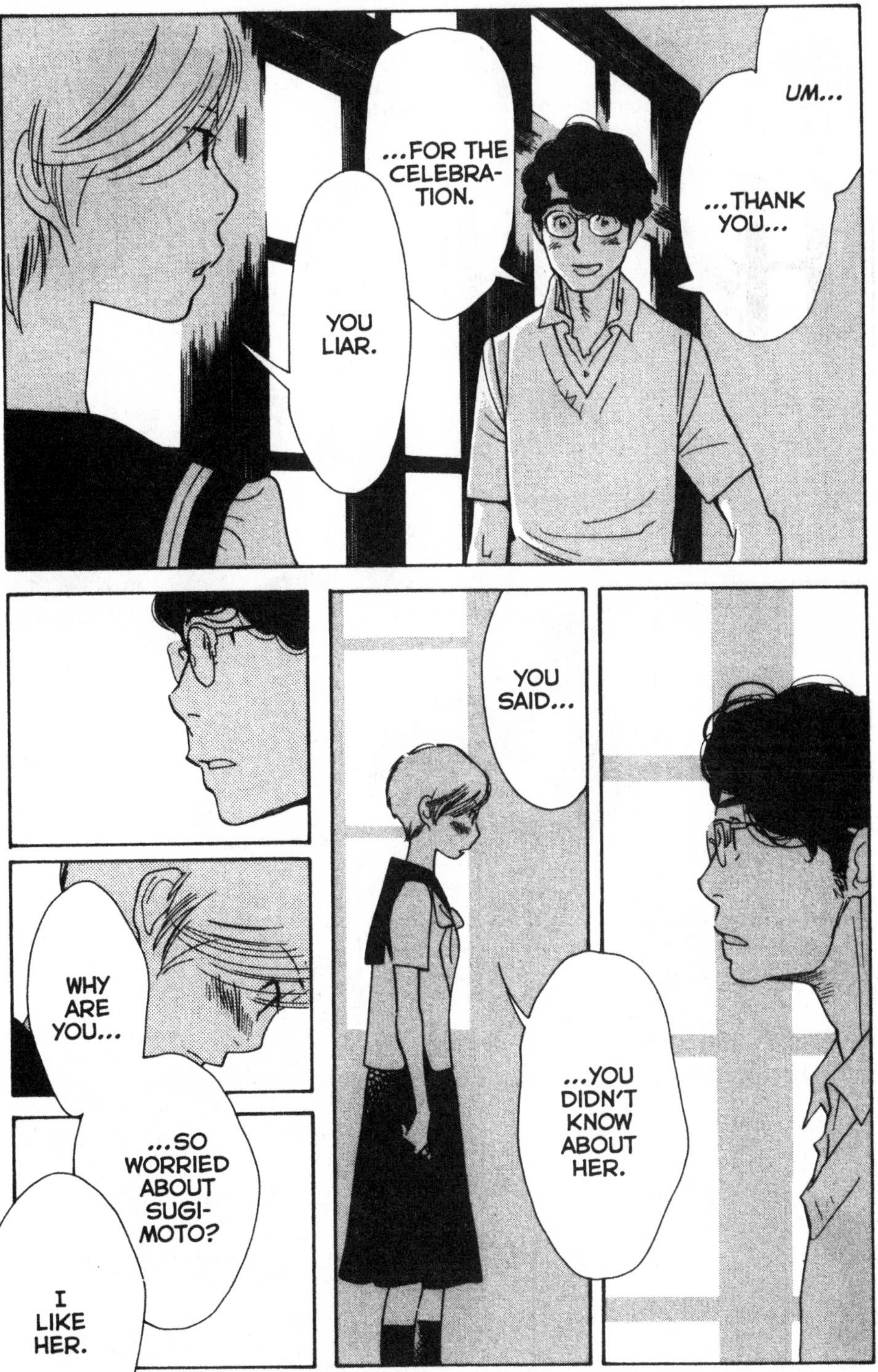
UM... ...THANK YOU...
...FOR THE CELEBRA-TION.
YOU LIAR.
YOU SAID...
...YOU DIDN'T KNOW ABOUT HER.
WHY ARE YOU...
...SO WORRIED ABOUT SUGI-MOTO?
I LIKE HER.

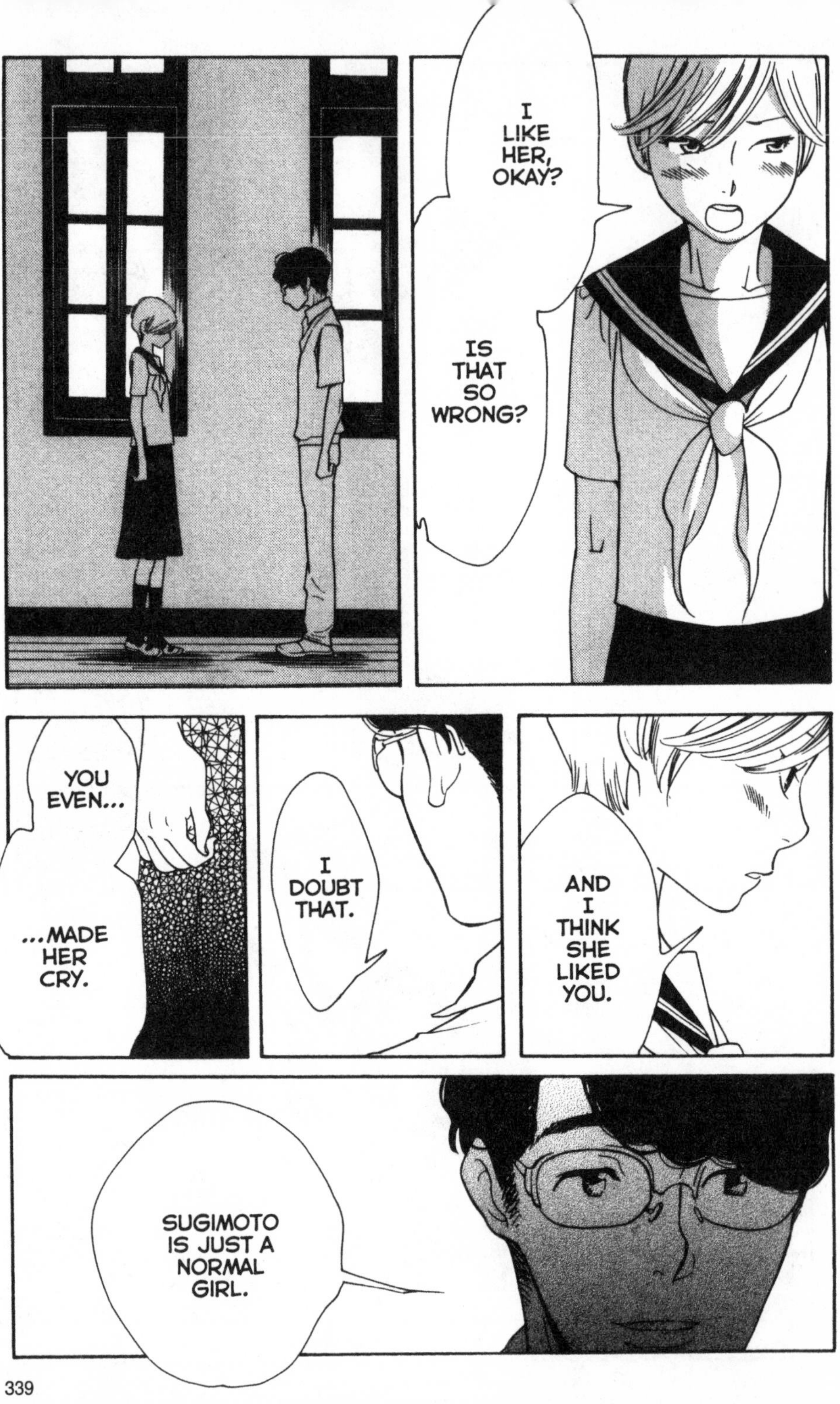
I LIKE HER, OKAY?
IS THAT SO WRONG?
AND I THINK SHE LIKED YOU.
I DOUBT THAT.
YOU EVEN...
...MADE HER CRY.
SUGIMOTO IS JUST A NORMAL GIRL.

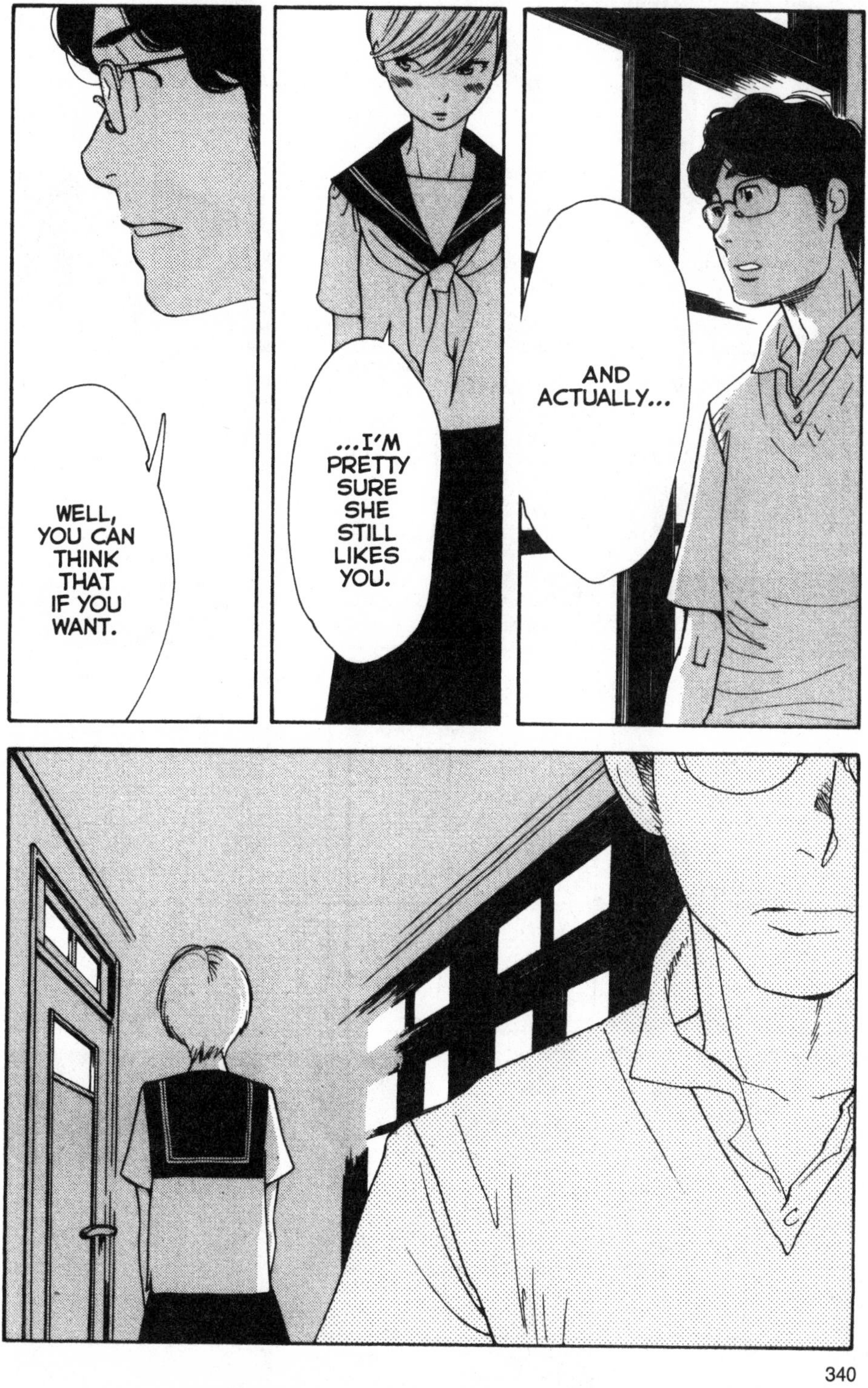
AND ACTUALLY...
...I'M PRETTY SURE SHE STILL LIKES YOU.
WELL, YOU CAN THINK THAT IF YOU WANT.

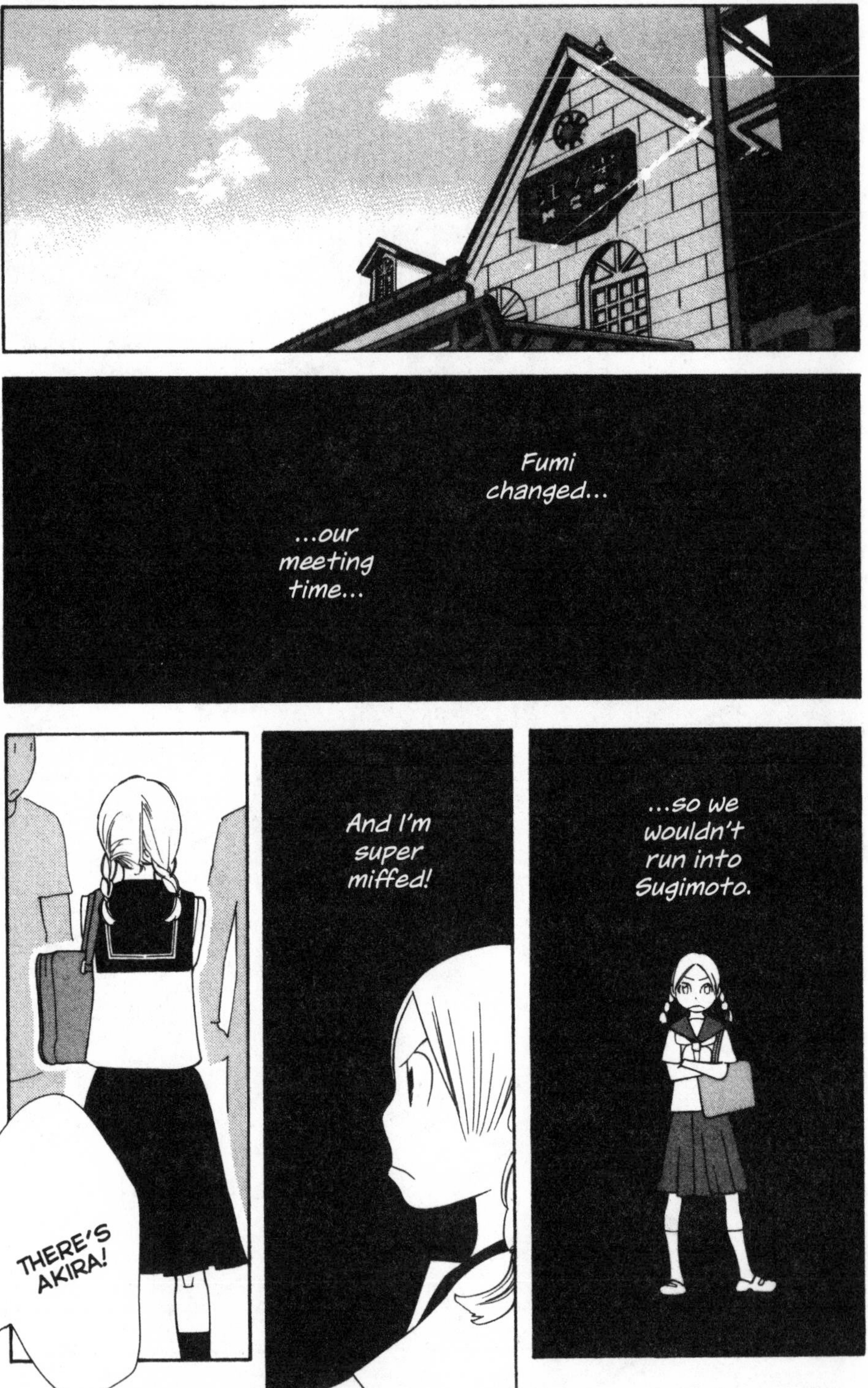
Fumi changed...
...our meeting time...
...so we wouldn't run into Sugimoto.
And I'm super miffed!
THERE'S AKIRA!

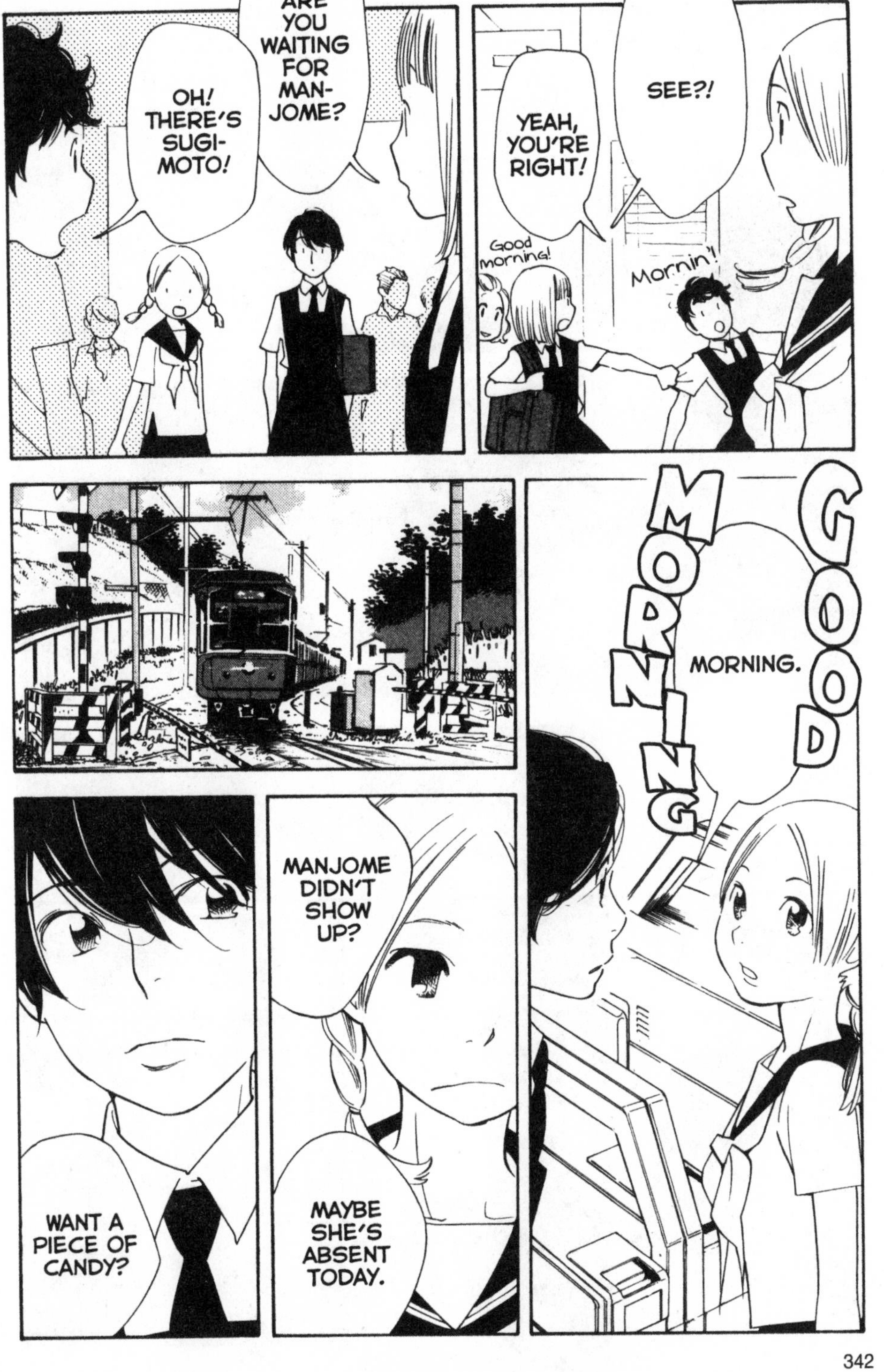
SEE?!
YEAH, YOU'RE RIGHT!
Mornin'!
Good morning!
ARE YOU WAITING FOR MAN-JOME?
OH! THERE'S SUGI-MOTO!
GOOD MORNING
MORNING.
MANJOME DIDN'T SHOW UP?
MAYBE SHE'S ABSENT TODAY.
WANT A PIECE OF CANDY?

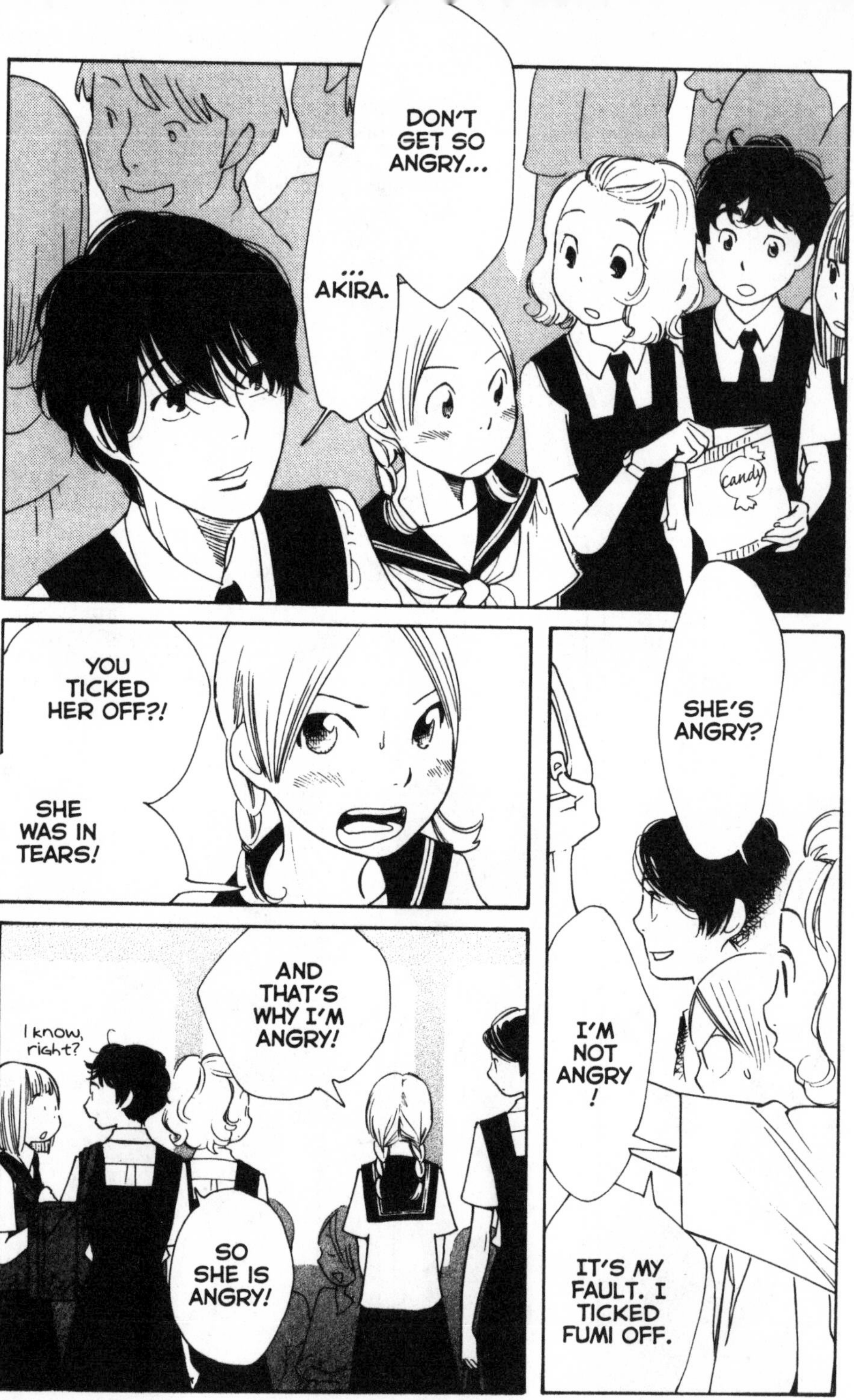
DON'T GET SO ANGRY...
... AKIRA.
SHE'S ANGRY?
I'M NOT ANGRY!
IT'S MY FAULT. I TICKED FUMI OFF.
YOU TICKED HER OFF?!
SHE WAS IN TEARS!
AND THAT'S WHY I'M ANGRY!
I know, right?
SO SHE IS ANGRY!

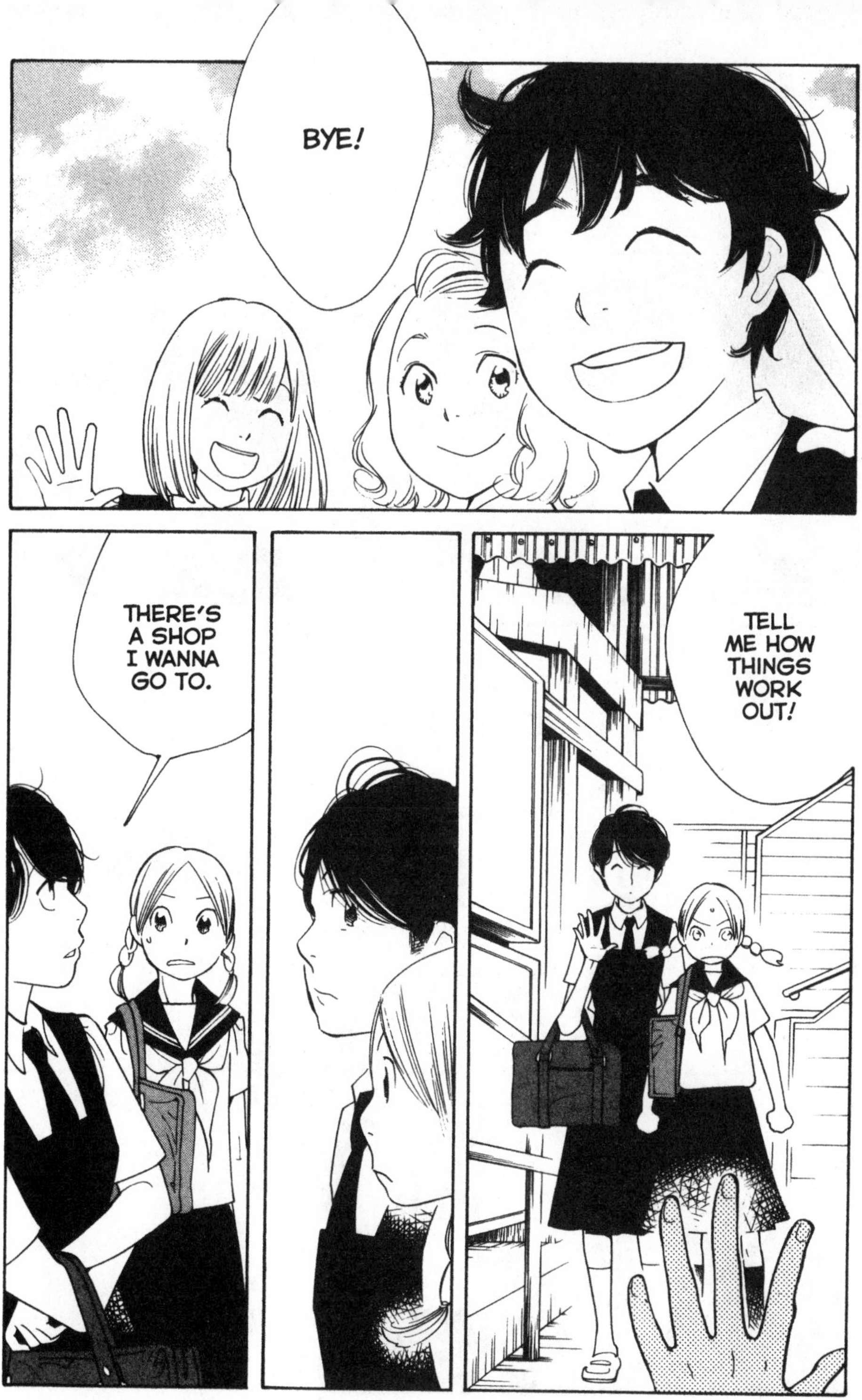
BYE!
TELL ME HOW THINGS WORK OUT!
THERE'S A SHOP I WANNA GO TO.

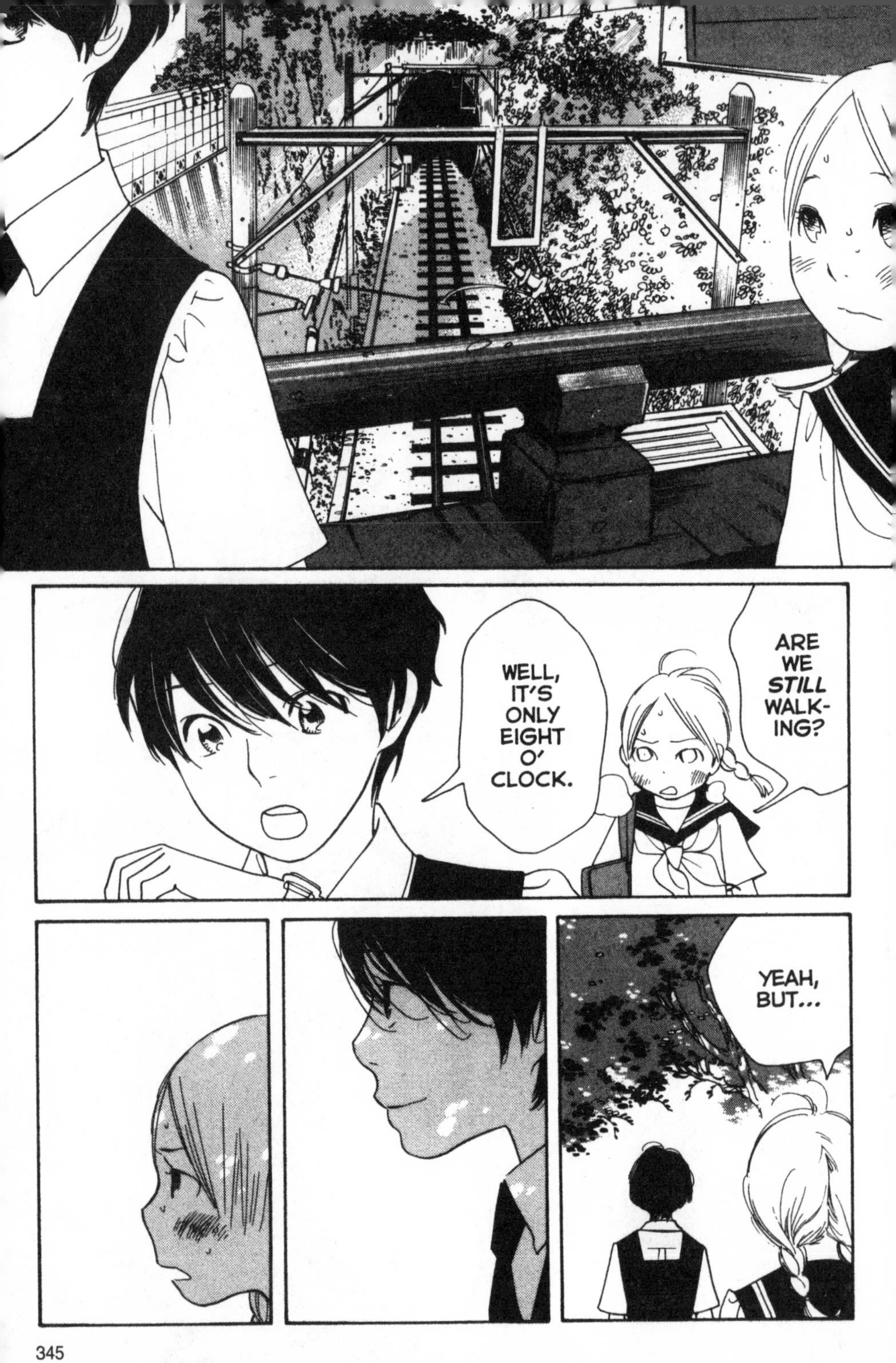
ARE WE *STILL* WALKING?
WELL, IT'S ONLY EIGHT O' CLOCK.
YEAH, BUT...

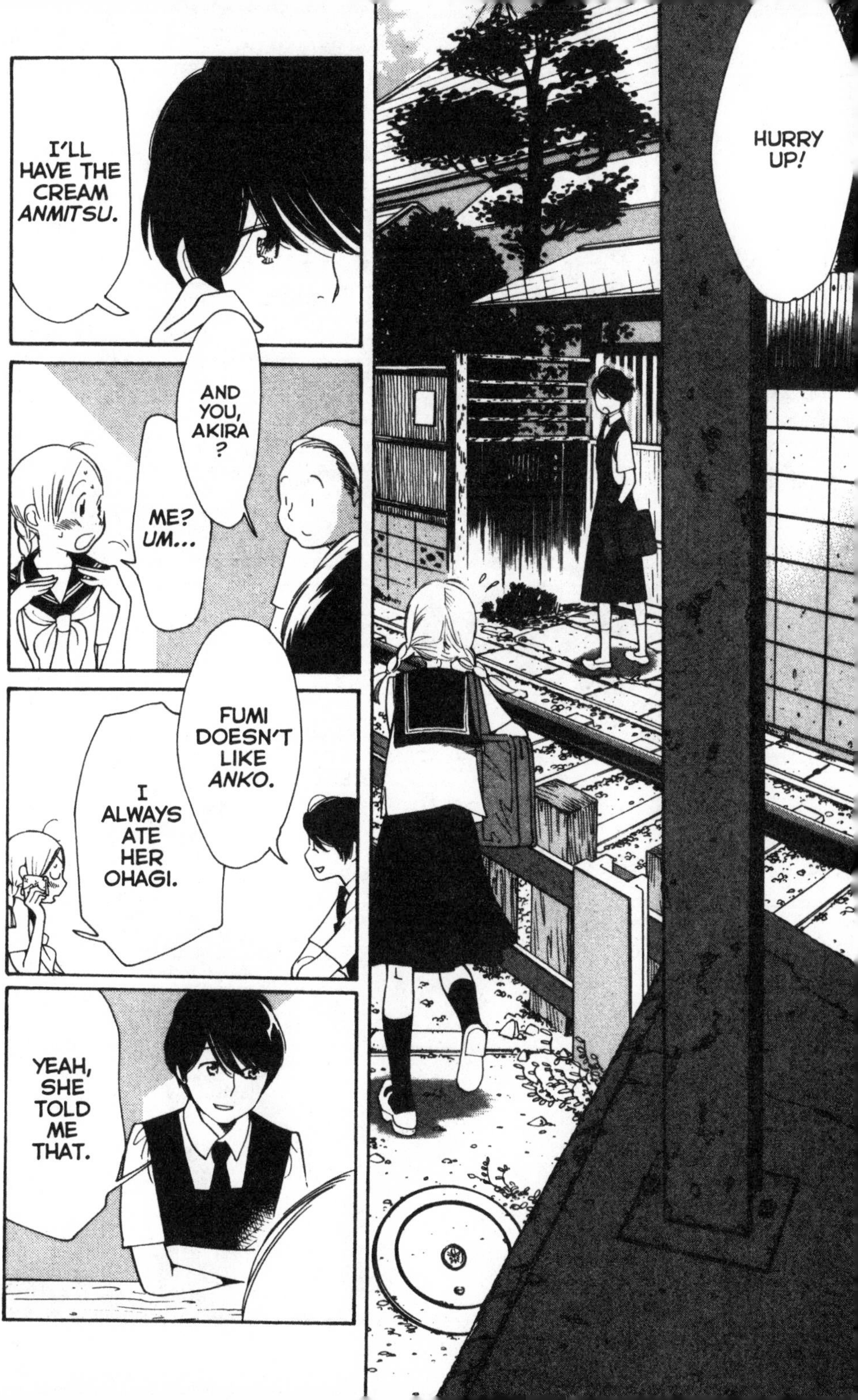
HURRY UP!
I'LL HAVE THE CREAM ANMITSU.
AND YOU, AKIRA?
ME? UM...
FUMI DOESN'T LIKE ANKO.
I ALWAYS ATE HER OHAGI.
YEAH, SHE TOLD ME THAT.

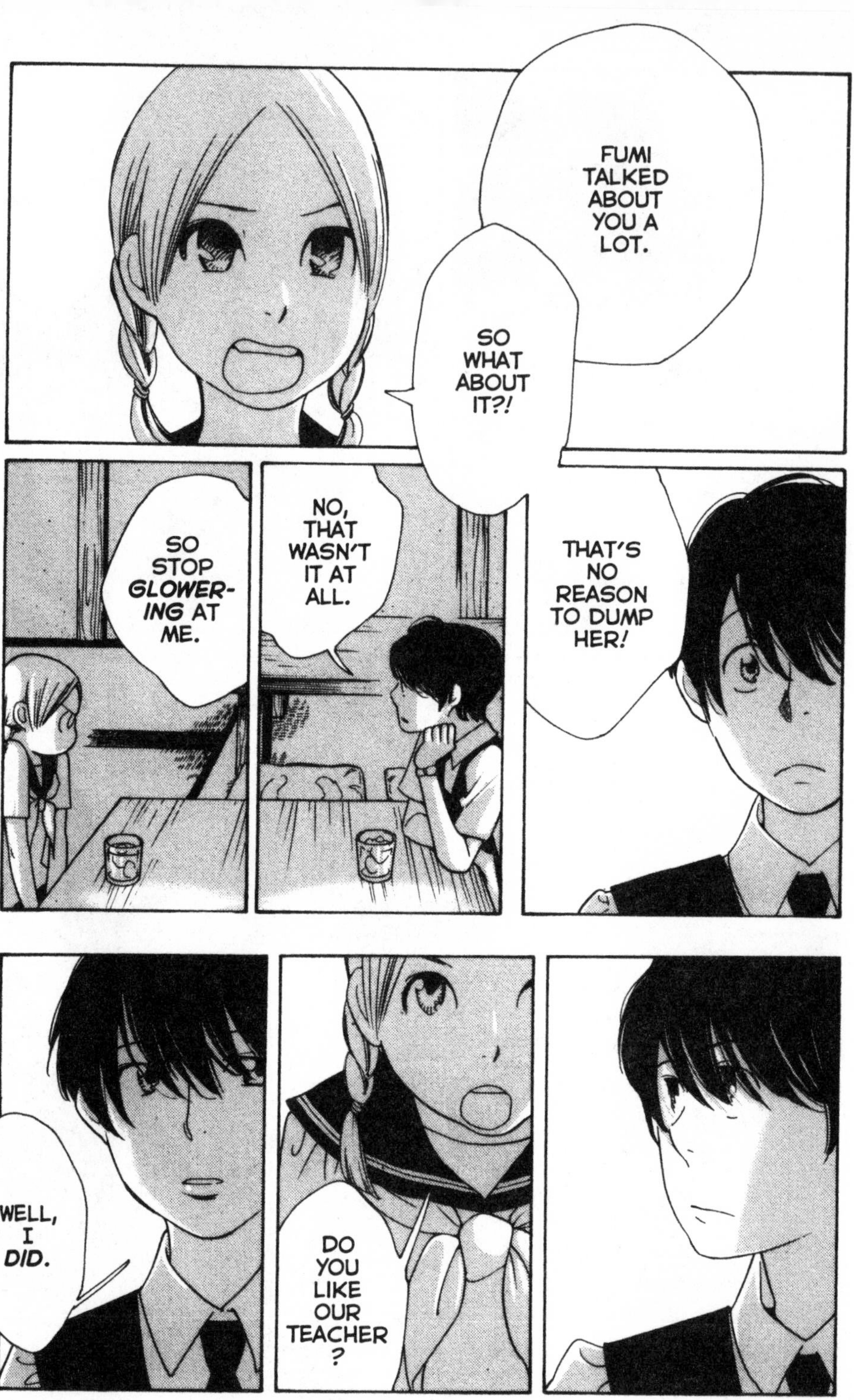
FUMI TALKED ABOUT YOU A LOT.
SO WHAT ABOUT IT?!
THAT'S NO REASON TO DUMP HER!
NO, THAT WASN'T IT AT ALL.
SO STOP *GLOWERING* AT ME.
DO YOU LIKE OUR TEACHER?
WELL, I *DID*.

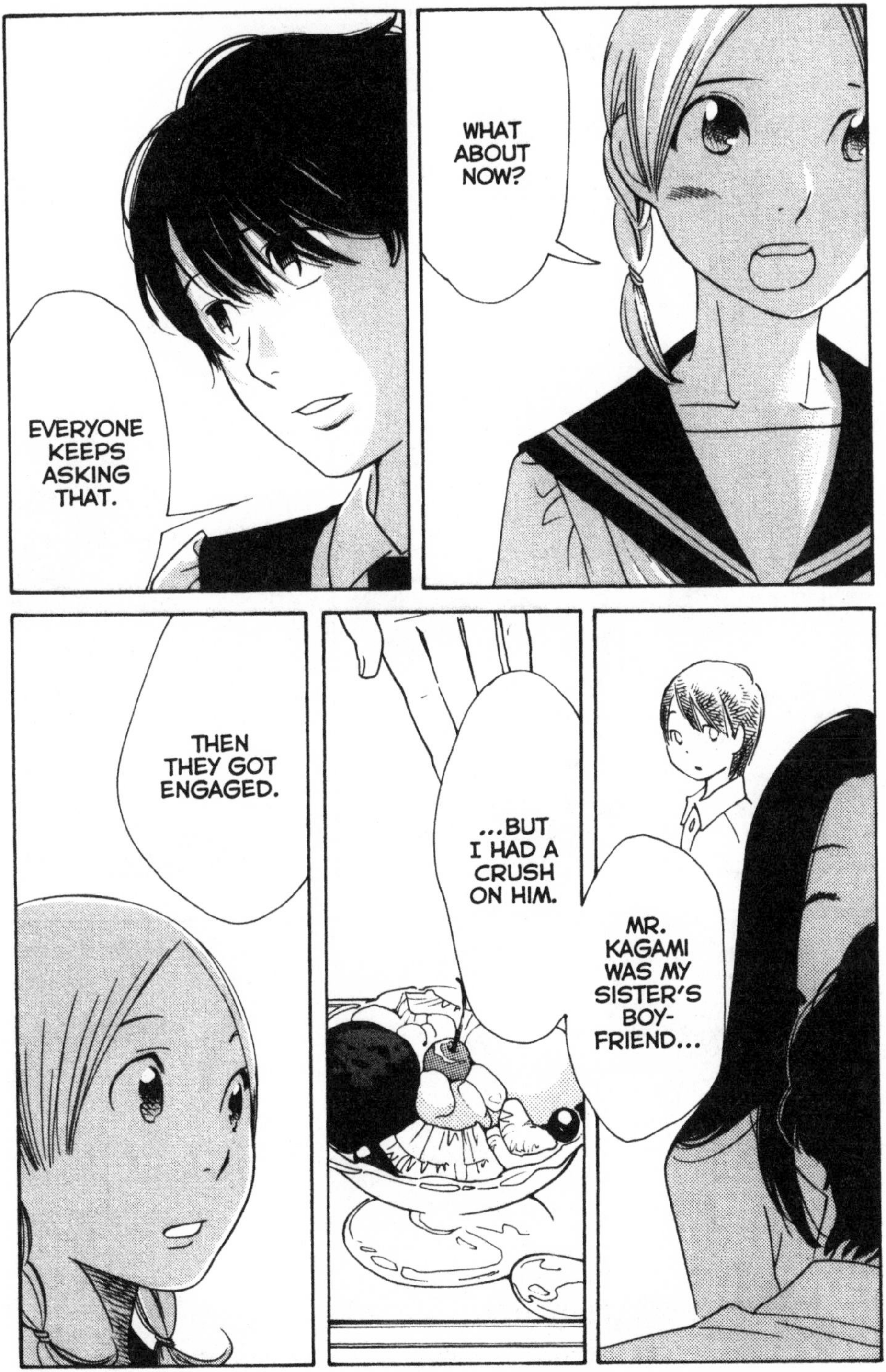

WHAT ABOUT NOW?
EVERYONE KEEPS ASKING THAT.
MR. KAGAMI WAS MY SISTER'S BOY-FRIEND...
...BUT I HAD A CRUSH ON HIM.
THEN THEY GOT ENGAGED.

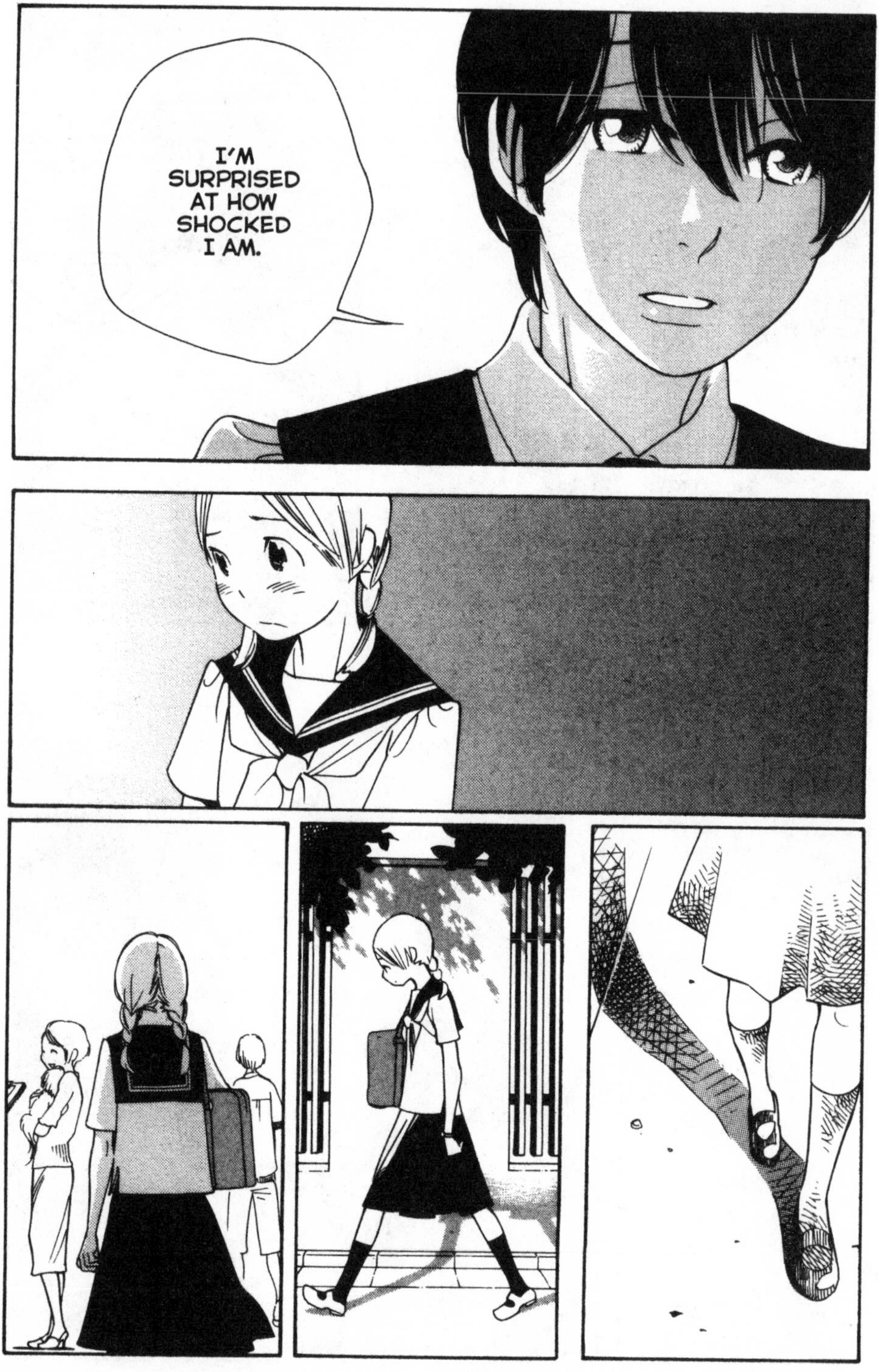
I'M SURPRISED AT HOW SHOCKED I AM.

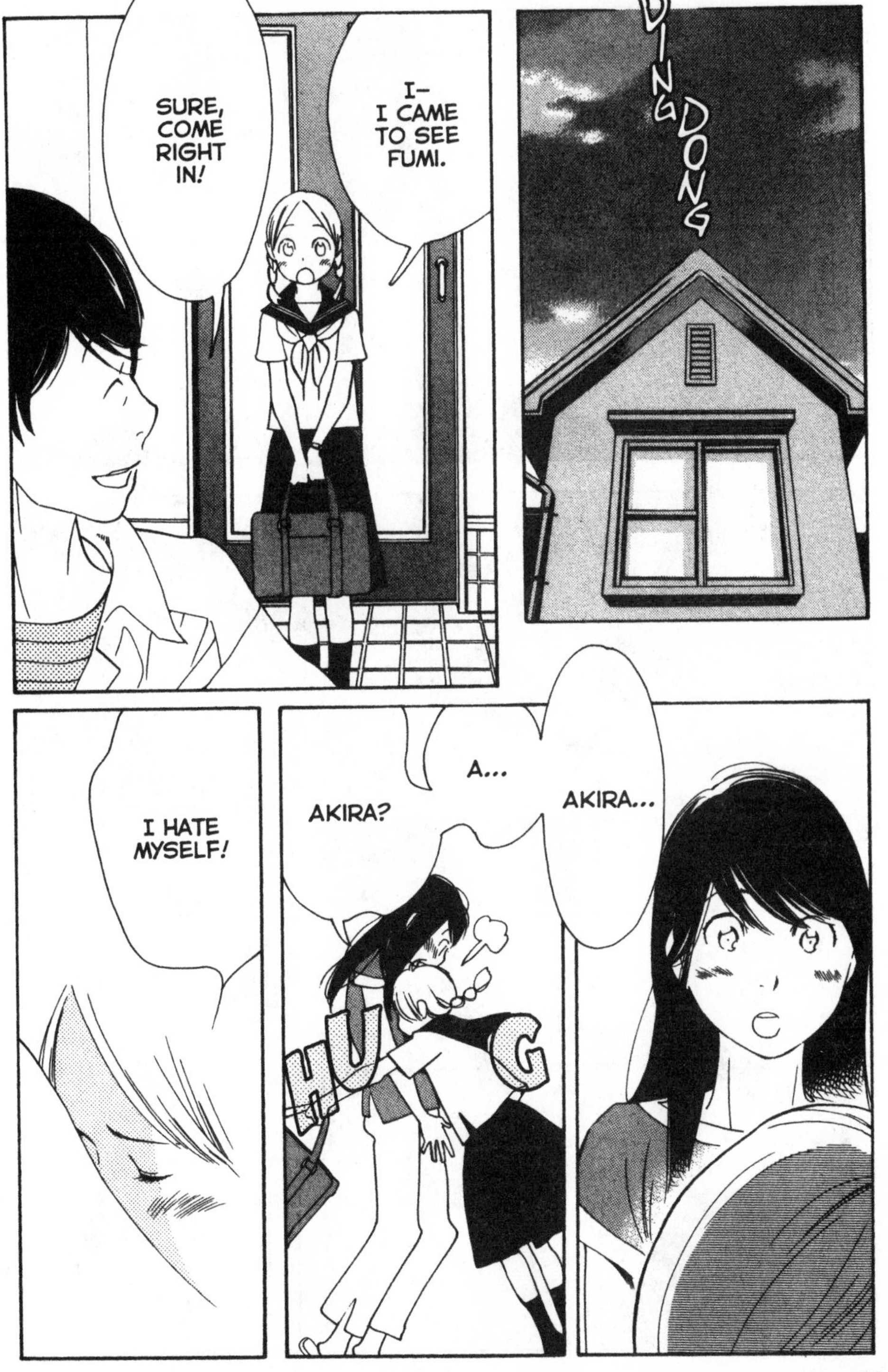
DING DONG
I– I CAME TO SEE FUMI.
SURE, COME RIGHT IN!
A... AKIRA...
AKIRA?
HUG
I HATE MYSELF!

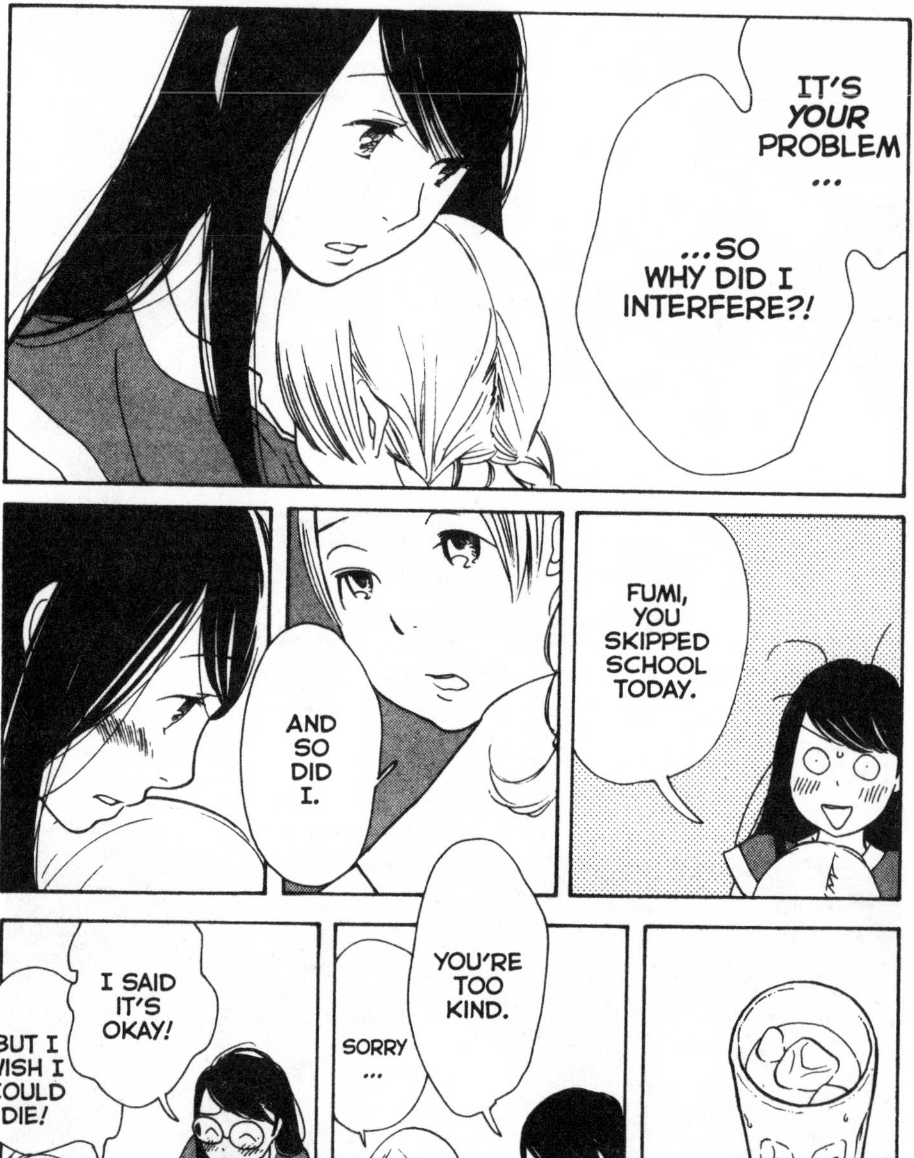
IT'S *YOUR* PROBLEM ...
...SO WHY DID I INTERFERE?!
FUMI, YOU SKIPPED SCHOOL TODAY.
AND SO DID I.
YOU'RE TOO KIND.
SORRY ...
I SAID IT'S OKAY!
BUT I WISH I COULD DIE!

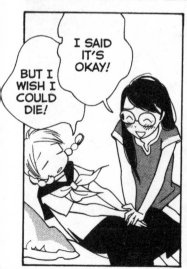

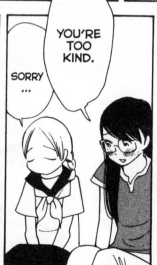

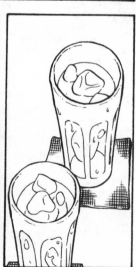

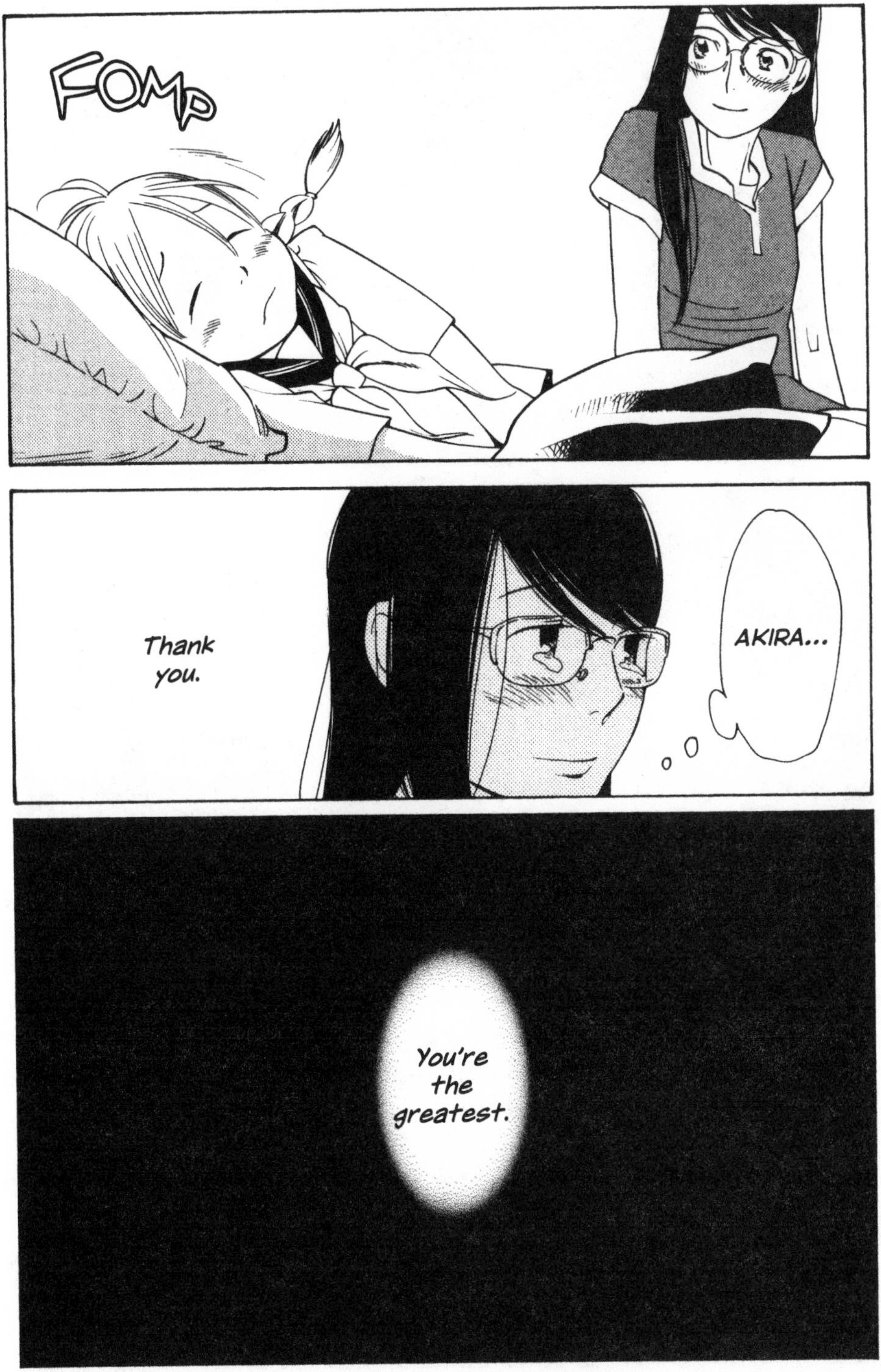
FOMP
AKIRA...
Thank you.
You're the greatest.

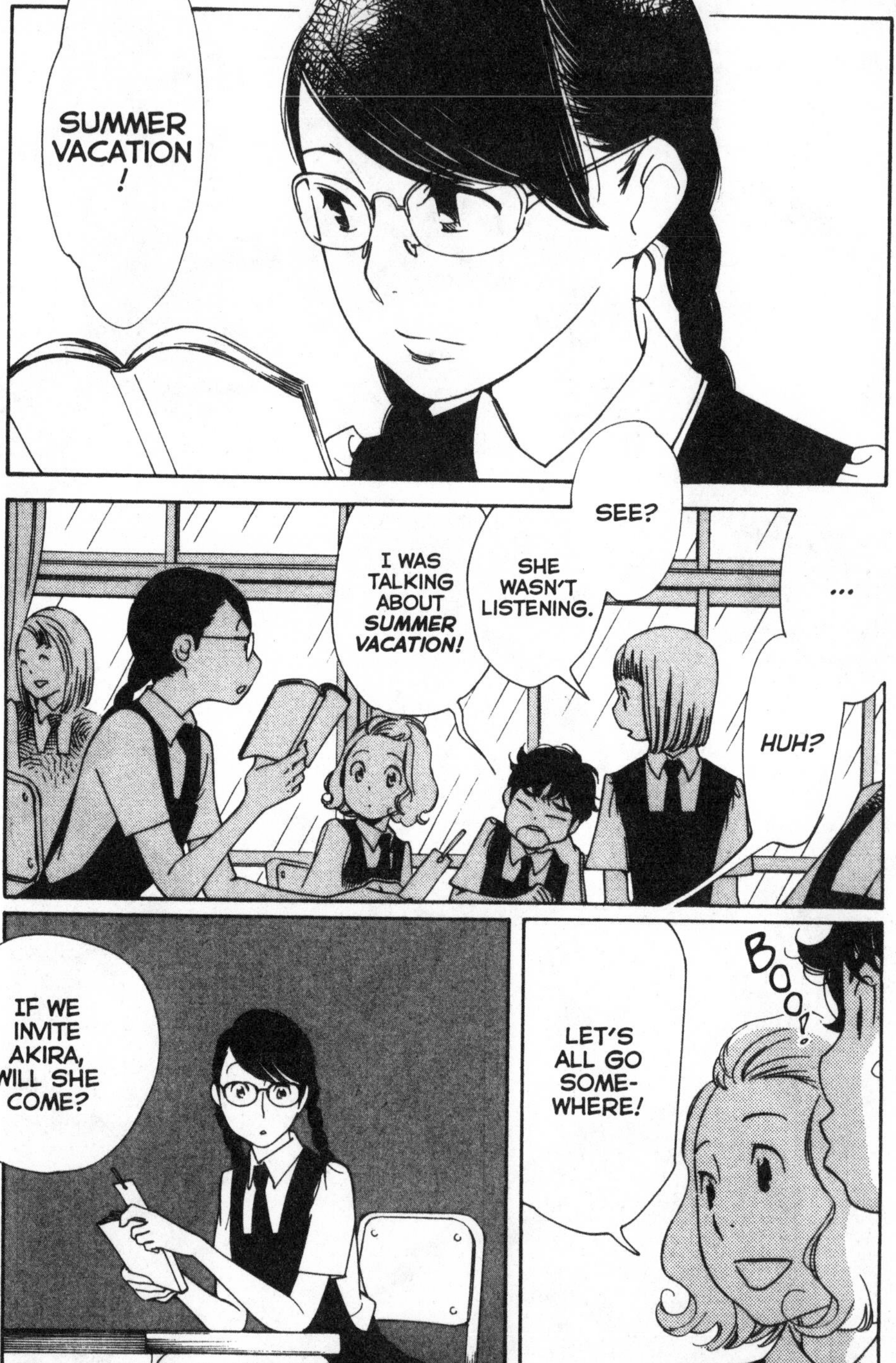
SUMMER VACATION!
SEE? SHE WASN'T LISTENING.
...
HUH?
I WAS TALKING ABOUT *SUMMER VACATION!*
LET'S ALL GO SOME-WHERE!
BOOO!
IF WE INVITE AKIRA, WILL SHE COME?

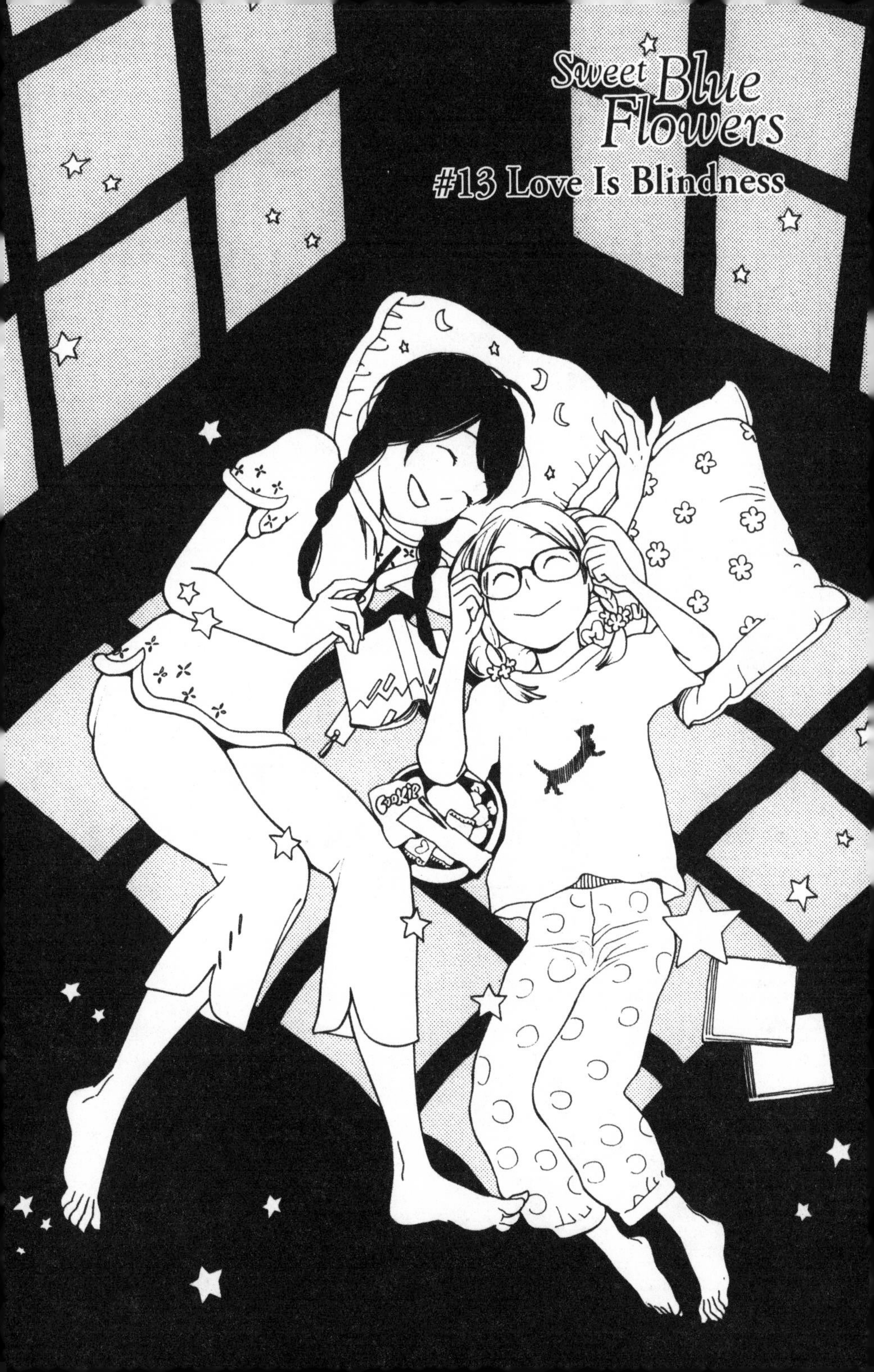
Sweet Blue Flowers
#13 Love Is Blindness

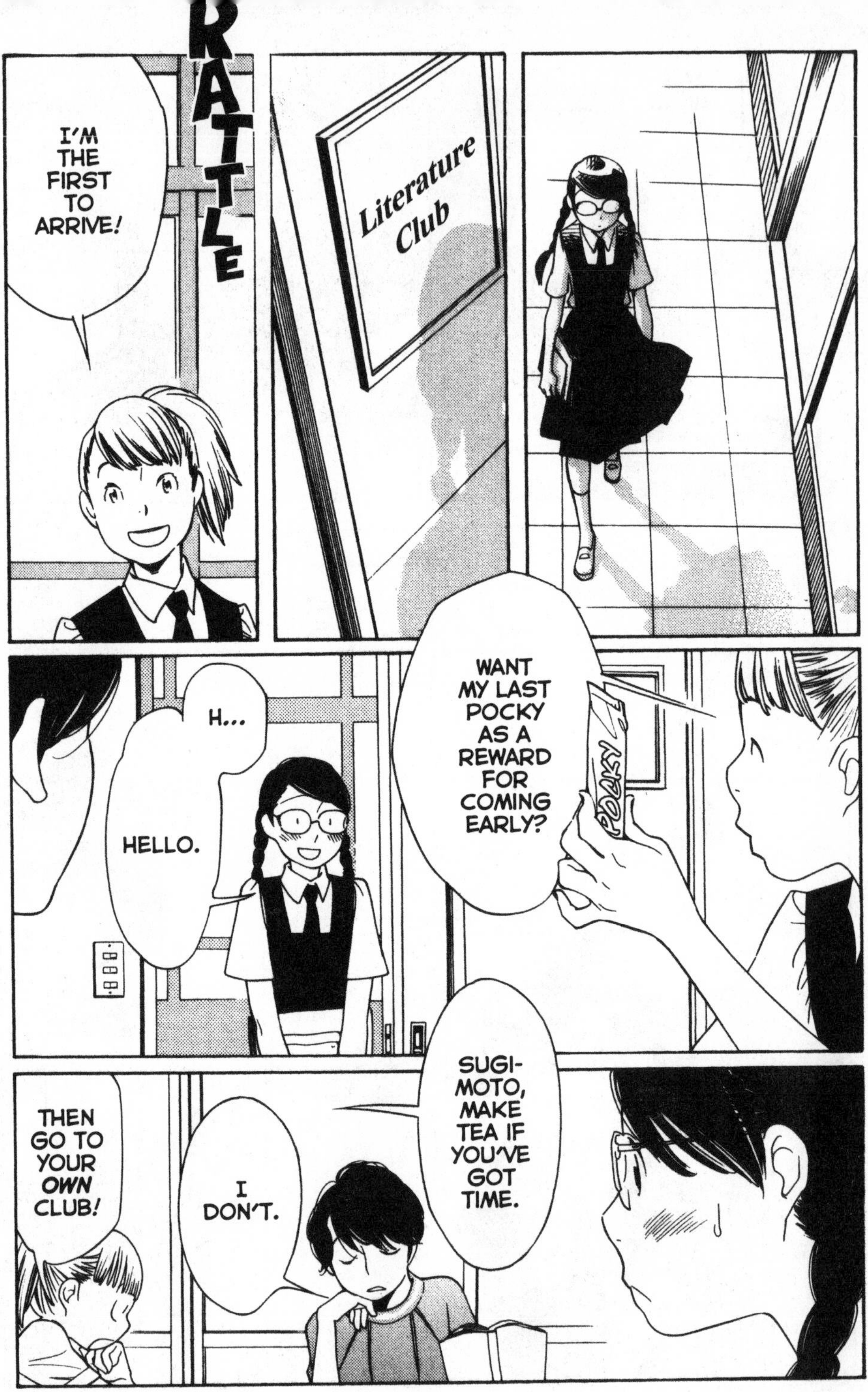
Literature Club
RATTLE
I'M THE FIRST TO ARRIVE!
WANT MY LAST POCKY AS A REWARD FOR COMING EARLY?
POCKY
H...
HELLO.
SUGI-MOTO, MAKE TEA IF YOU'VE GOT TIME.
I DON'T.
THEN GO TO YOUR *OWN* CLUB!

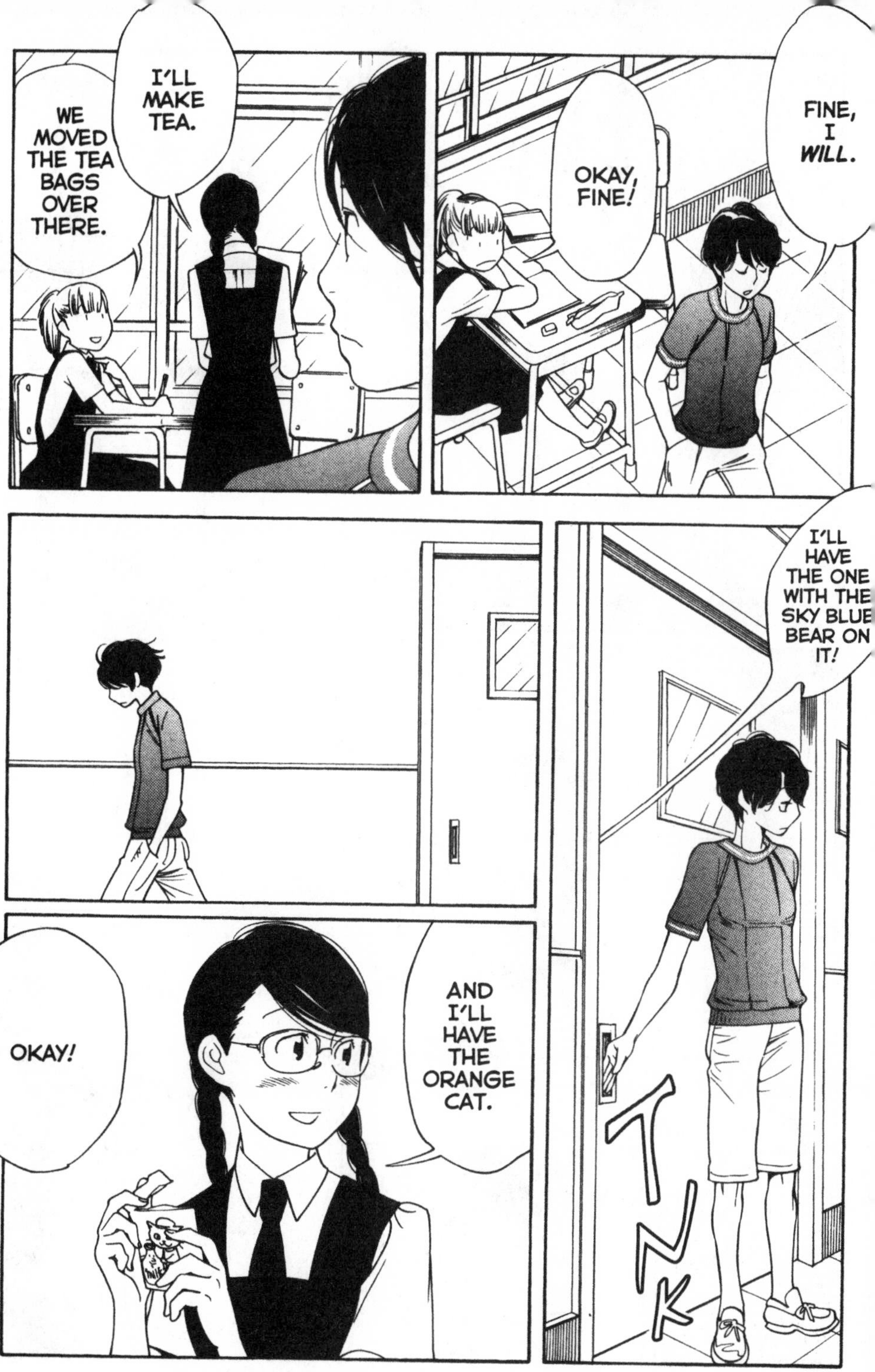
FINE, I *WILL*.
OKAY, FINE!
I'LL MAKE TEA.
WE MOVED THE TEA BAGS OVER THERE.
I'LL HAVE THE ONE WITH THE SKY BLUE BEAR ON IT!
TINK
AND I'LL HAVE THE ORANGE CAT.
OKAY!

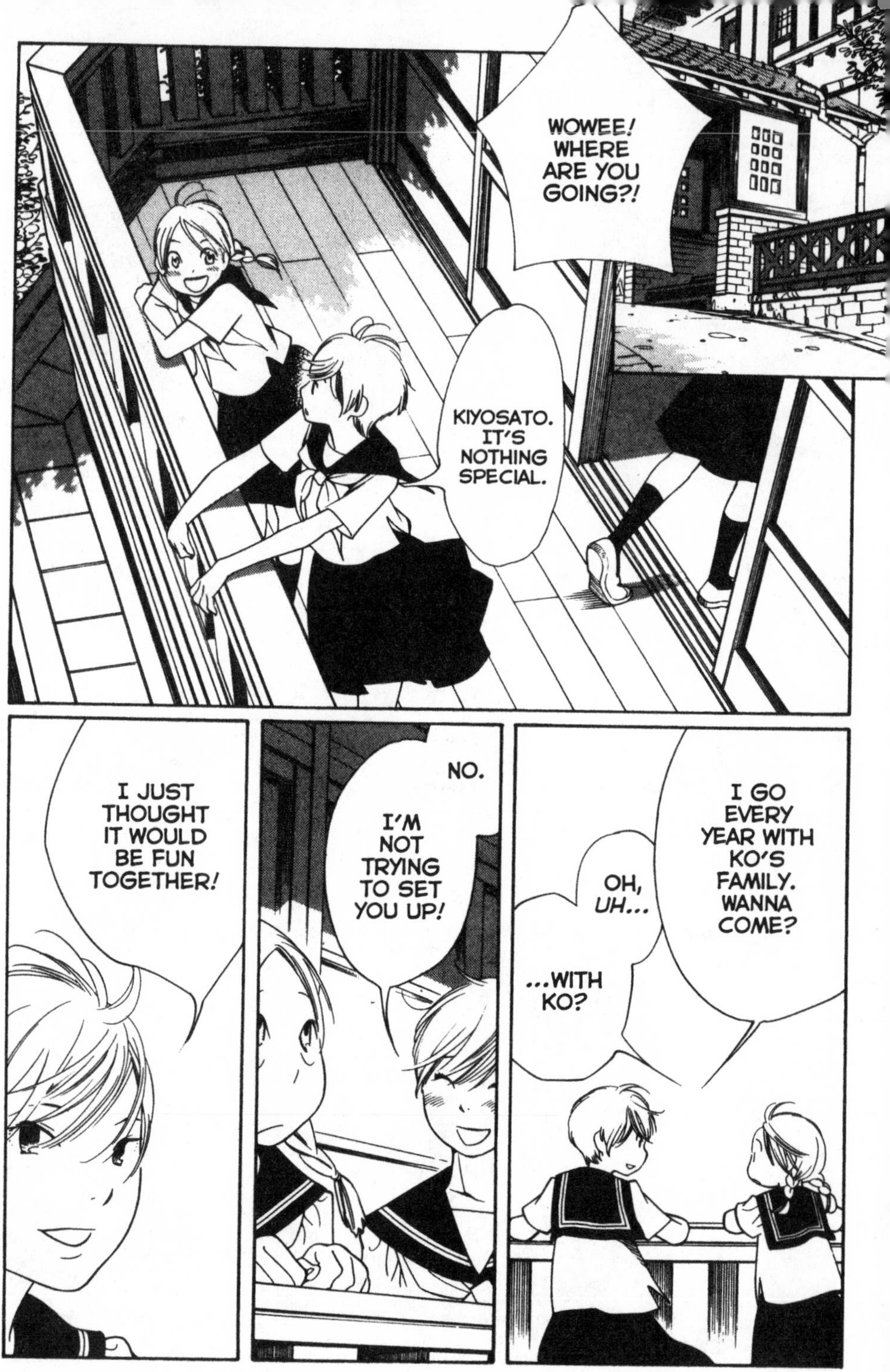
WOWEE! WHERE ARE YOU GOING?!
KIYOSATO. IT'S NOTHING SPECIAL.
I GO EVERY YEAR WITH KO'S FAMILY. WANNA COME?
OH, UH...
...WITH KO?
NO.
I'M NOT TRYING TO SET YOU UP!
I JUST THOUGHT IT WOULD BE FUN TOGETHER!

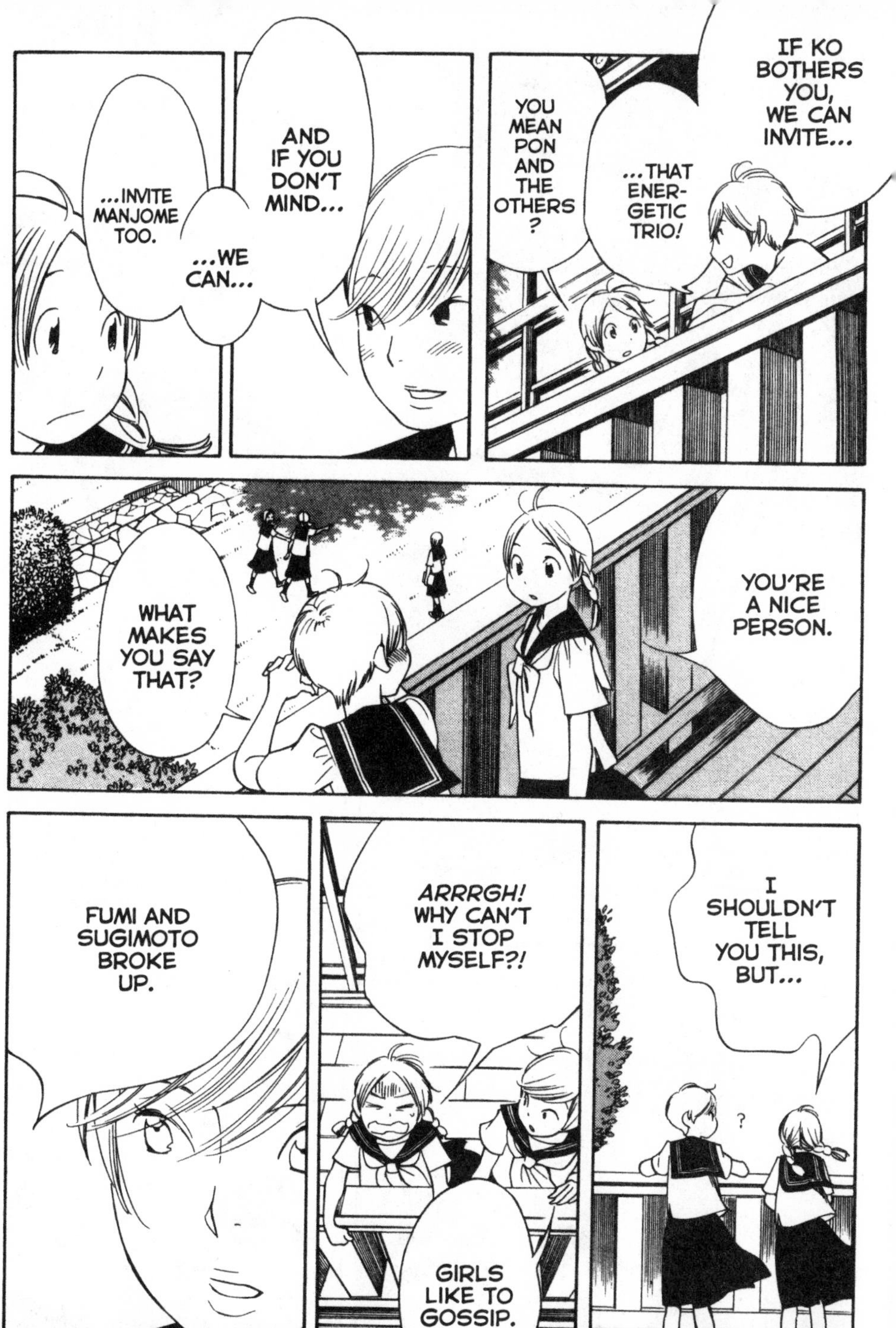
IF KO BOTHERS YOU, WE CAN INVITE...
...THAT ENERGETIC TRIO!
YOU MEAN PON AND THE OTHERS?
AND IF YOU DON'T MIND...
...WE CAN...
...INVITE MANJOME TOO.
YOU'RE A NICE PERSON.
WHAT MAKES YOU SAY THAT?
I SHOULDN'T TELL YOU THIS, BUT...
*ARRRGH!* WHY CAN'T I STOP MYSELF?!
GIRLS LIKE TO GOSSIP.
FUMI AND SUGIMOTO BROKE UP.

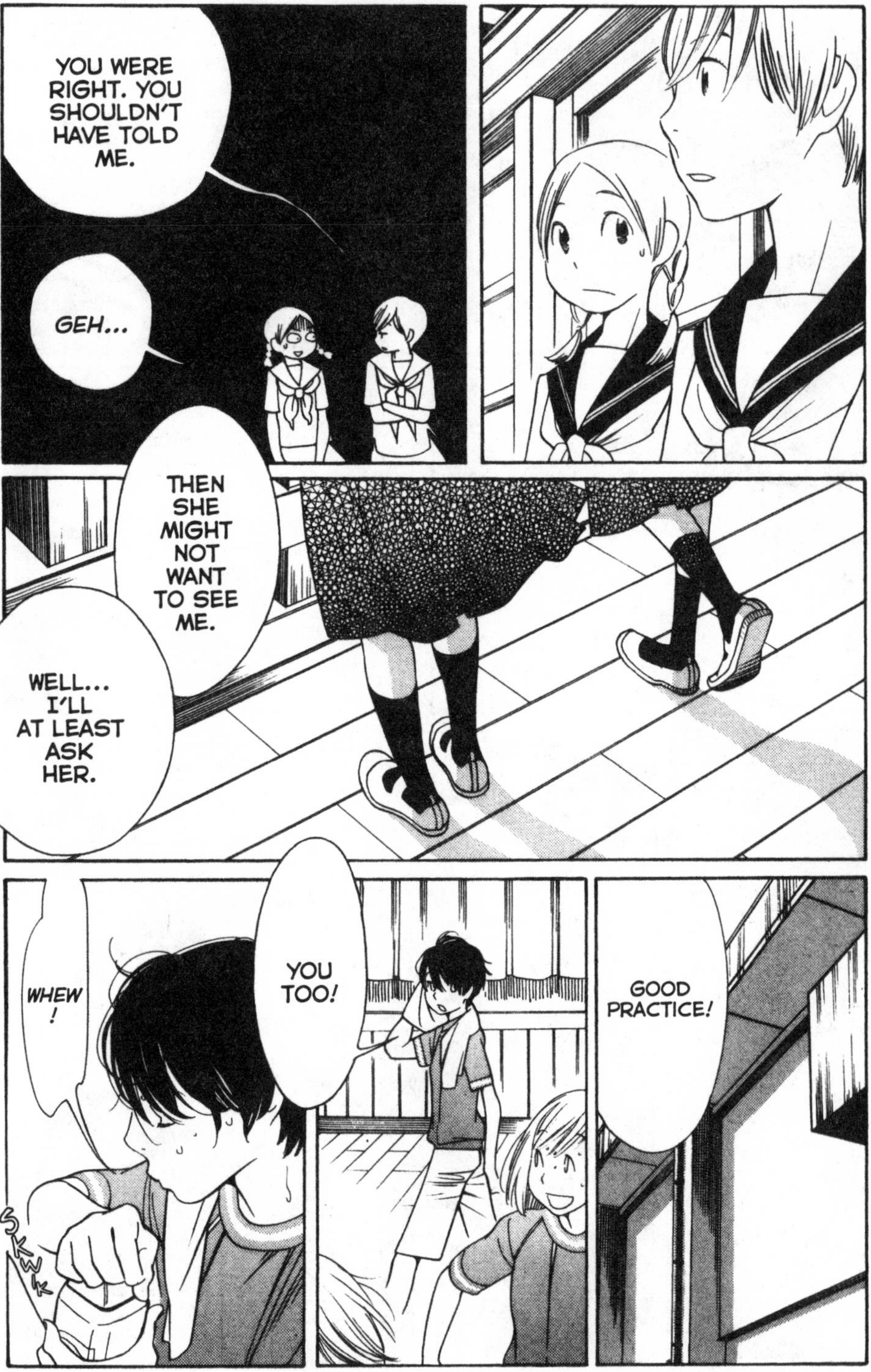
YOU WERE RIGHT. YOU SHOULDN'T HAVE TOLD ME.
GEH...
THEN SHE MIGHT NOT WANT TO SEE ME.
WELL... I'LL AT LEAST ASK HER.
GOOD PRACTICE!
YOU TOO!
WHEW!
SKWIK

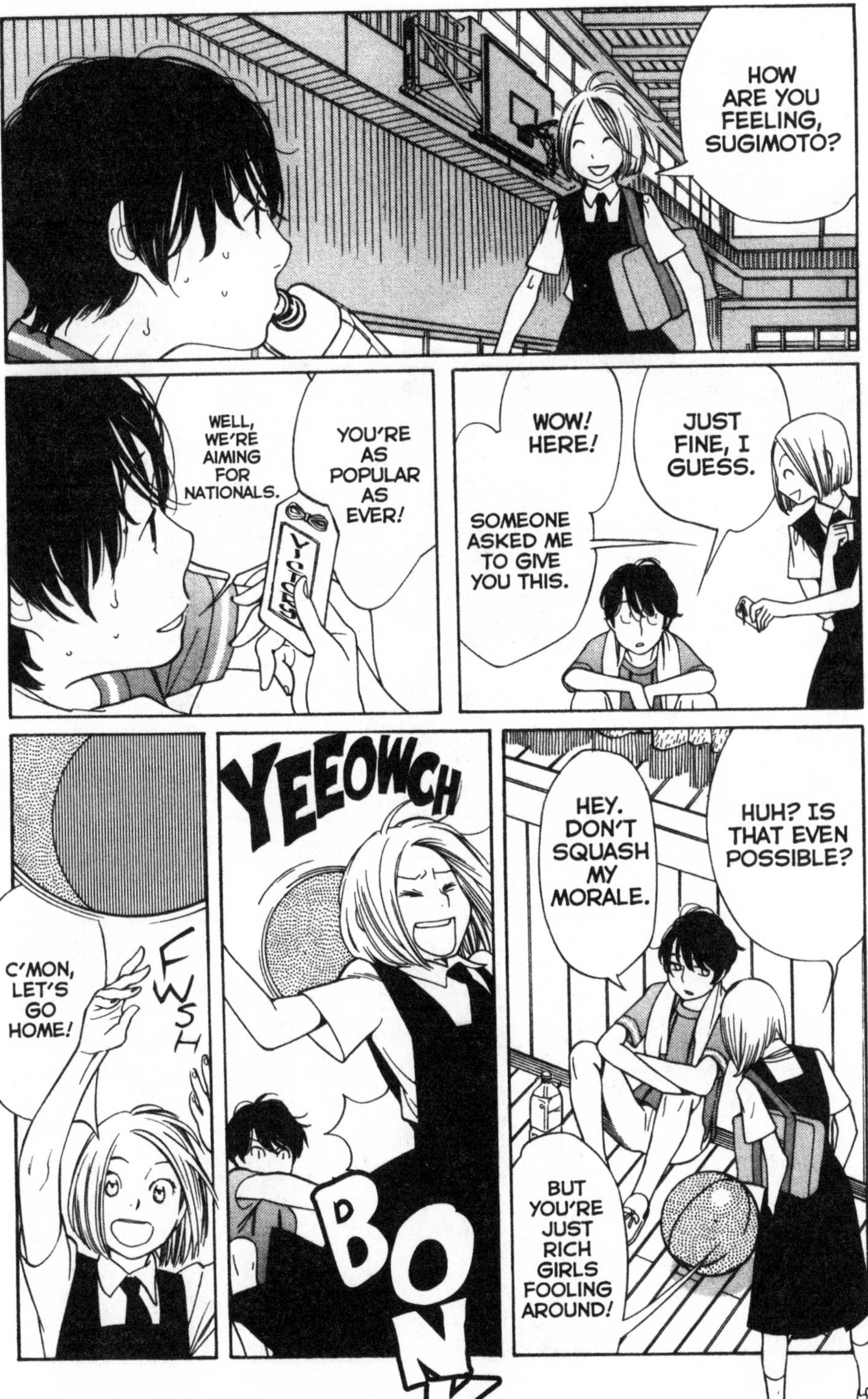
HOW ARE YOU FEELING, SUGIMOTO?
JUST FINE, I GUESS.
WOW! HERE!
SOMEONE ASKED ME TO GIVE YOU THIS.
YOU'RE AS POPULAR AS EVER!
WELL, WE'RE AIMING FOR NATIONALS.
HUH? IS THAT EVEN POSSIBLE?
HEY. DON'T SQUASH MY MORALE.
BUT YOU'RE JUST RICH GIRLS FOOLING AROUND!
YEEOWCH
BONK
FWSH
C'MON, LET'S GO HOME!

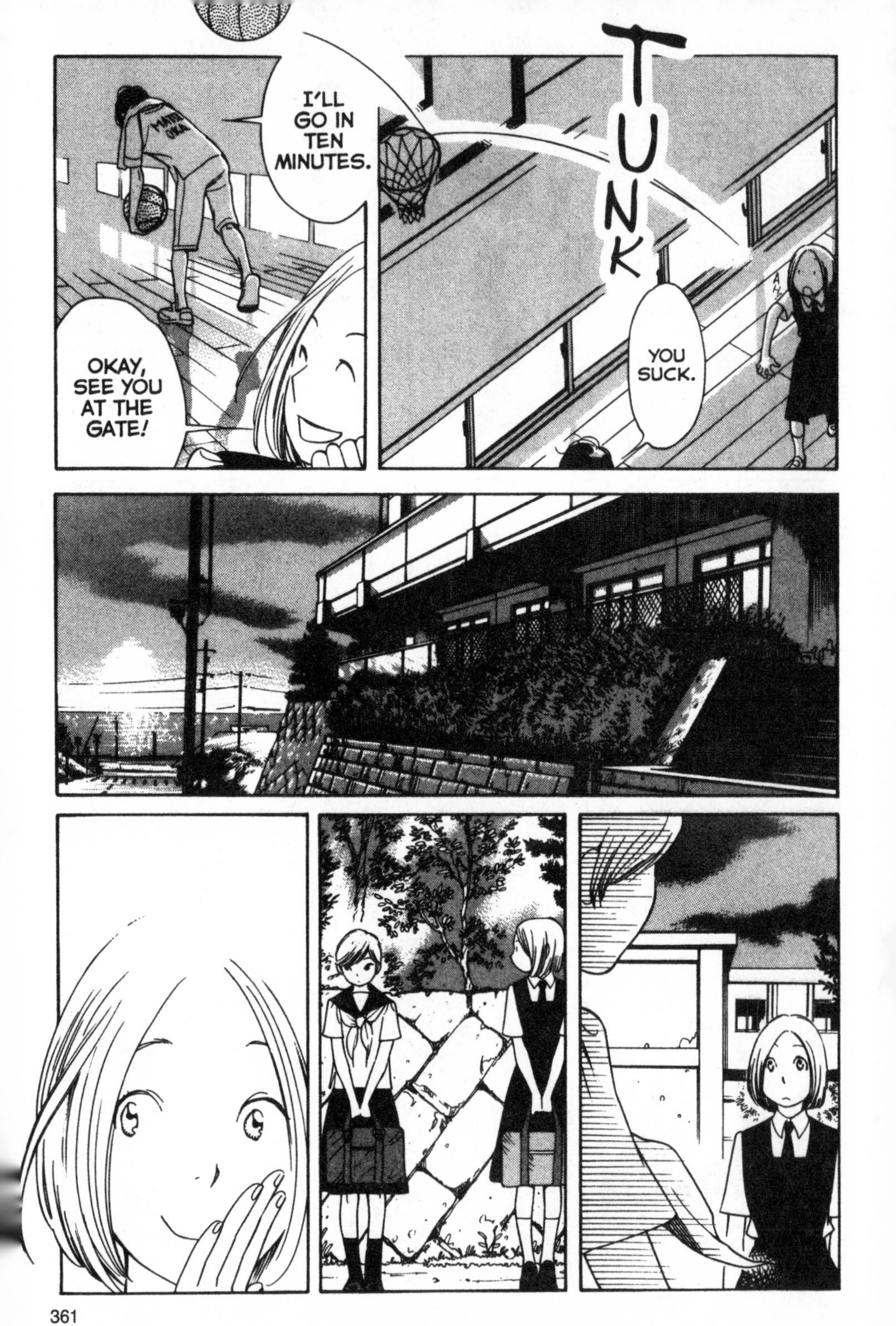
TUNK
YOU SUCK.
I'LL GO IN TEN MINUTES.
OKAY, SEE YOU AT THE GATE!

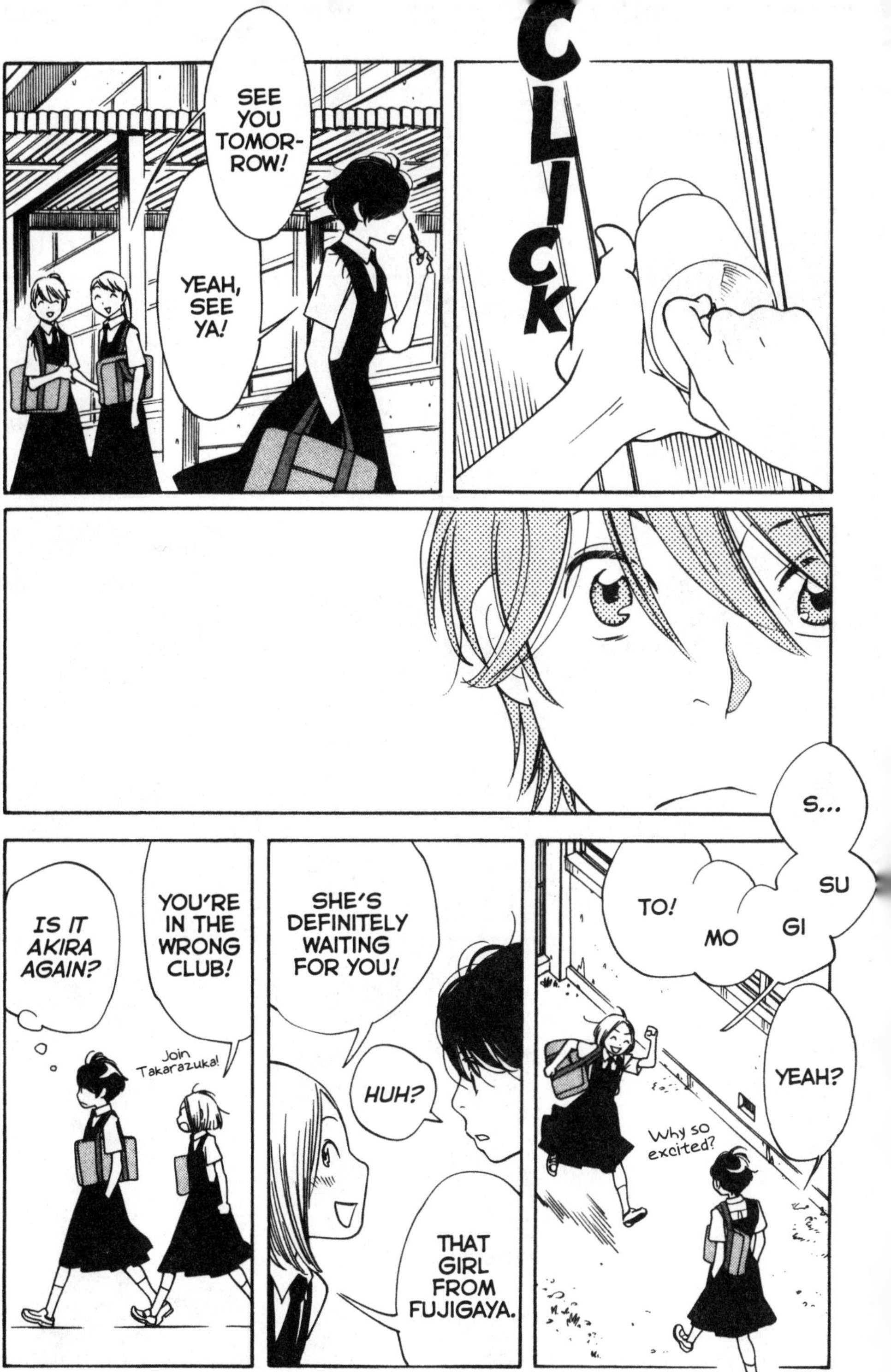

CLICK
SEE YOU TOMORROW!
YEAH, SEE YA!
S...
SU GI MO TO!
YEAH?
Why so excited?
SHE'S DEFINITELY WAITING FOR YOU!
HUH?
THAT GIRL FROM FUJIGAYA.
YOU'RE IN THE WRONG CLUB!
Join Takarazuka!
IS IT AKIRA AGAIN?

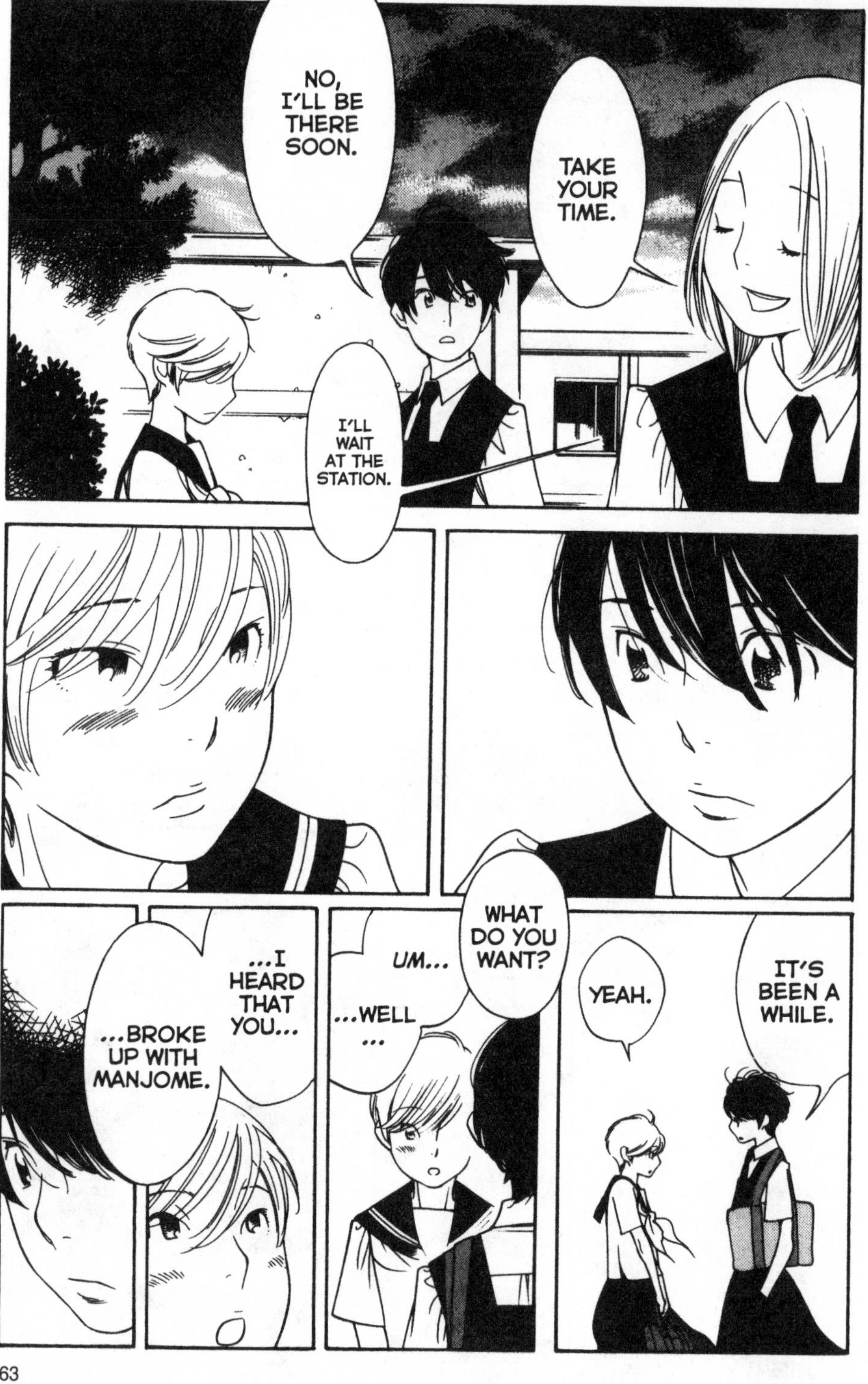
TAKE YOUR TIME.
NO, I'LL BE THERE SOON.
I'LL WAIT AT THE STATION.
IT'S BEEN A WHILE.
YEAH.
WHAT DO YOU WANT?
UM...
...WELL ...
...I HEARD THAT YOU...
...BROKE UP WITH MANJOME.

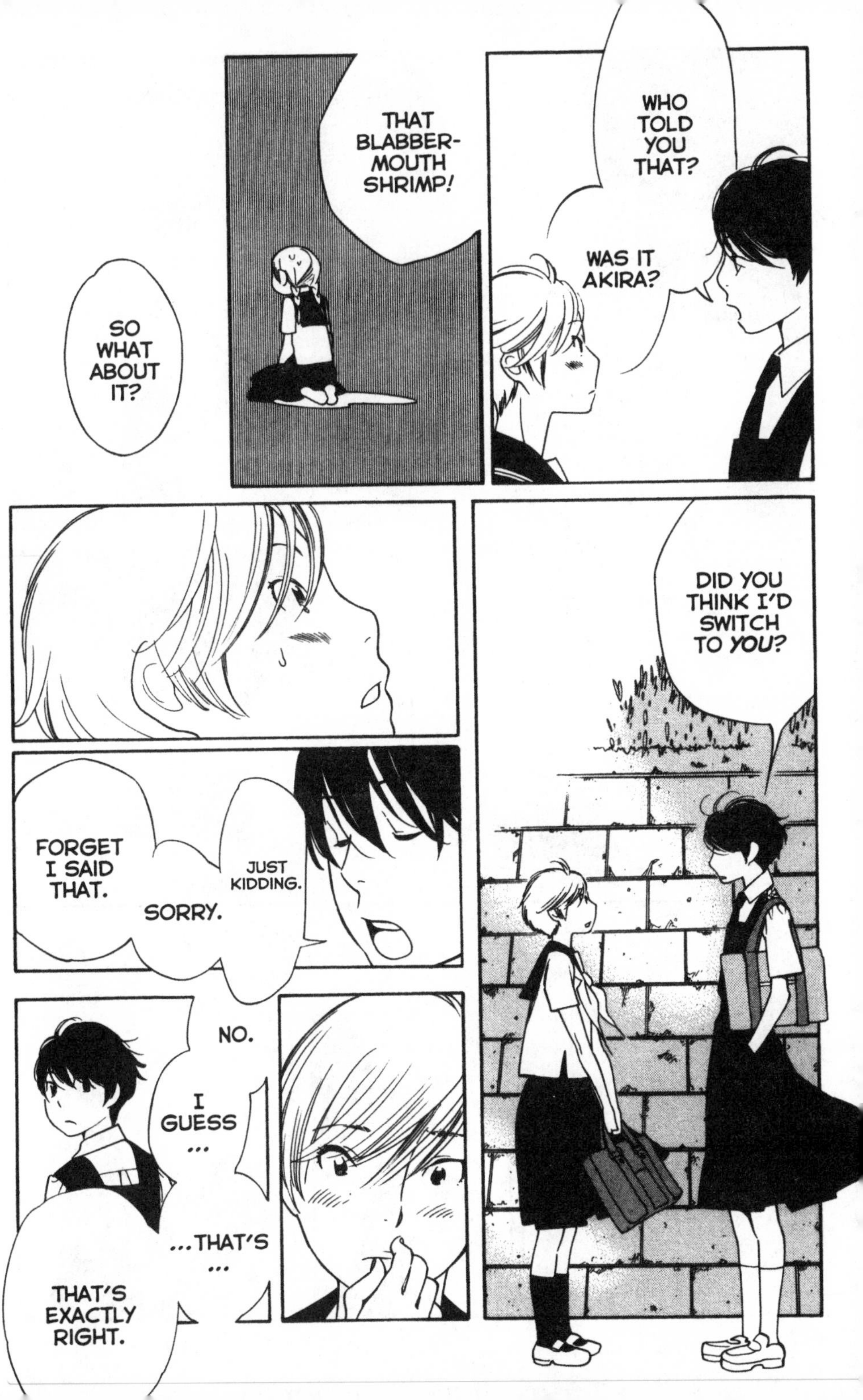
WHO TOLD YOU THAT?
WAS IT AKIRA?
THAT BLABBER-MOUTH SHRIMP!
SO WHAT ABOUT IT?
DID YOU THINK I'D SWITCH TO *YOU*?
JUST KIDDING.
SORRY.
FORGET I SAID THAT.
NO.
I GUESS...
...THAT'S...
THAT'S EXACTLY RIGHT.

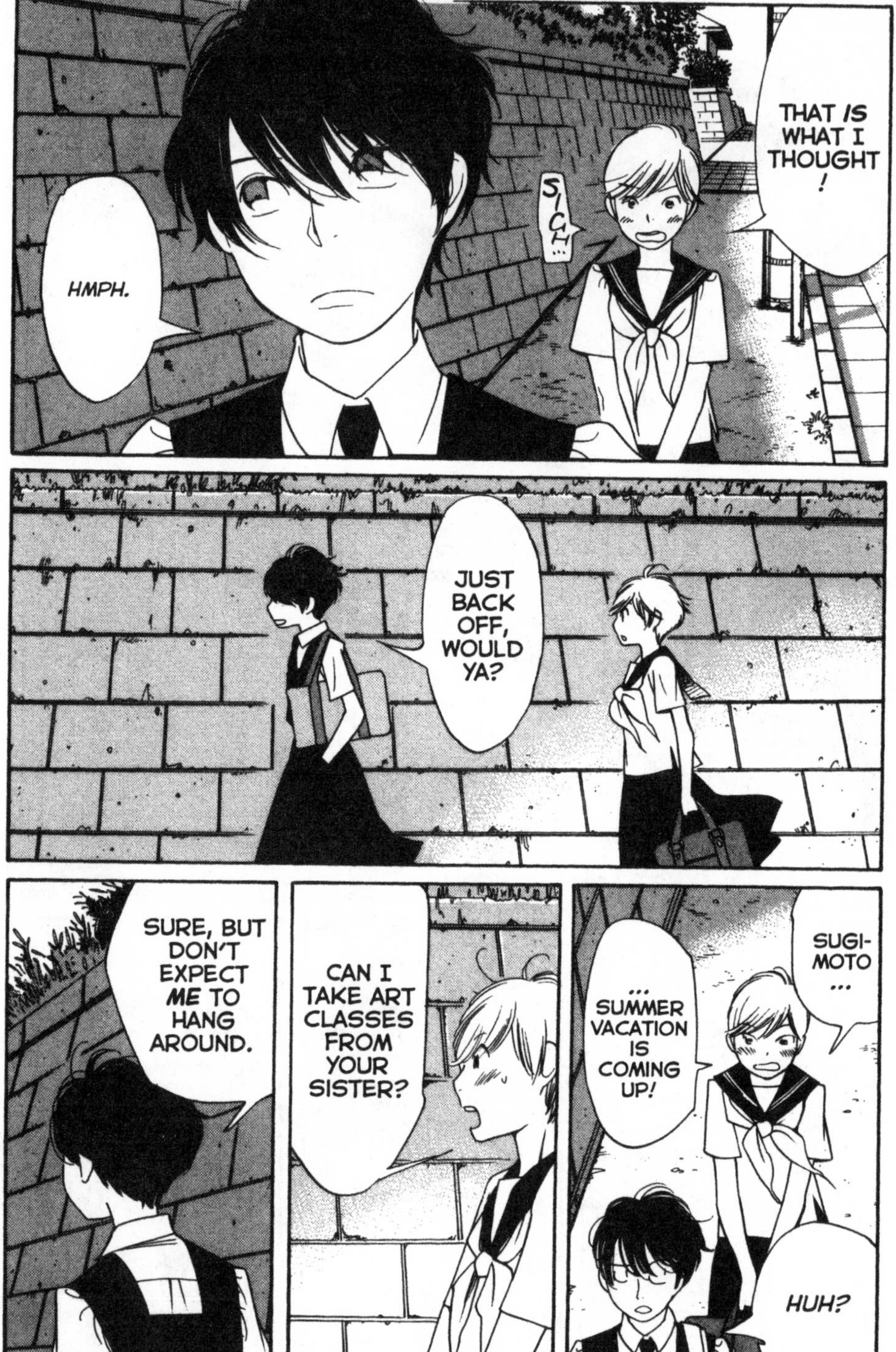
THAT *IS* WHAT I THOUGHT!
SIGH...
HMPH.
JUST BACK OFF, WOULD YA?
SUGI-MOTO...
...SUMMER VACATION IS COMING UP!
HUH?
CAN I TAKE ART CLASSES FROM YOUR SISTER?
SURE, BUT DON'T EXPECT *ME* TO HANG AROUND.

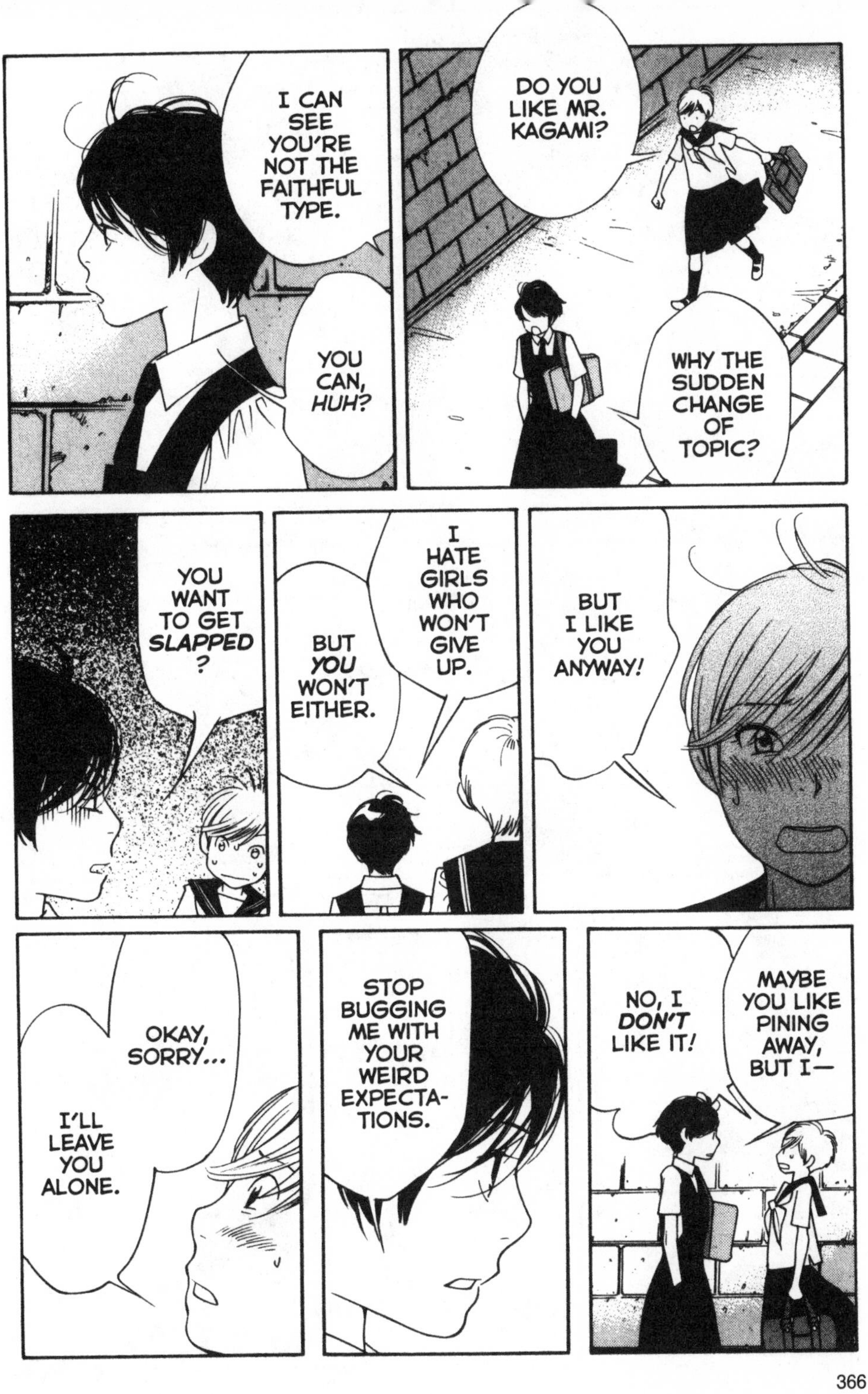
DO YOU LIKE MR. KAGAMI?
WHY THE SUDDEN CHANGE OF TOPIC?
I CAN SEE YOU'RE NOT THE FAITHFUL TYPE.
YOU CAN, *HUH*?
BUT I LIKE YOU ANYWAY!
I HATE GIRLS WHO WON'T GIVE UP.
BUT *YOU* WON'T EITHER.
YOU WANT TO GET *SLAPPED*?
MAYBE YOU LIKE PINING AWAY, BUT I—
NO, I *DON'T* LIKE IT!
STOP BUGGING ME WITH YOUR WEIRD EXPECTATIONS.
OKAY, SORRY...
I'LL LEAVE YOU ALONE.

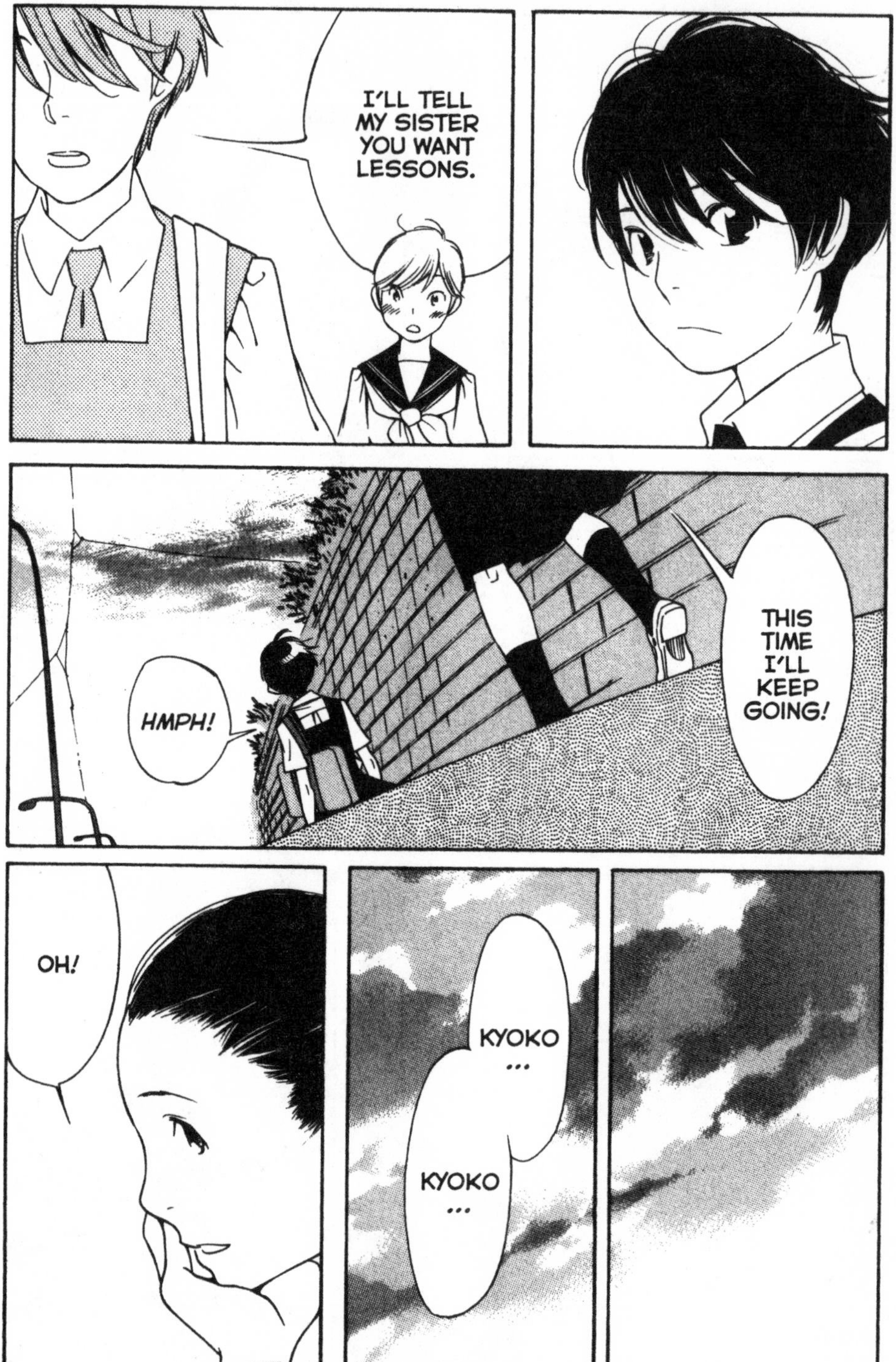
I'LL TELL MY SISTER YOU WANT LESSONS.
THIS TIME I'LL KEEP GOING!
HMPH!
KYOKO...
KYOKO...
OH!

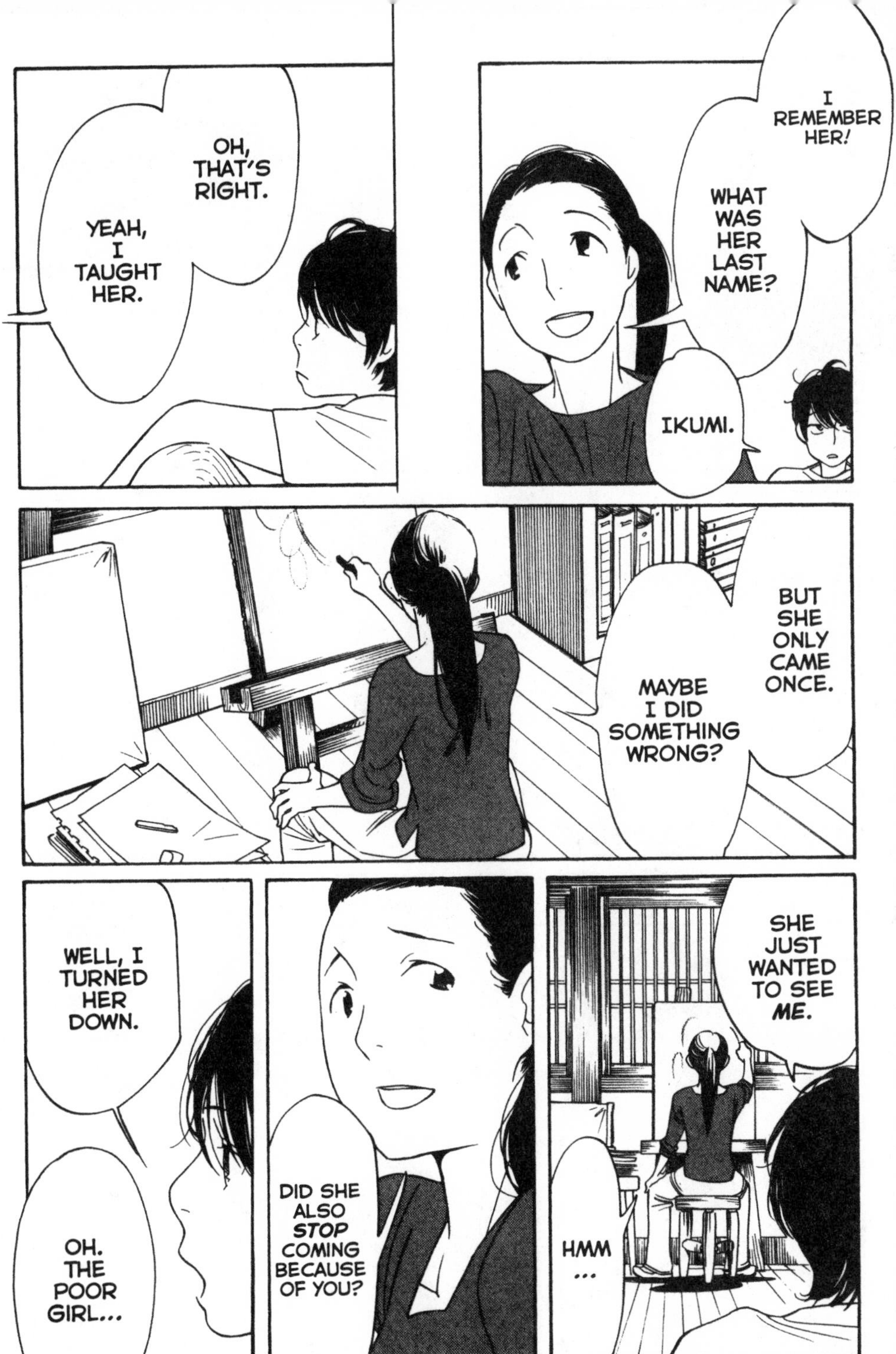
I REMEMBER HER!
WHAT WAS HER LAST NAME?
IKUMI.
OH, THAT'S RIGHT.
YEAH, I TAUGHT HER.
BUT SHE ONLY CAME ONCE.
MAYBE I DID SOMETHING WRONG?
SHE JUST WANTED TO SEE *ME*.
HMM ...
DID SHE ALSO *STOP* COMING BECAUSE OF YOU?
WELL, I TURNED HER DOWN.
OH. THE POOR GIRL...

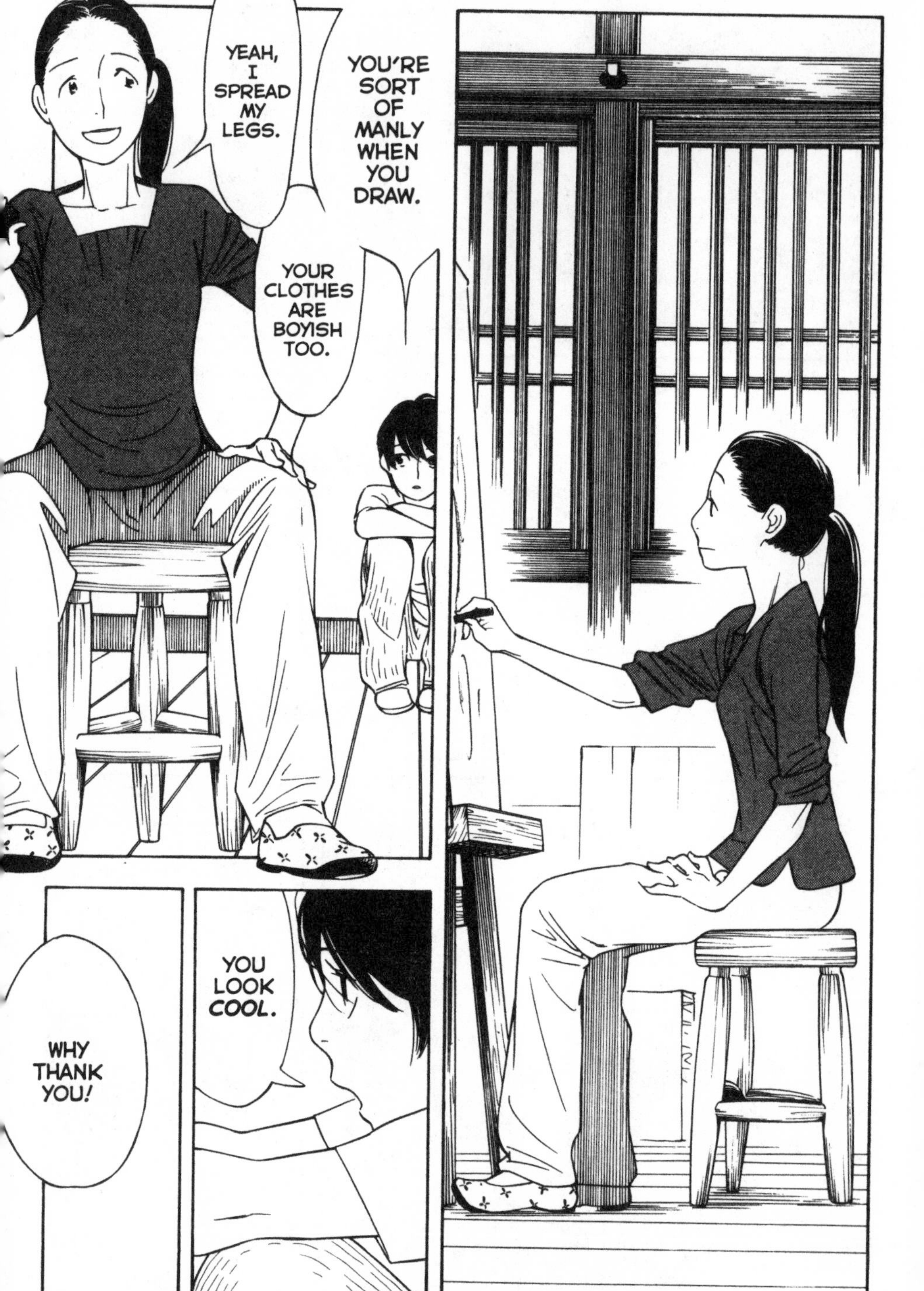
YOU'RE SORT OF MANLY WHEN YOU DRAW.
YEAH, I SPREAD MY LEGS.
YOUR CLOTHES ARE BOYISH TOO.
YOU LOOK *COOL*.
WHY THANK YOU!

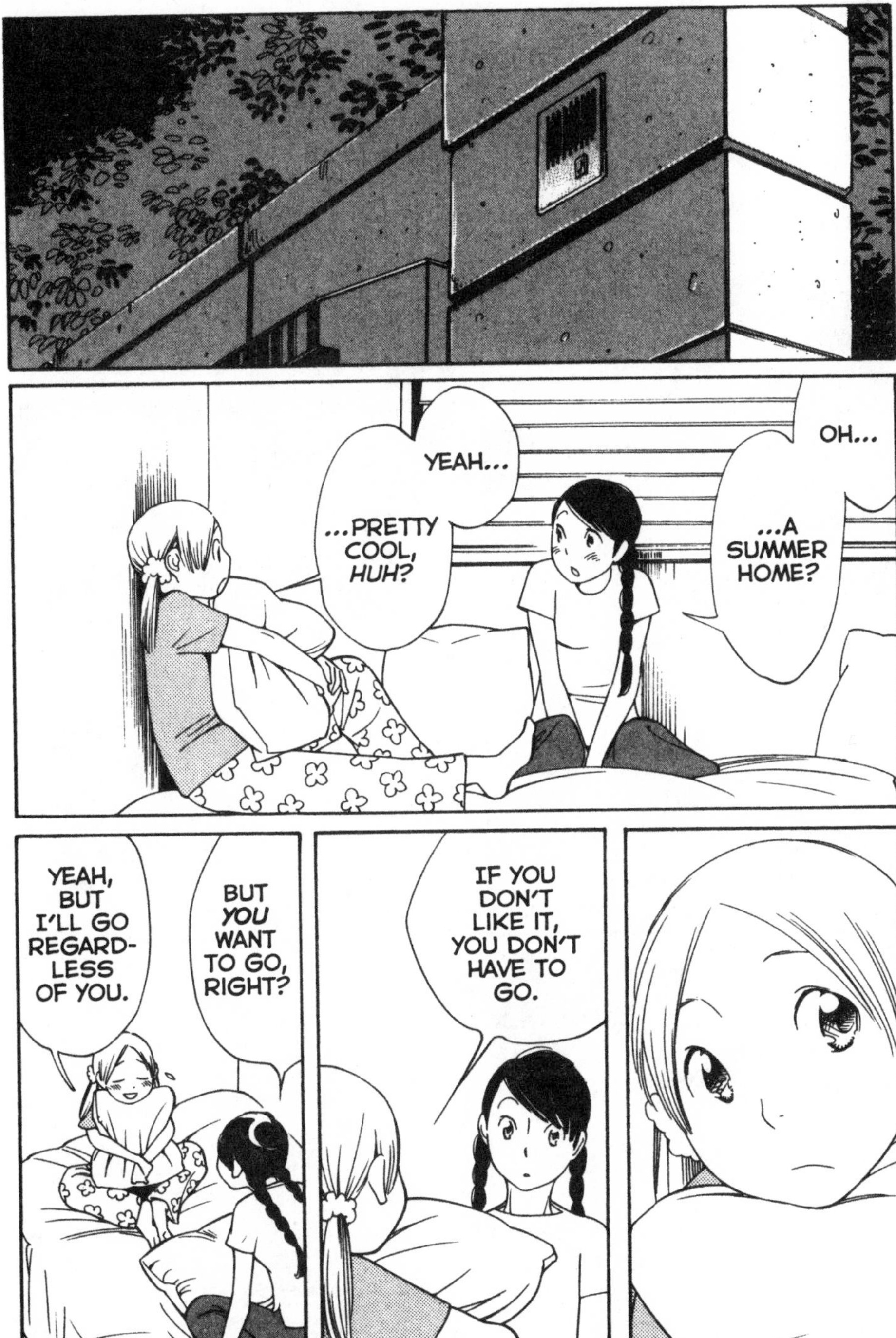
OH...
...A SUMMER HOME?
YEAH...
...PRETTY COOL, HUH?
IF YOU DON'T LIKE IT, YOU DON'T HAVE TO GO.
BUT YOU WANT TO GO, RIGHT?
YEAH, BUT I'LL GO REGARDLESS OF YOU.

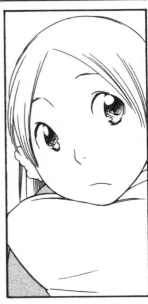

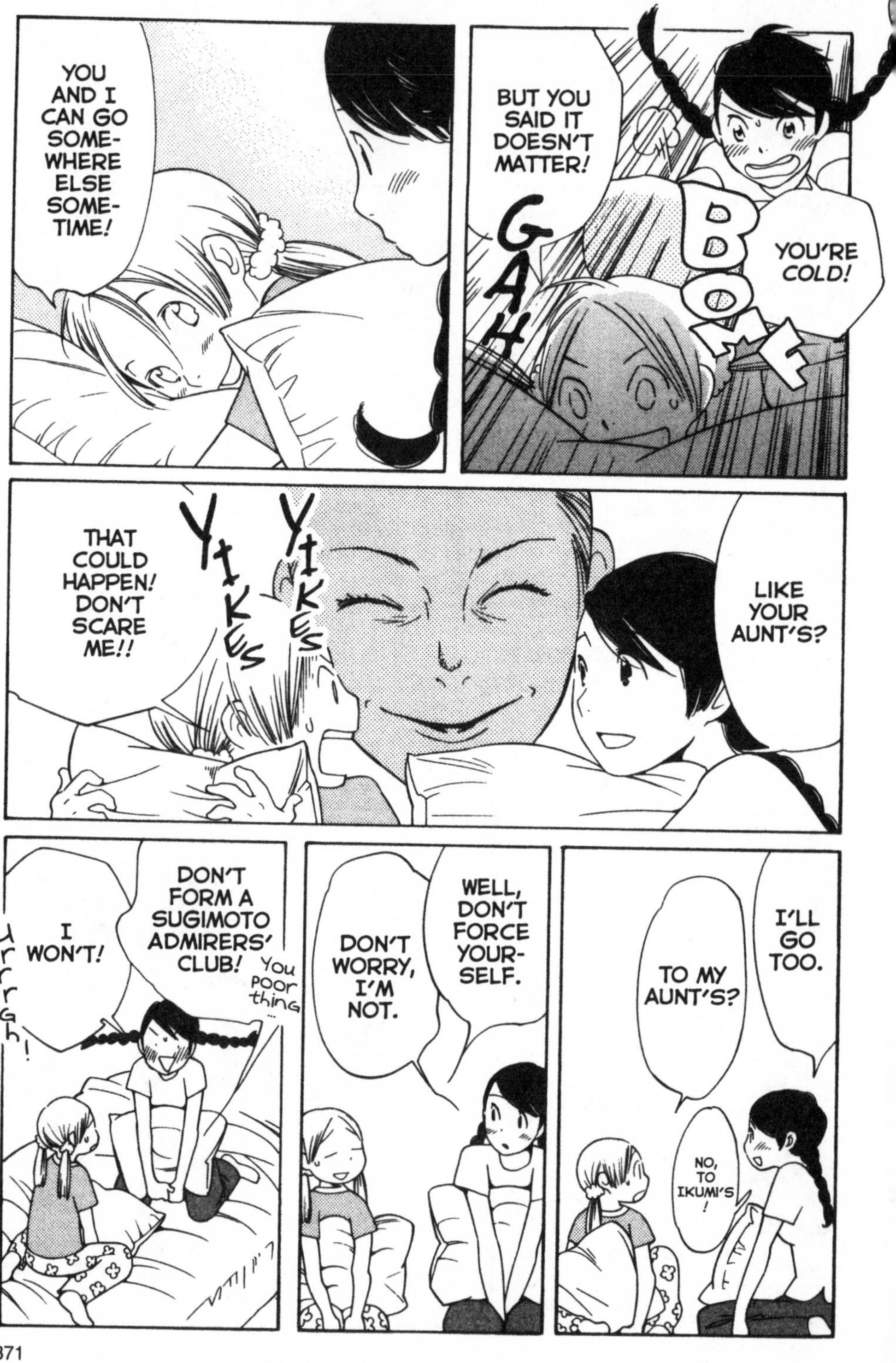
BUT YOU SAID IT DOESN'T MATTER!
GAH
BOMF
YOU'RE COLD!
YOU AND I CAN GO SOME-WHERE ELSE SOME-TIME!
LIKE YOUR AUNT'S?
YIKES
YIKES
THAT COULD HAPPEN! DON'T SCARE ME!!
I'LL GO TOO.
TO MY AUNT'S?
NO, TO IKUMI'S!
WELL, DON'T FORCE YOUR-SELF.
DON'T WORRY, I'M NOT.
DON'T FORM A SUGIMOTO ADMIRERS' CLUB!
You poor thing...
I WON'T!
Urrrgh!

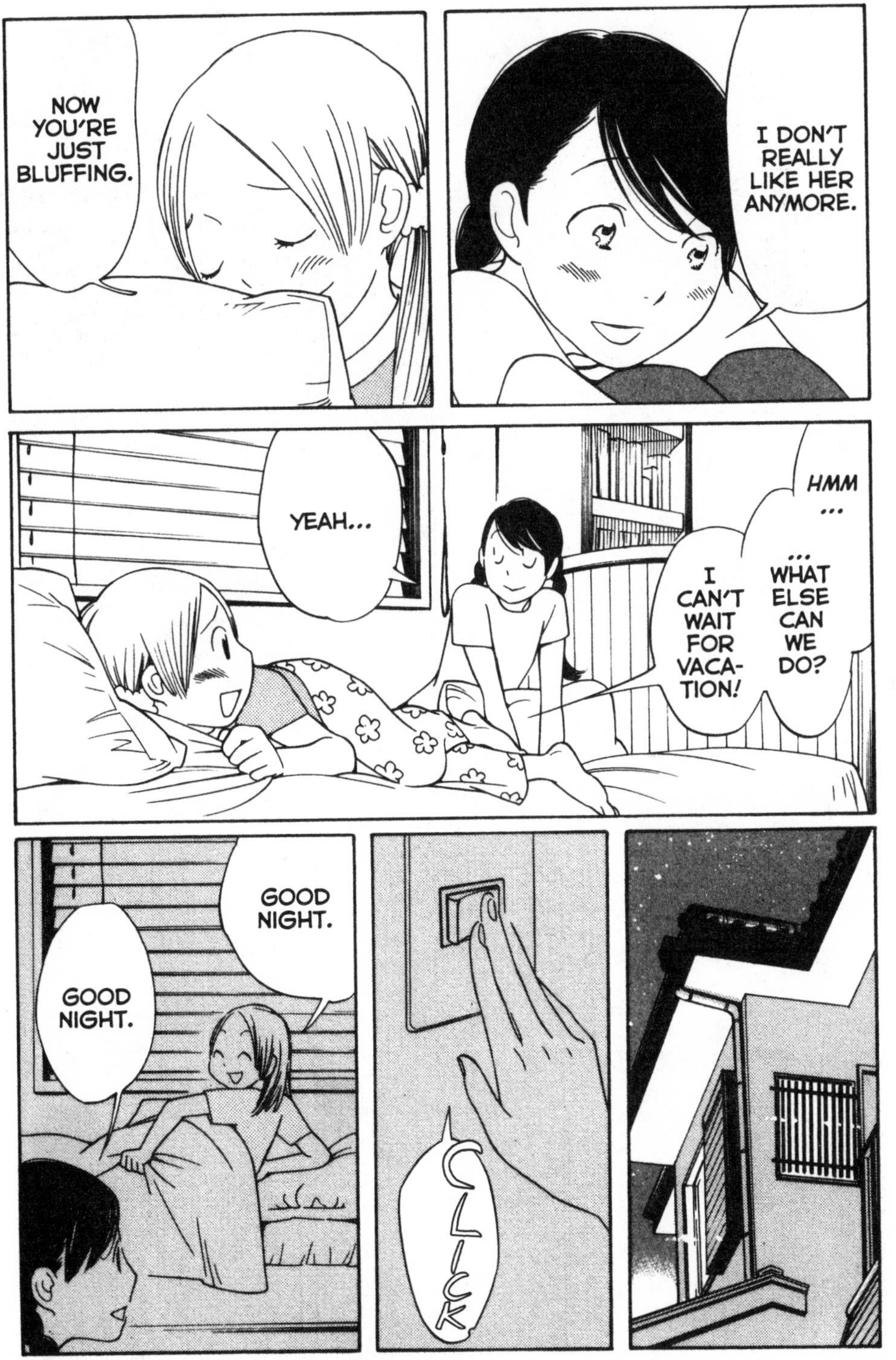
I DON'T REALLY LIKE HER ANYMORE.
NOW YOU'RE JUST BLUFFING.
HMM ...
... WHAT ELSE CAN WE DO?
I CAN'T WAIT FOR VACA-TION!
YEAH...
CLICK
GOOD NIGHT.
GOOD NIGHT.

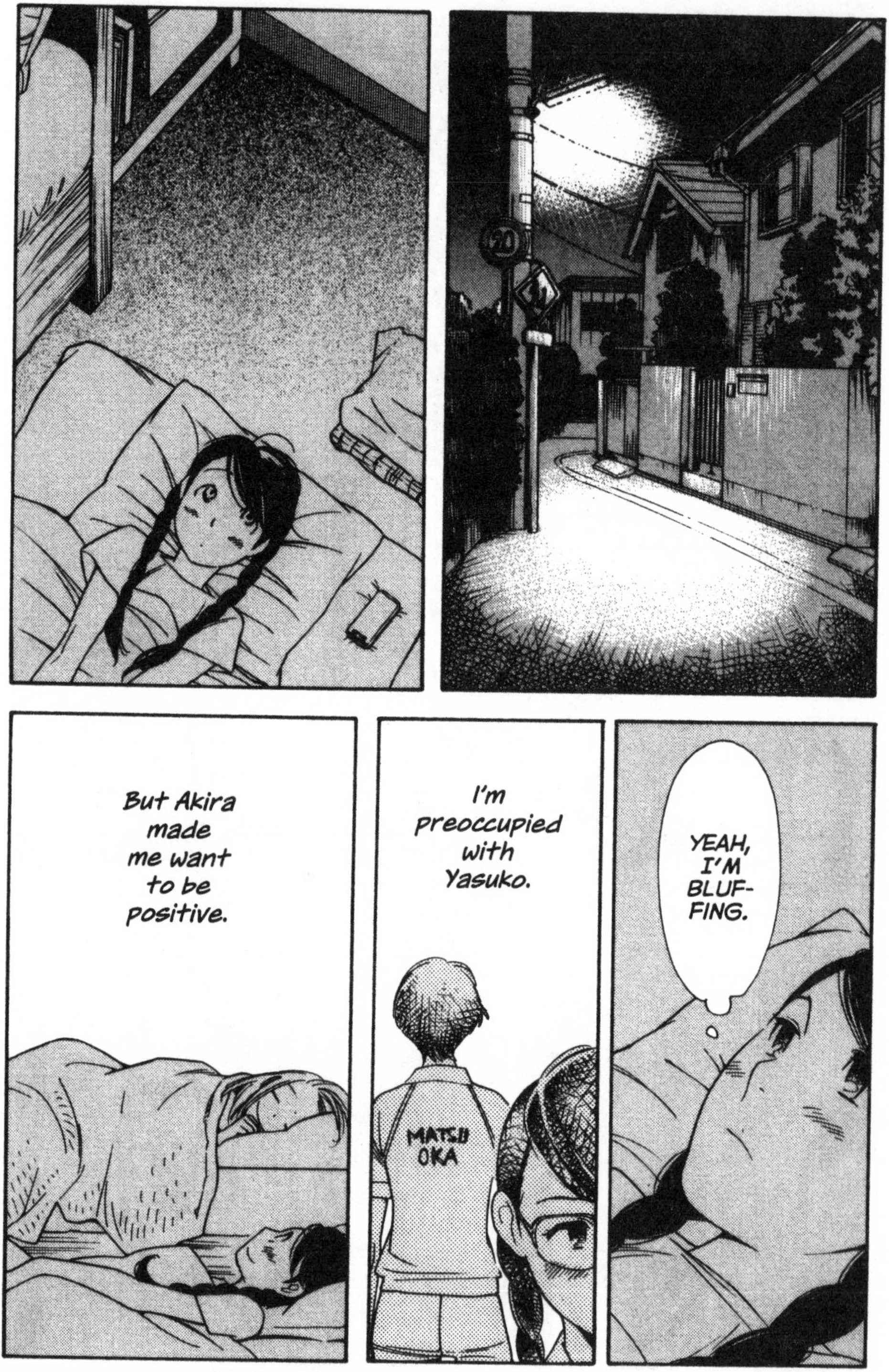
YEAH, I'M BLUFFING.
I'm preoccupied with Yasuko.
MATSU OKA
But Akira made me want to be positive.

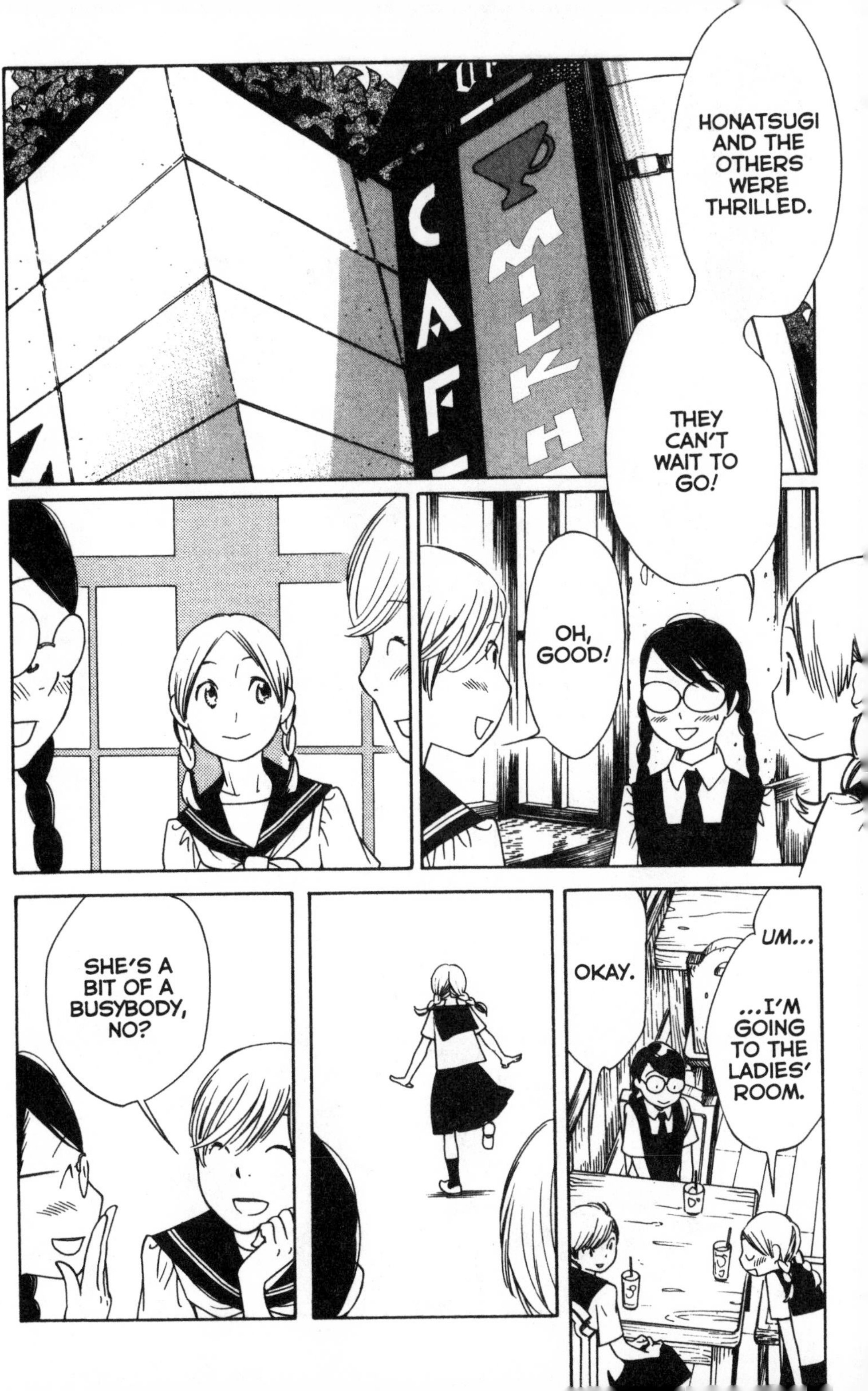
HONATSUGI AND THE OTHERS WERE THRILLED.
THEY CAN'T WAIT TO GO!
OH, GOOD!
UM...
...I'M GOING TO THE LADIES' ROOM.
OKAY.
SHE'S A BIT OF A BUSYBODY, NO?

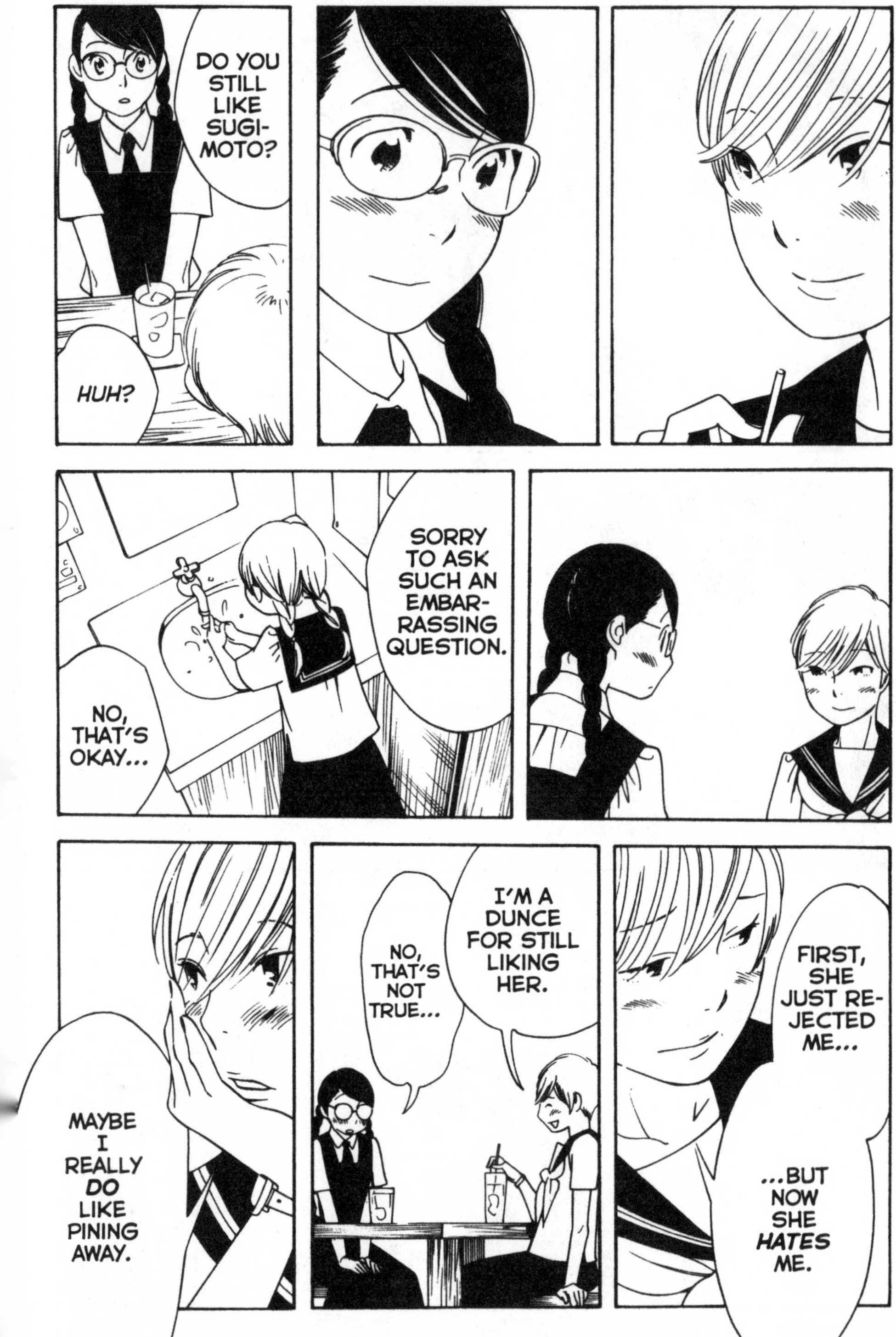
DO YOU STILL LIKE SUGI-MOTO?
HUH?
SORRY TO ASK SUCH AN EMBAR-RASSING QUESTION.
NO, THAT'S OKAY...
FIRST, SHE JUST RE-JECTED ME...
...BUT NOW SHE *HATES* ME.
I'M A DUNCE FOR STILL LIKING HER.
NO, THAT'S NOT TRUE...
MAYBE I REALLY *DO* LIKE PINING AWAY.

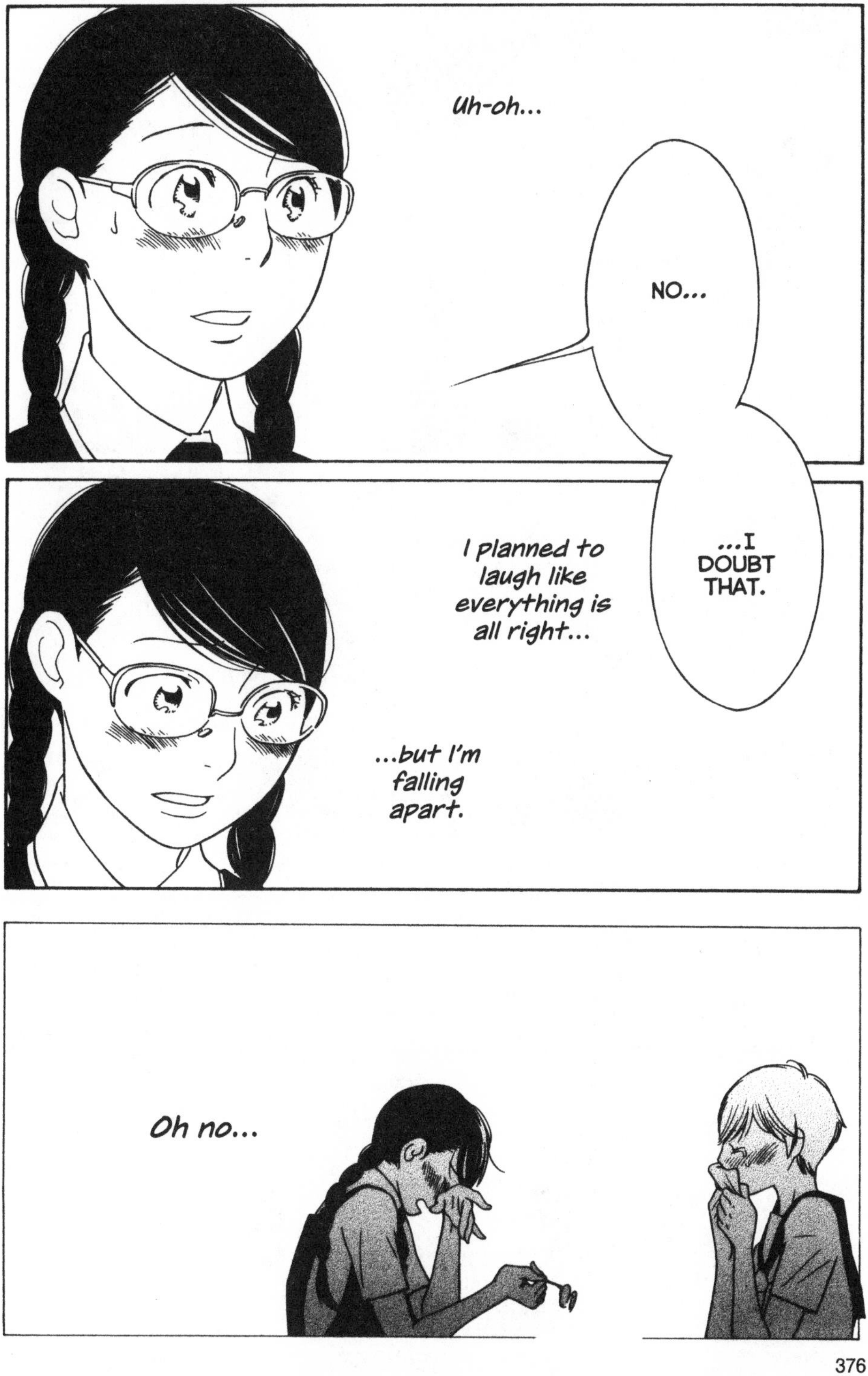
Uh-oh...
NO...
...I DOUBT THAT.
I planned to laugh like everything is all right...
...but I'm falling apart.
Oh no...

*Sweet* **Blue** *Flowers*

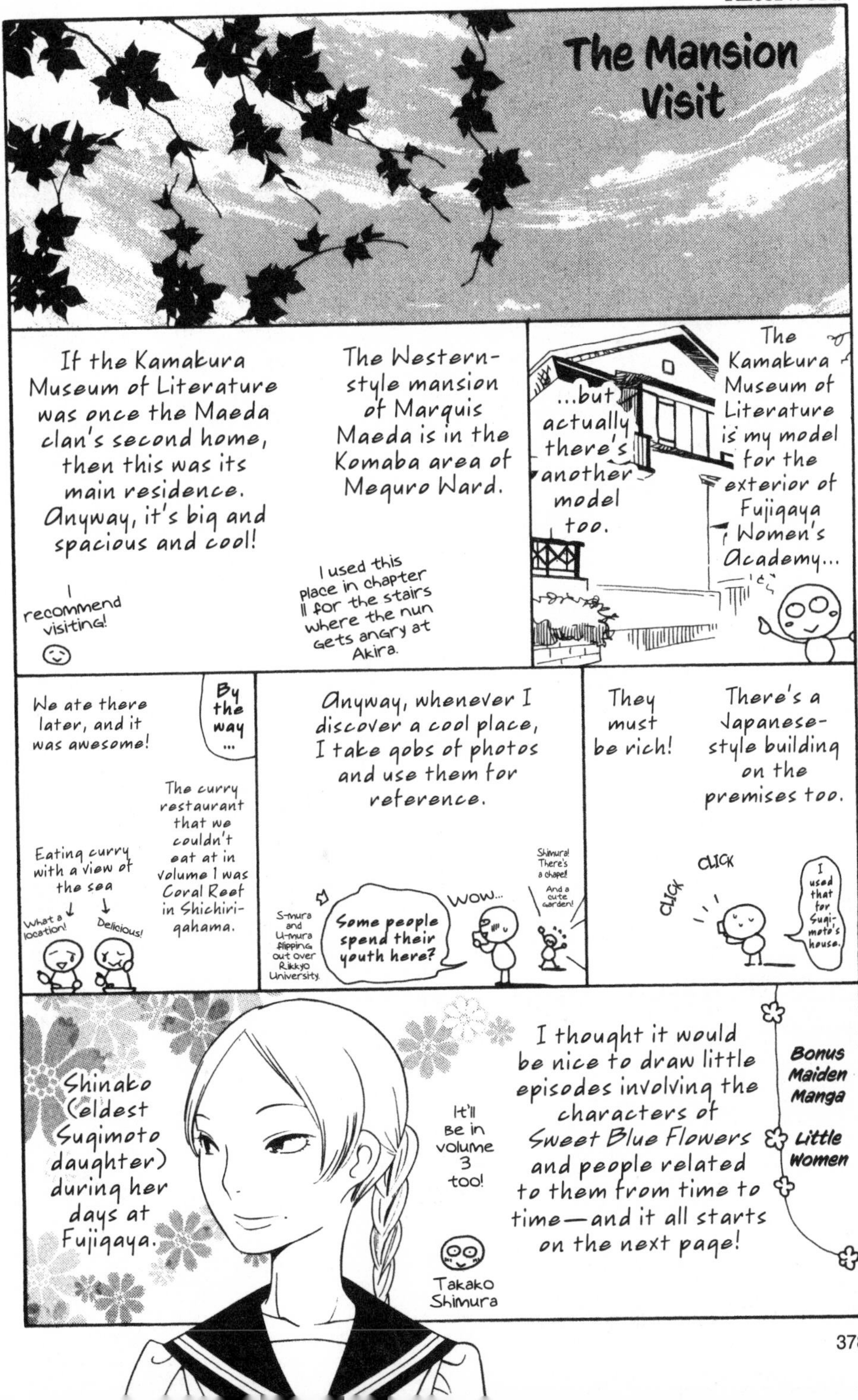
The Mansion Visit
The Kamakura Museum of Literature is my model for the exterior of Fujigaya Women's Academy...
...but actually there's another model too.
The Western-style mansion of Marquis Maeda is in the Komaba area of Meguro Ward.
I used this place in chapter 11 for the stairs where the nun gets angry at Akira.
If the Kamakura Museum of Literature was once the Maeda clan's second home, then this was its main residence. Anyway, it's big and spacious and cool!
I recommend visiting!
There's a Japanese-style building on the premises too.
They must be rich!
CLICK
CLICK
I used that for Sugimoto's house.
Anyway, whenever I discover a cool place, I take gobs of photos and use them for reference.
Shimura! There's a chapel!
And a cute garden!
WOW...
Some people spend their youth here?
S-mura and U-mura flipping out over Rikkyo University.
By the way...
We ate there later, and it was awesome!
The curry restaurant that we couldn't eat at in volume 1 was Coral Reef in Shichiri-gahama.
Eating curry with a view of the sea
What a location!
Delicious!
Bonus Maiden Manga
Little Women
I thought it would be nice to draw little episodes involving the characters of Sweet Blue Flowers and people related to them from time to time—and it all starts on the next page!
It'll be in volume 3 too!
Takako Shimura
Shinako (eldest Sugimoto daughter) during her days at Fujigaya.

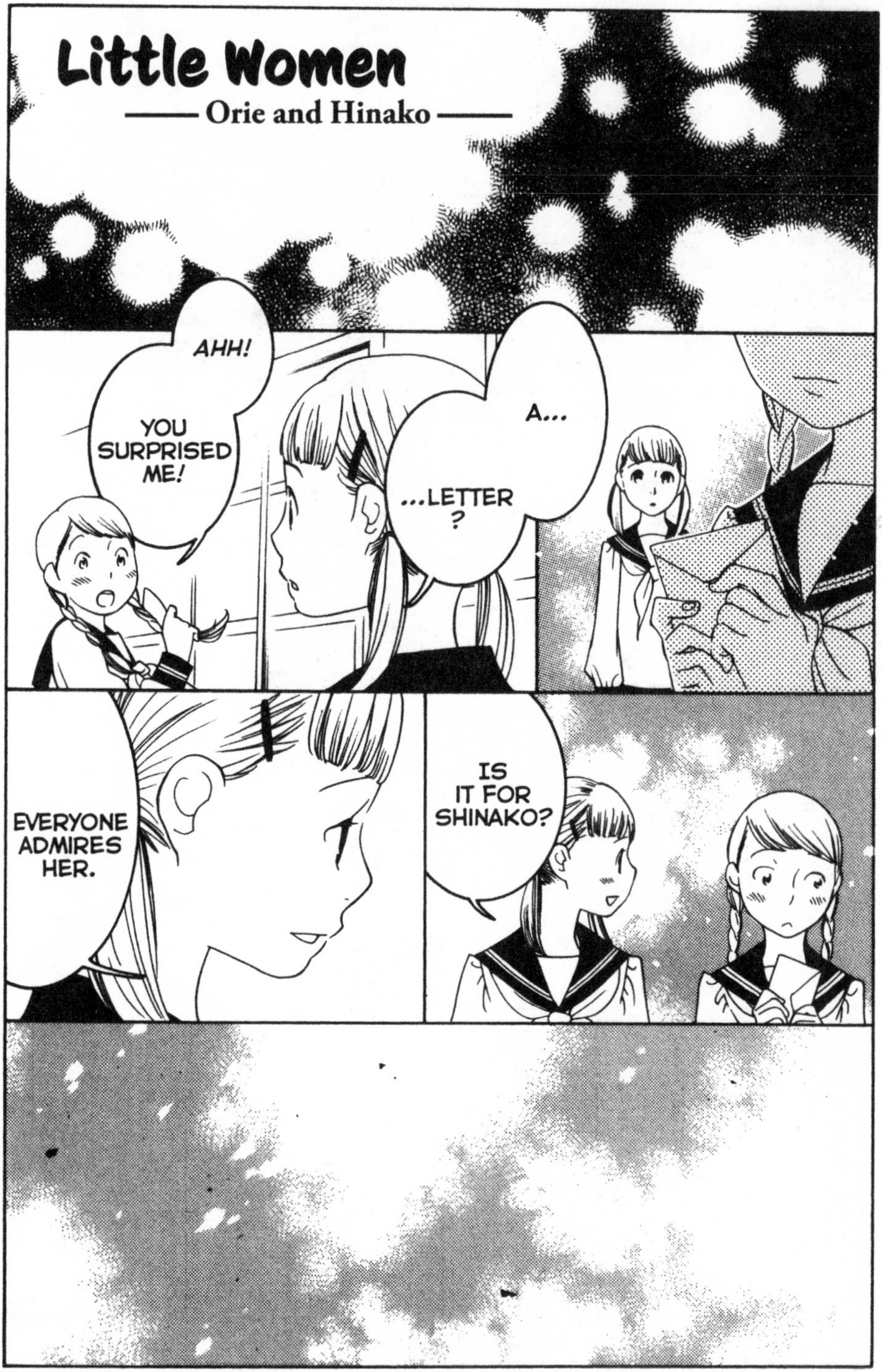
Little Women
—— Orie and Hinako ——
A...
...LETTER?
AHH!
YOU SURPRISED ME!
IS IT FOR SHINAKO?
EVERYONE ADMIRES HER.

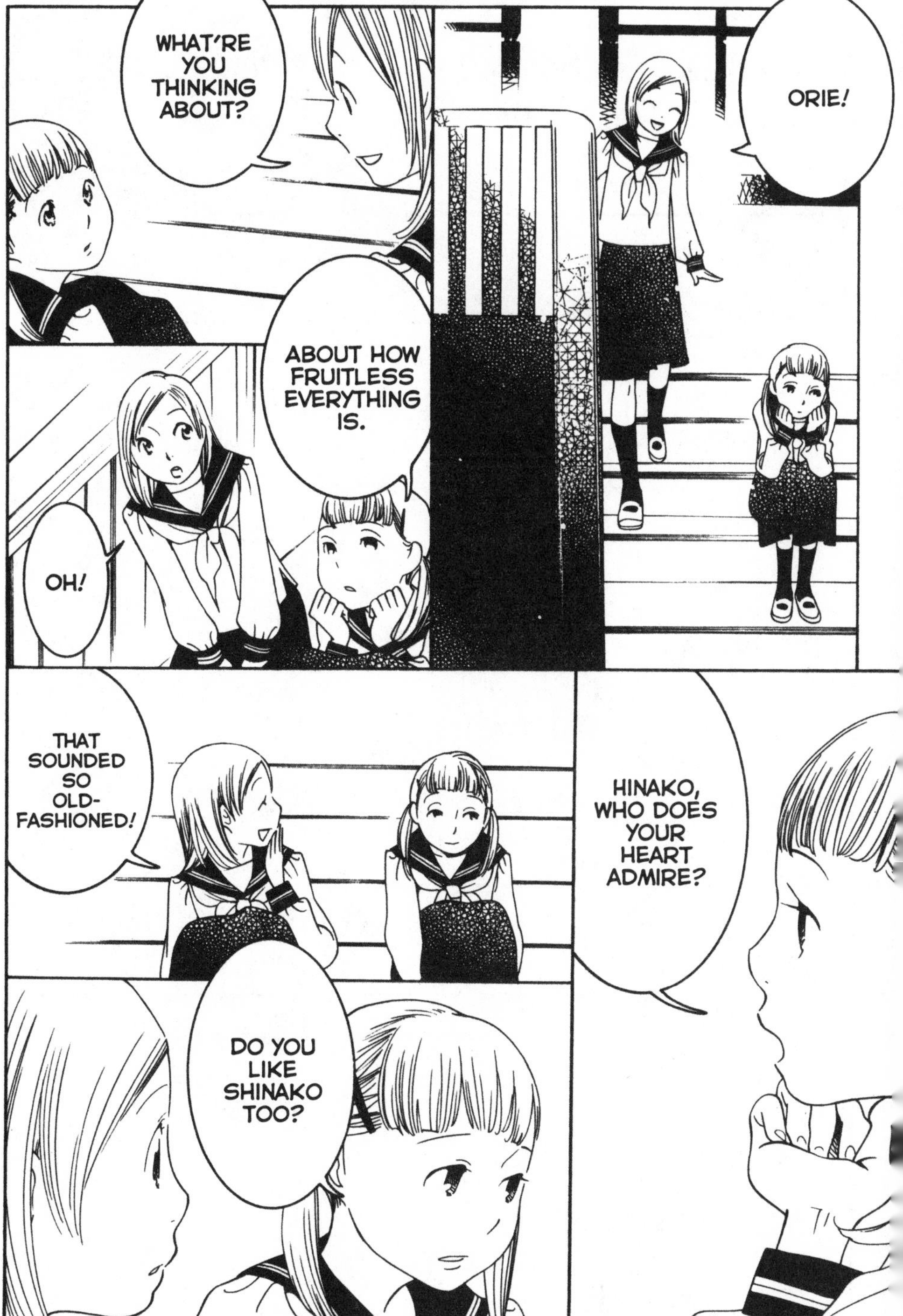
ORIE!
WHAT'RE YOU THINKING ABOUT?
ABOUT HOW FRUITLESS EVERYTHING IS.
OH!
HINAKO, WHO DOES YOUR HEART ADMIRE?
THAT SOUNDED SO OLD-FASHIONED!
DO YOU LIKE SHINAKO TOO?

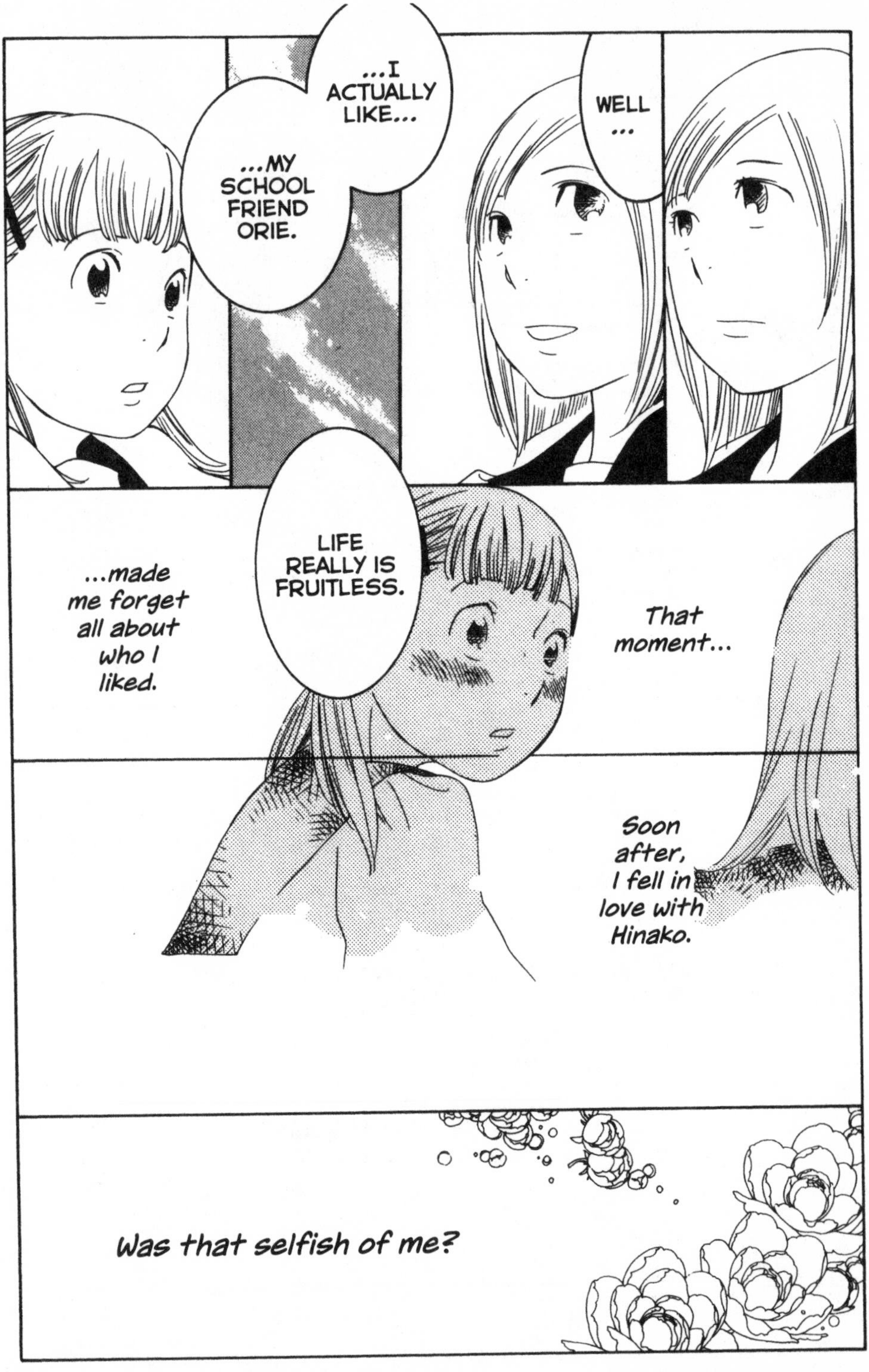
WELL ...
...I ACTUALLY LIKE...
...MY SCHOOL FRIEND ORIE.
That moment...
LIFE REALLY IS FRUITLESS.
...made me forget all about who I liked.
Soon after, I fell in love with Hinako.
Was that selfish of me?

# End Notes

**Page 46, panel 2: Asahi Cider**
A soft drink, not an alcoholic beverage.

**Page 49, panel 4: Ohagi**
A Japanese confection enjoyed in the autumn and made of sweet rice coated in sweet red bean paste (*anko*).

**Page 52, panel 6: Amazake**
An ancient traditional sweet drink made from fermented rice. It has low to no alcohol content.

**Page 55, panel 3: Takarazuka**
Takarazuka Revue is a famous all-female theater troupe based in Takarazuka, Japan.

**Page 114, panel 5: Library maiden**
The stereotype of a pretty girl who spends all her time in the library.

**Page 159, panel 5: Lady of the White Lilies**
The nickname of the poet Tomiko Yamakawa (1879–1909), a lesbian/bisexual icon.

**Page 167, panel 5: Anpan**
A sweet roll filled with red bean paste.

**Page 190, panel 4: Nobuko Yoshiya**
A novelist (1896–1973) who specialized in romance and YA fiction and was a pioneer of Japanese lesbian literature.

**Page 243, panel 3: Maya**
Maya Kitajima is a character in the manga *Glass Mask* who is devoted to acting.

**Page 286, panel 4: Taisho 10**
The year 1921.

**Page 288, panel 1: Meiji period**
A Japanese era spanning 1868–1912.

**Page 346, panel 2: Anmitsu**
A popular Japanese dessert of sweet agar jelly, red bean paste (*anko*) and various fruits. It is served with black sugar syrup (*mitsu*).

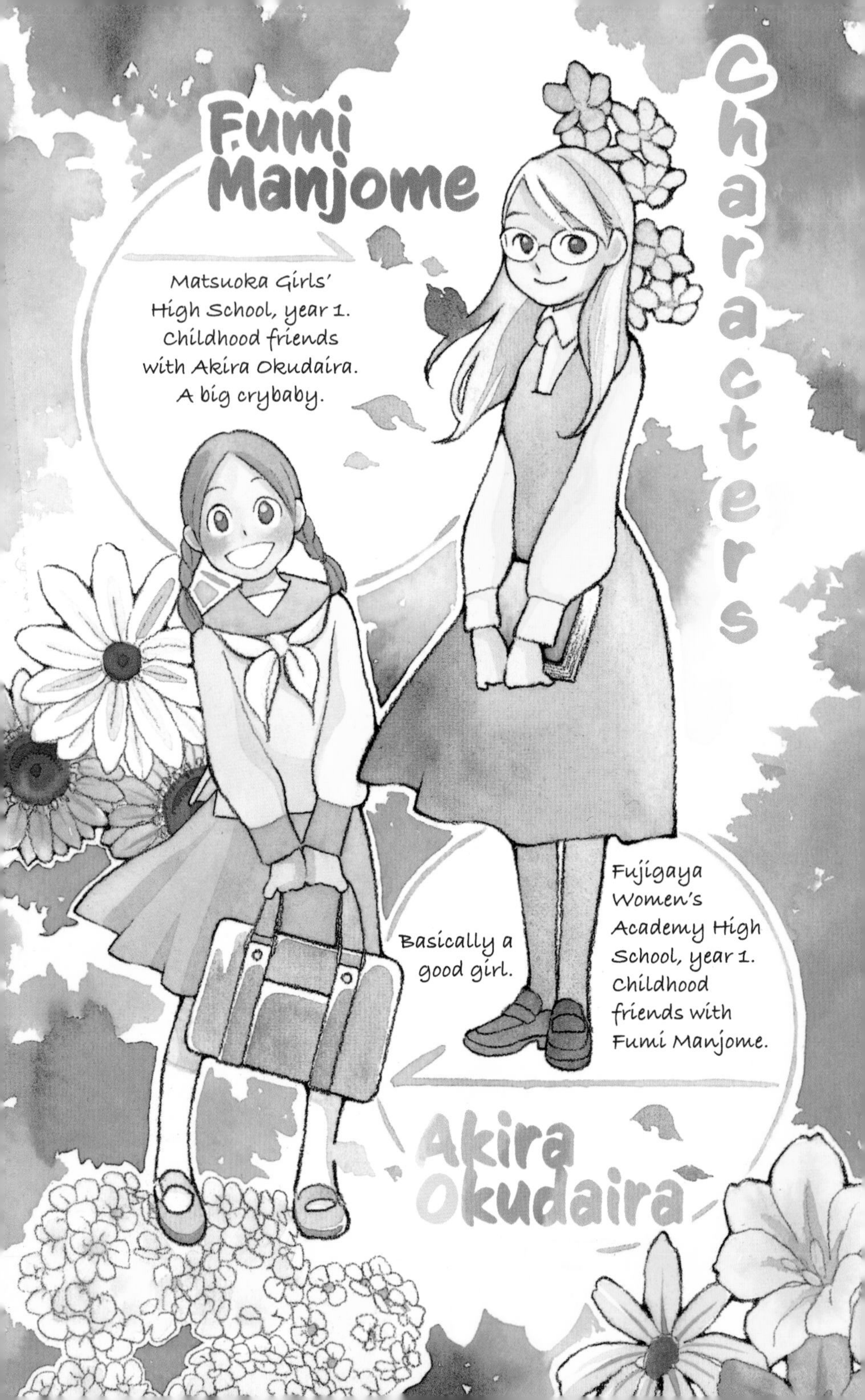
Characters
Fumi Manjome
Matsuoka Girls' High School, year 1. Childhood friends with Akira Okudaira. A big crybaby.
Akira Okudaira
Fujigaya Women's Academy High School, year 1. Childhood friends with Fumi Manjome.
Basically a good girl.

# Sweet Blue Flowers

Part One

1

Story and Art by
Takako Shimura

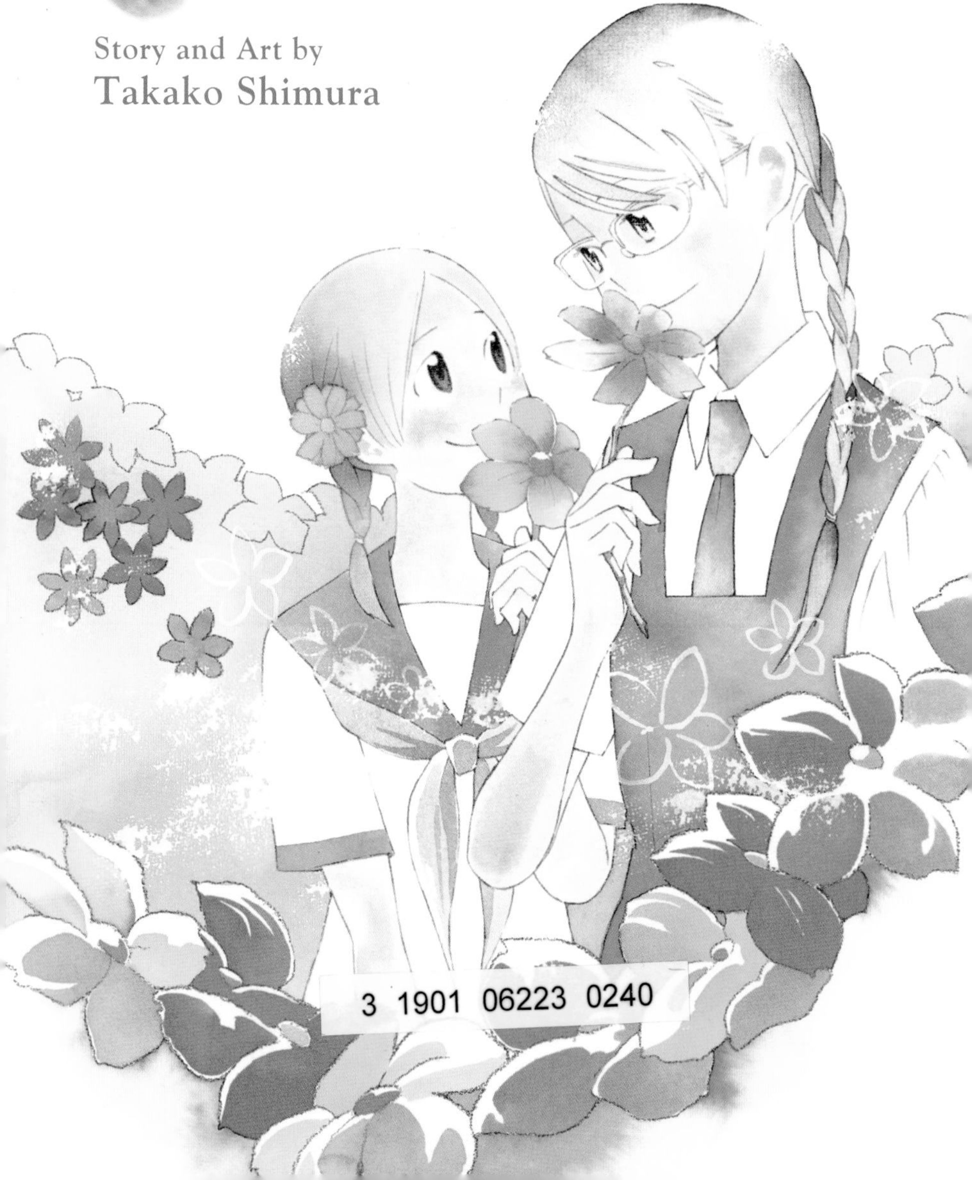

# SWEET BLUE FLOWERS
## VOL. 1
### VIZ Signature Edition

Story & Art by
## Takako Shimura

Translation & Adaptation/John Werry
Touch-Up Art & Lettering/Monalisa De Asis
Design/Yukiko Whitley
Editor/Pancha Diaz

AOI HANA Vols. 1, 2
© Takako Shimura 2005, 2006
All rights reserved.
First published in Japan in 2005, 2006 by Ohta Publishing Co., Tokyo
English translation rights arranged with Ohta Publishing Co.
through Tuttle-Mori Agency, Inc., Tokyo

Printed in Canada

Published by VIZ Media, LLC
P.O. Box 77010
San Francisco, CA 94107

10 9 8 7 6 5 4 3 2 1
First printing, September 2017

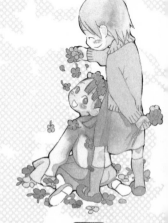

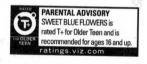

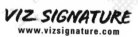

VIZ SIGNATURE
www.vizsignature.com

www.viz.com

This is the last page. *Sweet Blue Flowers* has been printed in the original Japanese format to preserve the orientation of the original artwork.

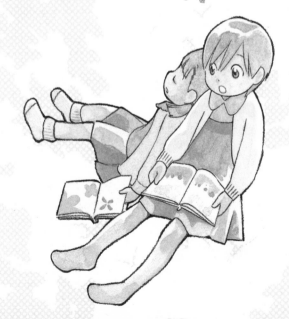